Andrew Ward

Andrew Ward lives in the United States, but his fascination with the Mutiny dates back to his childhood in India. His novel about Cawnpore, *The Blood Seed*, was published in 1985 to critical acclaim. He has been a contributing editor at the *Atlantic Monthly* and a regular contributor to *National Geographic* and the *International Herald Tribune*.

OUR BONES ARE SCATTERED

THE CAWNPORE MASSACRES AND THE INDIAN MUTINY OF 1857

ANDREW WARD

JOHN MURRAY

FOR ZOË YALLAND

◆   ◆   ◆

CONTENTS

LIST OF ILLUSTRATIONS

PREFACE

To write about the British in India is to ask what they were doing there. It was a question many of the European victims at Cawnpore must have asked themselves as they huddled with their children amid barrages of rebel round shot and musket balls in the disintegrating barracks and sweltering ditches of their pathetic Entrenchment, or as they waded in the bloody shallows at Sati Chowra Ghat or huddled in the swelter of the Bibighar while their slayers heaved their shoulders against the door. And it was the question Indians must have asked themselves as East India Company troops drunkenly attacked their villages, looting and burning their huts and shops, raping women, hanging men by the hundreds along the roadsides or tying them to the mouths of cannons and blowing them to pieces.

The cycle of massacre and retribution was a kind of imperial rite. Just as Custer's debacle at Little Big Horn presaged the slaughter at Wounded Knee, the Zulus' annihilative victory at Isandhlwana led to their own massacre at Ulundi, and General Gordon's death and the sack of Khartoum brought about the extravagant carnage at Omdurman, Cawnpore led to a terrible vengeance. The truth is that more than the retribution they engendered, these massacres advanced the imperial purpose. During the nineteenth century Europeans laid claim to the strangest and remotest places, but imperialism was never a unanimous impulse. To a good many people back home the acquisition of such places seemed gratuitous and immoral, not to mention expensive. Grand imperial schemes were always in peril; even the most acquisitive of Western statesmen, be they British prime ministers or American presidents, had to shroud their expansionism in pious rhetoric about spreading civilization, enlightenment, Christianity, trade, or some convenient combination.

But concocting a sustaining moral basis for the appropriation of other peoples' lands was difficult, and an occasional massacre—indeed, any unfortunate skirmish that might be passed off as a massacre—could at least temporarily unify Europeans in their essential contempt for the moral condition of native peoples, buttress their belief in their own cultural superiority, and obscure their own ambivalence with the fire and brimstone of their vengeance.

I have tried to depict the massacres at Cawnpore unflinchingly because though they were more terrible than anything I hope you can imagine, they were less atrocious than the British public was encouraged to think, and more complicated than either imperialist or nationalist historians have made them out to be. I have tried not to spare the reader the horrors of British retribution because they were *more* atrocious than the British public was encouraged to think. No one can say how many thousands of Indians—including women and children—died during the suppression of the Indian rebellion, but many times more, certainly, than the Europeans who died at Cawnpore: so many that it seems almost incredible that ninety years later the British and the Indian people should have taken leave of each other so amicably.

The following is the fullest account yet written of the Cawnpore tragedy, and yet it cannot be definitive; instead it is a reformulation of the sparse documentary evidence that survived the looting and razing of the station, the destruction of post offices, the sinking of home-bound ships, the censoriousness of bureaucrats and grieving relatives, the carelessness of some of their descendants. I shall leave a discussion of my sources for a later note, but it must be said at the outset that the overwhelming bulk of primary material remains Anglo-Indian, and what little survives from Indian sources comes through a British filter: the depositions of native witnesses afraid they might be hanged, the testimony of rebels at their trials, the journals of Indians eager to demonstrate their loyalty to the ascending Raj. But I have tried to give their evidence its due, for even after I discounted some of it as too incongruous, too convenient, too self-serving, enough remained at least to suggest the Indian experience of the Cawnpore uprising and its aftermath.

No nation has the right to conquer another, and the British had perhaps even less business laying claim to India than the Aryans, the Timurids, the Afghans, or the Mahrattas who preceded them. But nineteenth-century history respected sovereignty to the same extent that the propagation of the species respects virginity, and looking almost a century and a half back I am less interested in deploring the East India Company and the Raj than in observing and trying to understand the individuals—Hindus, Moslems, Eurasians, Europeans—whose bones are scattered throughout these pages.

Though the Mutiny, even the Great Mutiny, is an inadequate name for what transpired in the Upper Provinces of India in 1857–58, it seems to have outlasted everything else that has been applied to it. Indian and Pakistani nationalist historians have called it, among other things, the First War of Indian Independence or the Freedom Struggle of 1857. For my part I would prefer to call it the 1857 Uprising. But whether in India, the United Kingdom, or the United States, whenever I sit down with historians to talk about 1857, no matter how fastidious we try to be, by the end of the evening we are all talking about the Mutiny. Even in India and England, every other appellation elicits blank looks from librarians and archivists and no doubt from much of the reading public. So, for better or worse, I have employed the term in the title of this book.

But I have tried to be more fastidious in the text, in which I have applied the term mutiny only to the revolt of East India Company troops or, for clarity's sake, wherever a discussion of the British reaction demands it. Otherwise I refer variously to the events of 1857 as a rebellion, revolt, or uprising, in the sense that whether one speaks of the mutineers or the landholders who were dispossessed by the British or the princes whose kingdoms the British annexed or the Mullahs and Brahmins who felt their power shrinking in the glare of Company reforms, missionary evangelism, and Western technology, these were all subject peoples rising up against a ruling power.

From the eighteenth to the early nineteenth century, the word *Indian* referred not to natives of the Indian subcontinent but to English people born or raised there. This was gradually replaced by *Anglo-Indian*, but toward the close of the nineteenth century *Anglo-Indian* became the term by which people of mixed native and English stock—*Eurasians*, as they were called during the Mutiny—chose to call themselves. In the pages that follow I have employed these terms as they were generally in use in 1857. Thus *Indian* and *native* refer to all non-European inhabitants of the Indian subcontinent; *Anglo-Indian* to British persons born, raised, or living for much of their lives in India; *Eurasian* to people of mixed Indian and European ancestry (especially since many were part Irish, Dutch, French, or Portuguese). When I use *Europeans* or *European community* I refer to any group that included not just the English but also the few French, Portuguese, Dutch, Americans, etc. who also resided in India at the time. If any derogatory connotation still clings to these terms it is not in any way intended.

I have tried to be strict in my use of Indian military terminology. I use the term *sepoy* only to refer to native infantrymen, and not as a generic term for native troops. Native cavalrymen are referred to as *sowars*, native artillerymen (of whom there were few) as *golundazes*. Where a rebel force was composed of any combination of these three, I refer to them as *mutineers* or *native troops*. Where, as at Cawnpore, they were joined by civilians, bodyguards, the soldiers of native chiefs, freelances, matchlockmen, I use the term *rebels*. *Rebels* was a pejorative in British histories of the period, but as an American writing in the twentieth century I simply apply it to any Indian who, for whatever reason, fought against the Company's rule.

My spelling of Indian and Anglo-Indian words and place names is based on Yole and Burnell's *Hobson-Jobson: A Glossary of Colloquial Anglo-Indian Words and Phrases*, the eleventh edition of *Encyclopædia Britannica*, and Thacker's *Reduced Survey Map of India*. Thus I employ spellings—including *Cawnpore* and *Oudh*—that were either generally employed or in the process of being formalized at the time of the Mutiny. Again this is merely for clarity's sake and to establish some continuity between my prose and the quotes I employ. *Cawnpore* is the spelling inscribed on the local contemporary memorials to the events of 1857, in the first-hand accounts of the uprising, and even in today's military cantonment that encompasses the site of the Entrenchment, and so it is the spelling I employ when referring to the city's history up to 1947, before the spelling (and the pronunciation) changed to *Kanpur*.

The barbarities of the nineteenth century have been grotesquely superseded by our own, but if all history is an argument with death, this is even more the case where so many people died with such terrible simultaneity. Before I can tell you how these people died, I must first tell you how they lived. Here, then, as close as I can come to it, is the story of Cawnpore.

Bainbridge Island,
Washington
April, 1995

ACKNOWLEDGMENTS

This book is dedicated to the late historian Zoë Yalland. No student of Cawnpore could have asked for a more authoritative, encouraging or generous mentor: her two volumes on Cawnpore/Kanpur—*Traders & Nabobs* and *Boxwallahs*—drawn from hitherto untapped primary sources, are definitive municipal histories, illuminated but never blinded by her abiding affection for her place of birth. Even during her final illness, Zoë never blinked at my endless inquiries about even the goriest details of my story nor stinted in her advice and assistance. My thanks also to Zoë's husband Basil for putting up so graciously with my many demands on Zoë's time and for providing many of the illustrations for this book.

Among those who assisted me in India I owe my greatest debt, as always, to Mrs. Sajni Thukral, for her wonderful friendship and generosity. I want to thank Dr. R. K. Perti, Director of the National Archives of India, and his equanimous staff for their help during my weeks of research in their wonderful collection. Divyabhanusinh Chavda, Vice President (Operations) Northern Region of the Taj Group of Hotels also gave me much pertinent advice and assistance. Thanks also to the Honorable Thomas Pickering, United States Ambassador to India; Alan B. Ammerman, American Consul in Delhi; and David K. Krecke, Counsellor for Cultural Affairs at the United States Information Service in New Delhi.

In Kanpur I wish to thank Dr. Munishwar Nigam, whose devotion to the history of Cawnpore and meticulous insistence on absolute accuracy has freed me from many misconceptions about the history of Cawnpore and saved me from many mistakes. I am also extremely grateful to the distinguished journalist S. P. Mehra and his son Suresh for their kindness and patient assistance. I wish also to thank Colonel Bhupinder Singh of the 45th Cavalry Regiment for permission to photograph the burial well in the military cantonment. I am especially indebted to Keith Shepherd, a great-grandnephew of

Jonah Shepherd, who shared his family papers with me; his brother
Ian Shepherd of Lucknow; and Mr. and Mrs. Ivan Shepherd, their
parents. Kailash Charan Wahal, a descendant of Sheo Prasad, was
helpful in providing background material. I also wish to thank V. V.
Subhedar, great-great-grandson of Subhedar Ram Chunder, father of
Narain Rao, for providing me with background material. I am also
indebted to Nand Kumar of Sati Chowra, a descendant of the boatmen who arranged for Wheeler's flotilla.

My stay at Kanpur was facilitated by Mrs. Mahendrajit Singh, pro-
prietress of the Attic Hotel, and a leading citizen of Kanpur. My
thanks also to her family and staff for their assistance and hospitality.
Some of this book is based on research I conducted for my novel
about Cawnpore, *The Blood Seed*, which brought me to Kanpur in
1982. Among those who assisted me during that visit were Farooq
Ahson, Shri M. M. Kapoor of Sati Chowra, and District Magistrate
A. K. S. Solanki.

Among those who kindly assisted me in Bithur was the late Narain
Rao Tope, nephew of Tatya Tope, who died two days after our interview. He devoted two hours to answering my obscure questions
about his family and Nana Sahib, and gave me permission to photograph his extraordinary gallery of paintings of many of the partici-
pants in the uprising at Cawnpore. My thanks also to his son,
Vanayak Narain Tope, for translating his father's Maharastran replies
into Hindi. During my visit I was taken in hand by Colonel P. P. Singh
of Bithur, descendant of Raja Bhagmal Jat, on whose *jagir* Baji Rao
settled in 1819. My special thanks also to Kochin Wu for devoting a
day to escorting me around Bithur and sharing his insights into the
events of 1857.

I also want to thank the following for their contributions: Dr. Hari
Prasad Thapliyal of Meerut; Thomas Smith of Agra; Frank Carroll at
All Souls Church; the novelist Manohar Malgonkar.

I wish to thank my researcher in London, Miss E. Talbot Rice of TR
Military Search; and Bridget Lakin for researching on my behalf at
the Isle of Wight County Record Office.

I am especially indebted to Dr. R. J. Bingle of the Oriental and
India Office Collections (OIOC) of the British Library for his always
patient guidance and pertinent assistance. I also want to thank
Secretary-Librarian Dr. Lionel Carter for guiding a very hurried and
demanding guest through the splendid manuscript collection at the
Centre of South Asian Studies at Cambridge University.

Dr. Peter B. Boyden, Head of the Department of Archives, Photographs, Film and Sound; and Dr. Linda Washington, Head of the Department of Printed Books at the National Army Museum, were very helpful to me in chasing down illustrations and military records.

I wish to thank P. J. O. Taylor for sharing with me his insights from his lifelong researches into the Mutiny, for reading portions of the manuscript and saving me from many embarrassments, and for providing me with several of the photographs that illustrate this book. Any reader interested in pursuing this story further would be well advised to read his upcoming Mutiny encyclopedia, and to follow his columns in the *Statesman*. His pioneering research into the Wheeler family has been especially valuable to me.

The American biographer Katherine Frank generously shared with me her discoveries among the letters and diaries of Lucie Duff Gordon, who championed Azimullah during his stay in England; Frank also alerted me to various other important sources and contacts. I am also grateful to Raleigh Trevelyan for his untiring guidance and introductions and for permitting me to quote from the Halliday letters in his possession. A. C. Hardcastle, local-studies researcher and historian of Addiscombe, kindly shared his material on the Vibart family with me and elucidated the Addiscombe ties of many of the young officers who died at Cawnpore. My thanks also to Theon Wilkinson for his assistance with illustrations and for addressing some of the issues raised in my correspondence with his late sister, Zoë Yalland. I am grateful to the Earl of Shelburne and the Trustees of the Bowood Will Trust for permission to quote from the Lansdowne Manuscripts.

Among the descendants of the victims at Cawnpore I especially want to thank Dr. and Mrs. Colin L. Forbes for graciously permitting me to quote from Dr. Forbes's great-aunt Emma Wyndham Halliday's letters and reproduce her drawings. My thanks to Dr. Forbes also for the genealogical material he provided concerning the Wyndham and Halliday families, and for introducing me to Miss Katherine Forbes, whom I thank for sharing with me, among other things, a photograph of her ancestor, Emma Halliday; and Alan B. Walker, who kindly provided copies of his elegant Wyndham family trees.

I shall always be profoundly grateful to Sir Ronald Lindsay, Bart. and Lady Lindsay of Dowhill for permitting me to review and copy stacks of their family papers. My special thanks also to Alexander Lindsay Binney, grandson of Major William Lindsay's eldest son and "mutiny orphan" William, for his reminiscences and his kind permission to quote extensively from his ancestors' letters and to reproduce the Lindsay portraits that appear in this book.

Colonel Vibart McArthur, O.B.E., great grandnephew of Major Edward Vibart of Cawnpore, not only generously shared his research into the Vibart family but pursued further investigations on my behalf and read portions of the manuscript to correct this civilian's misconceptions about military life and terminology.

My thanks also to Mrs. A. Regan for generously providing me with material relating to her ancestors the Jacobis of Cawnpore, and to her brother, Gerald Fisher, for his kind assistance; and to Andrew Shepherd and Mrs. Lorraine (Shepherd) Menon, descendants of Jonah Shepherd. Thanks also to Mrs. Mollie Mallaby and Lieutenant-Colonel P. St. G. Maxwell MC for portraits of Gavin Jones and Peter Maxwell.

I consulted many collections in the United Kingdom and Ireland and wish to thank the following archivists: Mary Guinan-Darmody of the County Tipperary Joint Libraries Committee; Allan Blackwood of the Public Record Office of Northern Ireland; E. M. Rainey at the Palace Green Section of the University of Durham; Zoë Lubowiecka of the East Sussex County Council Library; Sarah Adams of the Law Society at Ipsley Court; Clare Brown of the Rhodes House Library, Oxford; Dr. Lesley Gordon at the University of Newcastle Upon Tyne; the staff of *Past & Present: A Journal of Historical Studies*; J. G. F. Stoy of the East Indian Devonshire, Sports and Public Schools Club; Dr. Chris Evans of the Royal Commission on Historical Manuscripts; Mrs. C. Boddington of the Humberside Archive Service; R. P. Jenkins of the Leicestershire Record Office; A. Geoffrey Veysey of the Clwyd County Council; P. R. Evans of the Gloucestershire County Record Office; W. Wexler of the Suffolk County Council Department of Libraries and Heritage; J. F. Russell of the National Library of Scotland; Jean M. Kennedy of the Norfolk Record Office; Roger Davey of the East Sussex County Council; the staff of the Royal Academy of Art; Mrs. M. M. Rowe of the Devon Record Office; Robert Hale of the Berkshire Record Office; R. J. Childs of the West Sussex Record Office; Dr. G. A. Knight of the Recreational Services Department of the Lincolnshire County Council; Ann Sylph of the Zoological Society of London; Penny Ward, Heritage Officer, Thanet, and D. C. Gibson of the Kent County Council Arts & Libraries Centre for Kentish Studies; Alison Fraser of the Orkney Library in Kirkwall, Orkney; Undine Concannon of Madame Tussaud's in London; Monica Ory of the

Warwickshire County Council Department of Libraries & Heritage; Guy Holborn, Librarian at Lincoln's Inn Library; and the staffs of the reading rooms of the British Museum, the British Library, and the National Army Museum.

My research into the Wyndhams and Hallidays introduced me to the Wyndhams of New South Wales, including Alward Wyndham, descendant of Emma Halliday's uncle George Wyndham. I also want to thank Margaret Kelly, Honourable Secretary of the Historic "Dalwood" Restoration Association, for providing me with Ella Wyndham's letter reporting Alexander Wyndham's grief over the loss of his daughter Emma Halliday, a letter from George Wyndham's son Alward describing his visit to the Wyndham family in 1852, and excerpts from a letter by Emma's Aunt Charlotte. I am also grateful to Mrs. G. A. Rink and James Wyndham of New South Wales for information regarding Trevelyan Wyndham's life in Australia, and William D. P. and Elizabeth Wyndham of Alberta, Canada for information regarding Emma's brother Alfred. I also wish to thank Russell Blaxland for sharing with me the Mutiny letters of J. Macansh.

My thanks also to the following archivists in the United States: Susan Miller and Kerry J. Norce of the department of history of the Presbyterian Church (USA); David Holifield and Douglas Johnson of the McAlister Library of the Fuller Theological Seminary; Martha Smally of the Yale Divinity School Library; the wonder-working staff of the Seattle Public Library Information Hotline; the staff of the Sterling Library at Yale; and Irene Joshi, archivist of the South Asian collection at the the University of Washington Library, which continually surprised and delighted me with the depth of its India collection.

My thanks also to Mary Ann Steggles of Acadia University in Wolfville, Nova Scotia, for information regarding the erection and removal of the Memorial Well.

The following people also assisted me in this country: John Gubbins, a relation of Martin Gubbins of Lucknow; Anne Toll; Drs. Julia and Herman Schweindinger; Huma Haque of the Department of Anthropology at the University of Washington; Richard Sorsky of Fresno, California; Judith Cuthbertson; and my criminal-pathologist brother-in-law, Dr. Robert Huntington III, who addressed many of the forensic questions that this gruesome story raised.

I also wish to thank Basil Yalland and the estate of Zoë Yalland for permission to use the plates of Savada Koti, the magistrate, Wheeler and Hillersdon, Hardeo Temple, British troops storming a rebel position, and the Memorial Gardens; Theon Wilkinson for the Bibighar photo and W. J. Shepherd; Dr. Colin Forbes for all of Emma Halliday's drawings; Katherine Forbes for Emma Halliday; Alexander Binney for Lillias Don; the Office of India and Oriental Collections for Major William Lindsay, Kate Lindsay's family, the spy, the ruins of Wheeler's barracks, Rao Sahib, and Mowbray Thomson; the Director of the National Army Museum for Wheeler, Neill, and Tatya Tope; Dr. Munishwar Nigam for Shepherd's map; the Presbyterian Church (USA) for the three American missionaries; Mrs. A. Regan for Charlotte Jacobi; Mrs. Mollie Mallaby for Gavin Jones.

My sincere thanks to my editor, Jack Macrae, for proposing this book and patiently disentangling me from the engulfing thicket of my research; and my agent, Ellen Levine, for her vigilance and encouragement.

As always, I am indebted to my godfather, Professor Emeritus Andrew Bongiorno of Oberlin College, for his editorial advice and corrections, his friendship and encouragement. Finally I want to thank various Wards, for whom India has always been a family affair: my parents, Dr. F. Champion and Duira Ward, for their careful reading of this manuscript; my sister Helen Ward; my brother Geoffrey C. Ward for his advice and assistance; and my sister-in-law, Diane· Raines Ward, for providing copies of Mutiny prints from various collections. Writing a history set in as complex a world as the Company's India and composed of so many hundreds of characters proved such a tall order for this writer of columns and essays that for the first time in his career he missed a deadline—by over a year, in fact. I wish to thank my wife Debbie for her love and support and forbearance, and my children Jake and Casey for putting up with the long extra days, weeks, and months I wound up devoting to what they came to call "Dad's dead friends."

MAPS

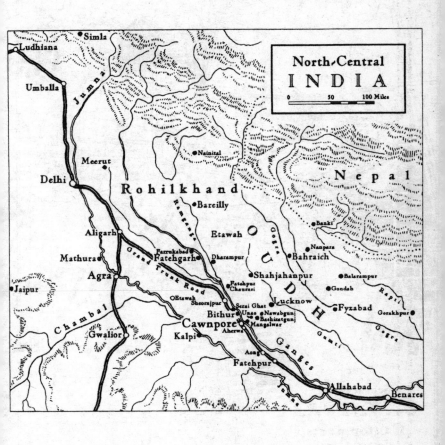

North-Central INDIA

0   50   100 Miles

Simla
Ludhiana
Umballa
Jumna
Meerut
Delhi
Nainital
Rohilkhand
Bareilly
Aligarh
Etawah
Mathura
Farrukabad
Fatehgarh
Dharampur
Ramganga
Agra
Grand Trunk Road
Jaipur
Shahjahanpur
OEtawah
Fatehpur
Chaurasi
Sheorajpur
Serai Ghat
Lucknow
Chambal
Bithur
Unao
Nawabgunj
Bachizatgunj
Gwalior
Cawnpore
Aherwa
Mangalwar
Kalpi
Anao
Fatehpur
Ganges
Gumti
Jumna
Allahabad
Benares
Nepal
Banki
Nanpara
Bahraich
Balarampur
Gondah
Rapti
Fyzabad
Gorakhpur
Gogra
OUDH

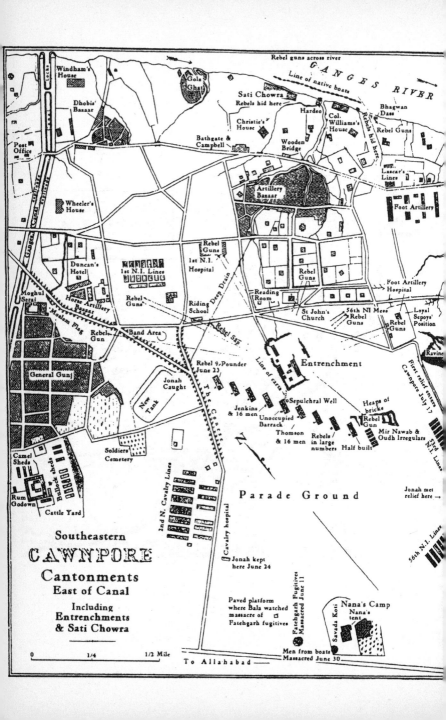

Rebel guns across river

GANGES RIVER

Line of native boats

Windham's House

Gola Ghat

Sati Chowra
Rebels hid here

Hardeo

Bhagwan Dass

Dhobi' Bazaar

Christie's House

Col. Williams's House

Rebel Guns

Foot Office

Bathgate & Campbell

Wooden Bridge

Rebels hid here

Lascar's Lines

Wheeler's House

Artillery Bazaar

Foot Artillery

Rebel Guns

Duncan's Hotel

1st N.I. Lines

1st N.I. Hospital

Rebel Guns

1st N.I. Hospital

Deep Drain

Rebel Guns

Foot Artillery Hospital

Moghul Serai

Horse Artillery Bazaar

Moslem Flag

Riding School

Reading Room

St John's Church

56th NI Mess

Loyal Sepoys' Position

Rebel Guns

Rebel Gun

Band Area

Rebel S&

Rebel Guns

Ravine

General Gun

New Tank

Jonah Caught

Rebel 9-Pounder June 23

Line of carts

Entrenchment

First rebel mine Cawnpore July 17

The Canal

Jenkins & 16 men

Sepulchral Well

Unoccupied Barrack

Thomson & 16 men

Rebels in large numbers

Heaps of bricks

Rebel Gun

Mir Nawab & Oudh Irregulars

Half built

42nd N.I. Lines

Soldiers Cemetery

Camel Sheds

Bullock sheds

Rum Godown

Cattle Yard

2nd N. Cavalry Lines

Cavalry hospital

Parade Ground

Jonah met relief here →

56th N.I. Lines

Jonah kept here June 24

Southeastern

CAWNPORE

Cantonments
East of Canal

Including
Entrenchments
& Sati Chowra

Paved platform where Bala watched massacre of Fatehgarh fugitives

Fatehgarh Fugitives Massacred June 11

Savada Koti

Nana's Camp

Nana's tent

0   1/4   1/2 Mile

To Allahabad

Men from boats Massacred June 30

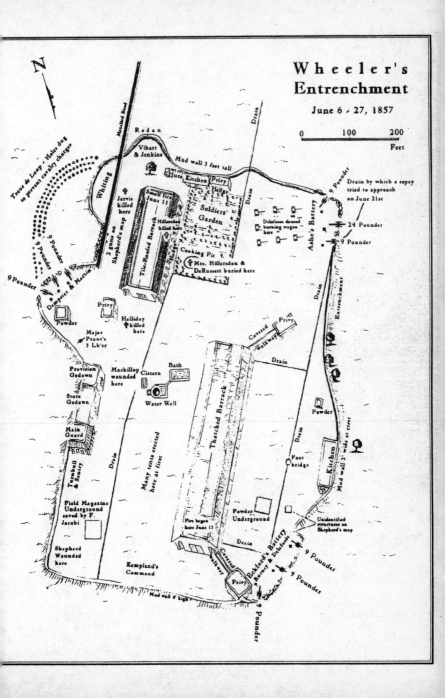

Wheeler's Entrenchment

June 6 - 27, 1857

0   100   200
Feet

N

Trou de Loup, Holes dug to prevent cavalry charges

Redan

Vibart & Jenkins

Whiting

Mud wall 3 feet tall

Huts Kitchen Privy
Hedge

Jervis killed here

Gun fired June 11

Soldiers' Garden

2 guns on Shepherd's map

Hillersdon killed here

9 Pounder

9 Pounder

Dalhouse dressed burning wagon here

Ashe's Battery

Drain

9 Pounder

Drain by which a sepoy tried to approach on June 21st

24 Pounder

9 Pounder

Cooking Pit
Mrs. Hillersdon & DeRussett buried here

9 Pounder

Dempster & Martin

Tile-Roofed Barrack

Privy

Powder

Halliday killed here

Major Prout's 3 Lb'er

Covered Walkway

Privy

Drain

Entrenchment

Provision Godown

Mackillop wounded here

Cistern

Bath

Store Godown

Water Well

Powder

Main Guard

Thatched Barrack

Turnbull & Beazly

Many tents erected here at first

Drain

Kitchen

Mud wall 2' wide at crest

Foot bridge

Field Magazine Underground saved by F. Jacobi

Powder Underground

Unidentified structures on Shepherd's map

Shepherd Wounded here

Fire began here June 13

Kempland's Command

Covered railway

Drain

9 Pounder

Privy

Eckford's Battery
Barney & Dehtrass

9 Pounder

Mud wall 6' high

9 Pounder

PART ONE

◆ ◆ ◆ ◆ ◆ ◆ ◆

HONOR AND FAME

Hugh Massy Wheeler: 1789–1806

At the throbbing heart of the rebellion that swept North India in the hot weather of 1857, sixty-eight-year-old Major General Sir Hugh Massy Wheeler sat at a low table in the middle of his room, writing amid the dust that sifted down from the shuddering ceiling. Beyond the walls of his barracks, over the booming of rebel cannon, the crash of round shot, the shrieking and bursting of mortar rounds, the native snipers' whining musketballs chipping at the shutters and window frames, the old general could hear a woman's hoarse cry, the sobbing of children, the imprecating groans of the wounded, a few officers barking commands. In one corner of his room sat his two unmarried daughters and Lady Frances, his Eurasian wife. In an opposite corner the blackening blood and brains of Wheeler's favorite son Godfrey drew flies to the stucco wall where, only the day before, a nine-pound cannonball had bounded into the room and torn his head from his shoulders.

Blowing the dust from his paper, Wheeler addressed a letter to his old friend Henry Lawrence at Lucknow, sixty miles to the northeast, where another European garrison was bracing for a siege. Shut off from each other by a rebel cordon, neither man knew for certain of the other's peril. Wheeler wrote to his friend bleakly, imploringly, on a scrap of tissue small enough to hide in the folds of the turban of a native spy or the crack in a bamboo walking stick.

On June 3, three weeks earlier, all four of Wheeler's native regiments had mutinied and marched for Delhi, only to be met by a local noble named Nana Sahib who had persuaded them to turn around and lay siege to Wheeler's garrison of over a thousand souls. The Entrenchment Wheeler had prepared "protected the men wonderfully," the old General wrote, and the barracks had stood up to the enemy's barrage "in a way never expected." But since then "we have had a bombardment in this miserable position three or four times daily" by rebel batteries that included two twenty-four-pounders

3

and three mortars against which his eight remaining nine-pounders were almost useless.

"All our carriages more or less disabled, ammunition short, British spirit alone remains," Wheeler reported, "but it cannot last for ever." Most of his senior officers had been killed or incapacitated by sniper fire, grapeshot, "the dreadful heat, fatigue or disease." Hundreds had died, many of them women and children, and there was still no sign of the eight hundred British troops Governor-General Lord Canning had promised him. His garrison had been "cruelly deserted and left to our fate. . . . We have all lost everything belonging to us, and have not even a change of linen. Surely we are not to die like rats in a cage. . . . The ladies, women and children have not a safe hole to lie down in and they all sleep in the trenches for safety and coolness. The barracks are perforated in every direction, and cannot long give even the miserable shelter which they now do."

Wheeler and Lawrence—especially the humane and judicious Lawrence—had seen all this coming, had known where their coun-trymen's ignorance and bigotry, arrogant reforms, and precipitous annexations had been leading these past twenty years. Still it hardly seemed possible that a gallant old sepoy officer like Major General Sir Hugh Massy Wheeler, Knight Commander of the Bath, should die at the hands of a rabble. Had not his sepoys proudly nicknamed him *Hamlah* ("Attack")? Was he not the same old warrior who had re-duced fortresses in Afghanistan, secured the Jullunder Doab in the Punjab, led ten thousand of the very same Sikhs he had just defeated up into the Himalayas to secure Kashmir?

Back in Calcutta, Lady Charlotte Canning, wife of the Governor-General, confided to her diary that though Cawnpore was "the most anxious position, . . . everyone speaks of Sir Hugh Wheeler and his brave spirit. There is not a better soldier," she assured posterity, "& all say, if any one *can* hold it, he will."[1]

✦   ✦   ✦

During his fifty-four years in the Bengal Army, Wheeler had been no stranger to Cawnpore. No Company officer could be, for it was the bulwark of North Indian defense and boasted the second largest Eu-ropean community on the entire subcontinent. Dusty and hot and poorly drained, Cawnpore had been a barbarous place.[2] "The coun-try is frightful," wrote one early visitor, "and the dust indescribable."[3] Wolves roamed the cantonments at night, crime was rampant, and on some bungalows "the doors, destitute of locks or handles," would not shut.[4]

Cawnpore had grown from a small village Indians called "Kanpur," a mere stopover between Bithur and Jajmau—ancient towns that were themselves no longer of much consequence. Though "Cawnpaw" and even "Cawnpwah" better represent how the British overconfidently pronounced it, they nonetheless spelled it "Cawnpore." They mangled the pronunciation and consequently the spelling of a great many places in what would become their Indian Empire, most notably substituting "Benares" for Varanasi, the holiest of Hindu cities. But perhaps in the case of Cawnpore it was right that the spelling should reflect the drawling British rendition of the Indian name, for the station was a British invention.

The East India Company first took notice of Cawnpore in 1770, when the semiautonomous Moghul governor of the neighboring province of Oudh asked for a Company force to protect the ford to his capital at Lucknow.[5] The British remained to establish Cawnpore as a staging area for their remote campaigns and "a watch-tower to awe down the royal Lucknowite."[6] But it was a haphazard affair. None of the officers who first camped at Cawnpore could have guessed that ten months or years or decades later the Bengal Army would still be returning to this bleak, sun-baked, dust-choked vacancy. But after each outlandish expedition they returned to find more Company soldiers encamped in tents and huts in its vast military cantonment, more officers' bungalows sprouting up with their roofs of pyramidal thatch along the bluffs overlooking the river, more stores and workshops and regimental bazaars spreading out across the barren plain. Eventually it would spread seven miles along the Ganges, a far-flung settlement occasionally punctuated by wells, ravines and drainage ditches, and solitary groves of trees.

Wheeler had taken command of the Cawnpore Division only six months before the uprising. A year before that, on his return from home-leave in Ireland, he had mustered an expedition at Cawnpore to enforce the annexation of Oudh; but his association went all the way back to the beginning of his remarkable career when, as a diminutive, wiry sixteen-year-old, he was first assigned to a native regiment. His father had been a captain in the East India Company's service who had returned home a full-fledged nabob and won the hand of the daughter of an Irish peer.[7] Their son grew up among the headlong gentry of County Tipperary, where he excelled at fox hunting. Indeed, at a little over five feet tall, young Wheeler seemed suited more to the cavalry than the infantry, but even though he evidently did not meet the strict standards of the engineers or the artillery, he had been too promising for the cavalry, where it was once said of an officer that he was so stupid even his comrades noticed it.

In the early 1800s sending sons to India was still a risky business. The East India Company had been founded in 1599 to cultivate trade with Sumatra. Thirteen years later it had persuaded the Moghul Emperor Jahangir to allow it to open a warehouse at Surat, the chief port on India's western coast. As representatives of only one of a number of European nations vying for trading agreements with the Grand Moghul, the English at first trod lightly. But by the end of the next century they had outmaneuvered their less audacious Portuguese, Dutch, and French competitors, often by allying themselves with the Mahrattas, a confederacy of Hindu warriors who were busily dismantling the Moghul Empire.

But even after the pugnacious Robert Clive conquered Bengal at the Battle of Plassey in 1757, the East India Company's hold on the subcontinent remained uncertain and incomplete. Various semiautonomous Moghul governors still entertained dreams of empire; the Sikhs held firm in the Punjab; the Mahrattas held sway over vast tracts of central India; bandits, tribals, and opportunistic freelances rampaged along the shifting boundaries of a thousand different domains; while the French, the Russians, the Afghans, and even the Burmese remained poised for the British to stumble. Now it fell to daring and ambitious young men like Hugh Wheeler to draw it all together.

After two years of training, Wheeler booked passage on an India-bound sailing ship, furnishing his cramped little cabin with a sofa, mattress, and pillows, a washstand, a hanging lamp, a looking glass with sliding cover, a chest of drawers in two pieces, and a bucket and rope to draw salt water up through his porthole.[8] He was expected to spend another £150 on his kit, which included his uniforms and linens, around 120 shirts, camp linen and crockery, condiments, saddles, boots, medicaments, "fowling pieces, rifles, fishing-tackle, . . . and an outline map of the route."[9]

In 1805 the route from England to Bengal was down the west coast of Africa, around the Cape of Good Hope, up the Mozambique channel, across the capricious waters of the Indian Ocean, and up the eastern coast of India to Calcutta. After four to five months and 14,000 miles of equatorial heat and Antarctic squalls, of sultry calms and treacherous currents, of whales and waterspouts[10] and St. Elmo's fire,[11] Wheeler joined his fellow ensigns along the deck rail to glimpse above the dull blue of the ocean the low, simmering coastline of Hindustan. The Black Pagodas of Juggernaut protruded from the pale shore "like old Russian churches," as the ominous swelter of the Indian land mass cast its heat across the water.

Finally they reached the vast, tattered mouth of the Hooghly River and gazed at fields so low-lying they put some passengers in mind of a kind of unmitigated Holland, despite the enormous bats that took papery wing in the sultry gloaming. The sounds from the shore were like music after months of the "monotonous splashing of water upon the ship's sides. . . . Even the howlings of jackals along the jungly banks of the Hooghly are music to a weary voyager," so much so that after many years in India "pleasant emotions" would still be "awakened by the hideous cries of these sneaking, detestable scavengers on their nightly rounds."[12]

From the lush villages at the Hooghly's mouth passengers rode boats upriver toward the cluttered harbor of Calcutta itself. Bamboo coastal huts gave way to dingy flat-roofed houses with narrow casement windows that seemed to follow the foreigners' progress balefully up the stream. "On either side jungle," an officer remembered of his first sail up the Hooghly, "cultivated plots of ground, palms, bamboos, buffaloes and cattle. . . . In slimy ooze gigantic garvials [long-nosed alligators]; in the river dead bodies of animals and human beings, vultures and crows perched upon and tearing their decomposing flesh."[13]

Finally Wheeler passed "the large handsome edifices of Garden Reach," the regal suburban compounds and Grecian verandahs of Calcutta's nabobs, and finally Calcutta itself: the City of Palaces, capital of the East India Company's ever-expanding domain. As soon as young Wheeler stepped down the gangplank, scores of native men surrounded him, tugging at his baggage, flourishing dubious letters of recommendation, and pledging their undying devotion in a bewildering tumult of obsequious broken English.[14]

Flush for the first time, many young men lavished their parents' savings or their shipboard winnings on fine horses, buggies, and other extravagances. It was the fortunate ensign who lived to enjoy them. If any of the myriad Indian hazards were to take a man, it was more than likely soon after he set foot on Indian soil. Some men were carried off the ship so weakened by vertigo, scurvy, sunstroke, and rum that the first whiff of Indian dust or sip of Indian water was enough to finish them.[15] Other newcomers managed to stagger up the country only to die miserably alone of cholera, dysentery, smallpox, malaria, or some virulent but nameless fever in the squalid gloom of travelers' bungalows, without family, friends, doctors, or clergymen—only curious villagers and palanquin bearers craning about the doorway to view the dying sahib, listen to his ravings and appraise his effects. The roads up the country were punctuated by the hasty graves of numberless young men.[16]

All this mortality made men callous; they might grieve an hour or so for some fallen comrade, but soon bid raucously and drunkenly on his effects. Families in England might never learn what exactly befell their sons; if they did it was often from some barnacled old Company hand. When a relative asked after a runaway named Nigel Gresley Fowler, a clerk reported back that young Nigel was "well meaning but uncouth but matters little since he has recently died."[17]

Ensign Hugh Massy Wheeler was assigned to the 2nd battalion of the 24th Bengal Native Infantry, a regiment of Oudh men that had recently been formed in the burgeoning Company camp at Cawnpore. Fresh from a triumphant campaign against Holkar, one of the most formidable and audacious of the Mahratta chieftans, the 2-24th was about to embark on a campaign to tame his rival, Scindia of Gwalior.[18] Wheeler and his chums voyaged up the Ganges in a special fleet of spoon-shaped hulks that were famous for "drinking and debauchery of every kind, varied by an occasional duel, or the homicide of some unfortunate Indian," with the result that villagers along the river fled at its approach.[19] In early 1806, after weeks of toiling upstream, Wheeler's boat drew up to the *ghats* of Cawnpore where, half a century later, he would meet his fate.

Here Wheeler first became acquainted with the sepoys or native infantry he would command for the rest of his life. They were in many ways superior to their British counterparts, who were often soldiers by default: detrimentals unsuitable for any other line of work. Sepoys tended to be taller and stronger, the cream of a bountiful crop of men from what the British called the "martial races": fierce Sikhs, towering Pathans, and rangy Rajputs who hungered for the Company's salt.[20]

The kind of Oudh men who lined the ranks of the 2-24th were especially impressive. "These men have a proud step, a stern eye, and a rough loud voice," observed one traveler, "such as might be expected from people living almost always in the open air, and in a country where, till its acquisition by the English, no man was sure that he might not at any moment be compelled to fight for his life or his property."[21]

Strangely enough, many of the men who joined the Company's Bengal Army were Brahmins from Oudh. No one has explained precisely why Oudh Brahmins were so eager to join the Bengal Army; the Brahmins of the south were too fastidious to join the Madras Army. Very few Brahmins ate meat or killed animals, and the time they spent in washing and praying and preparing their food "would break the heart of any sergeant-major."[22] But they made magnificent, if irascible, soldiers; a sepoy with only "a brass pot to draw water from the wells as he passes, . . . will be perfectly cheerful and comfortable," wrote one officer, "and will march at the rate of 30 miles a day."[23] During one nine-year stretch of the native army's history, writes Philip Mason, "in a force of about 55,000 soldiers, 35 cases were taken as serious enough for court-martial, and none of them involved drunkenness, malingering, or going over to the enemy. Perhaps no other army in history was as well behaved.[24]

A Company officer's pride in his men translated, of course, into a pride in himself. Though even the most inexperienced king's officer of ostensibly equal rank outranked his Indian Army counterpart by one grade—a king's captain, for instance, was equal in rank to a Company lieutenant-colonel—every officer of native troops believed, with some justification, that he was the better campaigner and his Indian soldiers the superior troops.[25] "Not one man in ten is fit for the command of a European regiment," one of them trumpeted, "but not one European in fifty is fit for the command of a Native regiment."[26]

HAMLAH
Wheeler: 1806–1853

From the very start, young Wheeler demonstrated that combination of discipline and empathy, warmth and dash that would eventually make him one of the most distinguished of the Company's sepoy officers. But Wheeler's career began, as it would end,

Cawnpore from the Ganges

amid the rumblings of mutiny. Though he would later be characterized as an officer of the "old school," by 1806 the affection and understanding between officer and sepoy that had characterized the
Company's first campaigns had begun to erode.

"Your duty as a soldier to the Honourable East India Company
which you serve," a guidebook advised young officers, "is to concili-
ate the native soldiery, pay attention to their prejudices, and respect
their forms of worship, at least as far as not ridiculing or making
yourself obnoxious to them by interference."[27] But at Cawnpore and
indeed in most of the Bengal Presidency, such advice was increasingly ignored. European officers no longer slept in the lines among
their Indian troops but at some distance, in bungalows, from which
they rarely stirred in the hot season except to go through the parade-
ground motions.[28]

Cawnpore was not so much a man's as a boy's world. The average
regimental officer was "a youngster who makes curry, drinks champagne and avoids the sun." Leaving their Indian troops to the care of

Indian officers and British sergeants, European officers became increasingly remote and disdainful.[29] "Anglo-Indian society was not given to indulgent views," wrote a civilian. "Sent into exile at an early age, before the traditions of the nursery had been modified by the better influences of education or by intercourse with cultured minds, the 'cadets' and 'writers' carried the moods of schoolboys into the work of men."[30]

There had been minor mutinies all through the history of the Indian Army, but the most dramatic occurred in the Madras Presidency the very same year Wheeler arrived in India, when sepoys defied a moronic order requiring them to remove their caste marks and jewelry and replace their turbans with European-style round hats incorporating animal skins and feathers that were anathema to their Hindu faith.[31] The sepoys rose up and shot down 129 Europeans and loyal sepoys at their fort at Vellore.[32] Though the British took back the fort, killing 350 mutineers (including many who had thrown down their arms) and reserving nineteen more for execution, the mutiny sent a shock wave through all three Presidencies, and ever afterward British officers were urged to keep an eye out for signs of unrest. Not that officers ever quite knew what to do if they did detect disaffection, for they were grotesquely outnumbered by their native troops.

Young Hugh Wheeler found himself soldiering in a medieval world of kings and castles. But it was no fantasy; the dangers were real. Wheeler saw his first action in 1806 against a Rana who clung so stubbornly to his mud-walled citadel that before his spiked gates were breached his knights and archers and matchlockmen had killed five of Wheeler's fellow officers and about a hundred of their men. Three years later Wheeler took part in the siege of a Jat fortress whose recalcitrant chief had raided a nearby British settlement. In these "mud wars" that filled the gaps between major campaigns, Wheeler's native troops repeatedly proved themselves courageous, disciplined, and almost religiously devoted to their regimental colors.

The British lumbered from siege to siege in vast caravans. In the Bengal Army each officer had as many as fifty people working for him: tent-raisers, bullock drivers, and coolies were added to the usual complement of household servants, and each sepoy had a few servants of his own, so that a single regiment might trail five thousand camp followers and their families, plus hundreds of elephants, camels, bullocks, horses, and goats. Such caravans could cut a ruinous swath, luring and in some cases forcing local farmers to abandon their fields and families to act as drivers and bearers. In fact, Sir Charles Napier would assert, "there is not a regiment here that moves whose march is not one of horrible oppression.

> We all pay respect to a cow in presence of a Hindoo—a respect he laughs at, for he knows we do not feel it. But at the same moment we take away his oxen and *himself* from the plough by force; we send him a thousand miles march with a regiment; he loses his harvest, his ground remains untilled, his family perish, his oxen, overloaded and overdriven by the soldiers, drop on the road, he is made to drive another, whose owner has fled in desperation, and after six or eighteen months—I knew one case of years even—he returns a ruined man to his once happy home.[33]

Landholders along the line of a march were required to provide some disposables for free—grass, firewood, and "earthen pots of the cheap and coarse kind used once for cooking a dinner and afterwards broken by all Hindoos of a respectable caste."[34] They were supposed to receive a tax abatement for such supplies, nevertheless they pressed "hard on the poor ryots."

Tenant farmers were not the only living beings to suffer when a regiment tramped through, for a march was a capital opportunity for sport. Officers crept off to shoot the cheetal, nilgai, and black buck peaceably grazing in the farmers' fields, rode elephants after tiger, fired volleys at every variety of fowl, galloped in pursuit of boar in the marshy stands of grass. Indeed, an expedition's route and pace was sometimes dictated entirely by a commander's shooting prospects.[35]

✦ ✦ ✦

Back at his station, Wheeler's first priority was to learn how to behave like a gentleman. "It is a serious business," observed a French diplomat named Fontanier, "the study of the thousand and one forms by which the regular gentleman shows himself; [how] he cuts up his meat, invites another to take wine, helps himself to salt. . . . The way to word a letter, fold it, seal it, despatch it, are the object of grave deliberations."[36] Much of this Wheeler had probably picked up at his family's estate at Ballywire. But to the usual niceties were added the peculiar cantonment protocols of calling hours, of precedence at mess, of managing servants and smoking water pipes and mastering the enormous lexicon of Anglo-Indian slang.

Anglo-Indian courtship was also complicated, and if a Company officer was not notable for his politesse around English ladies, it was because there were so few. The Company's India began as a male domain and had struggled to remain that way; during its first fifty years of rule the Company prohibited English maidens—with very few exceptions—from emigrating to India, and hoped its officers would seek out Indian brides and mistresses.[37] In fact, in its early days John Company actually provided European soldiers with a subsidy to marry Indian women, and encouraged officers in the higher echelons to marry native noblewomen.[38] After all, it was easier and certainly cheaper to marry men off to Indian women than to import a lot of frail, pious, and homesick English ladies for whom, if worse came to worse, the Company would be ultimately held responsible.

But Indian brides were never as numerous in Company stations as Indian mistresses. Officers' courtesans were called *bibis* in the Bengal Presidency, *bubus* in Bombay, and for decades they were well regarded.[39] It was argued that bibis not only steadied men but rooted the Company in the Indian soil and served as a hedge against unfortunate unions with Portuguese Roman Catholics. Though by the early 1800s actual marriages with Indian women were no longer encouraged, Anglo-Indians still believed that the Company's empathetic ties to its subjects were reinforced by its officers' bibis, who, reclining on their perfumed pillows, taught them the languages and customs of the country amid their giggles and sighs.[40]

But most bibis were hard-bitten, and no wonder. They tended to live in separate quarters called *bibighars*, and were escorted after nightfall into the house to wait in bed for their besotted sahibs to stagger home from their mutton clubs and regimental messes.[41] Though there were certainly exceptions—and even some of the most respectable marital arrangements in India were governed chiefly by caste and economics—Indian women had to be sold, coerced, or bribed into a sahib's service.[42]

The inevitable consequence of these arrangements, of course, was mixed-race children, and no one seemed to know what to do with them. No one even knew quite what to call them. In the early days of European settlement in India, the French and the Portuguese had mixed even more freely with Indian women than their British successors. So Eurasians had been dubbed everything from creoles, mustees, and Portuguese, to Anglo-Asiatics, East-Indians, Indo-Britons, half-castes, tchi-tchi, eight-annas, four-annas, and worse.[43]

Even after it fell out of fashion for officers to marry Indian women or employ them as mistresses, British soldiers continued to marry Eurasian girls or frequent Indian and Eurasian prostitutes.[44] As the number of English women in India increased, the British came to regard Eurasians as shameful vestiges of a vanishing way of life. Eurasians "with the slightest taint of half-caste are ignored completely," wrote a visitor, "and in India the eye gets educated to detect the least trace with a celerity that is astonishing."[45]

Eurasian women were believed to be promiscuous, uncultivated and a little ludicrous with their English lady-like affectations.[46] But one such woman would marry two Company officers, lose them both to the two worst calamities in the Company's history, and die a bona fide Lady. Her name was Frances Marsden, and she was the daughter of a newly retired Irish major and his Indian—probably Moslem—bibi.[47] Frances had been cut adrift by her home-bound father at the age of fourteen: the very age at which the abandoned Eurasian daughters of British officers lost their government stipends. From then on their only alternatives were marriage, prostitution, or starvation.

Most of these girls were described as having neither "the bodily formation nor the mental development" to fit them "for the functions, duties, and responsibilities they are called on to perform."[48] Be that as it may, at her wedding at Cawnpore in 1810, Frances was about fifteen years old, exactly seven months pregnant, and already the mother of another man's child.[49] Her groom was a contemporary of Wheeler's named Thomas Oliver, himself of mixed descent. Brusque and cantankerous, Oliver had arrived in India a year before Wheeler and for many of the next thirty-eight years Oliver's life would parallel Wheeler's. Whether young Frances had been a victim of rape or had ensnared a husband by the only means at her disposal, there appears to have been little love lost between her and her twenty-six-year-old bridegroom and, perhaps to escape an unhappy marriage, in 1813 Oliver volunteered for service in Java.[50]

Here the lives of Frances and Oliver and young Lieutenant Wheeler fatally intersected. Within months of Oliver's departure, Frances was pregnant again, but this time apparently by Lieutenant Hugh Massy Wheeler. Wheeler was twenty-four by now, Frances about eighteen, and whether young Hugh started out simply as a "peacocking" (cuckolding) opportunist or had intended merely to extend his sympathies to a shamefully neglected young woman, he became so devoted to Frances, and she to him, that they would remain together for the rest of their lives.

In 1818, Oliver and Wheeler served together amicably in Ceylon, where their little force was honored and rewarded for good conduct. Two years later, Wheeler and Oliver were back in India again and stationed, off and on, at Cawnpore. In 1823 Oliver sired a second son whose mother's name was not recorded.[51] It is unlikely she was Frances,[52] for in the meantime she and Wheeler continued to live together and would eventually produce no less than eight more children out of wedlock: six boys and two girls, for a total of nine offspring illegitimately conceived over a period of twenty-six years.[53] Divorcing Oliver appears to have been out of the question; perhaps Oliver would not agree to it. Wheeler resolved simply to brave the disfavor of his fellow officers and their appalled wives and try to lead the rest of his life as respectably as possible.

But the scandal was tremendous, and as an adulteress and a Eurasian, Frances Marsden Oliver was not a welcome guest at cantonment functions. She kept so much to herself that many took it for granted that she must be Indian. There were probably other indications: she may have inherited her mother's dark complexion and, like Wheeler, sometimes wore Indian dress. The peculiar protocols of cantonment life may also have deemed it more acceptable for Frances to live like a bibi or native mistress in separate quarters behind the house than to pass herself off as a lady. But there is no overestimating the ignorance of Wheeler's contemporaries, nor their iron-clad sense of propriety, both of which would have conspired to prevent them from ever discovering the complicated truth about Wheeler's lady. For whatever reason, the rumor that Frances Marsden Oliver was Indian hardened into accepted fact, and has endured up to the present day as an explanation of why, in May 1857, Major General Sir Hugh Massy Wheeler, commander of the garrison at Cawnpore, placed his trust in the likes of Nana Sahib.

Despite his unusual domestic arrangements, the peppery little warrior's star continued to rise. By the age of thirty Wheeler was a captain, by forty he was a major, and six years later he was lieutenant colonel of the 48th Native Infantry. It seemed that nothing could impede his fortune, nor the Company's for that matter. By 1826, Calcutta was positively smug with triumph.[54] Having defeated the Burmese in 1825 and the Jats at Bhurtpore the following January, the Company was enjoying unprecedented security and unrivaled prestige. The governor-general was the sickly Lord Amherst, whose early diplomatic career had been notable mainly for his refusal to kow-tow before the Chinese Emperor, for which he had been denied a royal audience. But now Amherst was capping his career with a most gratifying tour of the upper provinces on which Eastern nobles kow-towed before him by the score, showering him with gifts at Cawnpore camp.

Relations with the Sikh Maharaja Ranjit Singh of the Punjab were warily cordial, and the British were beginning to consolidate the three presidencies into which the Company had divided the subcontinent. Though the King of Delhi was still exalted by his Indian subjects—especially the Sunni Moslems, who saw him as a kind of pontiff—politically he was nothing more than a figurehead. Tippu Sultan of Mysore was long dead; Madras was entirely secure. The formidable Mahratta Daulat Rao Scindia and the vanquished Vizier of Oudh were both mere months away from their deaths; and though the deposed regent of the Mahrattas was not above trying "to keep alive in his former territories an interest in his fate," the Peshwa was now a pampered prisoner at Bithur.[55]

And so in its Bombay, Madras, and Bengal Presidencies the Company's agenda had turned from conquest to governance: the collection of revenues, the regulation of commerce, the dispensing of justice, the building of roads, and the digging of canals. The swashbuckling merchant adventurers who had conquered Hindustan were passing away, and a new breed was taking their place: pious, prudent, animated by Christian duty and the prospect of a pension.

But for all their complacency, the British were always anxiously scanning the western horizon for Russians and Persians. In the late 1830s the newly arrived Governor-General Lord Auckland thought he detected agents of the Czar and the Shah plotting with Dost Mahomed, the Amir of Afghanistan, and decided to replace him with his elderly predecessor Shah Shuja by means of a lumbering and overconfident thirty-five-mile caravan grandly dubbed the Army of the Indus. "No red-blooded officer wanted to miss the action," and Lieutenant-Colonel Wheeler and his 48th N.I. were proud to pass in review with the Army of the Indus before old Ranjit Singh himself and march off to glory in the mountainous wastes west of the Indus River. But five months later they were still bribing their way through countless fiefdoms toward Kabul, parched, half starved, their numbers depleted by disease and cold, snipers and precipitous climbs, as plump jackals fed on the thousands of camels and camp followers who dropped by the wayside.[56] On a stormy night in July 1839, about eighty miles shy of Kabul, Wheeler and the 48th N.I. took part in the first significant engagement of the campaign—the storming of the mountain fortress of Ghazni.[57] In August he rode into Kabul itself, expecting jubilant throngs to welcome Shah Shuja, only to find a sullen and ungrateful citizenry scowling from their doorways. Nevertheless the mission seemed accomplished, and the Army of the Indus was dispersed. A portion remained in an improvised cantonment on a plain outside Kabul, while other regiments were sent to various Afghani outposts. Wheeler was posted to Jalalabad, from which he made such successful forays against the chiefs of the Waziri Valley that he was made a Companion of the Bath, permitted to accept the Order of the Durani Empire from Shah Shuja, and selected to escort Dost Mahomed, the captured amir, back to India.

Who should he meet on the road home but Lieutenant Colonel Thomas Oliver and his sepoys as they marched into Afghanistan to reinforce the garrison at Kabul. One imagines the fathers of Frances Marsden's children saluting each other as they marched off to their tragic destinies: one imminent, the other still seventeen years away. It is possible that Oliver already knew that he would never return to Frances, or to Cawnpore, for after a year of the Afghan campaign he appears to have given up all hope. One of the few survivors of the siege of Kabul remembered Oliver as immensely obese and one of the "great croakers [complainers]" of the garrison.[58] When some of his men managed to forage some grain for the starving garrison, Oliver replied that "it was needless, for they would never live to eat it."

He was right, of course. There is no room here to account for the awful completeness of the disaster that would follow: the senile dithering of General William Elphinstone, the assassination of his hapless politicals, the siege of the cantonment, the uprising that grew and grew until the starving garrison was forced to flee in the middle of winter, the stragglers picked off by snipers, the wounded slaughtered by Afghani maurauders, the soldiers and camp followers frozen to death in the bloody snow, the surviving ladies given over as prisoners, until all that was left was a lone doctor on a wounded pony staggering into Jalalabad.[59]

At least Lieutenant Colonel Thomas Samuel Oliver was spared the final horrors of Auckland's misadventure. Declaring that in the event of a retreat his bulk would doom him anyway, on November 23, 1841, Oliver volunteered to lead his men against the Afghani snipers perched on the frozen heights overlooking the besieged cantonment. His less encumbered sepoys refused to follow him.

"Although my men desert me," Oliver was heard to cry, heaving himself up the gravel slope, "I myself will do my duty!"

Seconds later, a sniper's ball came buzzing through his brain.

Oliver's remains were not retrieved until the following morning, when his comrades found that after chopping off his head the Afghanis had been unable to wrench his wedding band off his chubby finger and so cut his hand off as well and carried it away.[60]

✦   ✦   ✦

News of the fall of Kabul was slow to reach India, and India was slow to believe it. It was the worst catastrophe in the Company's history, and would not be surpassed until 1857.[61] The debacle put the lie to British invincibility, dismaying the Company's allies and emboldening its foes, especially the restive Sikhs, many of whose brethren had died in the debacle.[62]

But at least the retreat from Kabul had this one happy result: three months after her husband's death, Frances Marsden Oliver married Hugh Massy Wheeler at Agra, and rebaptized three of their youngest children. The fertile Frances was about forty-seven by now, and over six months pregnant as she swayed down the aisle. By the age of fifty-three Lieutenant Colonel Wheeler had won a reputation as a cool and courageous officer: too precipitous, perhaps, for the kind of civil appointments the Lawrences obtained, but nevertheless a first-rate military man.[63]

It was in the Sikh Wars that Wheeler rose to prominence. Shortly after reviewing the doomed army of the Indus, Ranjit Singh, the monocular, inebriate, and canny Lion of the Punjab, had passed away. His barons had never appreciated the genius of his ambiguous alliance with the British, whom they darkly (and correctly) suspected of harboring designs on the Punjab. Like so many great men's sons, Ranjit Singh's heir proved a weakling, and his ferocious Sirdars scrambled to fill the vacuum. In the ensuing chaos, the European-trained Khalsa Army took charge and eventually championed the dynastic claim of a little boy named Dhuleep Singh. Alarmed, the British began to reinforce their adjacent garrisons south of the Sutlej River, and the Khalsa, in turn, concentrated their soldiers along the opposite bank. Both sides saw war as inevitable, and on December 12, 1845, the Khalsa crossed the Sutlej.[64]

A day later Lieutenant Colonel Hugh Wheeler was appointed brigadier of five thousand men and twelve six-pounder guns, and on December 18, at a little village called Mudki, he helped lead a British

The Battle of Mudki

force of ten thousand against a Sikh army twice its size. He must have plunged into the thick of it, for a Sikh sabre cut through the small bones and tendons in the back of his left hand, nearly severing his thumb and leaving his hand crippled for the rest of his life.[65] Though still suffering from his wound, the following January Wheeler "most gallantly" led a full-scale charge in the Battle of Aliwal in which "the 48th Native Infantry," writes one military historian, "fully justified Wheeler's faith in it."[66] Ever afterward his sepoys would fondly refer to him as *Hamlah*, or "attack."[67]

The Sikhs abandoned all but one of their outposts south of the Sutlej, and, for his contribution to the Company's victory, Wheeler was awarded a medal with two clasps, and in recognition of his wounds and his "soldier-like and judicious arrangements" the governor-general named him Aide-de-Camp to the Queen.[68] There were still so many Sikh soldiers in the Punjab that in order to avoid stirring them up the British decided not to annex the Punjab but to collect reparations and try to establish with young Dhuleep Singh a version of their old arrangement with Ranjit Singh.[69] The Sikh Durbar was unable to come up with the reparations money, and instead ceded Kashmir to the British.[70] When the old Moslem Governor of Kashmir refused to hand over his province, Wheeler and Henry Lawrence set off on an extraordinary expedition to enforce the arrangement, commanding ten thousand of the very warriors they had fought just months before.[71] In the end the governor surrendered the vale without a shot being fired, and for helping Lawrence work such magic, Wheeler was appointed Brigadier General in command of the field force on the newly annexed Jullunder Doab, which the commander-in-chief, Sir Charles Napier, regarded as one of the most important positions in India.

Wheeler had evolved into one of the most highly respected sepoy officers in the Indian Army, worshipped by sepoy and European officer alike. Though he was "so very small," he seemed to "swell visibly" when angered, and one glare from his "gory eyes" reduced more than one subordinate to jelly. Nevertheless his junior officers learned to watch for the "playful twinkle" in his "dexter orb," that betrayed his fundamental empathy and good humor.[72]

Governor-General Lord Dalhousie's confidence in Wheeler was emphatic—now that "Brigadier Wheeler is back to his district," he wrote, he did not "much care" if the Sikhs attacked. A year later Dalhousie followed Wheeler's advice to distribute large concentrated forces of British troops throughout the Punjab.[73] Thus Wheeler set the stage for his own doom, for these large deployments in the Punjab would drain Cawnpore and the Doab of its British soldiers, leaving it all but defenseless nine years later when the native soldiers mutinied.

Despite these concentrations, the Punjab was soon in flames again, and in the Second Sikh War Wheeler found himself excluded from the main field of operations. Though he saw action against large bodies of desperate Sikhs, Wheeler was entirely neglected in dispatches and had to remind his departing commander of his services.[74] In 1850, the Company belatedly recognized Wheeler's contributions in the Punjab, but the little general agreed to attend his investiture as Knight Commander of the Bath only on condition that it be private—"so strong is my repugnance to any public display concerning myself"—and that he not be required to speak. "I think if allowed the chance," he told Dalhousie, "I would sooner lead a charge than have to stand up, and attempt a speech in a public company. I have ever felt it a most distressing, and painful duty, even at a Mess Table, where my Health has been proposed."[75]

With the dubbing of her gallant little husband, the fecund Frances Marsden, teenaged mistress and disgraced Eurasian widow of

Thomas Oliver, became Lady Frances Marsden Wheeler. Insulated by her title from her in-laws' contempt, in 1853 she set off for a home leave with Sir Hugh and three of her children to the family's estate at Balliwire in County Tipperary.[76]

THE CHARITY BOY
Azimullah Khan: 1837–1851

Droughts in the North-Western Provinces usually followed eleven-year cycles and lasted a year or two. One year without rain meant shortages, but usually not famine, especially after improved roads, and later railways, made the distribution of food from unaffected areas feasible. But two years of drought meant devastation for a people already perched so precariously that "a breath of misery blows them away in thousands."[77] Many Anglo-Indians believed that since famines were natural and cyclical they should simply be ridden out. But for even the most oblivious Company servant, famine was at least an unnerving reminder of the preposterous immensity of their charge.

The old Moslem province of Bundelkhand to the south of Cawnpore suffered a devastating famine in 1834 that sent starving victims up into the city begging for food.[78] A relief society and orphanage were established, assisted by government donations of £500 per month,[79] but the province was still reeling three years later when the autumn crop was declared a failure. With the exception of a single light shower, no rain had fallen in some areas since March, and by December "there was an entire absence of vegetation, even the trees being stripped of their leaves, and the cattle were dying by thousands." Abandoning their villages, a dusty procession of emaciated peasants staggered toward Cawnpore.[80]

Emily Eden, touring with her brother Lord Auckland,[81] saw corpses "lying together by fifties," and between Cawnpore and Fatehpur a member of her entourage counted one hundred dead bodies putrefying in a single field.[82] "You cannot conceive the horrible sights we see," Emily wrote, "particularly children; perfect skeletons in many cases, their bones through their skin. . . . The women look as if they had been buried, their *skulls* look so dreadful."[83]

"The relief society feeds about 1500 daily," wrote *The Englishman*, "but then owing to the villainy of those who have to serve out the food, the flour is so adulterated with lime and sand that heaps upon heaps have died from eating it."[84] The sluggish Ganges became littered with dead bodies, which the wolves at Cawnpore grew so accustomed to eating that they developed a taste for human flesh and became notorious for attacking and occasionally killing armed sentinels and dragging babies away from their sleeping mothers' arms.[85] Cawnpore's Civil Magistrate appealed to the government for help, but Calcutta agreed to pay only those sufferers who were fit to labor on such public works as the digging of a "famine tank."[86]

Forty years later a commission would estimate that eight hundred thousand people died in the famine of 1837–38, but conceded that even this monstrous figure was probably conservative.[87] Whatever social coherence Cawnpore ever had dissolved. Some of the starving tried to sell their children for a rupee each,[88] or took to committing small crimes in order to be fed in the jails;[89] it was even said that "large numbers who were too proud to beg poisoned themselves and their families sooner than endure the pain of starvation."[90]

✦ ✦ ✦

In late 1837, a starving boy named Azimullah Khan staggered with his mother to the door of Reverend Carshore, founder of the Cawnpore mission of the Society for the Propagation of the Gospel in Foreign Parts (S.P.G.)[91] Carshore was a dynamo.[92] By the time of the famine of 1837–38, he had gathered a congregation of over sixty regular worshippers and oversaw six schools. The famine had already swelled the mission's orphan flocks, but the missionaries of the Doab were discovering that they could not expect too much of the boys and girls who stumbled into their stations. "The bad health that results from their early privations," an American missionary complained, "and the helplessness of character that often is produced by such a secluded education, operate as a hindrance to their usefulness" in spreading the Gospel among their people.[93]

Azimullah Khan and his mother were only two out of the hundreds of dusty, skeletal souls who managed to evade the watchmen of the station and creep weakly into British compounds begging for food and shelter. But there must have been something intriguing about this particular boy. He was certainly a handsome child: slender,

fair, and well proportioned. His father had evidently been a table servant, possibly Pathan, but no one knows whether he worked for an
Indian or a European.[94] If the latter, his son may have already picked
up a little English by the time he reached Cawnpore; he might even
have flourished a letter of introduction at Carshore's door. Or it may
be that his mother, shrouded though she probably was, had somehow captured the headmaster's imagination. She was evidently a
fierce and dignified woman of haughty bearing: pitiable, perhaps, in
her reduced circumstances, but obviously seeking more for her small
son than a *chupatty* (wheat patty) and a bowl of lentils.

Reverend Carshore employed them in his household, providing
them with a safe haven from the nightmare that still obtained on the
plains beyond the compound, where, "under a perpetual cloud of
dust," people continued to die in the hundreds. That Azimullah's
mother accepted a position in Carshore's house as nursemaid was an
indication of either her desperation or her humble origins.[95] The
British believed that these nursemaids or *ayahs* were apt to be dull
because they were generally of low caste; high-born Moslem women
of the period generally would not accept employment that involved
interacting with male servants. But the boy, at least, proved quick-
witted, with a facility for languages so remarkable that three years
later, when a Reverend and Mrs. Perkins succeeded Carshore,
Perkins encouraged Azimullah to attend classes at the Free School,
where, while his mother cared for the Perkins's son, Azimullah became fluent in both English and French.[96]

Reverend Perkins was a ruthless evangelist and must have brought
all of his zeal to bear on Azimullah.[97] The British believed generally
that "the boy who had been instructed in the morality of the Gospel
and had tasted the literature of the West, grew up as a man into the
admirer and often the partisan of the English."[98] A fatherless boy as
gifted as Azimullah must have seemed ripe for conversion, but his
mother would not have it. Moslem women were especially fierce
guardians of the faith, and no matter how many hours Azimullah
spent each day in the company of Europeans and Christians, his
mother never allowed him to forget his faith.[99] During his years with
the zealous Reverend Perkins, Azimullah's gratitude toward his
British benefactors degenerated into what would later manifest itself
as a genocidal loathing.[100]

He was a pretty child, and there may have been among his men-
tors an Englishman who made some tortured libidinous overture. He
may have witnessed too many unfortunate interactions between

sahib and servant, officer and sepoy. He might have formed a friendship with Perkins's son, only to run up against the narrow limits of
such a friendship when they got older. Perhaps he blamed the British
for the famine that may have claimed his father.[101] Perhaps the horrors of the famine itself had left in his starved belly an appetite for
the apocalyptic. Or maybe the only way he could reconcile his
mother's ferocious Islamic faith with the generosity of his Christian
sponsors was to see their philanthropy as a sign of despicable weakness. But throughout Azimullah's unique odyssey through almost
every outpost of English life—from the evangelical world of the
Cawnpore Free School to the bedrooms of Belgravia and even, by
one account, to the sitting room of Queen Victoria herself—familiarity bred a lethal contempt.

✦   ✦   ✦

As Azimullah continued to attend classes at the Free School, he followed in his father's footsteps into domestic service as a *kitmutgar* or
table servant, for which he was paid three rupees a month.[102] At first
blush kitmutgar may seem a natural position for an English-speaking
Moslem; all the servants who had anything to do with food tended
to be Moslems.[103] But in those days Anglo-Indians preferred their
servants to be non–English speaking so that as the kitmutgar passed
the tea cakes or the *syce* (groom) loped beside the buggy or the
sweeper duck-walked along the verandah with his broom, sahibs
and memsahibs could freely converse about everything from station
scandals to "horrid natives."[104]

It was the kitmutgar's duty to serve food at the table, but the less
prosperous his sahib the wider the range of his responsibilites: bachelors of moderate means even employed them as footmen and
valets. Something like a butler, the kitmutgar was the drum major of
the household staff, the most elegant and conspicuous of the servants. Guests would bring their own kitmutgars to banquets "where,
standing behind each chair, dressed in liveries of Eastern fashion,
commonly pure white linen with white turbans, which amongst the
higher classes are sometimes decorated with a narrow silver band,
surmounted by the crest of the family," they presented "a very extraordinary and imposing array."

Most guests arriving for dinner at the home of Azimullah's employer probably would have been apprised of the young native's facility with languages. They would have congratulated his sahib for
encouraging a native boy to better himself and, for the first half-hour

or so, must have occasionally glanced over at this handsome young Moslem as he gracefully made his rounds with the tureen, and wondered what he could be thinking behind his enigmatic smile.

But later, perhaps after Azimullah had circulated with the trifle, they would have forgotten all about his comprehension of the English language. As they snapped their fingers at him for another round of claret, there would come that unbuttoned moment in the evening when, their gossip exhausted, they began to regale each other with their folk tales about the cook who served egg curry with the eggs in their shells, the laundryman who wrung out his master's clothes under the wheels of an ox cart, or the grass cutter who poisoned his masters' horses and sold their cadavers to the leather works.

While the guests climbed into their carriages in the cricket song of the Doab night, and Azimullah closed the doors behind them, he may have already understood that underlying all this bluster was the fundamental anxiety of dislocated rulers overwhelmingly outnumbered by their subjects, as well as a chronic exasperation with a native culture which, no matter how long the British lived in India or how strenuously they extended themselves, remained closed to them and strange. They were the ruling power—the agents of progress, Christian civilization and all that—and yet to the humblest tenant farmer the British were outcastes, the lowest of the low. The Moslems called them heathen idolators, Hindus recoiled from their touch, even untouchables declined their table scraps.[105]

✦ ✦ ✦

Azimullah was probably never comfortable in service. His fluency in English would have made him an object of suspicion among his employers and of envy among the rest of the staff. In any case, he did not remain a kitmutgar for long. By some accounts he spent a brief period teaching at the Free School, but it is certain that in the late 1840s Azimullah entered the service of Brigadier John Scott, C.B., a hero of the Sikh Wars who hired him on as a *moonshi:* a translator and language tutor.[106] The Scotts were a merry couple, and evidently took a great liking to Azimullah, even teaching him to play Mozart on their Broadwood piano and encouraging him to perform the parlor trick of reciting Shakespeare in Urdu.[107]

At Cawnpore moonshi to a brigadier was a plum job. A community of moonshis had sprung up to translate the correspondence and improve the Hindustani and Urdu of the local officers. Most of them were *babus*—Bengali scribes—who interposed themselves wherever

Anglo met Indian. It was a thankless position. The natives despised them; the British ridiculed them as fussy, pompous, and effeminate.[108] No character in station theatricals was as certain to bring the house down as the ink-stained little babu in his *dhoti*, English shoes, and generic bottle-bottom spectacles, toting his writing kit and his frayed umbrella and mangling the English language. "What the milk was to the coconut," Lord Macauley was supposed to have said, "what beauty was to the buffalo, and what scandal was to woman, Dr. Johnson's Dictionary was to the Bengali Baboo."[109]

The babus of Cawnpore must have resented Azimullah Khan's ascendancy, for the engagement of a fatherless houseboy as moonshi to the Brigadier was a definite slap in their faces. As moonshi, Azimullah would move in high circles, reacquainting himself with the adopted sons of the former Peshwa, for whom he had conducted classes at the S.P.G.'s academy at Bithur in his peculiar drawl, leading Nana Sahib and his brothers in their erratic English conjugations.[110] He accompanied Scott on his visits to Baji Rao's palace as a guide and translator and, as moonshi to the doting brigadier, may have giddily suggested to Nana Sahib that he was more than a moonshi, really: that he actually exercised some considerable influence with the British that might eventually be turned to Nana's advantage.

In any case, Scott was so pleased with Azimullah that in May 1850 he recommended him to his successor, Brigadier Ashburnham.[111] But here something seems to have gone wrong. According to Jonah Shepherd, Azimullah Khan "misbehaved himself and was turned out under an accusation of bribery and corruption." Perhaps he was, but in the Byzantium of Cawnpore, it may have been more complicated. Perhaps the babus poisoned the water for him, or Ashburnham glimpsed the contempt lurking under the young Moslem's courtly manners, or got a whiff of his insinuations at Bithur. Perhaps Azimullah's sheer presumption, his brilliance at the billiards table, his insistence upon being treated as a native of consequence, perhaps even some audacious flirtation with a young lady of the station incurred the wrath of his new employer.

Whatever Azimullah's sins of greed or pride, his dismissal would have been the end of a lesser man, the final comeuppance for rising too far too fast, for never knowing his place. But Azimullah Khan had taken care to cushion his fall, and on the death of the Peshwa in 1851 he landed comfortably in the upholstered court of Nana Sahib, heir to the ghostly throne of the extinct Mahratta confederacy.

A LATENT
WARMTH OF TEMPER
The Mahrattas: 1620–1818

Looking back at the rajas, ranas, nawabs, and nizams who tried to stand in the Company's way, it is tempting to dismiss them as negligible obstructions to the British Empire's inevitable dominion. But some of them represented older dynasties, ruled greater kingdoms, amassed richer treasures, and commanded larger armies than any European prince. Up until the mid-1800s the Company treated its defeated foes not as rebels but as monarchs with whom accommodations must be made. If they survived their defeats in battle they were not hanged but sent off into exile or, if it seemed expedient, reinstalled on their thrones as figureheads beholden to the Company. These native pageants proved useful buffers between the people and the Company. The Moslem Moghuls who had ruled North India since the late 1500s had once been the wealthiest potentates on the face of the earth, and without the network of roads, canals, markets, and provincial bureaucracies the Moghuls had developed the Company would have found India neither governable nor profitable. Though the British had taken the Moghul capitals of Delhi and Agra in 1803, and a succession of invaders had reduced the emperor to an impoverished figurehead, the Company always took care to pay him tribute and invoke his name.

The most formidable of the Company's adversaries were the Mahrattas, its archrivals for dominion over the shards of the Moghul Empire. It was at Cawnpore that the Company's burgeoning army had first girded its loins to do battle with them; until the time of the Mutiny itself the fates of Cawnpore and the Mahrattas were inextricably intertwined. From the time of their first great chief, Sivaji, to the reign of their last leader, Peshwa Baji Rao II, the Mahrattas' courage, cunning, nationalist vision, and jealous venality had unmanned the armies of the Moghuls, absorbed their far-flung territories, separated their provincial governors from the throne at Delhi, and reduced the successors of Babar and Akbar to impotent figureheads.

The Mahrattas came from "dense forests, steep hill-sides and fast-nesses hard of access" in the Western Ghats, the rocky range of mountains that run along the middle of India's western coast.[112] They seemed unlikely conquerors: "inferior in height, good looks and dress."[113] But those who knew them better spoke of their "bright and piercing eyes," "desperate courage" and "unsurpassed endurance." Unlike the Rajputs, who claimed descent from the sun and the moon, they cultivated a strange, democratic pride in their humble origins. But they were by no means easy-going nor long-suffering. "They have a latent warmth of temper," warned an admirer, "and if oppressed beyond a certain endurable limit, they will fiercely turn and rend their tormentors."[114]

Until the seventeenth century the Mahrattas had been dismissed by India's various conquerors as mere brigands who might occasionally ride down onto the plains to loot a town or harass a camp but who could always be counted on to slip quickly back into their mountain strongholds. So long as the Afghani kings and Moghul governors of central India left them alone, they seemed content to follow a seasonal cycle of husbandry and petty plunder.

Their leader was a short, pale man named Sivaji Bhosla. Born in the late 1620s to a Mahratta freelance, Sivaji was romantic and incorrigible, charmed by Mahratta ballads and the marauding Mavalis—the people of the hills—whose expeditions he joined furtively in a variety of disguises. On a visit to the Moghul court Sivaji's keen nostrils had detected the unmistakable odor of decay. The last great Moghul, the brilliant and bigoted Aurangzeb, saw himself as the Moslem king of a Moslem empire, upon whose subjects—Moslem and infidel alike—he was obliged to impose the law of Allah. He alienated his forefathers' Rajput allies, slaughtered the Sikhs, expended his dwindling treasury on elephantine expeditions into central India and, perhaps most disastrously for his dynasty's posterity, disturbed the Mahratta hornet's nest.

Sivaji dreamed of restoring a Hindu empire such as the Brahmins had described to him in his lessons, but he was no bigot. During his campaigns he forbade his soldiers to destroy mosques or kill Moslem ascetics, to whom he sometimes turned for spiritual guidance. If one of his soldiers stole a copy of the Koran, he took pains to return it to the local Moslem scribes and teachers. He severely punished anyone who raped women or abducted children. And though Sivaji was probably unable to read or write, he was capable of great tact and stirring eloquence. "Why remain content with the gifts conferred by foreigners?" he asked his nobles. "We are Hindus: this whole country is ours, and yet it is occupied and held by Muslims. They desecrate our temples, break our idols, plunder our wealth, forcibly convert our countrymen to their religion, kill cows openly. We will suffer this treatment no more. We are as brave and capable as our ancestors of yore. . . . There is no such thing as good luck or bad luck. We are the captains of our soil and the makers of our freedom."

After Aurangzeb destroyed the Vishneshwar Temple at Benares in 1669, Sivaji raided so close to the Moghul stronghold of Aurangabad that the emperor had to send an army to chase him back into the mountains. But the lumbering Moghuls were no match for Sivaji's guerillas. They struck without warning, at the most improbable times and places; one year they even collected a large fleet and attacked Moghul ships bound for Mecca.

After a string of victories against local kings and Moghul armies, Sivaji crowned himself King of the *Kshatriyas*, or warrior caste, in a splendid ceremony at Raigurh in 1674.[115] By the time of his death in 1680 his empire would encompass not only the Western Ghats and the Concan—the region between the Western Ghats and the Arabian Sea—but dozens of individual estates scattered along their periphery, as well as the vast tracts in the Carnatic and the Deccan that he claimed as his paternal *jagirs*, hereditary estates from which he expected yearly revenue. But Sivaji's "territory and treasures," wrote Grant Duff, "were not so formidable to the Mahomedans as the example he had set, the system and habits he introduced, and the spirit he had infused into a large portion of the Mahratta people."

✦ ✦ ✦

The line that runs from Sivaji to Nana Sahib of Bithur was laid down in Sivaji's boyhood, when Sivaji's father entrusted his rearing to a Brahmin from the Concan. Sivaji's devotion to his guru had eventually extended to all Concanist Brahmins, to whom he and his successors entrusted their ministries. It was from these Brahmins, and not Sivaji's rough and ready little warriors, that Nana Sahib was descended. "Of all the Brahmins with whom I am acquainted," wrote Grant Duff, "the Concanists are the most sensible and intelligent."[116] "The climate," wrote another chronicler, " . . . for some unknown reason, has intensified their brain power to an amazing extent."[117]

Between Sivaji and Nana Sahib lies a morass that would appall a Machiavelli and dizzy a Gibbon. Suffice it to say that Sivaji's death encouraged Aurangzeb to venture southward into the Deccan. But the little chieftain's ghost haunted and mocked the last quarter century of the emperor's life, and Mahratta horsemen finally forced Aurangzeb to retreat with a ruined army, a nearly empty treasury, and half his kingdom in rebellion. "Among the ruins of his hopes," the old Emperor passed away in 1707, leaving orders that his empire be divided among his three sons.

He might as well have left orders for his sons to eat each other, for that, in effect, is what they did. As the descendants of Babur and Akbar the Great sank into barbarity, the Mahrattas galloped merrily onto the playing field, buying off or overthrowing the Emperor's restive governors and ministers and jockeying for position with invading Persians and Afghanis. Power gravitated toward the Peshwas or prime ministers and away from Sivaji's descendants, who were confined to the hill fortress of Satara.[118]

The Peshwas did not entirely dispense with Sivaji's dreams of a Mahratta nation, but as priestly bureaucrats they preferred to act as power brokers: free-ranging interventionists with armies in every corner of what still passed for the Moghul Empire. By playing one Moghul minister against another they acquired the right to collect a quarter of all revenues from the Deccan, Rajputana, and even the environs of Delhi itself.[119] In the process, of course, they became spectacularly rich. But when the Peshwa's subjects could not afford to pay him his extravagant tribute, the Mahratta armies enriched and sustained themselves by dispensing with Sivaji's humane constraints and letting their troops loose to plunder. Soon the Peshwa's generals had staked out vast territories and founded mighty dynasties of their own. Mahadaji Scindia of Gwalior, descended from the Peshwa's slipper bearer, was the most powerful of these vassals and invaded northward and eastward into Bengal, always acting with mock humility as a servant of the Moghul, of Satara, of the Peshwa himself.

◆ ◆ ◆

Scindia's adventures brought him into collision with the latest entrants in the contest for India's riches: an enterprising and curiously persistent race of pallid islanders who had settled inexplicably along India's coast. Sivaji himself had met up with a few of them. A representative had even attended Sivaji's coronation, and though the trader's tribute of a few jeweled knickknacks must have seemed paltry in a ceremony that cost millions of rupees, Sivaji and his ministers suspected that the East India Company's resources vastly exceeded appearances.

The appearance of these Englishmen was one of the strangest things about them. Indians at first believed that they "had no skin, but a thin membrane covering their body, which made them appear abominably white. . . . Most of them still worshipped images, and they ate everything, and particularly things forbidden by the holy Moses. . . . Only one [thing was said] in their favour—that they were not unjust; but in the administration of justice, they never deviated from the sacred book of the ancient law of Solomon, the son of David, etc."[120]

The lesson the English eventually learned from their adventures in India was that in order to sustain their monopoly they would have to expand their domain. But in the early days the Company's directors still hoped that by supporting this or that prince in their territorial and dynastic squabbles, they might strike a balance of power such as obtained in Europe. They intended eventually to hold that balance, especially vis à vis the French, but they wished to leave the dangerous and unprofitable administration of Indian principalities to the nizams and nawabs, rajas and chieftains of the Great Moghul's shattered empire.

Viewed from the directors' headquarters in London or even the governor-general's mansion at Calcutta, it seemed feasible enough: a matter of diplomacy, vigilance, and an occasional show of force. But the Company had no patience with the elegant machinations that among Indian princes made life worth living. To the brilliant, proud, and ruthless Mahrattas the British proposed stability and continuity, but to the great chieftains of the confederacy these were contemptible goals that would not only inhibit their princely dreams of riches and glory, but prove stupefyingly dull. Each prince might dream his own dream of supremacy, but what the Mahrattas would fight for was *chout* and plunder, the fluidity that had obtained before the Europeans asserted themselves, the labyrinthine game of deadly perils and exalted opportunities that had animated India's kings for centuries. "Intrigue," wrote their Machiavelli, "is better than power."[121]

Such was the credo of the last of the Peshwas, Baji Rao II. He was the son of Peshwa Rughonath Rao, a ruthless Mahratta Macbeth whose wife had arranged his predecessor's assassination in 1773. The British had championed Rughonath briefly in order to frustrate the French, but after a nearly incomprehensible affair known as the First

Mahratta War, they saw fit to abandon him.[122] The Company's betrayal festered in both the father and his son Baji Rao, who for many years was kept a prisoner of the Peshwa's court.

"Graceful in his person, with a handsome and youthful countenance which ensured favourable impressions," wrote Grant Duff, "Baji Rao had the mildest manner, and an address so insinuating that he gained the good-will of all who approached him." He was nobody's puppet, however, and secretly promised riches and vast territories to Scindia's young successor for bullying the court at Poona into crowning Baji Rao the ninth Peshwa of the Mahratta confederacy. When Scindia marched on Poona to collect his reward, however, Baji Rao tried to raise the money with fines and taxes, including a "contentment tax" that he levied on the "popular delight" of his succession. All the shopkeepers closed down in protest.[123] At Baji Rao's disgraceful suggestion, Scindia plundered the city.

It proved characteristic of Baji Rao. In the name of keeping his options open and his rivals disarmed and befuddled, Baji Rao was always making promiscuous and contradictory commitments. He was addicted to intrigue but lacked the will or the integrity to back up his plots and counterplots with decisive action. He sensibly treated the Company with wary deference as a guarantor of treaties, a mediator, an ally to be brandished against his foes.

Among these was the hard-riding Mahratta chieftain Holkar of Indore, who broke from the confederacy in 1802 and marched on Poona, defeating the combined forces of Baji Rao and Scindia and sending the young Peshwa fleeing ignominiously in a Company ship. Baji Rao traded away his power for the Company's protection, signing away his right to lead the Mahratta confederacy. The Company approached its treaties with tiresome literalness and terrible finality, but to Baji Rao they were mere respites from a game—not prescriptive so much as descriptive of a moment's circumstance, a fleeting inconvenience, a mere predicate for the next intrigue. No sooner had the Company reinstalled him at Poona than he secretly induced Scindia and other Mahratta chiefs to rescue him from the Company's thrall. By now none of his former feudatories had much use for the Peshwa, but they liked the British even less, and in exchange for promises of territories and chout, prepared to unite with him against John Company.[124]

Seeing a French hand in all this, Governor-General Wellesley sent General Gerard Lake to Cawnpore to prepare for war. When Scindia and his allies defied Wellesley's command to return to their own domains, His Excellency's little brother, the future Duke of Wellington, defeated fifty thousand Mahrattas with less than a tenth as many men, Lake routed Scindia in the Punjab, and the Second Mahratta War came to a close.

Baji Rao promptly returned to his intrigues with Hyderabad, Indore, and formidable bands of brigands known as the Pindharies. When the Company sent their forces sweeping across India to subdue the Pindharies, Baji Rao assembled a large army of cavalrymen on the pretext of assisting the English. An extraordinary man named Mountstuart Elphinstone was then the British Resident at Poona, and, in order not to provoke the inscrutable Peshwa, he removed his own force to a village four miles off. Taking this as a sign of weakness, Baji Rao attacked Elphinstone and his little garrison with twenty-six thousand men and fourteen cannon.[125]

They were quite a sight. "Those only who have witnessed the Bore in the Gulf of Cambay," an observer testified, "and have seen in perfection the approach of that roaring tide, can form the exact idea presented to the author at the sight of the Peishwa's army."[126] "Grand beyond description," sniffed Elphinstone, "but perfectly ineffectual."[127] With less than three thousand men he repulsed the army of Baji Rao, and when a second British force reached Poona and prepared to attack, Baji Rao fled the field, as he would flee from battle after battle over the next few months while his soldiers and followers fell away.[128] Peevish, treacherous, "a dupe of his own pretensions," he had destroyed not only his claim to the Peshwaship but the Peshwaship itself and with it the last hope of Sivaji's Mahratta nation.[129]

At last, in June of 1818, Baji Rao and his starved and tattered dependents surrendered unconditionally to the genial Sir John Malcolm, who informed the exhausted Peshwa that "no event short of the downfall of the British Government could restore him to Poona, or to power." Baji Rao burst into tears, and Malcolm was so shocked to see the greatest of all Hindu rulers "houseless and harassed" that at a time when Napoleon himself had been banished to penurious exile on a rock in the Mediterranean, Sir John agreed to pay Baji Rao an annual pension of £80,000 and find him a suitable home in Benares "or any other sacred place in Hindustan."[130]

SATURDAY HOUSE

Baji Rao and Nana Sahib: 1818–1853

Baji Rao feared that if he were exiled to Benares the thousands of Mahrattas who lived there and the hundreds of thousands of pilgrims who journeyed there each year would expect more charity of him than he could afford. So the deposed Peshwa chose the ancient town of Bithur, a minor place of pilgrimage that was nevertheless auspicious enough to suit his Concanist followers and close enough to the vast Company garrison at Cawnpore to keep him out of mischief. There was symmetry to this arrangement: Cawnpore had been founded as a bulwark against the Mahrattas, now it would be their sovereign's guardhouse. But the Company's Intelligence Department evidently did not recognize the significance of Baji Rao's selection. Among Brahmins Bithur was reputed to be "the accomplisher of every man's object" and was "well known among Hindus as the especial place of resort of those who have a grievance."[131]

Heralded by a cloud of dust, Baji Rao's bedraggled thousands arrived at Bithur in February 1819 and collapsed in a seedy heap on the adjacent plain as his carpenters and masons went to work.[132] His palace at Poona, *Shanivar Bara* or "Saturday House," had been enormous. Wrapped in heavy iron chains to ward off lightning and evil spirits, its exterior had looked "more like a gaol," but its vast rooms had been covered with exquisite carvings; the ceiling of one of its halls of audience was entirely composed of ivory.[133] The palace he constructed at Bithur was not so grand, but the homesick ex-Peshwa named it Saturday House as well. He filled it with carpets, tapestries, European chandeliers, and "twenty-five chiming clocks." There were shrines and verandahs and vast ghostly halls of audience, and apartments of shimmering marble and mirror glass. Baji Rao's sprawling compound was enclosed in a high wall and included orchards, fountains, color-thematic gardens, and stables and menageries watered by seven masonry wells.[134]

Even the commissioners the British assigned to watch over Baji Rao found it impossible to determine precisely how rich he was. Every year his territory had yielded about 120 million rupees in revenue, a sixth of which he had kept for himself, and in his heyday at

Poona he was supposed to have amassed a treasury of fifty million rupees.[135] Though he had fled Poona in a hurry and on his ruinous retreat lost vast sums to pilferers and extortionists, one witness to his flight counted ten royal elephants and thirty camels, all laden with "gold mohurs and bullion, gold and silver plates and dishes, gold ornaments and jewels."[136] With these treasures and his eight-hundred-thousand-rupee pension, Baji Rao was initially able not only to build palaces for himself but support the thousands who now flocked to join him at Bithur.[137]

Brahmins migrated to Bithur in droves, lured by Baji Rao's legendary altruism.[138] He was philanthropic by compulsion—driven, it was said, by a primal guilt over his mother's role in the murder of her husband's predecessor.[139] So many Brahmins pressed Baji Rao for grants that he appointed a Mahratta named Vanayak to head a kind of foundation through which he renovated ashrams, restored ghats, constructed temples, schools and rest houses, fed and sheltered countless priests, mendicants, and calligraphers.[140] Suddenly what had been a ramshackle town dozing between festivals awakened to the ringing of masons' hammers and temple bells.[141]

Nevertheless the British would not address Baji Rao as Peshwa nor even permit him the honorific *Pant Pardan* or Prime Minister, which cut to the core of his identity. The last Peshwa of all the Mahrattas was to be called simply Maharaja Baji Rao Bahadur: the sort of hollow title an upstart *zemindar* (landlord) might have adopted. Out of pride and crashing boredom he took to riding in state into Cawnpore every month, and made quite a spectacle of himself "surrounded by a troop of Mahratta horsemen with their long lances dashing along and a crowd of peons or footmen scampering away and struggling to keep pace with the quick shuffling walk of the elephants."[142] (His own elephant was one of the largest in India, owing, it was said, to a diet of sugar and ground almonds.)[143] But he steadfastly refused to attend any public functions unless the British accorded him the honor of a salute, which the British just as steadfastly refused to do. They allowed him to keep a small horse-guard and some musketmen armed with blank cartridges[144] and a few "old pieces of artillery," but only as "a sort of child's play of regality."[145]

Baji Rao entered middle age an enthusiastic debauchee. Saturday House was said to contain apartments "horribly unfit for any human eye; in which both European and native artists had done their utmost to gratify the corrupt master."[146] At Poona it was customary for appointment seekers to offer up their wives and daughters to his li-

bido, which was evidently not satisfied by his many wives and le-
gions of concubines.[147] Though Baji Rao was only forty-one when he
surrendered, he appeared so reduced that even as the British handed
him his pension they comforted themselves that he would not live
long to collect it.[148] He was reputedly impotent from venereal disease, hopelessly addicted to opium, and despondent over his lost
glory. But the British were always overestimating the debauchery of
Indian princes or the severity of its consequences.[149] By 1818 he had
already outlived four of his six wives, and after moving to Bithur
married five more,[150] all the while servicing three troupes of dancing
girls.[151] Despite his many wives, Baji Rao had sired only two sons
during his reign as Peshwa, both of whom had died in infancy.[152] His
marriages at Bithur had failed to produce any more, and as he entered his fifties he began to fret not merely about his failure to produce an heir but the terrifying prospect of not having a son to
officiate at his funeral,[153] for it is believed by Hindus that only a son
can release the father's soul and propitiate the souls of his ancestors
in annual memorial rites.

Fortunately Hindu law recognized adopted sons for this purpose,
and so Baji Rao looked around for a likely candidate. He did not have
to look far. On May 19, 1825,[154] deep in a valley in the Western
Ghats, the first wife of a learned Deccani Brahmin named Mahadev
Rao had given birth to a boy named Nana Govind Dhondu Pant:
"Nana" being a term of endearment meaning "few in years," for he
was their second and apparently favorite son.[155]

Reduced to poverty by the Peshwa's flight, Nana's father had
brought his family seven hundred miles from their home to attach
himself to the Peshwa's court-in-exile, where, toddling charmingly
in his father's yard, Nana caught the old king's attention. The boy's
pedigree was impeccable: his father and the ex-Peshwa bore the
same caste name; his mother was a sister of one of Baji Rao's
wives.[156] So in 1827, with the approval of his astrologer, the Peshwa
asked Mahadev if he might make little Nana his heir.[157] Whatever
dishonor Baji Rao had brought upon the Mahrattas during his cruel
and hapless reign at Poona, in their hearts he remained the Peshwa,
and to be asked to contribute a son to Baji Rao's line was an inestimable honor. Mahadev retained his rather homely oldest son Baba
to perform his own *shraad* but gave the Peshwa two others: Nana and
Bala.[158]

By Hindu law the adoption severed Nana's legal ties to Mahadev,
and he now took his place on the outermost limb of the Peshwas'

family tree. From the austere world of his father's house Nana was suddenly immersed in the luxurious trappings, chivalric lore, plots, and counterplots of Saturday House. His adoptive father, pausing between his devotionals and bacchanals, still doted on Nana, but his wives abhorred him, embodying as he did their failure to produce a natural heir. A Benares Brahmin was hired to tutor him in Sanskrit so he could join Baji Rao in his Vedic readings, and occasionally Nana and his brother would attend the S.P.G.'s little academy at Bithur to acquire just a smattering of English.

Among his playmates was Tatya Tope, the son of Baji Rao's dispenser of charities. A stout youth about six years Nana's senior, Tatya was affectionately known as "Benny" by his regal playmate[159] and evidently took part in what passed for Nana's martial training.[160] It is also believed that another of Nana's playmates was a bold, slight girl named Manu Bai, who would later become the Rani of Jhansi, the Joan of Arc of the Indian rebellion.[161]

A frequent guest at Saturday House remembered playing billiards with Nana when he was "a lad of fifteen years old, of pleasant and agreeable manners, a good physique, and gave promise of being a pillar of the state."[162] Though he may have tended toward corpulence in later life, Nana was also said to have been an excellent rider and such a vigorous swimmer that he and his brothers used to paddle across the Ganges and back when the river was in full flood.[163]

Nana Sahib so pleased his adoptive father as to revive Baji Rao's dynastic dreams, for in 1841 the old man named Nana "master and heir to the *guddee* [throne] of the Peshwa" and "sole possessor of his wealth and property."[164] But the ex-Peshwa never completely resigned himself to his own sterility. When receiving Company officials he made a point of stationing Nana not beside his throne—the customary position for the Peshwa's heir—but well behind it "to avoid all questionable matters" and "the possibility of giving offences."[165] And in 1841, in the same will in which he had bequeathed his estate to Nana, Baji Rao still held out some hope that he might yet "beget a son of my natural body" who would displace Nana Sahib as his heir.[166] Fortunately for Nana the old man proved everlastingly sterile, but for years Nana Sahib had to keep close watch on Baji Rao's *zenana* (harem) to prevent his aging wives from putting forth some imported infant as natural heir to the Peshwa's throne.

In 1851, at the age of seventy-six, Baji Rao II, deposed Peshwa Bahadur of the Mahratta confederacy, finally passed away.[167] With his philanthropy and pageantry and patronage of the arts the old man had become a far more beloved figure at Bithur than he had ever been at Poona. During his final illness "his residence and the roads about" had been literally filled by people anxiously enquiring after the state of his health."[168] To Nana Sahib fell not only "the throne of the Peishwa, the Dominions, Wealth, . . . family possessions, Treasure" and all of Baji Rao's "real and personal property," but the filial task of escorting the Peshwa to his next life. Within hours of Baji Rao's death his corpse had been bathed and perfumed, daubed with butter, and carried from Saturday House over a mile to the wayward bank of the Ganges where, as his widows smashed their bangles and the Brahmins who crowded the mud flats moaned and chanted, Nana Sahib circled the old man's pyre with a fire pot and set his remains ablaze so that his soul might find its incarnation. Until his flight from Bithur over six years later, Nana Sahib would sleep in the room in which the Peshwa passed away and maintain his deathbed as a kind of shrine.[169]

As the Ganges carried off his father's ashes, Nana tried to determine exactly what remained of the Peshwa's treasury. The old man's pension had been delivered by bullock cart in quarterly installments of gold coin with which Baji Rao had supported himself and his retainers and the vast religious establishment that had sprung up around Saturday House.[170] By the time of his death he had collected over twenty-five million rupees, two million of which he had managed to invest in public securities for an additional yearly income of eighty thousand rupees.[171] Baji Rao had apparently believed that the pension would extend to his heir, but Malcolm's wording of the Peshwa's terms of surrender had been so vague that in 1837 Baji Rao had asked the governor-general for a clarification. Lord Auckland had replied that the pension was "purely personal" to Baji Rao and would not descend to his heirs. Baji Rao had pressed the issue, and three years later the government of the North-Western Provinces reiterated that Nana would inherit only the Peshwa's personal property and would not be entitled to "any consideration of the Government."

The Directors upheld Auckland's ruling and maintained that the millions of rupees Baji Rao had presumably accumulated would provide Nana with "an ample patrimony." At this point Baji Rao evidently toyed with the idea of sending an agent on his behalf to London, but decided instead to rest his hopes for a new ruling on the "favourable impression" he hoped to make on the new governor-general, Lord Hardinge. Hardinge was as unmoved as his predecessors by Baji Rao's benignity. But Nana Sahib made such a favorable impression on the commissioner at Bithur that on the ex-Peshwa's death he recommended to Dalhousie that at least a portion of the old man's pension should be extended to his adoptive heir. After all, Nana had hundreds if not thousands of retainers to look after, and though the Peshwa's treasury was considerable, according to Mahratta and Hindu tradition not even a deposed regent could liquidate such assets as gold, jewels, and silks without bringing dishonor on himself and his ancestors.[172]

Ever annoyed by matters native-princely, the impatient and imperious Lord Dalhousie had no intention of spending another rupee on the late Peshwa's establishment or the adopted heir-presumptive to a vanished title. In a brusque minute he declared the commissioner's suggestion "uncalled for and unreasonable," urged that the old Peshwa's retainers be dispersed,[173] and instructed Nana Sahib to support the remainder of his establishment with the fortune he had inherited.[174] But in his haste to dismiss Nana Sahib's claims Dalhousie made the mistake of asserting that Baji Rao had "left no sons of his own," thus inadvertently holding out the hope to Nana Sahib that if he could prove that an adopted son had as much legal standing as a natural son the Company might decide the issue differently.[175]

On Baji Rao's death Nana Sahib was immediately stripped not only of his father's pension but of his seal, his hollow titles, even his yearly allocation of blank rifle cartridges. Nana subsequently fashioned a new seal and badges for his attendants which, "by the rules of Oriental etiquette," referred to him as Maharaja, but the commissioner disallowed the use of any such title.[176] In 1852 Nana's secretary, a Mahratta named Raja Piraji Rao Bhonsley, submitted a petition to the government that referred to Nana Sahib as Maharaja; the government summarily returned the document on the grounds that no petition that made "such an assumption" would be entertained.[177] In a memorial to the governor-general Nana later argued that since the Peshwas had owed their "dominions and greatness" to neither the Moghuls nor the British but "to their own enterprise" they ought to be allowed to call themselves whatever they pleased. What would it cost the Company, he wondered, to grant this one "liberality" that would be "a source of consolation" to Nana Sahib in his misfortune?[178] But Calcutta was determined to eradicate every vestige of the Peshwa's regency, and declared that "the Governor-General in Council recognized no such person as Maharaja Sreemunt Dhondoo Punt Nana Sahib."

Hundreds of Baji Rao's followers now loaded their household goods onto carts and began the long exodus back to the hills of Maharastra.[179] But Nana Sahib would not give up on his father's pension. Citing references in the terms of Baji Rao's surrender to the Peshwa's "successors" and the support of his "family," he reminded the Company that their courts had always treated adopted sons as legal heirs and indeed recognized eleven adoptive heirs to Indian thrones, including Jaiaji Rao Scindia of Gwalior. Why, Nana Sahib asked, was the Company so determined to make an exception of the successor of the most powerful of all of Hindustan's fallen kings, a man who had spent his retirement in good works, sustaining his family, loaning vast sums to the government, and in every way demonstrating an uwavering loyalty to the power that had removed him from his throne?[180]

In December 1853 Calcutta reasserted that "the Ex Peshwa's adopted son is not a Maharaja or a Raja," and that his memorials were therefore "wholly inadmissible."[181] But by then Nana Sahib had given up on Lord Dalhousie and resolved to go over his head.

MON CHER GOODY
Azimullah Khan: 1854–1856

Though Nana appears to have toyed with going to London himself, as a Brahmin he dared not pollute himself by crossing the "illimitable" black water.[182] He had considered sending Narain Rao, the son of the ex-Peshwa's chief minister, Subhedar Ram Chunder, but he was embroiled in a fight over his own father's estate.[183] This left only one other candidate: his secretary, Raja Piraji Rao Bhonsley of the fallen house of Nagpore, who had prepared his petitions to the Company.[184] Piraji had proved a dogged, loyal, and erudite servant, but Nana Sahib recognized that the mission would require charm as well as determination.

So Nana asked handsome and plausible young Azimullah Khan to accompany the Mahratta and apply his mastery of English manners and morals to the case. Azimullah had already established himself as

Nana Sahib

Savada Koti, Nana Sahib's headquarters

one of Nana's most valued advisers. Having spent most of his life among Anglo-Indians—civilians, missionaries, memsahibs, army officers—he accepted happily, confident of his ability to ingratiate himself with the Board of Control, Parliament, the Privy Council, and the Queen herself if it came to that.

Since neither he nor Piraji had ever visited England, however, Azimullah suggested that they might require an experienced guide and recommended a highly educated young Rohilkhand noble named

Mohamed Ali Khan who had once visited England in the employ of the King of Nepal. If Azimullah still had any sympathy for his British benefactors it would not have long survived the company of Mohamed Ali Khan. As a young man Ali had conscientiously studied for Calcutta's civil-service examinations and passed with flying colors. But the British made him a mere foreman in the Engineers and placed him under the command of a brutal and ignorant European sergeant who so humiliated him that Ali came to regard British "pretensions to liberality and sympathy as mere hypocrisy." In 1850 he resigned the service and returned to Rohilkhand, intending to offer his services to the King of Oudh. But that same year, "being well backed by recommendations both from native princes and English officials," he accompanied Jung Bahadur of Nepal on a three-month tour of England.

"Well supplied with money to engage the best lawyers," as Ali would recollect, "and also to bribe high officials, if necessary," Nana's three emissaries set off on their mission to England. But by the time their ship reached Southampton, only two were left to stagger down the gangway onto cold and solid ground.[185] The freezing gales and sweltering calms had proved too much for Piraji, and despite Azimullah's best efforts to revive him, the Mahratta noble had died in his cabin and was buried in the black water he had risked his caste to cross. Now Nana's suit was entirely in Moslem hands.[186]

Ten years earlier an Indian Moslem named Lutfullah had accompanied a dispossessed Nawab to London to plead a case similar to Nana Sahib's. To Lutfullah England had seemed "the end of the world, where the sun appears, far to the south, as weak as the moon" and "where the destiny of our sweet native land lies in the hand of some twenty-five great men."[187] Indians were still so rare a sight in London that they were all assumed to be princes. But Azimullah had resolved not to make a spectacle of himself as he checked into a suite of rooms on Hanover Square and began to make his rounds of London officialdom. He dressed in Western clothes, "trusting to his own education instead of to show,"[188] and apparently made an excellent impression, striking one guest who dined with him "in gentleman-like style" as "a well bred agreeable person of good intelligence about English matters."[189]

Nana Sahib's British friends had provided Azimullah with letters of introduction, names of lawyers, hotel recommendations and the like, but Ali also introduced him around, capitalizing on the connections he had made in Jung Bahadur's retinue three years before.

They were said to have employed a barrister named Biddle to prepare Nana Sahib's petition to the powers that be, and proceeded to East India House, the Company's imposing Grecian headquarters on Leadenhall Street.[190] There they met the great utilitarian philosopher John Stuart Mill, then the Company's liaison officer with the Indian states. Though Mill would have been discouraging about Azimullah's prospect of overturning Dalhousie's edict, he was apparently so taken with Nana's emissary that he introduced him to his boyhood playmate and lifelong friend, Lucie Duff Gordon. Through Lady Duff Gordon Azimullah would be introduced to many of the great writers and thinkers who passed through her salon, including Dickens, Tennyson, Thackery, Carlyle, Meredith, and Macaulay.[191]

A brilliant and empathetic translator and xenophile, Lucie Duff Gordon was the wife of the prime minister's cousin, Alexander Duff Gordon, Bart., a clerk at the Treasury and Gentlemen Usher to the Queen. Though Lucie smoked cheroots, dressed, according to Emily Eden, in clothes "half-way between a German student and an English waterman," and bore a decided resemblance to the Emperor Napoleon, she was still regarded, at the age of thirty-three, as a great beauty, with a knack for turning overly ardent admirers into "happy, crust-munching devotees."[192] But by 1854 she had been dispirited by her husband's languishing career and the commercial and critical failure of her most recent translations that seemed inevitably to consign her to a mere footnote in the biographies of her illustrious friends.

Enter Azimullah Khan. He and Ali arrived at her house at Esher one snowy afternoon, startling her small son as he was "quite knee deep, snowballing the dog and garden."[193] Azimullah was properly dressed in Western winter wear—"a British frock coat and top hat with a brass-buckled Gladstone"[194]—and settled happily into the "Gordon Arms," occupying a small sitting room behind the dining room where Lucie once wrote her translations.

"I have got my Musselman friend [Azimullah] Khan living here, and he quite provokes me by his delight at the beauty of the snow," she wrote a friend.

> You wd be amused at the incessant questioning that goes on—I have gone through such a course of political economy & all social sciences day after day & had to get so many books for my pupil to devour that I feel growing quite solemn & pedantic. [Azimullah] who came over with a strong dislike to the English has become an

enthusiastic Englishman & will go home with very reforming notions to his own people.[195]

She championed her "very grand-looking and very amiable,
charming young Mussulman Mahratta" and urged her influential
friends to obtain tickets for him for the opening of Parliament.[196] "He
of course wants to see the Queen & would much like to hear her
voice," she wrote Lord Lansdowne. Azimullah had actually asked
Lucie's husband if he might be formally presented to Her Majesty,
but Alexander Duff Gordon had replied that it would be improper to
present someone to Her Majesty who had come to England solely in
order to advance a claim against the Company. Lucie was indignant.
"Begging my husband's pardon," she fumed, "I can hardly believe
that our court can take upon itself to prejudice a question of the kind
or so openly to favour the E.I.C." Certainly it would be in the
Queen's interest, she wrote Lansdowne, to encourage Azimullah in
his attempt "to behave like a civilised man." What would it say to en-
lightened Indians if he were neglected "because he has left his barbaric 'pomp and circumstance' behind at Calcutta . . . ?"

Lucie believed she had convinced her protégé to set aside entirely
his "oriental notions" and "Eastern ideas of making interest and
gaining favour" and instead "either come to terms with the Company or go to law with them if he is willing to risk the money."[197] But
Azimullah had already learned from the example of the annexed
kingdom of Satara's failed emissary that supposedly Western ideas of
hard work and fair play would get him nowhere.[198] Despite his "laborious, untiring conscientiousness," Satara's man had failed in his
mission and returned to his country in disgrace.[199] Better financed
than his Mahratta counterpart, Azimullah believed that where "laborious, untiring conscientiousness" had failed, substantial bribes
might yet succeed. "The Company [has] bribed the Board of Control
and the Privy Council," he wrote home to Bithur, and "if his Highness [expects] to succeed, he must bribe over the head of the Company. Three lacs [three-hundred-thousand rupees or £30,000]," he
assured Nana Sahib, "would do it all."[200]

However successfully he may have hidden his contempt for English society and political institutions from his enthusiastic benefac-
tress, Azimullah seems to have reciprocated Lucie's devotion, and
certainly some among her circle must have whispered that they were
lovers. But it seems unlikely that their relationship was ever
amorous. He was in his early twenties, she was thirty-three: old

enough at any rate for him to call her his "European Mother, as the civillest thing he can say."

Nevertheless, during the summer of 1855 they were inseparable. She encouraged her young friend Henry Phillips to paint his portrait. Azimullah accompanied her to Lord Lansdowne's estate at Bowood while her husband and children went their separate ways, and tagged along with her to dinner parties and even to the opera.

There is no record of what Azimullah made of the opera. Perhaps, like Lutfullah, he was scandalized when "the females whirled round in their dancing" and "their short gowns flew up to the forbidden height."[201] Lutfullah was less supple than Azimullah, less of a chameleon, but the two men shared the same opinion of English women. Lutfullah pitied them their freedom to "enjoy the society of men in public and private. . . . Poor creatures! naturally weak, how many of them fall victims to the brutal intrigues of men! How many families of high name have been ruined by this unreasonable license!"

A great many, if the rumors that swirled around Azimullah had any foundation. A chronicler later envisioned Azimullah adorning "London drawing-rooms, or cantering on Brighton Downs, the centre of an admiring bevy of English damsels."[202] Another described him as "an accomplished rascal of the Gil Blas, or Casanova, type."[203] But Azimullah himself was more modest, and ascribed his conquests to the laxity of Western morals. Unless English ladies were restrained as they were in the East, he later warned, it was inevitable that "like moths in candlelight, they will fly and get burned."[204]

One of those he singed was a certain "Miss A." of Brighton, who would address her letters "Mon cher Goody" and pledged never to reveal the secrets of their passionate rendezvous, not even to her "father confessor."[205] "Such rubbish I never read," reported young Fred Roberts after discovering her letters in Azimullah's apartments. ". . . How English ladies can be so infatuated."[206] A civil servant who saw some of this correspondence reported that Azimullah "had actually been attempting to tempt distinguished ladies who had entertained him in London to visit his master in India,"[207] but whatever promises Azimullah may have breathed at Brighton, Miss A.'s friends evidently "interfered and saved her from becoming an item in the harem of this Mahommedan polygamist."[208]

"So far as London drawing-rooms went," recalled Ali, Azimullah's mission "proved a social success, but as far as gaining our end, a political failure." Azimullah kept sending Nana encouraging notes about the reception he received at the home of this or that luminary, alternating with despairing accounts of the rampant corruption that thwarted him at every turn. But all this was wearing as thin as the dwindling interest of Lucie's friends and the infatuation of impressionable young girls. Even his impersonation of an Eastern prince was coming unstuck. In late 1855, the barrister John Lang, a frequent visitor to Cawnpore, arrived in a Belgravian drawing room one evening and was offered the honor of an "introduction to the Prince," i.e., Azimullah. "Prince indeed!" scoffed Lang. "He has changed my plate fifty times in India."[209]

Azimullah had nothing to show for the tens of thousands of Nana's pounds he had expended hiring lawyers, paying confidence men, bribing clerks, entertaining dignitaries and sending them gifts. There could be no more convincing Nana Sahib that throwing picnic parties and presenting shawls and jewels to the wives of Company functionaries might regain his father's pension. There was no one left to whom to appeal. The pension was lost. Now what? In the greatest capital in the world Azimullah had been treated like a prince. Now he had to return in defeat to a disappointed master of dwindling means; to provincial, moribund Bithur; to an India ruled by what he conceived of as a very different breed of Englishman from Lucie's set: fatuous bigots who knew him only as the son of a servant, a disgraced moonshi, a facile impersonator of his betters.[210]

"It cannot be, I am sure," wrote Lutfullah after his first glimpse of England, "without the will of that one Supreme Being that this small island, which seems on the globe like a mole on the body of man, should command the greater part of the world, and keep the rest in awe."[211] But nothing could shake that awe like a visit to England. In India the British struggled to keep up appearances: restricting their ladies to cantonments, shipping their paupers and detrimentals home. Calcutta deemed it useful, perhaps even essential, to sustain the illusion that the Queen was like a goddess and her ministers sages, that their native land was the emerald paradise Anglo-Indians wistfully evoked; that London was a splendid city whose streets, if not actually paved with gold, were nevertheless broad and clean and orderly; that God had chosen the British to rule the world.

Azimullah had seen the Queen, however, and she was no goddess but a squat little woman in the sway of her German husband. And he had met some of her ministers, and they were not only devoid of anything Azimullah could recognize as human feeling but dismally ignorant of the nations and peoples the Company had subjugated.

The exalted English countryside with its bleak moors and snows and penetrating winds was harsh and forbidding. Industrial smoke and waste and the frigid, incessant rain made the slums of London worse than anything India's cities had to offer.

Azimullah was a scrambling self-made man of aristocratic pretensions, and there is little reason to believe that his moral imagination was particularly stirred by the predicament of the poor. But Britain's pretensions to civilization and magnanimity were belied by the ghastly conditions under which their own working men, women, and children labored in mills and mines. Azimullah may well have wondered what the British had in mind for the Indians they so despised if they were willing to subject their own people to such degradation. Was this the superior English way of doing things that the sahibs were always citing? Did the Company intend to displace India's graciousness and continuity and pastoral simplicity with this darkling world of grinding gears and roaring engines and blinding, poisonous fogs? And if God had chosen Britain to rule the world, why was it entirely populated by shopkeepers, dilettantes, bureaucrats, and their foolish, corruptible wives? Where were England's soldiers, its armaments, its great conquering generals? It seemed to Azimullah that it was only through sheer brazenness that this "mole on the body of man" had convinced the people of India that its power was infinite, its armies inexhaustible.

If Azimullah distrusted his own observations, he could always read the fretful editorials in the *Times* about the country's dangerous overextension around the globe, and listen to the imperialists and anti-imperialists debate each other in Parliament, at dinner parties, in Lady Duff Gordon's salon.[212] Britain seemed less and less the monolithic giant Azimullah had been led to expect and more a divided and depleted island nation. Already the British had been chased out of Afghanistan. Now, trusting in their native troops to hold down India, they were fighting an incomprehensible little war in Persia and embarking on a hazardous affair in the Crimea.[213] No wonder Azimullah, shamed by his failure with the Board of Control and dreading his return to his stymied prince, began to brood on what had once seemed too outlandish a notion to consider seriously: the expulsion of the British from India. Here was a theme that might turn his mission from a disgraceful failure into a historic success and satisfy his by now insatiable hatred of the English.[214]

✦ ✦ ✦

In June 1855, Azimullah checked out of his hotel in Hanover Square, muttering to the proprieter that "England would yet regret the manner in which it had used his master."[215] He and Ali sailed from Southampton, intending to proceed home via the Cape and Calcutta.[216] By now Azimullah had divested himself of the everyday Western wardrobe he had affected in Lady Duff Gordon's company and in the summer heat happily bedecked himself in Moslem "rings and finery." But as his ship paused at Malta to take on coal, he heard the news of the British disaster at the redan before Sebastopol and immediately changed his plans, arranging for a passage to Constantinople, from which to travel to the battleground at Balaklava.

Azimullah and Ali arrived at Constantinople in early July and reserved rooms at Missirie's Hotel, where they "dined at the *table d'hôte*" and made the very useful acquaintance of Mr. William T. Doyne, Chief Superintendent of the Army Works Corps, who was heading for the front.[217] Doyne kindly assisted Azimullah in acquiring the necessary permissions for a visit to Balaklava, and one lovely evening on the Missirie's rooftop invited him to smoke cheroots with William Howard Russell of the *Times*. The intrepid Russell was then on the brink of immortality as the first and perhaps greatest of all war correspondents: a reputation as the ultimate "man on the spot" that he would advance with his humane and fearless reporting from the Crimea, the Indian Mutiny, and the American Civil War.[218]

Russell remembered Azimullah as "a handsome slim young man, of dark-olive complexion, dressed in an Oriental costume which was new to me. . . . I recollect that he expressed great anxiety about a passage to the Crimea, 'as,' said he, 'I want to see this famous city, and those great Roostums, the Russians, who have beaten French and English together.'" As they puffed on their cheroots and gazed upon the Bosphorus, Azimullah "boasted a good deal of his success in London society, and used the names of people of rank very freely, which, combined with the tone of his remarks," Russell recalled, "induced me to regard him with suspicion, mingled, I confess, with dislike."

But Russell did not give Azimullah much thought until a few weeks later when he was startled to find the young Moslem standing outside his tent with a letter from Doyne asking the correspondent to "assist his friend Azimoola Khan in visiting the trenches." A little put out, Russell nevertheless went off to fetch a pass from headquarters and when he returned found Azimullah watching from a nearby cemetery as the Russian batteries pounded away at the British position.

Russell presented Azimullah with the pass and rather disingenuously expressed his regret that he would not be able to accompany Azimullah, as he was expected at dinner that evening at the Light Division's mess.

> "Oh," said he, "this is a beautiful place to see from; I can see everything, and, as it is late, I will ask you to come some other day, and will watch here till it is time to go home." He said, laughingly, "I think you will never take that strong place;" and in reply to me, when I asked him to come to dine with me at my friend's, where I was sure he would be welcome, he said, with a kind of sneer, "Thank you, but recollect I am a good Mahomedan!"
>
> "But," said I, "you dined at Missirie's?"
>
> "Oh, yes: I was joking. I am not such a fool as to believe in these foolish things. I am of no religion."

When Russell came home that night he found Azimullah asleep in his camp-bed, "and my servant told me he had enjoyed my stores very freely." Azimullah departed the next morning, before Russell awoke, and left the following note: "Azimoola Khan presents his compliments to Russell, Esquire, and begs to thank him most truly for his kind attentions, for which I am most obliged."

It is possible that there may have been more to Russell's side of his conversations with Azimullah, for it was the correspondent's unflinching description of disease and starvation among the British soldiers in the Crimea and negligence and incompetence among their officers that helped to rouse the British public.[219] In any case, Ali would remember how Azimullah had been "much struck by the wretched state of both armies in front of Sebastopol." While in the Crimea he also conferred with the Turkish general Umar Pasha, who asked Azimullah to keep him apprised of "the condition in India."[220] And when they returned to Constantinople Azimullah was approached by "certain real or pretended Russian agents" who according to Ali "made large promises of material support if Azimullah could stir up a rebellion in India.

"It was then," Ali would recall, "that I and Azimullah formed the resolution of attempting to overthrow the Company's Government."[221]

THE GENTLEMAN OF BITHUR

Nana Sahib: 1855–1857

By the 1840s Cawnpore boasted the second-largest European society in India, and though most of its civil and military residents were, like Wheeler, itinerant, a great many merchants and their families, supplemented by a growing number of pensioners, were finding Cawnpore an "agreeable residence."

"In consequence of there being so many settled residents," wrote Emma Roberts, ". . . the gardens rank amongst the finest in India," giving Cawnpore "a very luxuriant appearance."[222] In the 1830s the station had undergone a building boom. Bungalows sprouted up everywhere and a horseshoe-shaped theater with massive Doric columns and luxurious seating had been erected,[223] along with a large Moghul Serai or rest house in the native city.[224] In 1835 the prison building was greatly improved in order to accommodate a growing population of convicts.[225] And in addition to the establishment of the S.P.G.'s orphan asylum in an old converted palace called the Savada House, the stones for Christ Church and the "Soldiers' Church" of St. John's Chapel had been laid in 1837.[226] Throughout the decade, warehouses, bungalows, barracks, and shops rose "where late a jungle spread its tangled dells," until the European cantonments alone covered ten square miles.[227] A family named Greenway had expanded their enterprises throughout the district, including a newspaper and an indigo plantation,[228] and in their cavernous shop offered "every article of European manufacture necessary for comfort, or even luxury."[229]

Cawnpore remained a dust bowl in the dry season, but a broad boulevard known as the Course had been lined with shade trees and was watered down every afternoon.[230] And there was always the stately Ganges herself. In full flood the river was as much as three miles in breadth. When the water was low Indians grew "melons, cucumbers, wheat, &c., on the islands in the centre of the stream." Cranes migrated to the sandbars in the dry weather, "looking, in the distance," William Howard Russell later observed, "like old gentlemen in white waistcoats over their wine." Pelicans hunted in flocks along the shore, beating shoals of fish into the shallows with their great gray wings before scooping them up in their livid pouches.[231]

Herds of buffalo swam across in the early morning to graze upon the islands and returned in the evening "of their own accord." They swam so deeply that at least one memsahib mistook their heads for the porpoises[232] that shared the Ganges with alligators, tortoises, cormorants, and kingfishers, not to mention the otters[233] that slipped along the muddy banks, keeping watch for the white-headed pallas eagles that swooped down from the sky to steal their prey.[234]

The station boasted a Masonic Temple, a library, weekly band concerts, picnics, and the famous Cawnpore races, where young men gambled extravagantly and disastrously on the Arabian and European horses "from the best stables" that galloped in such popular heats as the Cheroot Race and the Merchants' Plate. If the wind blew the dust in the right direction, reviews and grand field days provided perhaps the most impressive spectacles. The "sandy wilderness literally [swarmed] with life" as regiments enacted mock battles complete with "the shock of contending battalions, the charge, the dispersion, the rally, and the retreat."

Though some deplored Cawnpore as "the most scandalous, gossiping station in all of India," others appreciated the station's liberality.[235] A civilian observed that though the divorced Lady Cardigan was "not received at Government House," and at Meerut "not a lady would meet her," at Cawnpore she was always greeted "with every kind attention."[236] At his first banquet at the Brigadier's, one lieutenant was delighted to find that everyone sat with "legs on the table" and "spittoons on the floor."[237]

To the tune of *Hare and Hounds*, one rollicking officer used to sing,

> For dancing and dressing,
> For sky[larking] and caressing,
> No Indian station can vie with Cawnpore.[238]

◆ ◆ ◆

A road slinked northwestward from Cawnpore, twelve miles along the Ganges to the little town of Bithur. The grade dipped so low in places that during the monsoon it was sometimes submerged by floodwaters from the convergence of the Ganges and the River Non.[239] But in the cool weather Bithur Road was a favorite carriage route for the Cawnpore garrison. Leaving behind the bustling and regimented contrivance of the cantonments, excursionists experienced a serene decompression as they rode through groves of tamarind trees and fields of mustard flowers, startling the green rose-ringed parakeets that bathed in the roadside dust.

After turning down a tree-lined boulevard, Nana's guests would arrive at the old Residency, now reserved as a "place of resort" for Nana's European visitors, and file into the dining room to down a full English breakfast off mismatched china under the disconcerting gaze of a row of life-size portraits of the Peshwas interspersed with "pictures of young children, English beauties and our noble queen."[240] They might stroll to His Highness's menagerie to admire his pigeons, falcons, peacocks, and apes, and then proceed to the elegant *parterre* gardens adjoining the Residency.[241] A picnic luncheon would be followed by an archery match in which officers' wives won cashmere shawls, gold lockets and chains. In the evening there would be a dinner and then a ball, at which Nana himself often made a half-hour's appearance.[242]

It is doubtful that any of Nana's guests were entirely won over to Nana Sahib's side by his elaborate displays of hospitality. But there were already a few Anglo-Indians who privately disapproved of Dalhousie's highhandedness. With his extensive experience with Anglo-India, Azimullah had convinced Nana Sahib that any outward display of petulance on His Highness's part could cost him their sympathy. Nana's establishment at Bithur would be an asset only if His Highness shared it with the British, a liability if he shut it off from them. He needed to persuade the influential Anglo-Indians who lived in and passed through Cawnpore that he was a modern and magnanimous prince with a grasp of politics and history and Anglo-Indian etiquette; in short, that he was a gentleman.

In some cases Nana evidently succeeded. One British visitor described him as "one of the best and most hospitable natives in the upper provinces."[243] Nana was invited to the opening of Cawnpore's telegraph office in 1854,[244] and inducted into the local Masonic Lodge Harmony reputedly as the first Indian Entered Apprentice.[245] But many returned Nana Sahib's hospitality with weary and ungrateful scorn, for to the British Indian princes were parasitic vestiges of a degenerate past: lazy, dull and useless.[246]

Nana Sahib did not fit this bill. He was, or at least had once been, athletic; he loved to swim, sometimes tried his hand at cricket, occasionally drilled his bodyguard, and in his thirties continued to ride and hunt. He was generous to his guests and lived in grand style, but one visitor described him as a "quiet, unostentatious young man, not at all addicted to any extravagant habits."[247] He had enough intellectual curiosity to have various English-language papers read to him every morning. Though he was never as popular as his father had been, his reputation at Bithur was of a pious man who always bathed before worship so as not to pollute the Ganges, and who gave as much as he could afford to the schools and priestly establishments his father had founded.[248]

Nothing could inflame the repressed imaginations of Victorian England more than an Indian zenana, but, despite Baji Rao's rapacity, Nana's domestic arrangements were rather mundane for an eastern prince. In 1854 he married a fourteen-year-old Deccani Brahmin girl named Krishna Bhai who lived in an apartment bleakly walled in by floor-to-ceiling mirrors and furnished with a trio of Bareilly couches.[249] He also especially admired a dancing girl named Bhima, but a young courtesan named Adala was evidently his most trusted female companion, upon whom he lavished hundreds of thousands of rupees' worth of jewels and silks.[250]

The visitor who left the most detailed account of Nana Sahib's court was the lawyer John Lang.[251] Lang had represented Nana Sahib's childhood playmate, the Rani of Jhansi, in her futile attempt to overturn Dalhousie's annexation of her kingdom in 1854. But his reputation among Indians rested on his spectacular success in suing the Company on behalf of Joti Prasad, an Agra banker who had loaned the British almost half a million pounds to maintain the Company's armies, both at Gwalior and during the war in Afghanistan. The Company had not only reneged but attempted to try Joti Prasad for malfeasance. Lang handed the government such a resounding defeat that at the conclusion of the trial, crowds of Indians had carried him and his portly client out of the courthouse on their shoulders.[252]

In Lang's honor, Nana Sahib pulled out all the stops. The attorney was greeted on the road by an escort of eight soldiers with drawn swords and four cavalrymen who "caused their horses to curvet and prance, and thus kick up a frightful dust." Lang was conducted to a suite of European guest apartments at Saturday House where he was surrounded by servants and offered "every kind of European beverage" and even a beef dinner if he so desired. Careful of Nana's Brahminacal sensibilities, Lang ordered rice and vegetables instead.[253]

He supped alone at a twenty-foot-long former "mess table of a cavalry regiment," dabbing at his mouth from time to time with a "bedroom towel." Lang was then escorted "through numerous narrow and gloomy passages" to the royal apartment in a corner of the palace, where, after removing his shoes, he found Nana Sahib sitting on a Turkish carpet and reclining slightly on a bolster. In front of him, on a floor covered with a sheet of immaculate white linen that had been drawn as tight as a drumhead and fastened at the four corners of the room, lay a sword, a *hookah*, and a nosegay.[254]

Nana Sahib was a wide, stolid, sallow thirty-year-old of middle height with a straight nose and large, restless eyes. His face and head were clean-shaven, "leaving only so much as a small skull-cap would cover," though as a youth he had sported a little upturned mustache. According to a Cawnpore surgeon named Tressider who once had the honor of lancing His Highness's infected toe, Nana was "an excessively uninteresting person" who "might have passed for the ordinary shopkeeper of the bazaar," but for his tight *kimkhob* (gold-embroidered) blouse through whose seams his chest hairs protruded, and his necklace of fat pearls, and his small bejewelled Mahratta turban shaped like a stout boat that floated at a tilt on the wave of his brow.[255]

Nana Sahib rose to greet Lang and show him to a chair. "The whole world," he said, "is ringing with the praise of your illustrious name."

"Maharaj," Lang replied modestly. "You are very good."

"From Calcutta to Kabul—throughout the whole of Hindoostan— every tongue declares that you have no equal. Is it true?"

Knowing that in India one "must not contradict his host, but eat his compliments with a good appetite," Lang ducked his head and murmured, "Maharaj."

A circle of attendants now formed around them. "The acuteness of your perceptions," Nana continued, "and the soundness of your understanding, have, by universal report, become as manifest as even the light of the sun itself." He turned to his attendants. "Is it true, or not?"

Oh, it was true, replied Nana's men, for how could it be possible "for a great man like the Maharajah to say that which was false?"

Nana Sahib asked if Lang's late father had been a great man.

"Maharaj," Lang replied, "you have honoured the memory of my father, and exalted it in my esteem, by expressing such an opinion." This was true enough; Lang's father had been a small-time Australian merchant who died before Lang's birth. Nana Sahib then asked if Lang's mother were a handsome woman. Lang demurred, but Nana Sahib claimed he could tell from Lang's "intelligent countenance" that simply to glimpse her would be worth a million pounds.

"I am going to England next year," Nana Sahib said. "Will the Sahib favour me with her address?"

"Laughing inwardly all the while," Lang dictated the fanciful address of a "Lady Bombazine, on the top of the Monument, in Piccadilly, Belgrave Square, St. John's Wood, Camberwell." Lang's mother was actually in Australia, where her convict origins had cost her son a place in Sydney society.

Nana promised to cherish her address and now offered him a "grand" hookah that had "evidently belonged to some European of extravagant habits."

As Lang drew in the hookah's "rose water fumes," Nana's courtiers issued compliments "in very audible whispers."

Nana Sahib told his moonshi to bring "the petition that I have laid before the Governor-General" which the moonshi began to read aloud. Nana seemed to listen "with perfect pleasure to its recital of his own wrongs," and Lang, struggling to stay awake, affected "to be astounded that so much injustice can possibly exist" and finally retired to bed and a massage administered by four attendants.

The next morning, after a breakfast of "Yorkshire pie, game pie, anchovy toast, mutton-chop, steak, sardines" and Fortnam & Mason marmalade, Lang accepted Nana's invitation to drive with him to Cawnpore, and the two men and five retainers climbed into his "very handsome landau" drawn by English horses in worn-out "country-made" harness. Nana chatted steadily as they trotted toward Cawnpore, assuring Lang that he had once owned a much better carriage and equipage worth twenty-five-thousand rupees. "But I had to burn the carriage," Nana sighed, "and kill the horses." He had loaned the carriage to a Cawnpore sahib to bring his sick child to Bithur for a change of air. But the child had died on the road, "and, of course, as a dead body had been in the carriage," explained Nana Sahib, "and as the horses had drawn that dead body in that carriage, I could never use them again."[256]

But why, asked Lang, hadn't he simply given the carriage away to a Christian or a Moslem?

"No," replied Nana Sahib, for then the sahib might have seen the carriage in another's possession and "his feelings would have been hurt at having occasioned me such a loss."

They arrived at Cawnpore in time to greet "the officers, civil and military, and their wives [who] were just coming out for their evening drive on the mall. Every soul saluted the Maharajah; who returned the salute according to Eastern fashion—raising the hands to the forehead. Several gentlemen approached the carriage near the band-stand and inquired after the Maharajah's health."

Nana embarrassed Lang by introducing him to all and sundry as "a great friend of the Governor-General, and . . . a relation of all the members of Council—a constant guest of the Queen of England . . . and of both Houses of Parliament."

On the drive back Nana Sahib reiterated his grievance with the Company and elicited Lang's promise that he would take it up personally with Dalhousie. "If I did not succeed in that quarter," Lang promised, "I would, on my return to England, take the earliest opportunity 'some day, quietly, after dinner' (this was his suggestion), of representing to her Majesty the exact state of the case, and that an adopted son of a Hindoo was entitled to all the rights and privileges of an heir born of the body."

Nana had grilled an earlier visitor "about the Hon. East India Company, and appeared exhaustless in his queries about the Board of Control,"[257] but now Nana told Lang not to bother with the Board of Control nor the Privy Council, for Nana "had the most positive proof that both these institutions had eaten bribes from the hand of the East India Company in respect of his claim." His "positive proof" of this turned out to be a letter from Azimullah Kahn.

After a *nautch* (a performance by dancing girls) three "slaves" came to Lang's apartment to sing him to sleep and whisper to him that "two women of rank were kept in a den not far from my apartments, and treated like wild beasts; and a third—a beautiful young creature—had recently been 'bricked up in a wall,' for no other fault than attempting to escape."

The "two women of rank" were probably Baji Rao's widows, whom their agents had repeatedly accused Nana Sahib of imprisoning.[258] The Commissioner had investigated such charges and found them baseless, but he must have been hard put to distinguish between imprisonment and the usual confinement of women in royal households.[259] They led lives of stifling insularity, and from all appearances serving girls, courtesans, and queens were all, in effect, prisoners and slaves.

On Lang's last morning at Bithur, Nana Sahib gave him a tour of his menagerie and showed him his collection of armaments—"his guns and pistols by Purdey, Egg, and other celebrated makers; his swords, and his daggers, of every country and age." Seeing that Nana appeared to be happily muddled by "some stimulant recently imbibed," Lang "took an opportunity of discoursing on the vanity of

human wishes, and especially with reference to his Highness's grievance. I translated many sentiments of Juvenal and Horace into Hin-
doostanee; but, I regret to say, they had no effect. . . .

"Such was the Maharajah," concluded Lang, "commonly known
as [Nana] Sahib. He appeared to me not a man of ability, nor a fool."
Indeed he was not very different, Lang said, from most Indian
princes. "During my rambles in India I have been the guest of some
scores of rajahs, great and small, and I never knew one who had not
a grievance."[260]

But in fact such regal grievances were Lang's bread and butter, and
few princes would have put up with his pretensions except in order
to sound him out. Nana carefully avoided discussing the matter directly with his other guests, even when the discussion turned to politics. In 1851 an anonymous official had also visited Nana Sahib, and
though he acknowledged that the Maharajah may have "cultivated
the acquaintance and friendship of the sahibs solely in the hope that
through their influence, direct and indirect, his grievances would be
redressed," nevertheless Nana "never once alluded to his grievances"
but talked entirely about "the Oude affair."[261]

THE EMASCULATE CAPITAL
Lucknow: 1764–1856

Lucknow, Oudh's capital, stood sixty miles to the northeast: an elegant and gracious sister city to drab and drudging Cawnpore.
The kingdom dated only from 1720, when the Emperor appointed a
Persian merchant governor of the Moghul territory of Oudh.[262] His
successors acquired the titles of viceroy and then minister, and thus
became known as the Nawab Viziers.[263] Seven years after the Battle
of Plassey Nawab Vizier Shuja-ud-daula took in the fugitive Nawab
of Bengal and with the Moghul Emperor Shah Alam made a bid to
seize Bengal back from the Company.[264] After an ignominious defeat
at the Battle of Buxar in 1764, the Nawab Vizier limped into the
British camp. Oudh became a Company protectorate guarded by a
British subsidiary force that Lucknow was forced to support by ced-

ing to the Company a portion of its provinces worth a million and a half rupees in yearly income.[265]

The office of Nawab Vizier was supposedly held at Delhi's pleasure, but in fact it became hereditary, and in order to diminish the Emperor further, Calcutta permitted the Anglophile Nawab Vizier Ghazi-ud-din to crown himself the King of Oudh in 1819 to the strains of *God Save the King*.[266] Though Lucknow was the center of Shiism in India, the King of Oudh was not the papal figure the Sunni Moghul Emperor was.[267] But he was tremendously wealthy, and, under the protection of the British force at Cawnpore, turned Lucknow into one of the most fabulous cities in the world.

"Not Rome, not Athens, not Constantinople; not any city I have seen," wrote William Howard Russell, "appears to me so striking and so beautiful as this; and the more I gaze, the more its beauties grow upon me."[268] Its limestone stucco buildings were a strange amalgam of western and Moghul styles: Corinthian pilasters, Saracenic arcades. But their proportions were exquisite and their effect sublime. Minarets rose from lush gardens and grand gilded domes swelled like suns over venerable groves of shade trees.[269]

All of this was paid for by land revenues collected by *chakladars*, contractors who received a "commutation of the estimated revenues and pocketed any surplus." These chakladars in turn farmed out the job to mercenaries who simply appropriated the lands in their charge and wrung the cultivators dry.[270] The chakladars and *talukdars*[271] were constantly at war, and as allies of Lucknow the British were obliged to side with the king's voracious agents and send their subsidiary force out to put down the talukdars, in effect enforcing the revenue contractors' reign of terror.

The British debated for years whether to withdraw completely from Oudh or annex it. William Sleeman, the last Resident of Oudh, was opposed to annexations on principle. "The native states," he wrote Sir James Hogg, "I consider to be breakwaters, and when they are all swept away we shall be left to the mercy of our Native Army, which may not always be sufficiently under our control."[272] But Oudh so horrified him that he recognized that some intervention, even the direct assumption of the government, was probably inevitable.

It certainly seemed so when in 1847 the last King of Oudh, the jug-eared and jowly Wajid Ali Shah, ascended the throne at Lucknow, and James Ramsay, the 10th Earl of Dalhousie, accepted his appointment as Governor-General.[273] Wajid Ali Shah was an accomplished poet and a self-styled virtuoso on the "tom-tom" who tried at first to be a conscientious king, but beyond the scent of his perfumed fountains the kingdom was a shambles. No novelist could have invented a more complete nemesis for His Highness than Ramsay.[274] His father had served under Wellington at Waterloo and later as Governor-in-Chief of Canada. His mother was a lady of celebrated erudition. He carried on his shoulders not only his father's legacy but the promise of two older brothers who had died in their youth.[275] Educated at Harrow and Oxford, where his successors Canning and Elgin had been among his classmates, after a promising start as a parliamentarian he was appointed by Peel to the vice presidency of the Board of Trade, where he had almost killed himself demonstrating "his remarkable ability and great capacity for work."[276] Even before he set foot on Indian soil, at thirty-five years of age Dalhousie was already dangerously whittled down by overwork, but he could still reduce the most formidable men to jelly.[277] He produced acres of documents in his own hand, and probably accomplished more than any other governor-general, or viceroy for that matter: building roads, laying railways, digging canals, reforming almost every aspect of the Company's rule. It was no wonder that years after Dalhousie's departure men still glanced nervously over their shoulders at the mere mention of his name.[278]

Dalhousie was an especially formidable advocate, articulating the directors' policies so persuasively that they seemed to emanate entirely from himself. In 1848 he defended a long-established but rarely exercised policy known as the Doctrine of Lapse, whereby the Company could automatically annex the principality of any Indian ruler who died without natural issue. "Where the right to territory by lapse is clear," he wrote, "the Government is bound to take that which is justly and legally its due, and to extend to that territory the benefits of our sovereignty, present and prospective." He did not want to be inflexible, he insisted, and yet he proposed that "on all occasions, where heirs natural shall fail, the territory should be made to lapse, and adoption should not be permitted, excepting in those cases in which some strong political reason may render it expedient."

With the majority of the directors' backing, Dalhousie put their dormant doctrine into practice. When Sivaji's descendant at Satara died in 1849 without a male heir, Dalhousie annexed the kingdom and on the same basis scooped up three more kingdoms while he was at it.[279] In 1852 he agreed to recognize the adoptive heir of the late boy-king of Karauli on the grounds that his state was politically insignificant, but when the "poor, worn-out, impotent" but otherwise benign Raja of Nagpore died without issue in 1853 of "a complication of disorders, of which debauchery, cowardice, and obstinacy were the chief," Dalhousie bravely refused "to admit that a kind and generous sentiment should outweigh a just and prudent policy" and annexed a kingdom one and a half times the size of the newly annexed districts in the Punjab.[280] That same year, when the latest in a succession of sterile, sickly Rajas of Jhansi passed away, Dalhousie ingeniously ruled that since Jhansi's regency had been the contrivance of the Peshwa, whose powers had long since been extinguished, the governor-general could eliminate it, despite the eloquent protests of Lakshmibai, Nana Sahib's childhood playmate and now the old king's widow.[281]

Most Anglo-Indians conveniently believed that the people of India did not care who ruled them; that it was religion, not politics, that gave them security and continuity. Indians seemed so jaded and fatalistic that their desires, even if discernible, could be safely ignored. "The people are but one people," wrote the founder of the Indian Civil Service. "It is indifferent to them whether they are under Europeans, Mussulmans or their own Rajas."[282]

The British were therefore shocked by how bitterly the subjects of even the most dissolute rulers grieved when Dalhousie dissolved their dynasties. "What they overlooked," wrote Zoë Yalland, "was the Indian need to have amongst them a figure whom they could revere; a king in their midst, and a king from their own people."[283]

✦   ✦   ✦

During his first and only home leave in over half a century's service, Sir Hugh Massy Wheeler was promoted to Major General, and on his voyage back to India he still hoped to cap his career with the ultimate honor of commanding the Bengal Army. Though commanders-in-chief of the Bengal Army were almost always appointed from the Queen's Army, the practice was under constant attack in the British press, and Wheeler dared hope that he might be just the Company general to break with this suffocating tradition.

No sooner had he and Frances returned to India, however, than he found himself at the age of sixty-seven riding in the cold rain of a January morning at the head of a large army of native troops, marching across the Ganges into Oudh.[284] Not since his foray into Kashmir ten years before had Wheeler embarked on a more delicate mission. The axe was finally about to fall on the Court of Oudh, and it was up to good old Wheeler to subdue the native country of so many of his Indian troops. Dalhousie could no longer tolerate the turmoil of the kingdom of Oudh. The King's soldiers ran wild through the countryside, whole villages had been abandoned, the King had almost entirely emptied his vaults into the pockets of his eunuches and minstrels.[285] But something else about the Court of Oudh rankled the Marquis, for as the newly widowed governor-general worked himself toward an early grave "the laughter and revelry of Lucknow," writes John Pemble, "seemed like a living affront to his own inner anguish; a mockery of his own self-mortification in the cause of duty."[286]

The Company's representative at Oudh was sixty-year-old William Sleeman, the exterminator of the Thugs and the Puritanical embodiment of the Company's emerging "moral duty."[287] He had once written that "annexation might some day render us too visibly dependent upon our Native Army," and if the sepoys recognized this dependency "accidents might occur to unite them, or too great a portion of them, in some desperate act."[288] But by the time he had been appointed to Lucknow his natural curiosity and empathy had given way to a mania for loyalty and correctness. Like so many aging crime-fighters, he was prone to bouts of paranoia.[289] After a series of fruitless, frustrating audiences with Wajid Ali Shah, Sleeman concluded that the government should remove the king's chubby, bejewelled fingers from the reins of power and set up a council of regency with himself at its head. Sleeman made a tour of the countryside to gather evidence of misrule, and from his interviews with obliging peasants assembled an incoherent but impassioned condemnation of the king's administration before retiring from India in a state of collapse.

At last Dalhousie composed his definitive minute on the subject. Whether by edict or force, the time had come to annex the kingdom and rescue not only the peasantry of Oudh[290] but the Company's purse while he was at it, for Dalhousie's reforms and construction projects had added £8,354,000 to the public debt.[291] On February 4, 1856, Sleeman's successor, James Outram, presented Wajid Ali Shah with an ultimatum: either sign over the administration of Oudh to the Company by noon of February 7, or the British would take his kingdom by force.

The king's mother pleaded with Outram to giver her son one last chance to mend his ways, but Outram was adamant, and as Wheeler marched across the Ganges and camped eight miles outside Lucknow's city limits, Wajid Ali Shah descended into bathos: weeping, pleading, baring his head to the appalled and embarrassed Colonel Outram. But at the urging of his fierce queen, the beautiful and brilliant Hazrat Mahal, he refused in the name of their son, Birjis Qadr, heir to the throne of Oudh, to sign the ultimatum.[292] The deadline passed, and the kingdom was officially annexed and occupied.[293]

Apart from the few cowed peasants who had paused in their labors to chat with Sleeman on his fact-finding tour, the people of Oudh had not been consulted. Conditions under Wajid Ali Shah may well have been every bit as bad as Sleeman had reported, but at least their oppressors had been familiar. The king's administration may have been corrupt, but it was also accommodating and above all Indian. The Company's promise of British efficiency and incorruptibility meant an alien inflexibility, incomprehensible laws, uncomprehending judges, a remote and inscrutable authority. Yesterday they had been the downtrodden subjects of a flesh-and-blood king from a splendid house, now it seemed they were to be the downtrodden subjects of the faceless, soulless *Kampani Jehan*.

✦ ✦ ✦

Among those who grieved the passing of the Oudh dynasty was an "inveterate and unscrupulous intriguer" named John R. Brandon, proprietor of the North-Western Dawk Company and publisher of the *Central Star*. Brandon had been a protege of one of Wajid Ali Shah's favorites, a larcenous barber named DeRusset who had arranged for Brandon's posting as a horticulturalist to one of Wajid Ali Shah's credulous predecessors. Brandon shared in the barber's banishment in 1837, but ten years later returned as a kind of impresario under the protective wing of a court minstrel, peddling mechanical toys and other amusements to the king, putting up with His Majesty's pranks, and bribing his eunuchs and minstrels to secure preferential treatment.[294] His primary competitors, the Greenway brothers of Cawnpore, owned something called the Lucknow Dawk, and yet, with his contacts at court, Brandon could undercut his competitors by charging half what the government levied for conveying parcels.[295] But now Brandon's cronies were streaming out of the emasculate capital, and in their place the Company's contemptuous Puritans were getting down to business.

Withdrawing to Cawnpore to look after his other enterprises—a store, a press, a railway contracting firm— in February 1857 he hired an agent named John Hampden Cook to look after his dwindling operation in Lucknow.[296] Cook had married a Eurasian widow and together they produced two sons and three daughters, who ranged from infancy to about ten. But his oldest charge was his seventeen-year-old stepdaughter Amy, whose natural father, Captain Frederick William Horne of the Royal Navy, had died when she was still a baby. A pretty, vivacious girl and a gifted pianist, Amy Horne detested Lucknow. "The place held out no inducements," she would recall. "It was so different from anything I had ever seen, the houses so strange, the streets so narrow, and the people so unlike those in the Bengal that I used to feel as if I had got into another world."

The Cooks lived near an iron bridge whose traffic was so dense that "night after night, without exception, was one of the merry making and rejoicing, and little sleep could we obtain." Moslem nobles still made their regal progress through the streets "arrayed in all the splendour [imaginable], their dress generally of the richest satins, and spangled over with silver and gold, . . . but this was shabby finery." Their cloaks and palanquin curtains were "filthy beyond description, the streets are never known to be swept; and flies abound in such numbers that sometimes the shops can only be opened at night." To make things worse, the streets were infested with monkeys that were always "unscrupulously walking off with all they could lay their hands on."

The people of Lucknow seemed to Amy "the most indecent, abusive set in the wide universe," and when, two months after their arrival at Lucknow, a band of young rowdies from the bazaar encircled her during an evening stroll and threw a garland around her neck, her outraged stepfather resolved to leave Lucknow. In April 1857, seeing "in the insolence of the natives," as he put it, "the shadow of coming events," he moved his family to Cawnpore.[297]

THE APPEARANCE OF DESIGN
Nana Sahib: 1856–1857

When the deposed King of Lucknow slouched down to Cawnpore to begin his eastward journey into exile, thousands of his dispossessed subjects followed him across the Bridge of Boats, weeping and singing dirges to the clatter of drums. But to Nana Sahib the king's predicament must have seemed almost enviable. Wajid Ali Shah had been offered a pension of some £150,000—almost twice what Baji Rao had received—plus all his titles and complete control of his household in a microcosmic kingdom on the Hooghly that would be reminiscent of the Peshwa's establishment at Bithur but infinitely more grand.[298]

With the failure of Azimullah's mission to London, Nana could expect nothing but the rapid dissolution of his own power, purse, and prestige. Except for a few souvenirs—including a letter from Queen Victoria, Azimullah's own portrait by Henry Phillips, a French printing press, and an amusing sheaf of love letters from "Miss A." of Brighton—Azimullah had nothing to show for the more than £50,000 of Nana's money he had spent in England and Europe. Though he apparently managed to elicit a letter from the Queen to Nana Sahib, all he appeared to have accomplished with his parlor allies like Lady Duff Gordon and his clumsy overtures was to annoy and alienate the Company further.[299]

Another Indian emissary living in an earlier time might have expected to lose more than his king's favor for returning such a failure. Sivaji might have beheaded him; even his flaccid descendant, the deposed ruler of Satara, had disowned his failed emissary, forcing him to apply to the Company for passage home.[300] But even if Nana Sahib had been disposed to scold or punish his agent for the spendthrift futility of his European tour, by the time Azimullah returned to Bithur in the early months of 1857, the "charity boy" was ready for him. He and Ali had spent their long journey through Europe—they did not reach Aden until October 1856—preparing their defense and developing their thesis. They had revisited Constantinople, where by some accounts they gained an audience with the Sultan and communicated with Russian agents. They are also said to have approached representatives of Napoleon III in Paris, traveled to Cairo and conferred with the Caliph of Baghdad. On the overland journey from Bombay Azimullah had made "a kind of tour of inspection to feel the temper of the Mahratta, Rajpoot, Seik Chiefs on his route from Bombay to enable him to report progress to his master."[301] He may even have paused at the court of Delhi, where, though the dreamy old emperor was a disappointment, his leonine wife, the Begum Zinat Mahal, was determined to restore the Moghuls to their former glory and place her son upon the throne.

On his arrival at Bithur, Azimullah apparently urged Nana Sahib to forget about his pension.[302] Why worry about a measly stipend when he might annihilate the English and recover his throne? His Majesty was to put out of his mind the fairy-tale picture the Company had painted of a vast and prosperous Emerald Isle teeming with soldiers and ruled by a wise and mighty Queen. Azimullah had seen the English in their frigid, filthy little lair. He had laid eyes upon the homely drudge they called a queen. He had seduced their noblewomen, toyed with their credulous intelligentsia, and seen their reforming liberality for the sham it was. At the Crimea he had seen England's vaunted army starved, diseased, defeated. John Company was merely a hollow serpent's skin that India could shake off with one shrug of its shoulders. If Nana Sahib could unite with the sepoys the British had betrayed, the princes they deposed, the zemindars they dispossessed, the Brahmins and Maulvies they disgraced—if he made common cause with the Emperor of Delhi in whose name the Peshwas had always ruled, he could drive these *Feringhees* into the sea.

Nana Sahib may have proved particularly receptive to Azimullah's thesis, for his guru, a centenarian named Dassa Bawa, had evidently divined that Nana Sahib would someday be "as powerful as the Peshwa had once been." Nana Sahib had politely thanked the old man for this prediction and casually promised to reward him with a jagir if it ever came true. But one night after an astrological ceremony Nana himself dreamed that the monkey-god Hanuman visited him and promised that he would reign victorious. The vision was so compelling that upon awakening Nana was said to have summoned Dassa Bawa and showered the ancient sage with twenty-five-thousand-rupees' worth of jewels.

But Azimullah was well enough acquainted with the culture of the Peshwas to know that Nana Sahib would not choose to fight the British unless forced. His Highness's early martial enthusiasms appear to have waned, and though he was not a coward, he had learned from his adoptive father that a Mahratta always kept his options open. He was a king, but from a line of Concanist Brahmins who had acquired their power by disguising themselves as mere servants of some greater power, whether Mahratta, Moghul, or British.[303] And so Nana would wink at Azimullah's machinations in case they bore fruit, while at the same time graciously welcoming his fellow Masons and British houseguests should the Company prevail. He would indulge Azimullah's fanaticism even if he did not share his secretary's bloody-minded hatred of the British. He would spoil his guests even if their government denied him his rights and titles.

Wishing no particular harm to anyone, Nana could be perfectly sincere in both cases. It was all a matter of statesmanship.

✦   ✦   ✦

As soon as the King of Lucknow was out of the way, Company civil servants fanned out across the newly annexed territory of Oudh, dispossessing the native proprietary landholders or talukdars,[304] raising assessments, collecting taxes, and demanding the immediate payment of arrears. In many cases land was assessed on past rates, but there was no time for even the most conscientious and humane collector to investigate the sometimes inflated figures the village accountants provided, and "past rates," of course, were often the ruinous rates the worst of the talukdars had collected in the first place. Though assessments overall were reduced, the egregious overassessments in some parts of Oudh seemed to the rest of the territory a precursor of things to come.[305] The talukdars had been reduced to rapacious caricature in Sleeman's reports to Dalhousie, but many had been, for better or worse, the lords and protectors of the villages they held. Now, stripped of their wealth and power, they could no longer intercede in bad times, support the priests in their rites and festivals, or assist families at marriages and funerals. In the name of rationality and fixed revenues, the entire agrarian system of Oudh had suddenly lost its flexibility and its human face.

Wajid Ali Shah's army had been dissolved, but a portion was reorganized into regiments of "Oudh Irregulars" under British commanders. Many of the king's soldiers were rejected as too old or too undisciplined; others vowed never to serve the infidels and stalked off into the countryside. Oudh had always hosted more than its share of idle soldiery, whose numbers increased as other kingdoms fell to the Company, and their renegade soldiery fled into the king's jurisdiction.[306] With annexation their numbers swelled dramatically, and in almost every village dismissed soldiers and disgraced talukdars brooded and plotted. The Company initiated a campaign of reducing all of the talukdars' mud forts and requisitioning all of their cannon. Some few small cannon came creaking in, but a great many more were disassembled and their components buried in walls or dropped into wells for some future dispensation.[307]

Among those the king left behind at Lucknow was his most ambitious Begum Hazrat Mahal,[308] the mother of the nine-year-old Birjis Qadr who, whether he was the legitimate son of Wajid Ali Shah or, as was whispered, the bastard of her paramour, she championed as the king's successor.[309] Hazrat Mahal was every bit as formidable as Begum Zinat Mahal of Delhi; indeed, had *purdah* not prohibited these two great queens from commanding troops in the field, the uprising of 1857 might have lasted much longer than it did. Whether Wajid Ali Shah had left Hazrat Mahal and her son behind because they had fallen out of favor or whether they remained at Lucknow to keep His Majesty's hopes alive, when the royal family approached Azimullah for advice about their appeal, he and the Begum appear to have formed a secret alliance. According to a letter Azimullah wrote to the Turkish general Umar Pasha, by 1856 they were "engaged in raising the country," and praying that "(please God) the next news would be of the expulsion of the infidels."

In his letter Azimullah also reminded the Pasha that "when they met in the Crimea, his Excellency had mentioned that he would be glad of information as to the condition of India; in pursuance of which [Azimullah] now had the honour to report that the British had sent an expedition to Persia, which was likely to fail, especially when the Persians were aided by a Russian army, as would surely be the case."[310] Such letters do not appear to have accomplished very much, but writing them must have been exhilarating for the former charity boy. In the perfumed seclusion of his apartments at Saturday House, Nana himself may have enjoyed them too, tilting his head to the rhythms of Azimullah's prose, just as he had once listened in John Lang's presence to the graceful music and unassailable logic of his late secretary's petitions to Calcutta: leaning back on his silken bolsters and dreaming of Sivaji's glory regained.

✦   ✦   ✦

Azimullah bestowed his new French printing press on his allies at Lucknow, who used it to publish eight-hundred copies of a pamphlet called the *Rissalah Jehad*, "a vehement exhortation to all true Moslems to take up arms and do battle for their Faith."

"You are always striving, by prayer and penance, and burdensome ceremonies," it read, "to wipe off your sins and arrive at Heaven at last. Why not scale it at once by dying in Battle with the Infidel? . . . Throughout Hindustan, let there be no sound but Allah." Later the press would crank out a journal called *Payam-e-Azadi*, edited by a grandson of the Emperor himself and regarded as so seditious that Henry Lawrence threatened to hang any Indian caught reading a copy.[311]

Azimullah also cultivated the allegiance of Jwala Prasad, the commander of Nana's bodyguard. Jwala was a tall, slight Brahmin with a whining, nasal voice and a hangdog, pockmarked face framed by long black curls.[312] His five-hundred-man force was all that remained of the vast army of French-trained troops Baji Rao had once led gingerly into battle. His elderly horsemen rode bony nags, feebly brandishing lances and rusted sabres. His infantry consisted of men dressed in a miscellany of uniforms and armed with clubs, pikes, and venerable, dragon-mouthed matchlocks from which they were permitted to fire only blank charges.[313] His artillery, intended solely for ceremonial purposes, consisted of about five small and venerable guns.[314]

Nana's little army posed no threat to anyone but the stray peasant or traveler from whom its soldiers sometimes extorted money, but over the years its commander had insinuated himself into the good graces of the native regimental officers at Cawnpore. In the old Mahratta universe allegiances were often tenuous, and few princes would initiate a campaign against another without first trying to buy off the other's army.[315] And so, with the furtive encouragement of Nana and the two Begums, Azimullah sent Jwala Prasad into Cawnpore to work on the sowars of the Company's 2nd Native Cavalry.

Raised in 1787, the 2nd had fought valiantly at Delhi, Laswari, Deig, Afghanistan, Ghuzni, and received an honorary standard for its role in Lord Lake's campaign against Holkar. But in 1840, two companies of them fled from what turned out to be a small body of Dost Mahomed's Afghan horsemen, and the expedition's outraged commander had disbanded the entire regiment and transferred all of its European officers to the 11th Native Cavalry. For ten years the 2nd simply ceased to exist, but the 11th fought so bravely at Mooltan—where an older cousin of the regiment's current Major Edward Vibart captured a Sikh standard—that in 1850 the Company restored the regiment's old number.[316]

Those ten years of disgrace had nevertheless soured the sowars of the 2nd Native Cavalry. Though the regiment was primarily Moslem, one of its rissaldars (lieutenants) was an Oudh Rajput named Teeka Singh[317] whose house in the native lines at Cawnpore became a gathering place for the disaffected.[318] Here Jwala Prasad met with a horse dealer and former sowar named Muddud Ali[319] and a former comrade named Raheem Khan, and assembled small cells of restive sowars who squatted in Teeka Singh's courtyard to vilify their officers.

"The men who cared least for all this," wrote a civil servant of the time, "were those most in danger, our young officers in the native regiments."[320] Even those European officers who knew of Teeka Singh's meetings shrugged them off, for it was an article of faith that the Hindus and Moslems could never unite against the British. The Moslems themselves were divided between the Sunnis of Moghul India and the Shias of Oudh, and certainly there could have been no love lost between the elderly Moghul Emperor of Delhi and Nana Sahib, whose adoptive ancestors had so reduced him; nor for that matter between the emperor and Wajid Ali Shah of Lucknow, whose ancestors had wrested Oudh from the Moghuls' grasp. But both the Peshwas and the kings of Oudh had always ruled in the name of the Grand Moghul. He had been their buffer, their validation. "The Nana," as a chronicler pointed out, "claimed to be Peshwa of the Maratha Confederacy; and . . . immediately before the introduction of British supremacy, the Maratha Peshwa had been the titular Viceregent of the Moghul Empire." Humiliated, disgraced, condemned by the Company to inconsequence and ultimate bankruptcy, Nana Sahib would have been "glad to fill" his ancestor's post.[321]

In April 1857 Azimullah guided Nana Sahib on a tour of Lucknow, bearing letters of introduction from "a former Judge of Cawnpoor" addressed to the financial commissioner, Martin Gubbins, and to Henry Lawrence's military secretary, the dashing and erudite Captain Fletcher Hayes. Apparently the heir of the Peshwa of all the Mahrattas was insufficiently awestruck by these two aspiring bureaucrats, for "his manner," Gubbins blustered, "was arrogant and presuming. To make a show of dignity and importance, he brought six or seven followers with him into the room, for whom chairs were demanded. One of these men was his notorious agent Azimoolla." Evidently Nana made a better impression on Henry Lawrence. The old man received Nana "kindly, and ordered the authorities of the city to show him every attention."[322] Nana paraded around Lucknow, Gubbins recalled, "with a retinue more than usually large," and may have visited with Azimullah's ally, Hazrat Mahal. "His demeanor at Lucknow," wrote Gubbins, "and sudden departure to Cawnpore, appeared exceedingly suspicious, and I brought it to the notice of Sir Henry Lawrence. The Chief Commissioner concurred in my suspicions, and by his authority I addressed Sir Hugh Wheeler, cautioning him against the Nana, and stating Sir Henry's belief that he was not to be depended on."[323] But Nana's "bearing and that of his followers was always arrogant," wrote another witness, and "it was only the subsequent events which gave their vulgarity the appearance of design."[324]

DEATH AND ABSENCE

The Lindsays: 1856–1857

By the 1850s generals of Wheeler's vintage had taken their place in out-station farces alongside the sputtering babus and over-aged maidens who came to India to troll for husbands. Their languor, their bluster, their fatherly indulgence toward the native troops they called their "children" were the stuff of endless jests and anecdotes. In their prime these old warriors had been nearly autonomous commanders who could punish and reward their troops with almost complete impunity. But as these old soldiers slowly rose in the ranks, nominal promotion seemed to go hand-in-hand with effective demotion. By the age of sixty or seventy they might command regiments, brigades, whole armies, but in the meantime, in the name of regimentation and reform, Calcutta had busily whittled away at their authority until they were mere figureheads, intermediaries between the Company and its Indian levies. Their troops came to realize that they could no longer turn to their "fathers" for protection from the chilly abstrusities and gratuitous indignities of the Company's proliferating regulations. For their part the old brigadiers groused in their cups about the Company's ingratitude, decrying the reformers, deploring their subordinates' ignorance, arrogance, and impatience.

A prime example of the new breed of Company man was Wheeler's adjutant at Cawnpore, Major William Lindsay. The short, portly son of a Dundee grain merchant, Lindsay was ostensibly attached to the 10th Native Infantry, but he had spent most of his career as a staff officer. "I have no ambition to become a character or at all conspicuous by any actions," he once wrote as a young ensign. Though he longed to feel that he was somebody, "in fact I like to be nobody."[325] He was one of those equable, literate, dependable men

Major William Lindsay   *Lillias Don Lindsay*

upon whom not only his senior officers but the continuity of the
Bengal Army depended. As acting assistant adjutant general, officiat-
ing sub assistant commissariat general, and assistant adjutant general,[326] he had overseen the correspondence and forborne the
tantrums and hesitations of colonels, brigadiers, and commanders-
in-chief. Reviewing the muster rolls; relaying orders from Calcutta;
dispensing keys; arranging tours of inspection; taking inventory of
stores and munitions; processing requests for leaves; attending
courts-martial; overseeing the crosslegged Indian writers who
scrawled their translations on the verandah, Major William Lindsay
had spent the past three decades on call at his desk under the
lugubrious waft of a *punkah*, drudging his way toward promotion.

He and his wife Lilly doted on their three children, but in 1854,
when their oldest child was only seven years old, Lilly took them
back to England. "My heart is full when I think of children being sent
home," William Lindsay wrote his sister from Cawnpore in 1851. "It
is the misery of this country."[327] But India was regarded as a spiritu-
ally and socially, as well as physically, dangerous place for children.
Anglo-Indian children were so indulged that parents worried that if

they were allowed to continue "prattling with all the artlessness of fearless childhood" they would never turn into proper young gentlemen and ladies.[328] Mothers feared that their offsprings' Christian lessons were "being mingled in their minds with the silly and abominable fables and images of the surrounding idols" and the sometimes lurid conversation of their native nurse maids.[329]

But the separations broke not only their children's hearts but their bonds with their parents. "After a long absence," wrote one chronicler, "parents and children meet as strangers. Death and absence," she concluded, "differ but in name."[330] Without the children, Lilly returned half-heartedly to India and her memsahib's existence at Cawnpore. Lindsay's devoted head babu, Lalik Ram, had hired servants for her and put everything in order, so that she arrived to find "the table laid and breakfast all ready," but she grieved for her children and despised Cawnpore society.[331] For reasons of modesty, respectability, and health, memsahibs had little freedom of movement, even in the hothouse confines of cantonments. Thus most female relationships in India, wrote Emma Roberts, were characterized by "a civil sort of indifference."[332] Lilly devoted herself to Christ Church, where the clumsy, muscular Reverend Moncrieff strained against the confines of his chaplaincy. His sermons were harsh, and he so favored his secondary role as director of the Free School that he sometimes neglected to open the church for major Christian holidays. The S.P.G.'s mission was in the hands of a pallid and hypersensitive widower named William Haycock, a former printer who had become a missionary "at some sacrifice of income."[333] He was evidently not one of he brightest of the S.P.G.'s New Lights (born-again Christians). Even after Haycock's death at Cawnpore, his brethren could not quite bring themselves to recall him with superlatives. His assistant Willis remembered his "constitutionally sensitive temperament,"[334] and the head of Bishop's College gingerly recalled him as a man of "patient, laborious, unostentatious habits,—not marked by any great intellectual endowments, but well acquainted with the language of the country, with revealed truth, and, I trust, with the power of religion."[335]

Such was Lilly's devotion to the church that when, at the age of forty, she lost a child in infancy, the Bishop of Calcutta himself sent her a book of sermons, inscribed with his "sincere condolences."[336] The major, seven years her senior, was overweight, plagued with lumbago, and fed up with India. But life in England was expensive, and he was determined to retire on a colonel's pension. "I only hope," he told his sister Mary, "I may be able to carry out my present wishes and intentions of leaving India for good in the end of 1858 so that I may still see them as boys and be able to enjoy some of their youthful frolics."[337] But now it appeared that before he left India the major was to pass the torch to another generation of Lindsays. His widowed sister Kate had decided to bring her son and three daughters to India, the son to seek a career in the civil service, where his father had been a magistrate, and the girls to find husbands among the eligible young bachelors of the Company's stations.

The nabobs had held out against such ladies as long as they could, but with each renewal of the Company's charter they had been forced in the name of decency, racial purity, and the prevention of venereal disease to open their dominions to English women and encourage young maidens deprived of suitors by the ravages of the Napoleonic wars to seek husbands in the Company's service. They were dubbed "spins"[338] and fell into two categories: the daughters of respectable Anglo-Indian families who had been sent off to England for their education; and the sisters, cousins, and schoolmates of Anglo-Indian brides who had been "induced to accompany them to the eastern world."[339]

Spins vastly complicated cantonment life. "The Anglo-Indian ladies," a civilian gingerly observed, "were not altogether suited to exercise the salutary effect on society that may be usually looked for at the hands of civilised woman. Such as the Anglo-Indian ladies were, the young officers were eager competitors for their smiles, and for this and other reasons were high-spirited, and, if the truth must be told, somewhat quarrelsome."[340] In fact, up until about 1855 and long after European gentlemen had found less hazardous means of settling their disputes, duels were still commonplace in India.

But a young officer need not have risked his life nor wasted his gunpowder, for Anglo-Indian courtship was characterized by ruthless calculations. When the first spins descended upon India, a junior officer of whatever promise stood little chance against the grizzled and "liver-decayed old Indian, with his parchment face" and treasure vaults of *mohurs* (gold coins) and rupees.[341] But by 1835, every rich old nabob and wealthy if "battered brigadier"[342] from "the days of sacks and sieges" had been taken, and the ambitious spin had to lower her sights to prosperous and often crapulous senior civil servants. The spins dubbed them "three hundred a year dead or alive"[343] because they were paid a starting salary of £300 and subscribed to a pension fund that guaranteed, after a few years' service, the same income to his widow.[344]

Kate Lindsay's son George put his mother's plans in doubt when he failed the stringent entrance examination for the Company's civil-service school at Haileybury. But eventually he had squeaked into the military school at Addiscombe, and Kate wrote William that she and her family would set sail in late July 1856 so as to arrive in India as the cool weather began. Lindsay hoped his rather imperious older sister would not be "disgusted and disappointed" with the changes in India since she had last lived there, "but I fully expect it." As Kate and George and the girls approached India like a juggernaut, the Lindsays pined even more for England and their children. They found it hard to get their minds off their return passage home, "yet we feel we may not set our hearts too fondly on any plan—it is so strange that we so crave to do the very thing *that Kate would not do*."[345]

In late October Kate and George and his sisters Caroline, Alice, and Fanny landed in India and immediately leaped into the social whirl of Calcutta and Barrackpore. At one officers' ball "the room was hung with flowers and the colors of the regiment," young Alice Lindsay breathlessly reported. It proved an ordeal to perform a quadrille "upon a clay ground, the thermometer up to a hundred, and in a perfect atmosphere of musquitos" at stations where the disproportionate number of men danced the ladies ragged.[346] The regimental musicians hired for these occasions were generally Eurasian, and at some stations a curtain was drawn across to shield the frolicking young couples from their sight.[347] The "superior domestics" who waited on their masters and mistresses dressed so splendidly that they often outshone the ladies, whose gowns were soon "tarnished, faded, lustreless" from the *dhobi*'s (laundryman's) ministrations.[348]

Kate had billed Alice as the beauty of the family, but Caroline seemed to catch everyone's attention. She appears ungainly in her only portrait, but was evidently more "finished" than her younger sisters and certainly more vigorous than George. And yet as the day of their journey upcountry approached, Caroline became strangely panic-stricken. Perhaps she had become smitten by some young officer, or overheard some worrisome scuttlebutt about disaffection among the troops, for when the time came to leave "she cried bitterly," recalled her host,[349] "and asked to be left with us, which we would have gladly consented to. From some presentiment she appeared afraid to go upcountry, but her mother would not hear of her remaining. At that time there was not even a shadow apparent of all that was to happen."[350]

After a slapstick journey up the Grand Trunk Road, Kate and her brood arrived at Cawnpore, where George's 1st Native Infantry had been posted. The girls seemed undaunted by the journey, Kate slightly the worse for wear. It was George who languished, keeping to his bed for two days with a fever complicated, perhaps, by a reluctance to plunge into the military career his mother had arranged for him. He struck his uncle the major as needing "to be drilled into some kind of method and arrangement as well as to have to think and act for himself" so that he would not make a fool of himself in front of his brother officers "who," wrote the major, "are quite a set of young men."[351]

George's 1st Native Infantry regiment had been raised as a battalion in 1757 by Robert Clive himself. It was known at first as the *Lal Paltan* or "red platoon" after their crimson European-style uniforms, but once red uniforms became the standard for many sepoy regiments the 1st dubbed itself the *Gillis-ka-Paltan* after its longtime commander, Captain Primrose Galliez. The regiment had been formed from the disparate material the Moghuls had employed in their armies—Pathans, Rohillas, Jats, Rajputs, Brahmans—but throughout its history they had been predominantly Moslem. It was a proud history. In 1758 at the Battle of Condore in Madras the sepoys of the 1st had "stood their ground nobly" against a French force three times their number and eventually sent them running, proving not only their own worth but that of native troops in general.[352] A year later at Masulipatam they pressed forward even when their European comrades had panicked and fallen back.

In 1803 they helped to rout the Mahrattas at the Battle of Laswari and were among the select regiments permitted to emblazon "Laswari" upon their colors.[353] In 1826 they had the further honor of adding "Bhurtpore" for their part in that terrible siege.[354] A native regiment's colors were almost religious relics, upon which a recruit was required to swear his allegiance, vowing, among other things, "to serve the Honourable Company faithfully and truly against all their enemies, while I continue to receive their pay and eat their salt." His allegiance to his colors was personal, the embodiment of his personal honor as well as the regiment's, and sometimes superseded religious beliefs. "We put our religion in our knapsacks," an old subhedar of the Madras Army once said, "whenever our colours are unfurled." The colors were brought forth during religious festivals, blessed before every campaign by Hindu and Moslem clerics, and even during the Mutiny the sepoys cherished them as emblems of their determination to remain soldiers, "faithful to their comrades and to each other."[355]

George's senior officer, Lieutenant Colonel John Ewart, had served at Bhurtpore, but not with the 1st. Like George, he was a newcomer to the regiment, having not taken command until 1855. He was fifty-three-years old and married to the former Emma Sophia Fooks. "Brave and clever"[356] and fluent in the vernacular, John Ewart was a strict and paternalistic parade-ground disciplinarian who addressed his sepoys as his "children."[357] George Lindsay would also be saluting Captains Turner and Elms[358] and five lieutenants, including thirty-year-old[359] Godfrey Richard Wheeler, the favorite son and aide-de-camp of Major General Sir Hugh Massy Wheeler himself. As a Eurasian Godfrey was something of an oddity among the Company's officers, but his connection to his legendary father and his capacity as an officer appears to have overwhelmed the scorn with which his Anglo-Indian comrades might have otherwise dismissed him.[360]

George could at least relax around fellow ensign J. C. Supple, who had just graduated with him from Addiscombe;[361] and he could experience the giddy pleasure of ordering around Sergeants Heron and Hilling and the grizzled Subhedar Major Radhay Singh and all his brooding sepoys.[362] By rights George had no business commanding these brave veterans of grueling marches and ferocious assaults, some of them thrice his age, most of them third- or fourth-generation soldiers in the *Gillis-ka-Paltan*. But now he was expected to shout commands in his tortured shipboard Urdu, mediate their Byzantine disputes, keep watch for signs of disaffection, all the while ingratiating himself with his brother officers by feigning (if he did not initially share) their contempt for the "niggers," as many of them called even the most decorated old Indian officers, and indulging "in those jokes at their expense to which young officers are prone."[363]

In the meantime George's sisters did their best to settle in at Cawnpore, where Caroline became the object of several officers' attentions. But she despised Cawnpore and longed to go home. "The station," Caroline confided to her Aunt Jane, "is a very ugly one and dreadfully scattered." Her uncle's house overlooked the river, but she found the view "by no means pretty or inviting to look at" except after a dust storm "when the grounds look as if covered with snow which I should not object to see.

"I have often and often wished I could be transported back to England to all my friends," she sighed, "but we must hope it is all for the best."[364]

✦ ✦ ✦

General Wheeler impressed Major Lindsay when, in late July 1856, he arrived to take command of the Cawnpore Division. "William likes Sir H. Wheeler very well," Lilly reported, but then other generals had been "very agreeable at first," only to prove irascible old martinets, "so we'll bide a wee before we say anything about the present Chief."[365] Nevertheless, Wheeler made an excellent impression on the station with his patient and diplomatic handling of a small crisis that arose when the occupant of the house he had rented, a Captain Bennington, refused to vacate until November, after his wife had given birth. "Now the Gen¹ *could* turn him out at once or at all events much sooner than in two months," wrote Lilly. "Moving from one house to another in this country is the work of a few hours & and [would] have been no fatigue at all to Mrs. Bennington! General Wheeler has shown great consideration not wishing to take any advantage of his position in the station."

At the age of sixty-seven Wheeler was now a vinegary, whittled-down man, "very grey," as one lieutenant described him, "of a sparing habit," and "not imposing in appearance except by virtue of a thoroughly military gait." But he had "a quick and intelligent eye" and despite his mangled left hand he was still a "first-rate equestrian," and vigorous enough to ride with his grown children through the outskirts of Cawnpore, chasing after jackals with his kennel of Scotch deer hounds.[366] "My service has been extraordinary," Wheeler himself would marvel. "With the exception of my two years in Europe—when unemployed—I have had but three months' General leave and was never absent on medical certificate."

Wheeler had understandably hoped he might be named commander-in-chief of the Company's army, but he had been disappointed to be named Commander of the Presidency Division at Barrackpore, and further demoralized by his subsequent appointment in June 1856 as Commander of the Cawnpore Division. He would do his duty, but it seemed clear to him that his career, like his life, was "on the downgrade."[367] Staff positions had eluded him for forty-one years, he concluded, only because he "had no Friends, and . . . had nothing from Govt that it could withhold from me."[368]

But in Calcutta's eyes Wheeler was still a creature of the regiment.

His distaste for ceremony and horror of public speaking had rendered him unfit for prestigious and well-paying civil-cum-military positions—residencies, commissionerships, lieutenant-governorships—that had been extended to old friends like the Lawrences. He was "Good Old Wheeler," one of the last of the sepoy officers: not quite *puckah* (proper) with his dubious lady and half-caste brood, but an excellent man in a crisis and, with his fluency in the vernacular and years of commanding sepoys, a very useful damper on the smoldering disaffection in the Company's native ranks.

✦ ✦ ✦

When their baby was stillborn in September, the Benningtons finally made way for the Wheelers.[369] The house was located across the street from Duncan's Hotel, a little over a mile from the river, with a long colonnaded verandah overlooking a vast yard and the tidy audacity of the new Ganges Canal.[370] The diversion of the sacred course of Mother Ganga had appalled the Brahmins and displaced and discomfited the native merchants, but by 1856 the Ganges Canal and its tributaries exceeded "all the irrigation lines of Lombardy and Egypt together."[371] Years would pass before they would make much difference to the farmers of the Doab, but eventually they did alleviate famine, and in the hot season of 1856 the swimmers and bathers who cooled themselves in the canal provided "one of the sights of Cawnpore."[372]

The smells of Cawnpore were not so delightful. In the native city "there were but six carts for carrying away filth, the sewers were generally defective and the house or subordinate drains so badly constructed that they often acted as mere cesspools."[373] Perusing the Canal Department's maps, the Quartermaster General envisioned the canal at Cawnpore as a kind of moat and proposed to move the westernmost boundary of the cantonments eastward along its edge, thereby protecting the military station from the encroachment of the pestiferous native city.[374] Now it fell to Wheeler to oversee construction of new barracks and dispose of the military facilities—barracks, godowns, the medical depot—now stranded on the other side.

The superintending surgeon at Cawnpore proposed that the old Dragoon (European Cavalry) hospital across from the soldiers' church of St. John's could be converted "with not very expensive alterations and additions" into a "commodious Medical Depôt."[375] In the meantime all three native infantry regiments then stationed at Cawnpore—the 1st, 53rd, and 56th—were to be moved to new positions and European regiments diverted to other stations while ground was prepared for the echelon of nine new barracks that the army proposed to construct close by the old Dragoon hospital.[376] Soon the plain surrounding the Dragoon barrack was aswarm with carpenters, masons, and coolies.

Overseeing all this construction was curious duty for a warhorse like Wheeler, and no less so for his brigadier, Colonel Alexander Thomas William Jack.[377] Erudite, handsome, impossibly brave, Jack was probably Wheeler's first choice as brigadier at Cawnpore. He was the beau ideal of an Indian Army officer and had proved himself to Wheeler again and again during the Sikh wars.[378] His classmates remembered him as a "tall, handsome, soldierly young man,"[379] and at fifty-one he was still a lean, Arthurian figure with greying mutton chops and a noble profile whose bachelorhood must have confounded the ladies of the station.[380]

But neither Wheeler nor Jack were miscast for the tacit role they were expected to play in the aftermath of the annexation of Oudh. While Wheeler held command in the Jullunder Doab, his 48th Native Infantry had been one of the very few regiments in the Punjab that had not threatened to mutiny over the withdrawal of two rupees' monthly field allowance.[381] And even Dalhousie's successor, Lord Canning, must have heard of the miraculous expedition Wheeler and Henry Lawrence had led into Kashmir. It must have seemed a stroke of genius simultaneously to appoint "Gunpowder" Lawrence Resident at Lucknow and old Hamlah Commander at Cawnpore.[382]

But it didn't seem so to the appointees themselves, who devoted their private correspondence to grousing about their careers.[383] By 1856 Lawrence was fifty years old, but with his long grey beard and narrow, sorrowing face he looked much older. Lawrence was a brave, humane and prescient civil servant, and no man predicted the catastrophe of 1857 with eerier specificity.[384] He was fed up with newcomers, reformers, and government itself, and toyed with returning to England. But in the meantime, as Commissioner of Oudh, he was once again faced with administering a territory whose annexation he had vehemently opposed.

Wheeler was confident of his sepoys' trust. Begging His Excellency's pardon for his "apparent egotism," Wheeler would later write Canning, but "I am well known to the whole Native Army as one who, though strict, has ever been just and considerate to them."[385] Nevertheless, he had been away for two years, and now the 48th

N.I., the regiment upon which that confidence had always rested, was stationed not at Cawnpore but at Lucknow with Henry Lawrence. His old subhedars still visited him across the Bridge of Boats, still brought him the *gup* from the native lines. But to the regiments stationed at Cawnpore he was a figure of some remoteness now: elderly, distracted, mulling over Calcutta's slights and snubs, doting on his daughters and his hounds, sagging a little in his saddle in the rising heat of the Doab spring.

AFFRONTS AND ALARMS
Wheeler: 1856–1857

In February 1857 small, grimy wheat cakes began to circulate among the Indian constables and village watchmen of the Doab. No one quite knew where the chupatties had originated, but it was widely believed among the Brahmins that the first of them had been concocted out of flour and lotus seeds by none other than Dassa Bawa, Nana Sahib's centenarian wizard, who had then distributed them among the watchmen of Bithur to circulate throughout the North-Western Provinces, declaring that Nana's suzerainty would one day extend as far as the chupatties reached.[386] India had seen such chupatties before. It was an old custom among local chiefs to distribute them to prepare the peasants for some imminent upheaval; any man who partook of the chupatties committed himself to obey whatever orders his chief might issue. Each watchman would hand a chupatty to his counterpart in the next village with the admonition that he bake five more and pass them on, and during the month of February the flames of the watchman's midnight cooking fires and torches flared in an ever-widening circle as the latest edition was baked and rushed off to the next village and the next, until they had spread across the whole of the North-Western Provinces.

The chupatties alarmed the British in the outstations,[387] but they failed to bestir Calcutta, where district officers "who dared to look gravely on the 'chupatty mystery,' were denounced as croakers."[388] Had the Company been "politically shaky," a newspaper editorialized, people might have been "disposed to detect a fiery cross in these local substitutes for a hot-cross-bun"[389] but it was hard to tell whether they would result in "an explosion of feeling, or only of laughter."[390]

But even the most complacent Calcutta bureaucrat had to concede that the cartridge business was more worrisome. The British had been slow to modify the guns and ammunition they issued to their infantry. The American Revolution had demonstrated the long-range inaccuracy of British smooth-bore muskets ninety years earlier, nevertheless they remained a mainstay of the British army because they were easier to load in close order than muzzle-loading rifles, whose grooved barrels required that powder charges be first rammed down the barrels and then bullets forced down the entire length with ramrods and mallets. But rifles were far more accurate, and after much experimentation the British decided to issue the muzzle-loading Lee-Enfield rifle, which reduced loading time by employing a paper cartridge containing both bullet and powder that could be rammed down all at once. According to army drills the cartridges had to be torn open with the teeth in order to expose the powder to ignition. But the first cartridges introduced to India were greased with tallow made from beef, whose ingestion was forbidden by Hindus, and pork, which was expressly forbidden by Moslems and regarded with disgust by both faiths.[391]

The history of the Company's army was replete with such blunders, but at a time of dangerous disaffection in the army's ranks this one proved colossal. A story circulated through the native lines of the Company's stations that at Barrackpore a sepoy had come upon an ammunition works where cartridges were rolled in animal fat.[392] Here was proof that the Company intended to destroy the caste and faith of its native troops and soften them up for the missionaries. The sepoys quietly resolved never to use the cartridges, and even looked with suspicion at the old musket cartridges that were still in use.[393]

At Barrackpore in late February the 19th Native Infantry refused even to touch their percussion caps, and after their colonel angrily confronted them with cavalry and artillery, they loaded their muskets and anxiously gathered on the parade-ground to defend their religion. At their demand the colonel withdrew his artillery and cavalry and canceled the next morning's parade. But as far as the government was concerned the 19th had committed mutiny, and Governor-General Canning ordered that as soon as enough European troops had been assembled, the regiment was to be disbanded.

Other sepoys were arrested for spreading sedition, and on March 29 an inebriated sepoy of the 34th Native Infantry named Mungal Pandy strutted before his regiment's lines at Barrackpore with a loaded musket, calling on his comrades to stand up against the forced conversion their officers were plotting. It was hard to argue that such a scheme was beyond the regiment's Colonel S. G. Wheler, an unabashed New Light who had been regularly thrown out of other regiments' native lines for berating sepoys with the Holy Word. And so Pandy's jemadar (second lieutenant) did nothing to restrain him, even after he fired at his British sergeant-major. When a lieutenant came galloping onto the parade-ground Pandy shot at him as well, felling his horse. In the swordfight that followed, Pandy badly wounded both the sergeant-major and the lieutenant, and, as the two men fled, other sepoys struck at them with their musket stocks.

The alarm spread up the ranks from Wheler—who deemed it "a useless sacrifice of life" to order a European officer to seize Pandy— to the station brigadier, Charles Grant, who seemed equally paralyzed by the crisis. Finally Hugh Wheeler's old friend General John Hearsey came thundering onto the parade-ground, and at the sight of this "enormous strong old man,"[394] as Lady Canning described him, Pandy turned his musket around and wounded himself in the chest.[395] On March 31, surrounded by artillery and troops of Her Majesty's 84th, Hearsey disbanded the 19th Native Infantry with as much compassion as Calcutta would allow: the sepoys were given their full pay, allowed to keep their uniforms, provided with transport home. As they piled their arms and limped homeward many of them wept, begged forgiveness, blessed General Hearsey for his unexpected mercies.[396]

All over India anxious officers issued orders that sepoys not only were no longer required to bite the cartridges but could grease them themselves "and therefore to their own satisfaction" with nutmeg butter, cocoa, cinnamon, or coconut palm oil. But all this seemed to many sepoys an admission that the Company had conspired to destroy their faith. That April furloughed sepoys, many of them from the Bible-battered 34th, returned home to Oudh and warned their comrades at Cawnpore that they would all "quarrel with Government presently; for new cartridges prepared with cows' and pigs' fat are going to be served out, and the sepoys refuse to receive them."[397]

"If an officer took *no* precautionary measures on receiving information of an intended plot, he was liable to the severest censure, [but] if he took precautionary measures he was accused of creating unnecessary distrust."[398] In every Company cantonment and camp officers debated "questions of novel and momentous sophistry. . . . Might a colonel call out his men, and then mow them down with grape if it was certain that the regiment was on the eve of revolt? Might he if it was almost certain? If it was most likely? If it was barely possible?"[399]

Congratulating his old friend Hearsey, General Wheeler wrote from Cawnpore that the Colonel of the 19th N.I. had "made a sad mistake in allowing himself to be dictated to instead of dictating, and his sending away the guns and cavalry before they (his men) had piled arms was most injudicious. I conceive that mutineers with arms in their hands should never be treated with or listened to. It is opposed to the first great principle of military discipline and subordination. He had the *power* to put them down, the want of which could alone justify his measures." Wheeler's approach would be to "counteract this system of terrorism and to induce the well-disposed (the great majority, I fully believe) to separate themselves from the disaffected. Effect this and you destroy mutiny." Though he had to concede that this was "easier said than done . . . that is no reason why it should not be attempted by every means and on every opportunity."[400]

✦   ✦   ✦

Following their husbands from post to post, officers' wives led an itinerant existence, and few were more itinerant than Emma Halliday. When Emma was a young girl, she had encountered a gypsy in the woods of Cranborne Chase near her home in Dorsetshire who told her that when Emma grew up she would marry the man she loved.[401] He would worship the ground she walked on and take her to "a far country across the seas," where they would be "very happy" and then meet a "terrible" death.[402] But she evidently disregarded this prophesy when the handsome Captain William Halliday of the 56th Native Infantry knelt before her and asked her to return to India with him as his wife.

Willie Halliday had seen action with the 56th against the Sikhs, and his faith in his sepoys was unbounded. Raised in 1815, Willie's regiment was known to its sepoys as the *Lambroon-Ka-Paltan* or "Lambroon Platoon," probably after one of its early commanders.[403] His men were a splendid sight in review order: rows of tall Oudh men in bell-topped shakos and red coats with white facings and gold lace, their polished bayonets and campaign medals shimmering in the rising light of morning. There might be a few bad apples in every

Edith Mabel Halliday

Emma Windham Halliday

Captain William Halliday

regiment, but with stalwart native officers like Rissaldar Major Bhowani Singh of the 2nd and Jemadar Khoda Bux of the 56th to look after them, Willie believed they could never spoil the barrel. His men were Pathans, Rohillas, Jats, and Rajput Brahmins whose ancestors had served in the armies of the nawabs and rajas of the Doab. Many of them were landholders of aristocratic bearing who, up until recently, had been treated with deference by their tenants and neighbors in their native villages, for not only did their army pay make them men of comparative substance, as soldiers of the ascendant Company they had been immune to the King of Lucknow's regulations and safe from the depredations of his revenue agents.[404] But now word was beginning to filter back from their furloughed comrades that they had lost all their status back home and all their privileges, and were now to be treated by the Company itself as no better than anyone else.[405]

Emma too admired Willie's sepoys. Many of them used to play with her delicate little toddler Mabel, carrying her on their shoulders and squatting around her in the garden as she read to them gravely from her ABC's, turning the pages and saying, "bow-wow-wow." But Emma despised her native servants. She probably understood even less of what her servants said than they understood of her mangled Hindustani, with the result that she would angrily bark at them for their misinterpretations. Her kitmutgar served plum pudding with the entrée and "used the finger napkins as dish clouts so I have had about 2 dozen spoilt."[406] "These people are so stupid," she declared after one particularly distressing supper, when her staff produced a hare laid out in a kind of racing posture, complete with tail, head and long singed ears.[407]

Imprisoned in cantonments, sweltering in the shuttered gloom of her drawing room, like memsahibs before and after her, Emma nursed unseemly grudges and suspicions, and even went so far as to poison her children's native nurse.[408] "I found some sweeties go very fast," she wrote her mother, "so I tartar emeticised them & today an *ayah* was sick & one [candy] gone, so I turned her off on the spot."[409]

But most servants were not dishonest, nor stupid, nor lazy. What was astonishing about them was their loyalty to employers who held them in such contempt, their honesty in the midst of such scarcity, and their supple mastery of Anglo-Indian protocols that were as complex as the most abstruse Brahminical texts: the orders of precedence, the dispensation of fish forks and butter plates, the circulation of calling cards. What many a languid memsahib before and after

Emma's time mistook for laziness and obstinacy was their servants' devout adherence to an ancient division of labor that prevented a cook from bringing food to the table, a kitmutgar from dusting the dresser, a groom from cutting grass for the horses.[410]

The Hallidays followed wherever the 56th Native Infantry led them: to the Punjab, Barrackpore, the hill stations of Simla and Darjeeling, and then to the Rajmahal Hills of Bengal to do battle with the aboriginal Santals. The Santals were nice people, usually: orderly, productive, and, according to Sir W. W. Hunter, full of "genial humanity." But droves of Mahajuns had used the Company's courts to steal their land, and in 1855 ten thousand of them decided to march on Calcutta to lay their grievances before Lord Dalhousie. The Santals had set out peaceably but soon ran out of supplies and began to plunder the countryside. Armed with bows and arrows, axes and very few guns, they swept eastward, burning and sacking towns, villages, indigo factories, railway stations. They slaughtered hundreds of Bengalis and five Europeans, including two ladies, and an expedition set off from Barrackpore to drive them back into the hills.

It proved a brutal and demoralizing campaign. The Santals learned not to engage the British directly but to melt back into the foothills until their lumbering foe had moved on.[411] Willie toyed with sending Emma and his daughter back to England, but found he could not bear to be away from them and brought them instead into Santal country. By then the campaign had reached the scorched-earth phase. Willie and a company of the 56th "utterly destroyed nine villages & immense quantities of grain and household furniture & implements. . . . Are you not ashamed of your husband?" Willie asked Emma. "I am almost ashamed of myself."[412] Emma had to be led around the corpses of hanged Santals, and at one camp, maddened by the scent of human remains, wolves carried away sheep, bit a man on the leg, and chased a sepoy up against Emma's tent.[413]

After seven months of burnings and hanging parties, the Santals finally shrank back into the hills, and the Hallidays retired for a few months to the hill station of Darjeeling before proceeding in February 1857 to the district of Banda, about sixty miles south of Cawnpore. Emma noticed along the way that "the milestones had been taken up and were lying on the ground": her first clue to the general disaffection that was about to overwhelm the North-Western Provinces.[414] Banda itself was impoverished, overtaxed, and ripe for rebellion, but Emma found the station pastoral, charming, and delightfully cheap. She assembled a menagerie, including a "Hausi" milk cow, a flock of pigeons, and two pet gazelles. The Halliday compound soon became "such a farmyard," as a neighbor described it, that "it quite reminded me of home."[415]

The local collector was the scholarly and devout F. O. "Foggy" Mayne who had been instrumental in persuading the Society for the Propagation of the Gospel to establish a mission at Banda. Under his influence Emma took a sudden interest in religion. She strove to bring her new ayah, a former Christian convert, back into the fold, and was pleased to find that one of her servants had a Bible "out of which he often reads." Perhaps simply out of a deepening affection for her husbands' native troopers, Emma began to take an interest in their salvation. "I want to know if you can get the Bible printed in Urdu and Nagari amongst the Christian Knowledge Society books," she asked her mother, "as I would like to get a lot to give away amongst the sepoys who read."[416]

Notwithstanding her ayah's malleability or her servant's curiosity, Willie's sepoys were Brahmins and Moslems and would not have appreciated the distribution of Bibles. Indeed it undoubtedly would have reinforced their growing conviction that the English were out to destroy their religion and caste and convert them to Christianity.[417]

THE FATEHGARH MISSION
1774–1857

Eighty miles upriver from Cawnpore, in the district of Farrukhabad, stood one of the most admired examples of Christian missionary work in North India: the Fatehgarh outpost of the Board of Missions of the Presbyterian Church.[418] Fatehgarh itself was the sudder, or chief civil station, of Farrukhabad district,[419] which the British had acquired from the Nawab Vizier of Oudh.[420] Near Farrukhabad the Company had resurrected the bleak and treeless fort of Fatehgarh: ten bastions linked together by a *kankar* (limestone mud) wall and surrounded by a fifteen-hundred-yard moat. Fatehgarh proved the dead end of many dead-ended military careers,[421] and the garrison's despondent officers acquired a reputation for bickering and petty graft.[422] Farrukhabad district itself was such a shambles that Europeans were enjoined not to trot beyond the parade-ground on their morning rides lest they encounter the bared sabres of banditti who "thought robbery insipid if it were not flavoured by murder"[423] and freely scoured the adjacent plain.[424]

Morale among the native troops stationed at Fatehgarh was notoriously low. They fitfully mutinied over petty slights and disappointments, and it was always a tremendous relief to officers and men alike when they were all periodically ordered off the simmering anvil of Fatehgarh Camp to perforate Pindaris, Mahrattas, Afghans, and Sikhs.[425] In 1857 the local regiment was the 10th Native Infantry, whose sepoys were still smarting from their service in Burma. With promises of rewards and honors, their officers, including Major Lindsay, had induced them to cross "the black water," as they called the sea, despite the danger to their caste. But in the end they were not even thanked, and the 10th had proceeded sullenly up the Ganges to Fatehgarh, whose whores and *pahn* sellers jeered them as the "Christian" regiment.

Out in the district, British settlement policies had put hundreds of native estates on the auction block, and in place of the ancient families who had cultivated the district for centuries came British indigo and opium planters who moved their families into Fatehgarh and began to pacify its rough and tumble.[426] They built bungalows in abandoned army lines, planted trees and gardens, established a gun-carriage factory, timber yard, and clothing agency, and paved the principal roads with convict labor.

The station's overextended merchants and disappointed officers were notorious for their nastiness toward Indians; everyone knew what a correspondent for the *Hindoo Patriot* meant when he described an Englishman he had observed abusing a native shopkeeper as "a gentleman of the Furruckabad breed."[427] The local magistrate, Robert Thornhill, was so fed up with India and Indians that he saw fit to recite the following doggerel in open court.

With a *puggree* [turban] on his head & a *talwar* [sabre] on his thigh
The stinking nigger mounts his gat to turn his back and fly . . .
Then let the conches' blast
To the loud tom-tom reply
A nigger must his *hookah* smoke
As without his *hookah* die![428]

The Nawab of Farrukhabad was now a pensioned figurehead who divided his time between watercolors and seductions. Bridging the chasm between the European and Nawabi establishments at Fatehgarh was a sizable community of Eurasians descended from the European officers of the Temporary Brigade and their Moslem wives and bibis. Their daughters attracted the attention not only of young subalterns but of the men of the Nawab's own family. In 1832 Harriet Birch, a mercenary's Eurasian daughter, caused a scandal by eloping with the Nawab's brother and becoming his second wife. Her family accused the Nawab himself of abducting her, but dropped the charge because Harriet was "just of age" and steadfastly refused to leave his zenana.[429]

No such objections obstructed the Nawab himself in his notorious affair with Bonny De Fountain, the daughter of a disgraced Eurasian merchant and his widow, Adolphine, who appears to have confused her maternal role with that of a procuress.[430] Adolphine evidently arranged and certainly encouraged the Nawab's afternoon visits to her fourteen-year-old daughter and even accompanied Bonny and his highness on hilarious carriage rides through the station. The scandal finally reached such a pitch that the authorities carted Bonny off to boarding school in Calcutta, where, at the age of nineteen, she married the rash young Ensign Reginald Sutherland Byrne. Unfortunately—disastrously—the Byrnes were posted back to Fatehgarh, where, with her mother's assistance, Bonny resumed her affair with the Nawab. As seems inevitable in these scenarios, Reggie returned unexpectedly one day to discover the lovers sparking in his parlor and kicked His Highness out the door, for which the Nawab, readjusting his dusty silks in the ensign's driveway, swore eternal vengeance.

He was not by any means the only disgruntled Indian in the district. The humane Acting District Magistrate W. George Probyn constantly pestered Calcutta to lower their assessments and sympathized with the dispossessed landholders who had lost their estates to the Company's courts.[431] But most of the populace were prepared to embrace Azimullah's theory that Britain was no larger than Farrukhabad district (England was actually fifty-six times larger), that its fighting men were all in India, and that the British intended to corrupt their caste by contaminating flour with bone dust and issuing leather rupees.[432]

✦   ✦   ✦

On the outskirts of this dismal station stood a thriving outpost of the Board of Foreign Missions of the Presbyterian Church in the United States. It may seem strange that in the early nineteenth century, before slavery had been abolished, before much of the American continent had even been settled, pious young Yankees would venture all the way to India to spread the Gospel. But now that India had been almost entirely "pacified," its heathen millions captured the imagination of hundreds of young Americans swept up in the evangelical fervor of the day.

Among these zealous and untested toilers was a handsome, square-jawed Princetonian named John E. Freeman, who with his wife Mary set sail for India in 1838, a year after the Board's founding.[433] "With nothing to regret," wrote John, "save my unimproved time and talents," the Freemans arrived in Calcutta in January 1839 and proceeded to the Board's mission at Allahabad, about a hundred miles down the Ganges from Cawnpore.[434] The Allahabad mission included a bustling printing shop, where Freeman was assigned to oversee the small boys who did "all the sewing and folding" of the mission's tracts, while Mary took charge of the orphaned girls.

A missionary's duties were far ranging: "preaching the Gospel, superintending schools, circulating Bibles, distributing tracts, arguing with Brahmins, mingling with the thousands who were congregating at annual festivals, and warning them of their sin and danger."[435] These tasks were difficult to rank. Everyone agreed that preaching the Gospel came first, but to whom and by what means? Many Europeans preferred Moslems to Hindus: they found their beliefs less inscrutable and respected them as fellow conquerors.[436] But American missionaries saw Moslems as their most obdurate foes. Hindus might be weighed down by the tyranny of caste, barbaric customs, monstrous superstitions, but "humanly speaking," wrote one reverend, they were "more hopeful as regards their conversion."

Occasionally a well-served village would welcome Jesus into their pantheon as a local deity. But this sort of equable acceptance was as rare as it was bewildering. Many Hindus found Christianity, and Christians, hopelessly simple-minded, and it did not help that the British themselves were so ungodly.[437] Hindus observed Anglo-Indian gluttony, drunkenness, and lechery, noted how sparsely British churches and chapels were attended, and came to regard Christianity itself as a degraded creed.[438] Many Indians believed that the missionaries were paupers who had agreed to come out only to collect a bounty for every Indian they converted. But others harbored darker suspicions that the missionaries were in the service and pay of the Company. "Hindoos and Mohammedans," wrote one missionary, "could not imagine a ruling power without a religion, or without zeal for diffusion of its own faith." Indians thus saw the government's disavowals as preparatory to "the most determined action against their castes and their faiths."[439]

Most missionaries acknowledged that evangelical tours produced "nothing that we know of, or next to nothing." But it was always nice to get away. They traveled in buggies and held meetings in mango groves and rest stations. But everyone agreed that the best places to preach were the holy ghats, where missionaries might find Indians in a more contemplative frame of mind and might even reach the ears of Hindu women. "They will usually not seem to attend," one American observed, "but if one chooses his place judiciously, they can hear him while they are undressing or dressing, or pretending to gossip." Marching along the burning ghats or stumbling amid naked and seminaked Hindu ascetics whose austerities included holding their arms aloft until they atrophied, devouring tidbits of human cadavers, and performing penile stunts for the faithful, John Edgar Freeman and his colleagues would spend weeks at Hardwar and Allahabad, cheerfully haranguing the pilgrims and providing the natives with "opportunities of witnessing the decencies and beauties of true worship."

They were not always well received. Priests sometimes sent out their best students to heckle the missionaries, often to a devastating effect. One Indian catechist was interrupted by a Brahmin who "suddenly uttered some sharp sarcasm, and followed it with a cry, 'Come, brethren, let us leave this infidel to himself. Victory to Mother Ganga!'" Moslem heckling often followed the same pattern: "You believe in two Gods," someone would call out. "You make Jesus to be God."[440] "Many a person who can fill a pulpit in America or England with respectability and credit," sighed Reverend Ferdinand De Wilton Ward of Madras, "would undoubtedly break down if called to make an attempt among the Hindoos."[441]

Missionaries were always complaining about the quality of the human material with which they had to work. In truth conversion did not seem to improve them. Hindus were patient, discerning, courteous, faithful to their families, and, unless aroused, incapable of cruelty. But once converted to Christianity many were said to become impetuous, blunt, arrogant, dissipated. Some even acquired a taste for liquor.[442] Missionaries were simply not prepared to concede that the goodness and gentleness of Hindus may have had something to do with their religion. Instead they theorized that the waywardness of Indian Christians was due primarily to the low caste of the Indians who found they had nothing to lose and perhaps something to gain from conversion. It was not enough for an Indian to become a Christian—the early Roman Catholic missions had produced Christians at a great rate. Inquirers had to strive to be Christians of the right sort: in this case, Presbyterians.[443]

In the 1820s Fatehgarh's Anglican religious establishment had consisted merely of a "Grecian" little church with a pyramidal spire and a succession of lackluster military chaplains.[444] But during the famine of 1837, an American missionary paused to declare the dreary station "a good centre for missionary work" and, gathering forty-eight orphans from the ragged droves starving along the roadside, arrived at Farrukhabad to open a mission.[445] On a former hunting preserve and parade-ground called Rakha, the Americans established a thriving school and carpet-weaving factory, and in two years had collected one-hundred-nine orphans,[446] though "they became so debilitated and diseased that the greater part of them died, although attended to most kindly and assiduously."[447]

The survivors formed what the Americans called a "Christian village" where they were expected to intermarry and breed new Christians for the mission's rolls. In 1844 these married orphans founded a tent factory which became famous throughout North India and grossed over sixty thousand rupees in its first two years.[448] Such factories were especially necessary to missions because practically no one else but another missionary would hire Indian Christians.[449]

However unhappy the native convert's lot, in 1846 the mission at Fatehgarh had become such a beacon to the Presbyterian church that the General Assembly in Philadelphia declared it the Farrukhabad Presbytery. Under the firm hand of a Reverend John Walsh the Americans established schools in and around the city itself, and their influence penetrated even into cantonments, where a new piety was taking stubborn root. They were befriended by Magistrate Thornhill's wife Mary, by Joint Magistrate Lowis, and by Rosa Monckton, devout wife of the supervisor of the district's portion of the Grand Trunk Road. The ladies of the station raised a subscription for "a very pretty, though very singular" Presbyterian church in the civil station that was dedicated in 1851. And the Americans all seemed to get on famously with both Mr. Shiels, the headmaster of the Company's school for European children at Fatehgarh, and the new Cambridge-educated Anglican chaplain, Reverend Frederick Fisher.

In fact by this time American missionaries in general had acquired a somewhat superior reputation to their English counterparts. One magistrate observed that the Americans were "such thoroughly practical, sincere men, the only missionaries that seem at all successful in conquering the deep caste prejudices of the North-West Provinces," perhaps because they were not quite so class-conscious as their British brethren.[450]

In the hard soil of Hindustan the graves of missionaries were always outnumbered by their wives'. Mary Freeman died ten years after her arrival in India, and her grieving widower returned to America to fetch another partner, the "excellent and admirable" Elizabeth Vredenburgh, who disguised behind a dimpled, doll-like face[451] a ferocious spirit bequeathed by her ancestors, two of whom had been shot to death in the American Revolution.[452] John escorted Elizabeth back to India in 1852, and four years later proceeded to Fatehgarh to oversee the orphanage and tent factory.[453] In 1856 Reverend David Campbell and his wife Maria, "a model of gentleness,"[454] were put in overall charge of the mission, which now included nineteen native schools.[455] Assisted by an Indian catechist named Dhaukal Pershad, the newly arrived and childless Reverend Albert Osborne Johnson and his wife Amanda had charge of the mission's high school.[456] Within a year of the Johnsons' arrival young Reverend J. McMullin, "a man of very considerable promise,"[457] arrived with his new bride Sarah to manage the Christian village and other country missions in the district.[458]

And so there in the dusty swelter of Farrukhabad district, in the heart of the Company's empire, these pious Americans stirred up the heathen. If theirs sometimes seemed a hopeless mission, if the results were meager, if "selfish Christians" said it was "an expensive undertaking to carry the Gospel to these ignorant masses," if "lazy Christians" called it "a discouraging undertaking," if the world declared it "foolishness" and "kings and rulers of the earth set themselves against it,"[459] the evangelicals of Farrukhabad could always remind themselves that "it took 250 years to convert the Roman Empire to Christianity, though the work was begun by the Apostles of our Lord and Saviour," and Rome, as one toiler pointed out, "contained fewer people than India."[460]

A CLOUD MAY RISE
Cawnpore: 1856–1857

In 1857 the civil administration of Cawnpore district was in the hands of Magistrate and Collector Charles George Hillersdon. The youngest man in his class at the Company's college at Haileybury, Hillersdon had served in India for sixteen of his thirty-five years, climbing the rungs of the civil-service ladder first as magistrate and then deputy collector of a string of outstations, where he was responsible not only for the tribunals of each district but "the collection of the dues and taxes by which it was replenished, and for the periodical transmission of the contents to headquarters."[461] He had even to inspect the public dispensaries, to direct the rude municipal management of large towns—and "to inspect and stimulate the national schools."[462] He was to regard himself as "the people's protector as well as the officer of the Company" and look on Indians as God's images, albeit "carved in ebony instead of ivory." He was to master the language and the idioms of his district and mix courteously (though never familiarly) with everyone.[463] No matter how respectably he comported himself or how fairly and efficiently he adjudicated cases, he was to expect to be the object of unrelenting scrutiny, envy, and speculation.[464]

Some civilians would look back with nostalgia on their grueling circuits through the countryside, but others found it unworthy work for such rarefied young men.[465] "Ears where the music of the brook flowed in," went a ditty of the period, "Are listening daily to the tales of sin./Fingers that wandered as the fancy told,/Draft off the dull biography of gold."[466] And of land. The Company thought it was being generous when it allowed cultivators to subtract their expenses and reserve their seed for the next planting before laying claim to about two-thirds of the remainder. But government collectors were so relentlessly efficient that for many peasants Calcutta's two-thirds of surplus proved more ruinous than the ninety percent the Moghuls had erratically collected. In the 1850s the Company's share was reduced to half of the surplus, but by then, in the Doab as in Oudh, thousands of hereditary chiefs and landholders and village cooperatives had lost their land to the Company's auctioneers.

"By fraud or chicanery, a vast number of the estates of families of rank and influence have been alienated," wrote a magistrate named William Edwards. "In event of any insurrection occurring," he warned Calcutta, "we should find this great and influential body . . . ranged against us on the side of the enemy, with their hereditary retainers and followers rallying around them, in spite of our attempts to separate their interests."[467] But voices like Edwards's were rare. "The character which an Indian officer dreads most," wrote one civilian, "is that of an alarmist."[468]

In February 1856 the job of commanding men like Hillersdon had passed from the exhausted hands of the Marquis Dalhousie to his old Oxford classmate, Earl Charles John Canning. Like Dalhousie, Canning had lost two older brothers and strived not only to fulfill their promise but live up somehow to the towering reputation of his parliamentarian father George, a liberal noninterventionist who by the time of his death in 1827 had made himself "the most powerful influence in English, and one of the most powerful in European, politics."[469] It was Charles Canning's fate to suffer by comparison: first to his brilliant father and then to his equally brilliant predecessor at Calcutta.[470] High-level bureaucrats at Calcutta found Canning a chilly stickler, and to the men in the field he seemed a naive and dithering drudge. Though he was occasionally paralyzed by anxiety, he publicly exuded a sometimes infuriating calm.[471]

Canning had hoped to oversee a period of consolidation after the shock of Dalhousie's reforms. He recognized, however, that continuing peace in India depended "upon a greater variety of chances and a more precarious tenure than any other quarter of the globe. We must not forget that in the sky of India, serene as it is, a cloud may arise, at first no bigger than a man's hand, but which growing bigger and bigger, may at last threaten to overwhelm us with ruin."

Though a few men like Edwards might detect such a cloud burgeoning over the Doab in early 1857, a collector's life was not all frustration and alarm. The collector was regarded, after all, as "the acknowledged head of the society of whatever place he may be stationed at," a role for which Charles Hillersdon and his young wife Lydia seemed perfectly suited.[472] Charles was "an active and judicious man," fond of shooting and the patron of the civilian cricket team.[473] At twenty-one Lydia was the soft-spoken and "accomplished" daughter of a Bengal Army major;[474] her sweet and gentle disposition had immediately endeared her to Cawnpore society.[475]

By the time Charles became magistrate and collector at Cawnpore in January 1857, Lydia had produced two children and was four months pregnant with a third. Fatehpur Magistrate and Collector John Walter Sherer and his wife, who would succeed the Hillersdons at Cawnpore, dined with them at their spacious bungalow in Nawabgunj in early May 1857, after which Lydia, "an accomplished pianist, . . . delighted us with some charming music," Sherer wrote, "both on her own instrument and on the concertina. She was fond of Mendelssohn's *Rondo Capriccios*, then not hackneyed," and the works of other "difficult" composers.[476] Together the Hillersdons seemed to embody the golden promise of the Company's Raj (rule).

"In many stations," writes Philip Woodruff, "there was conflict between civil and military,"[477] but General Wheeler would praise Hillersdon's "most cordial co-operation,"[478] which may have been due in part to the influence of his older brother William, the bachelor major of the 53rd Native Infantry that had arrived at Cawnpore in February.[479] Many evenings the major used to follow Charles and Lydia home from the course for supper. His *Castor-Kee-Paltan* had been raised in 1804 as the 1st Battalion of the 27th Regiment of the Bengal Native Infantry and had seen action at Kabul in 1842 and in the Punjab. They were Oudh men, the vast majority high-caste Brahmins of aristocratic bearing. In their "British red" uniforms with yellow facings,[480] they were regarded as some of the staunchest and best disciplined of all the Company's native troops, due in large part to Major Hillersdon himself, who was "personally intimate with many of the men."[481] Before the Mutiny, his lieutenants could detect "no appearance of reserve or sullenness" among their sepoys.[482] They had discussed the cartridges with their major and declared themselves willing to use them so long as they were permitted to tear off the ends with their fingers.[483] "Should there be any intention on the part of Government to christianize you," the Major had jokingly assured his sepoys, "I shall be the first to tell you."[484]

Nana Sahib pulled out all the stops for the Hillersdons, offering his guest house to Lydia and the children should they ever be indisposed.[485] In the cool weather they attended Nana's parties, picnics, weekend shoots, and other "costly festivities." An officer[486] recalled attending a party given by Nana Sahib in early May that was "the most magnificent ball ever given at Cawnpore."[487] Others continued to testify to Nana Sahib's "mental accomplishments, and to his polished and gentlemanly manners."[488] Louisa Chalwin, wife of a cavalry veterinary surgeon, was grateful to the "Gentleman of Bithur" for loaning his piano while hers was being tuned,[489] and a senior officer passing through the station remembered seeing Nana Sahib "driving about, and hearing on all sides of his attention and hospitality to Europeans."[490] His generosity and friendship were special comforts to Charles, who had come to regard him as a "great friend."[491] If anything happened to Charles, it was a relief to know that his family could always find refuge at Bithur.

✦ ✦ ✦

In the early spring of 1857 a strange quiet had fallen over the Doab. For all the alarms about chupatties, cartridges, and contaminated flour, the judges' dockets were practically empty. "Though our courts and office were open," Sherer wrote of his court at nearby Fatehpur, "yet there was no business. Only the opium-eaters were constant [and] came at the stated hour for their supply of the drug." In the outlying districts crime seemed to cease altogether. "Amongst the peasantry around us, there was a general expectation which paralysed all activity. The thief sat down by the doorkeeper, and the bad characters sought the shelter of the miser's wall; all were waiting— waiting—they certainly had no idea for what."[492]

The delicate illusion of security seemed to disintegrate unaccountably. "Driving through the streets," wrote a civilian at Agra, "I remember the singular feeling as if we had suddenly become strangers in a strange land,—as if, in fact, the people were pitifully regarding us as shortly, like all around, to be swept away."[493] The daughter of a Fatehgarh trader named Sutherland noticed a change "in the demeanor of the domestic servants [and] a falling off in Pa's business." Indian traders who had formerly required payment by check "because of the security insured on their return journey" insisted on "cash payments in every transaction" and "refused to have anything to do with paper money in any form."[494]

In the early months of 1857 Reverend Haycock of the Cawnpore S.P.G. took his two motherless sons up to the hill station of Mussoorie and deposited them in school. On his return a Moslem cleric warned him that the English would "soon feel the sharpness of the Mussulman's sword," whereupon Haycock's servant begged him to flee India before it was too late.[495]

For the officers' wives of Cawnpore, however, life went on as before. Shielded by their husbands from the ominous rumors of native disaffection, ladies like Louisa Chalwin filled her calendar with parties and balls. She stitched children's dresses, sang duets at the piano she had borrowed from Nana Sahib, tried to act the matchmaker for

Isabel White, a girlhood friend who had accompanied Louisa on her return from home leave. Louisa fretted over her hair loss (which she tried to remedy by rubbing onions on her scalp), contended with a steady stream of houseguests, enjoyed the company of her husband's fellow officers, and all in all found "the society in this station very pleasant and sociable."[496]

Cawnpore "was unusually thronged with ladies."[497] Some were the wives of officers stationed at Lucknow who had alighted at Cawnpore because "Oudh having been but recently annexed," they could not yet obtain houses near their husbands.[498] Other ladies had come to Cawnpore for April's round of officers' balls. "We have visitors constantly coming and going," wrote Major Lindsay, "as they pass up or down country." Their current houseguest was a Miss Bissell who had stopped off on her way up the country to troll for a husband.[499] But the Lindsays kept to themselves, aching with the absence of their three children, cherishing their increasingly dutiful little missives and drawings; sending home instructions for their instruction; scrimping and saving to hasten the day they would all be reunited in England.

Their yearning for home had apparently infected Emily Vibart, the skinny, stay-at-home wife of fifty-year-old Major Edward Vibart of the 2nd Native Cavalry. Major Vibart was a short, balding, overbearing man with a doughty chin protruding from beneath heavy black muttonchops. The Vibarts had three small children at Cawnpore whom they intended "next cold weather" to reunite with two of their oldest daughters now living in England with the parents of Willie Halliday,[500] whose brother was married to Emily's sister.[501] The Vibarts' oldest child Edward, whom the family had nicknamed "Butcher," had been posted to the 54th Native Infantry at Delhi.[502] In April Butcher had come down to Cawnpore to attend the 2nd Native Cavalry's regimental ball, where one young officer found "the floor very bad and the dancers fewer and not so good as those in Lucknow," but was delighted to dance "some polkas and a Lancers" with Alice and Caroline Lindsay.[503] Perhaps to divert the ladies' attention from whatever gloomy mutterings they might have overheard from their ayahs or houseguests or some inebriated "croaker," the officers declared the social season such a success that they announced plans to throw a "reunion ball" every month, even in the hot weather.

Despite the semi-mutiny of the 19th Native Infantry and the one-man rebellion of Mungal Pandy of the 34th, most of Cawnpore's officers deemed it inconceivable that their own soldiers would betray their salt. They insisted that something about the 19th and the 34th must have set them apart from other regiments: idleness, lax command, a disproportion of pampered Brahmins or ill-disposed Islamic fanatics. *Very different from* our *chaps*, they assured their wives. Besides, the natives were too lazy to launch a campaign in hot weather.

This was not just complacency talking. Their strength as sepoy officers always lay in their unshakable belief in themselves, their discipline, their continuity of purpose; in their capacity to cow, charm, cajole a thousand discontented men with a silent glare or a few fond words of praise, to pass off some desperate improvisation in the field as time-honored military procedure: in short, to brazen their way through the fundamentally preposterous imperial mission of commanding tens of thousands of Indians to subdue hundreds of millions of their own people for the greater glory and profit of a few thousand Europeans.

In April 1857 a vigilant officer might send a few more spies into the lines to listen for hints of disaffection, and he could quietly emphasize to newly arrived subalterns that they were to do nothing to inflame the superstitions and suspicions of their restive troops. But the main thing was to sweep the men along in the pull of one's supreme self-assurance, to observe the protocols of the mess and the parade-ground and the ballroom, and never to betray to his sepoys or his wife and children the bloody possibilities that sometimes flung him gasping from his dreams.[504]

JONAH
William Jonah Shepherd: 1825–1857

Eurasians in India dangled in limbo between the rulers and the ruled. And yet they were "zealously loyal" to the Company and the Queen and often contemptuous of their mothers' and grandmothers' people, who returned their scorn with hatred and sometimes even joined in the calls for their deportation. Many Eurasians were themselves exquisitely color-conscious, and could detect "an adulterated European by his knuckles, his nails, his eyebrows, his pronunciation of the vowels, and his conception of the propriety in dress, manner, and conduct."[505]

"They are an orderly and intelligent, and in one line, an industrious race of people," allowed *The Englishman*.[506] That one line was clerical, and it was very nearly the only line open to them. Unless championed by distinguished officer-fathers, Eurasians generally found the ranks of the Bengal Army closed to them.[507] Military officers declared Eurasians too epicene for combat duty, and allowed them to enter the army only as fifers and drummers, while civil authorities regarded them as too dull and compromised for high positions and assigned them to labor as "crannies"—mixed-race clerks—under an oppressively low ceiling of advancement.[508]

Such was the fate of William Jonah Shepherd. Jonah, as his family called him, became one of only three survivors of the siege of Wheeler's Entrenchment to publish his memoirs. As befit his middle name, he would be swallowed up by the Mutiny and miraculously spit back out. Jonah's grandfather John served with the Bengal Army; Jonah's father James was born in Burranpore in 1789 to John's probably Indian wife. In 1820 James served first as a quartermaster sergeant and eventually as regimental sergeant, and in 1825 at Allahabad his Eurasian wife gave birth to Jonah, the third of their four sons:[509] a tall, earnest, pious boy who nevertheless thrilled to the tales of his father's exploits.[510]

Jonah's grandfather may have been a brawling adventurer and his father a parade-ground bully, but Jonah studied to be a writer, and rose steadily through the ranks of the Commissariat Department. Infuriated by his people's treatment, routinely humiliated by his Anglo-Indian employers, Jonah nevertheless clung to the belief that God intended his "peculiar race" to inherit India from the British, but only if they worked hard, lived respectably and strictly adhered to the Christian faith.[511]

When it came to religion Jonah was a lion. He did not shrink from reproaching his superiors for their accommodations to Indian customs and beliefs, and he championed the evangelizing Colonel Wheler whom other regimental commanders sometimes ordered run out of camp at bayonet point for preaching to their sepoys.[512] But Jonah was otherwise a mild, meticulous, and rather hesitant man, the very model of the "methodical and trustworthy" cranny.[513] In June of 1850,[514] he married a kind and "very fair" Eurasian girl named Ellen.[515] She was only fifteen years old, but, like Frances Marsden Wheeler before her, she had found a husband in the nick of

Mary Ann, the Hallidays' ayah *(nursemaid)*

Ajodhya Prasad, banker

A spy whose hands and nose were amputated by Nana's court

time.[516] A year after her marriage, Ellen gave birth to a daughter they called "Polly": a calm and cheerful child and "fairer," boasted her color-conscious father, "than native children."[517]

In 1853 Jonah was promoted to head clerk of the enormous Commissariat Office at Cawnpore, and moved with his family to a small house beside the parade-ground. At twenty-eight he had already reached the ceiling of Eurasian opportunity, and though he may have hoped that other doors might one day open to him, within the Eurasian community he was a man of means and influence. He thought he might make a name for himself by writing a definitive guide to Commissariat regulations, otherwise he was prepared for the sake of his wife and daughter to devote the rest of his life to cultivating his pension, raising his family, and praising the Lord.

✦ ✦ ✦

The Commissariat office at Cawnpore dealt in enormous volumes of goods, swallowing up some of the mountains of wheat, cotton, and tobacco that tied up in barges along Cawnpore's waterfront. In 1853 there were over eight-hundred-thousand acres under cultivation in the district, and at harvest time their crops swelled the bazaars, crowded the river with towering barges, and jammed the roads with creaking carts.[518] As head clerk Jonah became acquainted with scores of local Indian businessmen and their agents. Along the halls of the Commissariat office bustled native bankers and traders, labor and livestock contractors, tanners, importers, tentmakers, and suppliers of harness and uniforms.

There were four great banking families in Cawnpore.[519] The wealthiest was headed by a portly, mustachioed purchasing agent named Ishwari Prasad who had assiduously cultivated his British customers and acquired a reputation for good manners and straight dealing.[520] Senior civil and military officers used to do him the honor of visiting his mansion in the native city to play billiards, attend his entertainments, and catch up on the news from the native quarter.[521] Some of his property had been acquired as payment on loans, for the native bankers of the time played the old usurer's game of coaxing the indigent owners of property they coveted into incurring enormous debts. They would forgive delays in payment until the debt had attained enormous proportions and then sweep in with decrees to seize their debtors' assets. It was a technique that made a banker more enemies than friends and required not only finances but reliable intelligence; eternal vigilance; familiarity with judicial procedure; cordial relations with Company officers, many of whom were often themselves his tenants and debtors; and, if all that failed, armed guards and fast horses.

Bankers jammed the district courts with suits and countersuits. The richest of them hired European lawyers but relied as heavily on spies and *mooktears*, legal advisers who worked the district magistrate's anterooms, courtrooms, and camps. One of these mooktears was the fidgety and self-promoting Nanak Chand who operated out of a house at Generalgunj.[522] He was himself a banker, and with Ishwari Prasad's financing mined the rich veins at the litigious court at Bithur, unsuccessfully but nevertheless lucratively pleading the cases of the late Peshwa's widows, who accused Nana Sahib of imprisonment and mistreatment.[523] Chand also litigated the case of Chimnaji Appa, Baji Rao's grandnephew, who tried to obtain a share of Nana Sahib's inheritance with a claim that the ex-Peshwa had intended before his death to adopt him as his son.

There seemed to be very few cases in which British magistrates could be bought off with gifts or bribes; by the 1850s the civil service rightly prided itself on the integrity of its judges.[524] Their Indian clerks were not always so incorruptible, and some could be persuaded for the right fee to alter land records, garble summonses, deport witnesses, mislay evidence, mistranslate testimony, declare old family documents forgeries. And yet it usually did not have to come to that. Judges were not without their prejudices and blind spots and fits of temper, and mooktears were experts in manipulating their crotchets. They advised their employers to take action against men unschooled in the bewildering procedures of British civil justice, and to choose lawyers who could represent their interests with the kind of nuance and attention to detail that won over British district magistrates who were so often perplexed and exasperated by the clamor of peasants with their ceaseless and inscrutable claims and counterclaims.

Most of Cawnpore's goods were transported by boat. The Ganges between Cawnpore and Calcutta was described in 1845 as navigable for boats of large tonnage throughout the year,[525] and "every description of vessel that can be imagined was collected along the bank."[526] The Commissariat contractor gathered fleets together for the local merchants, working with foremen who arranged for crews. They were all Hindus, and most lived in the beneficent vicinity of their Hardeo Temple at Sati Chowra Ghat.[527] Their centuries-old guild was on the decline. British-owned steamers had begun to ply the river, the railway from Calcutta that now terminated at Raniganj would soon extend into Oudh, and the Grand Trunk Road was already siphoning off the boatmen's business. Indeed, everything the British introduced to Hindustan—canals, even the telegraph—seemed calculated to rob them of their business.

As the busiest junction of British and Indian interests, the Commissariat Office acted as a kind of intelligence center.[528] The anterooms and verandahs of Cawnpore's commissariat swarmed with spies, some under contract to the civil and military authorities. Entire castes dedicated themselves to spying. There were reckless men who hired themselves out as messengers and learned to carry infinitesimal coded notes in the cracks of their bamboo staffs, in their hair, between their teeth, under specially cut flaps of skin or even in more private portions of their anatomies. And there were money carriers disguised as mendicants and sweepers who conveyed small sums of cash to other stations; and playacting spies who ventured out to eavesdrop in the native lines posing as peddlers and artisans.[529]

The contractors themselves were expected to provide the British with not only supplies but intelligence: the gossip from the bazaars, the alarms in the villages and native lines, warnings of bandits and renegade soldiery on the roads, rumors of secret deals and seditious scheming in the princely courts. Even a clerk like Jonah had to learn to pan for facts among their sometimes giddy fictions before troubling his superiors.[530] It was a skill that would eventually save Jonah's life in the uprising at Cawnpore and later stand him in good stead as the most dependable firsthand chronicler of the station's doom.

✦　✦　✦

In early March 1857, a merchant sent over eight tons of *atta* (ground flour) from Meerut down the Ganges Canal.[531] By the time it got to Cawnpore, word had already reached him of a second, larger shipment of flour approaching the markets. So he sold off the atta as fast as he could, eventually charging even less than the going rate for unground wheat. His customers naturally suspected there must have been something wrong with the flour, and when a native soldier spread the word that it had been adulterated with the ground bones of cows and pigs, people believed him. The rumor caused such a panic that for several days all trade in atta had to be suspended.[532]

The British tried to assure people that the flour was ground entirely under Indian auspices and that the government had not interfered in any way in its production or transportation, but nothing they said could reassure their customers. A native contractor and almost a hundred native troops returned from observing the grinding process at Meerut to declare the atta pure as snow, but their testimony "only did this much," reported one official: "that a small quantity of atta was taken off the dealers' hands at the reduced rate of 28 seers per rupee." Finally the British threw up their hands and closed all further sales of the Meerut flour.

Under the circumstances, Jonah Shepherd's request for leave from the Commissariat must have struck his superiors as ill timed. But Jonah had received a letter from his sister at Calcutta announcing the death of her husband and begging Jonah to bring her and her extended family back to live with him at Cawnpore.[533] So Jonah left his wife and two daughters in the care of their ayah and sailed down the Ganges to fetch his destitute relations. When his budgerow bumped up to the ghats at Calcutta, seven of them welcomed Jonah as their deliverer, and they all piled together onto the train for Raniganj, where they hired two carriages to take them the remaining six hundred miles to Cawnpore.

Traveling in the terrible heat and choking dust of May, the Shepherds hardly paused long enough to take food at the dawk bungalows. There must have been signs of trouble along the way: European women and children hurrying in the opposite direction, sullen parties of sepoys on furlough, insolent servants and peddlers, a few overturned mile markers, cryptic scrawlings on the bridges. But it was not until they reached Fatehpur on May 16 that they would first learn that the Company's native troops had mutinied at Meerut and that like doors closing behind them the mails had shut down along the road they had just traveled. Jonah hurried his exhausted and now panic-stricken relations the last forty-eight miles to Cawnpore. All would be well if they could just get home.

A TOWER OF STRENGTH

Cawnpore: April–May 1857

Though seasoned old sepoy officers like General Wheeler had refused to force the cartridge issue, others were inclined to address it head on. One of these was Colonel Carmichael-Smyth of the 3rd Native Cavalry. He was stationed forty miles from Delhi in the military camp at Meerut, where leaves and furloughs had reduced the ratio of European to native troops from the ideal of one in three to one in six. On Friday, April 24, the Colonel called out ninety of his elite sowars and told them that though there was no truth to the rumor about the animal fat, they would be permitted to tear the cartridges with their fingers so as not to defile their caste. When the time came to distribute the cartridges, all but five sowars refused to take them.

Flabbergasted, the Colonel hurried off to confer with General William "Bloody Bill" Hewitt, the obese and arteriosclerotic commander of the station, who ordered all eighty-five of the recalcitrant sowars imprisoned in an old hospital building to await court-martial. During the week it took Hewitt to assemble his court, placards appeared in the bazaars calling for the slaughter of all Europeans, and mysterious fires broke out in the town. All eighty-five sowars were found guilty of gross disobedience and marched out in front of an open square composed of armed European troops and Indian soldiers with empty weapons. The sowars were sentenced to life imprisonment and for several hours stood under darkling clouds as blacksmiths laboriously shackled them in irons. Most bore this humiliation in silence, but others pitched their boots at their officers and shouted, "For the faith!" and "Remember us!" as they staggered back to jail.

The next day, May 10, was a Sunday, and officers returned with relief to their Sabbath routine, riding in the early light, attending church, retiring to their beds to strip down and sleep through the unusually intense midday heat. But out in the bazaars a rumor circulated that European troops were about to swoop into the native lines and disarm the sepoys and sowars. Suddenly, in the furnace blast of the afternoon, the native troops buckled on their sabres, grabbed their guns and raced on horse and foot to the hospital building to release their comrades. When no British officer appeared to oppose them, they began to rage through the cantonments, setting fire to barracks and huts, breaking into the magazines, trailing a mob from the bazaars.

Officers started from their sweltering slumber to see fire and smoke spreading from the barracks to the European bungalows. As "Bloody Bill" trembled in his rooms, a few officers rode out to face the mob, only to be chased off or cut down. Others tried to hide in latrines or on rooftops. European soldiers returning from the bazaars were assaulted, and many killed, with knives and stones. Officers' wives desperately tried to flee from their houses only to encounter the rampaging mob: a pregnant infantry wife was eviscerated by a Muslim butcher; an officer's wife was stabbed to death after trying to escape in a *bhurka*; another, sickly with smallpox, was pelted with flaming torches until her clothes caught fire. As night descended the European soldiers finally managed to regroup on the parade-ground, firing ineffectually into the mango groves and the roiling smoke from the bungalows. But by then about fifty European men, women, and children lay dead, much of the station was in flames, and most of the rebels had galloped off to Delhi.

The first of them turned up below the emperor's balcony at about seven o'clock the next morning, their horses lathered from the forty-mile ride. "Help, O King!" they shouted up through the stone lattice that shielded the old emperor's apartments. "We pray for assistance in our fight for the faith!" The Emperor of Delhi was a henpecked octogenarian named Bahadur Shah whose dominion had receded in stages from the walls of his fort to his staterooms to the gilded borders of the miniatures he liked to paint. At the sight of the mutineers he shrank back into his apartments and summoned Captain Douglas, the commander of his guard, who ordered the rebels to stop annoying His Royal Highness.

Exhausted and confused, the rebels trotted around the walls of the Exalted Fort and swarmed into the city. Soon a second wave of Meerut rebels thundered in, and as the Emperor crept deeper into the fort the mutineers hunted down and killed Captain Douglas, decapitated the commissioner, chopped up the collector, and cut the throats of the manager of the Delhi and London Bank and his family, though apparently not before his wife had killed two sowars with a hog spear.[534] Women and children were killed in their rooms and gardens; fifty Europeans were taken prisoner, tied together in a great mass, and slaughtered by the emperor's servants.

A few survivors came scrambling the two miles northward to the Company's Delhi garrison to find the local sepoys standing by as the Meerut rebels massacred officers and rampaged through the cantonment church, sending its bronze bells clanging to the ground. The British managed to kill a rebel storming party by blowing up their magazine, but when the surviving rebels attacked the main guard the sepoys of the garrison joined in the attack, opening fire on officers, civilians, and their families as they tried to flee.

Some managed to escape, many of them spirited through the mobs by faithful servants and loyal sepoys. Butcher Vibart, recently returned from Cawnpore, scrambled off with a party of men, women, and children, while in the city's telegraph office an English signaler tapped out a few last desperate lines. *"We must leave office. All the bungalows are being burnt down by the sepoys from Meerut. They came in this morning. . . . We are off."*

✦   ✦   ✦

The news from Meerut and Delhi came crackling fitfully through an atmosphere of congested dread. Amy Horne recalled how it "threw our province into a state of panic."[535] On the morning of May 15, the Collectorate was in "a tone of alarm," and in the afternoon the station's principal Indian judge conferred with Collector Hillersdon about how best to quell disturbances.[536] Charles issued proclamations that the Company's government was still firmly in power, and placed his police on the alert "to detain suspicious characters."[537]

But Amy Horne would recall that "the shopkeepers, fearing a loot, closed their shops, and could not be prevailed upon by the authorities to resume business. Some servants absented themselves from their work on the plea of sickness, while others sent rude messages to the effect that our *raj* was over, and that they did not wish to serve us any more."[538] "There was much excitement amongst the troops at Cawnpore," a Mahajun would testify, "and reports were rife that they would follow the example of the troops at Meerut."[539] According to Amy Horne some were even "seen to rejoice openly."[540] A native bookseller reported hearing the son of a sowar of the 2nd Native Cavalry brag to his schoolmates that "the force here would act as that at Meerut had done."[541]

On Friday, May 15, the *Mofussilite* carried a proclamation from the Governor-General threatening to confiscate the land of any landholder who joined the uprising and to transfer their property to their loyal brethren. "The powerful British Government," said Canning, "will in a marked manner recompense its friends, and punish its enemies."[542] Perhaps no proclamation issued from the relative safety of Calcutta could have reassured the Europeans of Cawnpore or put the fear of the Company into the rebels. But this one seemed especially feeble and confirmed the native fear that the Company was planning mass confiscations of their property. The best that could be said for the proclamation was that at least it demonstrated that Calcutta recognized the real danger—that if "the dispossessed princes and people of the land, farmers, villagers, and ryots" joined in the rebellion, the entire Bengal Army would revolt.[543]

One dispossessed prince acted quickly to allay such fears. On Saturday, May 16, when the station first heard of the rebellion at Delhi, Nana Sahib drove into the civil station to confer with Charles Hillersdon. Along the way he told an officer "who knew him intimately" that he "lamented the outbreak. . . . He could hardly believe it," he said. "It was most shameful."[544] Hurrying to the Collectorate, Nana reminded his "great friend" Hillersdon of how exposed his family was in their compound in Nawabgunj and reiterated his offer to take the expecting *burra memsahib* and her two small children under his protection at Saturday House. Though Lydia hoped to remain with her countrywomen, her husband agreed with Nana "that it would be better for me and our precious children to be at Bithoor."[545] Indeed, Charles had even asked Nana Sahib to arrange safe passage to England for his wife and child.[546]

✦ ✦ ✦

General Wheeler did his best to quiet the station with "calm and expert policy." Colonel John Ewart of the 1st Native Infantry thought people were "needlessly" terrified because the old General was "on the *qui vive*, and is said to be equal to the difficulties of his position: cool and determined."[547] Wheeler was so "determined, self-possessed, and fearless of danger"[548] that the formidable Henry Lawrence deemed him "a tower of strength to us at this juncture."[549] "Such was our fatal belief in our security," recalled a visitor, "that no amount of warnings alarmed us."[550]

To demonstrate his confidence in the cantonment's security the little gray general showed himself everywhere, trotting cheerfully from place to place, sometimes in the company of his two daughters, and sleeping with his windows open and unguarded. He "visited the lines daily, chatted with the sepoys, and encouraged their confidence," and could not uncover any positive evidence "of anything like plotting in their midst." But each regiment nursed its own grievances, its peculiar anxieties. The Brahminical prophesy that the Company would last only a hundred years from the Battle of Plassey in 1757 weighed heavily on the sepoys of the 1st Native Infantry, whose infant regiment had taken a leading role in Clive's victory over the Nawab of Bengal. The 56th had been disabused by their part in the sordid campaign against the Santals, indeed "there was not a Sepoy in [that] war," wrote an officer of the 56th, "who did not feel ashamed of himself."[551] The predominantly Moslem 2nd Native Cavalry had been especially demoralized by the annexation of Oudh, and though the 53rd Native Infantry seemed the most staunch, it consisted primarily of Oudh Brahmins who, like the Moslem sowars, had lost their status in their home villages with the fall of the King of Lucknow.

Sometimes the men did strike Wheeler as "surly."[552] Many of the sowars of the 2nd Native Cavalry had decided, without permission, to send their families home, and there were rumors of midnight meetings in their lines.[553] But Wheeler marveled in his letters at "how this belief that the Government is bent on making the whole population Christians could have extended as it has done." For instance, "it was believed to be the intention of Government to transport to India the numerous widows whose husbands had perished in the Crimean campaign. The principal zemindars of the country were to be compelled to marry them; and their children, who would, of course, not be Hindoos, were to be declared the heirs to the estates, so that the Hindoo proprietors of land were to be thus supplanted." Whenever Wheeler demanded proof of the government's treachery his sepoys replied "that they do not apprehend force, but that it is to be done by artifice (*hikmat*) and cunning."

At Lucknow the men of Wheeler's own 48th Native Infantry had received a letter from a sepoy of the newly formed 7th Oudh Irregulars. "We should be of one mind," it said. "Cartridges have been given to us at three parades. You are our superiors. What you order that we will do. This concerns our religion." When Wheeler's own subhedar-major relayed the letter to Lawrence he faced down the 7th with artillery until the irregulars either fled or laid down their arms. But the loyal old subhedar's hut was burned down, as was the bungalow of Wheeler's ailing regimental surgeon, who had made the mistake of absently sipping from a bottle of medicine in their hospital godown.

Wheeler found that separating "the well-disposed" native troops from the disaffected was "easier said than done," when he "had neither troop nor battery here, and have been obliged to extemporize one on the chance of requiring it."[554] His senior artillery officer, fifty-year-old Major George Larkins, asked him for permission to place a guard over the few assembled guns in the station. Wheeler agreed only on the condition that Larkins do so "quietly" and assign only native gunners to stand guard.[555]

Wheeler's force now consisted of 3,450 native troops and sixty-seven European officers—plus three companies of artillery composed of eighty-eight European gunners and 152 natives, and one hundred of her Majesty's 84th Foot, many of them confined to the hospital with heat stroke, smallpox, and cholera. A decade earlier Wheeler himself had seen to it that most of the Company's European troops were deployed around the Punjab to overawe the Sikhs; now the ratio of European to native troops at Cawnpore was not one in three, nor even Meerut's one in six.[556] Even including the invalids among the European troops, by May 10, 1857, the ratio had plummeted to one in fourteen.[557]

✦ ✦ ✦

Despite Wheeler's best efforts the station remained in a state of alarm. On the night of Saturday, May 16, the cantonment awoke to shouts and the pounding of horses' hooves and rushed to their windows to see flames flaring from the lines of the 1st Native Infantry. The fire was quickly extinguished, and if it had been the signal for an uprising no one heeded it. But at dawn a great many Europeans rushed to the ghats in hopes of sending their women and children downriver to Calcutta. Among them was Wheeler's own adjutant, Major Lindsay, who feared that if "the city people at Lucknow [broke] out with the object of erecting the fallen Mahommedan state anew," others at Cawnpore "of the same class" might cause "a commotion, the extent of which no one could foretell."[558]

"Oh Jane," wrote Lindsay's gouty sister Kate, "such a day . . . I hope never to pass again. . . . Willie said I must go with the girls & he was anxious for Lilly to go with me, and also Miss Bissel." At last at about four o'clock the telegraph reported that the rebels were not descending upon Cawnpore after all but massing around Delhi. A native infantry regiment had refused to mutiny, and the major told Kate that "Queen's troops were marching downwards as fast as they could. . . . This gave us a more cheering feeling and we all went to church at ½ past 6 in the evening, and I think we all felt our minds calmed and comforted, and trusted that God, who is a good God, wd. not quite forsake us."[559]

But Lindsay was evidently sparing his womenfolk the truth. The real reason he turned them back was because he had received news (which proved premature) "that an outbreak had taken place at Benares" which had "at once put a stop to all proceeding in that direction."[560] And yet Lindsay could not bring himself to believe that the native troops at Cawnpore would turn on the ladies and children. "The human heart," he insisted, "is not always so diabolical."

On May 17 a telegram from Agra reported that a large British force was about to descend on Delhi to destroy the rebels. Agra declared that "the plague is stayed," a phrase at which several ladies of the station clutched in their anxious letters home. "All well at Cawnpore," Wheeler immediately wired Calcutta. Though "excitement continues among the people . . . the insurgents can only be about 3,000 in number, and are said to cling to the walls of Delhi, where they have put up a puppet-king. I grudge the escape of one of them. . . . The plague is, in truth, stayed."[561]

THE FORT OF DESPAIR
May 17–20, 1857

After taking a day to settle his extended family in his house, Jonah Shepherd arrived at the Commissariat on May 17 to find the office alive with rumors. "Every body in the station seemed to think that something dreadful was to occur, but were unable to see what it was." Jonah realized that he may have made a tragic mistake bringing his sister to Cawnpore and tried to send his entire family to safety. "Some of the European merchants and others engaged boats, intending to leave the station for Allahabad the moment any danger should become apparent. Others made arrangements to start by *dâk* [relays of horsecarts and palanquins], leaving house and property to the care of servants. Every person, according to his means and ability, entertained more [watchmen]."

Jonah's wife Ellen would not leave Cawnpore without him, however, and he had used up his leave. But where would they be safe? "There was no fortified position anywhere," he said, "save the Magazine, which was on the banks of the river, having a high *pucca* [brick] wall all around, and a spacious compound with several large roomy buildings in it, and in every way adapted for our purpose under existing circumstances." But not quite. The magazine stood five miles northwest of the native lines, and Wheeler and his staff "did not consider it safe to leave the troops to themselves at so great a distance, particularly as at that time they did not show any open signs of rebellion."[562] Wheeler expected troops to arrive any day from Allahabad and wanted to be in a position to meet them as they came marching into the southern end of the station. If by that time his native regiments had mutinied he did not want his garrison stuck in a position that the relief force would have to battle through narrow and unfamiliar city streets to reach. Large-scale preparations at the magazine might also dangerously alarm the city people as well as the native troops, and insult the increasingly sullen and defiant sepoys who guarded its gates. Besides, the magazine was the hottest place in the station, a huge clay oven whose great walls stymied the feeble breezes from the neighboring Ganges.[563]

Wheeler believed that if his troops did rise they would behave like the regiments at Meerut: wreak a little havoc for a few hours and then race off to Delhi. Calcutta urged Wheeler to "begin immediately to make all preparations for the accommodation of a European force, and to let it be known that you are doing so."[564] Wheeler tried to hurry the completion of the row of nine European barracks that were now under construction, and for the first time contemplated digging an entrenchment around the nearby Dragoon barrack and its tile-roofed neighbor, now occupied by the women, children, and invalid soldiers of Her Majesty's 32nd.[565] The site was already conveniently heaped with bricks, sand, and other construction materials and swarming with coolies whom he could redirect without making a spectacle of his preparations.

The barracks were substantial buildings with walls from eighteen inches to two feet thick.[566] The tile-roofed barrack housing the wives and children was about fifty feet wide and 190 feet long. The older thatched building containing the invalid soldiers was sixty feet wide by over 350 feet long with two outhouses connected by roofed and pillared walkways. The barracks consisted of a long central row of rooms flanked on either side by two rows of verandahs. The outer verandahs were shaded arcades each consisting of a sloped roof supported by a series of brick pillars. The inner verandahs were more substantial, but their windows and doors were open to the terrible dust that blew so thickly in May.[567] Only the central rooms had doors and window screens.[568]

Within a few hundred feet of the two barracks there were a number of other buildings, including a kitchen, two more of "those sani-

tary out-houses and conveniences which would be so essential a feature of a place of refuge in hot weather," a large masonry godown,
and a row of huts.[569] If you lived in cantonments and accepted
Wheeler's premise that the troops would not lay siege to the garrison, the position made a kind of sense. But the logic failed to impress
the merchants and civil servants stranded on the far side of the
Ganges Canal. What would become of them, they wondered, if the
troops rose up and the hooligans of the bazaars joined in?

One of the most prosperous businessman at Cawnpore was John
Hay,[570] whose father had established himself as the station's auction-
eer of choice, an especially lucrative occupation in a military station
full of itinerant officers.[571] As "an indistinct, undefinable feeling of
alarm spread among the European community," Hay and a small delegation of his colleagues called on Wheeler to urge him to prepare
the magazine as a refuge.[572] The unruffled old general heard them
out and then assured them that "there was no immediate cause of
apprehension." The soldiers were quiet, relief was on its way, and
even if the troops were to rise they would quickly flee the station.
Wheeler advised Hay and his fellow merchants to arm themselves,
and suggested that should it become necessary for them to flee the
city they would always be welcome to join the "ladies and children
of officers and Christian military followers" in the barracks.

Wheeler firmly, politely drew the meeting to a close, but the merchants emerged dissatisfied.[573] Hay offered his own establishment as
a kind of secondary refuge for any merchant unable to reach the barracks. But "we did not like the idea of remaining dispersed in our
several quarters," wrote Jonah, "knowing that at the moment of actual danger great confusion would ensue." It was all right for the
general to be contented with the barracks, the merchants muttered,
as they were so near the old man's house; there was even a rumor in
the native quarter that the general had chosen the site at the insistence of Lady Frances Wheeler, who did not want her elderly husband riding great distances in the heat.[574]

As the military engineer at Cawnpore, Lieutenant Swynfen C.
Jervis of the Bengal Engineers must have played a key role in the fortification of the Entrenchment, for "Engineer officers were long the
experts on everything to do with a siege."[575] Jervis's conception, no
doubt endlessly modified by Wheeler, Jack, and various other senior
officers, was of a "semi permanent" fortification, "the best imitation
of permanent defences that can be made in a short time, ample resources and skilled civilian labour being available."[576] However

ample the resources or skilled the workmen, the sun had baked the earth like a kiln, and despite double wages[577] and the supervision of the barrack master's office, the coolies were loath and jittery as they chopped at the hard crust and toted dusty chunks of baked clay in wicker head-baskets.[578]

If the dirt could be properly tamped and wetted, a wall three feet thick could protect soldiers from bullets and shrapnel, but there was neither enough labor to pack the clay nor enough water to set it. The efficacy of trenches also depended on their having open ground in front of them, a condition Wheeler met by demolishing the scattered bungalows in the Entrenchment's vicinity.[579] The trenches were just "deep enough to give shelter from high angle shrapnel, and narrow enough to minimize the chance of a common shell dropping into it," and beyond the parapet an incomplete series of cavalry-proofing perforations had been dug called *troup de loup*.[580]

Had the Entrenchment been occupied solely by soldiers it might have withstood an extended siege. But most of the occupants would be women, children, and invalids who would have to find shelter in the barracks, where the sun and wind exerted its own remorseless attrition. Swirls of hot wind and dust swept unimpeded across the parade ground, flaying the parched scrub in the soldiers' garden, moaning among the verandah pillars, slapping and rattling the window shutters. By midday the earth grew so hot it fried the soles of men's boots and cast up a sweltering, dizzying glow.

The Entrenchment did not extend to the unfinished barracks, nor to the well that lay between; Wheeler seems to have assumed that with enough troops to occupy them the outer barracks themselves would form a first line of defense and that the only protection the outer well would require was a line of overturned carts and carriages and piles of storage crates. After four days of labor[581] the trench formed a rough nine-acre rectangle with a few bulges, as though paced out by a staggering, sunstruck officer.[582] In the northern corner was a redan[583] protruding far enough out to permit a battery of guns a 180° east-west sweep. A bulge midway down the western wall commanded the 2nd Cavalry lines that lay a half mile away; the eastern wall was bent outward to encompass the regimental kitchen; and, to supply the artillery positions in the remaining corners, four underground powder magazines were dug.[584]

Coolies laid roofing tiles on the thatch of the hospital barracks and heaved sandbags along as much of the parapet as they could cover, but as the days passed fewer and fewer of them turned up for work.

The artillery positions with their pyramids of roundshot remained unfortified, the thatched roof was only partially covered over with tiles, the sanitary facilities for a prospective population of more than a thousand men, women, and children were grossly inadequate.[585] The two staggered barracks, the crude outbuildings, the lone well, the bare plane in between seemed like some nightmarish lunar outpost, uninhabitable by even the hardiest native soldiers, let alone Europeans, let alone their women and children.

"Like most old Indians [Wheeler] despised the enemy who appeared before him, or at all events he disdained abandoning the station as if from fear of anything they could do, and prepared to defend a position which he scarcely thought they would assail."[586] Anxious family men like Jonah Shepherd who strolled over to inspect their prospective refuge from the coming storm returned to their houses shaking their heads.[587]

One evening Azimullah Khan rode out to see Wheeler's preparations in the company of Lieutenant Daniell, a cavalry officer who had been a frequent visitor to Saturday House.

"What do you call that place you are making out in the plain?" Azimullah asked Daniell.

"I am sure I don't know," he replied.

Azimullah proposed dubbing it the "Fort of Despair."

"No," Daniell stoutly replied. "We will call it the Fort of Victory."

"Aha! Aha!" said Azimullah.[588]

✦   ✦   ✦

By the twentieth of May, the native troops were muttering among themselves that "the cavalry horses were to be shot, that Europeans were coming from England, and that 300 horses and 300 swords were to be taken from the cavalry regiment at Cawnpore, and given over to them. The men of the regiment," remembered a subhedar, "were frightened because the Europeans had come, and their arms were to be given over to them."[589] "I need not add," wrote Wheeler, "how entirely [this was] without foundation; but reports of the most absurd kind are constantly circulated; and one is no sooner disposed of, than another takes it place."[590]

Wheeler congratulated Colonel Ewart and Major Hillersdon for volunteering to sleep in their respective regimental lines on the night of May 20 "to show the Sepoys that they placed implicit confidence in them."[591] But just in case the men mutinied anyway he simultaneously sent off a plea to Henry Lawrence asking him for three hundred British troops. Lawrence could not spare so many men, but "resolved to despatch immediately a party of Europeans and of Irregular Cavalry to aid General Wheeler. "All the post carriages were accordingly collected, and by great exertion, fifty men of the 32nd Regt. under Captain Lowe were put into carriages, and sent off at an early hour on the 21st."[592]

Meanwhile planters, traders, missionaries, and engineers continued to pour into cantonments and huddled with their families in tents[593] and makeshift shacks close by Wheeler's Entrenchment, forming what Lilly Lindsay described as "a sort of camp."[594] It held no charms for Collector Hillersdon, who on the eighteenth sent a letter to Nana Sahib asking if he would "forward his wife and children to England."[595] Nana graciously agreed, and apparently encouraged Hillersdon's swashbuckling plan to organize a force of fifteen hundred fighting men at Bithur and personally "bring them into Cawnpore to take the insurgents by surprise. This is a plan of their own," Lydia had breathlessly written home on the 18th, "and is quite a secret, for the object of it is to come on the mutineers unawares."[596]

On May 20 the Collector himself had moved his wife and child into the Ewarts' bungalow near the barracks[597] and dispatched an opium contractor with government elephants[598] to fetch the treasury from Nawabgunj.[599] But the sepoys guarding the treasury would only allow the officer to remove one hundred thousand of the eight hundred thousand rupees[600] in the vault, insisting that "they were perfectly loyal and would guard the treasure to the last."[601] If Hillersdon tried to carry away any more of the treasury "they would consider that the officers had lost all confidence in them, in which case it would be just as well for them to go away to their homes."[602] "The sahibs have lost all confidence in us," a sepoy told one officer, "and we shall never get over it."[603]

Charles threatened to replace them with a European guard.

"That shall not be done as long as we are alive," they replied, "because in these two posts a guard of Europeans never was, and never shall be, placed; and, moreover, if the magazine or treasure should go on command, we will accompany it."[604]

Hillersdon backed off, and Wheeler refused to confront the sepoy guard with European troops. But the general agreed to allow Hillersdon to ask Nana Sahib to bring a small force from Bithur to watch over the treasury. Nobody knows if there was a quid pro quo between Nana and Charles. Some thought Wheeler and Charles had merely been "easily flattered in their pride of race," into accepting

Nana Sahib as their "influential" ally.[605] But Hillersdon's colleagues in the civil service assumed that Charles could only have procured the Mahratta's services "by promising to obtain the concessions" Nana had "so long pleaded in vain": his father's pension, title, seal, and salutes.[606]

After obtaining Wheeler's assurance that Agra would pay his men,[607] Nana left his establishment in the care of his nephew Rao Sahib[608] and on the morning of May 21 set off toward the city station[609] riding the largest elephant of a string of elephants and trailing two brass guns[610] and four hundred lancers and matchlockmen[611] under Jwala Prasad's command.[612]

As Nana and his men rushed toward Cawnpore they encountered Baji Rao's younger brother, Chimnaji Appa, who had allied himself against Nana with the Peshwa's widows.[613] As Nana's men hurtled down the road, they ran Chimnaji and his entourage into a ravine, beat up his guards, stole a sword and rushed on, warning Chimnaji that in a few days Nana would settle with him for good when the Company's raj was over.[614]

A SUDDEN FLIGHT
May 21–22, 1857

To protect the Commissariat's cash, Wheeler moved the Commissariat Office across the canal to Superintendent Williamson's bungalow in the middle of the cantonment. At around 9:30 on the morning of May 21, Captain Williamson's wife was sitting on her verandah, no doubt discomfited by the influx of her husband's staff, when someone ran up to her with a letter. After tearing it open she let out a scream, grabbed her child and ran down the road with her ayah hobbling along behind her. As the Commissariat babus hurried to the windows of their makeshift offices, Williamson himself appeared in the driveway and without a word to his writers pounded unceremoniously after his wife, pausing only to order his groom to prepare a carriage and bring it at once to the Entrenchment.

When Jonah Shepherd arrived the babus were in a terrible state "and ready to run for their homes." Jonah sent a note off to John Hay, who replied that he too was fleeing to the barracks and urgently advised Jonah to do the same. Jonah raced back across the canal to fetch his already panic-stricken family and joined the rush to the Entrenchment. "On our way we met several of our acquaintances going in the same direction," Jonah recalled, "who wished to know the cause of this sudden flight." But no one could say.

The Shepherds were among the very last to straggle into the Entrenchment, which they found "crowded to excess." Families like John Hampden Cook's rushed about as well, searching for space. The Shepherds had to settle for a portion of the outer verandah of the thatched-roofed barrack, where "our infants, who had only half an hour ago been enjoying the cool of the *khuss tatties* [wetted grass screens] and *punkahs,* were . . . almost smothered in the laps of their mothers" and exposed not only to the "hot winds" but the contagion of smallpox, dysentery, and cholera from the soldiers languishing in the hospital barrack.[615]

Even in the best of times the barracks had been miserable places. The two flanking rows of verandahs did little to cool the air of the interior rooms, which were serviced by punkahs. The wives and children of married soldiers usually occupied the inner verandahs, marking the boundaries of their living quarters with blankets and tatties hung from the ceiling. They shared these inner verandahs with the barrack urinals: long tubs that teams of sweepers carried out periodically on long poles, slopping their contents on the tamped clay floors.[616]

Within these wretched confines Wheeler's garrison had arranged itself hierarchically. The families of senior officers reserved the interior rooms of the newer and more fire-resistant tiled barrack, families of somewhat less standing occupied the inner verandahs, everyone else was left to scramble for space along the exposed arcades. The inner verandahs along one side of the thatched barrack were already occupied by the families of not only the musicians and the invalid soldiers languishing in the hospital but of soldiers stationed at Lucknow: about fifty women and seventy-three children in all. A surgery occupied many of the airless interior rooms of the thatched barrack, others were set aside for storage. As at the tiled barrack, traders, Eurasians, Indian Christians, and servants crowded into the vulnerable arcade of the thatched barrack's outer verandahs. The ladies tried their best to domesticate these premises by installing tatties and punkahs and bringing their servants with them to cook and tend the horses and fetch clean clothing, fresh sheets, combs, brushes, sewing boxes, writing desks, sofas, chairs, tubs, and camp beds. Though they were all Christians, these "many little factions" had been cast together for the first time in one compound and forced to coexist despite the "gulfs of incomprehension" that separated them.[617]

Huddled together in the blistering heat, the garrison realized that someone had mistaken Nana Sahib's force for an army of *goojurs*, marauding husbandmen whom they may have resembled with their matchlocks and bucklers and pikes.[618] But the Europeans' servants were appalled and alarmed by their sahibs' and memsahibs' behavior. A servant of Colonel Williams could not see "what took the officers into the entrenchments, as there was no active demonstration on the part of the troop to lead me to suppose that it was from fear of an immediate attack."[619] What had become of their masters' self-confidence? And if the sahibs had lost heart, what was to become of their servants and clerks? The Mahajuns were also alarmed, and Hillersdon grudgingly had to allow them to hire their own guards, providing that his police chief selected them and the Mahajuns paid their wages.[620]

At noon there were sounds of a commotion to the west of the Entrenchment, and the Europeans rushed to the wall to watch through the shimmering midday waves of heat as a guard of troopers emerged with a prisoner from the lines of the 2nd Native Cavalry. He turned out to be the servant of a native sergeant or havildar of the 56th Native Infantry named Khan Mahomed, who had sent him into the lines to warn the sowars that Wheeler was readying guns in order to fire into their lines at the next parade.[621] The havildar was summarily court-martialed and sentenced to be hanged for "spreading false reports."[622] Wheeler wisely decided that the grim spectacle of a military execution was the last thing he needed just then and ordered the hanging indefinitely postponed.[623] But by now all the sowars had "taken it into their heads that they [were] to be convicted" and became so "ripe for revolt" that Wheeler himself warned Khoda Bux that his life was in danger.[624] When a delegation of native cavalry officers reported that the sowars intended to mutiny that very night, Wheeler replied that he would hold them personally responsible for the sowars' disaffection.[625] "Every man who cannot prove that he . . . actively opposed the disturbers of the peace," he wrote, "should be, for that inertness, sent about his business."[626]

The sowars retired quietly to their lines at about half-past seven, having "consented to relinquish their intentions at least for that night."[627] "Can you imagine such a state of things," Lydia Hillersdon wrote disgustedly, "—our own troops threatening us with an outbreak, and then moodily putting it off for a few nights?"[628]

◆ ◆ ◆

On Saturday, May 16, Captain William Halliday had decided to send his wife Emma and their child Mabel ahead of him to Cawnpore. "The country is getting rather dangerous," Emma wrote her mother from Banda. The rebels were fast taking control of the roads, and if Emma and Mabel were to reach the safety of the Cawnpore garrison, there was no time to lose. Packing her Colt revolvers, Emma bade what she feared might be a final good-bye to Willie, and with Mabel and her ayah and a lieutenant to protect them, she left Banda early on the morning of May 18.

They arrived safely in Cawnpore in the middle of Tuesday night and drew up to the gate of her old friends the Vibarts.[629] She asked first about their oldest son, Butcher, and rejoiced with Emily at the report that young Edward had been spotted among a band of survivors fleeing to Kurnaul.[630] On May 22 Emma boasted that she and the Vibarts "were the *only* people who did not sleep in the Barracks last night," though Major Vibart did keep "his horses shod to be in readiness if wanted," and Emma confessed she slept with "two six-barreled pistols" under her pillow.[631]

Lilly Lindsay and Kate and her three girls held out at Kate's house through the morning and the long afternoon and deep into the sweltering night. After breakfast that morning Wheeler had advised Major Lindsay to keep his family in readiness for the firing of a gun: his signal for all Europeans to come to the Entrenchment. Perhaps Lindsay questioned the old man's judgment, or would not subscribe to the rest of the station's alarm. In any case, Lindsay rode back to the Main Guard after supper, leaving his womenfolk at the house to await the general's alarm. But a little after midnight Lilly and Kate decided to climb into their carriages with the girls and Miss Bissell and trotted the mile to the Entrenchment. "The scene of confusion and fright everybody was in [passed] description," wrote Caroline. Some of them managed to find beds in the tiled barrack, where crying and wakeful children "added much to our distress and anxiety," while the rest—Caroline included—slept in their carriages.[632]

In the evening John Ewart had left his wife and the Hillersdons at his house and gone off to sleep in the lines of his 1st Native Infantry. But when Hillersdon was called away, the two women decided at last to take their children to the Entrenchment.[633] "Accordingly," wrote Mrs. Ewart, "we took our little unconscious children out of their beds, and with the ayahs off went we in the carriage to the European barracks [for] a night of awful suspense."[634] The children wailed in the terrible heat, and Lydia Hillersdon "did not lie down all night."

Emma Larkins fretted about the health of her husband, George, who as Field Officer of the week had been obliged to remain in the saddle through the long day, guarding the nine-pounders in the artillery lines and watching the bridge for some sign of reinforcements from Lucknow. She repeatedly drove out to persuade him to come in out of the sun, but he refused to move until the reinforcements had arrived. At last, just before midnight, the garrison started at the sound of wheels and horses' hooves and peered into the darkness to see fifty-five dusty soldiers of Her Majesty's 32nd stepping heavily from their Lucknow carriages with 240 Oudh Irregulars sullenly bringing up the rear. The arrival of even this little force "delighted" Wheeler, who gratefully deployed them around the cantonments and welcomed their officers, including Lawrence's aide, the erudite Captain Fletcher Hayes, into the Main Guard.[635] "It was such a comfort," wrote Lydia, "to find ourselves surrounded by English soldiers, who we know would shed the last drop of their blood in our defence."[636] But rumors of an uprising persisted, and Captain Hayes was shocked to see how residents of the garrison hectored the old general "until nearly one A.M., on the 22nd, when we retired to rest."[637]

The garrison returned to their improvised beds—palanquins, pallets, rope-strung beds, chairs, tables, carriage cushions, piles of quilted blankets—until three in the morning of the twenty-second when a thunderstorm whirled through the station with such force that it tore the door off one officer's room, blew down tents and rocked Caroline about in her carriage.[638]

Early the next morning Mrs. Ewart joyfully rushed out to greet her exhausted husband John as he and Major Hillersdon returned blearily from their lines. She was proud that "the move of the officers/at least of two/to sleep amongst their men seemed to have checked the ardour of the mutinously disposed."[639] Indeed Wheeler and Brigadier Jack believed that their gamble had paid off so handsomely that in the morning Jack gave orders[640] that until the alarm had entirely passed every officer would be required to sleep in his regimental lines.[641]

Wheeler now ordered the women and children to remain in the barracks in case the Moslem sowars might decide to mark their festival of Eed by mutinying.[642] The Lindsay women obeyed Wheeler's command,[643] but others found the barracks too awful and returned to the cool interiors of their homes.[644] The wind and rain had cooled the station somewhat, but soon the sun would turn the mud to dust again; and, after all, the Lucknow troop had arrived, as had Nana Sahib's guardsmen who, "being Mahrattas," as Wheeler saw it, were "not likely to coalesce with the others."[645]

At six o'clock Friday morning the newly arrived Captain Hayes emerged from his tent and gazed around for the first time at the rain-washed Entrenchment. What he found was the most terrible scene of "confusion, fright and bad arrangement" he had seen since coming to India.

> Four guns were in position loaded, with European artillerymen in nightcaps and wide-awakes and side-arms on, hanging to the guns in groups—looking like melodramatic buccaneers. People of all kinds, of every colour, sect, and profession, were crowding into the barracks. Whilst I was there, buggies, palki-gharrees, vehicles of all sorts, drove up and discharged cargoes of writers, tradesmen, and a miscellaneous mob of every complexion, from white to tawny—all in terror of the imaginary foe; ladies sitting down at the rough mess-tables in the barracks, women suckling infants, ayahs and children in all directions, and—officers too! ... I saw quite enough to convince me that if any insurrection took or takes place, we shall have no one to thank but ourselves, because we have now shown to the Natives how very easily we can be frightened, and when frightened utterly helpless.

Now came the news that the troops at Aligarh had mutinied[646] and that the dilettante commander-in-chief, the elderly and sickly George Anson, had not yet reached Delhi but was paralyzed "for want of tents and carriage."[647] Far from the plague being "stayed," the rebellion was spinning down the Ganges like a burning boat, setting fire to station after station along its banks.[648]

"My darling mother," Emma Halliday wrote on the twenty-second, "I trust we shall meet again on earth, but, if not, I pray we may in another world, and though you may never see Willie, Baby or me, you can still remember us, as we shall only have left this world of care and gone to our last home." During her four years in India, Emma had traveled three thousand five hundred miles and occupied six houses in as many different stations: Cawnpore was to have been the seventh. And so it occurred to Emma to assure her mother that even if they should be killed "it won't be so like dying as going home, as we have always been moving about. . . ."[649]

"I will sell my life dearly," she promised, for she had "two six-barreled revolvers loaded under my pillow every night." She "awoke at every little noise," but took pride in the fact that she and Emily Vibart still slept in the Vibarts' house and refused to believe that Willie's 56th would join in the uprising.[650] "Oh Willie, dear," Emma wrote her husband at Banda, "if it is true! . . . *I pray God to preserve us all.*"[651]

But how could it be true? How could the same men who had protected Emma on her journeys through Santal country, who had brought lilies to her baby, who had gathered around Mabel in the evenings at Banda and kindly listened to her read from her alphabet book—how could these fond and upright men turn on their captain, his wife, and little daughter? "I wish so much that I could see some one of our regiment or some sepoy," Emma wrote Willie. "I would like to see Peer Bux. Surely *he* would not murder us."[652]

PRAY GOD

May 22–31, 1857

After his encounter with Nana's men on Bithur Road, the ruffled Chimnaji Appa had scrawled a note to his mooktear Nanak Chand. Nanak Chand, hoping to curry favor with the collector, promised to relay the Mahrattas' warning to Hillersdon sahib himself. By now Charles had staked everything—his reputation, his treasury, his defenses, even his home and family—on the fidelity of his "great friend." He had installed Nana Sahib in a bungalow across from the treasury,[653] and though men from his brother's 53rd[654] had relieved the sepoy guard, Nana was now in possession of the magazine and a treasury containing over seven hundred thousand rupees.[655] Hillersdon was therefore in no mood to entertain some insinuating slander about Nana Sahib's men predicting the end of the Company's rule. Disgusted, exhausted, Charles silently waved Nanak Chand away and returned to the papers on his desk.[656]

No doubt exhilarated by Hillersdon's trust, Nana Sahib held court at Nawabgunj, receiving merchants and grateful well-wishers from the civil station, and assuring officers "with joined hands" that he would be faithful to his covenant with Wheeler.[657] A writer would later recall that "on one or two occasions" Nana even sent his men out "to apprehend runaway sepoys from Delhi and Etawah who had plundered Government money," though they never seemed to return with any captives.[658]

Nana had to congratulate himself on how well he had positioned himself for a Concanist double game. If the troops did not mutiny—or even if they mutinied and fled the station—the British would have to reward Nana Sahib with his father's pension, titles, and honors. If the rebels remained and beat the British, the sepoys would restore him to the Peshwa's throne.[659]

All the while Azimullah made his rounds, commiserating with various officers and merchants while secretly corresponding with Turks and Russians. As his agents continued to meet with the disaffected officers of the native regiments, he kept in direct touch with the Begum of Delhi and Hazrat Mahal of Lucknow, where he had installed his traveling companion, Mahomed Ali. Heartened not only by the spread of the uprising but the Persian war, which "seemed to him a part of the advance of Russia," Azimullah "had just enough knowledge of the political drama to be 'a dangerous thing,' first to Hillersdon, and ultimately to himself and [his own] cause."[660]

✦ ✦ ✦

On Friday the twenty-second, the Moslem festival of Eed, "the shops in all the bazaars were shut four or five times," Hayes wrote, "and all day the General was worried to death by people running up to report improbable stories, which in ten minutes more were contradicted by others still more monstrous."[661] "The same uncomfortable reports came pouring in," wrote Emma Ewart, "news of fresh defections of corps at other places," and "threatening words" uttered by the men of the 1st Native Infantry, who now seemed as disaffected as the sowars.[662] Wheeler did not like the look of the recently conscripted Oudh Irregulars, either, whom he had deployed around the station.

Every midnight the old general would climb on his horse and ride through the dark station on what he called "subaltern duty," consulting with the havildars and British sergeant-majors, making the rounds of the regimental lines, softly speaking Urdu to the native pickets as they stood to salute him, gently teasing them about their undress in the heat of the night, asking after their families, reminding the old native officers of the battles in which they had marched together, fought together, bled together for the honor of the colors and *Kampani Jehan*. "I felt that I gave confidence," Wheeler wrote of his nocturnal rounds, "that I saw all [was] right with my own eyes, and that doing my own duty I had a right to exact it from others."[663]

Brigadier Jack and his brother slept at home that night; Deputy Judge Advocate-General Wiggins remained at his house because his very pregnant wife Christian was on the brink of hysteria, and Major Lindsay returned home at night, perhaps because he was not affiliated with any Cawnpore regiment.[664] But all the other senior officers slept in the native lines. As Major Vibart set off for the lines of his 2nd Native Cavalry, Emma Halliday presented him with one of her six-barreled Colt revolvers "as I think one Pistol is enough for me."[665]

"When my husband left me," wrote Mrs. Ewart, " . . . I never expected to see him alive again, for some of his men had been overheard wildly talking of mutiny & murder & had made a proposal to destroy their officers!"[666] But the night passed without incident, and Colonel Ewart returned to the Entrenchment to fetch his wife and child back to their "comfortable house. . . . God grant,"Mrs. Ewart prayed after riding away from the teeming barracks, "that we may not be exposed to such suffering as a confinement within that entrenchment would entail. Even should we be able to bear it, I know not how our poor little ones could go through the trial."[667]

On Saturday, Wheeler wired Calcutta that Cawnpore bore "a calm appearance; more favourable, but not to be depended on."[668] The native troops continued to bristle at the sight of the Entrenchment guns aimed in their direction, and resurrected the rumor that Wheeler, with his cannon ready aimed, intended to call them all out on the parade-ground and force the cartridges upon them.[669] Fletcher Hayes continued to admire the old man's equilibrium. "I believe that if anything will keep the Sepoys quiet, it will be, next to Providence, the great respect which they all have for General Wheeler, and for him alone." The Wheelers continued to keep all their "doors and windows open all night," and the old man "never thought of moving or of allowing his family to move."[670]

 But by the night of the twenty-third the tide of rumors had begun to overwhelm the old man, and he did move Lady Frances and his daughters into the Entrenchment after all, installing them in the tent he occupied by the Main Guard.[671] Without warning the rest of the garrison, he ordered a large body of Oudh Irregulars out of the station to chase the phantom goojurs on the Grand Trunk Road, and the receding clatter of their galloping horses momentarily convinced the refugees in the stifling barracks that the cavalry had mutinied.[672] He ordered his regimental commanders to obtain the keys to the Bells of Arms, thus humiliating the old native officers who traditionally safeguarded them.[673] He sent Lawrence two or three telegrams a day, declaring in one that he was "almost certain that the troops will rise to-night," a bulletin Martin Gubbins took so seriously that he kept a vigil on his roof in Lucknow Saturday night, watching and listening in vain for the flare and rumble of rebel guns in the dark southwestern sky.[674]

Sunday was the Queen's birthday, but Wheeler decided to forego the traditional artillery salute for fear the troops would mistake it for an attack.[675] This "frightened us not a little," recalled Amy Horne, "for it was something so strange allowing the day to pass unnoticed." Especially disappointed were "the merchants who, expecting liberal orders, had calculated on turning a penny."[676] "Oh!" exclaimed Lydia Hillersdon, "what a humiliating state of things. Fancy us, the governors of the country, obliged to shelter ourselves behind guns."[677]

Hillersdon posted matchlockmen at every boundary post, and a Lieutenant Barbour arrived from Lucknow with more Oudh Irregulars whom Wheeler intermingled with a picket of the 2nd Native Cavalry on the outskirts of the station.[678] The old man must have sensed by now that his constant alarms might be wearing thin at Lucknow. That Sunday he conceded in a telegram that "all is quiet here," but felt compelled to remind Lawrence that it was "impossible to say how long it will continue so,"[679] especially now that the telegraph line to Agra had been cut.[680]

That Sunday the Vibarts had felt so secure that they had guests for dinner and afterwards drove with Emma Halliday to Christ Church to say their prayers. The ladies were shocked to find that the gates to the church had been padlocked and so drove to the house of the muscular Reverend Moncrieff, whose watchman informed them that "Padre sahib" had fled into the Entrenchment. Emma and the Vibarts indignantly turned their carriage around to drive the two miles to the barracks and give Moncrieff a piece of their minds. As a servant hurried off to fetch the chaplain, Emma got out to see for the first time "what sort of room there was" in the barracks, and found that already "every room was crowded with beds" and the inner and outer verandahs filled with "groups of Ladies & Gentlemen."[681] Guns were "ranged round" the Entrenchment, European sentries posted along the walls, and Oudh Irregulars "picketed round beyond."[682] As she strolled through the Entrenchment Emma recognized the Australian Dr. Bowling, whose wife "started up just beyond" from the doctor's folding "iron chair," a standard piece of equipment among physicians of the time, who erected them during their house calls for teeth-pullings and minor surgery.[683] Emma was also greeted by young officers of Willie's 56th who assured her "our sepoys have sworn to keep by us."[684]

Emma lingered long enough to sit by the soldier's garden and roughly sketch the teeming sprawl of the Entrenchment that af-

Emma Halliday's sketch of the barrack exterior, showing the garrison assembled on May 25[685]

ternoon: the provision godown flanked by Wheeler's tent, a privy, carriages; a syce squatting by a horse, a stout man with a cane exchanging rumors with his neighbors.

When Reverend Moncrieff informed the ladies that General Wheeler had forbidden Sunday worship, Emma returned with the

Vibarts to their compound.[686] But no sooner had they stepped into the parlor than a Captain Seppings suddenly galloped up, "rushed in, and said an attack was decidedly going to be made during the night . . . and no time was to be lost, as may be it had begun already." Everyone else had left their houses, including Wheeler and Brigadier Jack, "so off we went," wrote Emma. She lifted Mabel out of her bed and raced off in the major's buggy, her small child sleeping soundly the whole way to the Entrenchment.[687]

There they joined Mrs. Bowling and Mrs. Larkins in a room in the tiled barrack. Tatties were kept wetted on the walls, and through the stifling night of the twenty-fourth of May, coolies tugged at the punkahs overhead. The officers' wives lay in rows, tossing and turning and gasping for breath, fearing for their husbands lying in their regimental lines amid their disgruntled sepoys and sowars. Emma thought of Willie then, separated from her by ninety miles of bleak wasteland and disaffected villages through which he would soon lead four hundred brooding native soldiers.[688]

All the officers posted at the Entrenchment "took it in turn to sit up all night," recalled Mowbray Thomson, "that we might not altogether be taken by surprise."[689] The next morning Emma Halliday and Emily Vibart returned to their house for a bath and were just settling down to breakfast when in rushed the major with another alarm. "Every one running from the bazar," he announced. "The

Emma Halliday's sketch of the interior of the tiled barrack: 1) wife of Surgeon Bowling, 2) Emma and her baby, 3) Mary Ann, the ayah, *4) punkah* coolie, *5) Mrs. Larkins, wife of the artillery commander.*

whole station risen! Run off whilst you can!" Scooping up Mabel, Emma fled once more to the Entrenchment. "Well," she reported to Willie, "we sat in the barracks, and at half past twelve all was so quiet that we returned. And I have determined never to believe a report without ocular demonstration. . . . All is perfectly quiet," she assured her husband, "and I really think there is nothing to fear. Five hundred men of a Queen's regiment passed Benares the night before last, so they ought to be here in a couple of days or so."

That very day, however, Governor-General Canning had wired Lawrence that it would be "impossible to place a wing of Europeans at Lucknow in less time than 25 days." A wing of Madras Fusiliers had arrived at Calcutta, and would shortly set off by bullock cart and train, but traveling at about thirty miles a day a full regiment of about a thousand Fusiliers could not reach Benares in less than nineteen or twenty days. Other regiments were due from Pegu, Bombay, and Ceylon, Canning wrote, but "this is the best I can do for you."[690]

Wheeler promptly ordered the Commissariat to supply the Entrenchment with twenty-five days' provisions.[691] Lentils, butter, "salt, rice, tea, sugar, rum, malt liquor, and hermetically sealed provisions were ordered, but peas and flour formed the bulk of the food obtained." The stock proved insufficient,"[692] for which Jonah Shepherd blamed an inexperienced native agent.[693] The officers, "who had no very lively confidence in Sir Hugh as a caterer," brought in their own supplies of mincemeats, joints, beer, brandy, cakes, tinned fish and fruit, jams, and biscuits.[694]

The magazine five miles upriver from the Entrenchment remained "full of military stores, many guns of various sizes and a store of ammunition . . . guarded by the sepoy guard, and . . . the usual staff of ordnance officers and warrant officers with *lascars* [artillery coolies]."[695] But Wheeler had gradually hauled an ample supply of powder and ammunition to the Entrenchment—some from the magazine, some from the regimental godowns. An additional store of weapons was collected at Savada House on the old mission grounds a mile southwest of the Entrenchment.[696] But Wheeler was careful not to issue any of his Enfield rifles and cartridges, not even to Europeans.[697]

By now the gunners had wearied of standing at their posts in various stages of alert, jumping to each of the general's false alarms. When Hayes joined Wheeler on his rounds Monday evening he was appalled by their lack of discipline. "We came upon one half battery without any challenge or the least exhibition of any alarm on the part of the gunners," Hayes reported.

> I walked up and put my hand on one of the guns, and could have spiked all three with the greatest ease. . . . Some little time afterwards the officer in charge was found asleep and was immediately put under arrest[698] . . . Dempster, the Adjutant of the Artillery, was so worn out with watching at night and performing other duties, that, seeing he was so done up and could not look after both batteries, I said I would take one, and accordingly remained in charge till daybreak.[699]

General Wheeler remained convinced that an attack was imminent. "Passed anxious night and day," he wired Calcutta on the twenty-fifth, "in consequence of a report, on very good authority, that there would be an outbreak during one or the other. . . . I rejoice to say that nothing occurred."[700]

By now Hayes no longer credited the relative quiet of the native troops to Wheeler but to the sepoys' own indecision. "They have been wrangling among themselves for some days," he said. A native officer had evidently tried to signal the cavalry to rise with a bugle call, but a subhedar had snatched the bugle away.[701] Mrs. Ewart heard that the rising had merely been "deferred" because "the infantry could not agree with the cavalry as to the mode of the outbreak."[702] On the morning of the twenty-fifth, the station was somewhat reassured "by all the implications of the 1st coming in a body according to custom, to salaam to Col Ewart after their prayers and [express] their intentions of fidelity etc." "It *is* most strange," observed Nanak Chand, "that all these men, whose hearts are estranged from Government, continue to do their duty under it."[703]

All through the station people buried their most precious possessions or entrusted them to servants. Lindsay left two boxes of "wearing apparel and small family relics, private papers, and little things he valued, amongst them a number of photographs" with his head writer, Lalik Ram.[704] Reverend Haycock entrusted the Cawnpore Mission's communion plate and altar cloth to a neighboring landlord.[705] A plump planter named Peter Maxwell put his possessions in the safekeeping of his native assistants and, leaving behind his Kashmiri bibi and four Brahmin female servants, moved into the Entrenchment. J. R. Brandon believed that the treasure he was holding for the deposed King of Oudh would protect his own trove, but his arch competitors the Greenways buried their fortune in their compound, as did wine merchant William Crump.[706]

As the Entrenchment filled with more and more "men, Officers women & children, beds & chairs all mingled together inside & out of the barrack, some talking & even laughing/some very frightened, some defiant others despairing,"[707] John Hay returned to Wheeler with his delegation of merchants. The two barracks were now so jammed with people that even a civilian like Hay only had to consider a single aspect of Wheeler's arrangements—the distance from the river, the shortage of privies, the impossible demand on the one protected well, the vast area the trench enclosed, the distance the exposed barracks stood from the merchants' establishments west of the canal—to see that it could never protect the civil population or sustain a prolonged siege. Some of the merchants "talked very bitterly" about the vulnerability of their property to attack, whereas the sepoys would not dare to loot the officers' houses within range of the Entrenchment guns.[708] With all due respect, Hay told the general, even if Wheeler and his officers decided to remain in the Entrenchment, Hay and his fellow merchants demanded the right to move themselves into the magazine.

Wheeler replied mildly that such a move would be extremely unwise because in the unlikely event that the troops did attempt to lay siege to the Entrenchment, he intended to blow the magazine to kingdom come. He did not tell them that the ordnance officer Wheeler had assigned to lay the charges had been followed so closely by the sepoy guard over the past few days that he had had no chance to "take the least step towards blowing up the powder," but his reply silenced the merchants, who left in gloomy silence, many of them resolved to flee the station.[709] "Alarming reports," recalled Jonah Shepherd, had "continued to fly about the station daily, and we lived in perpetual anxiety and dread." Jonah himself placed so little confidence in the Entrenchment that he had rented two houses in a native contractor's name to which the Shepherds might flee dressed as Indians. Ellen and his sister sent a servant off to buy coarse cloth and, patterning their clothes after their ayah's costume, secretly sewed disguises and rehearsed the family in their roles as Indian women and children. Jonah congratulated them on their handiwork, but secretly found their preparations "pitiful," for his wife and daughters, in whose fair skins he had always taken such pride, could probably never pass for natives.[710]

◆ ◆ ◆

The next morning Wheeler woke up in a cheerful mood. He had survived both the festival of Eed and the Queen's birthday, and he began to conclude that if the troops had not risen by now they never would. "All tranquil here," he wired Calcutta, "and I think likely to continue. The disaffected, disconcerted by the efficient measures coolly, but determinately, taken to meet any outbreak that might be attempted, are sobering down. I have had a most anxious and tried time of it; nor is it at an end . . . I have intrenched our position, and can hold it against large odds, but now I hope I may preserve the peace of this very important station without bloodshed. . . . All well, very well," he concluded, "and I think likely to continue so, unless some startling event should occur."[711] In a separate note Wheeler thanked Lawrence for his reinforcements and especially for the "extremely valuable" services of Captain Hayes. But he hoped that "we may consider the crisis passed; though the disease is by no means cured." Indeed, he had decided to return the fifty-five men of the 32nd Foot "as soon as 150 men of Her Majesty's 84th arrive; and shall be ready to aid and support you, as you have me. Letters tell," he grandiloquently reported to Lawrence, "that all look to Cawnpore."[712]

SOME GAY ASSEMBLY
May 18–31, 1857

In the middle of May, a Mrs. Fraser had arrived from the pandemonium of Delhi with an Indian driver who had "brought her faithfully to the end of her hazardous journey of 266 miles." People crowded around to examine the rebel bullet hole in her carriage and listen to her firsthand account of the horrors of Delhi.[713] But Mrs.

Fraser was just one of the many who now converged on Cawnpore. On May 14 Lieutenant Frederick Cortlandt Angelo had been appointed deputy superintendent of the Canal Department and a week later arrived in Cawnpore with his pregnant wife Helena and two daughters to find the garrison fleeing into the barracks. On the twenty-sixth they gave up the boat on which they had been living and moved into the Entrenchment, where Angelo accepted a post at one of the batteries. By now Wheeler's optimism must have infected the garrison, for Helena found the Entrenchment "a singular scene—parties of officers and ladies singing and laughing in one place—gentlemen assembled in the open air—all noise and bustle and one would imagine it some gay assembly."[714] But Lieutenant Angelo grew "thoughtful and serious" as he cast his engineer's eye upon Wheeler's defenses. Though the river was low and the sandbars treacherous, Angelo announced on the twenty-eighth that he was "absolutely determined" to send his family to Calcutta. By six o'clock that evening, he had hustled his wife and daughters into a native boat and waved them off from the city ghats. "Oh! my God," Helena prayed as she hid with her daughters in the bottom of the boat, "keep and protect my beloved husband."[715]

Another memsahib who passed quickly through the station was the somewhat unhinged Elizabeth Sneyd. In early 1853 Mrs. Sneyd had accompanied her son, Captain Henry Sneyd, on a grimly portentous journey to India. Shipwrecked en route, she had not reached the North-Western Provinces until 1854.[716] The Sneyds joined Henry at his posting at Shahjahanpur, but after a series of mysterious fires, Henry sent his mother, his pregnant wife Louisa, and Mrs. Sneyd's lap dog Topsy down the road to Calcutta in sedan chairs because all the good horses in the area had been requisitioned by local nobility. On May 25 they stumbled into Cawnpore to find that Nana Sahib's soldiers and retainers had taken every hotel room. The proprietor, "a shabby half-caste," could only offer Mrs. Sneyd a place on the verandah and served her the leftovers of the native soldiers. They not only refused to stand when she passed but pointed at her and sniggered. Irate and alarmed, Mrs. Sneyd and Louisa pressed on toward Calcutta.[717]

Several residents of Cawnpore happened to be out of station that month. Dr. Tressider had gone home to England to visit his family. Peter Maxwell's brother Hugh had just left for Calcutta to meet his family returning from England.[718] Mr. Willis of the Cawnpore Mission was in Calcutta for his ordination. And the coachbuilder Frederick Jacobi had sent his petite thirteen-year-old daughter Charlotte to Fort William to recuperate from a chronic illness.[719] But others had fled purposely. A milliner wrote off the £500 her customers owed her and sailed downriver with her four children.[720] A captain of an irregular Sikh regiment slipped down the Ganges with his family in late May,[721] and against Wheeler's advice the merchant Eduard Williams, finding his "suspicions regarding the sepoys daily strengthened," sent his family off to a remote village where they huddled together in a mendicant's hut, disguised as Moslems.[722]

✦   ✦   ✦

The garrison continued to bombard Wheeler with stories of the native troops' "wild speeches." A sowar had bragged to the head of the telegraph office[723] "that the means which he adopted to convey intelligence, and which was nothing but witch-craft, would soon be destroyed, and they would take care to attack this office first."[724] A visitor overheard sowars boasting openly of the services they intended to render "the *New Government*."[725] A sergeant's wife returned from marketing in the native bazaar to report that she had been accosted by a sepoy in his native clothes.[726] "You will none of you come here much oftener," the sepoy sneered. "You will not be alive another week." She hurried back to the Entrenchment to report the sepoy, "but it was thought advisable to discredit [her] tale"; another court martial might be just the spark to ignite a general uprising.[727] When Nanak Chand ventured to warn a deputy collector that five sowars had gone over to the rebels, the civilian simply shrugged it off. "What can we do?" he wanted to know. "If these people kill us, England will not be depopulated. More than 60,000 European troops are on their way from England. You will see what will happen."[728]

Perhaps it was Hillersdon's own nagging doubts that accounted for the reception he gave Nanak Chand at his office that afternoon. Or perhaps he was simply fed up by now with Nanak Chand's endless suits, which the mooktear continued to press even in the midst of the emergency. For the past two days Nanak Chand had been receiving reports that Company troops had been seen mingling with Nana Sahib's Mahratta soldiers, that Teeka Singh of the 2nd Native Cavalry continued to meet with Nana's agents, that the Maharaja of Bithur and his agents were plotting the downfall of the British Raj. Summoning up all his courage, Nanak Chand once again crept into Hillersdon's office and ventured his suspicions.

Hillersdon exploded. "You have all along been speaking ill of the

Nana, and filing suits against him in the civil courts," he shouted, pointing to the door. "I cannot pay attention to any representation from a person so hostile to the Nana."[729]

When a self-styled raja[730] entered the district with hundreds of followers Hillersdon shot off a warning that if the raja or his men caused the slightest disturbance he would be hanged.[731] By the time the message was delivered the raja's men "had plundered travellers and dak bungalows" and burned down a village, but they receded for the time being into the countryside.[732] Wheeler's pickets occasionally brought in natives suspected of instigating rebellion, and the police had caught several Meerut and Delhi mutineers en route to their villages laden with plunder: one sepoy of the 9th Native Infantry was found carrying one thousand rupees in his bag.[733] "Mr. Hillersdon has them confined in his gaol," wrote Mrs. Ewart. "We feel it rather dangerous work," for it might provoke their comrades.[734]

✦ ✦ ✦

Only two months earlier a promising young Anglo-Irish engineer named Robert Garrett had arrived in India "to examine into and report upon the merits of a proposed line of Railway in Oude."[735] The railway was essential to the development of the new territory, so Garrett had been given the royal treatment, including a tour of Lucknow by Lawrence himself. Crisscrossing Oudh by elephant and palanquin, Garrett had struggled to maintain his "gravity under difficult and [ridiculous] circumstances in a manner that would not disgrace a disciple of Allah and the Prophet" as he prepared his estimate of the railway's cost. But his surveyor soon fled, and his agent was stuck in Allahabad, where "all Europeans . . . look upon themselves as marked men." Garrett had hoped to have all his business "in a very favoured state," and it seems likely that he met with Azimullah. But by then it seemed "the fates have not prospered my business or indeed any other business properly so called in these parts," and he remained stranded at Cawnpore.

By the twenty-eighth Garrett had volunteered to join "a band of chosen warriors (ten in number) called the Railway Rifle Corps, whose mention," he dryly noted, "no doubt strikes terror into the hearts of the disaffected." In fact there were at least twenty-four railway men in the Entrenchment. Wheeler must have been surprised by the number, for the terminus of the East Indian Railway Company (EIRC) was still six hundred miles from Cawnpore, and its completion was years away. The "Railway Rifle Corps" consisted of

resident engineers, assistants, overseers, clerks, a surveyor, a plate
layer, an "articled inspector," and about fourteen other men, some of
them employees of J. R. Brandon, who ran thirty miles of his own
track through Cawnpore district.[736]

Though railway men were known as a rough lot, Garrett deemed
the upper-echelon railway engineers of his little corps "very decent
Fellows" with whom he was getting on "splendidly." They camped in
the redan and had been so "honored so far by the confidence of the
General, as to be placed as an advance or outer guard in one of the
most responsible positions." This "most responsible" position was
the echelon of nine unfinished barracks that ran about a half mile
northwest-by-southeast and at their closest point stood perhaps one
hundred yards from the southwestern corner of the Entrenchment.
The unroofed barracks were composed of bricks that had not yet
been stuccoed over and were still fitted with bamboo ramps and scaf-
folding. The nine barracks, in various stages of construction, were
each about two hundred feet long, and only the fourth from the
southern end had a roof. Two of them had walls some forty feet high,
the rest had only been raised to seven feet, and the half-built southernmost barrack was flanked by a pit-kiln and heaps of brick.[737] All
the barracks were littered with bricks and debris "incidental to the
progress of large works."[738]

Wheeler positioned his Railway Rifle Corps in the three nearest
barracks, hoping that the rebels could be kept out of the rest by artillery fire. Garrett had been "out on ground" every night all week,
"performing sentry duty. . . . We go out at 7 o'clock p.m. and return
shortly before 5 a.m. and as we are obliged to have always 3 sentries
on it comes to be rather heavy work for a small party. My share of
sentry work has varied from 3 to 4 hours per night," and to pass the
time he drew a tidy little map "shewing position of the Native & European Troops on the 27 May 1857 at Cawnpore."

Garrett believed that "the worst is over at least in this district," but
assured his brother that if it came to "a scrummage by day, I hope
and expect that we will be able to pick a lot of the devils off before
they know what they're about."[739] "We are all quite prepared," another of his corps would write, "and if the fellows break out there
will be wigs on the green."[740]

Wheeler might have despaired of Garrett and his Railway Rifle
Corps as they lined up before him in their sporting ensembles, looking, as Garrett himself put it, like "a set of jolly fellows out on a
shooting excursion." But through the long nights they took turns

keeping watch from the unframed windows of the outer barracks, resting their shotguns and hunting rifles on the brick sills as bats swerved and dove through an antic, gloomy atmosphere of bugs.

◆ ◆ ◆

By May 27 a note of exhaustion and despair had entered the letters of the officers' wives. "My dear little child is looking very delicate," Mrs. Ewart grieved. "My prayer is that she may be spared much suffering. . . . It is not hard to die oneself but to see a dear child suffer & perish, that is the hard, the bitter trial, the cup which I must drink should God not deem it fit that it should pass from me." She was no longer reassured by the presence of Nana Sahib at Nawabgunj. "There are . . . some 150 Marattas with the Rajah of Bhittoor come to our *assistance*," she wrote, "but I can scarcely feel comfort at their presence.[741] . . . I cannot conceal from myself that my husband is likely to be the first to fall," for the colonel had vowed that "if his Reg^t mutinies it may walk over his body, but he will never leave it."[742]

Several young officers implored them to flee the station for Calcutta. Veterinary surgeon Edwin Chalwin told his wife that "he would thankfully send me home now, if it could be easily done," nevertheless she hoped "that there may be no need for such precautions" because "every thing is so quiet here now and we all hope security will soon be reestablished."[743] Others refused to go "so long as General Wheeler retained his family with him."[744] Besides, it was "too late now," as Amy Horne recalled. The river was low, "there was not a carriage to be had, and . . . the roads were no longer considered safe."[745]

Many memsahibs, some for the first time, began to question their husbands' military judgment. Most were at least a decade younger than their husbands, to whom they had heretofore shown almost filial deference. The ladies might learn the orders of precedence, manage the servants and the household accounts, support the church, organize charity bazaars. But it was their husbands who knew the India that teemed beyond cantonments, and the Company that determined their fates. At other stations men like their husbands had betrayed their trust and allowed the unthinkable to happen, and even the most obtuse Cawnpore matron could see that they were all teetering on the brink of disaster.

Though Mrs. Ewart still admired the way "John goes to his perilous duties as a soldier and a Christian should do, and keeps up an excellent spirit" marching off to sleep "on his couch in the midst of

his Sepoys," she no longer believed he could hold his regiment together. "No commandant seems to believe that his men can be false.
But alas!" she groaned, "the most trusted have proved the worst, and
there is not any dependence to be placed upon them. . . . We are living face to face with great and awful realities—life and property most
insecure, enemies within our camp, treachery and distrust everywhere."[746]

The gaunt, careworn Lilly Lindsay tried to hope that the terrible
heat would keep the native soldiers idle. "We have fortunately very
hot weather for the season," she wrote, "[and] constant dust storms
to keep it so & no sickness so on the whole we have many things to
be thankful for."[747] But this was wishful thinking. No one had ever
thrived in Cawnpore's hot weather, but the heat posed a far greater
threat to the British garrison than to the more or less acclimatized
native troops. At Cawnpore the hot weather was aggravated by the
dust storms that whirled through the station, coloring the air with a
"hot yellow tinge," blowing the shutters off windows, heaving beds
across the room, "shutting out the view entirely."[748] What was most
unnerving about these "Cawnpore Devils" was that, like the blast
from a furnace, they seemed only to turn up the heat. "Under the influence of the hot winds everything suffers," wrote an officer. "A
sharp crack announces that a tumbler has broken in half; you find
your table one morning with a huge fissure in it, which shows the
wood was not seasoned up country; . . . everything is horribly hot,
a wineglass or tumbler, or plates etc. feel as if they have just been
filled with hot water, the knives and forks are hot, the chairs and
tables are hot, the walls of the house are hot; & the hot wind blows
steadily on."

In better times people could shutter their windows, wet down
their floors, install wetted tatties in every door and window, order
the punkah coolie to tug with more vigor on his hanging fan, if only
to agitate the flies in the daytime or the mosquitoes at night.[749] For
even the most stalwart British ladies and their most resilient children
the hot season was unthinkable without their shutters, tatties, punkahs, frequent baths and vast, dark bungalows.[750]

Mrs. Ewart regarded the hot weather as perhaps the garrison's
worst enemy. "Even should our position be strong enough to hold
out, there is the *dreadful* exposure to the heat of May & June together with the privations & confinement of besieged sufferers to
render it very unlikely that we can survive the disasters which may

fall upon us any day, any hour."[751] Senior wives like Mrs. Ewart actually had the better of it, of course, because their homes were close enough to the Entrenchment for them to spend the hottest hours of the day in their own bedrooms, in tubs or on clean sheets under the lazy waft of their punkahs.[752] But the civilians who lived across the canal had no such luxury. To secure their quarters in the Entrenchment they had to abandon their houses and spend their days jammed together in tents and along the verandahs, veiling their mouths against the dust. Nevertheless, every effort was made to keep the Entrenchment "dry and clean,"[753] and "with a little needlework," wrote Amy Horne, "we passed our time during the idle days, spending our evenings a little less wearily by stepping out to hear the band, and discussing our plans for the future."[754] "We manage very well with our meals," wrote Caroline Lindsay. "All our meals are cooked at home & brought here."[755] They still received fitful deliveries of mail. Mrs. Ewart described the curious sensation of receiving a long-awaited biography of Charlotte Brontë and reading her sister's letters "by the last gleams of daylight in my dressing room, feeling strangely and sadly the contrast" between her sister's "peaceful even life and this terrible state of disorganization by which we are surrounded."[756]

So many people were "crowding and inconveniencing the European soldiery and their families"[757] that Wheeler moved the families of the Christian gunners to Savada House and directed the families camping out in the verandahs to move to a few empty bungalows next to St. John's.[758] "This we gladly did," wrote Amy, "without loss of time. My little step-brothers and sisters; small as they were, even lent a hand to clean the bungalow which was allotted to us, and which we tried to make as comfortable as we possibly could. A few ladies were brave enough to venture forth to their homes to bring away requisites for housekeeping, but on the General learning of this piece of recklessness, he forbade them to repeat the act."

"Our new bungalows near the barracks were soon filled," Amy wrote, "and we had established quite a little colony of our own." But when John Hampden Cook sent his servants off to fetch some of his furniture, they returned to report "that the house was occupied by a native, who had made himself perfectly at home in it!"

◆　◆　◆

On the thirtieth of May news arrived of "the worst thing that could have happened for us," wrote Mrs. Ewart, a "partial *émeute*" (riot) at

Lucknow that was bound to "create a commotion amongst the troops here."[759] The brigadier and three other officers had been killed, and now European refugees from Oudh rumbled across the Bridge of Boats into Cawnpore in a dusty fleet of "dâk carriages and other conveyances."[760] Later in the day the Agra telegraph brought more bad news: Commander-in-Chief Anson was still stuck somewhere in the vicinity of Umballa and would not reach Delhi until June 9. "Scarcely anything short of a miracle can keep people quiet for so many days," wrote Mrs. Ewart. ". . . We want a Napier now, not a cautious calculating speculator."[761]

The best that could be said of Anson's delay was that it might further encourage the native troops at Cawnpore to proceed to Delhi as soon as they rose up, but even so they would very likely kill their officers first. "If the troops break out here," wrote Colonel Ewart, "it is not probable that I shall survive it. My post and that of my officers being with the colours of the regiment, in the last extremity some or all of us must needs be killed. If that should be my fate, you and all my friends will know, I trust, that I die in the execution of my duty." At least Wheeler would protect the women and children. "He is an excellent officer, very determined, self-possessed in the midst of danger, fearless of responsibility—that terrible bugbear that paralyzes so many men in command."

The Ewarts had earlier sent their oldest boy, Harry, to Mrs. Ewart's sister in England "with the utmost confidence that you will ever be a mother to him and do your very best for him." But her infant daughter "will share whatever is my fate, most likely." Mrs. Ewart could only "trust to our Almighty Father, without venturing to look forward beyond the present hour."[762]

✦ ✦ ✦

On the eve of his departure for Cawnpore, Captain William Halliday's neighbor at Banda asked if he were "as fond of your regiment as other officers, and will never believe they are mutinous?"

"I would sleep in the midst of them," Willie had replied, "and have no fear."[763]

Before Willie could set off northward for Cawnpore, Collector Mayne had presented him with a portion of his treasury to take to Fatehpur, but Collector Sherer, fearing such an amount would make his station a center of rebel attacks, refused it.[764] When Willie ordered his native lieutenant[765] to take four hundred thousand rupees of it to Allahabad, the jemadar asked for a European officer to act as his escort. But Willie refused, assuring the old veteran that there was "nothing to fear, for if you don't plunder it, no one else will."[766]

Willie finally reached Cawnpore on the morning of May 31, relieved to find Emma and little Mabel "all safe and well." He was appalled to find that "so many reports fly about daily to the prejudice of one regiment or another that it is enough to make men revolt," nevertheless "all the regiments at Cawnpore appear staunch," and Willie challenged any "croakers" to explain why, if the sepoys were so disaffected, they had not cut him down en route from Banda.

The 84th Foot was "coming up as fast as they can," Willie wrote his sister, "so I don't think we have really anything to fear at Cawnpore. . . . At any rate," he said, "we are in the Hands of the Almighty, and it is very little we can do without *His Will*."

On the evening of May 31 Willie gently commanded little Mabel to say her prayers. "She replied, 'Baby say prayers,'" he reported, "and she knelt down at my knees, joined her hands and said, 'Pray God preserve dear Mama, dear Papa, myself and all the Vibarts, for Jesus Christ's Sake, Amen.'"[767]

MAKE WAY

June 1–3, 1857

In the middle of May Wheeler wrote a letter to Anson praising his Cawnpore Division staff, especially the "cool calmness" of Major George Larkins and the excellence of all his "precautionary measures." But according to Mrs. Larkins all Wheeler "got for this was that general Wheeler was an 'Alarmist' at which he was most *wroth* and wrote back his mind to his Excellency" asking "who has shewn wisdom and who not."[768]

It did not matter. A few days later, Anson was dead, struck down by cholera while still awaiting transport for his siege train. Wheeler did not mourn his passing. In fact, it revived the old man's hope of capping his career as commander-in-chief. On hearing of Anson's death, Lieutenant-Governor Colvin at Agra immediately urged the governor-general to replace Anson with somebody of "Indian ability and experience," qualities Wheeler possessed in unrivaled abundance.[769] Certainly Canning had to have been impressed by the old general's success in "staying the plague" at Cawnpore.

Wheeler immediately sat down at his desk in the Main Guard to write a status report for the governor-general. He could not suppress a note of self-congratulation. Troops at Meerut, Delhi, Ferozepur, Aligarh, Etawah, Mainpuri, Roorkee, Etah, Naisirabad, Lucknow, Mathura, Bareilly, and Shahjahanpur may have revolted to one degree or another, but despite the alarms and panics, warnings and threats, Wheeler had kept the native troops of his Cawnpore Division true to their salt. Any day now Wheeler expected two companies of Her Majesty's 84th and 15 "Lambs"[770] of the Madras Fusiliers, to whom he had just sent eighty bullock carts to speed their arrival.

"In a few—a very few days," Wheeler assured Canning, "I shall consider Cawnpore safe—nay, that I may aid Lucknow, if need be." Though the heat was "dreadful," he was proud to report that he had left his house "and am residing day and night in my tent, pitched within our entrenched position, and I purpose continuing to do so until tranquility is restored." The native lines remained volatile, but his "difficulties have been as much from the necessity of making others act with circumspection and prudence as from any disaffection on the part of the troops." He had succeeded so far, he thought, because it was his "good fortune in the present crisis, that I am well known to the whole Native Army as one who, although strict, has ever been just and considerate to them to the best of his ability, and that in a service of fifty-two years I have ever respected their rights and their prejudices. Pardon, my Lord, this apparent egotism," he said, laying it on a bit thick. "I state the fact solely as accounting for my success in preserving tranquility at a place like Cawnpore. Indeed, the men themselves have said that my name amongst them had alone been the cause of their not following the example so excitingly set them."[771]

✦ ✦ ✦

By the end of the following day Wheeler expected not only to have increased the size of his European force but just as importantly to have reduced the number of native soldiers in the station by sending detachments off to patrol the outstations. Many of Lawrence's surly Oudh sowars had trotted off with Captain Hayes to relieve the jittery station of Fatehgarh, 240 sepoys of the 1st had proceeded to Banda, and about 160 soldiers of the 53rd were already eighty miles off at Urai, to which Wheeler was about to send 160 more sepoys of the 56th, thus subtracting almost six hundred men from the native regiments' ostensible force of 3600: a number he had further whittled down by means of a liberal dispensation of furloughs.[772]

It had been Lawrence's idea to send Fletcher Hayes and Lieutenant Barbour with the 2nd Oudh Irregulars up the country to Fatehgarh. Though Wheeler was sorry to lose Hayes, he was glad to be rid of the grumbling 2nd Oudh Irregulars, and for the very same reason that the ungrateful Collector Probyn of Fatehgarh so dreaded their approach. The last thing he needed was a large body of disaffected irregulars contaminating his troops with their discontent.

But they never reached Probyn. On the road to Fatehgarh, Hayes and Barbour bumped into two Englishmen named Fayrer and Carey, and on the thirtieth of May they camped at a village some fifty miles from Fatehgarh. Hayes and Carey rode into a nearby town to confer with the Civil Magistrate, expecting Barbour and Frayer to proceed up the road with the sowars. But they did not move, and after a night at the magistrate's house Hayes and Carey sent a letter back to camp demanding an explanation.[773] Hours passed without an answer. Finally a villager reported that the sowars refused to march, but then two sowars trotted in to insist that all was well. As proof they flourished a letter from Lieutenant Barbour that "appeared like the continuation of a letter previously despatched," Carey would recall, "and as if the writer were unable to express his meaning fully."[774]

It was not until after breakfast on June 1 that Hayes and Carey rode off with the two sowars to rejoin their squadron. It was a simmering Doab morning, and the dawn chirping of the sparrows in the sparse trees and thorn bushes was already receding in the rising heat as Hayes and Carey trotted along the dirt road, trying to keep ahead of their own dust. After riding eight miles, they caught sight of their squadron drawn up in a scattered line and paused, bewildered, when a native officer suddenly broke ranks and galloped toward them. Skidding to a halt, the old man begged them to turn back. The sowars had mutinied, he panted. Barbour and Fayrer were dead.

At dawn Fayrer had apparently dismounted to drink at a village well when a sowar rode up, silently drew his tulwar and nearly decapitated him with a single blow to the back of his sunburned neck. As Fayrer lolled to the ground in a fountain of blood, Barbour had tried to gallop up onto the road, but immediately ran into an advance guard of Irregulars blocking his path. Holding his revolver in one hand and his sabre in the other, Barbour had galloped directly into the troopers, shooting two of them and running another one through before the others closed in and hacked him to death in his saddle.

Now, with a shout, the rest of the squadron charged Hayes and Carey, and even the two sowars who had accompanied them from Mainpuri lunged forward with their sabres. The two young officers managed to pull their horses around and began racing back down the road with the sowars charging after them, "yelling," remembered Carey, "and sending the bullets from their carbines flying all around us."

But poor Hayes was no horseman. As he desperately spurred his Arab on, a native officer drew up alongside and with a graceful, contemptuous slash of his curved sword cut him across the face and sent him toppling to the ground.[775] Glancing back, Carey saw the rag-doll corpse of Captain Fletcher Hayes—scholar, linguist, indispensable advisor to Sleeman, Wheeler, and Henry Lawrence—tumbling among the hooves of the pursuing sowars.

Years of pigsticking had made Carey a skilled equestrian. Slight and nimble, he jumped his horse across a ditch, shaking off all but two of his pursuers. For two miles, with Hayes's riderless mount lagging behind, Carey outraced the sowars until at last they too fell back. Regaining the road, he galloped four more miles until his wheezing, lathered horse collapsed. Certain he was doomed, he set off on foot on his bowed, exhausted legs, but within a few minutes a lone mounted sowar came trotting along in the opposite direction, and with what little authority he could muster Carey ordered him to a halt and climbed up behind him, commanding him to turn his horse around and trot back toward Mainpuri. The sowar was loath and grumbling and seemed likely to turn on him at any moment, but a mile or so shy of town, Hayes's blood-spattered Arab appeared, and Carey scrambled into its saddle, galloping the last yards to safety and leaving the muttering sowar in his dust.[776]

On May 26, Lawrence had decided to unload another detachment of Irregulars by sending them across the Ganges to secure the Grand Trunk Road. The force was commanded by a Major Gall and consisted of a squadron of cavalry, four companies of the 4th Oudh Irregular Infantry, a company of the 1st Oudh Irregular Infantry, and the 3rd Oudh Horse Battery with three[777] guns under the command of Lieutenant St. George Ashe.[778] No sooner had they crossed the Bridge of Boats at Cawnpore than the 1st Oudh Irregular Infantry refused to go any further and had to be sent back across the Ganges to Unao. The rest of the Irregulars proceeded grudgingly through the civil station to the Grand Trunk Road, trudging north toward Fatehgarh. But the combination of the heat and the defection of the 1st Irregular Infantry seemed to take the stuffing out of Major Gall and his officers. When, on June 3, they learned of the mutiny of the Oudh Irregular sowars and the murder of Barbour and Fayrer and Hayes, Gall turned his column around and, glancing over his shoulders at his own mercurial troops, hurried back toward Cawnpore.[779]

In late May Wheeler sent yet another expedition out into the countryside. Ever since the middle of May two companies of the 53rd Native Infantry had been performing "detached command duty" at Urai;[780] on June 2 Wheeler assigned Lieutenant H. T. A. Raikes and Ensign Browne with two companies of the 56th Native Infantry to replace them, thus neatly trading two companies from the disaffected 56th for two from the staunch 53rd.[781]

✦ ✦ ✦

In his sunny letter to Canning, Wheeler had omitted to mention the alarming condition of his batteries. "The way the country is left without artillery!" he exclaimed to General Hearsey. "We have guns and a European company, but no carriage for them."[782] By now he had collected seven guns in the Entrenchment: six nine-pounders and a little three-pounder that had been recently rifled and could only be loaded with grape.[783] There were twenty-four-pounders languishing unassembled in the magazine, but Wheeler could not remove them without dangerously agitating the sepoy guard, whose brethren still suspected their officers of plotting to annihilate them at parade with one blast of grape.

Wheeler tried to pass off his defenses at the Entrenchment as a refuge not from his own troops but from some external threat—mutineers from other stations, Goojurs, rebel matchlockmen—but he could not conceal the truth forever. At the beginning of June he would have to pay his troops. But he did not dare remove their entire cash allotment from the Entrenchment to the native lines nor allow armed native troops to file into the chaos of the Entrenchment. So he ordered his paymaster[784] to require any native trooper who desired his monthly pay to enter the Entrenchment out of uniform and without his weapons.[785]

The troops were outraged by this indignity. Clearly Wheeler intended to disarm them so that the European force hurrying toward the station could force them into submission. They refused to collect their pay in the Entrenchment, and to keep them from obtaining their pay by other means and from other sources, Wheeler had the Commissariat treasury—almost one hundred thousand rupees in cash and government notes—moved from Captain Williamson's bungalow to the Entrenchment.

✦ ✦ ✦

In the meantime Nana Sahib had secretly gone off at dusk to a crumbling old ghat a few yards upriver from the magazine, accompanied by Azimullah and Nana's little brother Bala Rao.[786] Bala was in his middle twenties: a tall, lean, dark man with a crooked nose and large, expressive eyes. He was certainly the fiercest of the adopted sons of Baji Rao, and, like the Peshwas of old, would ride a war elephant into at least one battle. But he was missing his front teeth, his face was badly pockmarked, and he was given to lisping fits of unseemly rage when he did not get his way.[787] Though Bala had mixed more freely with the British than Nana did, to know them was not necessarily to love them, and he had made common cause with Azimullah from the beginning.

Perched on the deck of a native boat in the cooling breeze off the river, Nana greeted his former guardsmen Muddud Ali and Raheem Khan and a delegation of sepoys from the 2nd Native cavalry. According to one account, Teeka Singh, rissaldar of the 2nd Native Cavalry, spoke first. "You have come to take charge of the Magazine and Treasury of the English," he told Nana Sahib. "We all, Hindus and Mahomedans, have united for our religions, and the whole Bengal Army have become one in purpose. What do you say to it?"

Nana replied, "I also am at the disposal of the army."[788]

The meeting did not remain secret for long. A court clerk immediately reported it to Hillersdon who confronted Nana Sahib about it.[789] But the Mahratta insisted that there had been nothing whatever untoward about his parley; he had merely met with the sowars "to pacify them and prevent further disturbances."[790] Charles seemed satisfied, and after the two men talked "in terms of great intimacy," Hillersdon assured his subordinates that Nana and Azimullah had merely been "remonstrating" with the sowars "on the part of the Government."[791]

But his own trust in Nana Sahib was shaken. The rumors of Nana's treachery were reaching a critical mass, and Hillersdon armed himself with a pistol before proceeding to the Collectorate, where he appeared anxious and agitated.[792] And though as late as June 2 "it was actually projected to send some of our ladies to Bithoor, that they might be lodged in safety," Hillersdon had decided not to entrust his family to his "great friend's" keeping after all.

Nanak Chand continued to collect evidence of impending mutiny. He heard that one of the sowars who had met with Nana Sahib had boasted to a middle-aged prostitute named Azizun "that the Peishwa's reign would soon commence, and the Nana in a day or two would be paramount," whereupon the sowar would fill Azizun's house with gold mohurs.[793] Chimnaji Appa reported that both of Nana's brothers had thrown in their lot with the rebels. But when Nanak Chand tried to share his suspicions with Major Lindsay and Deputy Collector Stacy they only shrugged and returned to their billiards.[794]

✦ ✦ ✦

In the wee hours of the morning of June 2, all such rumors were drowned out momentarily by the jubilation that greeted the two dust-caked companies of Her Majesty's 84th and fifteen men of the Madras Fusiliers who finally came marching into the station from Allahabad.[795] Elated, Wheeler saw a chance to demonstrate to Canning his gallantry, magnanimity and masterful command, and sent to Lucknow one company of the 84th and all the able-bodied men of the 32nd whom Lawrence had sent to Cawnpore at the end of May. Indeed, Wheeler wrote Calcutta in his last telegram before the line was cut, he did not send more only because "conveyance for more [was] not available." He kept just the fifteen Fusiliers (armed with the only Enfield rifles in the station);[796] forty-nine men of the 84th; fifty-nine gunners; plus seventy-nine men of the 32nd, many of whom were sick with smallpox, cholera, and malaria: a total of two hundred two European soldiers, plus forty-three fifers and drummers and a bugler named Warcoat: all of them Eurasians whom the Company had long refused to tutor in the art of combat.[797] "This leaves me weak," Wheeler conceded, "but I trust to holding [our] own until more Europeans arrive."[798]

Unless, of course, "a single injudicious step" should in the meantime "set the whole in a blaze."[799] Even in the best of times Cawnpore had been notorious for its parade-ground mishaps, precipitated usually by officers suffering from senility or puerility mixed with homesickness, fever, fanaticism, and rum. So perhaps it was inevitable that during the worst of times one out of the thousand or so

Europeans in the station would take that "single injudicious step" Wheeler had so dreaded.

In November 1856, twenty-one-year-old Lieutenant William Edward Cox had cashed out of the "Dirty Shirts" or 1st Bengal European Fusiliers.[800] His military career had been restless and brief. At the age of fifteen he had been suspended from Addiscombe for idleness, and within a month of his posting to a native infantry regiment in 1854 he had managed to get himself transferred to the Fusiliers as an ensign. He had been a lieutenant for only a month when he resigned, whereupon his promotion was canceled, probably on account of drunkenness.[801]

Certainly he was royally drunk on the night of June 2 when a patrol of Native Cavalry sowars heard him staggering around in the dark outside his bungalow and ordered him to stand and be recognized. With a slurred curse, Cox fired his weapon somewhere in the picket's direction.[802] He missed, apparently, and the sowars quickly disarmed him and dragged him to the Main Guard, where he was promptly and publicly charged with firing on his own soldiers: a crime for which men were commonly executed or transported.[803]

Contemporaneous accounts speak of Cox's court-martial, but he was no longer a soldier and may have been tried as a civilian by Sir George Parker, the cantonment joint magistrate. In any case, Cox was the son of a knighted officer who had served as a general in the Portuguese army during the Napoleonic wars, and by the time he stood up to face the music he was sober and contrite.[804] Out of racial solidarity and chivalric deference to his father (mixed, perhaps, with a desire to preserve every able-bodied European in the garrison), the court ruled that his crime had been mere drunkenness and that his musket had gone off by mistake.

Outraged, the sowars declared to each other that soon "their muskets might go off by mistake in the same way."[805]

✦ ✦ ✦

At the news of the aborted uprising at Lucknow, Jonah Shepherd had moved his family from his house to a bungalow on the old parade-ground across from Christ Church and instructed his servants to keep an eye on the sowars picketed just outside his back gate, lounging about and smoking hookahs as their grass cutters fed their horses.[806]

On the evening of June 3, Jonah sat down with his family for sup-

per, famished from his day's work of transferring the Commissariat
records to the Entrenchment. As he tucked into his soup, his kitmutgar approached and asked if the sahib would please come look
at something with him. Jonah snapped that it would have to wait
until dinner was over, and for a while the kitmutgar fretfully stood
by as his master slurped his soup. Finally, unable to contain himself
any longer, he approached Jonah again, leaning forward now
and urgently whispering that "something dreadful is about to happen."

Ellen Shepherd overheard him and rushed to her feet, and before
Jonah could rise she was frantically summoning him to the window.
Out of the west a body of native horsemen were galloping down the
Delhi Road on lathered, dust-caked horses with three guns and sev-
eral horsedrawn gun carriages careening and clattering behind them.
The troopers at Jonah's gate stood up from their hookahs and began
to shout at each other in a panic, loading their pistols and saddling
their horses.

Shepherd's frightened family rushed from the table to don their
Indian costumes, but Shepherd spied a European officer riding
among the sowars: Lieutenant St. George Ashe, as it turned out, and
his 3rd Oudh Battery[807] galloping ahead of Major Gall's retreating
column. As the riders hauled one twenty-four and two nine-pound
guns past the parade-ground,[808] the sowars realized they were not
under attack and began to calm themselves.[809] So Jonah ventured
out to converse with the mob of sowars and townspeople who had
gathered excitedly by his gate.

Someone in the crowd must have mentioned the deaths of Hayes
and his comrades, for Jonah asked the first trooper he encountered if
he knew what had induced the Oudh sowars to kill them. His question "was the cause of eliciting a great many others from the troopers," Jonah would remember, "who just at that time were thrown off
guard and commenced mentioning everything that was working
upon their minds."[810]

One declared that their officers were treacherous, otherwise why
would they try to disarm the sowars and take away their horses and
demand that they report unarmed to the Entrenchment for their
pay? Another broke in to ask why, if the officers did not plan some
treachery, they were entrenching themselves? "If the officers deal
fairly with us, as before," he said, "we will never do anything wrong.
But they want to take away our caste by many stratagems."

Major General Sir Hugh Wheeler with a hookah

Turning to address his comrades, this second trooper urged the others to "see what deep plots are being laid against us. They know that we will never receive the new cartridges, and therefore flour mixed with cows' and pigs' bones are sent from Roorkee to make us outcastes."

"I see it all quite clear," declared another. "The officers have no faith in us. . . . They tried to remove the native guard and place Europeans over the Magazine and Treasury. The native corps have been considered trustworthy for so long, and now all of a sudden we're to be mistrusted."

By now troopers had entirely surrounded Jonah, who did his jittery best to argue with them. With a clerk's acuity he pointed out that the government didn't stand to gain anything by taking their caste away—the troopers would still demand the same pay for the same work. But they only grew more adamant. One reminded Jonah about Meerut, where, "because some of the troopers had refused to bite the new cartridge, they were severely punished and degraded in irons and sent to work on the roads with 10 years imprisonment."

"Thus we'll all be treated," continued another, "as soon as a European force is sent to Cawnpore. So we're not going to wait until then." He mentioned Cox's acquittal for firing on the sowars. "If we natives had fired on a European, we would have been hanged."

"You are all bent upon your own destruction," Jonah scolded them. "Where will you get so good and honourable service as with the British?"

"We are all Mussulmen," a sowar replied, sticking out his chest, "and we will serve a sovereign of our own creed who will know how to treat us as we deserve."

At this a sowar with ferocious whiskers and an elaborate mustache waved his hands over his head and began to chant "*Suffun suffa, suffun suffa* (Make way, make way)."[811] He and his comrades had made up their minds, he declared—they would sweep away all who came in their path, even their own wives and children, many of whom had already removed to their villages.

"But even if you are determined to do all these things," Jonah pleaded, "why should you hurt or molest those who are in no way connected with your affairs, such as merchants, clerks, and others and their families? They have done you no harm."

"Oh, you are all one," the whiskered man replied. "You are serpents, and not one of you will be spared!"

At this a native sergeant stepped forward to quiet his troops.

"Don't listen to what this foolish fellow says," he told Jonah. "You go about your business, and don't come among us."

By now several other soldiers were telling Jonah to go, and he moved back slowly and deliberately to conceal his overwhelming relief that they had not cut him down.

As he stepped toward his house another sowar began to jeer him. "Oh, you have nothing to fear from us," he called out. "Just put on the garb of a Mussulman, take a short stout stick in your hand, and come out boldly."

The soldiers burst out laughing as Jonah stepped through them.

"All you have to do," the trooper continued at the top of his voice, "is twist your mustachios and repeat the word *Ul-hum-do-lillah-rub-ala-lamy* (Allah be thanked), and you will do well."

Jonah pretended to ignore them, but as he neared his house he could hear an old subhedar-major bawling the others out. "Don't you know he is one of them," he heard him ask, "and will go and inform against us?"

Jonah rushed into the house and told his family to flee with him to the barracks. The women were so terrified that they did not even take a change of clothing for themselves, only a small box of cash, jewelry, and baby clothes. As they rushed for their carriages Jonah thought to grab a water jug and a nine-by-seven carpet, and they raced off, skidding into the Entrenchment at half past seven.

Nobody in the Entrenchment paid Jonah's encounter much attention. It was just one of scores of stories circulating through the camp. The few officers who deigned to listen simply shook their heads. There were no European troops to spare; in his unseemly haste to impress Lord Canning, the old general had seen to that. Now all they could do was watch and wait.

PART TWO

THE EVIL PROGRESSES
Wheeler: June 4–5, 1857

By June 3 the flow of fugitives fleeing downriver to Calcutta had almost entirely dried up. But the living were never the only travelers down the Ganges. Even in times of peace so many corpses washed up along the river's banks that sahibs hired special servants from the scavenger castes to push them back into the current. "In some parts," wrote an early resident of Cawnpore, "the stream forms a little bay [where] numbers of these dreadful objects are collected together by the eddy, and render the air pestiferous, until a strong current carries them onwards."[1] Now the dumped corpses of Europeans slaughtered up the country joined the Hindu dead in the fitful flow of the wide and shallow river, pausing on the sandbars until a thunderstorm flushed them free. On June 3 a crowd gathered around the first of these harbingers of murder and mayhem: the corpses of a European lady and gentleman that had floated down the river and snagged in the locks of the Ganges Canal.[2]

"The evil progresses," General Wheeler told his old friend Henry Lawrence on Thursday, June 4, writing in an atmosphere of dust and flies. The 2nd Cavalry was now "in an almost acknowledgeable state of Mutiny and ready to start at any moment for Delhi" and "the 1st N.I. is sworn to join and they now speak of going off this night or the next, doing all the mischief in their power first, this to include an attack on our position—I fear them not altho' our means are very small" and "the other two Native Infantry Corps may be carried off by the excitement to join the others." Whatever happened, he assured Lawrence, "we will do our best."

But he was past doing his best, and wrote "with a crushed spirit." Sweltering in his room with Lady Frances and his two daughters and his servants to fuss over him, hampered by the hundreds of women and children it was his duty to safeguard, harassed at every hour by brash young officers and fretful merchants, exhausted by his nightly rounds through the regimental lines, sixty-eight-year-old Hamlah devoted the rest of his letter not to his want of European troops, his lack of artillery, his exposed position, the worrisome rumors about Nana Sahib, the cutting of the Lucknow telegraph, or the bloody uprisings in the surrounding districts. Instead he dilated on the death of his hopes for promotion. For no sooner had Wheeler grandly relayed half his European reinforcements off to Lucknow than the news reached him that Calcutta had again passed him over for commander-in-chief and chosen instead, as Wheeler put it to Lawrence, "Lt. General, *Lt. General* Sir Pat Grant" of Madras, who was "long, very long my junior."[3]

Grant had neither the "experience nor the trials that I have had,"[4] Wheeler fumed, and it was Grant's "connection with Lord Gough" (his father-in-law)[5] that had "carried him over me on every occasion. . . . Whilst I wear the Cloth I will endeavour not to disgrace it" but once "tranquility is restored" Wheeler would "then take the course which I feel due to my professional Character and soldierly feelings," and resign.[6]

Now the rumors and alarms that had rolled off the old man's back began to penetrate him to his bones. Fed up, demoralized, slumping now in the furnace blast of the early afternoon, the old general entirely lost faith in his native troops and bleakly ordered all of his officers to give up their beds in the native lines and spend the night on watch in the Entrenchment. Only the 53rd's Major Hillersdon managed to persuade the weary general not to give up on his regiment. His lines stood closest to the Entrenchment and his native officers still insisted on their sepoys' fidelity. As dusk fell, Major Hillersdon proudly led his officers back to the quarterguard of the anxious 53rd.

✦ ✦ ✦

That day a thirty-year-old Pathan sowar of the 2nd Native Cavalry named Jehangir Khan returned from a two-week furlough to find his regiment in turmoil.[7] Now that Major Vibart and his European officers had abandoned the lines, it was left to the elderly rissaldar-major, Bhowani Singh, to hold the regiment together. A ferocious veteran of the Sikh Wars and the only sowar to be readmitted to the regiment after the 2nd's disgrace at Mooltan,[8] the old Rajput scolded his subordinates for their unmanly plotting and infidelity to their salt.[9]

His ears stinging from Bhowani Singh's warnings and threats, Jehangir Khan was posted to a night picket near the Entrenchment under the command of none other than Rissaldar Teeka Singh himself.[10] It was a sweltering night unrelieved by the strong wind that blew across the parade-ground, and the dust stung like hot cinders as he squatted in his dhoti and field coat with a small detachment of his fellow sowars.[11]

After his furlough Jehangir had difficulty matching his comrades' indignation. Speaking in muffled voices from behind the dust-screen of his turban's tail, Teeka Singh reviewed the regiment's litany of grievances: the insulting fortification of the Entrenchment; the menace of the guns; the flight of the officers' families; the attempt to empty the treasury and mine the magazine; the shameful order to collect their pay unarmed and out of uniform; the sinister acquittal of the drunken Mr. Cox. And now came reports that the officers had spiked the guns at the magazine and mined the parade-ground and in the morning intended to assemble all of the regiments and blow them to pieces.[12]

Obviously Jehangir's comrades were ready to follow Teeka Singh wherever he led.[13] But was Jehangir? Peering through the blowing dust at the lamplight flaring dimly from within the Entrenchment tents, he knew he would have to decide whether to stand by his comrades or his commanders.

Around 1:30 in the morning of June 5,[14] Jehangir was shaken out of his drowsy revery by three cracks of pistol fire from the direction of the cavalry lines.[15] As if at a signal, Teeka Singh and the rest of his picket rushed to their feet, mounted their startled horses, and galloped off to join their comrades. Jehangir reined in his mount and paused for a moment on the plain. The hot wind carried a murmur of alarm from the Entrenchment, and Jehangir could make out shouts of jubilation and the pounding of horses' hooves from his lines. Tentatively, he turned and trotted his horse to a nearby tent.

Jehangir did not recognize the harried-looking officer who emerged to confront him, demanding to know where the picket had gone.

Back to their lines, Jehangir replied.

"Then why are *you* still standing there?" the officer shouted over the wind.

Jehangir said he intended to stay at his post.

The officer mounted his horse and spurred it toward the Entrenchment, ordering Jehangir to flee before the other regiments turned on him. Jehangir paused a moment as the officer trotted off, and then a bugle sounded, and at last Jehangir Khan did as he was told, heading off in the opposite direction at a walk, then a trot, then a giddy gallop to the cavalry lines.[16]

At the cavalry's bell-of-arms Rissaldar-Major Bhowani Singh was angrily declining his men's invitation to join the rebellion, declaring that he "would only obey and serve Government."[17] Drawing his sword, he refused to hand over the colors the regiment had so recently regained. He held off his men for a few minutes, but they closed in on him, jabbing at his arms with their tulwars.[18] Still the veteran of Mooltan would not back off, and at last an exasperated trooper[19] brought his blade down upon the back of the old man's head and sent him crumpling unconscious to the floor.[20] Leaving their rissaldar-major for dead, the sowars grabbed the treasure, tenderly gathered up their colors and ran out to their horses.

✦   ✦   ✦

In the Entrenchment General Wheeler staggered out from the tile-roofed barrack as his officers rushed about, barking orders to the pickets and gunners. Here was an end, at least, to all this damnable suspense. Whole families rushed up from their makeshift beds. Jostled out of sleep on the barrack verandah, Jonah Shepherd found his family already awake and trembling to the "great sound of horses' hoofs and noise of men, some calling to one another," others shouting, "For the faith!"[21]

The sowars set fire to a heap of stable refuse and tossed a brand upon the thatched roof of the bungalow of their riding master.[22] In the gusts of wind the flames seemed to explode into the night sky.[23] Silhouetted against the blaze, sowars galloped northeastward "by twos and threes" along the tree-lined course.[24] As if hypnotized by the spectacle, "the gentlemen went outside the entrenchment and stood looking on."[25] And Lieutenant St. George Ashe, glancing over at his Oudh gunners, saw a secret delight play across their faces in the glow from the distant flames.

Scanning the cavalry lines from the bulge of the redan, Wheeler realized that a few bold horsemen might be tempted to continue their depredations southeastward to the exposed tents and bungalows of the European encampment that had grown up around St. John's Chapel. As a body of sowars, "mounted and accoutred,"[26] assembled on the tree-lined high road, the General ordered the alarm gun fired, at whose report most of the sowars changed their direction, racing up the course toward the city and clattering across the bridge that spanned the Ganges Canal.[27]

At the first crackle of pistol fire, John Hampden Cook tried to hustle his family out of their bungalow behind the church and hurry them to the sanctuary of St. John's.[28] But for the first time since they had left their house, the women of his family had undressed for bed, and now Amy Horne and her mother and half sisters took so long pulling on their clothes that by the time they ran from the house they no longer dared go around to the gate that faced the road. So the railway workers who had shared the Cooks' bungalow with them "unceremoniously" pitched the ladies and children over the wall. They found the church filled with soldiers of the relief company of Her Majesty's 84th, for whom Wheeler had not yet made room in the Entrenchment. Almost as soon as Amy and her family burst into the brick church the alarm gun sounded, and everyone—soldiers, merchants, servants, women, children—tore across two hundred yards of exposed ground, flung themselves over the parapet and scrambled for refuge along the already overcrowded verandahs.[29]

Jehangir Khan raced to catch up with his comrades, turning north across the canal and on to Nawabgunj. All along the way sowars were celebrating their liberation and urging the townspeople to stay calm "as they were not going to molest any one just then; but . . . after reaching Delhi and paying their respects to their lawful and mighty king," they would be back by the end of the month under the command of one of the Delhi princes, "and then they would see if they could not keep Cawnpore for their great king."[30] Despite these reassurances, the matchlockmen whom the Mahajuns had hired to protect their shops immediately demanded their pay and either fled the city or joined the mob,[31] whereupon a few young men from the regimental bazaars began looting whatever stalls they could break into,[32] and a body of sowars rushed to the abandoned barracks of the 3rd Native Infantry west of the canal and set them all ablaze.[33] The sowars sent a delegation to the lines of the 1st Native Infantry and, speaking in the name of the subhedar-major whom they had just left bleeding and unconscious at the bell-of-arms, demanded to know why the sepoys had not joined them.[34]

Colonel John Ewart now rode out of the Entrenchment in sleepless disarray, galloping past the riding school and into his regiment's lines to find his sepoys buckling on their cross-belts and grabbing their muskets.[35] "My children!" he called out to them. "My children!

This is not your way! Don't do this!"[36] But they did. Ewart had pledged that his men would have to ride over his dead body before he would let them mutiny, but now they merely ran around him, leaving him blustering in their wake.[37]

Trembling with rage and shame, Ewart galloped back to the Entrenchment and urged Wheeler to send Lieutenant Ashe and his Oudh Horse Battery after his sepoys. Wheeler agreed, but no sooner had Ashe and his native artillerymen begun to rattle down the metalled road than Wheeler received word that the 56th and 53rd, encamped in their lines to the south of the Entrenchment, might break out at any moment and charge the Entrenchment on their way north toward Nawabgunj. Before Ashe could reach the canal, Wheeler summoned him and his artillerymen back, and their twenty-four-pounder and two nine-pounders were rolled back into position in the northeastern corner of the Entrenchment.[38]

✦ ✦ ✦

Khoda Bux, Subhedar of the Grenadiers of the 56th Native Infantry, was sleeping soundly through the first minutes of the cavalry's mutiny when his havildar came rushing into his house.[39]

"What, are you not awake?" the havildar shouted. "There's a row in the cavalry lines, three reports of a pistol, and the quartermaster-sergeant's bungalow is on fire!"

Hurrying into his uniform, Bux ordered the regiment to turn out in front of the bell-at-arms and raced off to inform Colonel Williams. As disheveled officers rushed from the Entrenchment to the lines, Williams ordered Bux to move the regiment to the quarterguard and to shoot "any cavalryman" who approached. All through the dark hours of morning Williams and Willie Halliday and their comrades stood with their backs to their assembled ranks of sepoys, watching vigilantly through the clouds of dust and smoke as the sound of the mutineers receded toward Nawabgunj.[40] Just to the east, in the lines of the 53rd, Major Hillersdon and his officers had emerged bleary-eyed from their tents and assembled their sepoys under arms. There they stood in columns for several hours as the glow from the fires retreated before the harsh glare of the morning sun.

At about five that morning, Williams received the news that Bhowani Singh had been attacked.[41] Convinced that the sowars and the sepoys of the 1st had fled for good, he marched his men directly across the parade-ground to search for the wounded subhedar-major and collect whatever arms and horses the sowars might have left behind.[42] Finding the old man "in a perfectly helpless condition,"[43] a few staunch sowars had picked him up from the bloodstained wreckage of the bell-at-arms, littered him across the road to the cavalry hospital, and fetched the regimental surgeon.[44] Declaring himself "very much pleased" with the old man's valor, Williams ordered Bhowani Singh carried to the Entrenchment depot for further treatment.[45]

The sepoys of the 56th returned from the cavalry lines with one hundred abandoned horses[46] and carts piled high with salvaged furniture and weapons.[47] In the intensifying heat Williams now permitted his men to remove their uniforms and prepare their breakfast. Pausing to congratulate Khoda Bux on the staunchness of his men, Williams trotted off toward the river to check on his bungalow at Sati Chowra Ghat.[48]

Taking his cue from the Colonel, Major Hillersdon dismissed the 53rd as well and led his native officers to the Entrenchment to confer with Wheeler.[49] Indeed, both Williams and Hillersdon apparently deemed their lines so secure that they allowed their junior officers to leave the lines and "go about their usual avocations."[50] The result was disastrous.[51] As soon as the Europeans had left their lines, sowars trotted around to the tents of the 56th and abused the sepoys "for remaining inactive like women,"[52] warning them that if they did not join them, they would be considered as infidels, and excommunicated from caste privileges."[53] "We will cut off each other's heads and sacrifice our lives upon this very spot," the sowars warned, "and you will bring dishonor upon yourselves."[54]

They then rode over to the lines of the 53rd and complained to the sepoys hunkered down around their breakfast fires that their comrades at the treasury would not allow the mutineers to enter unless their entire regiment joined the rebellion.[55] Loyal native officers from the 53rd rushed back to Wheeler's headquarters to report that the sepoy guard at Nawabgunj was under attack, and certainly it sounded that way from all the musket fire Wheeler could hear miles off to the north. Wheeler wisely refused to allow their officers to ride to their assistance, but he was persuaded to send several loyal sepoys to Nawabgunj "to see if any arrangements could be made" to relieve the sepoys of the 53rd.[56]

Jemadar Khoda Bux of the 56th had returned to his house to remove his uniform and smoke his hookah, when his havildar pounded on his door and declared, "Jemadar, the regiment is turning out."

Bux asked by whose order and why, but the sergeant could not say. Bux hurried to his company's tent, "and saw that the Havildar was dreadfully frightened, and was buttoning his coat." He found his men rushing to and fro, some "packing up their clothes and others throwing them away."

"The 53rd Regiment is getting ready," they explained, "and so are we."

"Your regiment is the 56th," Bux snapped back. "What have you to do with the 53rd? It would be better for you first to shoot me and then do what you like afterwards."

"You are our senior officer," they told him. "We will not kill you. Come with us."

"Very well," Bux replied. "I will get ready and come with you." Bux left their tent and proceeded toward the Entrenchment "very slowly for about 100 yards" and then broke into a run to tell Colonel Williams that his men had mutinied.

Thus betrayed, a few of the sepoys of the 56th surrounded the rest of their native officers and threatened to murder them if they did not join. The officers immediately covered their heads, "fell at the feet of the sepoys and asked for their lives to be spared." The sepoys relented, but as soon as the 56th swarmed out of their huts the native officers raced for the Entrenchment.[57]

Colonel Williams refused to believe that his men had risen and ordered Khoda Bux to follow him and his officers back to the lines so he could see for himself. Bux begged them not to go. "Oh! Gentlemen," he told them, "all the regiment has mutinied, and are your enemies. It is not right for you to go to them."

Williams and his adjutant refused to listen and galloped toward their lines, but a few hundred yards from their men they heard three muskets fire and beat a hasty retreat to the Entrenchment.[58]

Two companies of the 53rd now converged on their bell-at-arms and, like the sowars, overwhelmed their defiant old native commander and grabbed their treasure and colors before joining the sepoys of the 56th, who now rushed from their lines, skirting the Entrenchment and heading for the canal.[59] The rest of the 53rd pulled their uniforms back on and assembled on the parade-ground.[60] Wheeler and his senior officers watched them through their field glasses, uncertain what to do. Hillersdon insisted that these men must be loyal or they would have run off by now. But Williams had just given Wheeler the same assurances about the 56th, and now his sepoys were pouring out of their lines with their kits and muskets. Lieutenant Ashe approached to voice his suspicions of his Oudh artillerymen. The only way he could commit them irretrievably to the defense of the Entrenchment, he told Wheeler, was to order them to fire on their comrades.[61]

Hillersdon protested, and Wheeler peered again through his field glasses at the distant ranks of the 53rd, standing in their red coats with yellow facings and silver lace. Behind them a few stragglers from the 56th chased after their comrades, ghostly in the intervening clouds of whirling dust. Other officers—Ewart perhaps, or Vibart, enraged by their own regiments' betrayal—joined in the call to fire on the 53rd. At last Wheeler lowered his binoculars and nodded to Ashe.

Ashe raised his sabre and signaled his gunners to fire. A golundaz reflexively touched his match to the torch hole of a nine-pounder and sent a ball arcing toward the lines of the 53rd and crashing into the sepoys' tents. Through his glasses Wheeler could see the men flinch a little, but they stood fast, thinking perhaps that Ashe was firing at the fleeing 56th. Now Ashe gave another order to fire, and a second ball came hurtling over the sepoys' heads and landed behind them with an earthshaking bounce. A third round landed even closer. Screaming that their officers meant to murder them, a sepoy at last broke from the stunned ranks of the 53rd, and the rest ran off in all directions. A few scuttled off to hide in their lines and in the hollows of a neighboring ravine, but most followed the 56th northward toward Nawabgunj.[62]

On the slim chance of holding on to a handful of wavering Oudh Irregulars, Wheeler had fired on the one loyal regiment in the station.[63] For Ashe it had been an act of desperation, but for Wheeler it may have been a decision born of sheer disgust. He was fed up with the lingering ambiguity of the 53rd's allegiance, sick of waiting all these weeks for the native troops to make up their minds. Not his name, nor his reputation, nor his nightly rides through the lines had subdued his native troops.[64] His superiors had scorned and humiliated him after fifty-two years of service. Now his sepoys had abandoned him. Sir Hugh had merely fired on the ruins of his honor and his fame.

◆　◆　◆

The sepoys of the 56th rushed up through the compounds that lay between the Entrenchment and the river, and by the time the sepoys of the 53rd caught up to them they had put the bungalows to the torch, including their colonel's mansion at Sati Chowra. But even on the morning of the fifth there were a few Europeans who still scorned the Entrenchment. The Deputy Commissioner of Unao, whose station lay directly across the Bridge of Boats, stoically remained at his post even as his "very nice"[65] wife and two children settled into the Entrenchment.[66] A captain named Lafout and his Indian Christian servant remained in their riverside bungalow, which they had fortified so effectively that the first rebels to attack it finally gave up "until they could appear in greater force." Before that greater force materialized, Lafout and his servant would manage to flee downriver to Mirzapore.[67]

Early in the morning, when it still appeared as though the 53rd and 56th regiments would remain staunch, a railway man named Murphy had ventured out to visit his bungalow on the railway line. Warned by his servants of the mutineers' approach, Murphy climbed onto his horse and tried to make a run for the Entrenchment, but a group of troopers spotted him, raised their muskets and fired. Two balls struck him in the back, a third in the head, and he tumbled to the ground some six hundred yards from his destination, the first European casualty of the Cawnpore uprising.[68]

✦   ✦   ✦

As the tide of sepoys receded across the canal, an eerie quiet fell over the cantonments. Walsh's house still smoldered, and the garrison could see other fires rising from the direction of the river and the Ganges Canal. Occasionally there was the distant sputter of musket fire from the civil station. Families stood along the Entrenchment walls, weeping as their bungalows went up in flames. And yet they had survived the mutiny of the native troops, and beyond the Entrenchment, as far as the eye could see, the vast cantonment appeared completely abandoned.

In the lull Captain Williamson of the Commissariat sent his contractor Bhudrinath and an elderly conductor named Berrill off to the godown in the Commissariat cattle yard to fetch a few barrels of rum and beer for the soldiers.[69] The four regimental commanders disguised their grief with manic activity. Major Vibart and Colonel Ewart devoted themselves to assisting Brigadier Jack in preparing the garrison's defenses, while Colonel Williams and Major Hillersdon set off to clean up after the mutineers and consolidate the cantonment's resources.

Enraged by Wheeler's order to fire on his men, Major Hillersdon latched onto the native officers of his regiment who had remained in the Entrenchment and asked them to bring in any loyal sepoys who might still be hiding in the lines. They returned with about thirty-five men, and his lieutenants[70] found seventeen more hiding in a ravine behind the artillery hospital.[71] Hillersdon ordered these sepoys back to their lines to collect any abandoned weapons or ammunition they could find, while Colonel Williams dispatched Willie Halliday and a detachment of European soldiers a mile away to Savada House to collect the weapons of the furloughed sepoys and the "baggage and property of the Christian gunners who had crowded into the Entrenchment."[72] Halliday returned with bullock carts piled with furniture and bristling with three hundred muskets, and the sepoys arrived with five or six carts of weapons, including their own, which they were afraid to bear "lest the Europeans should fall upon us."[73]

The major expansively insisted that they retain their muskets, but there was no room for the sepoys in the Entrenchment; the barracks were overflowing with Europeans and Eurasians, whose servants had taken up every inch of shade.[74] Emerging from the tile-roofed barrack and squinting in the harsh sun, Wheeler mounted his horse and led all that remained of his native army to the artillery hospital over six hundred yards[75] to the southeast.[76] But the sepoys were as dubious about this position as the Europeans had been about the Entrenchment. "We said in such a building we could not manage to save our lives," recalled a sepoy of the 53rd, "as the round shot would reach us from all sides." But Wheeler assured them there was nothing to fear and asked that they keep a sharp lookout for reinforcements from the rear of the building, which commanded a branch of the Allahabad road.[77]

Despite Ashe's disastrous attempt to "implicate" his Oudh gunners in the Entrenchment's defense, by noon they had grown dangerously defiant. Returning from the artillery hospital, Wheeler assembled the gunners and declared that any of them who "did not wish to serve the Government any longer . . . were at liberty to depart." Glaring at the European soldiers who had circled around them with their muskets at the ready, the Irregulars put down their arms, mounted their horses and rode out of the Entrenchment.[78]

At two o'clock that afternoon a bullock cart rolled in with a melancholy cargo: the stiffening corpse of the hapless Mr. Murphy.[79] The sight of his perforated body, caked with blood and dust, outraged the officers, who ordered it interred in the yard of St. John's in a coffin they scrounged from the hospital barrack.[80] He was buried in the same shallow grave that coolies had scraped out of the baked earth for a Mrs. Wade, who had died of fever some days before. There, surrounded by "his friends and companions" of the Railway Rifle Corps, with "the minister performing the usual ceremony," Mr. Murphy was laid to rest.[81]

Now that Wheeler had cleared the Entrenchment of almost every native soldier who might turn against him, it began to occur to the garrison that the old man may have played his cards well after all. As he had steadfastly predicted, the mutineers were pouring out of the station, heading for Delhi, and it seemed certain that by the time they returned from the emperor's court, reinforcements would have arrived to defeat them.[82]

A KINGDOM OR DEATH

Nana Sahib: June 5–6, 1857

At the sound of the cavalry's approach, Nana Sahib and his entourage had fled into the treasury[83] and the protection of the company of the 53rd who steadfastly guarded its gates.[84] Outside hundreds of Nana's own motley guardsmen, urged on by their commander Jwala Prasad, danced around the grounds of the Collectorate waving their blunderbusses, pikes, and swords and welcoming the mutineers who came stumbling in. As the sowars milled about, shouting threats and imprecations at the sepoy guard, Nana did not want to bring his double game to a premature conclusion. If all the regiments mutinied his course was clear: he would turn down the path Azimullah had so assiduously prepared for him. If the other regiments did not follow, he might yet advance his interests with the British.

Within a few minutes the matter was decided, for as soon as the sepoys of the 53rd came marching into Nawabgunj their comrades threw open the treasury gates, and Nana Sahib emerged like a regal host welcoming his houseguests. Angered and frustrated by the long wait outside the treasury and perhaps a little giddy with success, Rissaldar Teeka Singh relieved Nana of his little brass cannon, berated him for aiding the British, and noisily demanded to know once and for all where the Maharaja stood.

Nana Sahib might have pointed out that only a few hours earlier Teeka Singh and the mutineers had been the Company's enforcers. But instead he gently replied that while it was perfectly true that he had been "apparently the friend of [the] English and offered them assistance," he had actually long been "at enmity" with them.[85]

By one account "the Native officers and troopers" told Nana "that a kingdom was prepared for him if he joined them with all his wealth: or death if he sided with the Europeans." But Nana had already determined that "if I went into the entrenchments my soldiers would kill my family," whereas if he joined the rebels the British would probably punish only him. Since it was "better for me to die" than his family, he had decided to cast his lot with the rebels. In any case, Nana Sahib had reached the end of his double game. "My ryots were urgent," as he later explained, "and I was obliged to join the soldiers,"[86] so he declared to the mutineers that "he was with them and had nothing to do with Europeans." The rebels cheered, and Nana, relieved, no doubt, that they had not cut his throat, pledged allegiance to their cause.[87]

The rebels began to load the treasury onto the thirty-six elephants they had purloined from the Commissariat, but there were not enough to carry it all.[88] Teeka Singh thereby presented Nana Sahib with over two hundred thousand rupees to safeguard at Bithur,[89] and though sowars like Jehangir Khan would complain that "none but those who plundered in person could get a share,"[90] the mutineers magnanimously left another ninety thousand rupees for the city folk to loot.[91]

Carrying Nana Sahib along with them as a kind of totem, the rebels proceeded to the jail and released all the prisoners. They made a bonfire of Charles Hillersdon's records, set fire to the entire civil establishment, and at the magazine helped themselves to as much of the military stores as they could carry. Leaving Nana and his guardsmen behind to guard what remained of the treasure until their return, and assigning a small body of cavalry to complete the destruction of the British bungalows, the mutineers began the march to Delhi.

As they surged up the Grand Trunk Road with their elephants festooned with plunder, Nana considered his situation. It seemed doubtful that Jwala Prasad and his guardsmen could hold out for very long against Wheeler's small but disciplined European force. It could be weeks before the mutineers returned from Delhi, and by then the British would have marched out of their Entrenchment, reclaimed the magazine, attacked Bithur, and hanged Nana Sahib as a traitor.

Nana may have considered that as yet he had taken no detectable part in the outbreak; like Wheeler himself he had been forced, against overwhelming odds, to stand aside and let the rebels do their worst. But Azimullah Khan knew there was nothing for it but to destroy the British in their Entrenchment, and for that Nana would need to bring the mutineers back into the station. The rebels would accomplish nothing by jamming into Delhi. If they were to prevail against the British they first had to secure Oudh, hold off the reinforcements rolling up the country from Calcutta, and thus maintain the momentum of the uprising's remorseless eastward sweep. If Nana could persuade the troops to remain at Cawnpore and crush his old friends in their "Fort of Despair," he could reclaim the Peshwa's throne, reawaken the Mahratta confederacy, and deal with the Emperor of Delhi from a position of overwhelming strength.[92]

As if called to witness by Azimullah's arguments, Lieutenant Ashe's dismissed gunners now galloped up to Nawabgunj to report on "the advantages likely to be derived by attacking the English in their intrenchments; since there was so large a quantity of powder and guns of different sizes, with other ammunition quite at hand" in the station and about forty boats filled with shot and shell moored in the canal.

Azimullah was right. There was no turning back. The time had come for Nana Sahib to take his place in the pantheon of Peshwas. Ordering his men to secure the magazine, Nana climbed upon his elephant and hurried up the Grand Trunk Road to turn the mutineers around.[93]

◆　◆　◆

Nana Sahib caught up with the rebels at eleven o'clock that night as they camped in their thousands at a staging bungalow in the village of Kalyanpur, about nine miles out of town, bartering their loot and guarding their colors as camp followers fed the horses, stoked the cooking fires, and crowded around the well.[94]

As Nana Sahib's state elephant knelt ponderously in the dust and the Maharaja stepped down from his silken howdah, Teeka Singh and his fellow officers emerged from the bungalow to greet him. Nana congratulated them on their day's success and on their patriotic desire to join their brothers at Delhi, but he asked them to consider for a moment what they were leaving behind: the treasure, the magazine, the boatloads of powder and ammunition moored along the ghats, and a growing British garrison with reinforcements arriving in vulnerable dribs and drabs. Why not destroy the British garrison at Cawnpore first? It would only be the work of a few hours, and then they could march to Delhi in triumph.[95]

The rebel officers objected at first. But Nana's agents spread the word through the camp that if the mutineers gave up on their long, hot, and uncertain march to Delhi, he would double their pay and provide them with all the food they needed; if they destroyed the British in the Entrenchment, he would award each man a gold bracelet worth one hundred rupees.[96]

Feeling the ground shift beneath him, Teeka Singh at last saluted Nana Sahib as his king, for which Nana promptly appointed him subhedar-major of his newfound army.[97] Gathering up their weapons, the cheering mutineers assembled behind Nana Sahib's elephant and marched back to Cawnpore to finish what they had started.[98]

◆ ◆ ◆

Toward the end of May, Eduard Williams had removed his family to a village a few miles north of Cawnpore on the Grand Trunk Road. On the night of June 5, roused by the sound of the mutineers marching en masse to Kalyanpur, Williams had hurried his family into native clothes and hustled them beyond the glow of the mutineers' torches, circling back to what he hoped would prove a safe haven in the city.[99]

But around eight-thirty the next morning there was a general rush toward the Grand Trunk Road[100] where, in the diagonal light of the morning sun, Nana Sahib now came swaying into view, riding atop his elephant "with his two brothers and other relatives, coming forward with all the pomp of a newly created king."[101] To the whine of horns and the pounding of kettle drums he led four regiments of mutineers, their geometric ranks muddled by swarms of young men from the bazaars and villages he had passed along the way. They halted at the camping ground beside the Subhedar's Tank, midway between Nawabgunj and the Ganges Canal, and suddenly Eduard Williams and his family found themselves in the very cauldron of the rebellion.[102]

Almost immediately Nana acted like a Peshwa of old. Laying claim to a bungalow next door to the theatre, Nana and his entourage began to issue a torrent of orders and proclamations.[103] Nana appointed his own commander of guards, Jwala Prasad, brigadier of his army, and named Azimullah Khan collector and his brother, Baba Bhutt, head magistrate and treasurer.[104] He commanded a body of his Mahrattas under Tatya Tope to raise a flag near the old Residency in Nawabgunj to mark the beginning of his rule,[105] ordered the chief agent of the Peshwa's widows blown to pieces at the mouth of a cannon, incarcerated the widows' supporters,[106] sent squads of sowars into the city to plunder and execute all the Christians who might still be hiding in the station, and condemned any native found harboring Christians to instant death.[107] He promised his troops that he would remain seated in his saddle until the Entrenchment had been taken, pressed the lascars and coolies at the magazine into service assembling artillery pieces and hauling them into position within range of the Entrenchment,[108] and with the civility of a true gentleman he composed a letter politely notifying General Wheeler that he should expect an attack at around ten that morning.[109]

The order to annihilate Christians and plunder their property seems to have been executed with particular enthusiasm.[110] Thousands of villagers and young men from the bazaars joined in the melee,[111] and "the whole of Cawnpore was in a state of great alarm and uproar."[112] The sowars, riding in groups of ten, thundered about with torches, setting fire to whatever remained of the European station.[113] Any shop in which a Christian was found hiding was instantly burned to the ground.[114] Along the ghats even the native boats heaped with European furniture and trunks were set ablaze.[115] The only European building the rebels spared was the Masonic Lodge Harmony, the House of Ghosts and Sorcery, which may have been under the protection of its most prominent member, Nana Sahib himself.[116]

In addition to torching the European bungalows, the sowars attacked the houses of various merchants and Oudh nobles who had not yet joined the rebellion.[117] Eight sowars surrounded the house of the Commissariat contractor Bhudrinath, Wheeler's chief spy, and began firing at his door. When a bullet struck one of his servants, Bhudrinath unlatched the door and, ducking the sowars' fire, fled to the roof. Bhudrinath asked disingenuously why they were shooting at him. A sowar replied that they suspected him of harboring Lady Wheeler and her two daughters. Bhudrinath told them they were free to search the house. When they came up empty-handed, the sowars debated whether to force their way up onto the roof and kill the contractor anyway. But a sudden roar of artillery fire distracted them, and Bhudrinath managed to flee into the city, eluding yet another squad of sowars who knew he was Wheeler's agent.[118]

The gunfire had come from the direction of Christ Church, where rebel golundazes had paused on their way to the Entrenchment to test their cannon on its Gothic perpendicular, battering its tower and rending its roof with their bountiful supply of cannonballs.[119] The church's shell would become the rebels' cookhouse.[120] Some of the native Christian families still residing at the mission south of Nawab-gunj managed to flee, but the rest were herded out onto the old parade-ground and massacred. Others were killed while hiding in native shops, and two more were discovered and cut down near the liquor godown, which must have struck the rebels as a particularly fitting Christian killing ground.[121] A European in the civil station was "worried to death in his garden."[122] An Englishman with his wife and child were discovered hiding in an abandoned house near the Grand Trunk Road and also brought before Nana Sahib, by whose orders they were taken to the plain opposite the staging bungalow and shot.[123]

Next the rebels brought their guns to bear on the nearby residence of Nunne Nawab, perhaps the wealthiest of the rich Lucknow nobles who lived at Cawnpore. Two of his brothers also lived in the station, each living off a portion of the twenty-five-thousand-rupee annual pension their father Agha Mir had been awarded for arranging a loan for the Company from the King of Oudh.[124] The Nunne Nawab's wealth, his prestige among the Moslems of Cawnpore and the extension of his father's pension past his father's lifetime galled the dispossessed Nana Sahib and made the Nawab an object of particular suspicion.

The mutineers immediately plundered the Nawab's brothers and ordered them to serve at Nana's batteries. But, by his own account, Nunne Nawab, poised on his roof with a telescope to track the mutineers' progress, put up some initial resistance, until the rebels fired their cannon and blew in his back door. On the strength of a rumor that he was harboring Europeans, a mob of city people followed the mutineers and the Nawab's own servants into his vast saracenic rooms and carried off his furniture, hangings, lamps, and paintings.

This time, at least, the rumor was true: breaking into one of the Nawab's apartments the mob came upon an old European with his wife and two teenaged children, whom they dragged off to the plain in front of the dâk bungalow and killed.[125] The rebels hoisted the Nawab onto his splendid Arab and led him and his followers to Nana Sahib's establishment at Duncan's house. There Balo Rao laid claim to the Nawab's horse, ordered him disarmed and his followers "plundered of the silver and other valuables they had on them." But when a crowd of soldiers threatened to shoot the Nawab, Nana Sahib himself interceded and ordered the ruined noble packed onto an elephant and imprisoned[126] with other exiled functionaries of the Court of Oudh.[127]

When the gunners crossed the canal, they paused again, this time to reduce the Moghul Serai,[128] where it was believed more Europeans might be hiding. But the shots managed only to injure a few sepoys who had evidently entered the building, and all they found in the serai were about five old native pensioners choking in the clouds of dust and heaps of debris. Embarrassed and exasperated, the mutineers dragged the old men out and killed them anyway.[129]

SHOT AND SHELL

June 6–7, 1857

At the Entrenchment the Europeans watched as the cavalry's rearguard darted among the last of the bungalows, setting them all ablaze.[130] From the northwest to the southeast fires raged in a nearly unbroken arc. "We were in suspense," remembered Mowbray Thomson, "peering over our mud-wall at the destructive flames that were consuming all our possessions. . . . Very few of our number had secured a single change of raiment; some, like myself, were only partially dressed, and even in the beginning of our defence, we were like a band of seafarers who had taken to a raft to escape their burning ship."[131]

Up to now everything seemed to have gone as Wheeler had predicted. But late in the previous afternoon a sepoy from the treasury guard had arrived at the Entrenchment with the news that Nana— who, Wheeler bitterly concluded, "appears to have been at the head of the movement"[132]—had defected to the rebels and plundered the

Wheeler and Hillersdon (to his rear) receiving the news of Nana Sahib's betrayal

treasury.[133] Hillersdon was so shamed and devastated by the betrayal of the "Gentleman of Bithur," the "great friend" in whose care he had been willing to entrust his family's lives, that even when "sweet, amiable" Lydia, lying in a room of the tile-roofed barrack, succeeded in giving birth to a healthy baby, he was desolate. Everything that had made Nana Sahib such a valuable ally made him a particularly dangerous foe. He had the resources to sustain a rebel army indefinitely, especially with the magazine and Collectorate treasury at his disposal. He was intimately familiar with the garrison's defenses. If he succeeded in persuading the mutineers to remain at Cawnpore there could be no doubt that they would lay siege to the garrison.

As soon as Wheeler received Nana Sahib's gentlemanly warning of the morning's attack,[134] he summoned back all the officers who had wandered off to what remained of their bungalows, and "with such expedition was the summons obeyed," wrote Mowbray Thomson, "that we were compelled to leave all our goods and chattels to fall a prey to the ravages of the sepoys."[135] Everyone who may have strayed beyond the Entrenchment to view the fires or save their possessions was summoned back, and not a soul was allowed to leave. Brigadier Jack even forbade Lieutenant Thomson to fetch coffee from his nearby mess because "the General's order was most peremptory that not a soul should be permitted to leave our quarters, as the attack was momentarily expected."[136]

Wheeler and Brigadier Jack dismissed the dwindling crew of coolies who, over the past weeks, had continued to dig the trenches and lay clay tiles[137] atop the thatched roof of the hospital barrack.[138] At 5 P.M. Wheeler assembled the hundred or so able-bodied civilian males of the garrison, mustered them into militias and assigned them to different officers. Under the mordant gaze of the professional soldiers who manned the batteries, mild clerks and stocky merchants lined up in their hats and wetted bandannas to obtain weapons from the cache the loyal sepoys had retrieved, and at candlelight that evening men like Jonah Shepherd bade their wives and children good night and took their places along the Entrenchment walls.

Lining up with the others, Jonah was still glad he had fled to the Entrenchment when he did, and tried to trust "in the Mercy of God." But he felt such "anguish of heart" looking upon the faces of his "poor wife and children, and the dear creatures whom I had so lately brought away from Calcutta to meet a fearful death."[139]

By now the Entrenchment's circumference ran almost half a mile around the barracks and cookhouse, godowns and powder magazines. Wheeler deployed men every fifteen paces,[140] with orders to relieve each other every four hours or so.[141]

"How vivid is the recollection to me of this night," wrote Jonah, "being the first time I was called upon to perform military duty." It reminded him of his soldier father, "and of the many small anecdotes of his military career, which he used to relate to us."

By now the two barracks had become so crowded "that the drummers and their families and native servants had to remain in the open air at night."[142] Under a moon enshrouded by passing clouds of dust, the gloom seemed to saturate men's hearts. That morning one of Wheeler's officers—"the only one who from the first had poohpoohed the idea of an insurrection"—had written a few lines to a friend in Calcutta, "ridiculing the precautions that had been made." But late in the afternoon he had written again to the same friend, "enclosing his will, and stating that the crisis had arrived, or would be upon them that evening. He, poor fellow, was among its first victims."[143]

✦   ✦   ✦

As the mutineers rampaged through the distant city, the hot breeze brought the acrid smell of burning thatch and the booming of artillery, the chatter of musket fire, the percussion of horses' hooves, the shouts and screams and laughter rolling across the drum-head plain.

Everything that Wheeler had assured the garrison would never happen was happening; all his calculations had backfired, yet he still refused to believe the worst. When Bhudrinath's agents brought the news that Nana was preparing the magazine's heavy guns for the siege Wheeler assured his officers that the twenty-four-pounders were too mottled and rusted to be "of any use," even as Nana's newly recruited lascars, spurred on by the prospect of a hundred-rupee reward, were handily brushing up their barrels on a lathe.[144]

That morning Major Hillersdon of the 53rd had distributed four hundred rupees among his loyal sepoys to stock up on food for themselves in their position at the artillery hospital southeast of the Entrenchment. But when the sepoys reached the bazaar, they heard the guns firing on Nunne Nawab's house and hurried back to their barracks, where four of their lieutenants offered them one hundred rupees each if they would help them retrieve four disassembled cannons that Larkins had inexplicably left lying on the plain near the foot artillery barracks. The sepoys did their best to heave the hot barrels onto their carriages in the morning sun, but they were "too much for us," remembered Bhola Khan, and the officers ended up having to spike all four barrels[145] and haul the carriages into the Entrenchment to hold in reserve as spares.[146]

As the thunder of the rebel guns echoed from Christ Church to Nunne Nawab's mansion to the Moghul Serai, Wheeler was prevailed upon to allow Lieutenant Ashe and two dozen volunteer horsemen[147] to ride off with a couple of cannons and attempt to blow up the magazine; something Wheeler now realized he should have done as soon as the mutineers had marched off to Delhi. But Ashe and his party had gotten no further than a quarter mile from the Entrenchment when they encountered a swarm of rebels crossing the canal. The mutineers opened fire with their muskets and Lieutenant Burnett Ashburner,[148] an artillery officer the garrison could ill afford to spare, charged into them, or perhaps lost control of his horse; in any case he was never seen again. The rest of the party pulled themselves around and ran for the Entrenchment in such haste that one of their equally indispensable cannon careened off the road and fell apart, its barrel landing with a thud on the hard earth, a wheel wobbling across the open plain.[149]

At ten-thirty in the morning, a fashionable thirty minutes past Nana Sahib's appointed hour, the rebels wheeled a nine-pounder behind the scorched rubble of the cavalry lines and opened fire on the Entrenchment.[150] The first ball flew half a mile across the parade-ground, bounced off a parapet, bounded over the tile-roofed barrack and bowled into the leg of a kitmutgar squatting near the barrack's kitchen.[151] As he lay bleeding to death, all but a few of the servants ran out of the Entrenchment; those who remained, said Jonah Shepherd, were so panicked "as to be perfectly useless."[152]

When the ball landed "a large party of ladies and children were outside the barrack," remembered Thomson, and "the consternation caused amongst them was indescribable."[153] Screaming, clutching their shrieking children to them, the women fled their tents for the suffocating refuge of the barracks. A bugler sounded "all hands to arms," and every man rushed off to his place on the trench's perimeter, "many of us carrying in our ears, for the first time," wrote Thomson, "the peculiar whizzing of round shot, with which we were to become so familiar."[154]

The cannon boomed again from the cavalry stable, firing with such precision toward the Entrenchment's western battery that a gunner named McGuire seemed "fascinated to the spot" as the black ball whirred toward him. Seconds later, when the dust cleared, his comrades wrapped his mangled remains in a blanket and tumbled them into the shallow trench.[155]

As the senior military wives fled their tents, the competition for space in the two barracks became ferocious. Some stepped over the Eurasians and box-wallahs jammed along the outer verandahs and laid claim to the interior rooms of the tile-roofed barrack; others crowded the families of the musicians and invalids in the hospital barrack. Many were received graciously by friends and acquaintances, others scuttled from room to room, begging vainly for places for themselves and their children.

The walls of the barracks were up to two feet thick and impervious to nine- and even twelve-pound balls.[156] But the rebels were hauling heavier guns across the canal and installing them in three more positions. The nine-pounder at the cavalry stables was moved up a few yards to the racquet court, another battery was erected at the Moghul Serai and a third installed near the horse artillery bazaar.[157]

As these guns were wheeled into position, hundreds of rebels appeared to be massing for an attack among the huts and shops of the horse-artillery bazaar.[158] To the clerks and box-wallahs in the trenches and to the engineers deployed without military commanders in the outpicket of the unfinished barracks it appeared as though the end had come.[159]

Wheeler banished the few Bengali babus and their families who had followed their employers into the Entrenchment, telling them that they stood a better chance hiding in the city or the neighboring villages. Men heaped the garrison's carts and carriages into a succession of barricades along the hundred-yard route between the Entrenchment and the unfinished barracks. The officers commanded that the panicked cows, oxen, and goats that the garrison had accumulated be slaughtered immediately and dragged into the godowns.[160]

The rebel batteries opened up simultaneously from the north and west, but they were still too far off to do more than terrify the women and children.[161] "Most of their balls hit and lodged in the mound which was thrown up round the entrenchment." At first the British tried to return round for round, and with one well-directed fire of grape and ball killed two sowars, five sepoys, and about a dozen hangers-on who had strayed within range of the garrison's guns.[162] But the rebel batteries remained out of reach of the Entrenchment's batteries.

By mid afternoon the rebels were rolling in more guns[163] and beginning to set up the miscellany of mortars that would eventually cause "frightful destruction within the entrenchment."[164] Coolies hauled cartloads of ammunition out of the magazine to Nana's batteries, along with the two hundred thousand pounds of gunpowder they had requisitioned from the regimental magazines in cantonments.[165]

✦   ✦   ✦

Jonah pitied the Englishmen who had been used to sitting out the sweltering afternoons in the fanned dark of their homes and offices and were now exposed to "the hot winds and scorching rays of the sun." Some lay wet handkerchiefs on their heads or fashioned shelters out of "empty boxes, sheets, &c.," but there was no real refuge from the heat.[166] By now the weeks of worry and uncertainty and desperate exertions in the gritty, windy glare of the Doab sun had exhausted about half of the garrison's senior officers. Lieutenant Colonel Ewart and Majors Vibart, Prout, and Hillersdon were still vigorous, and Lieutenant Colonel Wiggins was well enough because he rarely ventured out of doors. But Wheeler himself was flagging now in body as well as spirit, and depending increasingly on his son and aide-de-camp Godfrey. Redfaced and short of breath, Brigadier Jack was on the brink of collapse, as were Colonel Williams and Captain Parker. Though Major William Lindsay's condition is not recorded, he despaired that he had not sent Lilly and Kate and his three nieces out of the station in time, and considering his weight, his lumbago, and his inexperience in combat, he could not have been thriving.[167]

Major George Larkins had nearly worn himself out preparing the Entrenchment's batteries and powder magazines. He now posted Major Vibart and Captain Robert Urquhart Jenkins of the 2nd Native Cavalry to the bulging earthwork of the redan on the northern corner of the Entrenchment, from which they faced the charred lines of their own regiment across rows of *trous de loup*.[168] Larkins replaced the dismissed Oudh Irregular gunners with a squad of recuperating volunteers from Moore's 32nd and put Lieutenant Ashe in command of a twenty-four-pounder and two nine-pounders in the eastern corner. Eckford and Burney of the Artillery were assigned to three nine-pounders in the southern corner, Major Prout of the 56th commanded a little rifled three-pounder by the main guard on the southwestern perimeter, and Larkins assigned the western redan and its three nine-pounders to Dempster and Martin of the artillery.[169] (Eighteen-year-old John Nickleson Martin had arrived just a few days earlier and, pointing to a heap of shells, had remarked, "I should like to see some practice with these things." "He soon saw far more of that practice," wrote Thomson, "than most soldiers three times his age.")[170]

◆   ◆   ◆

With so many of the senior officers faltering in the terrible heat, the garrison began to turn for leadership to a new arrival at Cawnpore: the spirited Captain John Moore of Her Majesty's 32nd (Cornwall) Light Infantry. As a Queen's Captain Moore was the equivalent of an Indian Army major, but his prominence in the defense of the Entrenchment was not just a matter of rank. At a little over thirty,

Moore was a tall, fair, vigorous Irishman with pale blue eyes.[171] He had served in the Sikh Wars at Mooltan and Goojerat, and had purchased his captaincy in 1851. His assignment as commander of the 32nd's invalids might appear to suggest that he did not enjoy the entire confidence of his regimental commander. But, like the late Fletcher Hayes, Captain John Moore would prove to be one of Henry Lawrence's greatest gifts to Wheeler's garrison. His service at Cawnpore would make him one of the most sympathetic heroes of the Indian rebellion.

At first Wheeler put Moore in command of only the outlying pickets in the unfinished barracks, but he played a part in every aspect of the garrison's defense. He was a daily visitor to all the pickets, batteries, and even to the families huddled in the barracks themselves. "His never-say-die disposition," wrote Thomson, "nerved many a sinking heart to the conflict and his affable and tender sympathy imparted fresh patience to the suffering women." His wife was equally indomitable, and used to scuttle across the plain to visit him in the unfinished barracks, where Thomson and his men "fitted up a little hut for her, made of bamboo, and covered over with canvas; there she would sit for hours, bravely bearing the absence of her husband, while he was gone upon some perilous enterprise."[172]

✦ ✦ ✦

Jonah Shepherd and his younger brother Daniel remained at their adjacent posts all through the sixth, exposed to the sun and the continuous wind, staring over the sandbag parapet of the Entrenchment's western corner in case some bold sepoy should sneak across the plain and take up a position in the brick kiln or the unfinished barracks.

Nevertheless, despite the masses of soldiers that Vibart and Ashe could make out in the northern distance, undulant beyond the glassy waves of heat rising from the interceding plain, the all-out infantry and cavalry assault that the garrison so dreaded did not materialize. If any muskets were fired at the Entrenchment it was from such a distance that they could not be heard over the firing in the city and the roar of cannon from the batteries, and their expended bullets never reached their destination. A couple of cannonballs thudded noisily but impotently against the barrack walls, whereupon "the shrieks of the women and children were terrific," recalled Thomson.[173] "As often as the balls struck the walls of the barracks, their wailings were heart-rending."[174] But most of the rebel rounds continued to land harmlessly on the parapets, sinking into the dirt or bouncing off the sandbags and waddling back onto the plain like misshapen bowling balls. A few crashed through the few parched, stubborn trees that stood here and there around the Entrenchment yard.[175] The rebel cannon remained at such a distance and their fire was so feeble that Larkins ordered his own batteries to save their ammunition and stand by with their matches burning in case of an all-out assault.

But the rebels had evidently convinced themselves that no sane officer, let alone as great a general as Hamlah, would have chosen so weak a position as the Entrenchment unless he had some trick up his sleeve. The likeliest theory was that the British had mined the Entrenchment and the parade-ground and intended to blow the rebels to bits as soon as they advanced across the plain.[176] For weeks Wheeler had denied this as a dangerous and seditious lie; now he may have found it convenient to confirm it. Seeing that the reduction of the Entrenchment would be the work of something more than a few hours, a saddlesore Nana Sahib ignominiously dismounted and spent the night sleeping on a carpet in a ditch.

At about seven that evening, as the sun eased down behind the unfinished barracks and cast the Entrenchment in long, merciful shadows, Jonah and his brother were allowed to rejoin the family they had never expected to see again, and "oh! how melancholy and yet joyful was our meeting!"

It was also brief. At midnight they were roused from sleep and instructed not to return to their places in the Entrenchment but to proceed to an outlying picket on the parade-ground beyond the unfinished barracks to replace some volunteers who had skulked off from their posts. So Jonah and Daniel bade their family good-bye, and as the careless cannonade continued, they crept out of the Entrenchment and along the broken row of overturned carts and carriages that protected the route to the unfinished barracks. There they met up with two British soldiers and a corporal with whom they formed a perilously strung-out picket, each man fifty yards from the next, the last soldier taking the westernmost position over two hundred yards out onto the parade-ground.

A little after midnight, this lone and jittery soldier called Jonah and the others over to report that he saw soldiers massing on the high road that ran in front of the cavalry lines. A mist of dust and smoke slipped by the moon that night, and in its faint and erratic glow they began to see what looked to them like the glitter of rebel bayonets.

The corporal took this opportunity to take Daniel and a soldier back with him to the barracks to report on what they had seen. Soon afterward the remaining soldier nervously announced he was also going to go back to the Entrenchment to get relief, and, urging Jonah to "keep a sharp look out," ran back into the gloom. Thus Jonah found himself "quite alone" on the exposed plain, and for half an hour lay there flinching at the spark and boom of the rebel guns as they dropped a few shells into the Entrenchment with a "tremendous crash." Finally, at about two in the morning, Jonah lost his patience or his nerve and began to call out for relief. When no one answered, he shot off his musket and was about to reload and fire again when his replacement arrived at last, and Jonah returned, exhausted, to his family.[177]

HOW HEAVY
THE HAND OF GOD
June 7–8, 1857

The next morning Nana Sahib raised a Moslem as well as a Hindu flag, and "all true Mussulmans were directed to join, and those who demurred were threatened, insulted, or fined."[178] In fact the Moslem community was divided between those who declared the rebellion a holy war and the followers of a local Moslem sage who "stoically [denied] that a Jehad can be proclaimed in such matters."[179] The exasperated rebels carried off the sage, but Nana realized that if Cawnpore's wealthiest Moslem remained a prisoner, the city's sons of Islam would never unify behind the rebellion.[180] The soldiers reviled Nunne Nawab as a Christian for not rallying to the *Jhunda* or Moslem standard and commanded him to attend the rebels' court or they would cut off his head and bring it to Nana. Teeka Singh "heaped abuses on me," Nunne Nawab would testify, "and threatened to have me tied to a tree and there mangled, as I appeared to be averse to the *Jhunda*. He caused me to be seated just close to their guns placed near the Saint John's Chapel, purposely to have me killed, as shots from the entrenchment were unceasingly fired at it, and I had very narrow escapes, shots passing over my head, sides, ears, &c."[181]

There were rumors that in exchange for Nunne's services Nana had "promised to make over Cawnpore to the Nawab" when Nana Sahib returned to his ancestral capital at Poona.[182] But even if Nunne Nawab's initial participation was coerced, to most people he appeared to serve willingly, and "had full authority"[183] over thousands of Moslem soldiers, including a phalanx of blue-coated sowars.[184] He proved a cool and conscientious artillery commander, and got a certain pleasure out of making Brahmins carry water and cannonballs to the batteries.[185] If the Nawab had "very narrow escapes" it was because he liked to sit at a little writing desk at his battery at St. John's and climb up occasionally to assess with his telescope the damage his guns were doing to the Entrenchment. Nana Sahib evidently distrusted the Nawab, suspecting almost from the start that he intended to take independent command of the Moslems at Cawnpore.

✦ ✦ ✦

By the dawn of June 7, the Entrenchment had been almost entirely surrounded and sealed off. During the night a sweeper had managed to sneak fifteen coolies through one of the gaps in the rebel cordon and deliver provisions to Wheeler and Majors Parker and Larkins,[186] but afterwards no more food got through.[187] "We had not a single good meal since entering the entrenchment," wrote Thomson, "from the first living on half rations."[188]

There was a gasp of sorrow from the soldiers when one of the first rebel balls struck several hogsheads of the rum and beer that Bhudrinath's coolies had managed to drag into the Entrenchment two days before.[189] But it turned out that "of this there was a large quantity," remembered Jonah, "and the loss was not felt."[190]

Many of the servants who had fled the initial bombardment or gone off to the city for supplies could not make their way back. Others preferred to return to their masters' compounds and dig up the treasure they had helped their sahibs bury.[191] Their absence from the Entrenchment was a particular hardship to the women and children.[192] "The morning and evening baths," wrote Sir John Kaye, "the frequent changes of raiment, the constant ministrations of assiduous servants in the smallest things, which are the necessaries of English life in India, were now suddenly lost to the helpless ones;

and, to intensify the wretchedness, the privacy and seclusion so dear to them became only remembrances of the past."[193]

During the night Eurasian musicians took the place of vanished punkah coolies, tugging the ropes to fan the dusty air as shot occasionally bumped against the barrack walls.[194] Many of the ayahs remained: some because they were Christians, others, like Shepherds' Thakurani, because they were devoted to their mistress's children. A crew of cooks labored in the two kitchens and over the cooking pit that Wheeler had ordered dug out of the soldiers' garden east of the tile-roofed barrack, trying to produce something resembling a meal for their anxious and exhausted sahibs, memsahibs, and *baba logue*.[195]

✦ ✦ ✦

In the night rebel snipers crept up to the roofs and upper-story windows of the surrounding ruins of the European bungalows to the east and the outermost of the unfinished barracks to the west, and as the sun began to sweep the plain their musket fire nicked at the parapets and shredded the mostly abandoned tents that still littered the Entrenchment yard.

It was then, wrote Amy Horne, "our troubles really commenced." To those who dared to peer out of the verandahs "the whole surrounding country seemed covered with men at arms, on horse and on foot, and they presented a most formidable appearance. They seemed such fearful odds to keep at bay from our Lilliputian defences."[196] Among them were a growing number of zemindars and matchlockmen eager to show their fealty to Nana Sahib by firing on the Entrenchment.[197]

At ten in the morning the rebels set fire to St. John's, the soldiers' church, which so demoralized Jonah Shepherd that he "could not help thinking how heavy the hand of God was . . . to bring this judgment upon us."[198] When its ashes ceased to smolder it would become one of the rebels' most effective artillery emplacements.[199] The cannonade steadily escalated until by noon a cordon of six batteries was pouring the heaviest fire that the indefatigable Captain Moore had ever witnessed. Rebel cannon had advanced on the Entrenchment from all directions, and now some stood in well-protected positions as close as 350 yards, and mortar shells and eighteen- and twenty-four-pound round shot began to tear into the barrack walls.

"Every shot that struck the barracks," wrote Amy Horne, "was followed by the heart-rending shrieks of the women and children, who were either killed outright by the projectiles, or crushed to death by the falling beams, masonry, and splinters. . . . Windows and doors were soon shot off their sockets, and the shot and ball began to play freely through the denuded buildings."[200]

A ball took away the feeble and elderly William Gee of the Inland Transit Company, another struck the wall against which schoolmaster Gill was leaning; he would survive an agonizing week more in the hospital barrack with his skull cracked open and his brain exposed. Another ball smashed the leg of Andrew Jack, the brigadier's visiting brother. When the shells burst in the verandah the effect on the women and children was indescribable. "The report was enough to burst their hearts," said Jonah, "and such was actually the case in some instances."[201]

Among those who probably died in those first hours was Emma and Willie Halliday's little daughter Mabel. High-strung and frail, she appears to have died of shock from the rebels' first salvos, tugging at her hair and screaming.[202] But in the cacophony and horror of the bombardment "gentle and calm" Lydia Hillersdon had somehow found the strength to recuperate from her labor. Sometime on the seventh Charles came to visit her from the Main Guard and in order to speak to her privately led her out of the room she shared with Mrs. Ewart and stood with her for a moment on the southern verandah of the tile-roofed barrack, out of reach of the rebel's batteries. This was the last of the Collector's miscalculations, for a new battery had just taken a position in the lines of the 56th and now sent a ball bounding into the Entrenchment. It struck Charles Hillersdon full in the stomach, and as Lydia shrank back in horror, her husband sank in a heap of his own entrails.[203]

♦   ♦   ♦

As Jonah Shepherd hunched down behind the low dirt parapet of the western trench, he heard a musket fire from the direction of the riding school and felt a sharp blow to his back, as though someone had struck him with a club.[204] Jonah fell back in a swoon, and when he came to found his brother Daniel helplessly fanning him, "quite at a loss to know the cause of my sudden indisposition." Jonah asked him to peel back his shirt and out fell a musket ball that had passed through several folds; it had left "a hole in them all, and penetrated about an inch deep in the body."

Daniel helped Jonah the few yards to the thatched barrack where a surgery had been established. The room was now filling with the wounded from the barracks and trenches, and Jonah thanked God that his own injury "was but a trifle compared to some of theirs." Jonah patiently waited his turn as the surgeons attended to people horribly broken and torn by shot and shell. Here the surgeons had to amputate what remained of the left leg of Andrew Jack, the brother of the brigadier; he died under the knife and saw,[205] only hours before his brother succumbed to heatstroke.

Near Jonah a soldier whose "left arm was shot off a little above the elbow" sat on a stool, gingerly peeling his shirt off the flesh that hung from his shattered stump.

"Well, you are a lucky man," exclaimed apothecary Twoomy when he finally got around to examining Jonah's wound.

Surgeon Arthur Wellesley Newenham, his apron spattered with blood, agreed.[206] "Nobody ever lives after getting a bullet in the part you have got," he told Jonah, "and as you have escaped this, you will live very long."[207] Jonah was excused from duty at the trenches and returned to recuperate with his family in the exposed arcade of the tile-roofed barrack.

Not all the wounded littered the gory floors of Newenham's surgery. The casualties among the Railway Rifle Corps in the outer barracks were tended to in an inner room of the fourth barrack by artillery surgeon Macauley, "who signalized himself by the most unremitting attentions and exertions on their behalf."[208] The jaunty Robert Garrett may well have been among his first patients. Garrett's family would try for some months to learn the exact circumstances of his death, but he had been so new to the country—in Shepherd's definitive list of casualties his first name is not even given—that no one could say for sure. But apparently he died in the first days of the siege—a victim of one of the rebel shells, perhaps, or one of the snipers' bullets that constantly plucked at his "set of jolly fellows."[209]

Garrett's comrades in the fourth barrack "distinguished themselves greatly by their skill and courage. Their sharp sight and accurate knowledge of distances acquired in surveying, had made these gentlemen invaluable as marksmen, while still higher moral qualities constituted them an addition to our force not to be estimated by their limited numbers." For three days they held the barrack without any "military superintendence whatever," but despite their best efforts hundreds of mutineers crept up at night under the cover of the echelon of unfinished walls to take sniper positions in the pit kiln, as well as the southernmost and northernmost barracks, from which they poured a steady fire. At last Wheeler assigned officers to the picket, placing Lieutenant George Glanville of the 2nd Bengal Fusiliers in command of the Railway Rifle Corps in the fourth barrack and sending Captain Jenkins of the 2nd Native Cavalry off with sixteen men to hold down the second barrack and prevent the sepoy snipers from moving any closer to the Entrenchment itself.[210] To supply the position with food and ammunition volunteers had to run a gantlet of sniper fire, ducking along the broken line of overturned carts and boxes that lined the route to the Entrenchment.[211] "Two men of the picket, who acted as cooks, performed this dangerous journey daily, when they went for our miserable dole of food. . . . If ever men deserved the Victoria-cross these poor fellows did."[212]

✦ ✦ ✦

In the meantime various detachments had remained out in the district. Lieutenant Raikes and Ensign Brown, whom Wheeler had sent out on June 2 with two hundred men of the 56th, proceeded southward toward Urai. On June 6, two days' march from their destination, the sepoys somehow learned of their regiment's mutiny and decided to join, but not before Raikes and Brown had managed to mount their horses and flee, "leaving every bit of our property behind," as Brown remembered, "with the exception of the clothes we wore and our swords and revolvers."[213] Raikes had made it through such scrapes before in the Santal campaign, but after days of parched and desperate flight from bands of mutineers and plundering villagers, he went mad.[214] "To cut the sad tale short," Brown would recall, "we had, when all hope was gone, to leave the poor fellow, and he must have died a pitiable death."[215]

The two restive companies of the 48th Native Infantry that Major Marriott and Lieutenant Hutchinson had abandoned at Mallawan had continued to march aimlessly and uselessly up and down the Grand Trunk Road. For four days they had become ever more loath and sullen, muttering among themselves in their remaining officers' dust. On the evening of June 6, as they camped near the town of Chaubepur, about fifteen miles from Cawnpore, word reached them of the mutiny of the native regiments, and through the night they furtively debated whether to join the rebellion.

By now Lieutenant Augustus Joseph Boulton of the 7th Native Cavalry had lost confidence in the sepoys and the few sowars of his own regiment who had accompanied him on this futile expedition. He positioned his horse and tent at some distance from the native troops' camp in case he might have to make a run for it. In the early afternoon the five officers were roused from their siestas by the blowing of a bugle and emerged from their tents to demand to know by whose orders assembly had been called.

"By the orders of Nana Sahib," the sepoys replied and opened fire, wounding their captain. Three officers jumped onto their horses and raced about a mile down the road, only to be surrounded and cut down by a body of sowars and villagers. Boulton managed to get to his horse and yank the wounded captain up behind him onto his staggering mount, but when they galloped off, a second volley from the troopers knocked the captain to the ground. As Boulton turned to see the sepoys cutting him to pieces, a ball tore through Boulton's cheek. Reeling, the young lieutenant nevertheless managed to escape the pursuing sowars, eventually jumping his horse over a ditch and losing them in the gloaming on the outskirts of Nawabgunj.[216]

◆ ◆ ◆

The sowars chopped off the heads of the three officers they had surrounded and were proudly carrying them to Bithur in a basket when they happened upon two more Europeans fleeing through the countryside.[217] Joseph Carter, a middle-aged tollkeeper from Sheorajpur, had remained dutifully at his post with his young and pregnant wife, but at the last minute had decided to make a run for it to Cawnpore. The sowars closed on them on the Grand Trunk Road and brought them to Bithur for Rao Sahib's dispensation: Mrs. Carter riding in a dooly, her husband staggering beside her in the sowars' dust.

A crowd of several thousand came to see the officers' heads displayed in the open air in front of Rao Sahib's house at Bithur.[218] Rao Sahib proposed to execute the Carters, but when their sentence—or perhaps Mrs. Carter's pleas—reached the ears of Baji Rao's widows, the old queens threatened to kill themselves if she was harmed.[219] Rao Sahib knew that his uncle Nana might have been relieved to be rid of Baji Rao's irksome widows, but their suicide would have brought disgrace on his house. And so the next morning Rao Sahib placed Mrs. Carter in the keeping of an old Moslem woman[220] and ordered her carried off to a room in the former Residency and placed under a cavalry guard.[221] The sowars, eager to collect their reward for their services at Chaubepur, led her sorrowing husband away to Nana's camp with the basket of trophies from their afternoon's work.

THE SEPULCHRAL WELL

The Entrenchment: June 9–10, 1857

Under the remorseless sun and incessant cannonade it was difficult to distinguish between heat stroke and shock. Thomson spoke of apoplexy, whose fatal symptoms were "headache and drowsiness, followed by vomiting and gradual insensibility, which terminated in death."[222] Whatever it was, it cut through the garrison's upper ranks like a scythe. Among its victims was the handsome and formidable Brigadier Jack, and Cantonment Magistrate Sir George Parker and Lieutenant Colonel Stephen Williams of the 56th, some of whose rebel sepoys still furtively visited his servants in his ruined compound to ask fondly after him and his family.[223]

Though the colonel had been wounded in the rebel barrage, it was the heat that had finished him, and he died late in the night of Sunday, June 8, surrounded by his wife and daughters.[224] As a regimental commander, Williams was entitled to be buried with full military honors. But it was almost impossible to dig proper graves, let alone conduct funeral services; the ground was too hard and the fire too intense. In the terrible heat his body could not be left inside the barracks, and so over his daughters' protests he had to be carried out to the ruins of the outer verandah and left there for later disposal.

During the siege of Lucknow the British dead would be buried wrapped in white sheets,[225] but at Cawnpore "not one of our killed was sewn in a bag," wrote Mowbray Thomson. "We had neither materials [nor] time for such labour. At nightfall each day the slain were buried as decently as circumstances would permit. Alas! it was little more we could do than place them under ground."[226]

On the night of June 9—two nights after her husband's eviscerated remains had been cleared away—another of the balls that constantly arced and bounced into the Entrenchment struck the inner verandah off Lydia Hillersdon's chamber and buried her in an avalanche of bricks. They managed to pull her out of the rubble, but her skull was crushed, and within a few hours, "in great distress," she died.[227]

Colonel Williams's corpse remained out on the verandah all day, but perhaps at Mrs. Ewart's insistence the Collector's wife was buried with more dispatch. Immediately to the east of the tile-roofed bar-

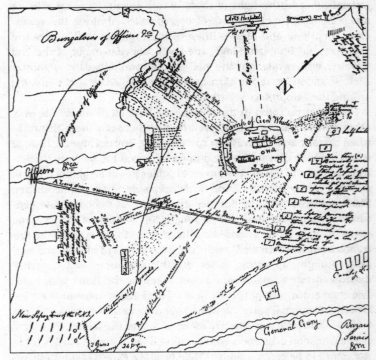

Jonah Shepherd's feverishly scrawled map, drawn just after his rescue, shows the intensity of the siege

rack was a soldiers' vegetable garden where Wheeler had ordered a cooking pit dug to a depth of three feet to prevent its glow from illuminating the Entrenchment and sending sparks "flying about." But in the barrage from the rebel batteries the pit was no longer of any use, and so it was there, in the mongrel morning hours of June 10, that the "gentle and calm"[228] Lydia Hillersdon was buried, probably attended by Colonel Ewart, her brother-in-law the major, and perhaps her children, too, if they were still among the living.[229]

On the night of June 10 they dragged Colonel Williams's remains out to the trenches and buried him there, covering him over with chunks of dirt from the parapet. But the shelling claimed many more that day, including five servants killed when a shell hopped into the ruins of Jonah's verandah;[230] their corpses remained entangled until candlelight, and the sight of them, wrote Jonah, "was dreadful to inexperienced eyes."[231] Rows of bodies collected along the verandahs: Mrs. Reid and Mrs. O'Brien of the Collector's office, dead of apoplexy; old Bhowani Singh, the loyal subhedar-major of the 2nd Cavalry, who while nursing his wounds was killed by a mortar shell;[232] and many of the garrison's gunners killed by shells bursting around their unprotected batteries.[233]

There was no room in the trenches to bury all of them. The only other option was the second well that lay between the fifth unfinished barrack and the western corner of the Entrenchment. Though it was a source of water to the outpickets, it was too far from the Entrenchment and too exposed to rebel sniper fire to be of much use to the rest of the garrison. And so Wheeler declared it a sepulcher. There the dead could be dumped after dark, "as nobody could venture out during the day," wrote Jonah, "on account of the shot and shells flying in all directions like a hail storm." Every evening the Entrenchment was "strewed" with "the dead bodies of officers and tenderly brought up young ladies of rank (Colonels' and Captains' daughters) put outside in the veranda among the ruin" with notes and mementos hastily tucked into their clothes "to await the time when the fatigue party . . . went round to carry the dead to the well, . . . for there was scarcely room to shelter the living."[234]

The Christian drummers who composed the "fatigue" parties could not afford to be ceremonious.[235] The heads of expired senior officers like Colonel Williams bumped and lolled as their dusty corpses were dragged by the feet down the verandah steps and slung onto hand carts or rolled onto litters.[236] As the outpickets intensified their fire on the rebel snipers in the unfinished barracks,[237] the drummers hurried the cadavers eighty yards beyond the parapets, lunging in the dark along the line of overturned vehicles and tipping their burdens into the well, turning to rush back to the Entrenchment as the dead tumbled sixty feet to the bottom and landed with a soft, echoing splash.[238] By the end of the siege some 350 bodies would accumulate in the dark throat of the burial well, and "the distress was so great," remembered Jonah, "that [no one] could offer a word of consolation."[239]

✦ ✦ ✦

By June 8 Captain Moore of Her Majesty's 32nd seemed immune to the hailstorm from the rebels' snipers and batteries. Before the siege he had broken his collarbone in a fall from his horse,[240] but with his arm in a sling and a pistol in his belt, this dashing, piratical figure was "the life and soul" of the defense.[241] He posted lookouts with spyglasses on the roofs of the barracks to assist the batteries in directing their fire, sent relief to the outposts, paused with words of reassurance for the women and children, personally and repeatedly led little squads of men out into the night to clear the fourth unfinished barrack of rebel snipers.

When the commander[242] of the seventh barrack was wounded, Lieutenant Thomson took his place, inheriting a motley crew of seventeen Fusiliers, soldiers of the 84th, and plate-layers from the railway works.[243] The son of a Bengal Army officer,[244] Thomson had entered the 53rd Native Infantry in December 1853. He had been a lieutenant for only two years and "had the bright face and laughing eyes of an undergraduate in his first term," wrote a friend. First and foremost, he was a soldier, and took "events almost surpassing the most romantic adventures of fiction, as if they were ordinary circumstances to be looked for in the day's work."[245]

"The orders given us were, not to surrender with our lives," wrote Thomson, and many did not. Within a matter of a few days all of Thomson's Fusiliers and several soldiers of the 84th had been shot at their posts, and Moore immediately replaced them with civil and military volunteers from the Entrenchment.[246] As each volunteer dashed to the unfinished barracks, "some scores of bullets were fired at him, which made him run as fast as ever his legs would allow," wrote Jonah, who, perhaps a little giddy from his wound, thought it "a very amusing sight."[247]

Thomson ordered a crow's nest erected some twenty feet above the roof of his barrack, where pickets spelled each other for an hour at a time, firing at every sepoy who dared show his face in the southernmost barrack. Twenty-year-old Cornet Walter Albert Stirling of the 2nd Native Cavalry proved himself such a master sharpshooter in his "elevated position," that it was "quite impossible to conjecture the results, in the number of sepoys brought down by his gun."[248]

Sometimes the sepoys moved in on the outpickets, "compassing us about like bees." Every evening "all hands were required on the look out, and we stood through the weary hours with muskets at the charge, peering out into the darkness, and as soon as a flash from the adjacent barrack indicated the whereabouts of the foe, we lodged our bullets in the same locality."

Their bugles sounded the advance and the charge, but no inducement could make them quit the safe side of Nos. 1 and 5; from the
windows of these barracks they could pepper away upon our
walls, yelling defiance, abusing us in the most hellish language,
brandishing their swords, and striking up a war-dance. Some of
these fanatics, under the influence of infuriating doses of *bhang*
[hemp], would come out into the open and perform, but at the inevitable cost of life. Our combined pickets always swept through
these barracks once, and sometimes twice a-day, in chase of the
foe. They scarcely ever stood for a hand-to-hand fight, but heaps
of them were left dead as the result of these sallies.

The pickets learned to divert the rebels' fire by piling their extra
muskets behind the parapets and bedecking them with hats and
shakos. As the rebels fired away at these straw men, the pickets
would move to a new position and open fire. They killed scores, perhaps hundreds of sepoys, inflicting "wholesale carnage," Thomson
recalled, "that nothing could have justified in us but the instinct of
self-preservation, and I trust the equally strong determination to
shelter the women and children to the latest moment." The outer
barracks stank with the decomposing dead, and on the parade-
ground, even in the midst of the rebel barrage, hordes of vultures
and adjutant birds closed on the rebels' corpses.[249]

After seeing how easily the rebel snipers could be chased off,
Moore decided to test the resolution of the rebel gunners as well.
Though Moore's audacity worried Wheeler, the old general could see
that the fair-haired Irishman's sorties worked wonders on the garrison's morale.[250] So he approved the captain's most daring plan to
date: a midnight foray northward to spike the guns of the nearest
rebel battery.

Donning dark clothes and smearing their faces with lampblack and
ashes, Moore and about two dozen volunteers crept out along the
echelon of unfinished barracks, across the drainage ditch and up to a
small battery in front of the 1st Native Infantry lines that was commanded by Nizam Ud Daula, one of Nunne Nawab's brothers. The
battery stood almost a mile from the Entrenchment and only two
hundred yards from Nana's own headquarters at Duncan's house.[251]
Moore and his men opened fire on the gunners and sent them running, killing perhaps a dozen rebel sepoys with their volleys, while
others of his party drove spikes through the torch holes of all the
cannon and detached the small guns from their ammunition car-

riages, working "as coolly," recalled Jonah, ". . . as if they were engaged in the most ordinary duties," and returning to the "hearty cheers" of the garrison.[252]

Nana heaped abuse on Nizam Ud Daula and relieved him of his battery.[253] In the morning Nana prudently moved his camp almost two miles south to a mango grove on the plain of Savada House, a large decrepit mansion of whitewashed stucco.[254] The British had used it as a godown—most recently for the belongings of the families of the Christian gunners and the weapons of furloughed sepoys—but it stood a mile south of the Entrenchment on a promontory that commanded the Grand Trunk Road. Here Nana erected his own personal battery, composed of two large guns manned by Ashe's disaffected Oudh Irregulars.[255] Pitching his luxurious tents in the shade of the mango grove, with Teeka Singh's sowars camped behind him along the road, Nana could not only direct the siege but watch for the approach of the British relief force rumored to be marching from Allahabad.[256]

PESHWA BAHADUR

Nana Sahib: June 8–10, 1857

The matriarch of the leading mercantile family at Cawnpore was the formidable Rose Anne Greenway, mother of Samuel, Edward, and Thomas. Samuel and Thomas had taken their families into the Entrenchment, but she had remained with Edward, who had taken an especially dim view of Wheeler's preparations and looked elsewhere for sanctuary. Burying his treasure beneath the imli, mango, and neem trees that shaded the family compound, he and his mother, wife, and four children had all fled to their indigo factory sixteen miles east of Cawnpore where they hid with Mr. Hollings, the rough and ready editor of the Greenways' *Central Star* newspaper.[257]

But by then the rebellion had spread throughout the district, and around the eighth of June a body of armed peasants attacked the Greenways' factory. Hollings immediately took command, leading the family up a ladder to their rooftop terrace where he had stocked a rack of double-barreled shotguns for just such an emergency. Drawing the ladder up, Hollings began to blast away at the surrounding crowd. Either the mob was dense and unusually bold or Hollings was a crack shot, for according to Jonah Shepherd he killed sixteen men and so terrorized his attackers that they sent for reinforcements from Cawnpore.

By the time a squad of Nana's soldiers arrived, Hollings had entirely run out of ammunition and was sitting out on the balustrade, contemptuously baring his chest and challenging the soldiers to shoot him.[258] The troopers opened fire, but it took several rounds before they finally hit the dangerous Mr. Hollings in the breast and sent him pitching headfirst to the ground below. The Greenways surrendered to the troopers, who probably would have allowed the enraged mob to cut them to pieces but for old Mrs. Greenway's promise of high ransom. And so the troopers led Edward and his family through the wrathful mob and piled them into a bullock cart and transported them into the presence of their former patron Nana Sahib, who "had been all along before the mutiny on social terms" with the Greenways, and had been "in the habit of frequently visiting the shop, and holding friendly intercourse with the brothers."

Amid the booming of his batteries, Nana agreed to provide safe passage to Allahabad on condition that they pay him two hundred thousand rupees.[259] The Greenways may have had some money on their persons, for by one account they immediately handed over a portion of their ransom. But the rebels were not satisfied and left the Greenways in an unprotected bullock cart in the blistering sun until more money was forthcoming. Perhaps Mrs. Greenway told the troopers about the treasure chest her son had buried, and they were left in the sun while the troopers searched unsuccessfully for it. In any case they could not come up with the full amount, and only when Mrs. Greenway promised to obtain the rest from her bank in Calcutta were she and her son and his sunstruck wife and children at last brought out of the summer glare and into a cool anteroom of Savada House.[260]

✦　✦　✦

As the rebels surged through the city, Ignatius Xavier DeGama, another of Cawnpore's principal merchants, hid himself in a perforated box he had installed on his roof as a hideaway, but he was soon found out and dragged off to Nana's camp. He must have expected mercy from his best customer, who had earlier warned him not to enter the Entrenchment. But unlike Mrs. Greenway, DeGama never got a chance to speak to Nana Sahib, for upon hearing the Portuguese merchant's name Nana merely averted his gaze and made a dismissive gesture that a guardsman interpreted as an order to kill. Drawing his sabre, the soldier slashed repeatedly at the little merchant, cutting through his mouth and sending him into the dust, where he rolled and writhed about "in a fearful manner" until "a few more strokes finished him."

Frederick Jacobi, the Swiss coachmaker who had recently sent his daughter Charlotte to Calcultta, took his family into the Entrenchment. But, like Edward Greenway, Frederick's watchmaker brother Henry declined to entrust his wife and two children to General Wheeler and hid with them in a native's house near the magazine. One night, as the troopers proceeded from house to house searching for Christians, Henry and his family somehow made their way across the Ganges and hid in some long grass on the opposite shore.

They intended to remain there until nightfall and then search for a hiding place in the countryside. But the next day, as the Jacobis huddled under the glare of the sun, some local landlords captured them and ferried them back to Permit Ghat. By now Henry was almost dead from heat stroke, so the rebels placed him on a ropestrung bed and conveyed him and his wife and children to Savada House.

They were about to share the same fate as poor DeGama when Mrs. Jacobi lost her temper and found her voice. Addressing Nana Sahib directly, she told him "that it was an act of cowardice to kill helpless women and children, when they had fallen in his power."[261] She declared that "the English always maintained those whom they deprived of their territories, and perhaps imprisoned, but never put them to death, and asked him in what scripture of his he found anything which sanctioned the commission of such acts of atrocity."[262]

"Our country," she declared, "will not be depopulated by our slaughter."[263] Perhaps Azimullah was not present to hear this dangerous challenge to his pet theory. Shame-faced, Nana ordered that the Jacobis be spared and sent them into Savada House as hostages. But Mrs. Jacobi's eloquence could not save her husband, who died of sunstroke, nor her grown son William, who had disguised himself as a native and hid in the city only to be hunted down and killed.[264]

✦ ✦ ✦

The Greenways and the Jacobis were apparently the only Christian captives Nana spared those first days. Fluent in Hindi, sixty-four-year-old Charles McIntosh, the wealthy landlord of several cantonment bungalows, disguised himself and his teenaged son as watchmen. "Not knowing what to do," they tried to hide under a bridge near the Greenways' compound, but some boys pointed them out, and that evening they were dragged off by a band of sowars and hacked to pieces with swords.[265]

McIntosh's elderly wife Amelia was discovered hiding in native clothes in her washerman's hut. She was taken to Nana's headquarters, where his guards decapitated her and placed her "bleeding head" under her arm, "in which position it was left to decompose."[266] The bibi of the elderly Superintendent of the Bridge of Boats tried to lead him in disguise to the Entrenchment, but as he hurried through the old native infantry lines he was recognized, led off to the parade-ground, and shot.[267] A discharged drummer held out with a few native Christians in a strong house and managed to kill half a dozen rebels before they were all burned to death when the sepoys torched the building. A Chinese shoemaker named Auchin "begged very hard for his life" when he was dragged before Nana, "saying he was a mere tradesman, a shoemaker, like the other natives, and not a European or a Christian."[268] He was beheaded.

An English lady whose husband had been killed on the road hobbled into the station with her children and tried to run for the Entrenchment. But she was discovered by a band of mutineers and brought before Nana Sahib. "The lady asked him to spare their lives," wrote one of Wheeler's spies, "but the coward refused to do so."

> The sun was hot, and the lady asked them to take her and her children into the shade. The wretch paid no attention to her request. The children clung to their mother, and asked her to take them to a bungalow; they said they were suffering from the heat of the sun. Eventually their hands were tied, they were taken to the middle of the *maidan* and fired on, all were killed at the first volley, except an infant. It was rolling about on the dead bodies and taking the hands of the corpses, was lifting them up and was saying, "why have you fallen down in the sun?" At last a trooper killed it with his sword.[269]

When the sowars presented Nana with the staggering, sunstruck tollkeeper Joseph Carter, his fate was already sealed. The three officers' heads evidently "pleased" Nana "much," and he ordered the sowars to add their captive's to their number.[270] Carter was taken out to the parade-ground opposite the Subhedar's Tank, shot and decapitated.

✦   ✦   ✦

Provoked by Moore's foray, Nana's commanders decided the time had come for an all-out assault. As Nana moved into his new quarters, he issued a proclamation that bore Azimullah's unmistakable touch. Delivered by heralds to the beat of drums, it declared that the British had resolved to send seven thousand troops up the country from Calcutta to murder fifty thousand Hindus and convert all of Hindustan to Christianity. To reinforce this army another thirty-five thousand British troops had been sent from England. But fortunately the Pasha of Egypt, shamed into action by the Sultan of Turkey, had sunk the British fleet at Alexandria and entirely wiped out the British force. "When the intelligence of the destruction of the army of London was received," the proclamation continued, "the Governor-General felt great grief and beat his head."[271]

The butchers of the city raised a Moslem standard with a star and half moon on a field of green, but only a few bazaar boys rallied to it. A local Moslem sage raised a second flag on the parade-ground near the Moghul Serai,[272] and Azimullah issued a proclamation urging all Moslem townspeople to assemble.[273] The British, he said, were trying "to deprive us of our religion and caste by many stratagems" and had "at last had recourse to open attempts, and thus incurred upon themselves the displeasure of the Deity, who has given the rule into our hands to punish them." It was therefore "incumbent on all true Mussulmen and the [natives] of all classes to join the good cause of exterminating the English people from India."

But even this second flag drew only a small crowd, and Azimullah had to resort to threats. "If you don't come," he is supposed to have told the residents of the city, "I will blow you from the mouth of cannon."[274] At last some Moslems gathered—watchmen, matchlockmen, rowdies from the city.[275]

Nana now raised a red Hindu flag bearing an image of Hanuman, the monkey god,[276] and circulated a proclamation declaring that every Hindu who did not "join in this righteous cause is an outcaste;

may he eat the flesh of cows, &c., &c."[277] At last a somewhat boggling crowd of two or three thousand townspeople gathered at the Moghul Serai,[278] flanked by a body of sepoys with mounted sowars following behind to prevent desertions.[279] Among the sowars was their favorite prostitute Azizun, a middle-aged madame who was "very intimate with the men of the 2nd Cavalry and was in the habit of riding armed with the sowars." Today she "joined the crusade . . . on horseback in male attire decorated with medals, armed with a brace of pistols."[280]

Silencing his drummers and calling for quiet, Nana Sahib and Azimullah commanded the mob to attack.[281] But the sage declined, perhaps suspecting that the sepoys intended to drive the crowd before them in order to trigger any mines the British might have laid.

"You attack them first," he told Nana, "then we will."[282]

The crowd was finally delivered from this impasse by Lieutenant Ashe, who fired one of his Entrenchment cannon at the mob. As the ball whistled toward the rest house they ran off in all directions;[283] "and a tremendous bolt they made of it," gloated Jonah, "the troopers of the cavalry giving the lead."[284]

✦ ✦ ✦

Nana Sahib was especially disgusted by the native merchants' lack of support. Many residents had been swept up in the short-term excitement of the rebellion, and some were willing to risk their lives for their faith. But the merchants of Cawnpore generally made unlikely revolutionaries. At first "many merchants expected that the sepoys would spare their property and that they would consequently be able to carry on business under the new Government."[285] But as the sepoys rampaged through the city, looting shops and godowns on the merest suspicion that they might be sheltering Christians, they were rapidly disabused.

"Sepoys plundered the shops of the cloth merchants and those of the manufacturers of brass and copper vessels," wrote one witness, plundering property worth an estimated one hundred thousand rupees.[286] The town was a shambles. Fires raged in all directions and mobs of laborers and hooligans, a few of them drunk on English liquor, stormed through the city "like swarms of locusts," looting British property and murdering native Christians, some of whom were betrayed by their own servants.[287] Babus were imprisoned, and if they were found wearing Western clothing they were killed on the spot.[288] Twenty-five cooks and bakers were caught baking bread to smuggle into the Entrenchment; some were executed for refusing to poison the loaves.[289] In the countryside "the *zemindars* rose up in arms and taking into their services numbers of armed men began to [take] revenge for old transgressions, dispossessing those who had acquired estates by auctions, by sale, by mortgage or by gift and plundering and burning the corn stored up in principal places."[290] The uproar extended even out into the river, where sepoys paddled about in boats, shooting their muskets at the European cadavers that kept floating by.[291]

When the batteries fired, townspeople "who had never heard such bombardment, except the artillery practice in peaceable times, trembled and crouched inside their houses."[292] Cawnpore had been a Company town whose richest natives had made their fortunes trading with the British. Rich or poor, the native residents had almost no other reason to be at Cawnpore except that the British were there. If the British detested the climate and had settled at Cawnpore only because of its strategic position, Indians found it just as hot and dusty and miserable. Most of the native establishment was as new to the place as the British; unlike the residents of India's ancient cities they were not bound to the place by feudal ties. Indeed if there was anything that distinguished the citizens of Cawnpore it was that most of them, or their fathers, had been willing to break such ties to make money off the British. Like the residents of almost every modern city, they were a variegated lot bound together by commerce; despite the rage of the sepoys and sowars, many of the leading native residents failed to see the logic of annihilating their best customers.

The revolution was proving bad for business. "During the two or three days of this outbreak all boats which had come from both directions were collected," wrote an opium contractor, ". . . to prevent any Christian or European escaping by means of a boat. The supply of grain [lentils] too was stopped from all directions, and prices consequently rose. Within four days the price of grain had doubled."[293] "Many of the natives suspected of aiding or serving the British force were put to death, and a list was made of all the bankers, who were mulcted[294] of their wealth."[295]

Nana at least tried to be scrupulous, as he would prove on an expedition to the chained doors of Ishwari Prasad's mansion, where, seated on his elephant, he demanded tribute of one hundred thousand rupees. The banker's mother called back from a window that her son had gone to stay with his brother at Agra. But in the end she was persuaded to throw down the keys to her son's basement vaults.

Nana's soldiers rushed in, but, according to Ishwari Prasad's own descendants, Nana would not allow them to carry away more than the one hundred thousand rupees he had originally demanded, and he returned the old lady's keys.[296]

On the night of June 10 a cavalcade circulated through the city, declaring to the beat of kettle drums that the Emperor of Delhi had conferred upon Nana Sahib the rights and titles that the Company had denied him for so long. Nana Sahib, the "gentleman of Bithur," was now to be known as Srimunt Maharaj Dhiraj Dundhu Pant Nana Sahib Pant Pardhan Peshwa Bahadur, ruler of Cawnpore and Bithur.[297] It was a start.

MYSTERIES OF THE BODY

The Entrenchment: June 11–13, 1857

Shortly after the bombardment began, Wheeler had ordered the garrison's horses set adrift, for "there was neither shelter nor food for them." Crazed with thirst, many of them had congregated around the well between the barracks, where they were struck by the rebel's most concentrated fire, "and fragments of their flesh fell in and polluted the water."[298] A few shellshocked animals still hung about the parade-ground, trapped by the encircling batteries booming in the distance. On the night of June 8 Captain Jenkins's pickets shot one of these bewildered beasts and dragged it into the unfinished barrack. They cooked "non-descript pieces" of it in a fire and reserved "the head, and some mysteries of the body" for a soup.[299] Though "it was nothing against the multitude," they stretched this grisly broth "as far as it would go."[300]

The next day the ever-solicitous Willie Halliday fetched a bowlfull for Emma and set off for the tile-roofed barrack to deliver it to her. Rushing to and fro to deploy pickets and redistribute ammunition, Willie had already distinguished himself in the Entrenchment's defense; survivors would later call him, with Ashe and Moore, one of the three "heroes of the wonderful siege."[301] But it is difficult to imagine Emma Halliday's condition as she grieved for her daughter beneath the listless punkahs in the smoking, shuddering, crumbling barracks, for she was already suffering the first symptoms—fever, backache—of the smallpox that would eventually carry her away.

Nor is it possible to gauge Willie's regrets as he scuttled across the yard. Why hadn't he sent his wife and child home when he had promised? Why hadn't he sent them to Allahabad when he still had the chance? Why, he may even have asked himself, had he let Emma talk him out of life insurance? Crouching low and moving out slowly so as not to slop his bowl of horse broth, Willie was making his way from the Main Guard to the tile-roofed barrack when a round shot found him, and Captain William Leonard Halliday exploded in a spray of blood and dust.[302]

✦ ✦ ✦

The garrison's gunners could do little to answer the rebel batteries. Their guns were too exposed, and Nana kept his batteries well concealed beyond the range of the Entrenchment's lighter pieces. All the gunners could do was stand by with their torches lit and their guns loaded with cannister in case of a rebel charge. Major George Larkins made the rounds of his batteries in the burning glare, hunkering down with his crews behind sandbags and parapets, bracing for the insurgents' fire, overseeing the repairs to the cannon that were knocked from their carriages by rebel shot. But he was soon done in by the suffocating heat and on June 9 collapsed shivering and vomiting in an apoplectic delirium.[303] "Dearest George . . . is, I grieve to say, obliged to abandon his post," Mrs. Larkins wrote in the last letter her servants would spirit out of the Entrenchment. "This is to me a grief." And now as there was "no hope of escape," she bade goodbye to her oldest children, whom she had sent back to England.[304]

After the first days of the siege, many of the most frail and frantic of the women and children had died of shock and exhaustion; many others had learned to suffer the barrage in silence "except when groaning from the horrible mutilations they had to endure."[305] By June 9 the shells had nearly decimated the arcades of the tile-roofed barrack and chewed at the doors and windows of the inner verandahs. Now the bullets and cannonballs roamed freely through the barracks' interiors, ripping through the sheets and screens women hung about for privacy, tearing away the punkahs, shattering the thin partitions and sending splinters flying. Women pressed themselves into corners, coughing through their prayers and trying not to stifle their small children in the shelter of their skirts.[306]

✦   ✦   ✦

In the Foot Artillery Hospital five hundred yards to the southeast, the fifty-two loyal sepoys had held out as best they could, exchanging fire with the snipers at St. John's and ducking the shot and shell that came whirring and shrieking into their little compound.[307] But their position was indefensible, and about four o'clock in the afternoon of June 9 a rebel cannon managed to fire an incendiary shell onto the thatched roof of the barrack.

As fire roiled through the compound, Subhedar Ram Buksh and a few sepoys raced the five hundred yards to the Entrenchment to beg permission to join the garrison, but Wheeler was adamant that no more native soldiers were to be allowed inside.[308] All Hillersdon could do was hand Ram Buksh a few rupees and a certificate attesting to his sepoys' loyalty, and urge them to look to their own safety.[309]

At six o'clock the sepoys fled the smoke and flames of their compound, and as they tumbled into a nearby ravine to hide until nightfall, one of them was wounded by musket fire.[310] These loyal sepoys, recalled Bhola Khan, "often said, 'Should the whole army mutiny, we never shall.' " And they evidently never did. Some were captured by rebel sowars;[311] some, stripped of their muskets by roving bands of peasants, managed to return to their villages; at least one headed east to join the British forces massing at Allahabad.[312] Incredibly, Ram Buksh tried to carry the regimental records to safety in a cart, but lost them to a band of peasants.

The sight of the barrack going up in flames was so fearsome that a Eurasian cornet player named Thomas Massey fled the Entrenchment that night and ran off into the countryside.[313] Others soon followed. A Christian drummer named Mendes disguised himself as a Moslem and managed to hide in a mendicant's garden on the banks of the Ganges.[314] And on the night of June 10, "seized with the insane hope that they would fare better if they left the entrenchment," an apothecary named Peters and a cattle sergeant named Ryan led a small party of women and children out over the parapets.[315] "Disguising themselves as *ayahs* and *bheesties* [water carriers], they were led out, while a volley of blank cartridges were fired on them to maintain the deception that they were natives,"[316] and they somehow managed to find a hiding place in a nearby village.[317]

✦ ✦ ✦

All night long "the ping-ping of rifle bullets" along the trenches "would break short dreams of home or of approaching relief, pleasant visions made horrible by waking to the state of things around."[318]

Spread out every forty feet or so along the Entrenchment's perimeter, crouched behind parapets a cow could have jumped, the garrison's pickets waited and waited for the rebels to charge. Surely they could see how vulnerable the garrison was. The continuous cannonade must have been intended to soften it up for a frontal assault. Through their field glasses the officers could see thousands of sepoys and matchlockmen swarming about, taking up positions in the burned-out chapel to the east, in the deep drainage ditch to the north, along the shaded course to the west. But hour after hour passed, and no attack materialized.

Then, in the early morning of June 10 as if to shame his fellow rebels into charging, a turbaned horseman began to gallop toward the Entrenchment. Squinting blearily into the dim light, the garrison's pickets raised their muskets and took aim at this distant, headlong apparition as it raced toward them from between the rebels' batteries. Several pickets fired, and the horse was seen to stagger slightly. But the rider kept spurring it forward, and suddenly someone was shouting at them to hold their fire.

The wounded horse pounded up to the parapet and with a groan lunged into the compound, carrying its "most distressed and exhausted" rider into the astonished garrison's midst. He was no sowar but Lieutenant Boulton, "to whom," wrote Thomson, "even our desperate fortunes presented an asylum."[319] His "turban" was a bloody rag, and despite the wound in his cheeks that had shattered his teeth, this sole survivor of Major Marriott's aimless detachment had somehow managed to creep through Nawabgunj and past the rebel batteries.[320] No sooner had the resilient lieutenant recovered a little of his strength than he joined the pickets in the fourth unfinished barrack.

✦ ✦ ✦

By June 10 Nunne Nawab's battery had cut the garrison off from a nearby tank,[321] and nearly all of the native water carriers had either died or fled, leaving families to fetch water for themselves from the one Entrenchment well.[322] Wheeler had surrounded the well with a parapet, but it was soon demolished by round shot, and the well remained the focus of rebel fire; even at night the creaking of tackle, like the pickets' "all's well," never failed to draw a hail of grape. But after the initial bombardment had eased off somewhat on June 9, the rebels stopped firing at candlelight and strolled back to their lines for a couple of hours' supper. During the lull people rushed out of the barracks to draw water up from sixty feet below.[323]

By now even the tackle had been shot to pieces, and men had to pull buckets up hand over hand, "and the labour . . . became much more prolonged and perilous. . . . Not even a pint of water was to be had for washing from the commencement to the close of the siege; and those only who have lived in India can imagine the calamity of such a privation to delicate women who had been accustomed to the most frequent and copious ablutions as a necessary of existence.

"The sufferings of the women and children from thirst were intense," wrote Thomson, "and the men could scarcely endure the cries for drink which were almost perpetual from the poor little babes, terribly unconscious they were, most of them, of the great, great cost at which only it could be procured." Children sucked on fragments of waterbags and leather straps "to try and get a single drop of moisture upon their parched lips."[324]

Drawing water "was always performed by volunteers," Thomson remembered, "and some of our privates of the European regiments made a trade of it, charging so much per bucket."[325] According to Jonah, when the soldiers' water jars ran out, some charged as much as ten shillings per bucket.[326] "To their credit it must be said," Thomson added later, "that when money had lost its value, by reason of the extremity of our danger, they were not less willing to incur the risk of drawing for the women and the children." But that was not Jonah's experience. Recuperating from his wound, he found that his most precious possession was proving to be the water jug he had brought from his house. But whenever his brother or his children's ayah ventured out to fill it they had to brave not only rebel fire but European soldiers who tried to wrest the jug from them for their own use.[327]

Joint Magistrate John Robert MacKillop was of a different breed.[328] Declaring himself a hopeless shot, this erudite thirty-one-year-old bachelor left his post in the trenches for the infinitely more hazardous job of fetching water for the women and children, cheerfully drawing bucketsful up from below and toting them to the barracks as the shells exploded around him and snipers' bullets flicked at the dust at his feet, chipped at the well's brick walls, and ricocheted eerily into its dark depths. The work was exhausting, and MacKillop asked Jonah if he might assist him. When Jonah declined on account of his back, he was "sorry to see [MacKillop's] disappointment."[329] One day, as MacKillop was rushing back from the well with his sloshing buckets, a shell exploded, and he clattered to the ground, clutching at his groin. Littered back into the barracks, the uncomplaining joint magistrate would survive the siege in agony.[330]

FUGITIVES

Fatehgarh: May 13–June 12, 1857

At the backwater station of Fatehgarh sixty miles upriver from Cawnpore, a regiment could pass months, even years, without seeing any more honorable service than a desultory expedition against a band of outlaws. An officer's chief duty might involve taking inventory in the timber yard or overseeing the manufacture of wheel spokes and trousers. So it was perhaps inevitable that in the spring of 1857 the garrison should have been commanded by so fatuous a mediocrity as Lieutenant Colonel George Acklom Smith.

By the time he took command of the 10th Native Infantry at Fatehgarh, Smith was sixty years old and his last battle was thirty-eight years behind him. Having spent most of his career with the 47th Native Infantry, he was an unknown quantity to the sepoys of the 10th and could do little to soothe their wounded pride after their unrewarded service in Burma. It is hard to tell whether he failed to keep his subordinates fully informed out of a lack of confidence in himself or in his subordinates. His officers were "conspicuous for their nullity." His second-in-command was fifty-one-year-old Captain Robert Munro who had somehow managed to serve in India for thirty years without ever fighting a battle, and his junior officers were bickering, undisciplined, and evidently none too bright.

Neither of the two most able officers at Fatehgarh in May 1857 had actually been posted there. The stentorian sixty-five-year-old Colonel Andrew Goldie, the military auditor general, was pausing at Fatehgarh with his three daughters, probably on a tour of inspection.

Reverend John Freeman

Elizabeth Freeman

Reverend A. V. Johnson

Despite his years, he would prove a resourceful and vigorous addition to Smith's little garrison. The second able officer was "the inevitable and invaluable" Captain Edmund Vibart of the 2nd Native Cavalry,[331] who had paused at Fatehgarh en route from Cawnpore to Naini Tal.[332] Teddy was a nephew of Major Edward Vibart of his regiment, and a great favorite of his toddler cousins, whom he sketched.[333] He certainly would have been familiar with Fatehgarh, and may even have formed a romantic attachment there, for the 2nd had been based at the station for almost twenty years, and as his boyhood verses show, he had a passionate disposition.[334] Despite his receding hairline and rather wispy mutton chops, there was a formidable resolve in his pale eyes and prominent jaw, and he stood head and shoulders above the bilious mediocrities of Smith's little backwater staff.[335]

✦ ✦ ✦

No station seemed more vulnerable to attack. The ratio of European to native troops at Meerut had been one in six, at Cawnpore one in fourteen; at Fatehgarh there were no European troops at all. Colonel Smith could be certain of the loyalty of only 150 sepoys, most of them Sikhs, and it seemed to many Fatehgarh residents that the rebels' "exterminating propensity might be indulged in to a great extent" at Fatehgarh, "and almost with impunity."[336]

"The panic was very great," wrote Mrs. Monckton, whose husband suspended work on the Grand Trunk Road and returned to his house to read Scripture with his wife. Carriages and buggies crowded Smith's and Probyn's driveways and "guns were entering into the Colonel's compound, and the whole place seemed in a commotion."[337] Mrs. Freeman of the American mission drove into the cantonment to find "all the ladies in tears, and their husbands pale and trembling."[338] The station was instructed to listen for the colonel's post gun: the signal for the European residents to take refuge in Smith's vast bungalow. But as Smith conferred with various delegations of residents, his emergency protocol seemed to change from hour to hour: people were to flee to the colonel's; no, to the fort; no, not to the fort—to the ghats.

Many Europeans now found a special solace in Scripture.[339] "The Lord reigns!" Mrs. Monckton wrote. "He sitteth above the waterflood. We are in the hollows of His hand, and nothing can harm us."[340] Nevertheless on Sunday the seventeenth, when Chaplain

Frederick Fisher stood up to deliver his sermon—"What time I am afraid, I will trust in Thee"[341]—"very few people were there," grieved Mrs. Monckton, "and fear seemed written on every face—it was most noticeable . . . Every countenance was pale."[342]

That afternoon Reverends Freeman and Campbell left their refuge in the civil lines and visited their mission church at Barhpur. They could offer their Indian congregation little comfort. Many of them had been converts from Islam, and "whenever they have gone to the city for the last two or three weeks," wrote Mrs. Freeman, "they have been treated with taunting and insolence."

"Where is your Jesus now?" people asked them. "We will shortly shew what will become of the infidel dogs."[343]

"In the service," recalled the Indian preacher Isuri Dass, "one or two of us native Christians were called upon to pray,"[344] and then the handsome, square-jawed John Freeman addressed them directly.[345]

"I feel that I am addressing you for the last time," he told them. "By fleeing to distant villages, you may escape; but I do not think that there is any hope for us. But whether we survive or perish, and whether the English rule remains or not, I know that the Church in India will remain, and that the gates of hell shall not prevail against it." Laying his hand on their heads, Freeman exhorted them all to be "steadfast, immovable, and to choose death rather than to deny their Saviour,"[346] after which the missionaries returned to their refuge, leaving the native Christians to "bury any money and jewels that we had" and find whatever sanctuary they could.[347]

For a while the missionaries thought of borrowing "some of the native Christians' clothes to slip on at a moment's warning," wrote Freeman, "and make our way to some of the friendly villages; for to attempt a defence against five or six hundred infuriated natives would be worse than useless."[348] Then they considered fleeing to Agra, and even arranged a down-country relay for themselves. But someone—perhaps John Monckton, who would have received reports of the perils on the Grand Trunk Road—talked them out of it.[349]

Rosa Monckton valiantly refused to flee without her husband, but the tension wore down many of the ladies of the station.[350] When a "thoughtless person" told a surgeon's expectant wife "that we were all going to be massacred, & that the mutineers were marching down on Futtehghur—She was very poorly indeed from the shock received, & if we continue to receive unfavorable intelligence may again be prematurely confined."[351] Magistrate Thornhill's plump and pretty wife Mary spent hours anxiously fashioning Indian disguises for herself and her two children, huddling with them in one of Dhuleep Singh's palatial houses.[352] As reports kept flickering in that mutineers, armed peasants, marauding herdsmen, banditti, and assorted rebels were about to descend on the station,[353] there was a constant rush back and forth between the cantonment and the fleet of boats the merchants now kept in readiness at the city ghat.[354]

✦ ✦ ✦

Like the sepoy guard at Cawnpore, the soldiers of the 10th refused to allow Probyn to remove the treasury from his vaults,[355] but Smith would not press the issue and insisted that they were acting not out of disaffection but soldierly pride.[356] He was determined to avoid doing anything that might betray a loss of confidence in his sepoys or further insult their dignity. But the vital thing was to keep them away from the disaffected troops of other regiments,[357] because for some weeks Smith's native informants had been warning him that the disaffected elements in the 10th intended to mutiny "as soon as another corps arrived."[358]

Now it seemed that everyone—Wheeler, Lawrence, even the authorities at Agra—was insisting on sending bodies of irregulars to Fatehgarh's relief. To Smith's relief, they never reached him. On May 29, despite Probyn's protests, the Commissioner of an extinct division of Oudh called Khyrabad had proposed sending him two companies of Wheeler's old regiment, the 48th Native Infantry, under the figurehead command of Major Marriott. Such was the Commissioner's confidence in the major that he had accepted Marriott's services only on condition that he not direct the line of march himself. So it was left to his disputatious junior officers, particularly a Lieutenant Hutchinson, to lead the column southwest to Fatehgarh.

Two troops of the 7th Bengal Cavalry and an escort of about twenty Sikhs completed the force, under a European staff of seven. The column's purpose was rather ambiguous, and "there is room for suspicion that the authorities wanted to place the troops where they could do no damage." In any case, they proceeded toward Fatehgarh in leisurely ten-mile stages, until the second of June, when they would reach a muddy backwater called Mallawan. As they passed through the station, Hutchinson did not like the way his men kept eyeing the treasury, and so he marched them some distance beyond the station to camp on the northeastern bank of the Ganges. By now Hutchinson and Marriott knew about the émeute at Lucknow, but the other officers believed their men would never mutiny, even as the troops balked and whispered and gazed back wistfully at Mallawan's unprotected riches.

After a supply run into town, Hutchinson and a fellow officer returned to find the troopers encamped on the opposite side of the river. One of the Sikh sowars now hurried up to warn Hutchinson that the troops had resolved to murder their officers, and Hutchinson sent the Sikh back to the camp to warn the others. But only Major Marriott and an assistant surgeon agreed to desert the column. The rest remained with their men, and the expedition, short its senior officer, gratuitously pressed on.[359]

❖ ❖ ❖

Just as Smith and Probyn had feared, the approach of Marriott's detachment (and Hayes' and Carey's ill-fated company) threw the sepoys of the 10th into turmoil. Convinced that like their comrades at Barrackpore and Meerut they were about to be disarmed, disgraced, and imprisoned, they assembled on the cloudy, still, and sweltering night of June 1 with their muskets loaded.

The garrison had just learned of the May 31 uprising at Shahjahanpur thirty-five miles to the north.[360] Bands of released convicts from Shahjahanpur's jail could be seen skulking along the opposite side of the river, and a body of Oudh rebels crossed into the district to loot the outstations. Their audacious advance guard even trotted into Fatehgarh, where they were warmly welcomed by various sepoys of the 10th.

"After strenuous exertions," Colonel Smith managed to dissuade most of the men from fraternizing with the rebels and sent them back to their huts, and when the skies opened up the tension in the lines seemed to dissipate like the steam that rose from the griddle of the parade-ground. To prevent more Oudh rebels from entering the city, Smith ordered the Grand Trunk Road barricaded with overturned carts and wagons, and Probyn commanded his police to sever the Bridge of Boats as Smith and his officers went off to sleep in the regiment's lines.

But by now most of the European community had given up on the colonel's hollow reassurances and fickle contingencies.[361] "Bad news," wrote Reverend Johnson to his family in America, "all is getting worse. The insurgents have arisen all around us, and we are trying to get a boat in which to escape. . . . Perhaps you may never hear from me again."[362] "The Europeans are in a state of the greatest panic," wrote Thomas Heathcote. "I never saw such fear in my life so exhibited. In spite of my greatest efforts—nay trust in God—my earnest prayers—it is with the greatest difficulty that I can retain my composure & presence of mind."[363] Even the Moncktons had begun to waver.[364] The road to Agra was closed, and the night was punctuated by the firing of matchlocks in the bazaars, where villagers and hooligans celebrated the Company's imminent fall.[365] Most of the merchants and their families spent the night on the boats that Probyn had collected for them along the Hospital Ghats, and it seemed to many of them that their last hope was the river, rising now beneath them through a night of heavy rain.

✦ ✦ ✦

On the evening of June 3, just before the uprising at Cawnpore, a rumor circulated through Fatehgarh that rebel cavalry were descending on the city. Colonel Smith instructed the Europeans to contain their panic and commanded his officers to remain with their families at their posts. But the civilians were fed up with Smith's complacency and the next morning hurried to the boats moored at Hospital Ghat.[366]

The American missionaries made one last visit to their establishment at Rakha to collect their effects and bid their native charges good-bye, leading their converts, including a number of blind orphaned girls, in prayer.[367]

"We have no place to flee," wrote Elizabeth Freeman, "but under the cover of his wings."[368]

"I am busy packing up a change of clothes for my husband, my children, and myself," the sickly Maria Campbell scrawled to a missionary's wife in another station. "We have determined to try to escape in the direction of Cawnpore, but I have only a faint hope that we shall succeed. And now, dear sister, farewell! If we should not meet again on earth, may we meet in heaven."[369]

Her husband David tried to persuade his fellow missionaries that they were duty-bound to remain with their converts, "whatever might be the consequence." But the others recognized that "so far from being able to assist their native brethren, should they remain with them, it would only render the destruction the more certain."[370]

"A few minutes before the missionary families left the premises," wrote Isuri Dass, Campbell's native preacher, "I had an interview with Messrs Freeman and Campbell.

Mr Campbell would have rather laid down his life on the spot. He did not seem much inclined to leave the place, and asked me whether they did right in going away.

I replied, it was their duty to do all they could for their safety.

He said there was merely a bare chance of escape, as the whole [riverbank] was lined with rebellious zemindars.[371]

When he was taking his leave, I reminded him that the Lord reigneth.

'That is very true,' he replied; 'but blood may be shed.'

I said '. . . The pain would be only for a few minutes.'

'For [my] part,' he said, 'I am ready to be cut to pieces, '[but] he was very anxious on account of Mrs Campbell who was always of delicate health, and at that time more so; and then he had two little children with him.

"Mr Freeman," recalled Dass, "had his eyes full of tears when we parted."[372]

✦ ✦ ✦

At the ghats Collector Probyn escorted his family to the lead boat with the Thornhills and the Joneses, while the Lowises piled into a second boat with their children and an ayah. Other boats dipped and rocked under the weight of twenty-four different families. The American missionaries with their children and three converts boarded a boat owned by a prosperous merchant named Maclean. The largest boat in the fleet was commanded by another merchant named Richard Brierly whom everyone knew as "Dick Sahib." A tireless entrepreneur, he brought along a cargo of wine he hoped to peddle to the Cawnpore garrison. Scattered among them all were ayahs, sweepers, and manservants, and in three boats servants and armed native guards sought roosts amid their masters' belongings and provisions.

By ten o'clock that morning some 157 souls were ready to set forth, including Collector Probyn's family, but as Probyn climbed back up the ghat to his office, the fugitives declared that they would not leave without him, and sent him a note pleading with him to join them in their voyage down the Ganges. He was the chief civil officer, and most of the civil population was fleeing; his place was with them. Probyn refused at first, but, convinced at last that his refusal was placing the entire party in jeopardy, he left a letter for Colonel Smith and returned to the Hospital Ghat. At one o'clock in the afternoon, the civilians finally pushed off into the sun-slapped, shallow stream of the summer Ganges.[373]

The fugitives' boats were mostly flat-bottomed grain barges with either deck cabins or areas shaded by roofs of planks and thatch. They made good time in a stream swollen slightly by the unseasonable shower, and at dawn on June 4 docked twelve miles downriver on the Oudh side of the Ganges. The servants had just disembarked to prepare breakfast when four officers of the 10th infantry appeared upstream, wheeling crazily toward them in a large, unnavigable boat. Their news was grim. When the 10th Native Infantry learned of the civilians' exodus they declared that their faces had been blackened, and at morning parade, as several officers and loyal troops were trying to transport the contents of the treasury to the fort, a sepoy had stepped out of ranks to hurl abuse at Colonel Smith, while another aimed his pistol at his head.

Smith had wheeled around and galloped to the fort with Ensign Henderson in tow as hundreds of sepoys swarmed across the parade ground, firing their muskets. Encountering a body of sepoys blocking the treasure at the gate, Smith and Henderson dismounted, and Smith began haranguing his men, ordering them to disperse. But they closed around him instead with their bayonets fixed, and backed him against a wall as the treasure was diverted to the parade-ground. The sepoys demanded two months' pay and six months' extra allowance while they were at it.

During the melee five officers found themselves cut off from the fort by the frenzied mob. One of them managed to commandeer a small boat and sail it to the fort, while the other four—including Reggie Byrne, whose wife Bonnie had found asylum in the zenana of the Nawab of Farrukhabad—had jumped into the clumsy barge and careened helplessly down the Ganges, in whose current they had now miraculously caught up with the fugitives' flotilla.

The officers climbed aboard the civilians' boats, and after sitting through the heat of the day they all pushed out into the stream again, peering into the gloaming as the river shredded into rows of narrow channels. After fourteen miles they reached the steep cliffs of Kusamkhor, home to a nasty aggregation of plundering Rajput converts to Islam who, in the best of times, were notorious for looting their neighbors. The fugitives' morning pause had given time for word of their approach to reach the inhabitants of Kusamkhor, who now lined the cliffs with matchlocks and blunderbusses mounted on pivots. As Dick Sahib, confounded by the dark, ground his great boat into a sand bank, they now gleefully opened fire, their matchlocks flashing with extravagant bursts of gunpowder in the gloom along the cliffs.

As the rest of the flotilla sailed ahead, the native guard splashed out of their boat to heave Brierly's barge into the stream. The firing from the cliffs was unceasing, but the night was so dark that only two men were wounded: a matchlock ball grazed the thigh of one of the Low boys, and Richard Brierly himself received a wound to his ribs.[374]

◆　◆　◆

At nine in the morning of June 5, after Brierly's barge caught up with the rest of the party, they docked at Meora Ghat, where they met another of Brierly's trading boats pushing its way upstream from Calcutta with a cargo of wine. Hailing his agent aboard, Brierly grudgingly abandoned his wine cargo by the ghat and the fleet pushed on in the midday heat. Some distance past the junction with the Ramganga, a man on the riverbank reported that a party of Oudh insurgents were crossing the river a few miles below. The flotilla anchored for a moment in the stream and sent a servant off to corroborate the story.[375] The servant returned to report that the story was false, but by now the leading men of the fleet were debating whether to accept an offer of refuge from Hardeo Baksh Singh, the proprietor of Dharampur. Some were for it, but many others protested that the larger boats could not be moved up the Ramganga, and men familiar with the area maintained that even if Hardeo Baksh could be trusted, there was not enough room in the Dharampur fort for the entire party.

So the fleet now divided itself into two parts: one bound for Dharampur under Mr. Probyn and Colonel Tucker, the other for Cawnpore under Mr. Brierly. Some believed that the Dharampur party stood the better chance, but only if their boat was not overcrowded. So a number of families decided to leave their youngest in Probyn's care, reserving the greatest risk for themselves: a Miss Sturt, for instance, was induced by her mother to join the Dharampur party while Mrs. Sturt pressed on to Cawnpore. All along the riverbank families bade farewell to their loved ones.

The Dharampur party numbered twenty-eight, of whom nineteen were children, and joined Probyn in the lightest boat that could accommodate them. They now had to work their way a mile back up the Ganges and twenty tortuous miles up the Ramganga, which was at that time of year a shallow maze of channels and sandbars. As their boat labored upriver in the fading light, the others waved a last farewell.

The Cawnpore-bound party remained docked at Meora Ghat and spent the night of the fifth and most of the sixth reorganizing itself. They decided to shed most of their cargo and consolidate themselves into six of the twelve remaining boats. But as they transferred their most precious possessions and left the rest scattered along the river's edge, Mrs. Sturt decided she had made a mistake allowing her daughter to proceed to Dharampur without her. And so, at the age of forty-nine, and over her companions' protests, she set forth alone and on foot in the broiling heat of the late morning, striding northwestward to catch up to Probyn's boat.[376]

Dick Sahib now led the way in his large boat with sixty-seven passengers, half of them children, and five smaller vessels jammed with women, children, servants, and various possessions the party could not—would not—leave behind. But their long halts had given time for word of their approach to precede them. Seven miles downriver,[377] as their boats bumbled along a shallow, narrow channel between a vast sandbar and the bank of the river, they were met by the inhabitants of the temporary and anarchic settlement of Beloi, who splashed out into the shallows with drums and muskets. Hundreds of them surrounded the boats, shouting and firing into the air.

Brierly kept his head and tied the boats together by the shore. The other families moved onto his barge, and there they all huddled through the steaming, cacophonous night. No villagers dared attempt to board the boats, but they kept up their terrifying din until morning, when Brierly sent a servant out to learn the intentions of the local landholders. A few hours later a pair of landlords arrived from an inland village to demand payment of two thousand rupees in exchange for safe escort to Cawnpore.[378]

The negotiations dragged on all day, but eventually Briefly saw there was no help for it and collected half the sum from his companions, promising the landlords the other half upon their safe arrival in Cawnpore. The landlords assigned five villagers to act as escorts, but eventually four of them jumped overboard and swam ashore.[379] Villagers plundered one boat,[380] damaging it so badly that when the little fleet departed on the morning of the eighth, Brierly had to leave it behind.[381]

Miles upriver, Probyn and his party were still toiling up toward Dharampur when they heard someone call out to them from the shore. There, waving from across the channel, stood the redoubtable Mrs. Sturt, who had managed to catch up to Probyn's flotilla and now climbed aboard to greet her daughter matter-of-factly as if returning from an evening stroll.

✦   ✦   ✦

Back in Fatehgarh "the sun arose upon an almost deserted station." The fugitive officers were "struck off the strength of the regiment"[382] and the civilians deplored for abandoning their offices, including the jail, the post office, Dhuleep Singh's estate, and the clothing agency where Colonel Tucker had abandoned "cloth enough to clothe the city of Furruckabad."

Colonel Smith had feebly but perhaps wisely agreed to leave the treasure in his sepoys' keeping, assuring his subordinates that they had not seized it so much as taken it under their protective wing. The troops appeared satisfied and melted away, leaving two guns and a guard to watch over the treasury. The native officers were appalled by Smith's capitulation, and that evening the colonel had tried to save face by ordering his contemptuous troops out on parade again, blaming the afternoon's outburst on a few new recruits among the 10th, whom he now fatuously forgave, declaring that from that day forward he knew that all of his "children" would be staunch.

During the next two days nothing had been "burnt, stolen or destroyed," nevertheless the native merchants of Farruckhabad considered European rule to be at an end, and turned to the Nawab for protection.[383] The Nawab issued a proclamation "that the peaceably disposed persons need be under no fear, that the Europeans would return the next day and that all wicked people attempting to make a disturbance would be apprehended and severely punished and that this was the order of the English Government and the proclamation made by their orders." But the merchants insisted that the hooligans "would not listen to the proclamation as it purported to emanate from the Europeans who they said had fled" and so the Nawab issued a second version "to the same effect and purport, only stating that it was by the orders of the Nawab."[384]

Evidently this quieted the city somewhat, and "the few ladies left drove out in the afternoon to show that they had not deserted the station."[385] But out in the district, police stations came under attack by *dacoits* (bandits), peasants, and bands of insurgents who worked the Grand Trunk Road. "Nothing," wrote Isuri Dass, "was heard during the night but the noise of fire-arms, insomuch that the very jackals ceased barking through fear." To protect the mission and its tent factory, the native Christians obtained swords and firearms, "and all the men were obliged to keep up the whole night, and though very few in number, compared with the adverse population of the surrounding country, and the extent of the premises to be guarded, were indeed successful in keeping them at bay."[386]

✦ ✦ ✦

Outraged by what he considered Probyn's desertion of his post, Smith appointed Captain Vibart to serve in his stead, and now Teddy sat at the Collector's desk issuing orders, signing papers, acquainting himself with Probyn's native assistants, including a writer named Karam Hussain, who absconded on a mission to hire two hundred irregulars. On the morning of June 7, Vibart was informed of a disturbance at the jail a mile outside of town. All 625 convicts had risen and overpowered the superintendent. Now, under the benign gaze of an inert sepoy guard from the 10th, they were busily digging their way out through a prison wall.

The Company's jails had always been hotbeds of rebellion. Sustaining an Indian prison population was an administrative nightmare, and over the past ten years North India had seen a plague of prison riots.[387] Whether or not the general Hindu population had any sympathy for prisoners as such, they were horrified by what they perceived to be British attempts to contaminate their caste, and for this reason prison riots often drew huge crowds of ordinary townspeople into the fray.[388] So Teddy Vibart buckled on his sabre and galloped off, hoping to quell the riot in the Fatehgarh jail before the prisoners could spread the contagion of rebellion to the already jittery town.

The jail itself was divided into eight wards, each designed to hold about sixty convicts, but many more than that had been jammed in.[389] The leader of the prisoners was a hooligan named Burriar Singh whom Probyn had imprisoned for a long list of crimes that included murder. Teddy, with his usual audacity, marched in with the ruffled superintendent to confront the convicts and order them back to their wards. But they were unimpressed by the thirty-two-year-old cavalry officer with his hazy whiskers and drove him back in a hail of stones. One bold prisoner even hurled a brick at him from close range and struck Vibart under the left eye, causing a severe contusion. His face streaming with blood, Vibart drew his sword and pistol and staggered back into the sunlight, ordering the sepoy guard to return with him into the maelstrom.

Teddy's bloody rage was so formidable that the sepoys obeyed him, and on his command opened fire on the convicts, killing sixteen and chasing the rest back into their cells.[390] Vibart had Burriar Singh dragged out into the yard, and, nursing his eye, ordered him executed on the spot. Leaving Singh's crumpled corpse in the yard, Vibart oversaw repairs to the prison wall, assigned a new guard, and led the sepoys back to town.

Smith's response was to line his troops up again and treat them to more of his histrionics, bawling them out for not quelling the riot on their own, and demanding that they all swear their allegiance to the Company on Ganges water and the Koran, and really mean it this time.[391]

✦   ✦   ✦

On the morning of the eighth of June, Probyn's party hauled themselves up to the fort at Dharampur. But to call it a fort, even in the subcontinental sense of the word, was an overstatement, for it merely consisted of a mud-walled pen containing a few sheds and shade trees. While settling his family into this dubious refuge, Probyn learned for the first time that contrary to what the officers had told him, Fatehgarh had not fallen to the rebels. Shame-faced, he commandeered a trio of horses from his host and with Lieutenant Fitzgerald and Ensign Byrne galloped the nine miles back to Fatehgarh to resume his duties.

Colonel Smith was not welcoming. He promptly placed the two officers under arrest for desertion and curtly informed Probyn that after he had "deserted his post and left 2½ acs [two hundred fifty thousand rupees] of treasure and 1,000 prisoners to our mutinous sepoys" he could not "receive his charge until reappointed by the Lieutenant-Governor."[392] Probyn endured this disgrace for two days but finally returned to his family at Dharampur, where they were joined by the family of his friend William Edwards, the prescient Collector of nearby Budaon.[393]

Once Dick Sahib's party cleared Beloi the day had passed uneventfully, and the bleary fugitives settled on the tilting deck, huddled against the hot wind, thanking God for their deliverance as they drifted southwestward through the night.[394] But at sunrise on June 9, as Dick Sahib's party cautiously floated up to Bithur, muskets opened up on them from the riverbank. Ordering the women and children below decks, several men in the party fired back. Perhaps three of their shots struck home as they finally drifted out of musket range.

At eight o'clock that night Brierly's overloaded barge ran aground again, this time on an island from which they could now see the smoke rising from their fancied refuge, and hear the guns thundering in the cantonments.[395] Brierly ordered the men to draw the four boats as far into the island's brush and tamarisk grass as they could haul them. Now everyone boarded Brierly's boat, and he sent a watchman and two servants into the city, the first with a letter for Wheeler, the others to gather information about the rebels' disposition.[396] The servants returned to report that the roads were closed and the garrison under siege. On the Oudh side opposite their position the refugees could see men darting about, but they did not attempt to push off, and waited for the watchman to return with help from Wheeler's garrison, not knowing that before he could reach the Entrenchment he had been captured by Nana's men.

Through the day and night of June 10, Brierly's party remained hunkered down on the pestilential island of Ganga Rui Katri, listening to the thump and whistle of Nana's artillery.[397] When the boatman did not return, Brierly sent another message, this time to Nana himself, but again received no reply. The rebels on the Oudh side of the river began taunting the boatmen, ordering them to bring the vessel around. But they refused, pleading that the boats were overloaded with seven hundred Europeans.[398] The mob grew into a swarm, but their shouts died off as darkness descended.

A harsh wind kicked up during the night, and was still blowing on the morning of the eleventh as Brierly and his party anxiously nursed their tea. For a day and a night they had watched antic figures flit obscurely along the shore, pointing, staring, as the fugitives huddled together in Brierly's barge. In the dark they had heard noises from across the water—an occasional shout, the stray firing of a musket, the creaking of wheels—faint against the muffled pounding of the distant siege. Perhaps Wheeler was on his way, or the rebels were too tied up in the cantonment to bother with a stranded ragtag boatload of civilians.

At about five thirty in the morning two cannons fired from upriver on the Oudh side of the Ganges and heaved two balls into Brierly's hull. Before the refugees could jump from the smoking, crumpled barge, a third shot turned the cabin roof to splinters, scattering the party's weapons into the river and crushing to death a Mrs. Ives, a child, and an ayah. The refugees leaped out and struggled ashore through the tepid, muddy shallows. A few of the men managed to retrieve a shotgun or a rifle as their wives frantically dragged their shrieking children into the grass, seeking whatever declivity they could find.

Swayed at last by the rebels' taunts and fortified by the cache of wine they had discovered in the night, Brierly's boatmen now turned coat, setting fire to the boats' thatch and charging around the island, clubbing several of the refugees to death and plundering their corpses. A few shots from the party scattered the boatmen, but the rebels only multiplied across the water, cheering as each round of cannon fire raised another spout of sand.

The fugitives could not last long under the broiling sun and ran for the shade of a sparse grove of sisal trees at the southern end of the island, where they stumbled upon a well. But the local landlord would not allow them to use it, and two of the native Christians set off to fetch water from the river. As the fugitives gulped down the muddy water, Dick Sahib proposed they hold a council "to determine what they should do, as they knew that the sepoys would soon find the means of reaching the island."

"My dear friends," intoned Reverend Freeman, "it is my belief that this is our last day on earth. Let us, before doing anything else, prepare to die."[399] And so the fugitives circled around him as he read from his Bible and led them in prayer and then, amid the intermittent roaring from the rebel cannonade, they sang a hymn. Brother Campbell felt called upon to make a few additional remarks of his own and led everyone in another prayer. Then, as cannonballs continued to plunge into the sand around them, and the women and children scurried back to their hiding places in the grass, the gentlemen held a council.

Resistance was obviously useless and escape impossible. "Their only hope . . . was to cast themselves, an unarmed band, upon the mercy of the sepoys." So the few men who had managed to grab weapons now dashed them against the trees and hurled the pieces into the shallows. But either a boatman's torch or the sheer intensity of the cannonade finally set the grass afire, and in a few moments the strong hot wind sent it roiling across the island, smothering and burning to death two more women and a child.

With a yell, a body of sowars from the 2nd Cavalry raced across the shallows. The servants scattered, and all escaped but two ayahs and five sweepers.[400] A local landlord now took charge, and plundered the fugitives of their jewelry, pocket watches, hats, shoes, even their stockings. They apparently overlooked one survivor: a daughter of a merchant named Sutherland who had remained with the garrison at Fatehgarh. While fleeing the flames she had fallen into a deep hole, where, her ankle broken, she would lie in a stupor until morning, when a subhedar of the 2nd Cavalry chanced upon her while "searching the [sand bars] for money and valuables which the Europeans in their flight had flung away."[401] The subhedar took pity on her, and brought her into the city.[402]

As the rebels closed around the rest of the survivors, Maclean begged to know what the sowars intended to do with them.

"Take you to Nana Sahib," one of them answered.

Maclean asked them why, seeing as how "many of them were merchants, planters, teachers, and missionaries, who were not connected with Government in any way, and especially seeing that they were unarmed."

"This is true," one of the soldiers said. "We should not injure these people. They have never injured us, and are not in a position to do so now."

"No," replied the others. "Away with them to Nana Sahib."

Maclean now offered them three hundred thousand rupees if the soldiers would release them and conduct them in safety to Allahabad. But the sowars would have none of it.

"It is not money we want, but blood," said one. "We don't want the seed of the English to remain in the country."

Hearing this, the missionaries turned to the native Christians in the party and urged them to flee. "You can be of no further use to us now," they said, "and to remain with us would be but to expose yourselves to certain death. Return to Futtehghur, and tell our native brethren, that though we die, the Saviour lives. Commit yourselves, soul and body, to His keeping; and, whatever befalls you don't deny Him."[403] The native Christians turned and lost themselves in the crowd.

The rest of the party was herded together. "Our hands were tied behind our backs," recalled an ayah named Hingun, "and then attached to a long rope."[404] They were hustled onto the smallest of their boats and thereby transported off the smoldering island and across to the Cawnpore side of the Ganges, where "the men were all bound with ropes and marched like French Criminals in chain-gangs to Cawnpore" with the women and children "forced along at the point of the bayonet."[405] The inevitable crowd gathered around them as they stumbled up to the road and staggered in the scorching wind and blazing midday sun, two miles past Nawabganj to the Subhedar's Tank.

"It took us a long time to get there," Hingun remembered, "for the ladies and children were without shoes and stockings, and their feet were bleeding." As the refugees passed Nawabganj, one of the native Christians, watching now from a distance, heard one sahib call out a farewell before disappearing from view among the houses of the town.

At the Subhedar's Tank the mutineers ordered them to a halt and they collapsed on the simmering ground. "The hard-hearted sowars would only allow a handful of water to each European and refused to give them more," and there they remained, bound and scorched and sunstruck, many of them wounded and bleeding, through the suffocating night.[406]

✦   ✦   ✦

In the early morning of June 12, a train of sixteen bullock carts rumbled to the Subhedar's Tank, and after an anguished night of praying, grieving, tending to each other's injuries, and comforting the children who now comprised half their number, the Fatehgarh refugees were ordered to their feet.[407] A guard announced that Nana Sahib himself had summoned them to his headquarters, where their fates would be decided. And so they were pushed and prodded into the carts and pulled through the city streets and along the Grand Trunk Road, three and a half slow, creaking miles as a growing mob of onlookers gathered to see the forbidden, unimaginable sight of sahibs, memsahibs, and baba logue bound and captive.

The accounts the fugitives had heard of the uprisings at Meerut and Delhi—of women stripped and raped in the streets, of children tortured, of men hacked to pieces—dogged their dismal progress toward Nana's headquarters, and some onlookers along the way taunted and threatened them. But Brierly and his party must have tried to console themselves that this was merely the ranting of an idle rabble. If the rebels meant to kill them surely they would have done so by now. The Maharaja of Bithur, like their own Dhuleep Singh, had been a well-known friend of the British, and even if he were now a rebel why would he do them gratuitous harm? No doubt he intended merely to hold them captive, to prevent them from carrying intelligence to Allahabad. Certainly the carts were a good sign, a mercy after the forced march of the day before.

As the bullock train neared Savada House the rebel guns were booming amid the erratic clatter of the garrison's musket fire over a mile to the east. The sepoys herded the refugees inside and seated them on the floor of the large central room, where they remained all morning: relieved, at least, to be out from under the blistering sun, but parched, starved, and exhausted.[408]

At two o'clock Nana Sahib summoned them out onto the plain between Savada House and the racecourse, and so the guards goaded them back out into the sun, now at its height, and drove them into a ditch, seating them down in two lines: the men in the back, the women and children in front.[409]

Nana emerged from his tent and walked a few yards past Savada House to inspect his captives when one of the party, probably Dick Sahib or Maclean, called out from the ditch. He declared that it was folly for the rebels to think they could exterminate all of the Europeans in the country. Why not keep them in confinement? he asked Nana Sahib. No good would come of murdering them; England would never be emptied of Europeans.[410]

Nana Sahib listened in silence, turned and walked back to his tent to confer with his courtiers. He declared that he was disposed to spare his captives, but Bala Rao was adamant that they all must die, and Teeka Singh agreed.[411] By now his soldiers were losing their patience with Nana Sahib. That day an attack had been contemplated that Nana proposed to lead, but the rumor was that he had previously arranged for his courtiers and commanders to beg him publicly not to risk a life so precious to the rebellion, to which Nana, with a great show of reluctance, would finally agree.[412]

Whatever the truth of the story, the reduction of the Entrenchment was supposed to have been the work of a few hours. But the rebels had been pouring fire into it for almost a week, and still the garrison showed no signs of capitulating. Here Teeka Singh's men finally had a chance to kill the infidel English, and the Peshwa was balking. If Nana Sahib didn't order the refugees killed, the voluble brigadier declared, then he would give the order himself.[413]

It must have pained Azimullah to hear his prince wax so equivocal. Whether Nana's ambivalence was born of his reflexive hospitality or his Concanist preference always to keep his options open,

Azimullah must have recognized that the only way to sever irreparably Nana's ties with his former houseguests and billiard partners was to annihilate these contemptibly ragged captives.

In the end, Nana Sahib was probably not so much swayed as worn down by the arguments of his brother, his brigadier, and his chief minister. The siege was not going as well as he had hoped, and he could not afford to exasperate the mutineers any further. And so, affecting a regal indifference, he apparently allowed himself to be outvoted, washing his hands of the whole business. The debate lasted no longer than half an hour, and it was Bala Rao who emerged to give the order. Through all that followed, Nana Sahib remained in his tent, though Adla, his favorite concubine, watched the proceedings through a tent flap.[414]

As Bala Rao and his fellow courtiers rode out onto the plain, a sepoy dragged Hingun and the other surviving ayahs away from the children and out of the ditch, and held them back some thirty paces from the refugees. By now a dense crowd of hooligans, low-caste *jullads* and sowars of the 2nd and sepoys of the 1st and 56th Infantry had encircled the ditch.[415] Some of the children were crying out for water in the midday glare, but their pleas were met with "horrible taunts and abuses and revilings of the grossest kind."

Jostled and spat upon by the surrounding crowd, a few men of Brierly's party asked the mutineers to tell Nana Sahib who they were and kindly send him their salaams.[416] "The gentlemen remonstrated," Nanak Chand was later told, "and said they should not be put to death as they were ready to do any sort of work."[417]

Some three hundred soldiers, lured by the spectacle from the 2nd Native Cavalry's camp and the siege line, had by now pressed their way to the rim of the ditch.[418] Bala Rao perched himself nearby on a paved platform a quarter mile north of Savada House, as the rest of the mob was shooed back so that the sowars and sepoys could aim their muskets.[419]

Over the missionaries' prayers, the children's weeping, and the men's indignant shouts, "Bala called out aloud," a witness testified, "saying it was Nana's orders that the Europeans should all be massacred," and the soldiers opened fire.

Despite their numbers, it took the mutineers two volleys to still all but a few of the refugees in the ditch, into which the jullads and a small complement of sowars now skidded down with swords.[420] Some mothers and fathers must have succeeded in shielding their children from the mutineers' fire, for according to Hingun a few children were dragged shrieking from among their parents' corpses and "cut in half," the rebels' sabres and bayonets "dividing them at the legs into two parts."[421]

Thus by a little after four o'clock in the afternoon of June 12, all four American missionary families and their neighbors lay dead. Sweepers moved in to loot the bodies. Some were buried, but most were loaded onto "common country carts," and conveyed the next morning to the river, where, until the coming of the rains weeks afterward, their sun-blackened corpses—torn by dogs and vultures, cranes and crows—snagged in the shallows and dotted the banks and sandbars.[422]

WE ARE IN DEATH
Cawnpore: June 11–13, 1857

On the morning of June 11 the siege of the Entrenchment intensified. Six to seven hundred yards to the north and northeast two pairs of mortars sent shells howling and bursting into the tile-roofed barrack. Two twenty-four pounders and an eighteen-pounder heaved their enormous round shot from the high banks of a tank five hundred yards to the east of the Entrenchment. Two more guns fired from a battery seven hundred yards to the southeast.[423] A nine-pounder took up a position by the brick kiln a mere 350 yards to the south. And two twenty-four pounders fired from positions 1100 yards to the north and northwest, entirely out of range of the Entrenchment's guns.[424]

By Jonah's count, during the heaviest bombardment each gun fired about twenty-five rounds every hour, which meant that a round descended an average of every eight seconds. Round shot rained through the roofs of the barracks or bounded through the doors, and even those that missed their targets shook the ground with such force that they dislodged the teetering bricks in the damaged walls.[425] Shells howled and burst among the barracks, tearing away at the last remnants of the outer verandahs.

228 + ♦ OUR BONES ARE SCATTERED

During that first week "fifty-nine artillerymen had all been killed or wounded at their posts" and the guns themselves were not "in much better condition; the howitzer was knocked completely off its carriage,—one or two of them had their sides driven in, and one was without a muzzle."[426] Nevertheless, the Entrenchment batteries, now almost entirely manned by artillery officers and assorted volunteers, managed to kill about a dozen rebels that morning with a few rounds of cannister.

But the rebels had seen what the fire had acomplished in the Foot Artillery Hospital, and now they concentrated their energies on setting the imperfectly tiled hospital barrack ablaze with round shot heated in braziers[427] and carcasses (shells) of flaming rosin.[428] These incendiaries succeeded in setting afire a few of the abandoned officers' tents; the rest of the tents had to be struck for fear they might turn the compound into an inferno.[429] Around noon, as Jonah paused to pour water over his wound, smoke was seen rising from a room at the northern end of the tile-roofed barrack where several merchants had stored their clothes and furniture. Despite the heavy shelling, people fled from their hiding places at the first alarm and stumbled and hobbled across the ground to squeeze into any space they could find in the thatched barrack, crowding the sturdier inner verandahs "to suffocation."

Some people were forced to gather under the thatched roofs of the central rooms, including an officer's wife who came in holding her small son by the hand. Suddenly out of all the roaring and howling an eighteen-pound cannonball came hurtling through the roof in a cascade of straw and splinters, wrenching the boy's hand from his mother's grip and crushing him to death. There was a silence, the horrified mother let out a scream, and people pressed themselves under the archways of the doors just in time to avoid a second ball from the same gun that came crashing through the thatch.

Near where the Shepherds huddled together, Paymaster Seppings knelt in a doorway, calmly leading his wife and children in prayer. He seemed "quite resigned," and after a time, as the mortar shells burst and the dust sifted down from the roof, he took out a pencil and wrote an inscription on the wall: "The following were in this barrack on the 11th June, 1857," it said. "Captain Seppings, Mrs. Ditto, 3 children; Mrs. Wainwright, Ditto infant; Mrs. Cripps, Mrs. Halliday."[430]

Emma had known Seppings since Willie's first posting at Neemuch and had dined with him and his wife at the Vibarts' just three weeks before.[431] By now smallpox had overcome Emma Halliday. Mabel and Willie had joined the dead in the burial well,[432] and Emma had been removed from the tile-roofed barrack and taken to a room in the hospital barrack to protect the others from contagion. It is possible that Seppings had stuck by her out of gallantry or fatalism, but it is more likely that having visited Emma in the hospital barrack he had reflexively rushed his family to her room for refuge.

Of all the ladies in Wheeler's Entrenchment it is hard to imagine any who suffered more than Emma Halliday. Craving water with the insatiable thirst that accompanies smallpox, rocked by the concussive roar of cannon, her pulse racing, her body convulsed with fever in the unremitting heat, her flesh erupting in pustules, everyone and everything she loved and cherished dead and gone, she was dying a more terrible death than even the old gypsy could have foreseen during Emma's girlhood walk in the woods of Dorsetshire.[433]

Suddenly there was a shriek from another room and Jonah turned to see two soldiers' wives cringing in a corner and pointing under a *charpoy* (rope-strung bed). A large, bluff road overseer known as Sergeant Parker barged in and, drawing one of his pistols out of his belt, reached a hand under the bed and dragged out a small native man coated with grease.[434]

Everyone immediately knew what he was. Not trusting entirely in their artillery's incendiary round shot, Nana's generals had evidently resorted to arson: perhaps the most common means of sabotage in India. In its early days Calcutta had been plagued by incendiary fires set by men who would oil themselves to escape capture and sneak around the city to hurl coconut shells filled with bricks and coals onto the thatched roofs of European houses.[435] Obviously the sergeant's captive had intended to set the second barrack ablaze but had been interrupted by the mob of people fleeing from the first. Now, as Jonah and the women looked on, Parker hauled the little man out of the verandah and promptly shot him through the head.[436]

There were eleven native prisoners in the Entrenchment, some from the regimental jails, some wounded and captured in the outer barracks, some suspected of sedition, including the condemned havildar of the 56th whom Wheeler had not yet seen fit to hang.[437] It was tempting simply to shoot them now that the Entrenchment's stores were running out and there were not enough men left to guard them adequately. But for the time being, as the crush in the hospital barrack became too great, they were tied wrist-to-wrist and led to the Main Guard and watched over by the wife of a sergeant of

Her Majesty's 32nd, a stout, muscular, sergeant-major of a woman named Bridget Widdowson[438] who, standing over them with a drawn sword, kept them "motionless upon the ground for more than an hour."[439]

A few of the prisoners had been captured in the unfinished barracks, but either because of the pickets' fire or the rebels' tendency to commit suicide, it was "strangely rare to see them otherwise than quite dead." Some of those who were dragged in apologized to their former officers for mutinying and blamed it on an adverse cosmic breath they called the Devil's Wind. "These prisoners," wrote Thomson, "always gave utterance to profuse exclamations of wonder at our holding out from day to day as we did, and looked upon the cause as something altogether supernatural; they had all felt sure that we must be overpowered by their numbers, or at least be utterly destroyed by the intense heat of the season."[440]

But after the first of these prisoners managed somehow to escape and report the condition of the garrison to Nana Sahib, no more prisoners were taken. As Thomson mildly explained, "It was not desirable that very frequent accounts of our destitute condition should be conveyed to the rebels, so in future, to remedy this evil, all we took were despatched without reference to headquarters."[441] These peremptory executions of former Company soldiers infuriated the rebels, who used them to justify their execution of almost every European they captured.[442]

If the rebels killed themselves to escape capture, suicide must have at least crossed the minds of the Europeans as well. There is no record of such understandings at Cawnpore, but at Lucknow husbands haunted by the tales of rape and torture at Meerut and Delhi made pacts to shoot their wives if the rebels closed in.[443] Men were equally terrorized by the tales of the horrors that befell officers captured by the rebels. When a party of sepoys found him hiding near Bareilly, Major Gall, the commander of the ill-fated detachment of Irregulars to which Lieutenant St. George Ashe had been attached, would fire two shots at the advancing rebels and then shoot himself in the head.[444]

✦   ✦   ✦

Late in the afternoon of the twelfth the small fire in the tile-roofed barrack was extinguished, and people began to scramble back through the barrage to their rooms. But in their desperation some of the ladies lost their way, and Jonah and his family suddenly found themselves sharing their room with a somewhat heavy but "very respectable looking European lady, of pleasing appearance, with grey hair." Jonah solicitously gave her a couch to lie upon, but after a time she moaned a little, turned to her side, and "brought up something that looked like the lungs of a goat." Somebody guessed that her heart had burst from fright, but no one could say who she was, and in the end the Shepherds carried her corpse to the verandah to await the fatigue party.[445]

Jonah's group was now joined by the wife of a Eurasian named DeRussett, son of the ginger-whiskered English barber who had made a fortune catering to the peculiar whims of the cross-dressing King Nasir-ud-din of Oudh. Unhinged by the bombardment, Mrs. DeRussett could not quiet her terrified children, whose shrieks pierced the thunderous booming of the rebel barrage. "Nothing could pacify them," said Jonah, until their young father, after a desperate search, finally found them, embraced them in "the most tender manner," and washed their heads with a wetted rag.

✦ ✦ ✦

Toward evening the rebels finally advanced on the Entrenchment, arraying themselves behind every ruined wall, digging a sap forward from the drainage ditch that ran east and west from the course to the artillery bazaar, pressing hard on the outpickets in the unfinished barracks, and, as the batteries intensified their barrage, pouring in the most murderous musket fire the garrison had yet experienced.[446] The volleys were "like hail-storms at times" as a ring of some five thousand mutineers fired as fast as they could reload.[447] From the windows of the barracks they could be seen "[peppering] away upon our walls, yelling defiance, abusing us in the most hellish language, brandishing their swords, and striking up a war-dance."[448]

"The din of this fearful cannonading and musketry was so incessant for nearly a couple of hours that it resembled continuous claps of thunder in a tremendous storm."[449] It may have been in this volley that a round shot smashed one of Wheeler's tumbrils full of treasure, "and its contents, consisting of some thirty or forty thousand rupees, were sent flying amidst the surrounding soldiers and their wives. Any circumstances less distressing than ours," wrote Thomson, "would have made the scramble that ensued a most humorous picture."[450]

Everyone in Jonah's barrack now lay flat on the floor "in fervent and earnest supplications to our Almighty Father."[451] At last a few well-aimed volleys of cannister from the Entrenchment batteries and the garrison's own rapid musket volleys combined to drive the sepoys back, and as the bombardment eased off again Jonah penciled his own message on a nearby wall. "Should this meet the eyes of any who are acquainted with us, in case we are all destroyed," he scrawled, "be it known to them that we occupied this room for eight days under circumstances so distressing as to have no precedent. The destruction of Jerusalem could not have been attended with distress so severe as we have experienced in so short a time."

Jonah concluded with a list of people in his party: his wife Ellen and their two children; his sister Rebecca with her infant and seventeen-year-old daughter; his orphaned niece; his sister's mother-in-law; his brother Daniel; his ayah Thakurani; plus a neighbor lady, an elderly commissariat colleague named Berrill and his wife and daughter—"together with other friends"—no fewer than sixteen people in Jonah's ostensible care. Just as all of those in Seppings's room had been Anglo-Indian, all of Jonah's party were Eurasian. Even in this desperate extremity the segregation of the Company's India stubbornly obtained.[452]

By then DeRussett had moved his mad wife deeper into the barrack, and no sooner had Jonah completed his inscription than Berrill and his family fled the barrack to find a haven in the trenches.[453] Either choice was miserable. The trenches were exposed, but the barrack rooms were "ovens," remembered Amy Horne. "Mothers who could not endure to see their little ones literally scorched under a burning Sun, had no alternative, but to keep in them, [but] it was only avoiding one evil to seek another, for alas death was everywhere."[454]

Despite Ellen's ministrations, Mrs. DeRussett died at seven o'clock that night of hysteria and heat stroke. Her disconsolate husband could not bear to leave her body to the fatigue party, but he was at a loss as to where he might bury her. Jonah told him of Mrs. Hillersdon's grave in the cooking pit and after dark feebly led him out to the soldier's garden. Jonah "could scarcely walk" and asked his oldest nieces to help DeRussett carry his wife to the garden. "It was a [moonlit] night," Jonah remembered, "an occasional mortar shell or two came riding in the air, like meteors, . . . and fell here and there in the intrenchment, but none very near us." DeRussett buried his wife next to Mrs. Hillersdon with a spade he had found, and Jonah read the burial service. "Man that is born of a woman hath but a short time to live, and is full of misery. . . . In the midst of life we are in death; of whom may we seek for succour but of Thee O Lord, who for our sins art justly displeased."

✦ ✦ ✦

Many officers distinguished themselves with their courage during the siege of Wheeler's Entrenchment, but there was one "craven-hearted" officer "of high rank, and in the prime of life who never showed himself outside the walls of the barrack, nor took even the slightest part in the military operations." He "seemed not to possess a thought beyond that of preserving his own worthless life,"[455] and his passing would prove "the only death," as Thomson put it, that his fellow officers "regarded with complacency."[456] Thomson withheld his name "out of consideration for the feelings of his surviving relatives," but the process of elimination points exclusively to Deputy Judge Advocate Edwin Wiggins.[457]

Wiggins had once served with bravery at Mooltan and Goojerat. But perhaps he had been too softened by an intervening decade of staff work to rise to the terrible occasion of the siege. It is possible that the presence of his wife and children had unmanned him; his wife Christian had lost her reason well before the siege began, leaving two children in his care;[458] perhaps their ayah had been among those who had fled the Entrenchment. Or it may be that Christian's endless ravings had eaten through his soldier's mettle.

In any case, "nothing could rouse him to exertion." In the name of taking care of his mad wife, Wiggins had kept indoors, but even after she died on June 12 of the same combination of dementia, heat stroke, and exhaustion that had claimed Mrs. DeRussett and many other ladies of the garrison, he remained out of harm's way, pleading the press of staff business as his fellow officers staggered back out into the maelstrom.[459]

There was no real haven, however, from the horrors of the siege. Amy Horne remembered an officer who "must have had a touch of the sun, as his face was very flushed." After returning from the trenches he sat in the verandah for a few minutes, resting himself in the broken shade of the shattered roof, "when a shot struck him full in the face, taking his head clean off. His body continued to remain seated, his hands falling by his sides, the blood gushing from between his shoulders like a fountain, and falling on those who rushed to his rescue."[460] The artillery officer and gifted linguist Lieutenant

James Eckford paused in the shade of the verandah to rest from his duties at the southeastern battery when, like some lethal medicine ball, a round shot caught him in the chest, crushing his heart against the wall behind him.[461] Elsewhere Captain Reynolds of the 53rd did not move quite fast enough to evade a round shot; it carried away his arm and sent him whirling to the ground in a spray of gore.

Very early in the morning of June 13, little Mercy, an orphaned native girl whom Jonah's grown niece had been raising, rolled too far into the middle of their shattered room and was shot through the brain. Mercy's corpse was set out beside a pillar of the inner verandah to await the evening burial party, but a round shot soon turned the pillar into a heap of brick, and "so that was her grave."[462]

During the siege the wife of a surgeon stationed at Lucknow[463] delivered a child in the barracks in a state of "most distressing publicity," as did Mrs. John Hay, wife of the merchant who had twice begged Wheeler to move the garrison to the magazine.[464] In a near reprise of the death of Charles Hillersdon, the proud Mr. Hay emerged for a moment after viewing his newborn only to spin to the ground with a bullet in his brain.[465] Two little girls were left for a moment in the comparative safety of their room, but when the parents returned they found "that a shell had come through the roof, and torn their dear ones to pieces—bones, brains and flesh were strewed all over, and not a step could you take without treading on some portion of their remains."[466] Captain Belson of the 53rd had recently taken into his care the infant of an officer of the Engineers whose wife had died at Cuttack. While a wet nurse was feeding the baby, a round shot fell from the sky and crushed both of the wet nurse's legs. "The little innocent was picked off the ground suffused in its nurse's blood," remembered Thomson, "but completely free of injury."[467]

"The mortality increased rapidly," wrote Amy Horne, "and sometimes a whole family would be found lying dead side by side." The stench not only from these corpses but "the dead bodies of the horses and other animals that had been shot in the compound, and could not be removed"[468] was "insufferable," and the "swarms of flies were a plague."[469]

FLAMES
June 12–13, 1857

Beyond the range of the garrison's guns, the executions continued. Sometime after the slaughter of the Fatehgarh fugitives, the Eurasian merchant Eduard Williams—who had spent the past week searching for his wife and three children—discovered their corpses near the native city. Cast out of their refuge and into the streets, they had been discovered and killed by a mob from the bazaars.[470] Apothecary Peters and his party of fugitives from the Entrenchment hid for three days in a nearby village, protected by a servant. But on June 12 Peters, Ryan, their wives, a Mrs. Purcell, and at least six children were discovered by the rebels, carted off to Savada House and put to the sword.[471]

In another village six miles east of Cawnpore, John Duncan, the superintendent of the Cawnpore section of the Grand Trunk Road, hid from the rebels under the protection of a local man named Ghunseram. But when Ghunseram heard that Nana was offering a reward for the heads of all Europeans and Christians he betrayed Duncan to the rebels, who ordered him to bring the superintendent's head to Nana. Ghunseram obligingly decapitated Duncan, but he was awarded a measly ten rupees, and when the rebels heard that he had kept Duncan's valuables for himself, Nana ordered him thrown into prison.[472]

Meanwhile, in a chamber of the old Residency at Bithur, guarded by sowars from the 7th Native Cavalry and protected by the Peshwa's widows, the young widow of the massacred tollkeeper, Joseph Carter, gave birth to a baby girl.[473]

✦ ✦ ✦

As the siege wore on, Nana scoured Cawnpore for money with which to sustain his army, to whom he had impetuously promised double wages. Thousands of soldiers from other stations were now pouring in, led by the embittered sepoys of the 17th Native Infantry. After plundering their station at Azimgurh they had been relieved of their loot at Fyzabad by fellow rebels from Jaunpore and Benares. "In high dudgeon" the 17th marched toward Cawnpore, venting their rage on any European fugitives they encountered along the way.[474]

Jemadar Durgah Prasad and the detachment of the 56th Native Infantry Willie Halliday had sent off with the Banda Collectorate treasure had somehow managed to keep his men in line. But now as they approached Cawnpore and heard the distant thud of the rebel batteries, his men began to burn and plunder along the road. It was obvious to Durgah Prasad that the younger men of his regiment had the bit in their teeth, and he had no choice but to join them. As his sepoys raced happily around the city, the jemadar reported to Nana Sahib.

The addition of the detachment seemed to pain Nana, who demanded that Durgah Prasad keep his men under control. The last thing Nana needed was another influx of arrogant sepoys drifting between the lines and the native city, looting, loafing, demanding their pay. The jemadar confessed that he could not control his men, but expressed his hope that they might settle down now that they had reached Cawnpore.

"If they don't obey orders here," Nana Sahib warned, "I'll turn them out."[475]

Nana was having a hard enough time keeping his own people under control. He had appointed one kotwal[476] after another to restore some semblance of order to the city. The Company's man had fled on June 7, whereupon Nana, or more likely Azimullah, appointed a Moslem named Wasi-ud-Din, who spent his first twenty-four hours in office riding happily about with the courtesan Azizun.[477] On the ninth of June Nana replaced him with Shah Ali, the son of another prominent Moslem, but Nana preferred to keep him close by as an adviser and installed him on the verandah of his tent.[478] A day later Nana finally turned to a Hindu: a disgraced Company policeman named Hulas Singh who had been nominated for the job by a committee of merchants who wanted to stop the plundering.[479] Like Nunne Nawab, Hulas Singh would later claim to have taken the job at gunpoint, but he proved a conscientious adminstrator. His job was to carry out the orders of Nana's court, which was composed of his predecessor Shah Ali, Azimullah, Bala Rao, the dour Baba Bhutt, and Brigadier Jwala Prasad.[480]

The police chief's first act was to collect together all the merchants and promise them that the city would not be plundered if they simply kept their businesses open. To supply the batteries with gunpowder, Teeka Singh, Nana's commander-in-chief, rounded up all the indigo merchants, demanding that they give over their supplies of saltpeter or face imprisonment.[481] And Nana put his father-in-law, Narunpunt Mama, in charge of destroying the telegraph on the Delhi Road and rolling the thick wire into vast coils from which the rebels snipped slugs for their muskets[482]—telegraph wire in India was "as thick as iron rod," explained Lady Canning, "because the monkeys used to swing on it, & break common wire."[483]

✦   ✦   ✦

Nunne Nawab's pensioned gunners were finding that preparing incendiary shells was dangerous business. In David Duncan's bungalow three men were killed and seven wounded when the embers from their hookah ignited a shell.[484] But in the gloaming of Sunday, June 13, as he squinted through his telescope at the parched roof of the thatched barrack, the "richly dressed" Nawab urged his gunners to bring all their ingenuity to bear on setting the barrack ablaze.[485]

It was dark when the son of one of the Nawab's pensioned gunners finally managed to roll a fiery carcass of rosin across the barrack roof, where it left a trail of flames before landing with a fiery splash among what was left of the officers' tents.[486] As a hard breeze sent the flames churning along the entire length of the thatched roof the rebels cheered and to the call of their buglers hundreds assembled around their batteries, in the drainage ditch, and in the ruined compounds of the European bungalows, preparing to charge.

The thatched barrack had been filled with groaning, writhing rows of the sick and wounded, curtained off with sheets and bamboo blinds from the musicians' and soldiers' wives and children and the European families who had remained after their flight from the fire in the tile-roofed barrack. Now in the glare of the flames, as the rebel sniper fire whined past their ears and chopped at the ground around them, the women fled in all directions, carrying their infants and whatever of their belongings they could grab. "The women and children were panic-stricken," recalled Amy Horne. "Confronted on one side by the burning building, and on the other by the shot and shell from the enemy's guns, which fell like hail on every side, they knew not where to run for protection." Some made for the unfinished barrack, some forced their way into the smaller and already crowded barracks.[487] Others flung themselves into the trenches while most of the remaining servants fled the Entrenchment entirely.[488]

They were all terribly exposed in the brilliant glow from the roiling flames, and easy marks for the snipers firing from the distant gloom of the northernmost unfinished barracks. "The livid blaze of that burning barrack lighted up many a terrible picture of silent anguish," said Thomson, "while the yells of the advancing sepoys and the noise of their artillery filled the air. . . .[489] In one place was the mother almost raving for the child which had just been shot in her arms and in another place a poor orphan weeping over the corpse of its Father or Mother . . .[490]

"From one portion of the barrack the women and the children were running out, from another little parties laden with some heavy burden of suffering brotherhood were seeking the adjacent building." Though many of the invalids were too sick or wounded to move, every able-bodied man was obliged to remain at his post in the trenches and prepare for the rebels' charge.[491] A few, unable to bear the heart-rending screams of the wounded, ran to their assistance. Lieutenant Warde of the 56th ran toward the barrack to help drag out the wounded, only to stumble and somehow run his sword through his leg.[492] Other soldiers darted across the yard to assist him, and "many a poor agonizing private was rescued from the horrible death that seemed inevitable." But the fire spread so quickly through the parched thatch and rafters, and there were so few men available to come to the rescue, that two maimed gunners died in the flames, and the rest of the wounded had to be dragged out "without any regard to the excruciating pain occasioned by their wounds."[493]

The rebels "poured a continuous volley of shot and shell into the burning building," and as the roof crashed down into the barrack rooms "several were burnt alive," recalled Amy Horne. "Mother and I were both wounded in the head. . . . My sister, a little girl of five, had her leg fractured by a falling block of masonry," and their ayah "had half of one foot torn off."[494] The flames incinerated not only Headmaster Gill of the Free School, who had been lying in agony with his head cracked open since the beginning of the bombardment, but his wife, who had just been confined.[495]

Jonah would put the number killed in the fire at about forty, but he was probably including all those who died of their wounds after all of the hospital supplies were lost.[496] "Every drop of medicine in the building was destroyed," wrote Amy,

and the consequences felt almost immediately, and bitterly too, for, putting recovery out of the question, no relief whatever could now be afforded to the sick and wounded. There was nothing now to soothe their dying moments, not even a drop of water to

moisten their parched lips. The heat affected their wounds, and
the flies settled on them and drove them crazy with their disagreeable presence. It was now that our skirts were in demand.
We tore every vestige, even to our sleeves, to supply bandages for
the wounded.[497]

After all that Emma Halliday had already endured it is almost inconceivable that she should have survived the fire as well. But according to Thomson she was among those dragged from the flames,
and she lay on the ground a few yards from the inferno, crying in
vain for a drink of water. No one knows how much longer Emma
lived,[498] but she had already been "sick unto death" when Willie was
killed, and must have died before the end of the siege.[499] Death
would have been a mercy, and perhaps in the delirium of her last
moments, before they carried her off to the burial well, she greeted
Willie and Mabel in her "dear little garden"[500] in Dorsetshire, or returned to the gypsy of Cranborne Chase, whose prophecy she had
fulfilled with such terrible exactitude.[501]

+ + +

Convinced that every man of the garrison would rush to assist the
women and children and the wounded, hundreds of rebels silently
advanced across the plain, one wing of them drawing within seventy
yards of Ashe's battery.[502] Ashe appears to have taken Larkins's place
as commander of artillery, and though Thomson never forgave him
for firing on the 53rd, he had to concede that Ashe was "a great
scourge to our enemies, in consequence of the surprising celerity and
accuracy of the firing from his battery." After every round Ashe
would "jump up on to the heel of the gun, regardless of the exposure, that he might see the extent of the damage he had inflicted."[503]

As the rebels crept forward, Ashe kept his men utterly quiet, hoping the enemy would believe they were catching his battery unawares. But just as they began to rush toward the parapets he
shouted, "Fire!" and sprayed the gloom with "a most destructive
charge of grape."[504] At the same instant all of the pickets opened up
with their muskets, each with a half dozen pieces "ready charged."[505]
Had the rebels thrown every available man into the attack they
would undoubtedly have taken the Entrenchment that night,
though not, Jonah believed, before the Europeans had killed half
their number. But even with the barrack afire and half the garrison
searching for refuge in the open yard, the rebels did not attack en

masse, and after half an hour of furious gunfire the plain was littered with a hundred rebel dead and at least as many wounded staggering and crawling back to their lines.[506]

ASHES

June 14–20, 1857

In the small hours of Monday, June 14, as the charred rubble of the hospital barrack smoked and crackled, the rebel snipers finally left off. All night long the mutineers' buglers had "continued to harass us," wrote Thomson, "by sounding the 'Assembly,' the 'Advance,' and the 'Double' so that our men could get no rest."[507] But now in the morning light the officers could see that in fact their enemy had receded from their advanced positions. The garrison's pickets, their faces black with gunpowder, blinked at each other in astonishment and exchanged bewildered congratulations. Incredibly, impossibly, they had survived.[508]

But the Entrenchment was a ruin. The smoldering wreckage of the hospital barrack amplified the heat of the day and added its smoke to the dust that blew across the plain. Bodies lay here and there, casualties that had been overlooked in the chaos of the previous night. In the trenches themselves whole families were huddled, caked with dust and sweat, trying to fashion shelter from the rising sun out of blankets, carpets, cots, crates,[509] "garments suspended on sticks and ramrods."[510] Men gathered up the struck tents and tried to erect "canvas stretchers overhead," wrote Thomson, "but as often as the paltry covering was put up, it was fired by the enemy's shells."[511]

Other women and children found shelter in the unfinished barracks, watched over by the bleary outpickets. In the battered barrack, families made room for the sick and wounded rescued from the flames. But even the tile-roofed barrack was a ruin, recalled Amy Horne, "the walls frequently perforated and every beam coming down." "The half-destroyed walls of the barracks," wrote Sherer, "or the temporary expedient of piling up tents and casks, formed the precarious but only shelter that could be obtained."[512]

With half their shelter gone and ever fewer men to spell each other in the trenches, wrote Delafosse, "we lost five or six men daily by sunstroke."[513] Now even the women were enlisted for sentry duty, "so that nearly the whole of the women and children also slept under the walls of the intrenchment, near their respective relatives."[514] "Not less than two hundred of them passed twelve days and nights upon the bare ground," wrote Thomson. "Many of these were wives and daughters of officers, who had never known privation in its mildest form."[515]

The blackened shell of the hospital barrack retained its heat "for no less than 4 or 5 days," Amy recalled, "and you [dared] not approach . . . within three feet."[516] The surgeons warned Amy that anyone who ventured too close would die from the heat or go mad, "and he was not wrong, for in one short day, death swept away Mrs. Captain Belson and child, Miss Campbell and Colonel Williams' daughter [Mary], [Mrs.] Yates, Mr. Christie, and child,"[517] all of them succumbing to a "maddening fever."[518]

Many of the rest went mad, including Amy Horne's own mother, seven months pregnant. "I used to sit and listen to her ravings, muttered in broken sentences. Her one theme was her mother whom she wanted to see. At one moment she would be calling for a conveyance to take her to her mother, and the next her mind would wander away to something else. Her dreadful affliction rendered me heartbroken, and her cries haunt me still." Sitting with her injured, raving mother and wounded half-sister, Amy sometimes "could not bear to look on their agonies, and often have I turned away, feeling my own mind bordering on destruction."[519]

It was enough to make outpickets like Thomson glad they were out in their soldiers' posts in the unfinished barracks. At least they were "somewhat removed from the sickening spectacles continually occurring in the intrenchment.[520] Sometimes when relieved by a brother officer for a few minutes, I have run across to the mainguard for a chat with some old chums, or to join in the task of attempting to cheer the spirits of the women; but the sight there was always of a character to make me return to the barrack, relieved by the comparative quiet of its seclusion."[521]

The surgeons had managed to save only two operating kits[522] and a small chest of medicine that was almost immediately expended, after which "no relief whatever could be afforded to the sick and wounded."[523] "The agonies of the wounded became most intense, and from the utter impossibility of extracting bullets, or dressing mutilations, casualties were increased in their fatality. It was heart-breaking work to see the poor sufferers parched with thirst that could be only most scantily relieved, and sinking from fever and mortification that we had no appliances wherewith to resist."[524] The widow of Captain Reynolds of the 53rd was wounded in the wrist by a musket ball, "and died of fever in consequence of there being no instruments or materials to alleviate her sufferings."[525]

Another casualty of the barrack fire was the storeroom.[526] "All the good clothes and other articles of the soldiers and children were burnt, for which reason they were reduced to the greatest straits, and very little food was cooked, as nearly all the servants ran away from fright."[527] For the first few days of the siege, soldiers had dined on tinned fish, jars of marmalade, even bottles of champagne. But after a week such delicacies had been entirely used up. Horse flesh became so prized that the garrison's snipers aimed their muskets not at the occasional inebriated sowar who would come galloping toward the Entrenchment but his mount, in hopes of creeping out at night to retrieve its carcass before decomposition could set in.

When the rebels installed a nine-pounder in one of the outer barracks the pickets salivated over their half-dozen artillery bullocks. But they watched "the ends of the distant walls in vain"; the rebels "artfully kept the horned treasure under cover." Finally a sniper shot a Brahma bull that came wandering innocently toward the parapet and a volunteer party under the indomitable Captain Moore ran out to drag it in. The killing of such an animal must have enraged the Hindus among the rebels, and they fired a "sharp fusilade, diversified with one or two round-shots," but "two or three ugly wounds were not thought too high a price to pay for this contribution to the commissariat" and Moore managed to tie a rope "round the hind legs and between the horns of the beast, and in the midst of the cheers from behind the mud-wall" he dragged the bull back to the Entrenchment, where the cooks made it into a soup. "None of it reached us in the outposts more palpably," groused Thomson, "than in its irritating odour."[528]

Otherwise everyone ate lentils and chupatties, "all without distinction."[529] "Our daily supply of provisions . . . consisted of half a pint of pea soup and two or three chupatties about the size of an Abernethy biscuit," for which the cooks charged a generous sum.[530] Jonah "repeatedly paid a rupee and two rupees for the cooking of one meal of dall and chupatties, and that too often not properly done."[531] Pampered and petted by their parents' servants, young children would ask their parents to punish the cook for serving "such a nasty breakfast."[532] "The soldiers," wrote an ayah named Mary Ann, "used to cook for the ladies and children, but for several days they took no food at all."[533] Hunger reduced the garrison "to a company of spectres" and according to Thomson at least two people died purely of starvation.[534]

The distribution of food was not altogether equitable. When the garrison's store of lentils began to run out, the servants were fed a gruel made from *gram*, a grain commonly used for horse feed.[535] A few servants still somehow managed to sneak food to their masters in the Entrenchment.[536] But eventually everyone ate gram, which was "steeped in four buckets, and placed in such a position that all could help themselves."[537]

◆ ◆ ◆

Like the water-carrying soldiers and the cooks, Wheeler's native spies and couriers worked for a fee, and their fees rose as the siege ground on. Eventually Wheeler would pay one spy six thousand rupees to carry a message to Lucknow.[538] But the risks were terrible. Many were caught, and though some were executed on the spot, the rebel courts ordered most of them mutilated and sent back without ears, noses, fingers, hands.[539]

At 8:15 P.M. on the fourteenth of June Wheeler wrote a note to Martin Gubbins, Henry Lawrence's Intelligence Officer at Lucknow. Since the thirtieth of May the Lucknow garrison had been preparing for a siege that would last for nearly half a year, becoming with Cawnpore one of the two great sacramental dramas of the rebellion. With his extraordinary prescience, Lawrence had spent months preparing a position for his garrison with every means at his disposal: filling a racquet court with cattle straw, burying his treasure, and employing thousands of coolies to demolish the palaces and huts that surrounded the European cantonment.[540] Into a miscellany of seventeen buildings, including a Begum's mansion and Lawrence's own Residency, poured three thousand Europeans and loyal sepoys surrounded by seven thousand mutineers and half a million city people still seething over the annexation of Oudh and the exile of their foolish but familiar king. Lawrence's supplies were ample and his position far stronger than Wheeler's, but the mutineers at Lucknow would be joined by thousands more, including mobs of matchlockmen sent by the zemindars of Oudh to avenge their dispossession.

"We have been besieged," wrote Wheeler, "since the 6th by the Nana Saheb." The rebels had two twenty-four-pounders and an array of other guns, but his own batteries had been reduced to only eight functioning nine-pounders. "Our defence has been noble and wonderful, our loss heavy and cruel. We want aid, aid, aid!" he concluded. "If we had 200 men, we could punish the scoundrels and aid you."[541]

Lucknow had known about the Cawnpore siege since June 7,[542] and Wheeler's urgent appeals for help "deeply affected us," wrote one of Lawrence's men, "and threatening as was our own position, we would gladly have gone to their rescue."[543] The precipitous Martin Gubbins even proposed a feint on Bithur and a crossing ten miles below Cawnpore. But Cawnpore was supposed to be Lucknow's watchtower, not the other way around. Two hundred men could never fight their way through the encircling rebels, and even if they accomplished such a feat, the bridge of boats was gone and all the native vessels scattered up and down the Cawnpore side of the river. Any remnant of such a force that managed to cross the river and reach the Entrenchment would be in no condition to do Wheeler any good.[544]

◆　◆　◆

Soon after Wheeler had set down his pen and wished his body servant God's speed, Captain Moore embarked on his most audacious sortie to date, this time to spike the guns of Nunne Nawab's battery in the ruins of St. John's, the soldier's church. It was imperative that the rebels believe that in spite of all the destruction of the day before, the garrison could still put up a fight. Besides, Moore argued, an attack on the rebel lines was the last thing the rebels would expect. The garrison's blood was up, and despite their exhaustion fifty men volunteered for Moore's sortie. Few of them would have required camouflage; their unwashed faces were already covered with gunpowder, their clothes filthy with dirt and sweat. Wheeler ordered utter silence throughout the Entrenchment as Moore led his volunteers along the storm drain that ran out of Ashe's battery and crept eastward across the corpse-littered plain. The sortie threw the women of the garrison "into agonies of fear" and "every sound was hushed. In no time the stillness of death seemed to be upon us, and the very infant to understand its danger."[545]

At the road the volunteers turned right, sticking to the culvert, astonished to find no rebel pickets barring their way. Three hundred yards from the Entrenchment they reached the compound of the soldier's church and slipped over the wall. As the others stood watch, a crew spiked a pair of guns the rebels had left unguarded. Incredibly, no rebels discovered them, and emboldened by their success, they made their way another 250 yards southeast of the church to the officers' mess of the 56th Native Infantry to take out the twenty-four-pounder that had battered the Entrenchment with such force and accuracy almost from the beginning of the siege.[546]

Here at last they met some rebels, pensioned gunners dozing at their battery, exhausted by the previous day's assault. Among them was Reuz Ali, the gunner who had fired the incendiary shell. He was now richer by ninety rupees,[547] his portion of the five thousand rupees Nana had awarded the Nawab for setting the barrack aflame.[548] Moore and his volunteers opened fire on the sleeping gunners as his crew spiked two more smaller guns and, jamming material into its barrel, put a torch to a charge in the twenty-four-pounder that blew it to pieces. But by now the sound of their gunfire had roused a swarm of snipers, who opened a blistering fire from the rubble of the church. Moore and his men scrambled back across the open plain, firing at their pursuers all the way, and collapsed, exhausted, in the trenches. It had all taken about an hour, but for the women of the garrison it had seemed like an eternity. Moore was greeted by "loud and hearty cheers," for it had been "a most brilliant, daring, and successful exploit."[549]

But "it availed us little," wrote Thomson. During their retreat one man had been killed and four wounded, and within a few hours the rebels had replaced the ruined guns and resumed their bombardment with a vengeance.[550] Wheeler could not afford such losses, and over the objections of his younger officers, forbade Moore any further sorties. Jonah believed Wheeler acted not only "from a false hope of receiving a reinforcement," but "the exceedingly great, though natural, attachment of the women to their respective husbands, fathers, and brothers." In retrospect Jonah believed that an attack on the insurgents "would, without doubt, have been attended with complete success, as I learn that latterly the cannons used to be almost entirely abandoned by the soldiery during the night, and only a few Golundazes kept loading and firing them; the musketry was kept up by a handful of Sepoys placed here and there, more for appearance sake than with any intention of doing us much injury."[551]

But Wheeler was a "poor victim of hope deferred."[552] He still expected a relief force on the morrow, and all next day he paced about, peering through his spyglass toward the Grand Trunk Road, squinting through the dust and smoke for a glimpse of a crimson corps of Highlanders, and—over the cries of the wounded, the taunts of the rebel snipers, the never-ending booming of the enemy's guns—listening for the skirl of pipers in the heat of the wind.[553]

OUR OWN KING

Nana Sahib: June 1857

Even Sivaji would have been hard put to mold an army out of the contentious hodgepodge of patriots, courtiers, priests, fanatics, peasants, watchmen, matchlockmen, mutineers, landlords, petty rajas, brigands, and opportunists who now flocked to Cawnpore to join the rebellion. Over ninety percent of Cawnpore District's approximately two hundred thousand[554] residents were Hindus, of which about twenty-seven thousand were Brahmins.[555] But there were eighty-four Hindu and fifty-six Moslem tribes and castes "excluding subdivisions" living in uneasy and insular proximity to their ancestral foes. Their obscure and relatively recent history had been punctuated by family feuds, swindles, land grabs, and mass conversions; over the centuries people had learned to bend with the prevailing wind. Property, religion, culture, and ancestry were entangled with dizzying intricacy, but more like vines than roots. Only the aboriginal Meos could claim deep ties to the district, and the Meos had been so persecuted by the Moghuls that most of them had long since passed themselves off as Rajputs.[556]

Many of the Moslems of the city were better off than the Hindus, owing to the demand for Moslem leather workers and weavers. The Hindu Mahajuns were the wealthiest residents, but the growing colony of Shiite Lucknow nobles were also extremely rich. Cawnpore had not seen the kind of catastrophic communal violence that afflicted Lucknow, but the city had a reputation for crime, and old antagonisms lurked beneath the surface.[557] The emergence of the Brahmin Mahratta from Bithur stirred the Moslem community's latent suspicions. Unlike Sivaji, the later Peshwas, including Baji Rao, had treated

Moslems with notorious contempt, so it fell to Azimullah to reassure his fellow believers—especially the voluble sowars of the 2nd Native Cavalry—that Nana Sahib was not a bigot like his father but a secularist like Sivaji: tolerant, generous, a friend of the King of Lucknow, a servant of the Emperor of Delhi. But among Nana's entourage were Brahmin fanatics, including his older brother Baba Bhutt.

For many years Baba had remained with Nana's natural father. "Bhutt" was a Mahratta word denoting "mendicant," and it is said that Baba had lived off alms until the time of Baji Rao's death, when Nana finally summoned him to Saturday House to serve as his treasurer.[558] An ill-tempered man with small, furtive eyes, he spoke in a "grumbling, croaking voice," and wore a large turban to cover his bald head. The sparse gray hairs that peeked along its sweat-stained rim and the green spectacles that sat askew upon his long thick nose made him appear twenty years older than his liege. But perhaps Baba's fiscal duties following upon his mendicancy had simply aged him beyond his years. As treasurer Baba had watched Nana's fortune hemorrhage from the vaults of Saturday House; he knew better than anyone else that if nothing were done about John Company, his brother and his dependents were headed for ruin.[559]

Looters, hoarders, and harborers of Christians were brought in for Baba Bhutt's dyspeptic dispensation, and one day in mid June a pair of Moslem butchers were brought before him on the charge of slaughtering a cow in the city bazaar. Invoking Brahminical proscriptions against bovicide, Baba Bhutt condemned the butchers to amputation, an ancient form of punishment that had been in wide use under the Moghuls.[560] The victim was pinioned and gagged and the hands removed "with an instrument like a carving knife, not at a stroke, but by cutting and hacking around about the wrist to find out the joint; and in about three minutes the hand was off," after which "the wounded parts were dipped in boiling ghee."[561]

In this case the procedure did not go well, and, when the butchers bled to death, the Moslems of Cawnpore were outraged. "Who has made this Nana a ruler over us?" the sowars of the 2nd Cavalry wanted to know. "Is he not a creature of our own hands; and can we not appoint anyone else we like? If he has already commenced interfering with our creed, and preventing cows being killed, which is not only lawful, but is necessary to our very existence, how much more will he not meddle with our other religious callings when he is firmly established in authority, and when our common enemy, the English, shall have been completely exterminated?"[562]

Swelled by the sowars camped along the Grand Trunk Road, a crowd of Moslems marched on Savada House to confront Nana Sahib.[563] Warned of their coming, His Highness emerged from his tent and stood before them in the glare of the sun with his feet and shaved head bared. The sowars "used much abusive language . . . and threatened to displace him if he did not do as they desired."

Nana begged their pardon and promised never to interfere again, asking only that they go about their business out of sight of their Hindu neighbors. Otherwise, "the Mahomedans were perfectly at liberty to kill as many cows as they liked." But the damage had been done, and from that day forward the sowars viewed Nana with suspicion and contempt.[564]

The Hindus' confidence in Nana Sahib was also waning. Among Cawnpore's Hindus, caste distinctions were of more consequence than sectarian differences.[565] Nana Sahib was a Brahmin, but a Mahratta Brahmin from the distant Concan, a very different species from the agrestic Kaunajia Brahmins of the Doab. Nana was not exactly a stranger to the Hindus of the district, many of whom had benefited from his charities, but his preoccupation with regaining his rights and titles and his diligent courtship of the local European community had distracted him from his philanthropy toward the Brahmins. It is not entirely certain that he even spoke Hindi with any fluency; in the bosom of his zenana he evidently spoke Maharastran and reverted to Urdu only in his public addresses and proclamations.

To the people of the Doab the Mahrattas had been invaders who had persecuted the local landowners during their brief expeditions through the region. And whatever deference the community might automatically accord the Peshwa's heir, Nana was certainly proving to be no better a general than his father had been. Some even whispered that he was of dubious origins, a mendicant's son unworthy of the Peshwa's throne.

"The English garrison could have subdued the discontented and disheartened mutineers" if almost all of the Rajputs of the District— "a fine body of men, sturdy, independent and dignified"—had not flocked to Nana's banner, including the turbulent descendants of the Meos, all of them determined to recover the wealth and power they had lost to the Company's collectors.[566] Only a few—perhaps a dozen self-styled rajas with substantial holdings—actually contributed soldiers to the siege of Wheeler's Entrenchment, but many more supplied food and transportation, and various landholders in Oudh sent their greetings, pledging to support Nana whenever he advanced on Lucknow.[567]

Despite the growing disaffection of the original four Cawnpore regiments, every day more mutineers, irregulars, and Oudh freelances came clattering into the city to join the rebellion, camping out of range of the Entrenchment's batteries and crowding the bazaars and sherbet shops. Beyond the siege line there was not a lot for them to do except man the pickets, supply the batteries, and thrill to the occasional alarm. On the sixteenth of June a rumor circulated that a fleet of boats crowded with British troops was approaching from Allahabad, and Teeka Singh led a force of sowars and sepoys and a couple of guns to the river to meet them. In fact a dozen boats did turn up downriver, but they turned out to be munitions boats stocked with much needed percussion caps and manned by native crews who had strained 126 miles upriver at the hapless direction of two Europeans who were now seized and executed.[568]

To slow the slaughter in the streets, Hulas Singh had offered all the city's babus amnesty if they vowed never to read, speak, or write the English language. But they remained objects of the deepest suspicion, and on June 16 he rounded them up at his prison and sent a deputation to Nana, who commanded them, on pain of death, to cease all communications with the British. Before Nana released them, Azimullah delivered a long speech to an assembly of Cawnpore's leading citizens at a kind of *durbar* (audience) at Savada House, declaring that he had been to Britain and knew it to be very scantily populated.

Here a few in his audience must have exchanged skeptical glances, for he asked them

> if it were not so, why would not more soldiers have been sent long ago? So many new countries the British have taken during the last few years, and have they increased their European troops? No! This is then the true reason for it. I have been at all their little villages, and know it for a fact, that no more soldiers can be spared; all that they can do is to send, now and then, with great difficulty, a few recruits to complete and keep up the strength of the corps already in India. What fools, then, we natives have made of ourselves, so quietly to surrender our country to a handful of tyrannical foreigners who are trying in many ways to deprive us of our religion and our privileges!

He commanded them to annihilate their enemies "root and branch," from the face of all India. Let not a soul escape, let not the name of a Christian be ever named in Hindoostan." He assured them that the rebel forces were strong and numerous, but that if they needed assistance he could always call upon his friends, "the Plenipotentiaries of France, Russia," and other states, who were "willing and ready to do anything" for him.

The speech was evidently effective, and turned the heads of many residents who had heretofore hoped for a return of British order. Whatever one thought of Azimullah Khan and his pretensions, the evidence of the Company's downfall was everywhere. There were stories of British soldiers burning and looting at Benares and Allahabad, but it was said that the Europeans were fleeing Calcutta, that the governor-general was helpless, that the Queen herself was faint with despair. Whether the British were finished or wreaking an indiscriminate vengeance, the time had come to unite against them.[569]

✦ ✦ ✦

By mid June Nana had managed almost completely to close Cawnpore to the outside world. "The southern road was entirely shut up," wrote Thomson, "and not a native was allowed to travel in the direction of Allahabad. Pickets of sepoy infantry were posted fifteen paces apart, so as to form a complete *cordon* around the position, and these were supported by cavalry pickets, forming a second circle, and the whole were relieved every two hours."[570] On the Agra road the spy and camel sowar Peer Bux passed five police stations within fifteen miles of Cawnpore, each with "ten sowars posted, who were the Nana's servants."[571] On the Oudh side of the Ganges, Captain Henry Lloyd Evans had remained at his post at Unao, agonizing over the fate of his wife and two children trapped in Wheeler's Entrenchment, but the Bridge of Boats had been severed, and all the native boats moored on the Cawnpore side.[572]

The rebels had stopped the mails, shut down the dâks, and cut the telegraph. All anyone could do to convey messages was entrust them, at great cost, to native spies, or hope that the few fugitives who had managed to slip downriver in time would inform Calcutta of the Doab's desperation.

One of these fugitives was Mrs. Elizabeth Sneyd, last seen on May 25, passing through Cawnpore with her daughter-in-law Louisa and Topsy, her lap dog. Mrs. Sneyd had found refuge at Fatehpur, fifty miles downriver, where in early June a native first brought her news of the fall of her son's garrison at Shahjahanpur. She hoped that since the news had come "through a native, it perhaps *might* turn out to be false." But it was true. On May 31 they had been attacked in church by the 41st Native Infantry. The chaplain had lost his hand to a sword stroke as he tried to bar the door, the magistrate was also cut and then killed as he ran across the courtyard. Others were killed and wounded, but the remaining men barricaded the doors as the women and children ran up the turret. When Elizabeth's son Henry arrived on the scene, the sepoys of the 28th returned to their lines for their arms. Devoted servants hurried their masters' weapons to the church, and in the company of a small party of loyalist Sikhs the remaining men, women, and children escaped—including Henry and his sister Anna, who as a small girl had dreamed of being killed in a church by black-skinned men. They were killed a week later near Aurangabad.[573]

At Fatehpur on June 4 Mrs. Sneyd started up from her friend's verandah at the sound of guns booming fifty miles away at Cawnpore.[574] Mrs. Sneyd immediately resolved to beat her way to Allahabad and that night set forth by carriage along the Grand Trunk Road. Traveling at night, she and her daughter passed a body of sowars with fine mounts and English saddles resting in the moonlight. Watching her balefully from their resting place, they silently let her pass.

By the time the Sneyds reached Allahabad, Louisa was nearly dead from exhaustion. The troops were on the verge of rising up and attacking their officers, and threatening crowds wielding broken earthen vessels and sticks already roamed the streets. At the post office, Mrs. Sneyd was told that the natives were intent on murdering every European man, woman, and child that very night. She fled to the fort, but the guard refused her admittance and advised her to secure steamer passage to Calcutta. The Sneyds now drove three miles back through the brawling city and down to the river to catch a steamer called the *Madras* that was stuck on a sandbar downriver from the city's ghats. But no one would take them to the *Madras* without a permit, and so Mrs. Sneyd was obliged to ride her carriage through the streets yet again, where sneering, contemptuous sepoys now "shook their ram-rods" through her carriage windows.

Finally, at midnight, after presenting their permit, Mrs. Sneyd reached the *Madras*. The steamer, armed with guns, freed itself from the sandbar and began to chug down river for Calcutta, passing burning vessels, stations in flames, mutineers yelling horribly and rushing about "in a most frantic state, as if they were mad!"[575] The *Madras* it-self was fired on once by grapeshot, which clattered onto the deck at Mrs. Sneyd's feet. Startled one night by the roar of coals being shoveled into the steamer's furnace, Louisa gave birth "to a remarkably fine little boy" while lying on a floor crawling with centipedes, cockroaches, and scorpions. Incredibly, the baby flourished, and Louisa, drinking milk from a goat requisitioned by the vigilant captain, recovered just as Mrs. Sneyd herself began to sink from exhaustion.

At last they reached Fort William and were all dropped off at a point on the riverbank of the Hooghly where a friend had promised to meet them. Hours passed and the friend failed to materialize, so Mrs. Sneyd paid two boatmen to fetch litters and bearers to carry them to a hotel. But the hotels were all filled with refugees from the "disturbed districts," and "not a spare corner [was] to be had" until the kindly proprietor of a men-only hotel finally took them in.

Calcutta itself was in "a dangerous state," wrote Mrs. Sneyd, "from the treachery and wicked machinations of the natives, particularly the Musselman party." Even the servants had become insolent. Sweepers were telling their masters to "fetch it yourself," and even Mrs. Sneyd's own ayah, who had stuck by her through their terrible river journey, disobeyed Mrs. Sneyd's orders and posed in the mirror with her memsahib's shawl, saying, "Ah, *your* rule will soon come to an end, and we shall have our *own* king!"

LAMBS AND SAINTS

Calcutta and the Column: June 1857

If Calcutta was in "a dangerous state" it was due in part to the Anglo-Indian community. On "Panic Sunday," June 14, the European and Eurasian communities, convinced that the troops at Barrackpore were about to rise, fled to secret hiding places and to boats they kept moored in the river. Merchants, tradesmen, civil servants entertained the most preposterous rumors, carried rifles and pistols into supper with them, rode together in improvised militias, met to swear vengeance on the sepoys and sowars and vilified the governor-general for his bland equanimity in the face of impending disaster. "All I can say," Canning wrote of the European community's unseemly flights, "is that in my life I never came across such a set of old women—some of them with swords by their sides—as those who fetch and carry the news of this town among the clubs and gossiping 'tiffin' rooms of their acquaintance." It was enough to make him "ashamed of Englishmen."[576]

To keep the blizzard of rumors from completely unhinging the Anglo-Indian community, Canning gagged the press, without distinguishing between Anglo-Indian and native papers. Canning himself appeared hardly ruffled by the mounting reports of mutiny and rebellion. To assure his countrymen, and more importantly the local native regiments, that he did not fear an uprising at Calcutta, he had steadfastly refused to cancel the Queen's birthday ball and would not replace his sepoy guard with Europeans. He prohibited Calcutta businessmen from forming corps of volunteers and not only delayed ordering a general disarmament until such a disarmament was virtually unenforcable, but extended it to the European as well as the native communities, demanding licenses of everybody.

On June 5 Lady Canning had reassured Queen Victoria that "the great towns in the valley of the Ganges about which so much anxiety was felt, have remained quiet. . . . A violent outbreak at Lucknow and the defection of several regiments did not inflame the country." But bushels of letters poured into Lord Canning's office from men in the outstations who desperately leapfrogged whatever was left of the civilian line of command in their ruined districts and wrote directly to the governor-general. Too many brave, dedicated, and sober men were sounding the alarm, begging for relief and painting the same pictures of murder and mayhem that Canning had been trying to dismiss as outlandish.

On June 6, Canning passed an act that empowered not only officers in the field but civilian "commissioners" to execute natives convicted of exciting or stirring up the native army. But this concession to the public cries for "wild justice" did nothing to rescue Canning's reputation. The Europeans of Calcutta took his evenhandedness for highhandedness, his deliberative scrupulousness for cowardly dithering. Cawnpore was supposed to be Calcutta's bulwark; if it fell, so went the prevailing wisdom, so would Bengal, so would John Company itself. When would Canning relieve old Wheeler at Cawnpore?[577]

But until fresh troops arrived from Persia, China, and Madras, Canning had to conserve his resources. He could weather the hysteria at Calcutta, though it was "enough to break one's heart," he wrote, "to have to refuse the imploring prayers of the Anglo-Indians at out-stations. . . . But to scatter our small force over the country would be to throw away every chance of a speedy success."[578] Nonetheless Cawnpore was never far from his thoughts. On May 31, Canning had ordered Commander-in-Chief Anson to detach a regiment of European Infantry and a corps of cavalry from his stalled Delhi expedition and send them down the country to retake Aligarh and relieve the "severely pressed" garrison at Cawnpore.[579] In almost every letter Canning wrote that June he expressed his anxieties for the fate of Cawnpore. At last European troops began to arrive at Calcutta's docks, including the ruddy, bearded 78th Highlanders whose kilts convinced some natives that the Queen had sent naked demons to wreak her vengeance.[580]

✦   ✦   ✦

First the naked demons would need a commander. Sixty-two year-old Brigadier-General Henry Havelock was a craggy, sun-browned little warrior with a churchy, parsimonious beard and a generous shock of snowy hair. Unlike the expansive and indulgent Wheeler, Havelock was almost concertedly unlovable. Dubbed "Old Phlos" by his schoolmates, who had regularly thrashed him for his priggishness, as a commander he proved "unpopular with his soldiers to an extraordinary degree. He was a martinet very formal and precise, and seems to have maintained a rigid and perhaps somewhat sour discipline which they could not bear."[581] Havelock had been converted to the Baptist denomination by his father-in-law, the Reverend Joshua Marshman, who would champion him in his weekly newspaper *Friend of India*.[582] Havelock exceeded even the pious Colonel Wheeler in his evangelical fervor, plaguing his British troops and officers with sermons, temperance tracts, prayer meetings, and notoriously long-winded battlefield orations that for forty-two years marked him as "a fanatic and an enthusiast."[583]

His men were ridiculed as "Havelock's Saints," but in an army plagued by drunkenness they were sometimes the only sober soldiers in the field. Havelock was almost supernaturally conscientious—and a lifelong student of languages, tactics, and the Bible, of course. In Burma, the Punjab, Afghanistan, and most recently Persia he had evolved from a brave if sometimes overreaching officer to a decisive and judicious commander. But he had yet to fulfill his boyhood dream of commanding an army in the field.

When news of the rebellion reached him in Persia he hurried to Bombay, hoping to join in the expedition against the rebel stronghold at Delhi. But as adjutant-general of Queen's troops in Bengal he was summoned to Calcutta with his old friend Patrick Grant, the son-in-law of Lord Gough who had leapfrogged Wheeler to become, however briefly, commander-in-chief.

"Your Excellency," Grant declared as he introduced Havelock to the governor-general, "I have brought your man!"

Havelock made a doubtful first impression with his tendentious self-assurance, his copious decorations jangling from his coat, his oversized sword dragging slightly as he stepped forward in his well-worn little boots. But Canning took Grant's word for it. "No doubt he is fussy and tiresome," Lady Canning wrote of Havelock, "but his little, old figure looks as fit and active for use as if he were made of steel."[584]

As far as Havelock was concerned his appointment had come not from Canning but the Almighty Himself. "May God give me the wisdom to fulfil the expectations of Government," he wrote, "and to restore tranquility to the troubled districts."[585]

✦ ✦ ✦

Havelock would need all of his mettle and sagacity just to contend with his leonine subordinate, Colonel James George Smith Neill, commander of the the 1st Madras Fusiliers—"the Lambs" as they liked to call themselves with a certain bloody irony. The colonel was a towering, ferocious, commanding figure ("the finest man I ever saw," wrote one of his subordinates). Behind his tangled, Old Testament brows and burning gaze lurked a complicated sensibility, by turns brutal and delicate. He had such dimension and charisma that whatever a man might look for in a commander—warrior, pastor, avenging angel, paterfamilias—he could find in Colonel Neill.

By the time Havelock set forth from Calcutta, Neill had been in the field for three weeks. He had already delighted the Anglo-Indian community by setting forth within twenty-four hours of his arrival at Calcutta and arresting the local stationmaster for refusing to delay a train for his tardy Lambs. He arrived at Benares on June 4, and at the rate he was traveling—some thirty miles a day—might have reached Cawnpore by the eleventh. But out of an entire lack of confidence in the sepoys of the Bengal Army and a conviction that to put down rebellion he must be utterly masterful, Neill persuaded the sunstruck local brigadier to permit him to disarm the apparently quiescent 37th Native Infantry.

Over the course of a disastrous parade, Neill directed his artillery to fire salvos of grape not only on the panic-stricken 37th but on a regiment of Sikhs and irregular cavalry, too. Believing that "the Word of God gives no authority for the modern tenderness for human life," Neill promptly erected gallows and hanged hundreds of suspected rebels, including a number of boys accused of romping around the city beating drums and flourishing rebel flags.[586] Neill let loose the Lambs' "Big Jim Ellicot" as "hangman-in-ordinary,"[587] and sent punitive parties into the surrounding districts, where they strung up hundreds of peasants from mango trees, playfully arraying one group in "the form of a figure eight."[588]

As a result, Neill did not leave Benares until June 8, and, as Mrs. Sneyd had discovered, by the time he and his Lambs reached Allahabad on the eleventh, the 6th Native Infantry, outraged by Neill's treatment of the 37th and his depredations in the countryside, had murdered most of their own officers, freed the prisoners in the jail, demolished the Presbyterian mission, plundered the city, and chased the remaining Europeans into the fort.[589] Prostrate from exhaustion, Neill loosed a combined force of Sikhs and European volunteers upon the city.[590] Their cannon, torches, and cross-firing muskets killed hundreds of natives, including old men, women, and children. They caught all the men "on whom they could lay their hands," wrote Bholanauth Chunder, a native traveler of the time, "—porter or pedlar—shopkeeper or artisan, and hurrying them on through a mock-trial, made them dangle on the nearest tree. Near six thousand beings had thus been summarily disposed of and launched into eternity. . . . For three months [would] dead-carts daily go their rounds from sunrise to sunset, to take down the corpses which hung at the cross-roads and marketplaces, poisoning the air of the city, and to throw their loathesome burdens into the Ganges."[591]

Rebel corpses, said Chunder, "hanging by twos and threes from branch and sign-post all over the town, speedily contributed to frighten down the country into submission and tranquillity." But Chunder was merely being polite. In fact not only did Neill's indiscriminate executions and floggings further inflame the rebels of the Doab, they lit fires "which he was compelled to stay and extinguish."[592] Colonel James Neill would still be at Allahabad, assembling transport, burning villages, and hanging natives, when Havelock finally caught up with him almost three weeks later.

BURDENS AND REGRETS

Wheeler: June 15–18, 1857

In a small, square, central room of the tile-roofed barrack, Sir Hugh Wheeler rose stiffly from his bed, haggard and hollow-eyed after another sweltering, cacophonous afternoon of interrupted slumber. The bed was nothing more than a mattress on which he and his family took turns sleeping. He had slept in his shirt and pants and boots, ready at the first alarm to return to the trenches.

Though Wheeler had sent most of the garrison's servants away, he had retained for his own family a staff of over half a dozen, including his kitmutgar, his bearer, and his cook.[593] Now that he had sent his valet to Lucknow,[594] it fell to his bearer to help him button his coat and buckle on his sword, feats Wheeler could not accomplish with his mangled left hand.[595] By now something like full-blown whiskers had sprouted beneath his sideburns, and his white hair lay flat upon his scalp in a plaster of dust and sweat. Drawing on his cap and wavering slightly in the hot blast of the Doab afternoon,[596] he said good-bye to Lady Frances and his grown daughters Eliza and Margaret,[597] and with his son Godfrey at his side he stepped out of the barrack to inspect the defenses.[598]

The old general rushed across to the shelter of the privy and then out to the western battery. The position had been commanded by Artillery Lieutenant Charles Dempster, assisted by his eighteen-year-old comrade John Nickelson Martin, but sometime in the middle of the siege Dempster had been killed between Whiting's battery and the remaining barrack, and Martin had been shot through the lung by a sniper and now lay in a barrack under the care of civil surgeon Harris's sister-in-law, Miss Brightman, who would literally exhaust herself trying to keep him breathing.[599] Major Prout of the 56th, who had commanded the little rifled three-pounder nearby, was dying of heat stroke in the tile-roofed barrack, and now a ragtag assembly of volunteers under the command of Captain Moore stood beside the three nine-pounders.[600] All three had been damaged by rebel shells, and though their barrels were loaded with grape against another assault, they were useless against the enemy's western batteries.

During the evening lull, husbands, servants, and a few entrepreneurial soldiers headed for the well, skirting the stinking, sunroasted horse carcasses that still littered the yard from the first cannonades.[601] Hiding with their jugs and tins behind what remained of the well and trough and bathing cistern, they waited their turn at the ropes and buckets. "Tattered in clothing, begrimed with dirt, emaciated in countenance," the pickets silently watched the general pass, quieting their wives and children who stirred nearby in the shallow trenches. "Worked to death," wrote Amy Horne, "underfed, and, in the later stages of the siege, starved; continually under a hot fire from the mutineers; their uniforms rotting on their backs; their faces unwashed; their hands covered with grime from the guns, which dried and formed a hard coating; they were such a pitiful sight to see."[602]

Along the drainage ditch that ran between the western trench and the burned barrack, other family groups hid from the sun under a hodgepodge shelter of crates, trunks, carpets, barrels, scraps of tent canvas, and mosquito netting stretched across splintered rafters and weighted down with bricks against the blistering wind. Within these shelters mothers "scraped away the floor to make hollows for their babes to sleep in."[603] Beds became so scarce and the sentries so exhausted that Amy Horne would sometimes wake up "to find a soldier sharing my charpoy (native bed), where the poor fellow had thrown himself down in utter weariness!"[604]

Wheeler had commanded soldiers under duress and could bear their reproachful stares, their half-hearted salutes. But the women and children were a different matter. Some gamely maintained their "modesty and delicate feeling" even as they set their dead children, husbands, sisters, and brothers out for disposal in the sepulchral well. Colonel Williams's wife had been wounded in the mouth by a sniper's bullet and her daughter Georgiana in the shoulder blade, but the "intrepid" Georgiana nursed her mother without complaint.[605] And Caroline Lindsay, the major's eldest and favorite niece, and her little sister Fanny were conspicuous in "servicing the fire and disease."[606]

Others "were sinking into the settled vacancy of look which marked insanity. The old, babbling with confirmed imbecility, and the young raving in not a few cases with wild mania."[607] Amid the carnage children mimicked the soldiers in their games. During the parallel siege at Lucknow "one was heard saying to another, 'You fire round shot, and I'll return shell from my battery.' Another, getting into a rage with his playmates, exclaimed, 'I hope you may be shot by the enemy!' Others, playing with grape instead of marbles, would say, 'That's clean through the lungs,' or 'That wants *more eleva-tion.*'"[608]

"Sometimes the little things, not old enough to have the instinct for liberty crushed by the presence of death," wrote Thomson, "would run away from their mothers and play about under the bar-rack walls, and even on these, the [snipers] would fire their mus-kets, and not a few were slain and wounded thus."[609] Some newly orphaned children were taken in by their parents' friends and comrades, others were left to wander about. The children of Head-master Gill and his wife, both killed in the barrack fire, became so "reduced from starvation . . . you would not have been able to make them out."[610]

Other children clung pitiably to their dying parents. "Assuredly no imagination or invention ever devised such pictures as this most hor-rible siege was constantly presenting to our view," Thomson recalled. A private's wife was walking with her husband, "looking for some covered nook in which to pass the night in safety.[611]

> Her twin children were one in each arm, when a single bullet passed through her husband; killing him, it passed also through both her arms, breaking them, and close beside the breathless husband and father fell the widow and her babies; one of the lat-ter being also severely wounded. I saw her afterwards in the main-guard lying upon her back, with the two children, twins, laid one at each breast, while the mother's bosom refused not what her arms had no power to administer.[612]

Some children met the crisis with as much gallantry as any of the garrison's adults. Shepherd's five-and-a-half-year-old daughter Polly used to sit in the corner of their apartment, "the very picture of pa-tience . . . struggling within herself in order not to cause her parents additional pain. I have often caught her eyes swollen with sup-pressed tears, fixed sometimes upon her mother's features and some-times upon mine, with an expression so full of the different emotions that worked within her, yet the desire not to pain us" was unmistak-able. "She would sometimes whisper her desires to our servant Thakooranee, at the same time begging her in a most pitiful manner not to mention to papa and mamma, as they would be grieved."[613] Thakurani herself was heroically faithful to the Shepherds, and often risked her life for them, especially for her "Polly *Baba*," for whom she once braved the midday hail of rebel fire and "stooping and crawling" fetched water from the well in her own water jug which, as a woman of caste, she was obliged to carry for her own exclusive use.[614]

Now that the rebels were concentrating their fire on the tile-roofed barrack, a few families had found a secret haven in the ruins of the burned barrack. Here and there soldiers of the 32nd ducked off from Eckford's battery to rake through the ashes for their campaign medals or scuttle into the shattered privies to relieve themselves.[615] Some soldiers and officers had become so contemptuous of the rebels' fire that they casually ducked the round shot as it whirred toward them. But it was a costly affectation. Out of "indomitable pride of race," Lieutenant Swynfen Jervis of the Engineers, chief architect of Wheeler's fortifications, steadfastly ignored his comrades' pleas to run and duck through the snipers' fire.[616] Walking slowly from Whiting's battery to the remaining barrack with his back straight and his head held high, he was promptly shot through the heart.[617]

Men lined up at the provision godowns for their families' rations of chupatties, lentils, and rum. At the Main Guard, where a grimy sentry gave Wheeler a tattered salute, the doctors had set up a surgery,[618] though it was no more than a holding area for the wounded and the sick now that all the surgical instruments and medical supplies had been lost in the barrack fire.[619]

Captain Turnbull, whose 13th Native Infantry had mutinied at Fyzabad, still commanded the western line south of the Main Guard, keeping watch over the native prisoners, providing covering fire for the cooks and volunteers who darted to and from the outer barracks, and protecting the underground field magazine from incendiary shells.[620] But the pale-skinned Captain Kempland had to command the southern wall of the Entrenchment in absentia, for he was "utterly prostrate and non-combatant" from heat stroke, and directed operations from the shell of a room in the burned barrack.

To the southeast stood what had been Artillery Lieutenant Eckford's battery, but after his death by round shot the three nine-pounders had been assigned to Lieutenant Burney of the artillery, assisted by the "pale and wiry" Lieutenant Henry George Delafosse of the 53rd. Proceeding northward along the Entrenchment's eastern perimeter, Wheeler passed the battered kitchen in which musicians' wives and children vied for space with the few officers' servants who had not yet run away. In the northeastern corner of the yard the parapet was interrupted by a gap where Lieutenant St. George Ashe still commanded a battery of one twenty-four- and two nine-pounder guns. The former had been battered out of commission, for this was the most exposed of the garrison's batteries, a special target of the nearest rebel guns at St. John's across the road. Ashe's was the one battery that was not served by an underground powder magazine and had to be supplied from perhaps a dozen carriages parked nearby in the open yard. It was a wonder that Ashe was still alive, still directing fire, still standing on the heels of his nine-pounders to watch his round shot arc toward the ruins of the soldiers' church.

At the beginning of the siege "the field magazines contained two thousand pounds of powder, with ball cartridge and round shot in abundance."[621] But after a week and a half Wheeler was paying coolies to collect round shot from the plain and tote it into the Entrenchment. (One coolie was caught by the rebels and "when asked why he would help the Feringhee in this way he replied simply that they paid him for it, for which answer his hands were cut off.")[622] Dinged and torn by rebel round shot, the bore of many of the guns could not accept even cannister, so the ladies were asked to donate their stockings "and other parts of our clothing,"[623] recalled Amy Horne, which the gunners filled with grape and rammed down the irregular barrels, sometimes with spectacular results.[624] Thomson remembered how Delafosse

> was much annoyed by a small gun in barrack No. 1; and as he was compelled to load his 9-pounder with 6-pound shot, he could secure no regularity in his firing. Thoroughly dissatisfied with his artillery practice, he at length resolved to stake his reputation as a bombardier on one desperate *coup*. He gave his worn out gun a monster charge, consisting of three 6-pound shots and a stocking full of grape, all well rammed down. The result was satisfactory beyond expectation; for the faithful old weapon did not burst, as might have been expected, and the sharp and troublesome little antagonist was never heard again.[625]

In the soldiers' garden where Mrs. Hillersdon and Mrs. DeRussett now lay buried, the low rows of thorn trees were merely charred stumps, and at the northern end of the Entrenchment pickets lined up to use the low privy that stood unwholesomely close to the garrison's second kitchen.[626] In the shambles of a row of coolies' huts left over from the construction of the outer barracks a few families sought refuge, including the wives and children of the men of Vibart's nearby redan that protruded northward toward the city.

The Entrenchment was no place for a cavalry man, but at fifty years of age Major Vibart was bearing up astonishingly well. His oldest daughters were in England, and his eldest son Butcher had made his way safely from Delhi to Meerut, but Emily and the major had brought their four youngest children with them into the Entrenchment.[627] His youngest child, Louisa, had already died of sunstroke, and Johnny, his oldest,[628] had been shot and killed by a sniper's bullet while running out to greet his father as he returned from his post.[629] But his thin and high-strung wife Emily had survived, and was now holed up in a central room near Wheeler's apartment, clutching little Willie and Emmie to her as the major greeted Wheeler at the redan.

Vibart's redan was perhaps the most hazardous position, vulnerable to fire from three directions. Here three young officers of the 1st Native Infantry assisted Vibart: Burney's Addiscombe classmate Supple, Lieutenant Henry Smith, and the overaged bachelor Lieutenant Frederick Redman, who had written home at the beginning of the siege that he was grateful "that he had no wife with him to share the surpassing horrors of his situation."[630] By the end of the siege all three of them would be beheaded by round shot.[631]

Southwest of the redan, across the metalled road that poked into the northwestern corner of the Entrenchment, Captain Francis Whiting of the Canal Department commanded another bulge in the walls that took the brunt of the fire from the northernmost rebel batteries. Here an exploding shell had landed in the trench, killing William Cox and Frederick Jacobi and maiming seven soldiers' wives. Cox was no loss; he was the detrimental cashiered Fusilier who had been let off for drunkenly firing on the sowar picket the month before. But Frederick Ernest Jacobi, the coach-building brother of the late Henry Jacobi, whose family languished with the Greenways at Savada House, was one of the civilian heroes of the siege. He had served under Turnbull by the Main Guard, and when an incendiary shell landed atop the magazine and threatened to ignite hundreds of pounds of gunpowder, he had climbed to the roof and removed it with his bare hands. Now, lying in the arms of his wife Sophie, he would survive the exploding shell in the trench for only a few minutes, bleeding from the bandaged shreds of his exploded legs.[632]

Wheeler's tours evidently did not extend to the outpickets. A man of his years could not have been expected to perform the broken-field running that a dash to the unfinished barracks required. So Wheeler had to content himself with reports from Captain Moore, whose wife still spent most days in a little hut the outpickets had fashioned for her out of bamboo and canvas. The outpickets held perhaps the most critical position of all, for if the rebels ever occupied the entire string of barracks they could fire from so short a distance and at such a commanding angle as to render the Entrenchment completely indefensible.

The rebels had settled more or less permanently into the south-ernmost barrack, and every day, recalled Thomson, they "resumed the old work of annoyance, by coming . . . up the lines of the unfin-ished barracks, and threatening us. Accordingly we had to resume the daily employment of expelling them, lest their unchecked inso-lence should lead to acts more decisive." The fighting was fierce.

> The frequency of our casualties from wounds may be best under-
> stood by the history of one short hour. Lieutenant Prole had come
> to the main-guard to see Armstrong, the adjutant of the 53rd Na-
> tive Infantry, who was unwell. While engaged in conversation
> with the invalid, Prole was struck by a musket-ball in the thigh
> and fell to the ground. I put his arm upon my shoulder, and hold-
> ing him round the waist, endeavoured to hobble across the open
> to the barrack, in order that he might obtain the attention of the
> surgeons there. While thus employed, a ball hit me under the
> right shoulder-blade, and we fell to the ground together, and were
> picked up by some privates, who dragged us both back to the
> main-guard. While I was lying on the ground, woefully sick from
> the wound, Gilbert Bax (48th Native Infantry) came to condole
> with me, when a bullet pierced his shoulder-blade, causing a
> wound from which he died before the termination of the siege.

Sometimes the combat was hand to hand. On one sortie Thomson and Daniell heard the "sounds of struggling in a room close at hand." Rushing in together, they found Captain Moore pinned to the floor by a powerfully built sepoy who was preparing to cut his throat. Moore, with his broken collarbone, was "unequal to such a *rencontre*" and "would certainly have been killed had not Daniell's bayonet in-stantly transfixed the sepoy."[633]

✦ ✦ ✦

On the morning of the sixteenth the bombardment resumed as usual, and the Shepherd family stood pressed against the walls of their apartment. But after a few hours of shelling the room had become such a perilous ruin that Jonah decided to lead them to new quarters. As bullets and shells continued to rain around them, they climbed over the heaped remains of the verandah and stumbled into an apartment that was only partially full. But the occupants, several of them Jonah's acquaintances, refused to let them stay, and they were forced back into the maelstrom.

At last they ducked into an apartment composed of two rooms: one well barricaded but occupied by officers and their families; the other less secure but evidently vacant and in any case better protected from the shelling than the ruin they had just abandoned. Thanking God for their good fortune, they began to settle into a corner when an "old grey-haired officer" rose with a start from his cot and ordered them out.

Jonah and his family "begged very hard to be permitted to remain there only an hour." But the officer commanded them to depart immediately, even "threatening personal violence" if they did not go.[634]

Before Jonah and his family returned to the yard they glanced into the second, barricaded room to find that the officers and their families had deserted it in the face of the rebels' concentrated fire. Rather than brave the hail of bullets and grapeshot in the open yard, the Shepherds decided to lay claim to the shuddering room for as long as they could. As his family settled in, Jonah returned to retrieve his valuables from his ruined apartment only to find that his locked chest had been struck by a cannonball and everything in it—pocket watch, jewelry, memorabilia—destroyed, including his niece Emmelina's dead parents' sole portrait, the loss of which "nearly broke the poor girl's heart."[635]

The firing on June 17 was especially intense. Nana sent two waves of mutineers across the parade-ground to attack the Entrenchment, and though they were both repulsed with a loss of fifty mutineers, the losses in the Entrenchment were also heavy.[636] Postmaster Roche, who apparently had taken Hillersdon's place as chief civilian officer in the garrison, was wounded in the right foot, knee, and shinbone,[637] and Godfrey Wheeler, manning a lookout on the roof of the surviving barrack, received such a severe contusion that he had to be littered into his father's apartment to be tended by his mother and sisters.[638]

Having recovered from his wound, Jonah joined Kempland's corps near the burned barrack, where he cleared a little space for his family. Because the roof had been destroyed, the enemy had all but ceased firing upon it. Nevertheless that noon, as Ellen sat with their infant daughter "answering her innocent smiles," a bullet came ricocheting into the room, passed through the flesh of Ellen's arm, and lodged under the skin behind the baby's ear. "The child shook a little," recalled Jonah, "and to all appearance was dead, but after a while, some signs of life appearing, I put a drop of water in her mouth, when she opened her eyes and began to writhe and struggle in great agony." A surgeon removed the bullet and placed a wet compress over the wound, but within hours she seemed to waste away before their eyes "until she resembled the bud of a delicate flower."[639]

✦ ✦ ✦

"Long and painful as this narrative of suffering may prove to the reader," wrote Thomson, "he will not forget that all this was but on the surface. The agony of mind, the tortures of despair, the memories of home, the yearning after the distant children, or parents, the secret prayers, and all the hidden heart-wounds contained in those barracks, were, and must remain, known only to God."[640]

Though Major William Lindsay outranked such line commanders as Kempland, Turnbull, Ashe, and Dempster, there was apparently no question of assigning him to one of the batteries. "I never have had a desire to Command anything or anybody," he once wrote, and a lifetime of desk work had left him overweight and crippled with lumbago.[641] According to his nephew George, the major had been "well but almost overpowered with work" before the siege began.[642] Lindsay spent his days in the Main Guard writing a profusion of "station and division orders" on torn slips of scarce paper with the whittled-down stubs of pencils, "for there was no ink or pens to be had for love or money."[643] The flow of dispatches, commissariat memoranda, casualty lists, and recommendations for medals and promotions sustained some semblance of order in the improvisational defense of the garrison. There must have been some officers who, amid exploding shell and mangled bodies, discarded Lindsay's memoranda in disgust, but others would have been reassured by at least the illusion of a line of command and the promise of honors and promotions.

Phlegmatic and deliberate, Lindsay had done his best to intercept the scores of petitions the garrison brought before Wheeler, facing down their demands, pleas, and indignant complaints with his deflating equanimity: calming the ladies, commiserating with the gentlemen, and sending them back to the trenches and barracks satisfied that everything that could be done was being done. But in truth there was so little that could be done, and when Lindsay returned to the barrack and saw his wife Lilly and his sister Kate and his nieces Caroline, Alice, and Fanny, Lindsay's latent melancholia, his chronic regret at ever having come to India in the first place, must have tortured him. Lilly was gaunt and prostrate with fever, her vitality guttering in the deep hollows of her eyes. The countenances of the others "assumed a stolid apathy, and a deadly stillness, that nothing could move."[644]

Why had he ever coaxed Lilly out to India in the first place? Why had he let her return to him after depositing their children at Rochester? Why had he not contented himself with a major's pension and returned to his three little children in England? Why had he not seen the death of his fourth child as the omen it was? And why had he allowed his sister Katherine to come out to India with her three daughters? Why had Kate herself not heeded Caroline's tearful forebodings at Calcutta? Why had he not put them all on boats for Allahabad when he still had the chance? It must have seemed to William Lindsay as he lay down to rest in the suffocating barrack, vibrating from the round shot pounding against its walls, that they were all to die of his own caution, reticence, and inertia.

On June 17, as he lay on his cot with his face to the wall, a round shot struck the opposite side and sent a spray of splintered brick into the room. The sharp shards struck Lindsay full in the face and when Kate and the girls pulled his hands away, they found that his eyes had turned to pulp. The sight of her husband's wound and the sound of his agonized cries was too much for poor feverish Lilly to bear, and within hours she had died of shock. "In total blindness and extreme pain," the major suffered one day longer under his sister's care, until, on June 18, after almost thirty-one years of service in a country he despised, death finally relieved William Lindsay of his burdens and regrets.[645]

TO THE LAST

The Entrenchment: June 18–20, 1857

Weakened by shock, heat, wounds, and hunger, many in Wheeler's garrison succumbed to fever. What kind of fever was rarely recorded; few survived the first flush long enough to manifest any specific symptoms. But in the presence of dead bodies, burst privies, offal scattered about the yard, mosquitos, flies, lice, dried blood, and contaminated water, it could have taken many forms: cholera, dysentery, typhoid fever, malaria, typhus, hepatitis, smallpox.[646]

In one day a Captain's wife[647] and child, Colonel Williams's married daughter,[648] a Miss Yates,[649] and the merchant Henry Christie and his child[650] all died "of a maddening fever."[651] Fever carried off Charles and Lydia Hillersdon's orphans, and Colonel Wiggins's motherless infant.[652] Miss Brightman collapsed with a fever while nursing the perforated Lieutenant Martin. Fever also rampaged through the improvised surgery in the Main Guard, killing surgeons Garbett and Newenham and Newenham's wife and children.[653] Captain Athill Turner's wife and children also died of fever, as did Turner's subordinate Lieutenant Richard Owen Quin.[654] The widow of old Mr. Gee had succumbed, and Thomas Greenway's daughter Louisa, Mrs. Samuel Greenway, Captain Jellicoe's wife, and Mrs. Wainwright, one of Seppings's party, who may have caught the pox from Emma Halliday.

Others continued to die of heat stroke. With its roof now broken through in places, its walls pitted by shot and its doors "breached and knocked down into huge shapeless openings"[655] the remaining barrack offered little shelter from the sun. In the exposed trenches the temperature reached 120 degrees,[656] setting off muskets and baking their stocks until they were too hot to touch.[657] "Across the plain, the mirage, which only makes its appearance in extremely hot seasons, painted its fantastic scenes, sometimes of forest scenery, sometimes of water, but always extending to a vast distance, and presenting a strange contrast in its unbroken stillness to the perturbed life within our mud walls."[658]

As terrible as the heat was the stench of excrement, vomit, sweat, and decaying flesh. The stink so permeated the barracks that despite the bombardment most families chose to spend their nights in the open air of the trenches.[659] During the lulls in the shelling, the widower Reverend Haycock of the Cawnpore Mission used to bring his mother outside to escape the fetor. Haycock had done his best to see to the safety of his native Christian charges, but by the time he had entered the Entrenchment "the excitement of the crisis, working on a constitutionally sensitive temperament" had already "disordered his intellect,"[660] and when his mother was wounded during one of her airings he became "a raving maniac."[661] For three or four days she tried to restrain him. "Poor old lady," wrote Jonah, "it was a pitiful sight to behold her solicitude and watchfulness over her son."[662] But every now and then the Reverend would wriggle free and run stark naked through the yard, insensible to the "iron storm" around him.[663]

Nothing was recorded about Henry Cockey's ministrations, and Father Joseph J. Rooney, the Roman Catholic priest, whom the Irish gunners supplied with food and rum from their "scanty rations," had died of sunstroke by the middle of the siege.[664] But the "vulgar and plain speaking" Reverend Moncrieff, long frustrated by the constraints of his chaplaincy, had finally found duties worthy of his fervor.[665] "Public worship in any combined form was quite out of the question," Thomson recalled, which would have suited the evangelical Moncrieff, who now "went from post to post reading prayers while we stood to arms. Short and interrupted as these services were, they proved an invaluable privilege, and there was a terrible reality about them, since in each such solemnity one or more of the little group gathered about the person of their instructor was sure to be present for the last time."[666] "Indefatigable in the performance of his ministry of mercy with the wounded and the dying," Moncrieff circulated among the mangled, feverish souls who, anesthetized with rum, writhed and babbled in the festering surgery.

After two weeks the survivors found they could usually hide from the sniper fire and even duck the round shot by merely stooping down or bobbing their heads.[667] But the shells the mortars lobbed into the Entrenchment found their way everywhere. One landed in the burned barrack among David Duncan's sleeping children and burst, instantly killing two but leaving one strangely unscathed.[668] "Our stress for water can be imagined," recalled Amy Horne, "when on one occasion we were obliged to drink some mixed with human blood, which had fallen into our vessel from the wounds of a native nurse or 'ayah,' who, while standing near by, had both her legs carried away by the bursting of a shell."[669]

A few men tried to take on John MacKillop's duties fetching water for the women and children. During his breaks from his duties in the outer barracks, Resident Engineer Heberden of the East India Railway Company circulated among the women and children, ladling out drinks of well water until a bullet passed through both of his hips. Heberden was littered into the surgery and "lay for a whole week upon his face," but despite his "extraordinary sufferings, . . . not a murmur escaped his lips."[670] A "very nice, well-made" gunner named O'Dwyer, unable to bear the cries of women and children, met a similar fate. Pausing on one of his runs to the well he poured a few buckets of water into the cistern and lay down for a moment to cool himself when a shell landed directly in the cistern and exploded, mangling his leg and maiming him in several places.[671]

O'Dwyer's more mercenary comrades used to pay the Christian drummers a "trifle" to fetch water that they would then sell to families by the jugful. One of these soldiers mistook Jonah's sunstruck brother Daniel for a drummer and threatened to run him through with his bayonet if he did not fetch water for him. The soldier was such an enormous, livid man that Jonah advised his frail brother to obey. But just as Daniel was rising to his feet, Apothecary Twoomy appeared and scolded the trooper for menacing his patient. The soldier backed off, muttering to himself, but evidently threatened a few others that day, for he was eventually pronounced mad and incarcerated in the Main Guard, where he died the next day of a cerebral hemorrhage.[672]

◆ ◆ ◆

Wheeler received word from Lucknow on June 18 that because the rebels had complete control of the river, Henry Lawrence could not send him any relief. "Pray do not think me selfish," Lawrence begged his old friend. "I would run much risk could I see commensurate prospect of success. In the present scheme I see none."[673] Desolate, Wheeler asked Moore to reply, hoping perhaps that an officer of his grit might convince Lawrence to reconsider. Even the gallant captain could not disguise the garrison's despair. "Sir Hugh regrets you cannot send him the 200 men," he wrote to Lucknow, "as he believes, with their assistance, we could drive the insurgents from Cawnpore, and capture their guns." The garrison had "acted most nobly; and on several occasions, a handful of men have driven hundreds before them. Our loss has been chiefly from the sun and their heavy guns. . . . We, of course, are prepared to hold out to the last. . . . We trust in God; and if our exertions here assist your safety, it will be a consolation to know that our friends appreciate our devotion."[674]

✦   ✦   ✦

On June 18, Jonah and Ellen Shepherd's seventh wedding anniversary, their wounded infant daughter passed away. The Shepherds could not bear simply to leave her out in the verandah for the fatigue party to pick up, and so, wrapping her in a scrap of clothing, Jonah carried her to the trenches after dark and by the light of the bursting shells scraped a grave for her out of the hard, dry earth with the blade of his Persian knife.

As he returned to the trenches and listened to the sentries calling the "All's well" on the quarter hour, Jonah began to meditate on the meaning of his own survival. To fetch his rations in the Main Guard, Jonah had been forced to cross sixty yards of ground every evening, through "shoals of bullets" that stabbed at the barrack steps as he raced back to rejoin his family. Once, as he awaited his ration of rum, a cannonball from an eighteen-pounder had come bounding off the archway of the Main Guard and struck the wall three inches from his head. On another occasion he came within inches of being crushed by falling bricks. It seemed to Jonah that the Lord was saving him for some special purpose, and it could not have been to serve as a soldier. Though he "longed to be able to render some service as might ensure the safety of so many poor suffering women and children and the sick and wounded," he was an indifferent marksman and too frail to be much use in hand-to-hand combat if it came to that. But he was a Eurasian fluent in Hindi and Urdu and dark enough after weeks in the sun to pass for a native. Lying for hours in the trench as the shells burst around him, Jonah began to fix on the idea of slipping out of the Entrenchment disguised as a laborer and setting fire to the magazine.

Captain Seppings told Jonah he was mad to consider such a scheme, and Assistant Commissary Reilly, who had fallen into disgrace for having failed to blow up the magazine in the first place, only repeated his insistence that the magazine was invulnerable to sabotage. But others encouraged him, even offered to accompany him if they could. At last Jonah finally decided to approach General Wheeler himself.

Furiously scrawling a dispatch, Wheeler only half listened to the tremulous little clerk's proposition, and before Jonah could explain the purpose of his mission the old man threw down his pen and ordered him out of his apartment. "If all the men were to leave," he snapped, "who would man the Entrenchment?"[675] Stunned and insulted, Jonah slouched back to the trenches.

Others continued to try to escape the Entrenchment. Demented by the shelling, a private's wife stepped over the parapets with a child in each hand, "courting relief from her prolonged anguish by death from the sepoy guns." But one of her husband's comrades ran after her and in a rain of sniper fire dragged her and her children back into the Entrenchment.[676] A Eurasian telegraph officer named Farnon escaped over Kempland's parapet and hid in the city, convincing one suspicious body of rebels that he was a Mahomedan by naming various Lucknow Moslems as his kin. Three ayahs had crept away, only to be captured by the rebels, most of whom disbelieved their stories of the garrison's desperation, afraid these loyal servants of the *sahib logue* had been planted by their masters to lure the rebels into a trap.[677]

✦ ✦ ✦

"Day after day," wrote Thomson, "throughout the whole period of our sufferings, . . . we were buoyed up by expectations of relief." Calcutta had wired Wheeler on May 25, promising troops by the nineteenth of June. Now that the nineteenth was upon them, the garrison "indulged the hope," wrote Thomson, "that they must have been expedited for our relief. Often we imagined that we heard the sounds of distant cannonading. At all hours of the day and night my men have asked me to listen. Their faces would gladden with the delusive hope of a relieving force close at hand."

After the nineteenth came and went, the pickets' faces sank back again "into the old careworn aspect." But the next day, as if conjured up by the garrison's frail hopes, a native water carrier suddenly appeared in the Entrenchment, dispensing fresh, cool drinks from his dripping leather sack. Declaring his devotion to the Company, he announced to Wheeler and the other officers that two companies of European soldiers with a couple of guns had reached the far side of the Ganges, "and might be expected in our midst on the morrow." Despite Lawrence's letter to the contrary, the desperate garrison believed the water carrier, and welcomed him back on the twenty-first when he returned to report that the troops had been impeded by the rising of the river but were building rafts and intended to cross the next morning. "The tidings spread from man to man," remembered Thomson, "and lighted some flickering rays of hope even in the bosoms of those who had abandoned themselves to despair."[678]

PLASSEY

June 21–23, 1857

The view from Nana's headquarters a mile away at Savada House was muddled by the glare of the morning sun, and in the evening the Entrenchment, already obscured by the echelon of barracks, was cast in shadows. Few rebels, not even the sepoys who surged through the unfinished barracks, had managed to approach closer than three hundred yards, and many of them had been killed by the garrison's sharpshooters and occasional bursts of grapeshot. Squinting through the same undulant glare that dazzled Thomson and his pickets, the mutineers could not see the garrison in any particular detail. Though the British excoriated the rebel snipers for purposefully firing on women and children, and no doubt some did, few snipers could have distinguished them from men as they darted across the yard. Most simply fired at anything that moved.

At night the garrison's lights were doused, and all the rebels could see of the Entrenchment were flickering glimpses in the sputtering glow from the mortar shells as they arced across the plain. One night a blazing light was seen in the Entrenchment, "from which it was supposed that the Europeans had set fire to their baggage with the intention of balking the sepoys in their hopes of plunder."[679] But it could have been anything: a cooking fire, an incendiary shell. None of the rebels could tell.

For Nana Sahib and his commanders the garrison's endurance was an exasperating wonderment. It was as if the sahibs had tapped into some magical, inexhaustible resource. No matter how much fire the rebels poured into the Entrenchment, Wheeler's pickets always fired back with a vengeance, and the outpickets in the unfinished barracks never failed to stave off the rebels' advances. Many of the rebels continued to believe that the Entrenchment and the surrounding plain were elaborately mined. There may also have been rumors of an impenetrable underground chamber in which the women and children were hiding; unbeknownst to the garrison itself—but perhaps dimly recalled by some aging coolie or pensioned sepoy—such a chamber, long covered over, actually did exist under the southern end of the burned barrack.[680]

Wheeler's officers had commanded these sepoys and sowars all their lives, and to see their men flounder in their preparations and balk in their attacks on so feeble a position filled them not only with disgust but shame. Had they been commanding the rebel forces, they told each other, they would have taken the Entrenchment in a day. Nevertheless, the Entrenchment's parapets, trenches, short-range guns, and ample supply of arms and ammunition combined to make a far more formidable position than it looked to either the rebels or the garrison. The men hunched down in the trenches were more or less impervious to anything but a direct hit from Nana's mortars, and in most places the parapets still stood up to the rain of round shot from his batteries. The barracks, even the honeycombed shell of the burned barrack, protected most of the pickets from crossfire.[681]

But it is not surprising that both the rebels and the garrison would have disparaged Wheeler's Entrenchment. Trenches and foxholes were alien to Indian sepoys and officers alike. They had been trained to reduce the occasional mud fort or chase down bands of brigands, tribals, and assorted upstarts, not dig in against assaults. In fact, the mere act of digging in had posed a special problem for the Brahminical sepoys of Oudh whose caste forbade them to so much as pick up a shovel. Trenches had played a significant role in the Crimea, but Lord Raglan had all but excluded Indian Army officers from his campaign; not one officer at Cawnpore had served there.[682] They had thus been denied some important lessons about the value of digging in against shrapnel and grape.

The romance of the Indian Army, as with most armies of the time, lay in its assaults: glorious, audacious, headlong rushes on the enemy. So it is hard to blame Moore for risking so much for so little result by attacking the rebels in his sorties, and difficult not to understand the rebels' shame for not having stormed Wheeler's Entrenchment. But against even the exhausted civilian snipers poised along the trenches and the garrison's makeshift charges of grape and bolts tied together in ladies' stockings, a frontal assault on a desperate garrison in a position like the Entrenchment could be suicidal.

✦   ✦   ✦

Time appeared to be on Nana's side. Supplies were running low and soon the monsoon would flood the trenches, devour the parapets, and turn the Entrenchment into a quagmire. But time was also Nana Sahib's enemy, for despite his exalted proclamations—the latest declared him the ruler of his father's old capital at Poona[683]—his wary troops were losing their patience with this self-proclaimed Peshwa and his entourage of zealots, opportunists, and dilettantes.

On June 20 the disaffection among Nana's Moslem troops reached such a pitch that the sowars arrested their own leader, Teeka Singh, for accepting an elephant and a pair of gold bangles from Nana Sahib and sending home two cartloads of requisitioned butter and sugar.[684] Like Nana, Teeka Singh had been obliged to humble himself before his sowars, and plead with them not to abandon Cawnpore for Lucknow and Delhi.

Azimullah kept assuring Nana that his troops could wipe out whatever feeble force Calcutta might send up the Grand Trunk Road, but Nana did not want to fight the British on two fronts. He had to subdue Wheeler's garrison before the relief force arrived. His gurus gave him the deadline of June 23, the centennial of the Battle of Plassey in which Clive had vanquished the Nawab of Bengal. The 1764 Battle of Buxar had been more decisive in establishing the Company's rule, but to the mutineers Plassey had greater significance. It was there that native troops had proved their mettle by standing firm through several hours of artillery fire, and at Cawnpore the anniversary had special significance for the 1st Native Infantry, the direct descendants of Clive's Bengal battalion, upon whose colors "Plassey" was still stitched in golden thread.

✦   ✦   ✦

After the fire on the thirteenth, Nana's gunners had concentrated their fire on the remaining barrack, but on June 20 the condemned havildar and a few of his comrades escaped the Main Guard, and slipped across the parade-ground. Bustled into Nana's presence, he reported that many in the garrison had returned to the shell of the burned barrack.[685] So the next morning the rebels redirected their fire, and shell and round shot hurtled into the charred ruins of the burned barrack.

As families scurried back into the exposed trenches and open drains, or found shelter in the remaining barrack, Wheeler asked Major Vibart to write another desperate plea to Lucknow. "This evening, in three hours," wrote the major, "upwards of thirty shells were thrown into the intrenchment. This has occurred daily for the last eight days: *an idea may be formed of our casualties*, and how little protection the barracks afford to the women. Any aid, to be effective, must be immediate. In the event of rain falling, our position would be untenable." They still expected a force of one thousand Europeans to relieve them at any hour.

> Any assistance you can send might co-operate with it. Nine-pounder ammunition, chiefly cartridges, is required. Should the above force arrive, we can, in return, insure the safety of Lucknow. Being simply a military man, General Wheeler has no power to offer bribes in land and money to the insurgents, *nor any means whatever* of communicating with them. . . . It is earnestly requested that whatever is done may be effected without a moment's delay. We have lost about a third of our original number. The enemy are strongest in artillery. They appear not to have more than 400 or 500 infantry. They move their guns with great difficulty on account of the unbroken bullocks. The infantry are great cowards, and easily repulsed.[686]

Vibart had grossly underestimated the number of rebel infantry at Cawnpore, but he was probably going on the evidence of the past few days, when fewer and fewer sepoys reported to their posts along the siege line and fewer snipers fired from the roosts in the unfinished barracks. Wheeler must have taken this as further proof that the rebels were falling away from Cawnpore and dispersing to their villages. But the primary reason was that the sepoys had fired so relentlessly during the early stages of the siege that, despite the boatloads of munitions that had fallen into Nana's hands, they had nearly used up their percussion caps and had to go to Nana's metalsmiths and gun makers to convert their muskets into flintlocks.[687]

On June 22 the mutineers gathered for a review at the Assembly Rooms, where their native officers pledged on the Koran and Mother Ganges to take the Entrenchment or die in the attempt.[688] Though Nana's guru divined that the next day would not be auspicious, Teeka Singh gave the 1st Native Infantry's Subhedar Major Radhay Singh the honor of leading the assault.[689] By now more than four thousand men had assembled, and, marching silently across the canal, they took up their positions for the next day's assault.[690]

After nightfall, a European sentry sitting in the crow's nest atop the second unfinished barrack counted seven hundred mutineers creeping across the plain from the abandoned lines of the 53rd and 56th Native Infantries.[691] Thomson desperately sent a request to Moore for reinforcements, but the captain replied that "not one could be spared." Thomson and his sixteen pickets braced themselves, cocking their hammers as the rebels approached, rattling and rustling in the distance like advancing locusts.

But suddenly Moore himself appeared in the barrack with Lieutenant Delafosse in tow. "Thomson," said Moore, "I think I shall try a new dodge. We are going out into the open, and I shall give the word of command as though our party were about to commence an attack."

Moore picked up a sword, Delafosse grabbed a rifle, and they set forth with a few outpickets to face the rebels. As they reached the second southernmost barrack, they came upon a large body of rebels who had left the security of the barracks and positioned themselves among the piles of bricks and debris that lay scattered about.

In a few more seconds the rebels might have subsumed Moore and his little band, but now the captain called out into the darkness, cupping his voice in different directions.

"First section, halt.

"Second section, right about and turn to the left.

"Steady, my men, and fire at the word of command!"

It worked. Their bayonet sheaths loudly rattling against their ammunition pouches, the rebels leaped over the "heaps of rubbish" and ducked back into the southernmost barrack.[692] "We followed them with a vigorous salute," wrote Thomson, "and as they did not show fight just then, we had a hearty laugh." But all through the night the rebel cannon laid a furious fire. The sepoys in the unfinished barracks kept up their feints and charges, and not a man in Thomson's picket "left his post for an instant."[693]

The rebel cannonade finally eased off, and as the morning sun rose Cornet Mainwaring persuaded Thomson to get some sleep. Crawling off into the lean-to shade of the second barrack wall, Thomson curled up on his side with his double-barreled shotgun close-at-hand. But no sooner had he shut his eyes against the sun than Mainwaring was shouting, "Here they come!" Thomson scrambled back to his post to see a smattering of distant daubs of color assembling along the horizon. Around the rubble of the riding school a mile to the north sowars appeared in blotted adumbration, reining in their mounts and drawing their sabres, and suddenly Nana's batteries opened fire from every direction.

Leaving his injured son Godfrey in his mother's keeping, General Wheeler pushed his way through an incoming tide of panicked women and children and emerged into the sunlight, buckling on his sabre.[694] Along the parapets the pickets took aim at the watery shapes of the sepoys as they advanced through the waves of heat "that made the horses appear twenty feet high, and riders in proportion."[695] A few battle-hardened ladies dusted their menfolk's stacks of guns and sat by with their ramrods and cartridges, poised to reload, but it must have seemed to most of the men who lay yards apart along the parapets, squinting into the rays of the rising sun and trying to choose a target from the onrushing multitude, that the end had finally come.

At the squawk of a bugle the sowars rushed forward with a great clanking of kits and a fulmination of hooves. Behind them an enormous cloud of dust rose into the hazy blue sky like a scrim, roiling with the dark gray smoke from the rebels' batteries. Waving tulwars and carbines above the flutter of their shirts and turbans and shouting "Deen! Deen!"—*For the faith! For the faith!*—they surged across the ditch and streamed around the bandstand to charge their old commander's battery.[696]

Splendid-looking devils, their officers must have conceded as the sowars approached. But they had forgotten some of their training, for they charged "all the way at a hand-gallop, so that when they neared the intrenchment their horses were winded." Wheeler kept his gunners poised with their matches burning, and not until the sowars had swarmed within fifty yards of the trous de loup did he allow his gunners to fire their three nine-pounders into his errant "children." A single round of grapeshot sent so many sowars and their squealing horses hurtling to the ground that it threw the rest "into hopeless confusion, and all who were not biting the dust wheeled round and retired."[697]

But there was no time to celebrate. Vibart's gunners rammed their stocking cartridges down their cannon's smoking barrels and turned them about to the east. For as the cavalry galloped off, the garrison peered over the parapets to behold a confounding sight: a row of large, pale objects that at first appeared through the smoke and dust to be ungainly whitewashed huts slowly advancing across the field.

They had crept some hundred yards before the garrison's officers finally figured out what they were: giant cotton bales the rebels had collected from the godowns at the ghats: mobile parapets behind which bands of infantry were scuttling along, popping up now and then to fire.

The bales had come within 150 yards of the Entrenchment when ranks of sepoys appeared along the compound walls and among the debris of the demolished church and surrounding bungalows, leaping up onto the road with a terrible roar. The officers in the garrison could recognize a few by their uniforms, for though most of the sepoys had sensibly reverted to their native clothes and "dressed like recruits,"[698] here and there among the "tag-rag-and-bob-tail" ranks a trooper of the 1st Native Infantry had donned his shako or his bright red coat.

They rushed across the ground with Subhedar-Major Radhay Singh in the lead, stumping heavily forward with his curved sabre flashing, exhorting his troops at the top of his lungs. A stream of rebels ran with their backs bent down, following the course of the storm drain, but the rest advanced in a bristling hodgepodge with their muskets at the ready, loping the 350 yards to the Entrenchment and shouting *"Deen! Deen!"*

The garrison's gunners and pickets fired as soon as the rebels came within 150 yards, and it probably came as no surprise to Nana's guru that the first volley caught poor Radhay Singh full in the chest. As the subhedar-major crumpled to the ground, a few of his men faltered, but most continued to advance, some kneeling or sprawling to fire. But another blast of grape from the garrison's batteries set a few of the cotton bales afire, and as their cover vanished into smoke and Wheeler's pickets fired at will, the advance party fled back toward the road, and the troops behind soon followed, leaving twenty-five dead on the field and many more wounded groaning and crawling across the scorched and splattered plain.[699]

In the unfinished barracks the swarms of sepoys tried again to take Thomson's position, approaching right up to the barricaded door. "Mainwaring's revolver despatched two or three," Thomson recollected. "Stirling, with an Enfield rifle, shot one and bayoneted another; both charges of my doublebarrelled gun were emptied, and not in vain. We were seventeen of us inside that barrack, and they left eighteen corpses lying outside the doorway."

In the melee a grapeshot caught Thomson in the thigh and "ploughed up the flesh, but happily, though narrowly, escaped the

bone." Captain Jenkins and his picket assisted Thomson in successfully clearing the sepoys out of the echelon of barracks, but as they
surveyed their morning's work, "a wounded sepoy, who had feigned
death while our men passed him, suddenly raised his musket and
shot Captain Jenkins through the jaw," Thomson recalled. "I had the
miserable satisfaction of first dismissing the assailant, and then [con-
ducting] my suffering companion to his barrack," but Jenkins was
forced to abandon his command.[700]

Captain Moore directed the Entrenchment battery to fire grape
from the north corner and took another couple of dozen volunteers
out to the fifth barrack, advancing southward until they had driven
the enemy out of the third. Another round of cannister finally drove
two hundred rebels back to their position at the brick kiln, where for
an hour and a half they "kept up a dreadful firing of musketry and
nine-pounder shot."

About midday a rebel mortar crew managed to hit one of the garrison's ammunition wagons in the southeast corner of the Entrenchment, and having found their aim exuberantly lobbed shell after
shell into the wagon's vicinity. To save the battery's nearest supply of
ammunition, Lieutenant Delafosse rushed out and crawled under
the wagon to pull away the burning splinters and throw them as far
as he could from the adjacent wagons. Two soldiers hurried to his assistance with buckets of water which Delafosse threw on the flames,
and despite the constant bursting of shells they managed to douse
the fire and return to the trenches without injury.[701]

By midday most of the rebels had melted away, and the sentries,
their faces blackened by gunpowder, their shoulders aching from
their muskets' kick, gaped at each other in astonishment. Here and
there a man lay dead or wounded, and the bodies of a few more
women and children killed in the barrage were set out along the
ruins of the outer verandahs, but the garrison had marked the anniversary of Plassey by surviving the worst the rebels could throw at
them. Could Wheeler dare to hope his valiant garrison had broken
the spirit of Nana Sahib's army? Brushing off the garrison's wan congratulations, the exhausted old man burst back into his apartment to
find Frances and his daughters grieving over the trunk of his "darling
son" Gordon who, in the preceding barrage, had been decapitated by
a round shot while pulling on his clothes.[702]

JONAH'S BID

June 24, 1857

That evening, as a few bold sentries were rolling some of the abandoned cotton bales back into the Entrenchment to fill shell holes in the parapets, a lone sepoy crawled along the storm drain that ran between the Entrenchment and the road.[703] He reached within ten paces of the Entrenchment before two sentries sighted him and shot him dead. When it was discovered that he was a Hindu and unarmed, everyone immediately surmised that he had been "coming to seek pardon for himself and his comrades without reference to the rebel authorities." Indeed, several sepoys had been watching his progress from the church, as if to see how he might be received.[704]

When a delegation of unarmed mutineers appeared on the field to ask permission to remove their dead and wounded, the garrison held their fire.[705] But many wondered how many mutineers might have followed that first lone sepoy had he crept safely into the garrison's custody. The officers wished there were some means of communicating with their wayward troops, "for they appeared to be very sorry for what they had done."

Jonah Shepherd survived the fray without a scratch and returned to his family in the barrack. Ellen almost fainted with relief at the sight of him, but he had a strange new glint in his eye and announced that he had finally divined the special mission God was saving him to perform; he would slip into the city and learn the condition of the rebel army after their ignominious defeat and return to report to Wheeler. Ellen desperately begged him not to go, but it seemed to him that the garrison could not survive another siege like today's, and the only weapons he had left were his wit, his fluency, and his sun-darkened skin.

In the morning the prostrate Captain Kempland again dismissed the proposition as too dangerous: to his knowledge everyone who had tried to sneak off had been captured.[706] But Jonah argued that this was because they had all slipped off at night. He told Kempland that he had made a study of the rebels' routine from his post in the southern trenches, and that between eleven and one their snipers invariably left their posts to take their midday meals. Jonah proposed to dart through the unfinished barracks at midday while the rebels were idle and make his way into the city.

Impressed by Jonah's careful reasoning and tantalized by the prospect of learning the enemy's condition, Kempland weakly jotted a note for Jonah to take to the redoubtable Captain Moore. Muttering "God's will be done" and strangely "callous to every danger" Jonah sought out John Moore, but the brave captain was not to be found. After scurrying back into the Entrenchment, Jonah was told by an officer on the northern parameter[707] that the captain was ill and had given up command of the batteries only an hour or so before.

In fact Wheeler had just refused to permit Moore to conduct another of his midnight sallies to capture the rebel batteries, and the captain had retired in disgust to take Jenkins's command in the outer barracks. Jonah believed that such a foray would have succeeded, for the enemy was demoralized, and though Moore's men seemed "quite worn out and reduced to a company of specters, so that they were not capable of standing their ground, [they] appeared quite resolute and willing."

Jonah was relayed to Captain Williamson, his old commissariat officer and now major of brigade, who in turn sent Jonah back into the barrack to confer with General Wheeler. He found Sir Hugh seated on a mattress in the corner of his room, looking old and feeble. Lady Wheeler and their two daughters squatted mournfully in another corner, and Postmaster Roche, who had been attached to the general since Lieutenant Wheeler's death, sat nearby, wounded in several places and looking very much "reduced." The old general looked up at Jonah and scowled. "You are the same person who wanted to leave me the other day," he said, grimly shaking his gray head. "I cannot trust you."

This time Jonah did not back off. "I would not desert the camp on any account," he declared—not with a large family in the Entrenchment who depended on him. If he had merely wanted to escape the Entrenchment, he told Wheeler, "nothing would be easier for me than to step over the wall at dead of night whilst standing sentry."

Suddenly the old man warmed to Jonah "and at once entered into my views." He confessed to Jonah that though he would gladly lay down his life to spare the women and children he was "quite at a loss what to do." Grasping now at this last shred of hope, Wheeler offered to reward Jonah for any intelligence he might bring back about the enemy or the prospect of relief from Lucknow or Allahabad. All

Jonah asked was for the right, if he chose to exercise it, to remove his family from the Entrenchment on his return. Wheeler agreed to this, and after thinking a moment, proposed that Jonah find Nunne Nawab and induce him to sow dissension among the rebel ranks, or, failing that, to go among the Mahajuns and offer them as much as one hundred thousand rupees and "handsome pensions for life" for sabotaging Nana's campaign.

As their meeting drew to a close, Jonah ventured to express to Wheeler how much everyone felt the loss of the general's son, whose blood and brains still marked one battered wall. At this the old man covered his face with his hands "and burst into a very severe paroxysm of grief." His "whole body shook, as if his heart were bursting" and pressing himself into the corner of his room "gave vent to his overpowering emotion in a flood of tears." When the general began to recover his composure, Jonah asked what he was to tell the rebels about the Entrenchment if he were captured.

"Do not let the enemy know that we are discouraged," Wheeler said, suddenly all business, "or that we have been short of provisions. Say that we are able to pull on very well for a month to come: and above all, let them know that we expect a speedy help from Allahabad."

On his way out of the Main Guard Jonah heard someone feebly call his name and looked down to find the heroic John MacKillop gazing up at him from his litter, much reduced by the wound to his groin. Once disappointed in Jonah for declining to assist him in his dangerous runs to the exposed well, the joint magistrate was glad to learn of Jonah's bold mission and wished him God's speed.

As soon as Jonah reached the burned barracks he was surrounded by a tattered mob of people weakly clamoring to hear his plans. Several elderly ladies commissioned him to bring back "some tobacco, and other necessaries." Jonah scrambled to assemble his disguise in time to take advantage of the mutineers' lunch break. He tried to buy clothes off of some native servants, but they refused, laughing when he offered to trade them for the filthy rags in which he had spent the past three sweltering weeks. Eventually Jonah managed to acquire a sepoy's loin cloth and a cook's coat smeared with grease. His hair was cropped close, with a tuft left in the center, over which a turban was wrapped; and "a small stick completed my disguise."

Just as Jonah was about to set forth, Postmaster Roche staggered out to reiterate the general's instructions. Jonah assured him that he entirely understood his mission and then, buoyant with hope, said

JONAH'S BID ◆ 283

good-bye to what was left of his family: his tearful wife Ellen, his beloved little Polly, his sister and her two children, his brother Daniel, her sister's aged mother-in-law, his orphaned niece.

One man gave him half of his rum ration, which Jonah rashly downed in a single swig. It made him so giddy that after obtaining a pass at the Entrenchment's northern battery he decided to test his disguise by dropping in on various British acquaintances. Elderly Conductor Berrill, who had shared the Sherpherds' quarters, jumped up angrily when Jonah peered in and bade him good morning. But Jonah's voice immediately gave him away to Mrs. Berrill and her daughter, who "had a most hearty laugh" and wished him "every success."

As Jonah passed the guard room, a European sentry called out to him to identify himself, but Jonah kept walking. Now others began to take notice along the way, standing and asking each other, "Who is that?" and "What is he?" until at last the sentry called out again in a threatening voice. Jonah stopped and two soldiers came out to command him in Hindustani to identify himself. At last a boy named Ball, whose father had died of sunstroke three days before, began to laugh, and, with a flourish, Jonah showed them his pass. "Their looks of astonishment amused me very much" although he confessed that Schorn's rum "had made me facetious."

Confident of his new disguise, Jonah crept back into the new barracks beyond the southern parameter of the Entrenchment and stole quietly into a room where a European piquet of five or six men was stationed. His appearance astonished them, and as he stood quietly in the middle of the room, one of the soldiers pronounced him mad.

"Who are you?" they all demanded to know. But Jonah merely grinned.

The commotion finally roused the officer on duty and a clerk who slowly recognized Jonah. Delivering the pass to the officer, Jonah accepted all their best wishes and as everyone kept quiet he stared a moment along the row of barracks and began to duck from one to another, passing the bodies of two slain sepoys, one "a mere skeleton, the other just getting decomposed."

◆ ◆ ◆

Jonah's plan was to go directly to a small tank north of the barracks and, if questioned, pass himself off as a Moslem leatherworker who had come to bathe. But as he paused in the last of the barracks, he saw two sepoys approaching from the west. Rushing northward a little way along the high, tree-lined course, he hooked down along a small ravine and ducked into the declivity of the tank, eager for a bath and a drink. But the tank was completely dry, and as Jonah stood bewildered in the midday sun, he turned to see that a cowherd had been following him with a heavy bamboo poised in his hands.

Before Jonah could get away, the cowherd was down in the tank and in a village dialect demanding to know who he was. Jonah tried to pretend not to hear him and began to move away, but the suspicious cowherd loudly persisted. Summoning up what he knew of village Hindi, Jonah said he was "an unfortunate traveller in great distress, going to the city of Cawnpore to beg for a morsel of bread."

"No such thing!" snarled the cowherd. "You're from the Entrenchment. I saw you coming out!"

Jonah tried to protest, but the cowherd described precisely how he had proceeded from barrack to barrack to the public road.

Jonah gaped at him a moment. "I don't know what you call the Entrenchment," he sputtered. "I'm a stranger. When I saw the first barrack on the roadside, I stepped into it to take a little rest from the heat. Besides, I'm quite starved," he said with unfeigned conviction. "I haven't had a morsel of food for some time past."

"But when did you come here?" the cowherd wanted to know.

"Only an hour ago," Jonah answered hurriedly, trying to get him off the subject. "Now do tell me the road to the city. I'm dying of hunger."

The cowherd now seemed to take pity on Jonah, and was about to show him the road to the city when four sepoys approached them, carrying swords.

"Who are you both?" they called out. "What are you doing here?"

The cowherd immediately recounted his conversation with Jonah.

"It's true," one of them snarled, turning toward Jonah. "He must be one of them. Look how his clothes are covered with grease and dirt. He must be a fugitive from the Entrenchment."

The soldier advanced on Jonah with his sword bared, muttering, "I'll cut off his head," and employing "a most disgusting epithet." Convinced that "all was up" with him, Jonah bowed his head and prepared to die, but at the last moment a second sepoy gripped his companion's arm.

"Let the poor fellow alone," he said expansively. "He looks so poor and harmless. Why take innocent blood upon yourself?"

The first sepoy paused.

"Let him go," his companion gently insisted. "You won't gain anything by killing him. He'll probably soon die of starvation anyway. He already looks half dead."[708]

The sepoy reluctantly sheathed his sword and, leaving Jonah where he stood, followed his companions toward the city.

Jonah "thanked God in my heart for His deliverance" and was about to strike off toward town when three more sepoys appeared from the same direction. Jonah hurried to catch up with the first four who had spared him, but just as they climbed out of the tank a Moslem orderly on an errand from Nana's headquarters at Savada House rode up to the four sepoys, who pointed Jonah out.

The orderly drew a gun and galloped up to Jonah, threatening to blow his brains out if he did not tell him who he was.

"If you spare my life," Jonah said, "I'll tell the truth."

The Moslem grudgingly agreed, but Jonah told him only part of the truth, which was that he had indeed escaped from the Entrenchment but only to escape the shot and shell.

"So now do not kill me," he begged the orderly, "but let me go away."

"You shall not be killed," the orderly replied. "But come along with me. You must give all the information about the Entrenchment to the Raja Sahib." Bending down from his horse, the orderly searched Jonah and took the two rupees Jonah had secreted in his makeshift turban.

Thus within less than half an hour of leaving the Entrenchment, Jonah Shepherd was Nana Sahib's prisoner. He nearly fainted walking barefooted and bare-headed across the stony, simmering plain. But the guards would not permit the curious passersby to mistreat him, and some in the neighborhood found him so pitiable that they brought him water, gram, and fried bread, which he eagerly consumed.

After a pause at a police station, he was taken to Nana Sahib's camp and led into a large bamboo enclosure guarded by four swordsmen. A couple of dozen other prisoners, male and female, squatted silently around him in the shade, and watched as Jonah was taken out to stand before an old man seated on a dirty carpet under a mango tree. Jonah had no answers rehearsed, but as a clerk he had taken depositions from natives and knew that the rebels would try to trip him up with detailed questions about his faith. So before the old man could wipe his glasses and arrange his papers, Jonah had already determined that he would pass himself off as a low-caste tanner who wouldn't be expected to hold to any "particular creed."

As other rebels gathered to listen, the old man asked Jonah to give his name.

"Budloo," Jonah replied, plucking up the name of a tanner who had worked for him once as a servant.

And his father's name?

Jonah faltered a moment, and then remembered the name of another of his servants. "Jhundoo," he said.

"And what is your caste?" asked the old man.

"*Chumar.*"

The old man asked Jonah his occupation.

"A cook."

The old man peered over his spectacles. "Cook of officers or of soldiers?"

"Soldiers," Jonah replied, for officers would never employ a tanner for a cook.

And where did he come from?

Jonah thought fast. If he named a neighborhood in Cawnpore, witnesses could be brought to expose him. So he told them he came from Allahabad, in whose cantonments he had spent his boyhood. When they asked him to be more specific he dredged up an area called Keet Gunj from his dim childhood memories, hoping they would ask no more.

"Where in Keet Gunj?" the old man asked.

Jonah swallowed hard. "I've just forgotten it," he said, stalling; he couldn't remember anything about Keet Gunj. The old man squinted at him and a few others who had gathered to hear Jonah's deposition leaned forward and glared. Jonah was on the verge of collapsing when it finally occurred to him that almost all native streets had wood stalls.

"Near the wood stall," he piped up, praying they would leave it at that.

They did, but now impatiently asked what he knew about the Entrenchment.

"I know nothing of the Entrenchment," he told them, trying to contain his relief. "I was kept entirely in the kitchen, and watched by the soldiers very carefully for fear of my running away. Very few servants are left there," Jonah continued, regaining his nerve. "Almost all of them deserted when the attack began. So I am quite unable to tell you its condition."

This reply infuriated his interrogators, who said he was lying and, with "disgusting epithets," demanded he be beaten.

"If he was so carefully watched," they asked each other, "how did he escape this morning?"

As they moved menacingly toward him, "a happy thought" occurred to Jonah.

"Soldiers went out very early this morning to the new barrack," he explained, "carrying their dead from the Entrenchment to throw into a well there. I bore a helping hand," he said simply, "but while their attention was engaged, I slipped away from the well, and remained hiding among the heaps of bricks nearby until I got the chance to get away."

Satisfied with this explanation, his interrogators settled back.

"But surely you must know how much provision is left," one insisted, "and the number of fighting men who are still living?"

"Well," said Jonah, "I will tell you as far as I know. I have often heard the soldiers say, while in the cook-house, that they can pull on with the provisions for another whole month."

The rebels exploded.

"This is altogether false," declared one.

"Don't believe him," another told the man. "We know full well the Feringees are starving. They have nothing but a little gram left, as the two women prisoners will confirm."

They now produced the two cowering ayahs who had escaped the Entrenchment on the twenty-first. To save their lives they had told the rebels the truth about the Entrenchment: that the inhabitants were desperate, that they lived on soaked gram; that most of the women, children, and able-bodied men had been killed; that those who remained were "in great distress and likely to die away shortly."

Jonah turned away from the ayahs and shrugged. "If you wish to believe these timid women who never stirred out of their hiding places for fear of the shots and who certainly got gram to eat . . . you are at liberty to do so, and it is not necessary for me to give you any further information."

Of course, Jonah had just told them that as a cook he never got out and around either, nonetheless the rebels shot glances back and forth between Jonah and the two ayahs, not knowing whom to believe. To tip the scales, Jonah provided them with some false details: that about twenty or twenty-five soldiers had died from sunstroke and "very few from the shot and shell," that "a good many women and children were dead from fright and heat, but that there were sufficient fighting men still left to defend the Entrenchment, and all were determined to fight to the last."

Once more the rebels shouted abuse at Jonah, but he stood his ground until at last they again backed off. Someone asked if it were true that the Entrenchment's parameter had been mined, and as Jonah pondered his answer the others leaned anxiously forward. Glancing from face to face, Jonah slowly realized why the mutineers, some of the bravest soldiers on earth, had laid such timid siege to Wheeler's feeble Entrenchment, herding townspeople ahead of them in their first grand assault.

Reminding himself that he was supposed to be a simple chumar, Jonah answered that he did not exactly know what they meant by "mined." Nevertheless, he told them, he was certain that there was powder buried all through the Entrenchment.

At this the rebels briskly brought his interrogation to a close, and, ordering that Jonah be returned to the bamboo pen, they hurried his deposition to Nana Sahib.

A group of mutineers lay around the grove, and from their "murmurings and suppressed whispers" Jonah eventually surmised that perhaps on the basis of his dissembling testimony Nana Sahib and his rebel council had finally given up on taking the Entrenchment by force.

In the middle of the afternoon an official of Nana's court approached Jonah and asked through the bamboo bars if he believed the garrison was "anxious to leave the station" and might accept an offer of safe passage.

Jonah answered that he wasn't sure, but he believed that the women and children were certainly eager to get away from Cawnpore and "for their sakes no doubt such an offer would be accepted if made in a satisfactory manner."

If Nana Sahib were to offer such a thing, the official inquired, would Jonah deliver a letter to the Entrenchment?

Jonah said he would, but answered perhaps too readily, for the official looked at him suspiciously and slowly walked away.

A wind began to blow dust through the mango grove, and a patch of rain cloud followed overhead, drenching Jonah and exciting his wound and the numerous sores that had erupted on his flesh during the past three weeks. His wet clothes began to reek so badly that he discarded his vest "and sat in the breeze," considerably keeping himself downwind of his fellow prisoners.

A few hours later another prisoner was brought into the bamboo pen with his arms tightly bound behind him. He turned out to be

Mendes, a Christian drummer who had escaped from the Entrenchment on the twelfth and hid in a mendicant's garden by the Ganges.
A sepoy had accused him of the capital offense of providing bread to
the Entrenchment, but Mendes, bursting into tears, had insisted he
was a Moslem and asked why, if he had been stealing bread, the
sepoy had not stopped him. This had so stymied his accuser that
Baba Bhutt had decided not to execute him immediately. Jonah
would later consider Mendes "a help-meet . . . though at that time
we had not the remotest knowledge of each other."

Jonah was not, as it turned out, the only man to escape the Entrenchment that day, nor indeed the only Eurasian to try to pass
himself off as a leatherworker. Not long after Jonah's departure
Wheeler sent a dark-skinned and temperamental Eurasian private
named Blenman with instructions to go to Allahabad "and make
known our desperate condition."[709] But Blenman did not get as far as
Jonah. "He managed to elude the observation of seven troopers who
were posted as cavalry pickets, but he was discovered by the
eighth. . . . They stripped him of rupees and pistol, and told him to
return to the place he came from." Blenman hurried back to the Entrenchment, the only one of Wheeler's spies that the general was
ever to see again. A third man, a sepoy named Ghouse Mahomed,
left the Entrenchment posing as a dead rebel's grieving brother who
had come to Cawnpore to buy burial clothes. But Ghouse Mahomed
lost heart and remained hidden in the city for the rest of the siege.[710]

Late in the afternoon at Savada House, Jonah overheard a rumor
that "an old lady from among the Christian prisoners"[711] would be
sent with a letter from Nana to the garrison, offering them safe passage downriver to Allahabad. Jonah was jubilant. The garrison was
to be spared, due in no small part to his own heroic masquerade. He
envisioned his family preparing for their passage to Allahabad, and
imagined their joy when he returned to the exultant garrison to lead
them to safety. Jonah became so agitated by his hopes that after several hours had passed he ventured to ask one of the swordsmen "if
he thought I would get my liberty soon."

But the guard replied with "a burst of the most shocking abuse,
accompanied by threats to beat me if I dared again utter a word."
At sunset Jonah and his fellow prisoners were removed from the
pen and led off to be incarcerated in the cavalry hospital, passing
through a shower of exhausted bullets from the distant Entrenchment's
fire.[712]

PART THREE

THE WHITE WAND

June 24–25, 1857

From her prison at Savada House, old Rose Greenway continued to buy time for her family with a promise of high ransom. But Nana was losing his patience. On June 23 Mrs. Greenway summoned her old friend Sheo Prasad and asked the Mahajun to advance her the money. But Prasad could only come up with a note for a little over half, and advised her to "settle with the Nana and let me know the result."

The widow of Henry Jacobi and her three children still shared the Greenways' room. Perhaps by now she too had promised Nana a ransom, or the rebels had simply lumped her together with the Greenways. But she had somehow managed over the past weeks to keep herself and her family out of the hands of Nana's executioners.

Though the Greenways' cook sometimes managed to sneak food to them, Nana's prisoners otherwise subsisted on a meager diet of chupatties and water. The guards had taken everything from them but a few articles of clothing: Mrs. Greenway was dressed in nothing but a gown;[1] after her capture her earrings had been wrenched out "through the flesh."[2]

In the afternoon of June 24 the guards unlocked the door to the prisoners' room and in walked Azimullah Khan, accompanied by the former police chief Shah Ali and the glowering, pockmarked Brigadier Jwala Prasad. Azimullah was probably gracious in his salutations, inquiring after the health of the ladies and Edward and the children and asking politely in English if Mrs. Greenway would accompany them to meet with Nana Sahib.[3] Probably assuming that Nana intended to inquire about her ransom, Mrs. Greenway covered her head against the sun and followed Azimullah across the yard to a vast tent where Nana waited, seated on cushions and surrounded by servants. With a nod from Nana, Azimullah now asked Mrs. Greenway if she might consider a proposition that could save not only her families' lives but the lives of the entire garrison. The siege of the Entrenchment, he explained, had been costly to both sides. Certainly the garrison had suffered terribly, but the rebels, too, had expended lives and ammunition on a goal that might now be achieved without inflicting further suffering on either side. The sole purpose of the uprising had been to rid Cawnpore of the Europeans. It made no difference to Nana Sahib how this might be accomplished, but little could be gained by prolonging the siege another day. He therefore wondered if Mrs. Greenway would be willing to convey to General Wheeler a letter from Nana offering the garrison safe passage to Allahabad in exchange for the surrender of the Entrenchment. Azimullah did not want to disparage Wheeler's noble defense, nor insult a proud old warrior with a demand for his unconditional surrender. But perhaps, if only for the sake of the women and children, he might consider accepting Nana's terms.[4]

Mrs. Greenway was probably too hardened a businesswoman not to set some conditions of her own, and may have agreed to carry Nana's letter only if, no matter what Wheeler decided, Nana waived the ransom and guaranteed her family's passage to Allahabad. Azimullah, in turn, insisted that during her negotiations Mrs. Greenway leave her family in Nana's keeping to assure his more suspicious comrades of her full cooperation. In addition she was forbidden to convey to the garrison any rumor she may have heard about the disposition of Nana's army or the British relief force that was still stalled at Allahabad, burning villages and hanging natives.[5]

◆ ◆ ◆

On the morning of St. John's Day, June 24, as the garrison at Lucknow toasted his health, a sleepless, grieving General Hugh Massy Wheeler scrawled another of his letters to Henry Lawrence.[6]

"All our carriages more or less disabled," he reported, "ammunition short, British spirit alone remains, but it cannot last forever." Yesterday's cannonade had been "tremendous," he said.

> I venture to assert [that] such a position so defended has no example—but cruel has been the Evil. Brigr. Jack, Coll. Williams, Majr. Prout, Sir G. Parker, Lieutenant [Richard Owen] Quin senr. and many ladies—also Major Lindsay died from the dreadful heat, fatigue or disease—Halliday, Reynolds, Prole, Smith, Redman, Supple, Eckford, Dempster, Jervis, Chalwin, and many more killed. Mr. Hillersdon and Mr. Jack killed. We have no instru-

ments, no medicine, provisions for 8 or 10 days at farthest and no possibility of getting any as all communication with the Town is cut off. Lieutenant Bax 48th killed—If Lord Canning's promises were performed we should have 800 men, with half the number we could capture their guns and drive them before us. We have been cruelly deserted and left to our fate. We had not above 220 soldiers of all arms at first, the casualties have been numerous. Railway gents and merchants have swollen our ranks to what they are, small as that is. They have done excellent service, but neither they nor I can last for ever. We have all lost everything belonging to us, and have not even a change of linen. Surely we are not to die like rats in a cage. We know nothing of Allahabad, to which place we have sent five notes, but whether they have reached or even gone we as yet know not. The ladies, women and children have not a safe hole to lie down in and they all sleep in the trenches for safety and coolness. The barracks are perforated in every direction, and cannot long give even the miserable shelter which they now do. God bless you.[7]

"Writing . . . on the floor," of the tile-roofed barrack "and in the midst of the greatest dirt, noise, and confusion," the pusillanimous Major Wiggins also wrote Lucknow that day:

The condition of misery experienced by all is utterly beyond description in this place. Death and mutilation, in all their forms of horror, have been daily before us. The numerical amount of casualties has been frightful, caused both by sickness and the implements of war, the latter having been fully employed against our devoted garrison by the villainous insurgents, who have, unluckily, been enabled to furnish themselves therewith from the repository which contained them. We await the arrival of succour with the most anxious expectation, after all our endurance and sufferings; for that, Sir Henry Lawrence has been applied to by Sir Hugh, and we hope earnestly it will be afforded, and that *immediately*, to avert further evil. If he will answer that appeal with 'deux cents soldats Britanniques,' we shall be doubtless at once enabled to improve our position in a vital manner: and *we deserve* that the appeal should be so answered forthwith. You will be grieved to learn that among our casualties from sickness, my poor dear wife and infant have been numbered. The former sank on the 12th, and the latter on the 19th. I am writing this on the floor, and in the midst of the greatest dirt, noise, and confusion. Pray urge our reinforcement to the Chief Commissioner [Lawrence].[8]

According to Vibart the garrison had lost about a third of its number by the twenty-first; perhaps another thirty had died in the meantime.[9] Thus only a little under seven hundred souls had survived out of the garrison's initial complement;[10] at least three hundred men, women, and children choked the sepulchral well. By now almost every gunner had been killed or wounded, and most of the cannon were too far gone to fire even the crews' ingeniously improvised charges of grape and shrapnel. The sentries had barely the strength to lift their muskets, and were reduced to using the pages of Bibles for gun-wadding.[11] But most desperate of all were the women and children. The burned barrack afforded them only the most precarious shelter, the walls of the surviving barrack were honeycombed; a few more days of bombardment and they would entirely collapse.[12]

For the past four days the garrison had been on half rations: even at that rate the Entrenchment's provisions could barely last another week.[13] People desperately improvised meals from whatever came their way. "Our last meal was a Horse," remembered Amy Horne,

> but neither myself nor my dear parents partook of any. My poor little brothers and sisters did, they were dying from hunger and would have eaten the most loathsome thing. . . . All we had to sustain us now, and to the day we capitulated, was parched gram and that insufficient to appease hunger. Of our family we were eight, and a faithful nurse who clung to us to the last, making in all nine, and our allowance of gram was about ½ a seer [a little over a pound] for all of us, and this we had once a day.[14]

Amy was especially moved by the plight of a soldier she had found "all but gasping his last for . . . a little *kicherie* [spiced rice], which actually I had hoarded up, as a miser would his gold." Amy gave it to him "at the bidding of my dear Parents, who could not bear to keep that which would have saved the life of a fellow creature. . . . Many a day had passed without his tasting food, and though hardly able to speak [he] thanked us over and over again in his feeble voice."[15]

Thomson's picket was reduced to eating dog. "Every possible blandishment was employed by my men to tempt the canine adventurer into the soup-kettle. Two or three minutes subsequently to my seeing him doubtfully trotting across the open, I was offered some of his

semi-roasted fabric, but that, more scrupulous than others, I was
obliged to decline."[16]

✦ ✦ ✦

On the evening of Wednesday, June 24, Nana's gunners ceased firing
on the Entrenchment, and for two tense hours the garrison's sentries
squinted over their riddled breastworks into the deepening gloaming.[17] The most battle-hardened vultures and adjutant birds had already swooped down to pick among the desiccated remains of the
rebel dead; now in the stillness their more timid comrades began to
flock. Peering westward from the crow's nest, Thomson's lookout
stared across the parade-ground toward Savada House and the old
cavalry lines but could see no troops massing in the hazy distance,
only the solitary figure of a woman approaching in the evening light.
He had seen many such women carrying supper to their husbands
and brothers along the siege line. But this one was walking directly
across the parade-ground with an ungainly stride and appeared to be
waving a "white wand."[18]

"There's a woman coming across," the lookout called down to
Thomson.

Probably another damned spy, the pickets thought. They had already
been fooled once by the water carrier; they were not going to be
fooled again. A picket cocked his musket and took aim, but before he
could squeeze the trigger, Thomson heard the woman call to them in
cultured English, and he pushed the picket's musket aside.[19] The lady
continued forward on her bare feet, wobbling slightly in the heat.
Thomson stepped forward to meet her, and she nearly fainted as he
helped her over the heaps of debris and into the barrack. When she
had recovered somewhat she handed Thomson a letter addressed "To
the Subjects of Her Most Gracious Majesty Queen Victoria."

By now Captain Moore had replaced the wounded Jenkins in the
adjacent barrack, and there, in the eerie silence of the rebels' ceasefire, Thomson handed him the letter. Moore opened it and read the
following brief message which had been written in English:

"All those who are in no way connected with the acts of Lord Dalhousie," it said, "and are willing to lay down their arms, shall receive
a safe passage to Allahabad."[20]

Moore frowned a moment and then hurried to the Entrenchment,
ducking instinctively along the line of overturned carts and past the
sepulchral well. Vaulting the parapet, he found General Wheeler
standing outside the Main Guard and handed him the letter.[21]

Wheeler gave the ambiguous little missive a quick, disgusted perusal and thrust it back at Moore. Though he probably recognized the meticulous penmanship of Azimullah Khan, Wheeler told the captain he would not dignify any communication that did not bear Nana's signature.

Back in the outer barrack Thomson and his men had gathered tenderly around Nana's mysterious courier. Though he was new to Cawnpore, Thomson thought he recognized her as Mrs. Greenway. The lady "cried most bitterly while enumerating her wrongs," and expressed her anxiety "to return to her little children." Thomson trepidatiously asked if she and the other women in Nana's keeping had been harassed, but "she most explicitly affirmed that no indignities or abuse had molested her honour."[22]

After nightfall an officer rushed to Thomson's outpost with the rejected letter in his hand and instructed the lady to tell Nana that if he intended to negotiate with General Wheeler the Mahratta had better at least take the trouble to sign his messages. As the lady tottered back into the darkness, Moore himself arrived to inform Thomson and his picket that if Nana replied with a signed letter Wheeler might be prepared to treat with the rebels. Wheeler, in the meantime, had apprised his officers of the letter's contents, and "the contents of this craftily worded note," Thomson wrote disgustedly, "instead of being kept secret was noised abroad to every one."[23] But it was not the kind of thing that could have remained secret for long as the garrison crowded around the Main Guard. Wheeler's orderly, Bugler John Bradshaw of the 56th, had overheard the general's conversation and immediately told his garrulous mother, and soon the entire Entrenchment was abuzz.[24]

In the strange silence of that evening families emerged warily from their makeshift shelters to debate the letter's portent. What did it mean by "all those who are in no way connected with the acts of Lord Dalhousie?" Would Nana spare only the women and children? What about the merchants? What of the officers and surviving civil servants? What of Wheeler himself? Hadn't he, after all, led a force to Lucknow to enforce the annexation of Oudh?

Many officers declared that they could not trust the Gentleman of Bithur; look what trusting in him had already cost them. But most of the women and many of the exhausted sentries disagreed. Thomson watched and listened as Nana's letter corroded the unity and resolution that had sustained his picket these three weeks. He could hear his men whispering, muttering, arguing about Wheeler's intentions.

What if the old fool flatly refused Nana's offer? What if the officers still clung to the catastrophic delusion that relief was on its way?

"Oh," Thomson overheard a picket declare, "if they don't make a treaty now as we have such a fine chance of saving our lives by laying down our arms we will not fight any more."

Enraged, Thomson drew his pistol from his belt "and walked up to the man who said this and told him that if he dared to use such an expression again he would shoot him."[25]

His pickets fell back into sullen silence. But Thomson could see how readily his exhausted men could redirect their grief and rage from Nana to their own officers. If Wheeler and Moore declined Nana's offer too precipitously they might have another mutiny on their hands. Thomson took Moore aside and reported his exchange with the sentry. Moore "seemed greatly agitated"; if he could not count on his sentries there could be no question of fighting on.

By the time Mrs. Greenway had returned to Nana Sahib she was worn out, and the next morning the job of courier had fallen to Mrs. Jacobi, who, to provide for her children on their passage to Allahabad, demanded the return of her jewelry from Azimullah Khan. In any case most witnesses agree that it was Mrs. Jacobi, the stout Eurasian daughter of a Bengal artilleryman[26]—not old Rose Greenway—who, a little after nine in the morning of June 25, arrived in a covered litter in the Entrenchment itself.[27] The women of the garrison surrounded her, for, as Amy Horne recalled, "it was a source of unbounded delight to us to see a white face from over the border." They invited her to remain with them, "but she said she could not, as the Nana had kept her children and would kill them if she did not go back."

Wheeler emerged from the barrack to meet Mrs. Jacobi, who handed him the same letter but this time bearing Nana's full signature, to which His Highness probably could not have resisted appending all his newfound titles. Wheeler and Moore and the remainder of his senior staff entered the Main Guard together and debated the merits of Nana's offer. Certainly it could not be accepted without clarifications and guarantees. Offhand it seemed a rather sly document, and it must have occurred to a few alarmists that they had no idea if there could be any such thing as a safe passage to Allahabad. What if the rebels had taken every district along the way? How did they know that Allahabad itself was not in rebel hands?

Wheeler himself "most strenuously opposed" capitulating.[28] "I conceive that mutineers with arms in their hands should never be treated with or listened to," he had declared to his friend Hearsey three months before. "It is opposed to the first great principle of military discipline and subordination."[29] He had already been duped once by Nana and Azimullah; he did not intend to end fifty-four years of honorable service by surrendering to a native. He proposed that they resume their places in the trenches and hold out, as before, until relief finally arrived.

He was not alone. "Many officers objected to any terms offered by this Nana."[30] Better to die honorably, they said, than risk Nana's treachery. "Moreover," recalled Amy Horne, "the thought of white men surrendering to the blacks was most abhorrent to British prestige. Most of the officers . . . were for fighting to the bitter end."[31]

But most of these officers were either bachelors or had already lost their wives and children in the siege. So it fell to Captain Moore to argue the case for capitulation. Moore hoped he had demonstrated that no one would sooner fight than he. But however much he detested the idea of surrendering, it was the only honorable course. Sir John Jones in his journals from the Napoleonic War argued that "the principle to be combated [was] the doctrine that surrender shall not take place when successful resistance becomes hopeless."[32] Well, resistance was hopeless, and the officers' first duty was not to their own honor but to the lives of the women and children. How could they hold out with only three days' rations? There were no instruments, no medicines. Another day of bombardment and their meager shelter would have completely collapsed. A single rain and the muskets would rust, the trenches fill, and the parapets wash away.[33]

Though the other officers[34] considered Moore "the very life sinews of our beleaguered band," he was "wholly inexperienced in native character," and the sepoy officers reiterated their profound distrust of Nana Sahib and Azimullah.[35] As a last resort Moore may have told the old general that his own European soldiers were on the verge of mutiny, but he probably did not have to. Exhausted by the siege, grieving for his son, fearing for the fate of his wife and daughters, shocked to learn that he had not ten but three days' rations left, Wheeler at last "succumbed to Captain Moore's expostulations, and consented to the preparation of a treaty of capitulation,"[36] perhaps consoling himself that if Nana accepted the garrison's terms, they might at least save the women and children. Even if Nana did not accept their terms, at least the guns would have been stilled a little while, and they might learn something of the rebels' morale.[37] Wearily telling Moore to do what he thought best,[38] Wheeler sent

Mrs. Jacobi back to Savada House to inform Nana Sahib that the general's men—Moore, Whiting, and Roche—would meet with Nana's representatives in front of the outer barracks.[39]

Azimullah Khan and Brigadier Jwala Prasad accordingly rode out onto the parade-ground about one o'clock in the afternoon with a few sowars of the 2nd Cavalry, and paused two hundred yards from Thomson's picket to await Wheeler's delegation.[40] Moore, Whiting, and Roche emerged from the outer barracks on foot and made their way across ground pocked by mortar shells and littered here and there by round shot and vulture-pecked rebel skeletons. Azimullah greeted Wheeler's delegation in English, no doubt conveying his prince's condolences for the frightful sufferings of the women and children and His Highness's hopes that some mutually beneficial arrangement might be agreed upon. But the scowling brigadier insisted that Azimullah conduct the negotiations in Hindi or not at all. With a helpless, complicitous shrug toward Wheeler's men, Azimullah laid out Nana's proposal. In exchange for the surrender of the garrison's money, guns, and ammunition, Nana would provide the garrison with a flotilla of covered boats for their safe passage to Allahabad.

Barely concealing his contempt for Azimullah and his brigadier, Moore told them that before Wheeler would even consider such a proposition, Nana would have to agree to supply the boats with enough flour to sustain them. Azimullah grandly offered to supply not only flour but "sheep and goats also." Moore also insisted on carriage to transport the women, children, and wounded the mile to Sati Chowra and permission for each man to proceed to Allahabad under arms and equipped with sixty rounds of ammunition. Azimullah replied that His Highness would probably accept Moore's conditions, and leaving Wheeler's men to draft the terms of the garrison's surrender, returned to Nana Sahib to make his report.

All this must have taken an hour or so, for it was not until mid afternoon that a sowar returned from Nana's camp to report that Nana had agreed to all the conditions but added a new one of his own: a demand that the garrison evacuate the Entrenchment that very night. Moore indignantly ordered the sowar to go back to Nana and tell him that the garrison could not possibly leave the Entrenchment until the following day. The sowar returned to Savada House and after a brief pause came galloping back across the parade-ground. This time Whiting and Thomson walked out to meet him. "He informed us that the Nana was inflexible in his determination that we should instantly evacuate, and that if we hesitated his guns would open up again." The sowar darkly reminded Whiting that Nana now knew exactly how things stood in the Entrenchment: that Wheeler's guns were shattered, his people starving, the barracks ruined.[41]

Whiting replied that the garrison was not afraid of the rebels. Nana had tried to take the Entrenchment in the past; let him try again. Even if the rebels succeeded, he said, Wheeler had men posted at each of the powder magazines, poised to blow themselves and the rebels to kingdom come if they somehow managed to storm the parapets.

Here was the old fear again, plaguing the rebels even in their hour of triumph. The sowar gloomily returned to Savada House, "and by and by he came out to us again, with the verbal consent that we should delay the embarkation until morning."

Whiting and Roche wrote out the terms of surrender in Thomson's barrack for Moore to sign in Wheeler's stead.[42] Among the haggard railway men in Thomson's outpicket was a Mr. Todd, who had abandoned the railways some years before for the more lucrative position of tutor to Nana Sahib. Todd volunteered to deliver the final draft of the treaty and to cast his expert eyes around Nana's court for any sign of treachery. About a half hour later Todd returned to report that he had been received courteously, and Nana had unhesitatingly signed the treaty. Expressing his regret that the garrison had suffered so much, Nana "swore by his gods," wrote Amy Horne, "and upon the Gunga to protect us and have us safely taken to Allahabad in boats."[43]

At eight-thirty that night Lieutenant Master of the 53rd jotted a hopeful note to his father at Lucknow. "We have held out now for twenty-one days, under a tremendous fire," he proudly reported. "The Raja of Bithoor has offered to forward us in safety to Allahabad, and the general has accepted his terms. I am all right, though twice wounded. Charlotte Newenham and Bella Blair are dead. I'll write from Allahabad. God bless you!"[44]

A PEACEFUL NIGHT
June 26, 1857

By nightfall of June 25 the rebel guns had been silent for twelve hours, and people emerged from their hiding places like resurrected corpses creeping up from their graves. Skeletal ladies hobbled out, a few in shoes split by the heat. Their bony arms and shoulders were livid with sunburn where their sleeves had been torn away for bandages. "All smeared with powder and covered with dirt," many wore no more than a bodice and a tattered petticoat, employing scarfs and handkerchiefs to cover their nakedness."[45] Their eyes had retreated from the sun into deep hollows, their teeth were yellow from a diet of lentils, their hair caked with three weeks of filth and blood. Some, like Amy Horne's mother, had withdrawn into babbling imbecility.

The children too were specters, their hair bleached and their pinched faces peeling from the unrelenting sun. Some had the nervous energy to celebrate their liberation from the confinement of the barracks and trenches and raced around the wreckage collecting splinters for their mothers' cooking fires. Some clung mutely to their parents; some who had no mothers or fathers straggled after the families who now stumbled through the debris to view the shattered defenses that had so improbably kept the rebels at bay. Blinking and staggering in the sunlight, families greeted each other, compared their losses, expressed their condolences, or mutely passed each other by in embarrassment over the times one chased another from a crowded room, accused another of shirking or hoarding, quarreled over the cries of an inconsolable child, or witnessed some intimate act in the teeming dark.[46] All afternoon women and children crowded the well to draw up bucketsful of water. "Draught after draught was swallowed," wrote Thomson, "and though the *debris* of mortar and bricks had made the water cloudy, it was more delicious than nectar [and] it was not given out by thimblefuls that night." At the cistern mothers washed themselves and their children for the first time in three sweltering, dusty, bloody weeks.[47]

Williamson of the commissariat, now the major of brigade, distributed double rations of chupatties, lentils, and rum. But it was a measure of the degree of mistrust between the garrison and the rebels "that no decent food was begged or bought on our side, nor was it offered or given on the other." Nevertheless, their shrunken stomachs swollen with food and water, the garrison lay down in the blessed silence of the night for their first unbroken sleep in three weeks.

On the morning of June 26 "a weight seemed taken off each heart," remembered Amy Horne. "The joy was general and everybody appeared to have at once forgotten their past sufferings—it was such happiness to quit a place so fraught with misery, and so fearfully haunted with the groans of those death had snatched away."[48] Nana intended to evacuate the Entrenchment that evening, so the garrison spent the day preparing for the journey, "though there was not much to do in that way."[49] Most of the women and children had lost everything they owned, but some had managed to retain a few items—combs, hand mirrors, portraits, notes, Bibles, lockets of hair—which they now tucked under their tattered skirts. Here and there men dug up what small treasures they had buried during the siege—medals, coin, jewelry. All day long sentries crowded the godown to stuff their pockets with cartridges "till they were walking magazines,"[50] and then sat cleaning their muskets and pistols and sharpening their knives and bayonets in the broken shade of the barracks.[51]

At about two o'clock in the afternoon Nana provided two elephants and a company of sowars to take a delegation of officers to the ghats to inspect the boats he had ordered for the garrison's passage.[52] At least three officers volunteered,[53] including the bachelors Delafosse and Goad and the widower Captain Turner who had commanded the sentries by the Main Guard.[54] They set out along the metalled road that began at Vibart's battery and made their way through the encircling crowd of townspeople, servants, and mutineers, plodding the mile northeastward past the artillery bazaar and then turning south at the charred shell of Bathgate and Campbell's chemist shop and across a wooden bridge to the shallow ravine[55] that cut down to the river from the Ganges Cliff.[56]

To the right, a row of gnarled trees marked the boundary between the dirt road to the water and the vast riverside compound of the late Colonel Williams. To the left the edge of the ravine was surmounted by a row of prickly pear and the walled estate of Henry Christie, a recent acquisitor of Bathgate & Campbell, now four days dead from heat and exhaustion.[57] Beneath Christie's compound, over a hundred yards upriver from the ravine, lay the boatmen's village of Sati Chowra, sitting low along the bank.

It was one of the loveliest spots in Cawnpore, a favorite destination of officers and ladies on their morning and evening rides: three years earlier, the river had "quite refreshed" Emma Halliday here, "and the trees looked so green."[58] At the mouth of the ravine, over three hundred yards from the road, stood a small Shivaite temple patronized by the boatmen of the area. Known as Hardeo Temple it was built into the riverbank, its upper level consisting of a domed shrine and two terraces that reached toward the Ganges like the arms of a chair, between which a wide row of steps led down to the water when the river was high.

But in June the Ganges ran some hundred yards from the lowest step. Along the top of the riverbank stood palm trees and neem trees leaning out over the sun-baked bank. South of the temple was a group of huts[59] with heaps of timbers[60] lying alongside "gardens with places on the banks to raise water from the river for irrigation."[61] Herders drove their buffalo here, and women lay dung cakes out to dry along the sloping bank. Plovers and monkeys fidgeted at the water's edge, and the mud was strewn with the flotsam and jetsam of the Ganges's flow: garlands, floating lamps, the shattered remains of ritual statuary. Occasionally a cadaver appeared in the mud, stranded by the receding current. But by now jullads had prodded the naked corpses of the Fatehgarh fugitives out into the current, lest they alarm the garrison's scouts.

Turner and his deputies proceeded on their elephants out into the mud flats to inspect the twenty-four boats moored in a long line up and downstream from the ravine's mouth. There they were met by the harried Goordial, one of Cawnpore's most prosperous contractors of boats, whom Nana's kotwal had enlisted to prepare the garrison's flotilla.

"Much vexed," Turner noted that only a few of the boats had been supplied with food, and several still lacked thatched roofs to protect the garrison from the sun.[62] "Why haven't you put the boats in proper order?" he demanded.

"I have only just come," Goordial pleaded, and bawled out one of Nana's underlings who had been superintending a crew of four hundred coolies from Bithur.[63] The complaint echoed from underling to underling in the usual declension, until the coolies themselves were snapping at each other.

Their task was formidable. The boatmen figured that whether or not the garrison ever reached Allahabad they would never see their boats again. They had therefore sensibly contributed only the meanest vessels. Gathering the boats together on such short notice had been complicated. The police chief had at first approached Lochun, the commissariat contractor, with "the strictest injunctions to get the boats ready," but Lochun demanded his money in advance.[64] For this he was apparently beaten and imprisoned and the boats were finally obtained from his rival, Budloo. Budloo assembled some two dozen boats at Permit Ghat and directed them the three miles down river to Sati Chowra Ghat.[65] Five boats were from Cawnpore, the rest from Farrukhabad and other outstations.[66] All of the boats needed "new bamboo *chalee* [flooring]"[67] installed across their deep, rimpled holds.

A traveler described the kind of boat that moored at Sati Chowra.

> It is decked over, throughout its whole length, with bamboo; and on this is erected a low light fabric of bamboo and straw, exactly like a small cottage without a chimney. . . . Upright bamboos are fixed by its side, which support a kind of grating of the same material, immediately above the roof, on which, at the height probably of six or eight feet above the surface of the water, the boatmen sit or stand to work the vessel. They have, for oars, long bamboos, with circular boards at the end, a longer one of the same sort to steer with, a long enough bamboo for a mast, and one, or sometimes two sails, of a square form, . . . of very coarse and flimsy canvass. Nothing can seem more clumsy or dangerous than these boats."[68]

They averaged about thirty feet long and ten feet wide and on their sterns the boatmen had painted large eyes to help them navigate.[69] Such boats required crews of four or five, but only about nine of Nana's vessels had full complements of boatmen, another ten had three, the five peddlers' boats had none.[70] But their hulls nevertheless floated clear of the river bottom and were tied to long bamboo poles driven into the mud.[71] The deepest part of the river ran along the Lucknow side of the Ganges, and Turner could see that as soon as the boats were loaded they would have to pole their way several hundred yards out into the water before they could catch the current. "We might and ought to have demanded an embarkation in deeper water," Thomson would write, "but in the hurry of our departure, this had been overlooked."[72]

As the officers inspected the boats from the altitude of their tottering howdahs, one of Colonel Williams's servants made his way down from his sahib's ruined compound and reached up to offer the officers a bunch of grapes from his master's vines. Goad informed the servant that the colonel and his daughter Mary were dead, as were many of his officers, but Mrs. Williams was alive, albeit wounded by a bullet to her lip.[73] The servant asked Goad for permission to enter the Entrenchment and visit his memsahib, but the lieutenant refused, handing him two rupees instead and advising him to prepare his family for the passage to Allahabad.[74]

Though Turner was evidently reassured to see teams of coolies carting food into the finished boats, he warned Goordial that unless every boat was fitted out satisfactorily the garrison would refuse to board. It was a hollow threat, of course, for there was no time for another inspection, and once the garrison left the Entrenchment that evening there could be no turning back.

As the officers' elephants lumbered back up the ravine, sepoys of the 56th walked alongside, conversing with the sowar escort, and unless it was merely a trick of the afternoon wind blowing off the river or the noise from the sparrows flocking in the trees, Turner swore he heard the word "*kuttle*" or "massacre" among the rebels' whispers.[75]

When the officers returned to the Entrenchment they found that the garrison's joy had dissipated, diluted now by deferred grief and growing foreboding. Groups of men, women and children had followed the trail to the sepulchral well to say prayers over the common grave of their comrades, friends, and loved ones, covering their mouths as they approached, disturbing the flies with the notes and mementos they dropped over the rim.[76] The Reverend Moncrieff conducted services a discreet distance upwind from the well,[77] and here Ensign George Lindsay, still vigilant with his musket, probably joined his mother and four sisters in their prayers for his dead Uncle William and Aunt Lilly, as their friends the Vibarts prayed for their two dead children and their annihilated kinfolk, Emma and Willie and little Mabel Halliday.

Entangled to a depth of sixty feet were the corpses of sergeants and corporals and privates; gunners and bombardiers, drummers and fifers and buglers intertwined democratically with officers, box-wallahs, civil servants, Eurasians, railway men, women, and children. Brigadier Jack, among the first to die, must have lain somewhere near the bottom, under the remains of the five native servants killed soon afterward by a mortar shell. Several strata below the corpses of Mrs. Reynolds and her child lay her husband the captain and his amputated arm. Above them lay hundreds of other bodies, including Captain Elms; Lieutenants Smith, Bax, Prole, Manderson, Quin, Chalmers; Louisa Chalwin's husband, Edwin; surgeons Collyer and Garbett and Apothecary Slane; one of the voluble DeRussett children; Thomas Greenway's daughter Louisa; Major Prout of the 56th; Cantonment Joint Magistrate Sir George Parker, third Baronet of Harburn.[78]

Still more were tipped into the well that day. Reverend Haycock, exhausted by his ravings, passed away in his wounded mother's arms. Captain Jenkins died "in excruciating agony" from his wound to the jaw, "as it was quite impossible, without the aid of instruments, to get even the wretched nutriment we possessed into his throat."[79] Other men lay comatose and so critically wounded that they could not be moved.

Convinced that Shepherd was dead, his wife, Ellen, blamed herself "for consenting to my undertaking so perilous a journey [and] lamented my loss, stooping down against the wall in the corner of the burnt barrack where I had left them, and where I used to sit, refusing to be comforted. My sword and my Bible, as well as the garments I had taken off on the 24th now became to her inestimably precious."[80] Ellen visited her infant's grave in Kempland's trenches, sought little Mercy's burial place among the rubble of the verandahs, prepared the long-suffering Polly and Mrs. Frost and Jonah's sister and brother and grown nieces and their steadfast ayah Thakurani for the morning's journey to the ghat, praying that by some miracle Jonah might meet them there.

As news of the capitulation circulated through Cawnpore, servants approached the Entrenchment to inquire after their employers. They bore worrisome tidings. Thomas Greenway's servant, Kalka Pershad, agreed to go into the city and obtain three hundred rupees from the Mahajuns, but told his master that he had heard that the rebels intended to massacre the sahibs at the river.[81] According to legend another family's ayah overheard the sepoys boasting in the bazaar that they intended to massacre the Europeans in the morning. The ayah hurried to the Entrenchment and told her sahib and memsahib what she had heard. They approached a senior officer who dismissed the story, but they believed their ayah and decided that though they could not escape whatever transpired in the morning, the ayah might at least save their baby daughter. So they wrapped the child in a cloth and laid her in a basket with her identification papers tucked beneath her and anxiously watched from the Entrenchment as the ayah spirited her through the rebel lines.[82]

The garrison's forebodings deepened when Nana's gunners arrived to take away the Entrenchment's batteries. Not that the guns were much of a loss: only two were still capable of firing even Delafosse's improvised charges of grape, two or three others were not even worth remounting.[83] But the garrison was disturbed by the presence of the same gunners whose merciless barrage had killed so many of their loved ones. And with the gunners came a party of sowars with a string of carts into which Nana's coolies loaded up what remained of the garrison's treasure—between 114 and 130,000 rupees[84]—but for the time being they left what remained of the stores and ammunition untouched.[85]

Nana had hoped to get the flotilla under way that night, but he had been unable to assemble enough palanquins and bearers for the women, children, and wounded, so he announced that the garrison would have to delay its departure until morning.[86] The delay made Wheeler uneasy, but Nana designated no less a personage than Jwala Prasad and two other functionaries as hostages: guarantors that the rebels would not attack the Entrenchment that night.[87]

As the great orange sun descended, and a slight breeze stirred across the Entrenchment yard, soldiers shared their rations of rum with each other and handed around secret caches of food. A few contrived to entertain the children by beating time on casks with sticks and dancing dusty, cadaverous jigs.[88] Mowbray Thomson, still suffering from his wound to the shoulder blade and limping slightly from his wound to the thigh, was the last to leave the outer barracks that night. Before departing he hid a gold pocket watch the late Captain Elms had loaned him, intending to retrieve it for the captain's family when, as Thomson vowed he would, he marched back to Cawnpore to punish the rebels.

Jwala proved an ingratiating guest, and "condoled in most eloquent language with Sir Hugh Wheeler upon the privations he had undergone, and said that it was a sad affair at his time of life for the general to suffer so much; and that after he had commanded sepoy regiments for so many years, it was a shocking thing they should turn their arms against him." Jwala promised Wheeler that he would personally see to it that no harm would come to the garrison in the morning.

His assurances were cast in the gravest doubt when, late in the evening, a rifle went off in the southernmost outer barrack, and suddenly the rebel batteries and snipers opened up. With groans and curses, the sentries scrambled to their positions as women and children, some of them sufficiently revived to resume their screaming, ran and crawled for cover. No doubt with an outraged officer's sabre at his throat, Jwala Prasad desperately begged Wheeler's permission to send one of his companions off to dispatch "a quieting communication to his uneasy principals." The man galloped off into the dark and after a few more volleys the firing ceased. A sepoy's musket had simply misfired in the heat, Jwala's man explained, and the sepoys had mistaken it for the garrison's fire. It would not happen again.

This episode actually reassured some in the garrison. Without cannon the garrison was virtually defenseless, and yet the rebels had ceased their firing. Surely if they intended to massacre everyone they would have done so that night. Here and there mothers sat together, repacking their scant possessions and worrying about the morning's journey.

"Do you think it will be all right tomorrow?" one of them asked.

Another wondered, "Will they really let us go down to Allahabad in safety?"

But most kept up their spirits, "and comforted one another with the prospects of rescue."

"After such an acclimation of the brain to incessant bombardment," Thomson found the stillness "actually painful," as if the "angel of death" were brooding over him. But "with a pillow of brickbats, made comfortable by extreme fatigue and prolonged suspense, and with a comfortable sense of having done all that he could, or that his country could require, many a poor fellow slept that night."[89] Outside the Entrenchment, beyond the circle of rebel pickets,[90] jackals returned for the first time to chew on the animal remains strewn across the parade-ground, and many in the garrison fell off to sleep to the howls and yips that had first greeted them after their voyages from England, the sound many of them had associated ever since with landfall and safe harbor.[91]

THE DAY IS COME

June 27, 1857

Before dawn many of the women rose to set fire to the heaps of splinters their children had collected and bake chupatties for the journey.[92] The sentries slowly, stiffly stood from their dusty beds in the trenches to find not only the parade-ground but the rubbled vicinity of the sepulchral well rustling with hundreds of vultures, adjutant birds, kites, and crows already "gloating over their carnivorous breakfast."

Here and there women helped each other "bind up and secure the clothing that could scarcely be made to hold together." The wounded in the Main Guard were given "cordials" of water and "hurried words of sympathy [and] many a hearty declaration . . . that, at all hazards, they should not be left behind." The garrison's transport arrived an hour or more later, advancing toward Ashe's battery and into the first light as the sun cleared the Ganges Cliff and the dismal rubble of St. John's.[93] Sixteen commissariat elephants led the way, followed by perhaps eighty palanquins and an assortment of horse and bullock carts.[94]

Fanning out to either side of this caravan was a multitude of native soldiers—some thought they numbered in the thousands—who now melded with the encircling line of sentries. At the sight of them approaching in a saffron cloud of whirling dust, people tucked a few last-minute mementos into their clothing. Mowbray Thompson found room among the cartridges stuffed into his pockets for his father's Ghuzni campaign medal and a portrait of his mother.[95] As their husbands stood by with their muskets poised, women pinned notes to their children, felt one more time for the jewels they had sewn into their skirts, and elicited more vows from their ayahs that whatever happened to them they would never abandon the children.

A few more servants entered the Entrenchment looking for their employers. One arrived to deliver his master's dog, which he had protected in his hut during the siege.[96] With the assistance of four sepoys Colonel Williams's servant found his widow and her daughters "in a wretched plight: scorched and blistered by the sun." Mrs. Williams "had a slight bullet-wound on her upper lip" and "asked about the property left in the house, and enquired about all the servants. . . . She told me . . . to make every endeavour to join her son [in the hills] as soon as the roads should be open, and to show [him] the spot where the colonel was buried."[97]

The women at the cooking fires gathered up what few chupatties they had managed to bake and distributed them among their children.[98] Otherwise "no rations were served out before starting, nor was any ceremony or religious service of any kind observed."[99] As the men of the garrison lifted their baggage into carts and helped the sick and wounded into the palanquins, thousands of mutineers streamed into the Entrenchment until "there was hardly any place to stand."[100]

In one corner of the yard sepoys of the 53rd meekly sought out officers like Thomson and Delafosse to commiserate over their sufferings. "The sepoys were loud in their expression of astonishment that we had withstood them so long, and said that it was utterly unaccountable to them. We told them that had it not been for the failure of our food, we should have held the place to the last man."

Thomson asked one of his native officers how many mutineers had been killed laying siege to the Entrenchment.

"About seven hundred to eight hundred," the sepoy replied, disappointing Thomson, who had guessed a thousand.[101]

"Are we to go to Allahabad without molestation?" Thomson asked another of his men.

Yes, replied the sepoy, such was his firm belief.[102]

According to Thomson, a group of Major Vibart's sowars "insisted on carrying out the property which belonged to him," helped Emily and her two surviving children onto their palanquin, and escorted them out of the Entrenchment "with the most profuse demonstrations of respect."[103]

But elsewhere in the crowd native officers made a point of brushing past their former commanders without saluting. "Come to the boats. All is ready,"[104] they commanded with grating officiousness, pointing toward the river with their sabres. Affecting their customary breeziness, a group of officers recognized a functionary among the rebels who had once worked for their regiment.

"Doubtless he is made a general," one officer remarked, "because he can speak English, however incorrectly."

"Is the Nana seeing us off?" another asked.

The native was strangely unruffled by his old sahibs' sneers. "Do you remember," he asked the officers, "that about eighteen months or two years ago I told you that the natives of India would like to have the Europeans make chupatties for them? Well, good morning, sir," he said, waving an arm toward the ladies at their stoves. "The day is come."[105]

Thomson heard a sepoy bark, "Give me that musket," and saw him grab for an officer's barrel.

"You shall have its contents, if you please," the officer replied, raising the barrel to the sepoy's chest, "but not the gun."[106]

The sepoy backed off.

But elsewhere in the yard Amy Horne watched in horror as the sickly Captain Kempland of the 56th Native Infantry was "severely beaten" by a group of his sepoys until they managed to yank his musket from him; according to her, "many other officers were treated in the same way." "These men," she wrote, "would rather have died a hundred deaths than have submitted to such indignities at the hands of the black devils, but to have resented the insults would have been folly, outnumbered as we were."

Only Captain Moore dared to protest. "Drawing himself up to his full height, and with a manner full of pride and courage, he told the mutineers that their triumph would be short-lived, and that every man would yet pay dearly for his misdeeds. Some of the rabble . . .[107] abused him in so gross a manner that it made the ears of all tingle, threatening in the bargain to spit in his face, if he did not observe perfect silence."[108]

Amid the "confusion and hurry" the soldiers terrified some of the women and children with "their rude and rough manner."[109] The Cook family's "bundles, money and what little valuables we had were forcibly taken away."[110] A trooper snatched Jonah's sword out of Ellen Shepherd's hand "and would not give it up, although she entreated him with tears to do so. She then appealed in the most pitiful manner to the by-standers all round, explaining how precious a relic it was to her. Her appeal was so touching that one or two of the men immediately recovered and restored the sword to her, with which she hastened to join the other ladies now ready to start for the river."[111]

General Wheeler's own elephant had been brought for him and his family, and Lady Wheeler and her daughters climbed into its howdah for the ride to the ghat.[112] But "not feeling disposed to have himself look conspicuous under existing circumstances" or perhaps choosing not to be restricted to such a ponderous beast, the old General elected to ride a horse.[113] Climbing onto a skinny galloway as the crowd closed around him, he bleakly muttered that he had once again been "duped."[114]

Because the other elephant drivers sullenly refused to command their beasts to sit on the ground to receive their passengers, the hackeries and shaded palanquins became the vehicles of choice. Some of the hackeries and ox carts were loaded with baggage and sent ahead,[115] but so many officers and their vestigial families climbed into the palanquins—including the badly wounded Colonel Ewart of the 1st Native Infantry; the "very gauche" Mrs. Kempland;[116] and the disfigured Mrs. Williams[117]—that Moore decided he would have to leave behind eleven wounded men with a promise to fetch them when the rest of the garrison had reached the river.[118]

Mrs. Cook, Amy Horne's pregnant and shellshocked mother, had to climb an elephant by pulling herself up on its tail, but "hampered as she was by her *enceinte* condition" she lost her hold and fell heavily. Some of the wounded also slipped off, landing excruciatingly on their wounded limbs.[119] Many ladies, among them Kate Lindsay and her daughters, climbed into hackeries, but everyone else, including Jonah's family, had to proceed on foot.[120] Nevertheless the garrison slowly arranged itself into a kind of funnel shape with Wheeler and Moore at the head and the others spread out, as ragtag as camp followers, waiting to enter the procession as it stretched down the road toward the river.

At about eight o'clock a sowar galloped up to convey Nana's apologies. His Majesty's underlings had evidently underestimated the extent of the garrison's baggage. If the coolies loaded any more onto the boats there would not be enough room left for the evacuees; Nana would have to send the rest along in a separate flotilla.[121] For the same reason, said the sowar, none of the garrison's servants would be permitted to accompany them to Allahabad.

The ladies raised a cry of protest.[122] Losing the baggage was bad enough: their boxes contained many of their valuables and their only change of clothes. But how could they manage without their ayahs, many of whom had raised their children from birth and pledged their lives to protect them? As the sepoys pulled the ayahs and assorted servants out of the column, the children themselves began to cry, and the Shepherds' long-suffering daughter Polly, "finding that Thakooranee was not allowed to accompany them, was greatly distressed and kept looking back and calling to her all the while, until she was hid from her view."[123]

"Our hearts now began to quail at the prospect before us," wrote

Amy Horne, "as the rebels had given us an earnest of what we were to expect at their hands."[124] But the Entrenchment was in rebel hands, and Wheeler had nothing to bargain with but a few sacks of rupees. There was nothing he could do. Promising a thousand rupees to each of his servants if his family should survive the embarkation and absently handing a sack of money to the Greenways' elderly ayah Mary Ann, Wheeler ordered, "Quick march," and led what was left of the garrison to the river.[125]

♦　♦　♦

"Never, surely," wrote Thomson, "was there such an emaciated, ghostly party of human beings as we."[126] Though Amy Horne would insist that "every woman retained her modesty and refinement to the last," Thomson was shocked by the garrison's undress.[127] "There were women who had been beautiful, now stripped of every personal charm, some with, some without gowns; fragments of finery were made available no longer for decoration, but decorum; officers in tarnished uniforms, rent and wretched, and with nondescript mixtures of apparel, more or less insufficient in all."[128]

"The old—battered and bruised," wrote Amy Horne, "like ships that come into port after being buffeted by storms—babbled like children; others had a vacant stare in their eyes, as if they beheld visions of the future. Many a little child was raving mad, and it was pitiful to see their singular behaviour."[129]

Alarmed by the size and temper of the crowd, Moore instructed officers not to wait for the whole garrison to board but to push off as soon as their own boats were loaded "and make for the other side of the river, where orders would be given for our further direction." Indeed, he ordered that no one attempt "anything like order of progress."[130]

Nevertheless there was a certain "order of progress" along what their countrymen would call "the Via Dolorosa of the Empire."[131] At least two senior officers—Williamson and Wiggins—rode up front with the Wheelers and Emily Vibart and her children, thus adhering to the same protocols that had obtained in ballrooms and banquet halls and, however imperfectly, in the Entrenchment itself.[132] Major Vibart was the last to ride out of the Entrenchment, but apparently caught up to his family at the head of the column, for his would be one of the first boats to push off.[133]

The heat was already asserting itself; by this hour, in another life, the ladies would have been returning from their morning rides to

take breakfast on their verandahs or bathe in their cool and shuttered rooms. Riding their elephant, Amy Horne and her family could
see the extent of the crowd, the rubble of the bungalows neighboring St. John's, the rebel pickets' abandoned stations along the drainage
ditch. But the passengers swaying low to the ground in the palanquins could see only the legs of the sowars' ponies, the faces of
the soldiers marching alongside, and the curiosity seekers who had
crowded along the compound walls to bid the English good-bye or
good riddance.

The sick and wounded ladies lying in their soiled bandages and
torn clothes slid the palanquins' shutters closed against the crowd's
stares. Some of the ladies who rode through the mob in hackeries
and ox carts must have thought for a moment of the French noblewomen who had been thus transported to the guillotine half a century before. Other women staggered down the middle of the road,
many of them barefoot, their clothes patched and pinched together
with string and pins as they jollied their children along. A few soldiers carried cases and bundles on their heads like coolies, others feebly marched like pensioners on parade.[134]

Some sahibs tried to resist the troopers as they yanked away the
loyal servants who defiantly persisted in marching with their employers, and "a great disturbance was the consequence."[135] Here and
there mutineers took hold of former regimental comrades who had
remained in the Entrenchment with their commanders. About three
hundred yards from the Entrenchment, in the middle of the column,
a group of mutineers from the 56th attacked their old jemadar
Khoda Bux and roughed him up, grabbing his musket and cartridge
box, knocking away his turban, and stripping off his uniform before
finally dragging him and his son toward their regiment's old lines.[136]
The rebels carried off four other sepoys[137] as well, including Govind
Singh, whom Lieutenant Goad had been leading by the hand.[138]

Palanquin bearers paused from time to time to shift their burdens,
and here and there a family called out pleas and instructions to
the few friendly and familiar faces in the crowd. The result was that
the column gradually stretched out for almost half a mile, with the
crowd closing around a few stray groups and shuffling along with
them toward the river. The front of the column was apparently
greeted with a measure of awe. The senior officers and the stately
elephants and the Vibarts' sowar escort caused the crowd to back
away, some reflexively bowing and salaaming. Indeed, from his van-

tage in front of the procession Delafosse concluded that the entire garrison was proceeding "without being molested in the least."[139]

But the evacuees marched in a kind of declension, with the crippled and destitute tending toward the rear, so that the garrison appeared to the crowd ever more helpless and degraded: contemptibly "old, haggard, desperate and imbecile."[140] As this spectral parade faltered past, the onlookers became more derisive and menacing. At St. John's the crowd began to jeer the stragglers. Standing by the artillery hospital the banker Ayodhya Prasad spotted Emma Ewart walking alongside the palanquin of her husband, Colonel John Ewart of the 1st Native Infantry. Nearly stupefied by grief and exhaustion, Emma had already experienced "the hard, the bitter trial" of watching her "very delicate" little daughter die of heat and shock, and had spent nearly the entire siege tending to her husband's mangled arm.[141]

"When [the Ewarts] had arrived abreast of the church," Prasad would testify, "seven or eight sepoys of the 1st Native Infantry came up and told the coolies to set down the bed and stand aside." The coolies immediately obeyed, prostrating themselves "lest they might be murdered too."

According to Shepherd, two of the sepoys then approached the colonel and, "pretending to feel very sorry for his sufferings, offered to carry him in their arms. They made him put his arms over the shoulders of each, and lifting him up by the legs, carried him to one side of the church."

"Is the parade well dressed up now?" the sepoys asked, mocking him with "the angry expressions he sometimes used towards them on parade." At last, as his wife watched in horror, they dropped John Ewart onto the ground and chopped him to pieces with their sabres.

"Go along. We won't kill you," the sepoys told Emma, lowering their bloody blades. "But throw down all you have." Emma Fooks Ewart frantically dug in her skirts and handed them a small parcel tied in cloth. But before she could turn and flee, they cut her down as well.[142]

The Greenways' elderly ayah stumbled after the garrison, carrying the sack of rupees Wheeler had given her. A sepoy grabbed it from her and struck her in the back with his sabre, leaving her for dead by the roadside.[143]

Back at the Entrenchment townspeople swarmed through the debris, inspecting "every mite of ground in search of spoil," digging wherever newly turned earth might betray a cache of buried treasure.[144] One of them even turned up the pocket watch Thomson had buried in the outer barracks.[145] A group of insurgents ducked into the Main Guard and emerged dragging the eleven wounded Europeans by their quilts, tumbling them into the middle of the yard where young men mocked them and knocked them about until at last some sepoys, weary of this dismal sport, killed them with their muskets.[146]

A mile away Wheeler and Moore reached the high road that ran along the top of the Ganges Cliff and turned south along the river. It hardly seemed possible, but thousands more onlookers now came into view, rushing for vantage points along the heights of Colonel Williams's yard. Wheeler crossed the whitewashed bridge over the ravine and turned down toward the water.[147] Some of the villagers in the crowd carried weapons—swords, spears, axes—but they did not flourish them as Wheeler stopped his galloway and dismounted to join his wife and daughters on their elephant.[148] The crowd meekly made way as the sowars rode ahead of the column, commanding everyone "to stand aside" and not to come down to the ghat.[149]

Riding behind the sowars, Moore and Turner stiffly posted down to the water to inspect the boats, only to find that either the river had receded in the night or the boats had been hauled closer to shore, for they now sat in a mere two feet of water, their hulls plumped down in the sand. "While the siege lasted," wrote Thomson, "we were daily dreading the approach of the rains,—now, alas! we mourned their absence, for the Ganges was at its lowest."[150]

SATI CHOWRA

June 27, 1857

On the southern terrace of the Hardeo Temple a group of well-dressed native gentlemen were seated on mats, conferring with each other. Azimullah, every trace of Western clothing discarded now for the immaculate white of a pious Moslem nobleman,

A dry-season view of the receded Ganges from Hardeo Temple, where Tatya Tope commanded the attack at Sati Chowra

nodded at Wheeler's officers as they passed. Nana's brothers sat nearby: the turbaned Baba Bhutt, the morning sun dully glinting off his generic spectacles, and the tall, broken-nosed Bala Rao. Perhaps a half dozen others sat among them, including Shah Ali, the former kotwal, and his successor Hulas Singh who had overseen the requisition of the boats. But it was the stout, vigilant Tatya Tope, Nana's boyhood instructor in the Mahratta arts of war, who seemed to be overseeing the embarkation that morning, for he was the calm nucleus of the rebels' restive, whispering circle, the one to whom Jwala Prasad and Teeka Singh of the 2nd Cavalry kept looking from their horses on the riverbank below.[151]

As soon as the garrison reached the river, people hurried out of their hackeries and palanquins and dashed and staggered for the water. "We found that the boats were not very close to the shore," wrote Amy. There were no gangways,[152] "and the task of getting on board was a most difficult one. We had to wade knee-deep through the water, and it was pitiful to witness the difficulty of the aged, the sick, and the wounded in clambering up the boats' sides."[153]

Lady Wheeler and her two daughters slid down from their elephant and into the lead boat, with the general himself following after them, accompanied, apparently in defiance of the sowars, by several of his servants.[154] Joining them were Wiggins, Williamson, and Whiting, as though the boat had been reserved for Ws.[155]

The other boats filled up according to rank and race, but each was provided with a guard of at least two European soldiers or junior officers to help the boatmen heave their hulls out of the sand and into the current. In one boat far upstream from Wheeler's flagship, Eurasian musicians and their families joined perhaps a score of girls from the Free School and a couple of European soldiers.[156]

Ellen Shepherd and Polly and the rest of Jonah's family clung together in one of the rear boats,[157] and in Amy's boat her stepfather, John Cook, and his two sons and two daughters settled under the awning while Amy and two wounded soldiers roosted on the bamboo foredeck with Amy's half-sister Florence,[158] who was writhing in such an "agony of pains" from her broken leg that "it was utterly impossible to take her inside."[159] In the "hopeless scramble and confusion" Mrs. Cook had been taken to a nearby boat.[160]

By Anglo-Indian standards the boats were only big enough to carry half a dozen people at most, but as many as fifteen men, women, and children piled into each vessel, crowding their jittery crews of nine boatmen and grinding the hulls even deeper into the Ganges's sandy bottom.[161] In some of the boats the ladies were pleased to find that the crews had thoughtfully lit cooking fires in their little clay stoves.[162] But much of the food Turner had watched the coolies load into the boats had apparently disappeared overnight. Some of the boats still had no bamboo floors;[163] others lacked oars or ropes.[164]

"All this time the enemy were looking on like so many fiends exulting over our distressing situation, taunting and mocking us, for at last having fallen into their hands."[165] Keeping an eye on the gathering crowd along the rim of the embankment, the soldiers and officers desperately heaved the women and children and the wounded into the boats as fast as they could, "busy and anxious when they should be able to start."[166]

Thomson, limping from his thigh wound, boarded a boat somewhere near the front of the fleet while Henry Delafosse climbed into the lead boat and, laying down his musket and discarding his coat, began to work one of the bamboo pilings out of the sand to pole the vessel into the stream.[167] A few officers apparently rode down the line of boats, directing the embarkation as best they could. But by nine o'clock all of the boats were full and a great many of the evacuees were still wading along the shore, still stumbling down the ravine, still crossing the wooden bridge a quarter mile away.[168]

If any officer approached Nana's men to demand more boats, none was apparently willing to wait to see they were provided. As the tattered survivors of three weeks' siege continued to scramble aboard boats already "crowded to suffocation,"[169] or desperately splashed upstream, searching and begging for berths in the tottering "floating haystacks" of Budloo's fleet,[170] Major Vibart joined Emily and his two surviving children in the lead boat. No sooner had he stepped onto the bamboo deck than someone gave the order to push off.[171]

Wheeler's elephant had remained in the shallows and may have given the general's boat a nudge as Delafosse and his comrades poled the boat away from shore.[172] Some said Wheeler had bribed his boatmen with one thousand rupees to free the boats;[173] Thomson believed it was simply of lighter draft than the others.[174] In any case, the vessel began to work its way free of the shoal.

This sudden motion seemed to agitate the sixteen sowars who had escorted Major Vibart to the river with such solicitude.[175] Two now galloped up the ravine, shouting to the crowd to disperse,[176] while another, his horse strutting nervously in the pale dun shallows, suddenly commanded all the native crews to "leave their boats, and come up to receive pay."[177]

In the far distance west of the river three guns fired,[178] and all along the riverbank the semi-naked boatmen hurled their oars into the water and leaped from their teetering vessels, which rose now and rolled sluggishly in the soft sand.[179] The officers on board the boats gaped a moment as the boatmen landed with a series of splashes and struggled toward the shore.[180] Men, women, and children stranded at the water's edge froze in confusion and then pointed in horror at the dense, green-gray smoke billowing from several of the vessels' roofs where boatmen had secreted embers from their cooking fires in the sun-parched thatch.[181]

Before most of the boatmen had reached the riverbank, a bugle sounded and three cannon boomed nearby. One fired from the heights of Henry Christie's compound, spraying the shoal with grape. The others sent cannonballs arcing from the tall grass on the Lucknow side and plunging into the river, splashing the flotilla with water and mud.[182]

As the cannonfire echoed from bank to bank across the Ganges's chop, the little band of sowars opened fire with their carbines and rode off, making way for the seemingly impossible number of sepoys who now swarmed out from between the village of Sati Chowra and Henry Christie's compound wall, running the one hundred yards toward Hardeo Temple and firing their muskets.[183] A second squad emerged from the fleeing crowd along the ravine,[184] some skidding down the riverbank's slope to take positions behind bushes and heaps of timber, others firing a round up toward the stragglers at the bridge.[185] And a hundred yards downriver yet another hive of mutineers began to funnel out from behind the southern wall of Colonel Williams's compound, where a team of gunners were hauling a fourth cannon into position.[186]

The two soldiers on Amy Horne's boat fell wounded by the first volley of musket fire and slumped off the roof and into the hull, leaving Amy and her injured sister "stupefied with terror and amazement."[187] Men struck desperately at the smoldering thatch with their discarded coats, cut with their sabres at the moorings,[188] grabbed spars to pole the hulls free, or reached for their muskets on the bamboo decks.[189] From some boats[190] enraged officers and soldiers shot a gratuitous round at the retreating boatmen, while others fired at the gathering sepoys, sending two toppling back into the brush.[191]

The sepoys arrayed themselves in no particular order, "but extended in a long line down the banks"[192] and began to lay on a tremendous barrage;[193] the first round fired from north of the temple killed over a dozen evacuees.[194] Soon the rebel gunners found their range and nine-pound shot[195] crashed into the frail old hulls.[196] "Some of the boats presented a broadside to the guns," wrote Thomson, "others were raked from stem to stern by the shot" as their desperate occupants tried to pole and push and rock them away from shore.[197]

Stoked by the hot wind that rushed unobstructed down the Ganges's course, the thatched roofs now burst into furious flame.

Here and there in the dense, engulfing smoke, boats slowly pivoted against each other or entangled themselves in each other's moorings. Flames from one roof leaped across and ignited another until most of the boats were ablaze. In the wind that raced downriver the fire consumed the bamboo decks and roiled into the hulls, igniting the clothing and bedding of the sick and injured,[198] including Mrs. Thomas Greenway and her children; Reverend Haycock's aged mother;[199] the wounded water carriers MacKillop and Heberden;[200] the battered, swooning Captain Kempland;[201] Ensigns Dowson and Forman of the 53rd;[202] the gasping, perforated Lieutenant John Nickelson Martin; Mrs. Darby and her newborn infant; and Amy Horne's demented mother, Mrs. Cook.[203] Their frenzied screams pierced the roll of gunfire and the clatter of muskets, but only for a few moments. "One mitigation only there was to their horrible fate," wrote Thomson: "the flames were terrifically fierce, and their intense sufferings were not protracted."[204]

Jonah believed that his wife, daughter, brother, sister, and the rest of their family were among those who, like many of the native Christian schoolgirls from the Free School, were consumed by the flames.[205] But some women and children, their hair and clothing ablaze, managed to tumble blindly over the sides of their boat and into the water.[206] Many who landed in the shallows on the Cawnpore side were cut down by the sepoys' fusillade. Others who jumped off the opposite side found refuge from the sepoys' muskets behind the hulls[207] or, "calling on God for help,"[208] waded far enough out into the river to expose only their heads to the rebel fire.[209] But even here they were vulnerable to the shrapnel and grape fired from the guns on the opposite shore.[210]

"The balls came whizzing past us as thick as hail," recalled Amy, "sinking many boats." As soon as one vessel was destroyed the survivors scrambled around to hide behind the shattered hulls or fumbled toward one another through the thick boil of smoke. Some boats escaped the flames but could not be budged. Though the water was still too shallow to float the hulls, it was deep enough to immerse the children whose mothers had pitched them overboard, and ladies scrambled desperately through the water and the smoke, feeling in the dun opacity of the shallows for their drowning children.

Not ten minutes from the first volley "the water was red with blood, and the smoke from the heavy firing of the cannon and muskets and the fire from the burning boats, lay like dense clouds over and around us."[211] Somewhere in the chaos Lieutenant George

Lindsay fell trying to protect his mother and four sisters, and as his mother fled through the shallows a bullet caught her in the back.[212] The air was filled with the trumpeting of panicked elephants, the squealing of horses, screams and shrieks of women and children, and the crashing of round shot into the burning hulls.[213]

✦   ✦   ✦

As rebel bullets cut through the surrounding smoke, skipping like scooning stones along the Ganges's surface, Thomson and his fellow officers struggled to shove their stranded boat out of the shoal. But it would not budge from its bed of sand. Crouching by the hulls of the enmired boats women sobbed and prayed, some of them sinking from the weight of dresses and gowns saturated with water and blood.

Peering through the smoke, Thomson spotted one vessel, Wheeler's boat, still sluggishly receding from the bedlam through the shallows. Thomson decided to save himself. "I threw into the Ganges my father's Ghuznee medal, and my mother's portrait, all the property I had left," he would write with as heroic a flourish as he could muster, "determined that they should have only my life for a prey," but at least as determined to discard anything—clothing, cartridge pouch—that might drag him down as he "struck out, swimming for the retreating boat."[214]

He was only one of a general exodus of able-bodied men, and to his comrade Henry Delafosse watching from Wheeler's boat it appeared that the men of the garrison had "jumped out of the boats and instead of trying to get the boats loose from the moorings, rushed to the first boat they saw loose."[215]

Perhaps a dozen swam with Thomson, "beating the water for life." Another group paddled straight across the river, trying to reach the far shore, but most of these were killed by rounds of grape or picked off by the Sultanpore sepoys of the 17th Native Infantry who now emerged from the grass along the Oudh side of the river, firing their muskets. Only a few managed to reach the shore and hide themselves in the tall grass.[216]

"Many a poor fellow I saw sink before me in that dreadful swim," wrote Thomson, "some from exhaustion and others from round shot grape or shrapnel."[217] Thomson, however, had spent a guinea two years before for swimming lessons at a pool at Holborn and now swam powerfully through the water.[218] Two hundred yards from shore he passed an islet where Lieutenant Harrison of the 2nd Cavalry had managed to lead a few evacuees. As Thomson paddled by, three sowars waded up and attacked, one of them cutting down a lady in Harrison's party before the lieutenant could fell him with a shot from his revolver. Another shot killed the second sowar, and as the third dashed back to shore, Harrison dove into the river and joined Thomson in his race for Wheeler's boat.[219]

Swimming close by Thomson's side were twenty-one-year-old Lieutenant Robert William Henderson of the 72nd Native Infantry and his newly arrived little brother John.[220] As Robert sank from exhaustion, his brother was struck in the hand by a grapeshot. "He put the disabled arm over my shoulder," Thomson recalled, "and with one arm each, we swam to the boat, which by this time had stranded on a bank close to the Oude side of the river. We were terribly exhausted when Captain Whiting pulled us in; and had it not been for the sand-bank, we must have perished."[221]

In the meantime a second boat had reeled out of the shoal and into the stream, only to be struck by a round shot below the water line. As its hull filled with water, its passengers jumped out and joined Thomson, Henderson, and Harrison in Wheeler's boat. "Now the crowded state of our poor ark left little room for working her." The rudder had been shot away, and the boatmen had thrown all the oars overboard. "The only implements that could be brought into use, were a spar or two, and such pieces of wood as we could in safety tear away from the sides. Grape and round shot flew about us from either bank of the river, and shells burst constantly on the sand-banks in our neighbourhood."

The women did their best to keep out of the men's way. Mrs. Swinton, a relative of the late Lieutenant Jervis, stood with her little boy in the rear of the boat when a round shot from the southernmost gun on the Cawnpore side whirred down the river and struck the stern, knocking her overboard.[222] One of her little boys ran up to Thomson and said, "Mamma has fallen overboard." Thomson held the boy for a moment and assured him his mother was beyond all pain.

"Oh, why are they firing upon us?" the boy asked. "Did not they promise to leave off?"

"I never saw the child after that," Thomson recalled, "and suspect that he soon shared his mother's death."[223]

According to one of Wheeler's servants the shot rocked Wheeler's boat so violently that "all the sahibs became terrified"[224] and several "gentlemen and some ladies,"[225] evidently including Lady Wheeler and her daughters, "took fright and jumped into the river."[226] But some apparently jumped not to flee but to try to lighten the load and shove the boat off the sandbank.

Two companies of sepoys ran along the embankment, following the lone boat's agonizing progress down the river.[227] In the sepoys' indiscriminate musketfire officers who had cheated death for three weeks of bombardment began to fall. As others tried to keep up a covering fire, the irrepressible Moore removed his cartridge pouch, dropped down from Wheeler's grounded boat into the water and despite his broken clavicle heaved his back against the hull. But a spray of musketfire caught him "in the region of the heart" and, as his wife looked on, the gallant Captain John Moore of Her Majesty's 32nd sank into the shallows.

Artillery Lieutenant St. George Ashe of the eastern battery and Lieutenant Augustus Joseph Boulton, still maimed from the facial wound he had received outracing his sowars three weeks before, jumped down to replace Moore in the shoal. They, too, were killed outright by another rebel fusillade, their bodies floating off in the dilatory current. A merchant named George Reid was killed,[228] Major Vibart was wounded in the arm, and as they struggled in the shallows a single round shot not only killed Lieutenants Burney and Glanville but reduced half of Lieutenant Fagan's leg to a shred of sinews.

None of which induced Major Edwin Wiggins to quit his hiding place deep in the hold of Wheeler's boat. "No expostulation could make him quit the shelter of her bulwarks," Thomson recalled, "though we were adopting every possible expedient to lighten her burden. It was positively a relief to us when we found that his cowardice was unavailing; and a bullet through the boat's side that despatched him caused the only death that we regarded with complacency."[229] Wiggins's corpse was dumped overboard, and at last the boat floated free.

Among those killed at the sandbar was the elderly Lady Frances Wheeler, shot down or drowned as she struggled with her daughters to flee through the shallows and up the embankment. What became of Eliza Wheeler no one knows, but a rebel apparently dragged Margaret Wheeler out into the depths and left her there to drown as the boat floated out of reach.[230]

♦　♦　♦

A third boat pushed away from the chaos at Sati Chowra, but its crew managed only to punt it across the river and onto another sandbar, where the gunners firing from the grass soon turned it to splinters and took the survivors captive.[231] But by now the rebel gunners had lost interest in the sunken, burning boats at Sati Chowra, and Tatya Tope signaled to Teeka Singh to order his cavalry into the shallows to finish off the stragglers and the wounded. Brandishing sabres and pistols, a stream of sowars came surging out from behind the village of Sati Chowra, shouting "*Deen! Deen!*"[232]

Europeans who had crouched petrified in the shoal now tried to flee toward the burning boats, hoping to lose themselves in the storm of smoke. Gasping and moaning, one man hurled himself through the water, trying to outrace a pair of cantering sowars. As they caught up to him, recalled Amy, "they made several cuts at his neck [and] chopped off his hands which he held up to protect his head. The swords being blunt & the blows awkwardly dealt, this poor man's tortures are beyond description," and he fell back, fountaining blood into the churning water.[233]

Other sowars spurred their horses around to the far side of the shattered flotilla, where they came upon the Reverend Moncrieff standing behind one of the ruined hulls with a group of drummers. Moncrieff, whose "nice, ladylike looking, delicate"[234] wife had been killed with their child in the rebels' first burst of gunfire, held a prayer book in his hand.[235] "If we English take prisoners," he told the sowars as their horses waded toward them, "we do not put them to death, but imprison them. Spare our lives, and put us into prison."

A sowar struck Moncrieff across the neck, and the muscular reverend slowly fell face forward into the water. Working their way through the huddled group, the sowars cut a drummer across his face and stabbed his pregnant wife in the stomach.[236] Mrs. Murray, wife of the pensioned drum major of the 56th, received a sword cut across the back after her pregnant daughters-in-law had been cut down as well: one of them, "being very far advanced, [expecting] daily to be confined, was ripped open, and the child came out of her womb [and] was cut on the spot."[237]

Along the slope of the embankment and up the length of the ravine all the way to the bridge some of the stragglers still tried desperately to get to the river. All they could see beyond the trees was smoke and the flicker of flames and the firecracker flashing of muskets. Most were shot by the two or three hundred sepoys who now fired upon them from the bridge;[238] but a few still managed to dodge the sepoys' fire and splash into the water.

Evidently several women were taken off by troopers—at least that was the rumor that spread through Nana's camp. Mrs. Jackson, wife of a lieutenant in the 67th, was carried off struggling in her green silk gown,[239] and Captain Belson's sister-in-law was abducted as well, along with several Eurasian girls, including a fourteen-year-old named Charlotte Spiers who was never seen again.[240]

Down on the riverbank a cavalryman named Ali Shah was said to have plucked Colonel Williams's youngest daughter, Fanny, from her sister's side and galloped up the ravine with her flung across his horse's neck.[241] Running into the shallows, a sepoy brandishing a bayonet then bore down on Fanny's older sister Georgiana who, de-spite the sniper's bullet that had lodged in her shoulder blade, had spent the siege tending her wounded mother.[242]

"My father," Georgiana reminded the sepoy, "was always kind to sepoys."

Ashamed, the sepoy turned away, but no sooner had he moved on than a villager came up behind Georgiana and "dashed her brains out" with a club.[243]

Other insurgents cut down a five-year-old and a twelve-year-old pair of brothers with sabres,[244] bayoneted a four-year-old child,[245] picked up others by the leg and hurled them into deeper water.[246] Mrs. Henry Christie was killed within sight of her own house.[247] But the sepoys and sowars concentrated on the males who still wal-lowed, wounded and exhausted, in the bloodening mud. According to Eliza Bradshaw, the mother of two Christian drummers of the 56th Native Infantry, a sepoy grabbed her two-year-old granddaugh-ter, but "on finding her to be a girl, . . . in a rage cast her away into the river." Mrs. Bradshaw threw herself upon her two sons and begged the sepoys of their regiment to spare them, "reminding them that they were of the same corps, and had always behaved kindly to-wards all in the regiment. [But] no notice was taken of me beyond pushing me aside and completing the foul deed upon my poor inno-cent sons."[248]

All along the bank sepoys and sowars paused to club the wounded with their musket stocks or chop at them with their sabres. A Euro-pean who had been stunned by a round shot's glancing blow had "floated down to the bank, and was standing behind a boat with up-lifted hands, and was looking about with intent to conceal him-self . . . when a boatman . . . struck him a second blow on the head, which split his skull in two."[249] While the sowars continued to slash at the men bleeding and floundering in the tepid water, mutineers and villagers squattered out to the boats to plunder them of weapons, treasure boxes, the little parcels of jewels and money people had tied into their clothing, dispatching any survivors who might still be crouching on the decks or hunched down in the shattered holds.[250] One villager retrieved a fine double-barreled shotgun from the shoal,[251] another led a whimpering dog off a boat and pulled it through the bloody water.[252] Others yanked rings and earrings off the women lying dead or wounded in the water.[253]

As the sepoys approached her boat, Amy Horne pulled Florence off the roof and down onto the deck and huddled with her there, mouthing her little sister's whimpering prayers "for mercy and help" and preparing "for that what was coming, feeling sure, the hour was not distant when we should have to stand before His dread presence." Suddenly the boat lurched and Amy looked down the length of the deck to see sepoys climbing up the side and dropping down into the hold. Shielding her sister, Amy watched the sepoys proceed methodically through the boat, shooting "two sweet little girls, sisters, who were between the ages of six and eight [and] clinging to each other," and then turning their muskets on a Eurasian produce trader named John Kirkpatrick, searching his pockets.[254]

When they reached Amy a sepoy grabbed her by the arm and commanded her to hand over "all I possessed." She gave up "a few trinkets," but the sepoys ran their hands through her gown, searching for more.

"My senses had very nearly forsaken me," wrote Amy. "I was in a sort of stupor. The search was made on my person while I was standing, but to speak more exactly I was made to stand while I was searched" as a sepoy "let off his gun over my head and shoulders in the most deliberate and cold-blooded manner." While the sepoys were searching her, a sowar riding saddle-deep in the water came up alongside Amy's boat and, leveling his carbine at her, ordered her to come with him. When she dazedly turned her head away, he barked an order to one of the sepoys to throw her over the side. As Florence scrabbled at Amy's hand, "I was thereupon brutally seized round the waist, and though I struggled and fought wildly, was quickly overcome and tossed into the river." Buffeted by the river's chop and haunted ever after by her sister's retreating cries of "Oh, Amy, don't leave me!" she floated downstream a hundred yards or so,[255] somehow found the strength to crawl out of the shallows, and collapsed upon the bank.[256]

✦ ✦ ✦

It was all the work of less than an hour, and at ten o'clock a messenger galloped down the ravine and handed a note to Tatya Tope.[257] Tatya signaled to his bugler who sounded the ceasefire, and the sowars and sepoys and plundering villagers[258] lowered their blades and barrels and began to retrieve the survivors from the water and drag and prod them up the bank.[259] All the men lying in the shallows were either dead or near dead;[260] on her scramble through the shoal Amy had seen that at least one, the gentleman with the severed hands, was still breathing. Beyond the line of smoldering boats bodies floated downstream, others lay snagged on sandbars or sprawled across the bank.[261]

Within an hour some 120 women and children had been assembled on the riverside, sobbing and praying in their torn, scorched, and gory gowns. "Many of them were wounded with bullets and sword cuts; their dresses were wet and full of mud and blood; [and] they were ordered to give up whatever valuables they might have hid upon their persons."[262] A few of the children but none of the women had been stripped of their clothing.[263] Some still wore soggy bonnets and straw sun hats with crumpled, dripping brims.[264]

Among this wretched party lay Kate Lindsay, reeling now with a bullet in her back, but attended, miraculously, by all three of her daughters: Caroline, Fanny, and the feverish Alice.[265] The indomitable Bridget Widdowson, the stout soldier's wife who had guarded the sepoy prisoners with a sword, marched defiantly out of the water.[266] Isabel White, her dark hair hanging in sandy scrags, clung to her friend Louisa Chalwin, the veterinarian's wife who had brought her to India to find a husband.[267] Mrs. Blair, an officer's widow who had never given up hope that her husband had survived the siege of Kabul, prayed with her last surviving daughter.[268] Mrs. O'Brien sat on the muddy ground, looking toward the shallows for her little boy's corpse.

After half an hour[269] the women were ordered to their feet and since "all of them were dripping wet and could hardly walk,"[270] some were led to a few of the same hackeries that had borne them down to the river. A few native and Eurasian women were let go. Shepherd's ayah Thakurani was spared "owing to her old age and miserable appearance."[271] A wet-nurse from Colonel Williams's household "came out of the boat almost naked [and] the mob were going to kill her," but some sepoys interceded. She stumbled back into Colonel Williams's compound to tell her fellow servants that her master—apparently the late colonel's relation—had thrown his child into the river when the roof caught fire, "and told her to leave the boat."[272]

Eliza Bradshaw was permitted to fetch her granddaughter from the shallows and escape into the city, where she disguised herself as a beggar. But for many days afterward her granddaughter "would constantly urge me to go to the riverside," Mrs. Bradshaw would recall, "and look for her father, and on being told that he is dead and not there, would beg me with tears in her eyes to put my hands under water, and search well, that possibly he may be hid under the waves."[273]

IF HE MUST DIE

June 27–30, 1857

When the firing ceased at Sati Chowra, the townspeople returned from their hiding places to watch as the mutineers[274] led batches of women and children up the ravine.[275] "Suffering under their wounds, and stupefied by the fearful ordeal through which they had just passed," they proceeded over the bullet-pocked bridge and back around the artillery bazaar, retracing their footsteps to the Entrenchment and then continuing past Vibart's battery and across the parade-ground to Nana Sahib's headquarters at Savada House.[276]

"The sowars were on both sides," recalled the captive drummer John Fitchett, "right and left of them, and some sepoys brought up the rear."[277] Some of the survivors rode in horse carts, but most walked the more than two miles under the harsh sun, many of them barefooted. Khoda Bux was brought out by his captors to watch the women and children pass. "On some was nothing but an under garment," he said, "on others but one gown."[278] Most of their muddy clothes were stained with blood, but it was hard to tell which was their own blood, which the blood of others they had tried to save. At least two appeared badly wounded, "and had their heads bound up with handkerchiefs." The oldest of the males among them appeared to be about thirteen.[279]

If any came to jeer the women and children as they staggered up from the river, apparently the sight of them struck many people speechless. Some sepoys were remorseful and declared that it had been "a crime to put to the sword such fair and tender creatures." They were especially moved by the youngest of the Blair daughters. "She had been wounded," wrote Amy, "and was lying on the cart with her hair thrown back. Its great length and dark colour, together with her delicate complexion, some of them said, gave her the appearance of an angel; others adding that they could compare her to nothing but a rose."[280]

When the tattered assembly of women and children reached Nana's headquarters, the Peshwa emerged from his tent and ordered them incarcerated in the main hall of Savada House[281] under a guard of his own Mahratta soldiery.[282] All sowars were obliged to hand over any British female they may have captured, and in the afternoon Ali Shah brought Fanny Williams to Savada House, reuniting her with her wounded mother. Other sowars brought in their British captives, including Mrs. Jackson and Captain Belson's sister-in-law, but none of the Eurasian girls were returned.[283]

Late in the afternoon the rebels brought in about seventeen male fugitives from the third boat that had drifted across the river only to be demolished by rebel fire. A party of sowars and matchlockmen brought them bound before Nana Sahib, who ordered them executed. As the women and children listened in the gloom of Savada House, all seventeen men were tied together with rope and taken out onto the plain to be shot.[284] "Those amongst them who were merely wounded by the musketry were decapitated by the executioners"[285] and dragged into the Ganges in trussed-up bundles of five or six.[286]

That night as the grieving women and children lay down on the stone floor of Savada House, as Caroline Lindsay found space for herself and her sisters and tore bandages from her damp clothes to bind her mother's wound, the rain the garrison had dreaded finally began to fall, raising a suffocating steam from the parched plain.[287]

✦   ✦   ✦

In the mayhem of the morning of June 27, Amy Horne had crawled up the embankment and hidden in the brush. "Gracious and merciful Father," she silently prayed as the slaughter continued in the shallows below. "Thou wilt not desert me in the time of need! Oh Lord, have mercy on me!"

Gradually she fell into "a sort of drowsy fit" from which she was soon wakened by approaching footsteps. Amy jumped to her feet to find not the rebels but "to my great relief, the well-known face and form of Miss Wheeler, the General's daughter," who, like Amy, had been left to drown in the shallows by "men who perhaps thought she was not worth a bullet."

Amy and Margaret Wheeler were too exhausted and terrified to be of much comfort to each other, but they cowered together in the bushes for an hour until a rebel party stumbled upon them. A mounted sowar apparently hauled Margaret up behind him and rode off with her into the countryside, while Amy was left behind with the others to be "pushed and dragged along and subjected to every indignity. Occasionally I felt the thrust of a bayonet, and on my protesting against such treatment with uplifted hands, and appealing to their feelings as men, I was struck on my head, and was made to understand, in language too plain that I had not long to live; but before being put to death, that I would be made to feel some portion of the degradation their brethren felt at Meerut when ironed and disgraced before the troops."[288]

She stumbled up from the river, crowds of onlookers gathering and jeering and then falling away. At last her abductors brought her to a cluster of huts that had sprung up during the uprising near the Assembly Rooms.[289] By now she was almost entirely naked, "for my clothes had been torn to pieces when I had been dragged along by the men, and I had the mortification of being made a spectacle before these heartless and cruel wretches." Swirling around her, onlookers clapped their hands and shouted, "Well done" as she sank to the ground and buried her face in her hands.

"At length I heard a voice speaking to my persecutors in rather a conciliatory tone. 'Spare the poor creature, and have compassion on her. Let her alone; she seems dead already.'"

Amy looked up to see an African, possibly a eunuch from the court of Oudh, staring down at her. "There was something mild and compassionate in his look," she recalled. Covering her nakedness with a cloth, he led her into a tent to rest, assuring her that he would do all he could to spare her life. Amy thanked him for his kindness.

"You are very unwell," he said. "Your eyes are bloodshot, and your face is very flushed."

For the first time Amy realized that a high fever was compounding her exhaustion. Conceding that "a little sleep would perhaps do me good," she lay her "aching head on the mattress and fell fast asleep."[290]

✦   ✦   ✦

By noon of June 27 as many as sixty people, many of them mortally wounded, had crammed into Wheeler's boat as it slowly reeled down the river.[291] Even under the most ideal conditions it took skilled and vigilant helmsmen to navigate the Ganges. The challenge was to avoid the capsizing gusts of wind that tormented the center of the river's course and stick to the steepest banks, ever alert to the latent menace—sandbars, tree stumps—that lurked beneath the river's surface.[292]

But Wheeler's overburdened boat had to navigate the shoals down the center of the Ganges, equidistant from the rebel squads and guns that continued to follow them along both sides of the river.[293] It was slow going. Even in the deepest channels of the river near the Oudh side, the current in the dry season ran only about two and a half miles an hour.[294] In the warm shoals the water was nearly stagnant, and here and there the men who paddled and poled the boat along could hear the hull grating across the sandy bottom.

There was no food in the boat, and its splintered gunwales dipped dangerously as people leaned down to slake their thirst with river water. The more able-bodied passengers rode on the bamboo deck or on the frame atop the thatched roof that had escaped the boatmen's embers. But "the wounded and the dead were often entangled together in the bottom of the boat" in a puddle of water and blood. Whenever a man died in the hold, his comrades had to wade down through the impossible press of passengers and pull his corpse out from among the groaning wounded and throw it over the side. It was "work of extreme difficulty," wrote Thomson, "though imperatively necessary from the dreaded consequences of the intense heat, and the importance of lightening the boat as much as possible."

Sometimes they were in such a hurry to lighten the boat that they hardly bothered to check for a pulse. That afternoon a bullet grazed Thomson's head and knocked him unconscious; the next thing he knew, two of his comrades were standing over him, reaching for his arms and legs. "We were just going to throw you overboard," they told him as he began to stir.[295]

Mrs. Fraser, who had fled to Cawnpore from the pandemonium at Delhi, bravely tended to the wounded. "She appeared alike indifferent to danger and to her own scanty covering; while with perfect equanimity and imperturbed fortitude she was entirely occupied in the attempt to soothe and relieve the agonized sufferers around her, whose wounds scarcely made their condition worse than her own."[296]

Rebel gunners straggled after the boat with two cannon, but the smallest was loaded merely with sacks of grape that clattered harmlessly around the boat, and the gunners could not figure out the elevating screw on the larger cannon.[297] A few round shot plunged into the nearby sandbars, but at last the gunners fell back, their bullocks bogging down in the soft sand along the bank.[298]

The boat floated only six miles downstream in at least as many hours, and at five o'clock once again snagged on a sandbar. By now General Wheeler was entirely incapacitated by exhaustion, exposure, and despondency, and command had fallen to Major Vibart. Vibart decided that enough men had died already at the first sandbar; this time they would remain huddled in the boat until nightfall, "in the hope that when darkness sheltered us we might be able to get out the women and lighten the craft sufficiently to push her off."

Nightfall was long in coming, and a large body of sepoys caught up to them on the riverbank and fired upon them with their muskets. But the officers and soldiers "returned the fire with their rifles from the boat, and wounded several of the sepoys on the bank, who thereupon drew off."[299] Once again the frustrated sepoys tried to let fire accomplish what their guns could not and sent a burning boat down the stream, "in the hope," wrote Thomson, "that she would fall afoul of us." When it missed the boat by "a yard or two" they fired "arrows with lighted charcoal fastened to them, to ignite, if possible, the thatched roof." So the officers tore the roof down, reserving any substantial bamboos they could pull from its frame and pitching the thatch overboard.

As soon as darkness set in, men jumped down to heave the boat off the bar, and though the sepoys kept up their fire until after midnight, the new crescent moon was so obscured by clouds that their firing had little effect. They finally gave up, leaving the boat to blunder downstream in the pitch dark, bumping another four miles from sandbar to sandbar, so that Thomson and his comrades had to spend "as much of the night out, as we did in the boat."[300]

In the morning the refugees woke to find that their pursuers had vanished. They spotted some villagers bathing by the river and sent a native drummer off with five rupees to persuade one of the bathers to bring them some food and a crew of boatmen. The villager exchanged the five rupees for his water jar "as a guarantee for his fidelity," but warned the drummer that a powerful landlord named Ram Buksh had pledged to capture the fugitives and return them to Cawnpore.

At this news Captain Whiting penciled a note saying that he had abandoned all hope, put it in a bottle someone had found in the hold, and threw it into the water. The river answered him by snagging the boat on a sandbar that afternoon, opposite a village called Nujuffghur, and as officers dropped down once again to push it off, two parties of sepoys caught up to the boat on both sides of the river and opened fire with muskets. The casualties were terrible. Whiting was killed. Major Vibart, already wounded in one arm the day before, was now wounded in the other. Lieutenant C. W. Quin and Captain Seppings were shot through the arms and Mrs. Seppings through the thigh.

As the wind picked up and the sky darkened, Blenman, Wheeler's temperamental Eurasian spy, was shot in the groin and begged the others to "terminate his sufferings with a bullet." They refused. When Lieutenant Harrison was killed, Thomson removed his rings and gave them to Mrs. Seppings, "as I thought the women might perhaps excite some commiseration, and that if any of our party escaped, it would be some of them."[301]

Now the rebels brought a field piece into position, and managed to fire a round shot that smashed Captain Turner's legs as he struggled in the shoal. But just then a sudden rain doused the gunners' matches and soaked their store of powder, silencing the cannon. At sunset "fifty or sixty natives came down the stream in a boat from Cawnpore, thoroughly armed, and deputed to board and destroy us." But fifty or sixty natives evidently overloaded their craft as well, and they too got stuck on a sandbar.

"Instead of waiting for them to attack us," Thomson proudly recalled, "eighteen or twenty of us charged them, and few of their number escaped to tell the story." The Europeans gained a new store of ammunition in the attack but no food, "and death was now staring us in the face from that direction. . . . Faint and weary, and expecting never to see the morrow," the fugitives fell asleep.

In the middle of the night a mass of fulgurant clouds came tumbling down the river, unleashing a torrent of rain, and the fugitives awoke to find their boat floating freely down the rising Ganges. "Some fresh hopes buoyed us up again; but daylight returned to reveal the painful fact that we had drifted out of the navigable channel into a siding of the river opposite [Sheorajpur]," and as the boat ground to a groaning halt on yet another sandbar, thirty or forty rebels resumed their musket fire.[302]

By nine A.M. of June 29 more rebels had massed along the river-bank, and Major Vibart decided that the fugitives' only hope was for a party of men to charge directly into them, drawing their fire as other men dropped into the water to push the boat free. It seemed "a forlorn enterprise," but Vibart invested eleven able-bodied soldiers in it, under the command of Lieutenants Thomson and Delafosse and Sergeant Grady of the 84th.[303]

If Thomson was any measure, "able-bodied" had become a relative term, for he had been thrice wounded by this time, with grapeshot in his thigh, a bullet in his back, and a gash on his head where the sniper's bullet had grazed him only the day before. But, as Delafosse put it, "there was nothing left but to charge [the sepoys] and drive them away."[304] With a few muttered prayers the fourteen men huddled down in the hold for a moment, readying their muskets, and then emerged with a roar, tumbling down into the shallows and, "maddened by desperation," rushing the sepoys on the shore.

The startled sepoys fell back in confusion, but as Thomson and Delafosse led the others further up the bank other rebels closed behind them, "until we were thoroughly surrounded by a mingled party of natives, armed and unarmed." Thomson turned his men about and tried to charge back toward the river, but by now too many rebels had caught up to them, and they had to approach the river obliquely, cutting their way through the rebels who tried to block their path and splashing down into the shallows a mile downstream from where they left the boat.[305] Thomson and his men ran a few more yards downriver, thinking the boat might have floated away, but they saw no trace of it. Giving up on ever seeing "either the boat or our doomed companions any more" they fled into the countryside "with a rabble of ryots and sepoys at our heels."[306]

✦　✦　✦

Back at the ghat a few Eurasian evacuees had escaped the massacre of the twenty-seventh. When the boats caught fire, a pensioned musician named James Stewart had hauled his wife and another woman overboard and dragged them out into deeper water, where they bobbed together for several hours until they could see the rebels leading the women and children up the ravine. Stripping down to their underclothes and "enduring incredible hardship, what with want and exposure" and the dread of running into parties of rebels, they were able to reach Allahabad twelve days later.[307]

A party of women from Stewart's corps that included a Mrs. Letts and her severely wounded daughter as well as Mrs. Bradshaw, her two daughters-in-law, and two granddaughters, were able to hide in the timbers along the riverbank all afternoon and then slip into the city in the dark. After being chased out of their hiding place in a Moslem cemetery they found refuge in an elephant shed, where Mrs. Letts's daughter-in-law died "in the utmost pain" from a stomach wound.[308]

As the others sought refuge in the sheds that rainy night, another musician named Benjamin Murray left his hiding place in the city and crept down to the ghat to search among the dead for his mother. The hundreds of corpses had been stripped of jewels and clothing and pushed out into the water beyond the broken line of charred boats, but up on the riverbank Benjamin saw a lone woman lying in a pool of blood. He turned her over to find she was his mother, "wounded in several places," but still breathing. Benjamin picked her up and carried her back to his refuge.[309]

Other fugitives were not so lucky. Sergeant Matthew Ogle of the Canal Department was captured and killed after trying to escape into the countryside.[310] Lieutenant Frederick J. G. Saunders of the 84th was captured after swimming away. He demanded to see Nana Sahib and in the Peshwa's presence withdrew a revolver he had hidden in his clothes, shooting five of his captors before firing his last round at the Peshwa. He missed, and the rebels seized him, whereupon, according to a cook-boy, they nailed Saunders to a plank, cut off his hands and feet, and ran over him with their horses, hacking at him "until he was literally hewed into pieces."[311]

During the attack on the boats Captain Frederick Angelo,[312] the newly arrived superintendent of the Canal Department who had managed to get his pregnant wife and two daughters out of Cawnpore on the eve of the siege, succeeded in swimming across the river and hiding in the reeds until nightfall.[313] Stripping down to a waist cloth, Angelo darted along a series of ravines, trying to make his way north toward Lucknow, when villagers surrounded him and took him to their landlord. The villagers gave him sugar and watched as he greedily devoured it "with both his hands."[314]

The landlord took pity on Angelo and promised to take him to Lucknow. But word of the feringhee's capture quickly spread, and on June 28 a party of sepoys arrived at the landlord's village to lay claim to him. The landlord refused to break his word to Angelo, but then more rebel zemindars descended on the village, overpowering his matchlockmen, and took Angelo to Baba Bhutt, who ordered him cut down on the spot. His rebel captors refused unless the captain was himself armed. "Our creed does not permit us to kill a bound prisoner," one of the matchlockmen explained, "though we can slay our enemy in battle."[315]

"Let him strike us," another suggested, "and then we will strike him in return, but we will not strike him in his present condition." A sowar put an end to this impasse by striking Angelo on the arm, whereupon the jullads "laid on with their swords, and he was despatched."[316]

That day Angelo's pregnant wife, Helena, and his two little girls were safely sailing for Calcutta in the rain; it was a Sunday, and the passengers held a service. "My dear Fred," Helena wrote in her diary, "I wonder whether my prayers have been answered and you spared in all these dangers!"[317] Two hundred miles upriver her husband's slashed corpse floated after her down the Ganges.[318]

✦ ✦ ✦

After Thomson and his party charged the rebels, more sepoys assembled along the bank, firing their muskets at Wheeler's boat. In the brief exchange that followed, Lieutenants Battine, Satchwell, Balfour, and Chalmers were killed in the shallows, and Master and Daniell were wounded. Major Vibart ordered that a white flag be raised, and what little was left of Vibart's party threw their weapons over the side. A body of sepoys waded out into the shallows to accept their surrender and collect their arms. Few of the passengers were capable of lifting their wounded compatriots out of the boat, and villagers had to lower them to the shallows and carry them to the riverbank.

The rebels assembled carts from nearby Sheorajpur to transport the women and children and the wounded. Apparently some of the rebels' ferocity had been spent, for they did not handle the women as roughly as they had two days before. They did not search them, bind them, or take away their valuables.[319]

The men were bound together with ropes, including old Wheeler, Lieutenant Fagan with his smashed legs, and the wounded Captain Seppings. On the eighteen-mile journey from Sheorajpur to Cawnpore, Major Edward Vibart evidently bled to death from his multiple wounds, leaving Emily and their two children to proceed alone. And

Lieutenant Master, who had written a hasty and hopeful note to his father on the eve of the garrison's evacuation, also succumbed to his wounds.[320] Their bodies were discarded by the wayside.

On the morning of June 30 the survivors and their sowar escort reached Savada House,[321] where Nana Sahib emerged from his tent[322] to congratulate their captors and command that the men be separated out for execution.[323] There were only four children and a few wives left: among them the wounded Mrs. Seppings, Mrs. Harris, and a Mrs. Boyes. Emily Vibart and Mrs. Reid were now widows, and Mrs. Fraser's husband was at Delhi, from whence she had escaped in May.

A few sowars stepped forward to plead for the life of Captain Seppings and his wife, but Teeka Singh overruled them, and Mrs. Seppings, wounded in the thigh, was dragged from her husband's side.[324] The sepoys pulled the other women away and sat the men down on the greening ground in their soiled clothes and bloody bandages. Nana ordered the sepoys of the 1st Native Infantry to shoot them, but they balked.

"We will not shoot Wheeler sahib," they told Nana, "who has made the name of our regiment great, and whose son is our quartermaster." Nor would they shoot the severely wounded Captain Currie of the 84th. They asked Nana Sahib to "put them in prison" instead.

"What is this?" the Oudh Irregular sepoys sneered. "Put them in prison? We will kill them all."

The sepoys of the 1st made way, and two companies of Irregulars closed around Wheeler and the others, cocking their muskets. But the wife of civil surgeon Horatio P. Harris suddenly broke through their ranks and stood beside her husband with her child in her arms.[325]

"I will not leave my husband," she said. "If he must die, I will die with him."

Other ladies tried to follow her example, crying, "We too will protect our husbands." But Mrs. Seppings was wounded, Mrs. Boyes was ill, and as their husbands desperately begged them to go back, they were soon dragged away. Only Mrs. Harris remained. "The child was asked of her," but she refused to give it up. "This provoked the mutineers," and at last the sepoys stood back and raised their muskets.[326]

Captain Seppings asked Nana if they could have a moment to pray.[327] Nana agreed, and ordered that the wounded Reverend

Cockey's arms be untied so he could retrieve a prayer book from his pocket.

The delay was too much for a gentleman who lay wounded in the arm and leg. "If you mean to kill us, why don't you set about it?" he snapped at the encircling sepoys. "Be quick, and get the work done at once! Why delay?"

But Wheeler and the rest painfully knelt down as Cockey read a few prayers, and then as they awkwardly tried to shake hands with each other through their bonds, the sepoys opened fire.[328]

"One sahib rolled one way," said a native witness, "and one another; but they were not dead, only wounded. So the [rebels] went on, and finished them with swords," including Mrs. Harris and her baby.[329]

As the remaining women and children were herded into Savada House, scavengers stripped the dead and dragged them off to a corner of the compound. But before they became "the food of wild beasts and birds of prey," Mrs. Seppings found a use for one of the rings that Thomson had given her, trading it with a sweeper for a lock of her husband's hair.[330]

THE SIRCAR
June 27–July 2, 1857

On June 27 a proclamation was issued in Nana Sahib's name declaring that "by the grace of God, and the destroying fortune of the King," all of "the white faces" who had fought against him had "entered hell."[331] That night the rebels held a grand review on the plain northeast of Savada House.[332] By now Nana's army consisted not only of the four resident Cawnpore regiments but the 12th and 13th Native Infantry, four regiments of Irregular Cavalry, detachments of sepoys from Fatehgarh and Allahabad, the 2nd Oudh Irregular Infantry, plus artillery batteries, a regiment's worth of newly recruited Cawnpore militia, and a "great mob" of matchlockmen.

A proclamation urged the people of the city to "celebrate this victory with rejoicings and peals of artillery," and that night the camp was illuminated with mustard lamps. As the troops assembled in their thousands, Nana Sahib Bahadur finally received the twenty-one-gun salute that the British had denied him and his adoptive father for almost forty years. His artillery roared in a positive orgy of salutes. Nineteen guns were fired for Bala Rao, his brother and governor-general, and seventeen for Jwala Prasad, his commander-in-chief. Nana heaped praises on his ministers for "the way in which he got possession of the entrenchment," and "extolled much Uzeemoollah Khan and Jowalapersuad, Ressaldar, saying that it was to their wisdom that so easy a conquest was owing."[333]

Bala Rao praised the soldiers for their great courage in obtaining a complete victory over the British at Cawnpore, promising them one hundred thousand rupees' reward, and distributing 4,500 rupees[334] to the contractors to pay the boatmen for the loss of their craft.[335] The artillery salutes were repeated, the soldiers dispersed into the bazaars, and Nana and his ministers returned to their tents.[336]

✦ ✦ ✦

The idea of simply offering the garrison passage to Allahabad had evidently been floating around the rebel camp all week. Nana Sahib preferred to allow the garrison to depart in safety. The later Mahrattas had been capable of committing certain outrages, but general massacres were not part of their repertoire. The Moghuls might wipe out the population of a town, but the Mahrattas were more pragmatic. Who would pay them their tribute if no one survived to farm, trade, and collect taxes? Rather than execute the princes they defeated, they had often reinstalled them under the Peshwa's aegis. This pragmatism was part of the ethos that Nana's shrewd Concanist tutors had inculcated. A massacre might satisfy a moment's passion, but it shut off your options. How could you negotiate with a foe that believed capitulation meant annihilation? How could you ever reason with enemies so outraged by their compatriots' slaughter as to put vengeance ahead of their own self-interest?

To this ethos Nana Sahib added a certain grudging fondness for at least a few individual Europeans. He had not been blind to most of his houseguests' contempt, but he had respected accomplished men like Wheeler and Charles Hillersdon; enjoyed hunting with the dashing Lieutenant Daniell; was amused by some of the ladies who paused in their dancing at Saturday House to admire his ancestral portraits, compliment him on his furnishings, or thank him for his gracious hospitality. None of these relationships compensated for the humiliation he had suffered from their employers in Calcutta and London, but enough Europeans like Lang had offered to intercede with the Company on Nana's behalf to immunize him from the genocidal loathing that animated his brothers, his generals, and Azimullah Khan.

For Azimullah the annihilation of the British had to be total. The British had already demonstrated what they could accomplish in even the most insignificant numbers. Not one European could be allowed to live. Every time a rebel asked for permission to spare someone—an aged Englishman, a pregnant memsahib, a Christian infant he proposed to adopt—Azimullah and his Moslem subordinates would cite an old Persian saw: "To extinguish the fire and leave the spark, to kill a snake and preserve its young, is not the wisdom of sensible men."[337]

What made this reasoning especially compelling to the mutineers at Cawnpore were the stories of what Colonel James Neill had done to their comrades in the 37th Native Infantry at Benares: firing salvos of grape into them as they peacefully assembled and hanging hundreds more after they tried to flee—a grotesque and inexplicable escalation of John Company's treachery at Barrackpore and Meerut. Now sepoys of the 6th Native Infantry arrived from Allahabad to tell of Neill's atrocities there, of bazaars looted and destroyed, of villages surrounded and torched. Neill's execution parties burned all the crops; hanged every man and boy they could catch; carelessly, sometimes purposely killed women and children in their crossfire. Everywhere the British went, said the sepoys who staggered into Cawnpore from down the country, they left death and destruction. The rumors extended to native babies bayoneted and women raped and tortured, counterparts to the exaggerated tales the British had circulated about rebel atrocities at Meerut and Delhi. And if in their outrage the feringhee made no distinction between male or female, old or young, mutineer or loyal sepoy, why should the rebels be any more fastidious?

And so by the time of Nana's defeat on the twenty-third of June the idea of offering safe passage had mutated into a ploy by which to lure the British to their doom. The Moslems solemnly debated the propriety of committing such treachery, but everyone concluded with Kazi Wasi-ud-din that luring the Europeans to the river and then murdering them was "lawful and proper."[338] A fugitive from the terrors of Allahabad, Maulvie Liaqat Ali concurred, as did Nana's advisor Shah Ali. Since the rebels had to kill the British "in the long run," it was only sensible to "induce the Europeans to come out and then despatch them."[339]

Nana could not see what would be gained by such treachery. The garrison was half dead already, and under the blistering sun, bumbling through the shallows of the receding Ganges, how many would ever reach Allahabad anyway? Let other rebels along the river attack the fleeing garrison if they wished, "he had taken a most solemn oath to allow the English to leave in safety, and therefore would not accord his consent to their slaughter."

But no one listened to him. He had opposed the massacre of the Fatehgarh fugitives, now he would deny his soldiers their last hope of victory. They did not need his consent. To the Hindus Nana was nothing but a figurehead. To the Moslems he was a nonentity. Even the ambivalent Nunne Nawab was preferable: at least he was a Moslem and a native of the Doab. Still bristling over the execution of the Moslem butchers, the corruption of Nana's generals, and their shameful defeat on the twenty-third, the mutineers "openly declared they did not care for the Nana" and directed that all of his proclamations end with the words "by order of the brave soldiery."[340] That they bore any allegiance to Nana Sahib at all depended entirely on the preeminence of Azimullah, whom they may have expected to turn eventually on Nana Sahib and lay claim to Cawnpore in the emperor's name.

Reading the temper of their troops, Bala Rao and Jwala Prasad sensibly sided with Azimullah and the Moslems of the 2nd Native Cavalry who "took it upon themselves to conduct the foul deed, saying that they had taken no solemn oath nor bound themselves by promises."[341] When Azimullah had returned from his last negotiation outside the Entrenchment he told Shah Ali and Jwala Prasad that he had arranged "a good opportunity for getting rid of the Europeans,"[342] and at sunset, "unmindful of the Nana's oath and promise," issued orders to wipe out the garrison as soon as it reached the river.[343]

All the rebel landlords were summoned to attend the European embarkation, and Hulas Singh ordered the contractors "to settle with the boatmen, that they must set the boats on fire upon a signal from them and jump off and swim to shore, the instant the Europeans get into the boats."[344] Lascars had been enlisted to bring guns to the river; they were already installed and hidden away "that suspicions might not be excited" when the officers inspected the boats on the twenty-sixth.[345] And Tatya Tope had been summoned to Nana's tent and directed to assemble five to six hundred sepoys and hide them in the interstices of Sati Chowra.[346]

At ten o'clock on the night of June 26 Nana's officers issued the following order to the 17th Native Infantry encamped across the river.

> There are absolutely no English troops remaining here; they sought protection from the Sirkar [Nana], and said, 'Allow us to get into boats and go away;' therefore the Sirkar has made arrangements for their going, and by 10 o'clock tomorrow these people will have got into boats and started on the river. The river on this side is shallow, and on the other side deep. The boats will keep to the other side, and go along for three or four koss. Arrangements for the destruction of these English will not be made here, but as these people will keep near the bank on the other side of the river, it is necessary that you should be prepared, and make a place to kill and destroy them on that side of the river, and having obtained a victory come here. The Sirkar is much pleased with your conduct, and it is very conspicuous, and the English say that they will go on their boats to Calcutta.[347]

During the attack Nana Sahib had remained in his tent, pacing anxiously as gunfire rolled and crackled up from the river.[348] When a trooper galloped up to report that the entire garrison was being killed Nana sent him back with an order to spare the women and children, a command Tatya Tope loyally enforced and the elated sepoys readily obeyed.

Two hours later Azimullah and Bala Rao returned to Nana Sahib to report that only one boat had escaped and the surviving women and children were on their way to Savada House. Imperial historians depicted Nana Sahib emerging from his tent to gloat over the sufferings of his captives, but there is no firsthand account of how he reacted when he saw the survivors brought back from the ghats.[349] More likely he was distressed, not only by the suffering of innocent women and children but by the enormity of what Azimullah and the soldiers had perpetrated.

✦   ✦   ✦

At the 2nd Cavalry Hospital Jonah Shepherd had been in "a fever of anxiety." When would the garrison depart? When would he be allowed to join his family? "What horrible dreams I dreamt! . . . Was I

awake," he asked himself, "or was I asleep?" By the twenty-sixth he
had become "very ill in mind and body," but after overhearing some
sepoys discussing the next morning's evacuation of the Entrenchment, Jonah realized that unless he revealed his true identity to
someone he might never be allowed to rejoin his family.

"I am not what I have stated myself to be," he confided to the
kindly commander of the guard. "I came out in this disguise merely
to find out a place of safety in the city where to hide my family, as
they were in great distress in the intrenchment."

Some of Jonah's fellow prisoners now claimed to recognize him
under his filthy disguise, and "the subadar at once believed my statement, and when he learnt my respectability and the number of my
family, he became favorably inclined towards me and pitied me very
much [and] promised to make a report about me, and have me released early on the morrow."

Overjoyed, Jonah finally fell off to sleep. But the next morning he
was puzzled to see "an immense concourse of people" covering the
parade-ground like "some great fair." He had been waiting an hour
for the subhedar to release him when he heard three guns fire.
Jonah and his fellow inmates assumed this must be the signal to
evacuate the Entrenchment, but then they heard a second round,
this time from the direction of the river.

"A deep silence ensued in the jail; all listened attentively, and the
idea of treachery for the first time glanced in my mind." Jonah "remained in the utmost state of anxiety for about two hours," but refused to believe the worst until a few sepoys from his guard returned
from the Entrenchments laden with booty. One man flourished
a pocket watch—possibly the same pocket watch Thomson had
buried—which he intended to melt down for ornaments for his wife.
As the sepoys passed by the cavalry hospital Jonah heard them say
"that they hoped not one of the 'Feringee Solas' had been spared, as
arrangements had been made to entrap and kill them."

Seeing his anguish, a few prisoners tried to comfort Jonah, but
others taunted him. "Where are your comforts now?" they asked
him. "No servants to come to your call? You folks always had the best
times; you never stirred out but a horse or a carriage was to take you;
see how the tables are turned now. Those of the Feringees who are
not killed will be turned into slaves."

Jonah began to weep and begged the subhedar to tell him what
had happened, but he refused. "You'd better keep quiet," he advised
Jonah, "and remain where you are. You don't know what has hap-

pened."[350] Not until later did Jonah realize that the subhedar was trying to protect him.[351]

That night at the Cavalry Hospital one of the guards rightly suspected Jonah of plotting an escape and tied Jonah's arm to his cot. Thus imprisoned among plunderers, hoodlums, hoarders, mendicants, spies, and captive ayahs and servants to the annihilated British, Jonah "felt but one desire, and that was to die." And yet if a great many women and children had survived perhaps his womenfolk were among them in Savada House, which "now became the centre of all my hopes and speculations."[352]

WE ARE FRIENDS
Mowbray Thomson: June 29–30, 1857

Under the burning sun of June 29, Thomson and his detachment ran barefoot for three miles, trying to elude their pursuers over a "rugged raviny ground. . . . To render us less conspicuous as marks for the guns, we had separated to the distance of about twenty paces apart; from time to time loading and firing as we best could upon the multitude in our rear." As the rebels grew bolder, Thomson ordered his men to make for a small temple he sighted in the distance, and they straggled in, all but Sergeant Grady, who toppled forward by the door with a bullet in his brain.

Thomson ordered four men to kneel down in the temple's single narrow entrance with their bayonets fixed while the rest stood in the darkness, firing into the crowd, deafening themselves with the echo of their musketfire in the little stucco shrine. The rebels charged with such violence that several of them were pushed against the foremost soldiers' bayonets and killed; their bodies formed a shield for Thomson and his men.

But the detachment's angle of fire was restricted to the one door, leaving the rebels free to creep in safety around to the back and try to dig their way through the temple's foundation. As they listened to the rebel bayonets chipping at the brick foundation, Thomson and his men found that in the temple's long-neglected altar a pint or two of water had accumulated "which, although long since putrid, we bailed out with our hands, and sucked down with great avidity."

At last the rebels gave up their excavation and decided to smoke the British out by heaping brush in front of the door and setting it afire. As they prepared to run from the temple Thomson gamely urged his men "to sell their lives as dearly as possible." But the wind carried the fire and smoke away from the door, "and we began to hope that we might brave our torture" until nightfall. The fire had burned down to a heap of burning embers when several sepoys came around the circular wall of the temple with bags of gunpowder and hurled them into the "red-hot ashes." Black, sulphurous smoke now rolled into the temple, and Thomson and his men rushed through the embers in their bare feet, firing into the engulfing crowd. Six of Thomson's men fell under the tide of rebels, the rest bayonetted their way down the embankment and hurled themselves and their muskets into the river.

The weight of their ammunition pouches dragged them under, but "while we were thus submerged, we escaped the first volley that they fired." Removing their pouches they bobbed back to the surface and furiously swam away, so that by the time the rebels had reloaded "there were only heads for them to aim at."

Nevertheless the rebels managed to hit two of these heads in the second volley, reducing Thomson's band to five. As they paddled downstream a pair of natives beckoned Delafosse and a private Murphy to a sandbar near the opposite shore, promising them protection. Delafosse and Murphy, "were so much inclined to yield that they made towards the bank," but as they neared the bar something about the villagers made them suspicious and they "suddenly and wisely altered their determination."

The two natives became infuriated and swung at them with clubs. One actually threw his club at Murphy and fell into the water; the other managed only to strike Delafosse on the heel as he kicked his way back into the current. But the two villagers had better luck with an exhausted private named Ryan. Swimming on his back to keep from sinking, Ryan inadvertently blundered up onto the same sandbar, where the two natives happily clubbed him to death.

Now all that was left were Thomson, Delafosse, Private Murphy of the 84th, and Sullivan of the 1st Madras Fusiliers, and for two or three hours these four somehow managed to stay afloat. Thomson wriggled out of his coat and trousers and swam in nothing but a pink flannel shirt. Delafosse stripped down to a waistcloth. Murphy and

The survivors of Thomson's party flee into the river.

Sullivan proceeded in the nude, pushing themselves along in the current and ducking the rebels' dwindling fire.

For the next few hours the rebels fell away, until all that was left was a lone sowar drawing his lathered pony to a halt and watching them drift away. At last the four fugitives—the only British men to have survived the massacre at Sati Chowra Ghat—crept into the shallows to rest, sitting in the wet sand with the water up to their necks and startling a trio of benign, long-nosed crocodiles that had been basking nearby in the afternoon sun.

Suddenly they heard footsteps and leaped with the crocodiles into the stream.

"Sahib! Sahib!" a voice called out as the four men desperately swam off. "Why swim away? We are friends!"

Rajput matchlockmen with swords and shields and towering turbans, they did not look like friends.

"We have been deceived so often," Thomson called back, "that we are not inclined to trust anybody."

The Rajputs offered to throw their weapons into the river if that would reassure Thomson, for they had been sent by their raja to take them to safety.

Thomson and the others had been swimming for six hours without resting. Another mile and they would drown. They decided they had no choice. "Partly from the exhaustion which was now beginning to be utterly insupportable, and partly from the hope that they were faithful," they slowly crawled up onto the bank.

They were too weak to stand when they reached the shallows, and the Rajputs had to lift them out and lay them down on the riverbank under four of their blankets.

> Murphy had a cap-pouch full of rupees tied around his right knee; but our generous preservers were not proof against the temptation, so they eased him of this load, and also of a ring which he wore, but when they found that this was made of English gold,— which on account of its alloy the natives greatly despise—they gave it [to] him back again.

Lieutenant Delafosse's shoulders "were so burnt by exposure to the sun, that the skin was raised in huge blisters, as if he had just escaped death by burning," and they were all so weak that even after they had rested a while, the Rajputs had to all but carry them to a nearby village, where the local zemindar "received us most kindly, commiserated with us upon our horrible condition, and gave us a hearty meal of dhal, chupatties, and preserves."

Fortunately they had floated into the domain of the elderly loyalist Raja Dirigibijah Singh of Moorar Mhow, head of the most powerful Rajput clan in all of Oudh. The old man had been feuding with a neighboring zemindar who had joined the rebels; if only to gall his rival, the raja had remained loyal to the British.

That evening the Rajputs and their emaciated guests set off to meet the old raja at Moorar Mhow. "The walking was exquisite torture from the condition of our feet," wrote Thomson, "and our progress was dilatory indeed until about half way, when guides met us with an elephant and pony." Murphy and Sullivan were the worst for wear, so Thomson and Delafosse gave them the elephant, climbing up together on the lone pony and proceeding through several villages where peasants gave them buffalo's milk and native sweets.

It was dark by the time they reached the fort at Moorar Mhow, where the raja received him "out of doors surrounded by his retainers; his vakeel was at his right; his two sons close at hand, and his bodyguard, armed with swords, shields, and matchlocks": a "strictly oriental company" picturesquely illuminated by torches. Thomson and the others dismounted and salaamed to the raja, who inquired about their military rank, asked them to narrate their adventure, complimented them on their bravery, "ordered us a supper with abundance of native wine, assured us of our safety, promised hospitality, and had us shown to our apartment."

Because their touch would have defiled the raja's beds, they were given piles of straw and carpets that were as welcome to Thomson and the others as "the choicest down." Temporarily deranged by his ordeal, Delafosse had somehow convinced himself that he had inherited £30,000 and vast estates in Scotland to which he now expansively invited all of his comrades.[353] Tipsy with native liquor, the two privates dozed off as Thomson lay on his "workhouse" bed, replaying the horrors and terrors of the past few days but returning, always, to the same "ludicrous" note of self-congratulation: "How excellent an investment that guinea had proved," he kept telling himself, "which I spent a year or two before at the baths in Holborn, learning to swim!"[354]

✦ ✦ ✦

For the first three days of their imprisonment the women and children at Savada House had been all but forgotten by their captors.[355] There were at least 180 women and children huddled together in the anteroom, encamped like tattered refugees at a train station. A corps of sepoys replaced the initial Mahratta guard, and cooks came in once a day to distribute a ration of one chupatty and a cup of lentils. But "they were in a most wretched state."[356] Many were wounded, stunned, deranged by grief and despair. Few had any decent clothes, and since no bedding had been provided they had to lie directly on the limestone floor.[357]

Only one guard actively harassed them, a sepoy who enjoyed throwing handfuls of grain across the floor and watching the children scramble after it.[358] But the captives were objects of curiosity, and people gathered to catch a glimpse of the captive memsahibs and baba logue. Jokhun, the Williams's servant, deplored the ladies' coarse rations and approached the havildar major[359] from his late master's regiment "and begged of him to supply people who had lived in a very different way with better food." The havildar gave Jokhun a few annas to buy sweetmeats and allowed Fanny and Mrs. Williams to come out onto the verandah to receive them. Fanny tried to impress on Jokhun the importance of finding her brother and showing him the colonel's resting place, but the visit was brief, for other ladies now tried to press their way out onto the verandah, and the sentries chased Jokhun away.[360]

◆ ◆ ◆

"As by the kindness of God and the good fortune of the Emperor," Nana's heralds proclaimed through the streets of Cawnpore, "the yellow-faced and narrow-minded people" at "Delhi, Poonah, Satarah, and other places [have been] destroyed and sent to hell by the pious and sagacious troops, who are firm to their religion; . . . and as no trace of them is left in these places, it is the duty of all the subjects of the Government to rejoice at the delightful intelligence, and to carry on their respective work with comfort and ease."[361]

Though things were not going as smoothly as all that for the rebels, they were proceeding well enough. A British relief force was stuck on a ridge at Delhi, harassed by a gathering army of rebels within sight of the seemingly inaccessible imperial city. Neill was still in Allahabad, his small force depleted by cholera and heatstroke. Nana's old playmate the Rani of Jhansi had taken arms against the British after their sepoys had massacred the European garrison in early June. On June 14 the superbly disciplined troops of the Gwalior Contingent had risen against their British commanders while their ostensible sovereign, the loyalist Maharaja of Gwalior, "wrung his hands in despair."[362] The deposed King of Oudh was still a British prisoner at Fort William, but his wife, Begum Hazrat Mahal, was proving a gifted leader whose forces had beaten back a British sortie and laid devastating siege to Henry Lawrence's entrapped garrison.

Now even the most loyal landlords and merchants began to doubt the might and main of Kampani Jehan. Station after station had fallen, and the tattered ghosts of British hegemony were scrambling back down the country for Calcutta. Was it truly possible that the British would fall back into the sea? What would take their place? The glory and continuity of the old Moghul Empire? Not with the doddering Bahadur Shah on the throne. More likely the Doab would come under the sway of a renewed and enriched Mahratta confederacy with Nana Sahib presiding.

On July 1, 1857, Nana Sahib returned to his palace at Bithur, and in an evening ceremony his Brahmins applied a sacred mark upon his forehead. Baji Rao's old throne was dusted off, and to another round of artillery salutes Baji Rao's adopted son was formally coronated with a "costly turban"[363] as Srimunt Maharaj Dhiraj Dundhu Pant Nana Sahib Pant Pardan, Supreme Peshwa of the Mahratta nation.[364] Cawnpore and Bithur were illuminated, including the sacred ghats, and children frolicked into the night with fizgigs and bottle rockets. Merchants sent gifts, and gold from the treasury was melted into the bangles Nana had promised his troops at Kalyanpur four weeks before.

His ministers amused themselves reviving elaborate protocols and devising tables of tribute Nana might expect to collect from foreign rulers. These were later dismissed as absurd, and the amounts they proposed were indeed playroom-fanciful, but Nana conceived of himself as Peshwa now, and at one time the Peshwa was the most powerful statesman in India and as mighty as any other potentate in the world. Thus Nana expected tribute of thirty-five million rupees from the Emperor of China, seven and a half million from the Sultan of Turkey, five million each from the rulers of Kabul, Kandahar, Balkh, Bokhara, and, incidentally, England,[365] which he intended to conquer with France's assistance as soon as he secured the subcontinent.[366]

He was "now everywhere victorious," he wrote his kotwal, Hulas Singh. "You are, therefore, ordered to proclaim these glad tidings in all cities and villages by beat of drum that all may rejoice on hearing them. All cause for apprehension is removed."[367] And yet for the next few days Nana's actions suggested not exuberance but anxiety, lassitude, even despondency. He lingered at Bithur, retreating into the quiet, upholstered apartments of Saturday House, ignoring his army's call to return to Cawnpore. It would require the threats of his own commanders finally to convince him that like the monsoon that now flooded the Ganges, the massacre at Sati Chowra had carried him out of the shallows and swept him into the swollen and inexorable current of his countrymen's rebellion.

THE WORLD IS GOD'S

Fatehgarh: June 9–July 11, 1857

Sixty miles beyond the glow of Nana's triumphal illuminations, Colonel George Acklom Smith, commandant at Fatehgarh, squinted in the light from the guttering candle and leaned over a tiny scrap of tissue with his finest-honed nib, trying to summon up whatever remained of his schoolboy French.

> Fort Futtehgurh, July 1st. Au magistrat de Mynpoorie, ou à un officier European attacé à une armée de soldats Europeens. Nous avons été fortement assiegés dans le Fort, de Futtehghur, par une force d'Insurgents, pendant la dernière semaine et nous avons peu d'espoir de continuer le siege si nous n'avons du secours de suite. Nous sommes en tout 100 personnes: 32 hommes, et 70 femmes et enfans. Nous vous supplions de venir de suite à notre secours, nous sommes en très grand danger.

With that, Smith had evidently exhausted either his patience or his French. "We are in great danger and plead for speedy help," he blurted. "We are more than one hundred—32 men, 70 women and children, against 1000 insurgents. G.A. Smith, Colonel Commanding." The colonel handed the tiny paper to Magistrate Robert Bensley Thornhill, now the senior civilian at Fatehgarh, who, though his left arm had been mangled by a musket ball, countersigned the note and handed it to a native courier who expertly rolled it up into a tiny cylinder, inserted it into a quill, and set off for Agra in the drizzling dark.[368]

It had been almost a month since the flotilla of merchants and missionaries had set off downriver from Fatehgarh and then divided into two parts: one fated for slaughter at Cawnpore, the other, under the phlegmatic[369] Collector Probyn, turning upriver to the mean little "fort" of Dharampur. By June 9 the conditions at Dharampur had become desperate. The band of fugitives now consisted of twenty-six, nineteen of them children, all baking in a few low huts in the middle of a small, mud-walled compound and subsisting on what little their native host could provide. On June 11 a letter arrived from Colonel Smith beckoning them all back to Fatehgarh and assuring them that he had secured the services of 150 loyal natives with whom, if need be, the garrison could fight its way down to Allahabad. By now Probyn had abandoned all faith in Colonel Smith's fatuous assertions. But the rest of the party longed to return to the comforts of their bungalows and voted to accept Smith's invitation. The next day, June 12, "in spite of all Mr. Probyn could say to break them of their infatuation," the others, including Magistrate Thornhill and Colonel Tucker, bade farewell to Probyn and William Edwards and their families and set off by bullock cart and palanquin for Fatehgarh.[370]

Thornhill's party returned not to their bungalows, however, but to a makeshift encampment on the banks of the river and new perils and alarms. In order at least to impersonate calm and normality, Thornhill returned to his magisterial duties, but in the process almost precipitated an outbreak by signing an execution order on a local native whom the High Court at Agra had condemned to death. When the sepoy guard refused to carry out Thornhill's orders, Captain Edmund Vibart buckled on his saber again and rode to the jail with only Thornhill and Dr. Maltby to back him up. But the sepoys were so menacing that Teddy acceded to their wishes and released the condemned man.

Meanwhile, at Sitapur, thirty miles west of Lucknow, the 41st Native Infantry had murdered both officers and civilians—including one of Thornhill's own brothers—and were now proceeding toward Delhi via Fatehgarh, where, half a century earlier, their regiment had been raised.[371] On June 14, they encamped across the river, where a local zemindar welcomed them with open arms and not only helped them assemble boats to ferry them to Fatehgarh but joined them in looting the vast undefended palace of Dhuleep Singh, the deposed boy-king of the Sikhs who had recently converted to Christianity and moved to England.

Two days later the native officers of the 41st sent a letter to their counterparts in Smith's 10th Native Infantry, ordering them to kill their commanders. A loyal sepoy relayed the letter to Colonel Smith who angrily dictated a reply. But a few native officers of the 10th intercepted his letter and replaced it with their own message indicating that though they would not themselves kill their officers they would not object if the 41st were to do so.

In the meantime Pathan nobles who had lost estates to the Company's courts were pressing the Nawab of Farrukhabad to throw in his lot with the mutineers. Among the most persistent was the Nawab's own coachman, Wazir Khan, who daily drove down to the lines of the 10th to champion the rebels' cause. The Nawab stalled them as long as he could, hoping Smith would show some resolution. But Smith's response to the discovery of rebel couriers and agents in the 10th's lines proved feeble, and all the colonel could do to keep the 41st at bay was to sink a few of the vessels from the Bridge of Boats that Probyn had severed at the beginning of the month.[372] When Colonel Smith asked the Nawab for men and ammunition, His Highness first "sent word that he had no armed men, and no guns" and then after repeated pleas from the Colonel merely posted a few matchlockmen to guard the gates and police station.[373]

Now rebel landlords began to trouble His Highness's leisure with unwelcome pledges of allegiance, while the district's mounted police entirely deserted Teddy Vibart and roamed around the station's outskirts as if restlessly awaiting their cue. Smith posted guns and sowars to guard the severed bridge, but on Wednesday, June 17 all such arrangements were finally deemed useless.[374] As a courtesy to their commander, Smith's native officers formally advised the colonel to retire with his garrison to the fort. At dawn on Thursday the eighteenth, a loyal subhedar rushed to the fort to announce that the 41st was crossing the river in boats, and the 10th had mutinied and released the prisoners from the jail.[375]

At first the garrison considered trying to flee in the boats Smith had collected by the river, but by now the water was even lower than when the civilians had bumbled off two weeks before, so there was no help for it but to try to hold out as long as they could in Fatehgarh Fort. Unlike Wheeler's Entrenchment, the fort at least boasted high, thick walls of limestone cement, an ample water supply, and immediate proximity to the river.[376] Panic-stricken, almost every European at Fatehgarh raced through the gate to seek shelter for themselves and their families among the buildings in the yard. But there was no problem finding quarters. The Fort covered more than twice the area of Wheeler's Entrenchment and encompassed relatively well protected barracks, godowns, guard rooms, mess houses, a vegetable garden, a cemetery, and a walled two-hundred-foot-square wood yard that projected off one corner; and yet the garrison's population was only a tenth of what Cawnpore's had been.[377]

A faction of the 10th Native Infantry now proceeded to Farrukhabad to coronate the loath Nawab, who received them blearily in his rumpled dressing gown.

"Up to this day," their subhedar declared, laying his regimental colors at His Highness's slippered feet, "we have been servants of the Company. We are now servants of the Emperor. Your ancestors were formerly tributary to Delhi also. So we have come to place you in your old position on the throne as Nawab under the King of Delhi."[378]

Annoyed at having his sleep interrupted, the Nawab groused that all this was unnecessary, as the English had already installed him on the throne. At this the sepoys accused him of being a Christian.

"Leave me alone," the Nawab groaned. "I am content as I am.

Since you say you are servants of the King of Delhi you had better *go* to Delhi."

"We are not to be got rid of in this way," the subhedar said. "If you do not do as we direct we will at once loot you and kill you."

After securing a promise of some share in the rebels' plunder, the Nawab relented, allowing two Pathan landholders to lead him to a chair and go through the motions of an improvised coronation. He agreed to distribute sherbet to the mutineers and purchase gunpowder for a salute, and the rebels emerged from his palace and proclaimed the new regime.[379] "The World is God's," declared the rebel heralds. "The country is the Emperor's! The Nawab, the ruler, is in command!"

A crowd of men from the bazaars now descended to plunder the bungalows. At the police station the Nawab's matchlockmen melted away, and the rebels auctioned off their plunder. Here and there a few Eurasians were surrounded and killed. A rich old landlady named Collins refused to give over her jewelry and was cut down; the next day the rebels discovered her daughter hiding in the bazaar and dragged her back to her mother's house where they showed her her mother's lacerated corpse, forced her to find the jewels, and then cut her down as well.

Some stragglers were imprisoned by the rebels, others escaped, including the dauntless Mrs. Sturt, who had returned to Fatehgarh with Thornhill's party. She might have been better off remaining at Dharampur, nevertheless her intuition had not entirely deserted her. Instead of fleeing with her daughter to the fort, she hid in a pile of straw in which she was conveyed by boatmen across the river. Traveling with her son, she eventually reached Agra, where she would survive the Mutiny by a year.[380]

One of the principal targets of the mutineers was the Presbyterian mission's thriving tent factory and native Christian village at Rakha. "About 10 A.M.," wrote the late Reverend Freeman's native catechist, "hundreds of villagers from the surrounding country began to pour in, and plunder the mission compound and the Christian village. Ready-made tents, timber, tables, sofas, chairs, book shelves, brass and copper vessels belonging to native Christians, . . . in short, all that could be carried off, was taken away in a few hours, and by the evening of that day, nothing was left but beams that were in the roofs of the houses."

On Friday the nineteenth, as the native Christians watched from the surrounding scrub, a band of sowars set fire to the mission itself.

"Our hearts were ready to burst with grief," recalled one of them, "as we saw the smoke ascending up to heaven." But for some reason there was not the general massacre of native Christians that had characterized the uprising at Cawnpore. So far none of the native Christians had been killed, and for the most part the villagers of the district treated them kindly, providing them with food and labor and protecting them from the rebels.[381] The blind girls from the orphanage would spend the duration of the uprising begging in villages.

On Friday sepoys of the 10th looted the treasury, but the mutiny of the 10th was not unanimous.[382] Some holed up in the Nawab's gardens, where they were hunted down and killed by sepoys of the infuriated 41st who then proceeded to burn the 10th's regimental lines.[383] A few joined the garrison in the fort, and a detachment under a Captain Bignell actually tried to flee into Oudh with part of the treasury, only to be killed by rebel villagers. A great many other sepoys simply dispersed into the countryside with their plunder, so that only one hundred out of perhaps one thousand 10th Native Infantry sepoys remained at Fatehgarh to fight alongside the 41st and the various Oudh Irregulars and freelances who now came clattering in on their bony horses to lay claim to the station's magazine.[384]

✦　✦　✦

The odds against the European garrison at Fatehgarh were even longer than at Cawnpore. The station's only trained fighting men were officers, and many of them were elderly. Smith could count on only thirty-three able-bodied European men, including civilians like John Monckton of the Road Department, plus a few loyal native servants to face almost two thousand rebels.[385] Almost immediately Smith's force was reduced to thirty-two, for it was while loading one of the garrison's three hundred muskets on June 19 that Magistrate Thornhill wounded himself "severely in the hand and arm, incapacitating him for further duty."[386] The garrison could muster seven guns, but found so little in the way of ball or shell that "nuts, screws, hammers etc." had to be assembled immediately to improvise charges.

"Everything remained quiet that day and night" as the garrison braced itself for a siege. At first looting distracted the rebels, and then they decided not to attack the fort without the Nawab's sanction. Furious at the sepoys for forcing his hand and thoroughly disgusted by the British, the Nawab stalled, refusing to buy the rebels ladders and sulphur. He eventually declined even to meet with the sepoys, who now demanded 125,000 rupees for reducing the fort.

On June 21 His Highness formally notified Magistrate Thornhill that "he was now utterly powerless, and in the hands of the rebels," who still suspected him of loyalist sympathies. Be that as it may, he was still harboring Bonny De Fountain Byrne, erstwhile wife of Ensign Reggie Byrne, who had once kicked His Highness down the steps of his verandah for dallying with his bride. Now, as the disgraced Reggie loaded muskets in Fatehgarh Fort, Mrs. Byrne and her procuress of a mother were safely tucked away in the Nawab's zenana, to which His Highness himself retreated for three whole days. On Wednesday, June 24, the rebels sent one of His Highness's Pathan courtiers to coax him out of his perfumed refuge, and after he grumpily emerged, his self-appointed commanders directed heralds to announce an attack on the fort at the dawning of the Christians' sabbath.[387]

The few sepoys who had remained with the garrison had slowly withdrawn from the fort, and though some occasionally returned to retrieve their water jugs and mess kits, by June 26 all but two had deserted their officers.[388] In the meantime Colonel Smith divided his defenders among the three of the fort's ten bastions that faced Fatehgarh's cantonment. Making sure that the rebels were watching, he ran a black train of ersatz gunpowder to a dummy mine of charcoal dust set conspicuously atop a wall: a ruse, wrote one defender, that was "as good as fifty men."[389] In order to deprive the rebels of cover, Smith paid coolies to demolish some adjacent buildings. Late in the evening rebel snipers fired upon the coolies, sending them running off into the station and raising a great alarm in the fort. But it wasn't until the small hours of the next morning—the same Sunday morning when, eighty miles downriver, Wheeler and his garrison were preparing for their journey to Sati Chowra Ghat—that the rebels opened fire on Fatehgarh Fort.

The first shots flew over the fort and splashed into the river, so the rebels held off until sunrise, when they began again with a great roar of guns and a chatter of musketfire, punching and nipping at the fortress's bastions so remorselessly that the thirty-two pickets posted along the wall could hardly fire back.[390] Parties of sepoys came into view toting scaling ladders, but they had miscalculated the depth of the surrounding ditch and when most of them reached the walls their ladders were too short to reach the battlements. Only in one corner did they prove long enough, but here the British had piled stacks of heavy wooden wheel naves from the gun-carriage factory which they now tumbled down upon the scaling parties, killing "many sepoys."[391]

As the rebels retreated, the defenders gave a great cheer, and their attackers retired sullenly for lunch. Over the next few days the firing was sparse and sporadic, and the Nawab's Pathan landlords ridiculed the mostly Hindu sepoys for their failure to storm the fort.[392] But snipers positioned in nearby buildings were nevertheless able to shoot at dangerous angles less than a hundred yards from the fort, depriving the Colonel's sunburned pickets of sleep and preventing the garrison's amateur gunners from firing their pieces.

Infatuated by his ostensible reign, the Nawab suddenly came to life, rushing supplies to his bickering troops and introducing a large force of Pathans to excite "a spirit of rivalry."[393] Now the sniper fire grew so furious that there were few pickets in the fort whose hats had not been torn by multiple musketballs. Indeed, some made a sport of holding up their hats on ramrods and counting the balls that passed through them.

During the siege Smith proved himself a deadly marksman, and the Clothing Agency's Mr. Ahern discovered he had a knack for cannoneering. Dhaukal Pershad of the Mission High School distinguished himself as a medic, and Teddy Vibart seemed to be everywhere at once, cheering the others on, a veritable Captain Moore of the Fatehgarh defense. But the barrage began to take its toll. Captain Phillimore, the merchant Sutherland, and several servants were wounded. A planter named Thomas Jones was shot in the head while providing covering fire for Ahern's battery, and the next day shared a grave in the cemetery with Colonel Tucker of the Clothing Agency, who was shot in the eye while peering through a loophole.[394]

Under their snipers' protective fire, the rebels began to construct a breastwork along the base of the wood yard. A blast from Ahern's cannon sent them fleeing, but before long they had run up to the wall and dug their way into the yard itself. Teddy Vibart begged Colonel Smith's permission to lead a midnight sortie against the miners, but Smith forbade it. Instead he waited until the attackers had assembled in the wood yard and then ignited a sentry box he had coated with tar and tumbled it into their midst.

As the sepoys scrambled back from the flames, the garrison gave another cheer, but their voices were fewer and weaker. The flames roared for twenty-four hours, baking Colonel Smith's adjacent bastion until it was almost uninhabitable. The seventy women and children gathered in the bungalow of Major Robertson, the gun-carriage agent, which had become the object of the rebels' ineffective but alarming fire.

Among Smith's pickets was the late Thomas Jones's brother Gavin, a tall and gawky twenty-year-old planter who kept his vigil with a loyal manservant standing by to reload his rifles and shotguns.[395] In the wee hours of July 1, the servant had just awakened Jones to show him a sputtering fire rising by the western bastion when there was a roar and a blinding flash that knocked Jones unconscious for a moment. When he regained his senses and rushed to the breach, he was relieved to find that nobody had been killed and the explosion had not quite broken through to the yard. But as the dust cleared, a storming party of almost 150 sepoys and Pathans could be seen assembling below the breach "as thick as bees," their swords flashing dimly in the predawn light.

Jones fired into this "teeming mass" as fast as his bearer could reload his two double-barreled shotguns and eight "foul" muskets whose recoil nearly knocked him unconscious. When other pickets ran to his aid, the sepoys fell back, leaving their dead in the ditch below,[396] but this time no one cheered their victory, for the gifted amateur gunner Ahern had been killed, and it was clear to all that another mine would finish the garrison.[397] By now the defenders' feet "were so swollen with the fatigue of standing night and day at their posts that they resembled those of elephants, while their eyes were starting from their sockets for the want of sleep."[398]

Around noon, as most of Smith's pickets retired for lunch, the Nawab's Pathans attempted to show up the Hindu sepoys by attacking the breach, but they ran into the station chaplain, Reverend Fisher, who stood up from the rubble with his shotgun raised and killed their leader with a single blast.[399] The Pathans fell back without firing a shot.

It was that night that Smith and Thornhill sent their tiny note to Agra. All the next day the enemy was quiet, apparently content after the slaughter of July 1 to starve the garrison out. But on the night of July 2 pickets resting on the ground could distinctly hear the chop and scrape of picks and shovels, and in the morning of July 3 sepoys could be seen rolling barrels of gunpowder toward the fort.

The garrison could try to countermine, but to what end? There were too few men to hold down the fort and at the same time manage a sortie against the sepoys. Someone suggested they fall back from the walls and fortify some of the fort's workshops and godowns. But they could not hold out long if the rebels commanded the surrounding bastions. It was young Gavin Jones who proposed the only remaining alternative: fleeing by boat to Cawnpore.

A SECOND FLOTILLA

Fatehgarh Fugitives: July 3–11, 1857

Unlike the fugitives in the first flotilla, Smith and his party should have been aware that the garrison at Cawnpore had been under siege; Probyn had already heard about it by the tenth of June. But either no one who remained at Fatehgarh had retained this information, or they supposed that Wheeler had holed up at Cawnpore in the magazine on the bank of the Ganges, where they might find refuge despite the rebel siege.[400]

In any case the exodus was an act of desperation. Only three of the eighteen boats Smith had assembled near the fort remained. Only four boatmen could be procured, and these had to be kept under armed guard. But at least the water had risen slightly in the first monsoon rains: indeed, it was still drizzling when, at the stroke of midnight of Friday, July 3, the garrison began to board their boats.

The women and children proceeded first, escorted by aged pensioners, the limping wounded, and ayahs and servants laden with baggage, as the remaining able-bodied men kept watch from the bastions. Then they too fell back from their posts in the dark, spiking their guns and leaving decoy muskets and hats along the ramparts.[401] Colonel Smith directed everyone to their positions in the thatched cabins and along the decks. Smith himself commanded the smallest boat, Major Robertson of the gun-carriage factory took the next, the aged but vigorous Colonel Andrew Goldie, the auditor-general of the Company's army, followed in the last and largest vessel. At two o'clock Saturday morning the three boats pushed out into the stream, their steersmen lying flat out on the decks.

Perhaps it was the wounded Colonel Goldie's stentorian "Let go!" that alerted the rebels, but before the boats had floated much past the walls of the fort, the mutineers were scrambling down the river-bank and firing furiously into the dark.[402] Smith led his tiny fleet behind the cover of an island and into a narrow channel that proved so shallow that every able-bodied man had to jump down to pull the boats through. Over the next six hours the party managed to float to a village only five miles downriver where, at eight o'clock in the morning, they moored their boats and prepared breakfast. Gertrude Heathcote, wife of the 10th's regimental surgeon, was in an advanced state of pregnancy, and it is possible that the party stopped so that her husband could help deliver her child.[403] As the men built their fires on the bank, a "freebooting" landlord named Mangal Singh turned up with about fifty matchlockmen, demanding to know who these Feringhee were. A young planter named David Churcher, thinking perhaps too fast, informed the landlord that they were reinforcements sent from Cawnpore to relieve the garrison at Fatehgarh.

Mangal Singh knew better, and with a contemptuous laugh ordered his men to open fire. But their shots went wild and as they blunderingly reloaded, Smith ordered his officers to charge them with fixed bayonets. Teddy Vibart, Major Munro, Lieutenant Swetenham, and Ensigns Eckford and Henderson marched forward, firing their muskets, shattering Mangal Singh's hand, killing one of his men, wounding two others, and sending the rest running into the countryside.

Smith evidently decided that in the wake of his little victory he and his men deserved an extended rest, and rather than press on they continued with breakfast, rummaging through the piles of baggage on the three boats for condiments and utensils. In fact they did not return to their boats until late in the morning, when they discovered that two of their boatmen had vanished.

Smith sent off a servant to procure more boatmen from his native village across the river, but pushed off before the servant could return with the news that the village directly across the river from them was infested with mutineers. Had Smith known, he might have released all of the servants in his party, abandoned Goldie's unwieldy boat and persuaded his party to dump the mountain of baggage they carried with them, including, incredibly, an enormous chest full of crockery and china. Instead the colonel and his officers retained their servants and their baggage and continued to try to navigate all three overladen boats, jumping out to shove the boats off the sandbars that lay hidden just beneath the Ganges's murky surface. Exhausted, they paused again on the Oudh side of the river, despite the matchlocks that now began to crackle and flash from the opposite bank.

At last the fugitives dismissed a few servants, but they allowed Gavin Jones's bearer to remain, and Mrs. Lowis's ayah,[404] the two loyal sepoys, and the catechist Dhaukal Pershad and his wife and four children. By now a body of Oudh Irregulars had appeared on the opposite shore and begun firing their field pieces from almost two miles off, their round shot raising spouts of mud along the intervening shallows. Peering through his telescope, Magistrate Thornhill spotted mutineers climbing into a pair of grain barges and beating their way across the river. The last stragglers now scrambled aboard in a panic. Goldie's party divided itself between Robertson's and Smith's vessels until there were sixty-five in Smith's smaller boat and only forty-four in Robertson's, which included Jones, Churcher, Fisher, and the Sutherland family. There could hardly have been enough room for all of them, and yet no baggage was removed from the remaining vessels, and the two boats dipped dangerously low under the added weight of Goldie's party.[405]

No sooner had the boats pushed off than villagers tumbled down the riverbank and swarmed over Goldie's boat, chasing off the servants, seizing the ayahs, and carrying away the baggage. With a father-and-son team of boatmen to guide it and four more men to work it through the shoals than Robertson could muster, Smith's boat raced some 150 yards ahead. By three o'clock in the afternoon a body of sepoys had crossed the river and were now chasing along the riverbank, trailing a mob of villagers and matchlockmen and pausing here and there to kneel and fire. A stray ball struck the younger of Smith's boatmen and sent him toppling into the river, which was now choppy from a "high and contrary" wind.[406] The remaining boatman—the father of the first—kept to the rudder and managed to hold the vessel to the center of the stream and well clear of the shallows. But Robertson's boat now lagged several hundred yards behind, and as it turned to clear the two-mile island of Manpur its hull ground into a sandbar.

Most of the able-bodied men on board stripped down and jumped overboard to push the boat free, struggling for over half an hour in the sandy muck as the sun clouded over and the wind kicked up a spray across the shallows. Two apparently empty native vessels now floated into view, but as they came within twenty yards of Robertson's boat, rows of sepoys suddenly jumped up from their holds with their muskets raised and opened fire. Still struggling on one side of the boat's hull, the already wounded merchant Sutherland was killed in the first volley, and Fisher slumped into the water clutching his thigh. As Gavin Jones turned to help the reverend, a bullet caught him in the shoulder, while above him, on the deck, David Churcher's older brother Thomas fell dead with a bullet in his chest.[407] A ball passed clear through Mrs. Sutherland's back, and another tore through the arm of Gavin Jones's fatherless niece and wounded her mother in the ribs.

On the opposite side of the hull, Major Phillott, Lieutenant Simpson, and Ensign Eckford fell in their turn like ducks in a shooting gallery.[408] The rotund Major Robertson, his hip pierced by a musket ball, now begged the women and children to jump into the water. The few who hesitated were killed in the next rebel volley, the rest tumbled over the side, only to find that the boat had by now perversely drifted into deeper water. Many of the wounded and the women and children simply vanished when they hit the chop. Despite the wound to his shoulder, Gavin Jones climbed back into the boat to find a musket and managed to fire once at the sepoys who now clambered over the stern. But he could not find another percussion cap, and by now there was no one left on board the vessel to defend. Hurling his musket aside, Jones grabbed a gourd and jumped back into the river.

Lieutenant Fitzgerald and his family drowned together.[409] Mrs. Robertson was dragged by the current out of the arms of her husband, who now struggled to keep his child atop his shoulders. A Miss Thomson at first found the bottom with her feet, but the current tugged at her skirts and dragged her downstream, where she was cut down by the advancing rebels.[410] Reverend Fisher, bleeding from his thigh, reached out to save his wife, who had leaped into the river with their "beautiful boy [of] eight or nine years" clasped tightly in her arms, but her dress ballooned out and dragged her and her son under the waves.[411] Major Robertson's child also slipped from his father's grasp, possibly struck by a sepoy's bullet. A few managed to find the shallows on the lee of the boat, but they too were shot down by the sepoys who had climbed aboard to plunder, until after only a few minutes only nineteen of the forty-four passengers in Robertson's boat were left alive.[412]

Delirious with grief, Reverend Fisher managed to float away by swimming on his back, as did Gavin Jones's bearer, whose master, clinging to the boatman's gourd, paddled eight miles downriver. Clinging to an oar, David Churcher managed not only to reach an island downstream but to keep the corpulent, desolate, and severely wounded Major Robertson afloat beside him.

Fourteen of Robertson's charges were immediately captured by the sepoys, including the late Mr. Sutherland's daughter, son, and wounded wife; Dhaukal Pershad and his family; the perforated Mrs. Jones, her mother, and injured daughter; loyal sepoy Kale Kahn; and the newly orphaned child of a gun-carriage conductor named Jons whose mother's and sisters' heads were among those the Moslem villagers of Bohjpur now severed and toted back to Fatehgarh to collect the Nawab's reward.[413] Except for the wounded, who had to be littered, all of the captives were forced to march fourteen miles on foot and then transported in Road Department bullock carts the rest of the way to Fatehgarh.[414]

◆ ◆ ◆

Two miles downstream, Smith's boat was pushing on below the steep cliffs of Singhirampur, where four companies of Fatehgarh mutineers were hurriedly erecting a battery. The sepoys now poured musket and cannon fire onto Smith's boat as it sluggishly passed below. In the worst hail of grape Smith had ever experienced, the rudder was smashed and the sole remaining boatman killed, along with Colonel Goldie's youngest daughter and a child of Conductor Rohan, who was himself mortally wounded.[415] Doctor Maltby also received a wound, and Lieutenant Swetenham was shot in the back. But even as the grape clattered upon the deck, Smith somehow managed to keep the boat in the center of the stream. At last they passed out of range and continued on for six more miles before running aground on a sandbank in the dark.

There they remained for the next few hours, waiting for Robertson's boat to catch up. Because they had passed through the rebels' fire, perhaps they imagined Robertson's party had survived as well. In any case, this is what the gentlemen told the women and children, for when Gavin Jones swam up to their grounded vessel he was enjoined not to mention the massacre at Manpur lest he unduly alarm the ladies and little ones.

Perhaps some of them were sleeping, for it was nine at night, and a steady rain was pouring when Major Munro pulled Jones from the water and laid him shivering on the deck, where Deputy Collector Lowis's indefatigable wife served him a restorative dose of brandy. Jones was in an agony from his wound and the great blisters the sun had raised on his back and arms, but he fell off into such a deep sleep that even the splash of Conductor Rohan's discarded corpse hardly awakened him.

Smith's men repaired the rudder and rigged up two blankets for a sail, and after hours of rain the river rose sufficiently to free the boat from the sandbar. The craft began to reel out into the current, and by dawn they had managed to drift another four miles downstream, where they were greeted by the impossible apparition of Reverend Fisher who, despite the bullet in his thigh, had somehow found the strength to float and stagger downriver all night and catch up to Smith's boat "more dead than alive, and [raving] about his poor wife and son."[416] He too was dragged up onto the deck, and "after rubbing him for some time" Smith's men gradually brought him to his senses.[417]

It now occurred even to Colonel Smith that if the injured and nearly demented Reverend Fisher could catch up to him, the rebels could not be very far behind. The wind had died down, and the blanket sail hung limply as the men pulled on their oars, but they pressed on through the cool, clear morning and a countryside already greening from the long night's rain. Now the boat neared the cliffs of Kusamkhor from which, unbeknownst to Smith, matchlock-men had fired on the first Fatehgarh flotilla the month before. But Kusamkhor had always had an evil reputation, and the colonel wisely kept clear of it, navigating the boat over to the Oudh side of the river where villagers brought them food and milk and even helped them heave the boat to shore.[418]

By now Jones was in an agony from his wound and, despite Mrs. Lowis's generous applications of "sweet oil," his sun blisters had become thoroughly inflamed. As Colonel Smith engaged a crew of boatmen and a guard of matchlockmen, Jones decided to leave the boat and spend the night on a native bed, vainly urging the wounded Lieutenant Swetenham to join him. A friendly Thakur led Jones to his hut in the nearby village of Chauchpur, gave him a bed, and offered him a meal from his personal plate. Though he was famished and exhausted, the young planter declined to contaminate the head man's plate with his defiling touch and endeared himself to the village by asking that his meal be served on a platter of leaves.[419]

At five o'clock on the morning of July 5 a party of villagers approached Smith, threatening to attack if he did not pay them money. Smith, with a crew of three newly hired boatmen, thrice sent word to Jones to return to the boat.[420] But by now Jones's wound had become infected, and he was too feverish to stand. At last, as the villagers glared from the riverbank, Smith's party pushed on without him.[421]

They bumbled downstream for four unaccounted days, snagging here and there on the river's shoals, stopping often among the long sandy islands that choked the Ganges like indigestible lumps of clay. Some days they sailed, some days they rowed and poled their way downstream. On the rainy afternoon of Tuesday, July 9, almost a month after the first Fatehgarh fugitives arrived at Cawnpore, the colonel's boat landed at the village of Fatehpur Chaurasi, opposite Nana's palace at Bithur, where Nana's batteries opened up as a rebel landholder sent his men down the Oudh bank of the river with their matchlocks blazing.

Resistance was useless. A round shot carried away Major Munro.[422] Dr. Maltby was killed by a musket ball.[423] Mr. Lowis, the deputy collector, was drowned. After a few minutes of fitful fire, Colonel George Acklom Smith raised a white flag of surrender. The matchlockmen surrounded and boarded the boat, collecting the party's discarded weapons and taking the survivors captive. A few were killed by the swarming villagers. According to Reverend Fisher's relatives Gertrude Heathcote's newborn baby "was seized by the brutal wretches in spite of the mother's shrieks, placed on a plank, and pushed out into the river and swept away by the stream," and when a native nurse named Nancy Lang[424] clasped one of the Lowis's children to her "and refused to give it up . . . the murderers instantly hacked nurse and child to pieces before the parents' eyes."[425]

Perhaps at the sepoys' insistence, the killing ceased, and the rebels towed the remaining prisoners across the river to Bithur.[426] There were now only sixty left out of the more than one hundred who had set off from Fatehgarh.[427] Soaked to the bone, many of them wounded, they were met at the Bithur ghat by bullock carts covered with thatch and transported a mile to Azimullah's home in the old Residency, where the local Anglo-Indian community had so often gathered to avail themselves of Nana Sahib's hospitality and deride his arrangements.[428]

There they were inspected by the Rao Sahib, Nana's nephew, whom the newly reinstalled Peshwa Bahadur had left in charge of Bithur.[429] Rao Sahib was by all accounts a decent man. Appalled by the state of his drenched and bleeding guests, he "treated them very kindly and sent food for them" and evinced "no evil intentions to-

wards these Europeans."[430] He ordered one of his most trusted retainers to look after them,[431] and sent a request for instructions to his
uncle at Cawnpore.

Smith's party remained at the Residency through the night, and on
the morning of July 10 were somewhat heartened to find breakfast
prepared for them. But then the guard's tone abruptly changed. Rao
Sahib's retainers tightly bound the men's arms behind them, ordering them all to their feet and hurrying them into a train of bullock
carts for the twelve-mile journey to Cawnpore.[432]

Villagers and townspeople joined the procession, walking alongside the Mahratta escort and peering under the thatched coverings of
the stifling little carts at the Europeans' darting eyes and sunburned
faces. By three o'clock in the afternoon a vast mob had gathered on
the plain southeast of the Assembly Rooms to witness their arrival at
Nana's new headquarters at the Old Cawnpore Hotel. The question
of what to do with these prisoners had been decided the night before,
and this time Nana had evidently prevailed: the women and children
would join their Cawnpore counterparts in a nearby building called
the Bibighar, only the men would be executed.

The fugitives' Mahratta escort now pulled the men from the carts,
and as they stood together on the grassy plain the carts continued
eastward toward the Bibighar and the women and children leaned out
from under the carts' thatch, calling out their prayers and farewells.
The mutineers closed around the twenty bound men with their carbines and muskets raised and shoved them northward toward the
Commissariat Office across the road. The sowars of the 2nd Native
Cavalry must have recognized their Captain Vibart as Teddy stumbled along in his muddy rags; out of kindness or cruelty they probably informed him of his uncle's family's fate. And a few sepoys might
have had the mordant wit to ask Reggie Byrne how his wife was enjoying the Nawab's protection. But most of the prisoners would have
been strangers to all but Cawnpore's native merchants, few of whom
had much taste for the spectacle that was now unfolding.

A native officer announced that the men would be executed, and
the mutineers began hustling the prisoners toward the road. But ferocious sixty-four-year-old Colonel Goldie[433] raised his bandaged
hand and declared this was utterly preposterous.[434] There were senior civil and military officers in the party. They could not simply be
executed in cold blood. Straightening up to his considerable height,
the old colonel ordered a sepoy to go at once to Nana and tell him
who he was.

As the execution squad continued herding its prisoners toward the Commissariat, the sepoy jogged back to the hotel. Begging His Majesty's pardon, he asked, but did Nana know that among the captives marching to their doom were not only Colonel Smith and the son of Director Thornhill of the East India Company but Colonel Andrew Goldie, the auditor-general of the Company's entire military establishment, a sahib of the first order?

Nana was evidently very glad to know. With Cawnpore and Fatehgarh and almost the entire Doab under rebel control, his attention had turned down the country. Maybe the senior men, and especially the distinguished Andrew Goldie, could be used as hostages. Perhaps, Nana's advisers giddily suggested, they could be coerced into arranging the evacuation of Allahabad in exchange for their lives.

Goldie, Thornhill, and Smith were now separated from the others and led back to the hotel, where Nana asked them what they would make of such a proposal. "They no doubt felt the utter impracticability of the thing," wrote Jonah, "yet wishing to prolong life, in the full assurance of a speedy deliverance, promised, it is said, to do all in their power, but that the acceptance or refusal of the offer would, of course, entirely rest with the Governor-General." This evidently satisfied Nana and his advisers, and the three men were led away to the Bibighar.[435]

The rest of the men were led to the rear of the Commissariat Office and lined up against the compound wall: the limping, half-demented Reverend Fisher;[436] Teddy Vibart, jutting his trembling, stubbled chin in defiance of his kinfolk's murderers; Captain Phillimore, comforted perhaps by the thought that his wife was safe in the hills; the severely wounded Lieutenant Swetenham; Adjutant Henderson; poor disgraced young Reggie Byrne; Assistant Opium Agent James; Donald senior and junior, planters who had fled Budaon with William Edwards but had refused to follow him and Probyn to Dharampur.[437] And then there were the family men—Doctor Heathcote and Sergeants Best and Roach, old Gibson and Pensioner Boscow—whose ears still rang with their wives' and children's receding cries.

The sepoys tried to spare two more men. But Wrixon, an elderly Eurasian musician, refused the sowars' offer to convert him to Islam, "saying he had not pursued Christianity merely for the sake of bread." This so enraged the sowars that they immediately pulled him away and "hacked him up to pieces." The sepoys also commanded Humphreys, the late Colonel Tucker's native manservant, to step away from the sahibs and save himself.[438] But he too refused. "I have served my master faithfully for years," he told the rebels. "I have eaten his salt, and have been to him as a son; how can I now forsake him in this time of trouble? I prefer to die with my master."[439] With that a native officer held a pistol to Humphreys's ear and fired a bullet into his brain.

For a moment the rest stood haggard and bedraggled, whispering prayers and staring up at the congested sky or across the yard at the Commissariat stables, now a skeleton of charred beams and rafters. Then the sepoys opened fire. A few survived the first volley, and as was by now customary in these matters, jullads moved in to pin down the sahibs' struggling bodies with their feet, severed their heads with a few practiced strokes of their sabres, and then supervised the sweepers as they stripped the corpses and searched for gold mohurs in the bottoms of their shoes.[440]

Their cadavers "were allowed to lie exposed for a couple of days," wrote Jonah

> for the troopers and other Mahomedans to try their swords upon. On such occasions these men were in the habit of bringing their own children—young lads—and instructing them . . . that a cut upon even the dead body of a Christian Kaffir was of infinite value, entitling a true believer (moslem) to a place in Paradise. After this the bodies were removed and cast into the river. Those of the inhabitants of the city who had occasion to pass that way, and saw the bodies of these unfortunate gentlemen, state, with wonder and admiration, that some of them looked of gigantic size and most athletic proportions as they lay thus exposed on the ground.[441]

The women and children of Goldie and Thornhill and Smith were not allowed to greet them as they shuffled past the Bibighar and disappeared into a separate room, but they must have glimpsed them through the shutters and called to them with anguished relief. Thank God, they told each other, their husbands were safe. But to some it must have seemed ignominious that the senior men were spared, for what of the husbands and fathers of the women and children who knelt in prayer in the Bibighar's courtyard as the muskets clattered in the distance? And who were all these other gaunt and spectral creatures who now shuffled toward them from the shadows?

THE HOUSE
OF THE LADIES
Cawnpore: July 2–15, 1857

The Bibighar stood on the periphery of Sir George Parker's ruined compound but had been spared the rebels' torches. At the time of the uprising, the baronet's babu had been living in it with his family, but, as its name suggests, the house had been built originally as the living quarters of an officer's bibi.[442] It was about forty by fifty feet and divided into three parts.[443] The middle section was an open courtyard with walls and doors at either end: one leading into an eight by ten foot anteroom and the other, obscured by a small mulsuri tree, to an adjoining complex of servants' quarters.[444] On either side of the courtyard a step led to a verandah fronting a ten-by-twenty-four-foot room with square pillars and cusped arches. At either end of each of these two open rooms were eight-by-ten rooms that had once served as kitchen, bathroom, godowns, and bedrooms.[445]

The house must have provided ample living space for a bibi and her extended family. But by European standards the rooms were small and poorly ventilated, for the door-sized windows were shuttered closed and the walls at either end of the courtyard combined with the surrounding compound walls shut the Bibighar off from any breeze that might have reached it from the Ganges a quarter mile to the northeast.

A couple of hundred yards to the west stood the Old Cawnpore Hotel, a large, yellow stucco inn overseen by a supple Moslem named Nur Mahomed.[446] Well before Nana Sahib returned to Bithur, some of his senior officers had already taken advantage of Nur Mahomed's hospitality, sleeping on the hotel's verandahs and building their cooking fires in its suites. Two doors down, across the Crumps' estate, Jwala Prasad occupied a bungalow, and next door to him was another house filled, like the Assembly Rooms, with plundered British property.[447] So when the time came to withdraw from Savada House and move Nana's headquarters into the hotel, it seemed sensible to install the women and children in the nearby Bibighar.

Azimullah might have remarked the irony of quartering English ladies in the former dwelling of an Englishman's Indian mistress, and some rebels might have gotten some grim satisfaction from the prospect of cramming more than 180 Anglo-Indian women and children into an Indian house.[448] But others fretted that in such close quarters these precious hostages to Nana Sahib's fortune might not survive the special hardships of a Cawnpore July.

Even back when they could change into clean cotton gowns and retreat into some vast, shuttered, high-ceilinged sitting room to be fanned by punkahs, veiled in mosquito netting, and steeped periodically in tepid baths, the ladies of Cawnpore had always dreaded July. The sultry, sporadic rains might temporarily settle the dust and produce a fickle, tantalizing breeze, but more often it was as if a dank and moldy blanket had descended on the station. In July "the Europeans experienced extreme lassitude; even those who were in the best health were unfit for exertion."[449] Those who did not flee to the hill stations used to give up on their morning and evening rides; cancel their appointments, tours, and military exercises; surrender their English assiduousness to the steamy, enervating damp that rotted clothes on the hook, spoiled food, buckled veneers, mildewed upholstery, and left the polished stucco floors warm and sticky underfoot.

At five o'clock in the afternoon of July 3,[450] as Nana luxuriated at Bithur, the rebels had herded the women and children down the steep steps of Savada House and carted them two and a half miles up the tree-lined course, across the canal, and through the ruins of the civil station,[451] "surrounded by an armed escort," wrote Jonah, "[and] a great mob of the city people and others [who] followed some distance on the sides and in the rear.

> Many of the helpless females covered up their faces as they sat huddled up with drooping heads. It is known how slow these bullock hackeries move, and what severe jerks they give. Many a poor woman and child was suffering from wounds received on the banks of the river, and the distress they must have undergone may easily be imagined. One of the ladies, I am told, got down to make room for others, intending to walk all the way, but a sepoy, having a rattan in his hand, gave her several severe cuts on the back, and loaded her with the most disgusting abuse.[452]

At last they reached the Bibighar and limped in to claim space for themselves and their children. But there were at least 180 of them, and only about two thousand square feet of room, including the courtyard that was open to the rain. The city people had looted the house of all of the babu's furnishings and there was "no furniture," wrote Thomson, "no beds, not even straw to lie down upon, but only coarse bamboo matting of the roughest make."[453]

Crowded together into this dismal, shameful vestige of the age of bibis and nabobs, someone had to take charge, and for the sake of their survival many of the captives probably observed some semblance of their old social hierarchy. Deputy Collector Stacey, Brigadier Jack, and Major Hillersdon had all been bachelors. Lydia Hillersdon, the collector's wife, was dead, as were the wives of Wheeler, Larkins, Ewart, and probably Vibart. Katherine Lindsay, the widow of a pensioned judge, was technically the highest-ranking civilian woman at the Bibighar, but she was suffering from a festering bullet wound in her back.

The senior military wives at the Bibighar were Mrs. Williams, Major Prout's widow, and Mrs. Moore. The widow of Colonel Williams was apparently a brave and dignified woman, but she had suffered a disfiguring wound that made speech difficult, and the widow of Major Prout was a mere girl newly arrived in India. So, just as it had fallen to her husband to sustain the Entrenchment's defense, it may have fallen to the brave Mrs. Moore to comfort the children and organize the ladies into rotations under the roofed verandahs,[454] for there was not enough room in the building for everyone to lie down at once.[455]

A corner closet was designated as a cooking room under the supervision of a drummer's wife named Mrs. Pair,[456] and apparently the anteroom was employed as a privy.[457] Rose Greenway's family and Mrs. Jacobi and her children had joined the exodus from Savada House, but they were evidently sequestered, perhaps to protect them from the wrath of the other ladies, some of whom may have been convinced by now of their complicity in Nana's treachery at Sati Chowra Ghat.[458]

Otherwise the groups of women and children occupied every inch of house and courtyard, sleeping on the coarse and moldy mats that covered the tamped clay floors and trying to cover themselves with their torn clothes against the swarms of flies in the daytime and mosquitos in the night.[459] The women and children were evidently not molested, but at first the rebels seemed to go out of their way to humiliate them in little ways. Their scant rations of lentils and chupatties—though no more scant than many Indians' meals—were served on earthen plates by members of the scavenger caste who came in to collect their offal. This was "the greatest indignity that Easterns could cast upon them" and was probably not lost on the caste- and status-conscious memsahibs of the station.[460]

The air hardly moved in the Bibighar's rooms, for the door-sized windows were fastened shut against escape, and every day the monsoon drenched the crowded open courtyard. Many prisoners, including children, had suppurating wounds. Many more suffered from dysentery, and, too weak to wait their turn in the designated privies, probably had to defecate into pots where they squatted. With no soap, clean clothes, or bandages, and the same scavengers' hands serving their food and carrying away their refuse, infection, dysentery, and cholera spread quickly—the latter had already infected Kate Lindsay's Alice, her "handsome" daughter whose ambitions for an "upper life" had brought them all to India.

The ladies tore their skirts to fashion hammocks for their smallest children and hung them between the hooks that lined the walls and pillars, and a few may have encouraged the fittest boys to climb into the branches of the mulsuri tree. Attempts were made to divert them with rounds, perhaps, or games of checkers and pachisi improvised on the courtyard floor with broken bits of pottery. But there was hardly an extra inch of space for them to play in, and many must have sunk into a stupor, clutching their mothers' skirts if their mothers still lived, or pressing their faces against the cracks in the window shutters, sucking in the outside air and watching the guards taking their tea, smoking their hookahs, and napping on their rope-strung beds.

Some of the Fatehgarh ladies had been allowed to keep a few of their effects from Colonel Smith's boat, and some servants of the Cawnpore prisoners had evidently been permitted to bring their mistresses' combs, brushes, and needlework, with which they numbly occupied themselves as the long hot hours passed. A few ladies still clutched Bibles and prayer books. They sang hymns and turned to the Old Testament for their comfort, reading aloud from the ferocious prophets and the "denunciatory Psalms," praying together for vengeance and deliverance.[461] "The Lord trieth the righteous," they assured each other, "but the wicked and him that loveth violence his soul hateth. Upon the wicked he shall rain snares, fire and brimstone, and an horrible tempest."[462]

But at least one passage might have appealed to the rebels themselves. "Come down," Isaiah seemed to snarl from beyond the gloom of the Bibighar,

and sit in the dust, O virgin daughter of Babylon, sit on the
ground: there is no throne, O daughter of the Chaldeans; for thou
shalt no more be called tender and delicate. Take the millstones,
and grind meal: uncover thy locks, make bare the leg, uncover the
thigh, pass over the rivers. Thy nakedness shall be uncovered,
yea, thy shame shall be seen: I will take vengeance, and I will not
meet *thee* as a man. . . . Sit thou silent, and get thee into darkness,
O daughter of the Chaldeans: for thou shalt no longer be called
the lady of kingdoms.[463]

NANA'S RAJ

Nana Sahib: July 6–10, 1857

By the time Nana Sahib returned to Cawnpore on July 6, there
were almost twenty thousand rebel soldiers in the city.[464] Many
had yet to be paid, and when the merchants in the bazaar could be
made to open their shops, they charged enormously inflated prices
for their goods. The new regime's first stab at consolidating its resources had backfired. When the townspeople ignored a demand
that they return all looted British property, Nana's agents had sent
squads out to search the native quarter. But among the houses they
raided were the homes of the golundazes, the artillery men who now
lived near the magazine. Outraged that Nana's agents should invade
the sanctity of their wives' living quarters, the golundazes marched
to Bithur and confronted Nana Sahib himself, leveling their guns at
him and threatening to shoot if the order was not revoked. Nana told
them it was all a misunderstanding, the fault of a few overzealous
functionaries whom he would duly chastise.

The golundazes marched back to Cawnpore[465] but joined with the
sowars to pledge their fealty to the Nunne Nawab and even raised a
green flag in his name, summoning all Moslems to unite with them
and join the Emperor of Delhi.[466] Already an object of Nana's suspicion and alarmed by the rebels' unwelcome pledges of devotion,
Nunne Nawab tried to flee into Oudh, only to be captured by Nana's
agents.[467] To mollify Nunne's adherents, Nana distributed "robes of

honor" among his Moslem courtiers at Bithur and officially announced their promotion, notably Wazi-ud-din to *Cazi* or chief law officer and Azimullah to the collectorship of Nana's dominions and the directorship of the Ganges Canal.[468]

The command of the army remained in the hands of Hindus. Teeka Singh was general, Jwala Prasad was brigadier, Raghopunt Apta commanded the artillery,[469] and Tatya Tope superintended the commissariat.[470] The Moslems remained restless and threatened to march for Delhi if Nana did not return and pay them what he owed. "Mahomedans," wrote Jonah Shepherd, "calling themselves the descendants of the Prophet, wearing garments of the most extraordinary devices, and many covered over from head to foot with armour, laden with five or six different kinds of weapons, poured in from Oudh, and other parts of the country by hundreds." Accompanied by sepoys and sowars, some "entered the houses of the inhabitants under different pretences, plundered them, and in some instances took forcible possession of their women."[471]

Rumors now reached Cawnpore that the British were approaching Fatehpur only fifty miles away, and as Azimullah and Jwala Prasad made ready,[472] townspeople began to flee into the district.[473] At last Teeka Singh persuaded Nana to bid the comforts of Saturday House good-bye, climb upon his elephant, and, to the beat of kettledrums, rejoin his restive army.[474]

"Clamorous for rewards," troops greeted him on the outskirts of the city. "To every man belonging to the Artillery, the Infantry and the Cavalry who has joined us or will join us in this contest," he hastily granted pensions. At last the mutineers received the gold bangles he had promised, and he agreed to supply them with raincoats and tents to see them through the monsoon.[475]

Nana sent off a small detachment of his most disruptive sowars to Lucknow "to slay the unbelieving Nazarenes, and despatch them to hell,"[476] but he was determined to keep the bulk of his army massed at Cawnpore to meet the British column if and when it reached the city. The Moslems suspected Nana of trying merely to protect his establishment at Bithur, but Nana was right. Cawnpore was, as it had always been, the key to the Doab; if the British regained it they could transport and supply their forces via the Ganges and the Grand Trunk Road and send them off in all directions.

On July 9,[477] Nana's scouts reported that a remarkably slight British force of about seven hundred men was approaching, laying telegraph wire behind them and extending the atrocities at Benares

and Allahabad up the Grand Trunk Road, setting every village ablaze
and "hanging people as they came along."[478] The next day Nana sent
off a force of 3,500 men under Teeka Singh and Jwala Prasad,[479] confident that "as the British force cannot be a large one, they will soon
be annihilated."[480]

In the meantime he kept issuing contradictory proclamations—
that all Europeans in India had been exterminated, that only one
"small body of Europeans had managed to escape," that his troops
had wiped them all out, that he was sending more troops out to
"check the Europeans either at Allahabad or Futtehpore." Cut off
from all other sources of information, Cawnpore's native residents
"easily believed" Nana's reports. "When they were told that the
whole of the Native army in Bengal, Madras, and Bombay had mutinied and killed all their officers . . . those few who were loyal to us
at heart began to waver, and many sought and obtained employment
under the Nana."[481]

It is hard to judge how far beyond the city Nana's raj extended. According to the Cawnpore District *Gazetteer* "the rule of the Nana was
of the most primitive description, being based wholly on force and
fear," and "beyond the immediate reach of the Nana's arm, little attention was paid to his authority and utter confusion prevailed." It
has been said that his regime relied entirely on extortion to collect
taxes, and that the "chief sufferers" were "the bankers and merchants of the city" who "at all events deeply lamented the disappearance of British authority."

But apparently his regime was chaotic only to the extent to which
chaos always reigns in wartime, and his agents were certainly no
more extortionate than the British relief forces that were now conscripting whom they did not execute and foraging what they did not
burn. In fact many more natives would flee Cawnpore at the coming
of the British than had fled during Nana's rule. A great many peasants enlisted in Nana's cause, and powerful landlords, most of whom
had suffered losses in the Company's courts, continued to pour into
the city to pledge their allegiance to the new regime until "practically
the whole Rajput community . . . joined in the rising."[482] If the
bankers and merchants of the city longed for a return to British rule,
it was only because the British had made them rich.

"The Nana," wrote Jonah, "felt himself fully established at Cawnpore. . . . Disciplined and well-trained troops continued pouring in
from all the neighbouring stations . . . laden with Government treasure, after murdering their officers, and in most cases these treasures

were presented to the Nana. Collectors of revenue were appointed to realize land rents from the [landlords]. . . . Courts of 'Justice'(!) were established, officers of State (selected from among the Maharattas) were appointed; attention was paid to both civil and military offices."[483]

✦ ✦ ✦

As Jonah Shepherd was to learn firsthand, Nana's "courts of Justice" were in the hands of Nana's dyspeptic older brother Baba Bhutt.[484] For nearly a week Jonah had remained disguised in his pen in the cavalry lines, trying not to give himself away to the other prisoners. It had not been easy. At one point his turban blew off in a sudden breeze, exposing his pale scalp, and an apparently crazed sepoy had struck him with his musket. According to family legend, he gave himself away on another occasion while eating his ration of parched gram; Indians pop it gingerly into their mouths, but Jonah brought it to his lips, touching his mouth with his fingers.[485] The kindly subhedar continued to protect him from the rest, including a bullying subhedar-major from Nowgong who had been brought in on a charge of desertion. "A more sly, prying fellow I have never seen," recalled Jonah. "When he learnt who I was, his rage exceeded all bounds." He threatened to crush Jonah's head against the prison wall, and vowed to expose him as a Eurasian clerk as soon as he came before Baba Bhutt.

On July 5 Nana's native prisoners had been "driven along like flocks of sheep" to the city jail at Putkapur. Jonah almost did not reach it. On the way the prisoners had to be escorted through a phalanx of sepoys who mistook them for some villagers who had earlier unburdened them of their plunder on the district roads. And a few yards farther on, Jonah spotted Wazi-ud-din, Nana's newly appointed Cazi, with whom he had been on friendly terms before the uprising. "Calculating upon our former acquaintance, I made up my mind to whisper to him my condition when near enough to be able to do so, trusting that he would help me out of my misery." But the Cazi ignored Jonah as he passed, and it was a good thing, too, for Jonah later learned that Wazi-ud-din had sworn a sacred oath "not to spare the life of a Christian in Cawnpore," and "had assisted in the massacre of many who concealed themselves in the city."

The diet at the jail disagreed with Jonah, and some nights he became violently ill and lay in a cold sweat, longing for Ellen's ministrations. Where was she? Where was Polly? Where was Daniel, his brother? Had they been killed? Or were they among the survivors languishing half a mile away at the Bibighar? He was sustained in part by Mendes, the diminutive captured drummer who managed occasionally to procure bread for them. On July 9 the guards brought in a number of loyal sepoys from the 56th, including Subhedar Khoda Bux and the sepoy Govind Singh whom Lieutenant Goad had tried to save during the march to the ghat. They had been severely beaten on the morning of the twenty-seventh and had been condemned to mutilation at a "grand parade of the entire army" that was still to be arranged. Among the other prisoners was the villager Ghunseram who had complained about his reward for decapitating Road Superintendent John Duncan and had been promptly imprisoned for hoarding.

In the afternoon of Friday, July 10, Jonah and twenty-four other prisoners were summoned to Baba Bhutt's court in David Duncan's old bungalow. But Nana's older brother, who now insisted on the more dignified appellation of Baba Sahib, had a weakness for pageantry and kept his prisoners waiting two days as he marched up and down the road under an enormous red umbrella, reviewing and drilling new corps of recruits. Finally, on Sunday morning, he alighted on a billiard table and called his court to order.

Jonah was the eighteenth case called, and by the time he stepped before Baba he knew the minimum sentence he could expect, for an authentic native cook had already been condemned to three years' hard labor for having "remained and assisted the Europeans in the entrenchment," the very same crime with which Jonah had been charged.[486] Already the diminutive Mendes had been condemned to six months' hard labor for stealing cotton, primarily because Baba deemed all short men "wicked." Another newly recruited sowar was convicted of extorting money from a local merchant and condemned to fifty lashes and a ride around the city seated backward on a donkey with his face blackened.[487] Over the past weeks men had their hands amputated for writing English and adulterating gunpowder.[488]

Jonah noted that almost all of the late Magistrate Parker's staff were in attendance: a "host of scribes, smartly-dressed," with their pens poised to record Baba's deliberations.

"What's the delay?" Baba Sahib snapped to his assistant as Jonah's case was called.

The assistant announced Jonah as "Budloo, son of Jhundoo—cook by occupation—"

"Well, well," Baba broke in. "What is his crime? Read that."

"Ran away from the English entrenchment on the 24th June," the assistant read.

"Three years' imprisonment with fetters," declared Baba.

"With labor?"

"With labor. Of course."

Jonah tried to speak, but Baba shouted, "Stop his mouth! Stop his mouth!" and he was immediately hustled out to a blacksmith on the verandah and clapped in five-pound fetters.

The kindly subhedar congratulated Jonah for being spared execution and "advised me to keep up my spirits." But the subhedar from Nowgong was outraged that Jonah had not been condemned to death. "Look at him how innocent he appears to be," he snarled as Jonah rejoined the other prisoners in Duncan's yard. "But he is very deep." Jonah was a snake, he told the other prisoners, and as soon as his own case was called he intended to reveal Jonah's true identity.

Jonah now prepared himself to die, "and arranged in my mind to beg one favor," that he be allowed to visit the Bibighar and tell his family, if they still lived, "that I had not deserted them when I came out of the entrenchment, as the circumstances of my not going back might have led them to believe."[489]

THE BEGUM

The Bibighar: July 6–10, 1857

On July 6 Nana moved into Nur Mahomed's Old Cawnpore Hotel with his Mahratta guard and turned his attention to his captives at the Bibighar.[490] It was rumored that by now he had received orders from Delhi to treat the prisoners decently, but more likely the Bibighar had horrified the Peshwa or at the very least injured his hostly pride.[491] In any case, he assigned a Bengali doctor (possibly Sub-Assistant Surgeon Koylas Chunder Mookerjee of the Government Charitable Hospital and Dispensary)[492] to look after the women and children, and ordered that they be supplied with fresh clothes collected from the sahibs' former dhobis,[493] hired cooks from the fish bazaar to prepare better meals,[494] including a meat course.[495]

"On one occasion beer and wines were given; on another rum was issued," and every day the children were served a swallow or two of milk.[496]

Perhaps most important, Nana permitted his prisoners to emerge from the Bibighar to sit in the evening air. Jonah claimed that Nana allowed this only so that he and his brothers could leer at their captives, and that he had provided them with food and medical care only in order to persuade the ladies to sleep with him. But Nana was evidently devoted to his native concubine Adla, and had never shown any prurient interest in English women.[497] According to Thomson, few men could have been attracted to the ladies of the garrison in the state they were in, and a fastidious Brahmin like Nana Sahib would probably have found them repulsive. But whether he was disgusted or titillated by his prisoners' wretchedness, the Peshwa would have been strictly prohibited by his caste from so much as touching them.

Azimullah would not have been under any such constraint, and certainly he had made his conquests in England, but his lust was apparently overwhelmed by his contempt. Had Azimullah been driven by mad passion there would have been nothing to prevent him from kidnapping any of the ladies of the Bibighar and installing them in his zenana. But there is no evidence of his having done so; indeed, unless his pathological hatred of the British had entirely subsumed his common sense, he would have fully understood their value as hostages and encouraged His Majesty, at least for the time being, to treat them with decency.

Despite Nana's mercies, however, by July 10 cholera had begun to clear space for the fourteen women and twenty-four children the sepoys brought in from Fatehgarh. Borne by contaminated food and water, cholera apparently originated in northeast India and in its severest form caused violent watery diarrhea that led to rapid dehydration and death. Of the fourteen casualties the Bengali doctor recorded by July 11, nine of them had died of cholera, among them Alice Lindsay and an orphaned infant whom he listed simply as dying "of itself."[498]

✦   ✦   ✦

Perhaps to underscore the irony of incarcerating upstanding Anglo-Indian ladies in the former house of a native mistress, but probably because she was the only candidate available, Nana assigned his favorite concubine's serving girl to oversee the prisoners.[499] She was a tall, fair Moslem woman[500] named Hussaini Khanum who had been one of Baji Rao's slave girls.[501] In her early thirties,[502] she was somewhat past her prime, with a temperament so fierce and imperious that people called her "the Begum."[503]

If Nana had hoped Hussaini Khanum would make life easier for his prisoners he was mistaken, for the Begum evidently nurtured a particularly virulent hatred for the ladies who, over the years, had haughtily stolen away the best customers from her guild of prostitutes and concubines.[504] Any lady who tried to treat the Begum as a mere servant must have learned quickly that she saw herself as the memsahib and the ladies as the lowest of the low. She chased off the servants who had heretofore bribed their way in to see their memsahibs and smuggle them food.[505] Like Isaiah's "daughter of the Chaldeans," a few of the women were apparently led off each day by the Begum to grind gram, and their feeble efforts proved a source of amusement for the guards and hangers-on at the stables at Nur Mahomed's hotel, from which some ladies nevertheless managed to smuggle handfuls of gram for the children.[506]

Only one *bhisti* serviced the prisoners, toting his dripping leather water sack between the Bibighar and the nearby well. There was not enough water to bathe adequately, and in the terrible heat some of the women snipped off each other's hair against infestations of lice.[507] Only two sweepers were assigned to clean the rooms and the teeming courtyard, and there was no privacy whatever:[508] no way to shield themselves from the sight of the guards of the 6th Native Infantry who peered at them through the shutters from time to time, or protect themselves from the prying eyes of the idle boys who used to sit along the compound walls.[509] Insanity anesthetized some of the ladies to the terrible crush in the steamy confines of the Bibighar, convincing them, perhaps, that they were back in some English grove or attending some regimental ball in the Assembly Rooms, exhausted by yet another quadrille, dizzied by the spangle of their partners' uniforms.

The ladies from Fatehgarh must have complicated the Bibighar's hierarchy, for Mary Thornhill was the wife of a magistrate from a distinguished Anglo-Indian family. Anna Smith was the wife of a colonel and a daughter of a major,[510] and Mrs. Tucker was a colonel's widow. But the status of Mary Thornhill and Anna Smith must have been compromised by their husbands' dubious arrangement with Nana Sahib. Both women had shown great courage in remaining at Fatehgarh after Collector Probyn and the first flotilla had fled. But like Mrs. Greenway and Mrs. Jacobi, they may have been shunned not only by their fellow Fatehgarh fugitives but by some of the Cawnpore widows who had seen their husbands killed in the Entrenchment, slaughtered at Sati Chowra, or executed at Sheorajpur and Savada House.

The Bengali doctor kept a list of the prisoners, and did what he could for the sickest women and children, apparently moving the terminal cases into a separate room from whence, after death, *mehtars* dragged their emaciated corpses into the yard, carted them to the ghats, stripped them of their clothes, and flung them into the river.[511] Among these dead was poor Louisa Chalwin, who died of cholera on July 10, leaving behind Isabel White, the girlhood friend whom she had induced to follow her to India to find a husband.[512] That same day cholera also claimed the brave Mrs. Fraser, who had escaped the horrors of Delhi and survived the siege of the Entrenchment ministering to the wounded, and deserved "rather to be commemorated for her virtues than her sufferings."[513] Two days later William Lindsay's ambitious, garrulous, and not altogether welcome sister Kate died of an infection from the wound to her back, leaving Caroline and Fanny to see themselves to the catastrophic end of their matrimonial *shikar* (hunt) and to record, on the merest scrap of paper, the terrible chronology of the Lindsays' extinction.

Mama died, 12th July
Alice died, 9th July[514]
George died, 27th June
Entered the barracks, 21st May
Cavalry left, 5th June
First shot fired, 6th June
Uncle Willy died, 18th June
Aunt Lilly, 17th June
Left barracks, 27th June
Made prisoners as soon as we were at the river.[515]

A few tried to leave some record of themselves on the Bibighar's walls, writing inscriptions with charcoal and pieces of pottery.[516] Others also tried to record their histories on what paper they could scrounge from their Bibles and prayer books. "We went into the Barracks on the 21st of May," one lady wrote on a crude map she had drawn, and went on to lay out the bare, impossible facts of the uprising, the surrender of the garrison, and the Sati Chowra massacre,

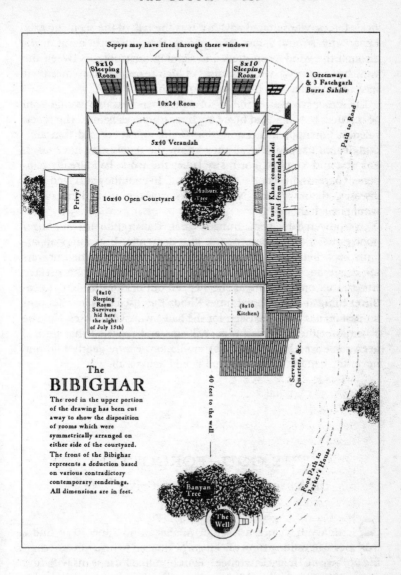

Sepoys may have fired through these windows

8x10 Sleeping Room

8x10 Sleeping Room

2 Greenways & 3 Fatehgarh Burra Sahibs

Path to Road

10x24 Room

5x40 Verandah

Mulsuri Tree

16x40 Open Courtyard

Privy?

Yusuf Khan commanded guard from verandah

(8x10 Sleeping Room Survivers hid here the night of July 15th)

(8x10 Kitchen)

Servants' Quarters, &c.

The
BIBIGHAR

The roof in the upper portion of the drawing has been cut away to show the disposition of rooms which were symmetrically arranged on either side of the courtyard. The front of the Bibighar represents a deduction based on various contradictory contemporary renderings. All dimensions are in feet.

40 feet to the well

Foot Path to Parker's House

Banyan Tree

The Well

breaking off at Savada House, where "we were taken prisoners and taken to a house, put all into one room."[517]

She left out her name, however, and thus may have intended her account not as a memorial but as an anonymous dispatch to Havelock's forces, whose rapid advance was the talk of the sepoy guards. Apparently several ladies, whispering their instructions at night through the window shutters and slipping their notes between the slats, had managed, with promises of high reward, to convince their servants to convey such messages to Allahabad.

The senior wives tried to reassure the others that they would soon be rescued, but they had heard such reassurances before. The rebels ruled at Cawnpore, Lucknow, and Delhi, and it seemed that anything could happen. For all they knew, the rebels may have taken Calcutta and Bombay. For many ladies the worst had already happened: parents, husbands, children dead. Even if they survived their diseases, their wounds, Nana Sahib's caprices, what kind of life would be left them?

Overpowered by heat, hunger, grief, claustrophobia, and sheer hopelessness, a few simply sank into dementia. But others apparently kept their faith, sustained their hopes, and raised their prayers for deliverance. One of these was Fanny Williams, who greeted Khoda Bux one evening as she stepped out of the Bibighar "to eat the evening air." In happier times Khoda Bux used to watch her canter past on her morning rides, for she had a way with horses. Now he asked after the wounded Mrs. Williams and reported that he had been sentenced by the rebels to mutilation. Fanny gently told him never to abandon hope, for "God would help us all."[518]

THE GOD—FORGOTTEN

The Moveable Column: June 30–July 17, 1857

Sir Henry Havelock arrived at Allahabad on June 30 to find a message waiting from Lucknow. "I am glad to hear you are coming up," wrote Henry Lawrence. "Four hundred Europeans with four guns, 300 Sikhs, with 100 cavalry will easily beat everything at Cawnpore, *as long as Wheeler holds his ground*; but if he is destroyed your game will be difficult."[519] It would not be made easier by the state of Colonel James Neill's expedition, which had preceded Havelock to Allahabad on June 11. Three weeks of burning houses and hanging natives had emptied the pool of Indian laborers Neill would need for his march to Cawnpore, and cut him off from the Indian contractors who usually supplied the Company's forces in the field.[520]

Back at Benares the hanging parties had continued to make their terrible rounds. Prominent in these punitive expeditions were the 78th Highlanders, one hundred of whom were sent out in carts "to scour the country." On June 28 a Highlander's detachment had been greeted at a village by a furloughed sepoy who "came running out to us . . . and saluted our officer.

> We shouted that he was a sepoy, and to seize him. He was taken, and about twelve more. We came back to the carts on the road, and an old man came to us, and wanted to be paid for the village we had burned. We had a magistrate with us, who found he had been harbouring the villains and giving them arms and food. Five minutes settled it; the sepoy and the man that wanted money were taken to the roadside, and hanged to a branch of a tree. . . . We came to a village and set it on fire. The sun came out, and we got dry, but we soon got wet again with sweat. We came to a large village and it was full of people. We took about 200 of them out, and set fire to it. I saw an old man trying to trail out a bed. . . . I saw the flames bursting out of a house, and, to my surprise, observed a little boy, about four years old, looking out at the door. I pointed the way out to the old man and told him if he did not go I would shoot him. I then rushed to the house I saw the little boy at. The door was by that time in flames. I rushed [into] . . . a sort of square, and all round this were houses, and they were all in flames, and instead of seeing the helpless child, I beheld six children, from eight to two years old, an old dotal woman, an old man, not able to walk without help, and a young woman, about twenty years old, with a [five or six-hour-old] child wrapped up in her bosom. . . . I took the lead, knowing they would follow.

At the far end of the village he found 140 women and about sixty children, "all crying and lamenting what had been done. I offered them some biscuit I had for my day's rations; but they would not take it; it would break their caste, they said." Out of the male prisoners that were taken, "we hanged ten of them on the spot, and flogged a great many—about sixty. Oh, if you had seen the ten march round the grove, and seen them looking the same as if nothing was going to happen to them! There was one of them fell; the rope broke, and down he came. He rose up, looked all around; he was hung up again." In the next village on the next day two thousand peasants and rebels united to avenge the Highlanders' atrocities, but the 78th surrounded them and set fire to the village, shooting everyone who came running out of the flames. "We took eighteen of them prisoners; they were all tied together, and we fired a volley at them and shot them on the spot. . . . In this country we are told that we had killed 500 of them: our loss was one man and one horse killed, and one man and one horse wounded."[521]

Neill had checked some of the looting in the city of Allahabad, where "lawless and reckless Europeans" had threatened any officer who stood in their way of plunder.[522] But he sent parties of his regiment out into the Indian settlements that bordered the British cantonments, where they "burned all the villages" and "hung every native they could catch." Another detachment burned down part of the native quarter "whilst volley after volley of grape and cannister was poured into the fugitives as they fled from their burning houses."[523]

Neill appointed commissioners to oversee the retribution, including one particularly homicidal civilian who on June 28 boasted that "we have the power of life and death in our hands, and I assure you we spare not." Each day he had strung up "eight and ten men," and after "a very summary trial," each prisoner was "placed under a tree with a rope round his neck, on the top of a carriage; and when it is pulled away, off he swings."[524]

The commissioner commanded thirty railway men who "cut down all natives who showed any signs of opposition," and "enjoyed these trips very much, so pleasant was it to get out of the horrid fort for a few hours. . . . The flames shot up to the heavens as they spread, fanned by the breeze." The Sikhs took part in the plunder, and many of them became falling-down drunk, but "no-one could blame them," the commissioner wrote admiringly, "for they are such jolly, jovial fellows, so different from other sepoys."[525]

"Retribution is going on in a very fearful way," a civilian wrote from Allahabad on July 3. "Fourteen men were hung here yesterday and fourteen the day before, and houses are burnt down at once—wherever any portion of stolen property—a strip of cloth even—is found."[526]

What had made it "so pleasant" to get out of the fort for a few hours was an epidemic of cholera that had carried away fifty-seven soldiers and civilians by the thirtieth of June. The garrison could not

Highlanders resting for the night after an execution.

obtain enough food from the terrorized Indian contractors, and though they sat through the heat with wet clothes over their heads "the deaths from sunstroke continue[d] large."[527]

Recovering from sunstroke and frustrated by the delays arising from his own retributive policies, Neill had tried to send Major Sydenham Renaud with a force of three hundred Europeans and four hundred Sikhs up the Grand Trunk Road the day before Havelock's arrival, but he could not assemble enough coolies and lascars.[528] Not until Havelock had arrived at Allahabad did Renaud march out to reassert "British authority." The means Neill proposed to Renaud were monstrous. All villages along the roadside were to be entirely destroyed, and certain other villages "were marked for destruction," writes Kaye, "and all the men inhabiting them were to be slaughtered. All Sepoys of mutinous regiments not giving a good account of themselves were to be hanged."[529]

Neill reserved the station of Fatehpur for a special vengeance. On June 2 Collector John Walter Sherer of Fatehpur had written to his wife that "the little canary bird is singing beautifully—old Sandy is asleep under the table—nothing in nature sympathizes with the dreadful political storm."[530] But within a week he had been "utterly beggared—without clothes, servants, house or furniture, having been turned out of Futtehpoor by a Mussalman conspiracy—property all stolen and house burnt."[531] Hundreds of rebels and released prisoners had converged on Fatehpur, and yet Sherer had escaped with all of the station's civilians but one: the pious and magnanimous Magistrate Henry Tucker. Tucker was already a particular hero of the "new lights" of the Doab for having installed road markers bearing the Ten Commandments and painted "Thou God seest me" on the wall above his courtroom bench.[532] The rebels eventually shot him to death on the roof of his flaming courthouse and then, reportedly by order of his native deputy, displayed his head in the bazaar.[533]

Neill regarded Tucker as nothing short of a Christian martyr and intended to make examples of his murderers. The city was to be attacked, he told Renaud, and the Pathan quarter and all its inhabitants destroyed.[534] "All heads of insurgents," Neill ordered, "particularly at Futtehpore, to be hanged. If the Deputy Collector [sic] is taken, hang him, and have his head cut off and stuck up on one of the principal [Moslem] buildings of the town."[535] Havelock apparently approved these marching orders, and Patrick Grant congratulated Neill for providing "for every possible present circumstances as well as all eventualities" and hoped Renaud would be guided by these "admirable" instructions, "and by them and them only."[536]

"Our first spring was terrible," William Howard Russell would write of Renaud's advance, "I fear our claws were indiscriminating."[537] According to an officer in his column Renaud's "executions of Natives were indiscriminate to the last degree." During the course of two days' march toward Fatehpur he saw forty-two men hanged by the roadside, "and a batch of twelve men were executed because their faces were 'turned the wrong way' when they were met on the march. All the villages in his front were burnt when he halted,"[538] which was often, as his orders were to keep his men "exposed as little as possible."[539] The officer "remonstrated with Renaud, on the ground that, if he persisted in his course, he would empty the villages and render it impossible to supply the army with provisions."[540] Renaud ignored him and continued marching his column, "fighting as occasion required, and tranquillizing the country by the very simple expedient of burning all the villages in the line of march and hanging everybody with a black face falling in his way."[541]

Meanwhile a Captain John Spurgin followed a parallel course in a steamer called the *Burrampoota*. Neill had ordered Spurgin and his force of 120 pensioned artillerymen and untried Fusiliers to "land nowhere, but if necessary and opposition is shown, open fire and destroy as many rebels as you can" and once at Cawnpore "bring down here [Allahabad] all the ladies and children, also sick and wounded officers," of Wheeler's garrison.[542] But after being fired on by roving bands of rebels, Spurgin landed twice, firing rather indiscriminately on the settlements along the river, including the village of a loyal zemindar who had harbored English fugitives.[543]

The condition of Wheeler's Entrenchment remained the subject of endless contradictory reports. Rumors of the fall of Cawnpore reached Havelock almost as soon as he arrived in Allahabad, but he dismissed them until July 2, when two Indian couriers claimed to have "passed through Cawnpore and [seen] Wheeler's force destroyed."[544] A message from Henry Lawrence confirmed the story. "You must not move with less than 1,000 Europeans," Lawrence warned Havelock. "The Nana will probably join the rebels at Lucknow; but we can stand them all for months. Civil or other officers of tact and temper, ought to join each regiment."[545]

"I don't believe this," Neill recorded in his diary, "but General Havelock does and his staff also have lost nerve." Renaud evidently also believed it, and decided to halt his column until Neill sent him two to three hundred more.[546] Neill was contemptuous of Renaud's "evident state of alarm," and commanded him "on no account to retire but hold his own boldly." Neill even took it upon himself to write a protest directly to the commander-in-chief.

Grant at first advised that Renaud stay put until Havelock caught up with him. But then he ordered the major "to push on thither,"[547] for he knew "Sir Hugh Wheeler too well not to feel convinced that while mind and body held together with him he never would put himself into the power of an Asiatic, thoroughly cognisant as he was of native character and native treachery."[548]

"They say now," wrote Sherer—who, "as a Civilian supposed to know something of the country," had been posted to Havelock's column—"[that] the Mahratta chieftain—the Nana Sahib—hearing bad news from Delhi moved off of his own accord and that Wheeler has come out of the Entrenchment and hoisted his flag at the Kotwalee."[549] If this falsehood had been spread deliberately by the rebels to slow Havelock's advance, it apparently worked. Renaud stayed put and two days passed before Havelock and his army finally lumbered out of Allahabad. Havelock forebore Neill's insubordination, but by now the two men were hardly speaking to each other. Sherer feared that "these delays will be thought very badly of, but they are wholly the fault of the military authorities," for the commanders could not agree on how many men should march with Havelock and how many should remain with Neill.[550] "If Sir Hugh Wheeler is still holding out," groaned Sherer, "he must think this failure to attempt to relieve him very cruel."[551]

✦   ✦   ✦

Havelock's army had been assembled hastily and supplemented by a corps of Sikh sowars and a miscellany of British volunteers who had stepped forward at Benares and Allahabad. In addition to the usual crapulous and semisuicidal deserters and derelicts dragged out of the grog shops and flophouses of Calcutta, the ranks of the Fusiliers had been swollen by teenaged Eurasians recruited from the Madras Military Orphanage.[552]

The Company's European soldiers lived in "a snarling animal world," with only alcohol to comfort them. Many if not most British troops could not get through a day without downing an entire bottle of liquor, preferably mixed with chopped pepper.[553] "Drunkenness and violence of temper," Bishop Heber had written, "made the natives of our own provinces at once fear and despise a *Feringee* soldier."[554] They were never fond of their Indian comrades. In wartime they might appreciate the native troops who fought bravely alongside them, but the sentiment rarely survived for long into peacetime. Few of the Company's British soldiers and even fewer of Her Majesty's could speak more than a dozen words in an Indian tongue. Aside from the haughty sepoys whose privileges—including immunity from flogging[555]—the British troops resented bitterly, the only Indians they knew were the lowest sort: camp followers, usurers, whores. Calling themselves the "God-forgotten," they regarded their service in India as a kind of perdition. "Let us eat and drink—especially drink," ran their motto, "for tomorrow we die."[556] Not for them the shoots and mutton clubs and seasonal balls of cantonment life. They would avenge the women and children, reassert British authority, join in Havelock's prefatory prayers. But they would also pay India back for their cramped barracks, bastard children, filthy bazaars, sunstroke, fever, and venereal disease.

Havelock's Highlanders were a somewhat different case. Half of them were English, but the rest were Scots whose families had been cleared from the Highlands by English lords and Anglicized clan chieftains to make way for lowland sheep. Many Scots had joined the army rather than starve on Scotland's coast or emigrate to New Zealand or North America. That they served the Crown at all was a wonder, that they soldiered with such bravery and forebearance was a triumph of tribal martial pride over their festering grievances with the English. The pride of the 78th Highlanders now mingled with an appetite for vengeance born of their regiment's losses in the flight from Kabul, in which the regiment suffered 669 casualties, including 47 women and 124 children lost to Afghanistan's snows and snipers.[557]

On the morning of July 7 "Old Phlos" assembled his column at the fort at Allahabad and indulged himself in a Napoleonic peroration that went on a trifle too long. "We are bound on an expedition," he told them, "whose object is to restore the supremacy of British rule and avenge the fate of British men and women. Some of you I know—others as yet strangers to me; but we have a common aspiration which knits us together as one man."

When he was done, the "disciplined yet opinionative" Highlanders of the 78th, who had come to know Havelock during their recent campaign in Persia, "remained grimly unresponsive, and a mutter ran along the ranks." The old general rode up to their commander and fondly observed that the dour "Ross-shire Buffs," as the regiment called itself, "like better to cheer when the bugle sounds 'Charge,' than when it sounds 'General Parade.' We'll try their throats by and by," he said, riding off. The 78th broke into loud hurrahs.[558]

Joining in the cheers were detachments of Her Majesty's 64th and 84th and the 1st Madras Fusiliers, whose comrades had fallen at Cawnpore; a battery of Royal Artillery; a few European volunteer horsemen, and 150 Ferozepur Sikhs who would eventually prove as brave and ferocious, and as drunken and atrocious, as their British comrades-in-arms.[559] And thus the Moveable Column set forth from Allahabad. "With nine guns and 1,200 European troops," Sherer exulted, "who can resist us?" But as they passed through the city streets the inhabitants of Allahabad scowled down at them from the roofs of their remaining houses, and no sooner had they cleared the outskirts of the city than a tropical rain began to pour, turning the tramped road into a quagmire.[560] Miles behind them, "saturated with rain, the tents doubled in weight, and under the burden of hauling piles of them in their oversized carts the bullocks collapsed and died."[561] For long stretches the road disappeared into "a sea of slush, knee deep now and now breast high."[562] After proceeding only eight miles the column encamped for the night on ground streaming with rainwater, waiting in vain for their tents.[563]

The next day the sun came out, only to illuminate the nightmare landscape Renaud had left in his bloody wake. "Many of the villages had been burnt by the way side," wrote Sherer,

> and human beings there were none to be seen. . . . The swamps on either side of the road, the blackened ruins of huts now further defaced by weather stains and mould; the utter absence of all sound that could indicate the presence of human life or the employments of human industry (such sounds being usurped by the croaking of frogs, the shrill pipe of the cicada, and the under-hum of the thousand-winged insects, engendered by the damp and heat); the offensive odour of the neem trees; the occasional taint in the air from suspended bodies, upon which before our very eyes the loathsome pig of the country was engaged in feasting: all these things—appealing to our different senses,—contributed to call up such images of desolation, and blackness, and woe, as few, I should think, who were present, will ever forget.[564]

Havelock shelled several reputedly rebel villages along the way, and apparently executed a few suspected spies,[565] but his exhausted men generally spared the peasants who dared to approach them to sell milk and sweetmeats.[566]

Convinced by now that Cawnpore had fallen, Havelock proceeded for three days in relatively easy stages. But on July 11 a rider galloped in to report that Nana's army was advancing in great strength on Renaud's camp. Havelock pushed his men on for fifteen miles, and then, after a few hours' rest, pressed on again until, to the skirl of "The Campbells Are Coming," Havelock caught up with Renaud and paused to confer with the major. Havelock knew that momentum was everything to the British soldier, that their worst enemy was not the sun or the rain or the enemy's fire but hesitation and delay. British troops were superb on the attack but easily panic-stricken in retreat. No matter what hordes of rebels he may encounter, Old Phlos must take the initiative.

So after only a few hours' rest, the combined column marched for sixteen more miles, halting at seven in the morning of July 12 by a vast swamp four miles shy of Fatehpur.[567] After sending a detachment of riders on a reconnaissance toward the city, Havelock ordered his men to rest on the dry ground of a low ridge overlooking the Grand Trunk Road. He had just dismounted to take tea "under the shade of some trees"[568] with two Indian spies from Lucknow when a round shot suddenly came hurtling down the road and struck a camp kettle with a tremendous clang.[569]

Havelock jumped onto his horse as more shot arced and bounced down the road, and his scouts came galloping back, pursued by a horde of jubilant sowars clad all in white.[570] They were none other than the sowars of the 2nd Cavalry, sent by Nana with two regiments of infantry and a battery of guns.[571] They had marched over fifty miles in two days to annihilate Renaud's little column, but now skidded to a halt and lowered their sabres, shocked to find the bayonets of Havelock's entire column bristling along the ridge.[572]

As the sowars reined their horses about, Havelock arranged his companies into four columns with Renaud on the right while one hundred men of the 64th took up a position a few hundred yards forward in a grove of trees just to the left of the road. Havelock's artillery opened fire on the sowars, and though "the first practice was not very good," wrote one officer, nevertheless "it emptied some saddles."[573] For a few minutes Havelock hoped he might be able to rest his exhausted troops in formation while the rebels decided what to do. But when the sowars pulled their horses aside they revealed a vast formation of mutineers and cannon hurrying around to attack the British rear.

Havelock ordered his guns to the copse to destroy the rebel batteries, and "it was refreshing," wrote a volunteer horseman, to "see the round shot ploughing them up, and the grape falling on all sides, and shells bursting over their heads."[574] Then, as the detachment of the 64th waded through the "rice swamps" to support them, his gunners hauled their artillery around to cut off the rebels' flanking movement as Renaud's Enfields poured fire on the rebels' left.[575]

"Knock over that chap on the elephant," an officer called out to Captain F. C. Maude of the artillery, who thereupon fired a round shot up the elephant's vitals, sending none other than Tatya Tope tumbling to the ground, unhurt but chagrined.[576] Now the Highlanders moved up the road, chasing the rebels from their damaged guns and advancing in a wavering line that straddled the road and dipped down into the adjacent swamps. The Enfields' accuracy and rapidity of fire demonstrated why the quartermaster general had been in such a hurry to introduce them to India. But a good many jammed, and the neophytes among the Fusiliers kept loading their cartridges backward and misreading their sights, sending their fire high over their enemies' heads.[577] Nevertheless they had an effective range of three hundred yards[578] and enough found their targets to terrorize the sepoys, whose own lighter-charged musket balls fell among the British "spent and harmless as autumn leaves."[579]

Beet-faced from the heat and filthy from the stinking swamps, the British beat their way to the barricaded gates of Fatehpur and broke into the city. As Maude's "well directed shrapnel" drove the rebels through the gardens and narrow streets, Havelock's infantry chased the sepoys from house to house.[580] The rebel musket fire was "wild and miserable," and merely "whistled over our heads," but exhaustion and the search for food and drink began to slow the Highlanders' progress.[581] The Sikhs halted to stuff their pouches with silver rupees from an overturned cart, which gave the retreating mutineers time to regroup on the far side of town, and for a moment it appeared that the rebel sowars, unopposed by Havelock's wavering Indian horsemen, might turn the general's right flank.[582] But despite the surprising accuracy of the rebels' gunners and the "astonishing rapidity" of their sowars, the mutineers could not hold their ground for long against Havelock's renewed assault, and they began to recede up the Grand Trunk Road.[583]

At a cost of twelve men dead—all of them from sunstroke—by noon of July 12 Henry Havelock had won not only his first battle as a commander in the field, but the first British victory since the uprising began.[584] "I have lived to command in a general action," he wrote his wife that night. ". . . But away with vain glory! Thanks to Almighty God who gave me the victory."[585]

His soldiers were less reverent and worked out a ditty for the occasion:

> With our shot and shell
> We made them smell hell
> That day at Fatehpur . . . [586]

Fatehpur "was given over to plunder and the firebrand,"[587] and every sepoy captive was hanged "without ceremony or delay."[588] There was ample plunder for everyone,[589] including the country people who tagged along as *syces* and grass cutters,[590] and helped the British hunt for fugitives.[591] The houses were full of "ladies' dresses, men's overcoats, saddles, pictures, etc." from "the sack of Cawnpore,"[592] including Wheeler's own white saddle-cloth edged with gold lace,[593] all of which "made the men yet more determined to punish the ruthless destroyers of English women and children."[594] "The inhabitants had fled to a man," wrote Sherer, "so the shops and houses were ransacked without remonstrance, and next morning, when we marched away, the Seikhs were left behind to set the town on fire in several places at once."[595]

As Havelock's bone-weary troops fell asleep a mile and a half beyond Fatehpur, a nearly naked man, "worn to a shadow, and much embrowned by exposure," came staggering into camp. He was Ensign Brown of the Cawnpore garrison, whom Wheeler had sent off under the late Lieutenant Raikes with a detachment of the 56th. For six weeks now, "wild and haggard," young Brown "had been swimming along the Ganges, tortured by the flaming sunshine, gnawed by hunger, . . . bereft almost of hope," but sustained by a few friendly villagers along the way.[596] Half mad from exposure,[597] Brown now asked permission to join Havelock's volunteers and return with them to Cawnpore.[598]

The rebels' defeat at Fatehpur enraged Nana Sahib. He ordered another force sent out, this time under the command of his brother Bala Rao, ordering him to "kill all those men in the dirty shirts and blue caps"—the Enfield-toting Fusiliers—for "they kill all my men before they fire."[599]

The next day, July 14, Havelock marched toward Cawnpore, with salvaged long-range rebel cannon and volunteer European horsemen scouting in advance.[600] At dawn of July 15, near the village of Aong, Havelock's scouts came upon a heavily fortified rebel position with two guns and a substantial body of mutineers preparing themselves for the column's arrival. The rebel gunners fired their cannon down the road, and as the scouts pulled their horses around, a detachment of sepoys came loping after them, only to swerve off into a nearby village.

Havelock sent a third of his column ahead to meet the rebels, retaining the rest to guard the baggage, threatened now by bold bands of rebel cavalry that trotted about in the distance, "hovering on both flanks."[601] Major Renaud routed the sepoys from the village, but during the attack one rebel at least had the satisfaction of shooting this wholesale arsonist and hangman in the leg, driving a portion of his scabbard into the muscle of his thigh.

In the meantime Maude's gunners fired so accurately at the mutineers' position on the road that a round shot not only killed a rebel gunner but "smashed the rammer, and jammed itself with the utmost neatness into the muzzle of the gun."[602] Back at Havelock's position the sowars tried to cut their way to the bullock train, but the British flung them back, and within a few minutes the rebels were fleeing the Enfields once again, rushing in such a panic that they strewed the road with weapons, plunder, tents, and carts.

As they poked through this flotsam and jetsam, a party of Havelock's officers came upon an abandoned palanquin. Drawing their swords and gingerly lifting the curtains, they discovered a feverish young woman cowering inside in Indian dress. It was Miss Sutherland, the sole survivor of the first Fatehgarh party's calamitous landing at Bithur, whom her protector's panicked servants had abandoned on the road. "Surrounded by white faces once more," Miss Sutherland thought her "heart would burst with gratitude" as she was gently relayed back to the baggage train to be tended by the expedition's surgeon.[603]

A few miles farther on, the Grand Trunk Road crossed a broad stream in full flood called the Pandu River. Lacking boats and pontoons, Havelock would need the bridge to get his troops across, but only two hours after the Battle of Aong, his spies reported that the rebels had fortified themselves just across the bridge and mined one of its three stone arches. If the bridge was destroyed it could take him days to get his troops across the river, so Havelock ordered his men back to their feet and marched them another two hours under the midday sun.

As they neared the river rebel artillery suddenly opened up, and they fell back, lying flat on the ground as the old general squinted through his telescope down the simmering road. The near end of the bridge jutted out from a high bluff at the apex of the river's curve, where the road followed the middle of three parallel ravines. Across the bridge in the crook of the river the rebels were entrenched in great numbers on a gradual slope, armed with twenty-four- and twenty-five-pounder guns.

Havelock sent his Fusiliers down the outer ravines, from which they spread out along the upper reaches of the riverbank and opened fire with their Enfields, biting at the cartridges that had helped to precipitate their enemy's mutiny in the first place, and managing to wound Bala Rao himself in the right shoulder. The rest of Havelock's Infantrymen lay on the ground with their arms over their heads as the rebel gunners fired in front of them, and Maude's battery, arrayed in a vast arc and firing from only six hundred yards, answered with a cannonade of round shot. The first rebel round struck three men in the legs, and another knocked off the head of a young soldier lying near Havelock.[604] As his horrified neighbors wiped their comrade's blood and brains from their shirts, Havelock felt called upon to remark that his had been "a happy life," for he had "died in the service of his country."

"For myself, sir," a Highlander replied, "gin ye've nae objections, I wad sunner bide alive i' the service o' ma cuntra!"[605]

His comrades' mordant guffaws were interrupted by a loud explosion, and the men peeked up from the ground to see a great cloud of dust and stone rising from the bridge.[606] But the rebel mine had only taken a bite out of the roadway. Havelock's gunners opened up on the rebel battery, firing so accurately that they killed Bala Rao's elephant[607] and broke the rebels' sponge staves.[608] A detachment of Fusiliers came thundering across the cratered bridge with the Highlanders following behind, stabbing the stymied gunners with their bayonets and heaving the rebel wounded into the turbid stream.[609]

As the sowars galloped away, Havelock hurried the rest of his troops across the bridge and halted a mile beyond. They counted thirty dead and wounded, and the damaged bridge so slowed the commissariat cattle that they arrived too late for the soldiers' dinner. That night another spy turned up with the urgent news that the Cawnpore garrison had not been entirely wiped out after all and that over two hundred women and children were prisoners of Nana Sahib.

At four in the morning of July 16, Havelock roused his exhausted troops.[610] "With God's help, men," he declared, "we will save them, or every man of us die in the attempt. I am trying you sorely, men," he called out, baring his head and gripping his sword. "But I know the stuff you are made of . . . Think of our women and the tender infants in the power of those devils incarnate!"

The bleary troops gave a hoarse cheer and began marching into the heat of the hottest day of the expedition, each man laden with sixty rounds of ball ammunition.[611] As the sun rose a few men dropped purple-faced to their knees and toppled over, vomiting, scrabbling at their collars from sunstroke. All their comrades could do was drag them into the wayside shade for the baggage train to retrieve. By noon they had gloomily tramped some sixteen miles.

As they paused to rest, Havelock's scouts returned with two fugitive sepoys from Nana's army. In the dirt by Havelock's boots they drew the fork in the Grand Trunk Road where a branch led off to the cantonments. Here, said the sepoys, five thousand rebels and eight heavy guns lay in wait, under the personal command of Nana Sahib himself. To the left of the fork was the swampy little hamlet of Aherwa, heavily fortified with three guns and four companies of troops. Four other walled settlements dotted the landscape: two in the crook of the fork, another to the right of the cantonment road, and a fourth behind a large, overflowing tank. All but the last were heavily fortified with sepoys, sowars, and guns.

To march directly into such a position would be suicide. Havelock's only chance was to attack the rebels' flank, and fortunately for him three groves of mango trees stood in a thousand-yard line in front of the rebel position. So he ordered his volunteer cavalry to the front to act as decoys by trotting directly toward the rebel center, as if leading the foot soldiers on a frontal assault, while the bulk of his infantry turned abruptly to the right and crept behind the mango groves to attack the rebels' left flank.

By now Havelock's men had flooded their empty stomachs with forty barrels of porter that the rebels had discarded, possibly on purpose, in a nearby swamp. Leaving the baggage behind, Havelock led them along the road for two miles. Now more men, reeling and dehydrated from alcohol, fell along the wayside, crying out for water, until the groves of mango trees came into view, and what remained of Havelock's infantry and artillery turned off the road and trudged silently across a flooded field as a rebel band, playing in the distance, performed an infuriating approximation of *"Cheers, Boys, Cheers."*[612]

Havelock's dodge worked at first. There was no telltale dust to raise as the infantry proceeded one thousand yards along the grove of trees, and the rebels kept bowling their round shot directly down the road. But through a gap in the trees one of Nana's gunners caught a glimpse of the soldiers' redcoats and tartans and ordered his comrades to redirect their fire, sending their shot whistling and tearing through the trees like flocks of monstrous birds. The British did not return fire at first, but continued tramping through the flooded fields and swampy groves as the rebel shot plunged around them, raising a great brown spray. The sepoys desperately wheeled about to meet the British, but were still scrambling into position when the column emerged from behind the third grove and advanced on the rebels' left.

Half of Nana's guns were now useless to him, for he could not fire to his left without hitting his own troops. But his three twenty-four pounders, positioned on high ground behind sturdy mud walls,

British troops storming a rebel position.

raked the British ranks as they charged forward. Havelock's field guns were proving too light to reach their targets, and his infantry lay down now as the rebels' shot skipped across the fields.

By now Havelock's horse had been shot out from under him. Bareheaded and erect on a hastily requisitioned nag, he ordered his Ross-shire Buffs to their feet, and to shrill Highland cries and the whine of bagpipes they quick-marched into the heat and the rebels' heavy fire, unleashing "one rolling volley" from their muskets.[613] "Never have I beheld conduct more admirable," Havelock reported.[614] "The men were very fierce," wrote one participant, "and the slaughter proportionate."[615]

Abandoning their guns, the sepoys fell back in two waves, one massing a hundred yards toward the cantonment, the other clustering behind a howitzer set in the center of the branch road. Almost overcome with emotion, Havelock called on his Ross-shire Buffs once again. "Now, Highlanders," he cried, "another charge like that wins the day!"

But with the 64th running alongside, the "petticoated devils," as the rebels called them, overran the howitzer, stabbing the gunners with their bayonets, as eighteen volunteer horsemen bloodied their swords on an advance party of sowars, scattering the rebels up the cantonment road.[616] Havelock's men were sinking in the terrible afternoon heat, and Nana was proving a more tenacious commander than his generals, flashing "his gaudy presence on his people in a last convulsion of courage" and ordering more artillery into the field. In the waning evening light Nana's gunners opened up an effective fire from two cannon set in the fork in the road.

Riding his nag among his recumbent troops, Havelock asked them, "Come, who'll take that village—the Highlanders, or the 64th?" Running now on nothing but alcohol and adrenalin, men of both regiments rose to their feet once again. Charging forward with a cheer that was "more like a howl," they took the rebel battery.[617] But as if drawing on some inexhaustible artillery supply, Nana somehow brought yet another heavy gun into play, and as his round shot whistled and bounded toward them, Havelock's exhausted and discouraged advance detachment could only lie flat on the ground until Maude's guns and the rest of the column could reach them.

Nana Sahib himself could be plainly seen riding to and fro, like some spangled mirror-image of Havelock himself, reviving his troops' spirits in a din of trumpets and cymbals and drums. Heartened by the sight of the Highlanders lying upon the field, the rebels rallied and regrouped, and Nana's sowars rode jubilantly forward to envelop Havelock's prostrate troops as Maude's panicked artillery bullocks struggled in vain to draw the guns across the swampy ground.

By now perhaps one hundred British soldiers had fainted from the heat, and Havelock could see that a few more minutes of prostration and paralysis could cost him the battle.[618] There was nothing for it but to order his warriors to their feet yet again, despite rebel fire of as perfect "precision and determination" as Havelock had ever witnessed. As the Highlanders formed ranks, the rebels' shot toppled them like bowling pins, spraying their hastily formed ranks with flesh and blood and strewing the field with the wounded. But strangely provoked by the rebels' music and leaning into the hostile fire as if against a wet winter wind, "Havelock's Ironsides," as they came to be known, kept marching in lockstep to within three hundred yards of the guns and then, with Havelock's own son and aide-de-camp leading the way, charged forward into the smoke and grapeshot belching from the cannon's muzzle.

"The mutineers fought fiercely and well," wrote an officer. But as the British infantry closed in with their seventeen-inch bayonets, the rebels fired high and Maude's guns finally moved up to pour round shot into Nana's ranks.[619] After ferocious hand-to-hand combat, the rebels fired one last wild volley and retreated toward Cawnpore for good.

"It was universally remarked," wrote another officer, "how much closer and fiercer the mutineers fought that day. . . . The sepoys always came into action very well," and if, "as the battle wore on, [they] got bothered, and made a mess of it," it was only because "the master-mind was wanting."[620]

As the rebels' mastermind retreated to Bithur to retrieve his family and his treasure, Havelock's men bivouacked on high ground, and "you should have heard the cheer we gave as our gallant commander rode down the lines."[621] Havelock declared that if he lived to be offered the command of a regiment, he would beg to be given the Ross-shire Buffs.[622] He ascribed his success to British pluck, Maude's artillery, the Enfield rifle, and Almighty God, of course, but, as one officer wrote, it had been the usual case of British "unity of purpose [prevailing] over multitudes."[623] After marching 126 miles through terrible heat and drenching downpours, Havelock and his column had won four major battles in eight days, earning a permanent perch in the schoolboy pantheon of the British Empire.

Searching in the gloaming the Highlanders came upon a pond entirely filled with the rebel dead, and in one of the little hamlets nearby they finished off three hundred wounded sepoys and sowars.[624] But Havelock's soldiers were utterly drained. "Cart-loads" of men had been laid low by "sore feet and sun-strokes," and almost a hundred more were wounded.[625] With "nothing but dirty ditchwater to drink," many more were suffering from dysentery and cholera that seemed to rise like a poisonous miasma from the trampled mud of their encampments.[626]

After collecting their wounded, Havelock's troops collapsed where they stood and fell off to sleep without tents or rations[627] but within sight of the "the roofless barracks" of Cawnpore's artillery lines.[628] Havelock himself lay down on the damp ground, "my waterproof coat serving me as a couch."[629] At midnight they were startled awake by the sound of hoofs plodding toward them, and reflexively fell into formation. But the rumble was merely the sound of commissariat bullocks arriving unannounced with cartloads of rum.

When reveille sounded on Friday, July 17, those of the Lambs and Ross-shire Buffs who were not hung over were probably still a little tipsy as they formed their columns on the cantonment road. A rumor was already rustling through camp that the women and children they had fought so bravely to rescue had been massacred at the last moment by Nana and his men. But they were sick of rumors. Captains Ayton and Moorsom led off with two doctors to minister to the women and children and a detachment of Her Majesty's 84th, selected perhaps in honor of their comrades who fell in the siege and massacre of the garrison.[630]

Marching up the road in the dim morning light, Ayton's men kept their eyes peeled for rebel snipers as the rest of the column followed with their artillery rumbling to the rear. With the sun peeking over the horizon, Ayton's detachment reached the abandoned lines of the 56th Native Infantry, and were just passing the neighboring 53rd's when a shackled, antic figure suddenly popped up from the plain, carrying his chains in one hand and shouting, "All right! All right!" in a croaking voice. Taking him for an escaped criminal, two of Ayton's men were about to shoot him when the man removed his turban and waved it in the air, shouting "Hurrah! Hurrah!" at the top of his lungs.

This seemed so un-Indian that at the last second Ayton ordered his men to lower their Enfields and trotted up to meet this lone figure standing in the rosy dawn rays that were now fanning across the desolate plain. "I am William Jonah Shepherd," stammered this gaunt and fettered apparition, and he had a tale to tell.[631]

THE BIBIGHAR

Cawnpore: July 14–16, 1857

For the past five days Cawnpore had thrilled and quaked to a barrage of bulletins and alarms. Nana had continued issuing his proclamations, squandering his subjects' credulity with blasts of hyperbole. Poona was in rebel hands; the British were evacuating Calcutta, Bombay, and Madras; not a single Englishman remained in all of Hindustan; Turks and Egyptians had cut off British reinforcements on the high seas; Nana was victorious; the emperor reigned supreme.

When, late in the afternoon of July 14, the rebel wounded first began to return "defeated and in confusion" from the debacle at Fatehpur, even the loyalist merchants who had resisted Nana Sahib began to tremble for their lives and property.[632]

Nanak Chand, the loyalist mooktear who had tried so unsuccessfully to warn Collector Hillersdon of Nana's intentions, had spent the entire uprising hiding in a nearby village. But at the news of the British advance he cautiously made his way toward the city and watched as a stream of townspeople filled the roads with their carts. Nanak Chand asked a passing merchant why he was fleeing his old customers' advance.

Because, replied the merchant, the Europeans "would spare nobody in their desire to avenge the massacre at Cawnpore."

"I thought to myself, this must be true," Nanak Chand wrote, "and the gentlemen must be very savage. . . . At a time like this the British were not likely to distinguish between friend and foe." So Nanak Chand hurried back to his hiding place, passing villagers "with their dresses changed coming along the banks of the Ganges." By now "the terror in the hearts of all was so great, that they asked each other no questions."[633] After Bala Rao's defeat at Aong the desertions from Cawnpore steadily increased.[634] Eventually three quarters of Cawnpore's population would flee, many times the number that had fled from rebel rule.

Now it was the rebels' turn to bury their treasure. "Dispirited and panic-stricken" mutineers "who possessed plundered property kept it to one side."[635] Hulas Singh buried one thousand rupees before fleeing with Nunne Nawab.[636] The complicitous boatmen fled to Bithur,[637] and even the guards at the prisons began to sneak away, leaving only the most committed of the mutineers to defend the city.[638]

Back when Havelock was still approaching Fatehpur, Nana Sahib had summoned his three Fatehgarh *burra* sahibs—Colonels Smith and Goldie and Magistrate Thornhill—from their cell near the Bibighar and demanded to know "what they had to say regarding the evacuation of the Fort of Allahabad, as, instead of this being effected, troops were coming to Cawnpore from that direction."[639] But the gentlemen "could make no reply."[640]

As the rebels raced to and fro along the Grand Trunk Road, they captured a few Indian couriers bearing notes that appeared to have been written by ladies at the Bibighar and by various loyalist Indian merchants.[641] According to Henry Fane, a fugitive civil servant privy to the collector's intelligence reports at Mirzapore, the rebels had earlier warned the ladies that if the British captured Cawnpore they would all be killed. Though Fane heard that the ladies "were not allowed to write to say so"—an odd prohibition from the rebels' point of view, unless it was predicated on a suspicion of anything written in English—it is possible that some of the messages they had apparently tried to send to Havelock contained this warning.[642]

The letters may have been forgeries Azimullah had concocted in order to persuade Nana Sahib that they posed a danger to his rule.[643] In any case, the rest of Nana's court wondered whether the ladies' ostensible messages—for others may have reached their destination—accounted in some measure for Havelock's outlandish success. In a furious rage Nana ordered the couriers decapitated on the following day,[644] and decreed that on July 16 the nose and right hand of every English-writing Indian in the station would be amputated,[645] Azimullah's excepted, of course.

A little after noon of Wednesday, July 15, Bala Rao returned from the battle at the Pandu River nursing his shoulder wound and demanding a conference of all of Nana's courtiers and commanders. Eventually the grumbling, impatient Baba Bhutt, the unflappable Azimullah, and the stout, ferocious Tatya Tope gathered with Nana Sahib in the garden of Nur Mahomed's hotel to hear Bala Rao confirm the terrible news of his defeat at the bridge over the Pandu. Panting, lisping through the gap in his front teeth, his large eyes bright and flickering with pain, Bala Rao told the others that the British "were coming like mad horses, or mad dogs—caring for neither cannon nor musketry, nor did these appear to have any effect upon them."[646]

It was just as Azimullah had warned Nana all along: leave one Feringhee alive, and he will destroy you. All Nana had accomplished with his mercies was to provoke the English into performing superhuman feats of courage and endurance. Had the British shown any such mercy to the people who lived along the Grand Trunk Road, the villagers whose homes and crops they burned, the furloughed sepoys and poor ryots they hanged, the women and children who had died by the hundreds in the flames and crossfire?

What had his mercies gained him? Nana had spared the Greenways and Jacobis for ransoms that never materialized. He had spared the three Fatehgarh burra sahibs in exchange for an evacuation of Allahabad that was now more remote than ever. And out of sheer kindness he had spared the women and children, only to have them spy on him and betray his secrets to the British at the cost of thousands of his followers' lives.

No one has determined what Nana himself made of these arguments. He may well have seen the logic of eliminating witnesses and would have felt betrayed by the prisoners he had saved, especially the obfuscating burra sahibs from Fatehgarh. And it is possible that the decision to destroy them may have contributed to his newfound resolution on the field of battle. But during their long flight from the British, Nana[647] and Tatya Tope,[648] even at their most defiant, would insist that they took no part in the decision to massacre the women and children. Mohamed Ali Khan, Azimullah's old cohort, would deplore their massacre—even blame it for the ultimate defeat of the rebels—but he ascribed it to his old friend Azimullah's fanatical desire "to see [Nana] so irretrievably implicated in rebellion that there would be no possibility for him to draw back."[649]

With Havelock's column menacing the city, there was not much time to dawdle over the matter; indeed it may have gotten lost among other questions more vital to the rebellion's survival. How many men could the rebels muster from their shrinking ranks of Cawnpore? How many had fled? Were there enough lascars and bullocks to bring the artillery to the fork in the road? Who would protect Nana's household at Bithur? Where would they go if they were defeated? Where would they go if they won? To Fatehpur? Allahabad? Benares? The British had defeated all of his commanders. Now Nana himself must lead the troops. Who would join Nana in his stand at Aherwa?

◆ ◆ ◆

Some one hundred yards away from Nur Mahomed's hotel, the Begum reigned supreme at the Bibighar. After the capture of the Indian couriers, she cut her staff of servants to two: a female sweeper and a cook. When even the fresh clothes Nana had provided became fouled with sweat, mud, and the offal from the sick and wounded, the women were obliged to do their own laundering. On July 14 a young Brahmin climbed to the top of the compound wall and watched several ladies washing their "filthy" clothes. Why, he asked one of the guards, couldn't anyone "get the ladies' clothes washed by a washerman?" The sepoy slapped the Brahmin across the face and confined him overnight on suspicion of loyalist sympathies.[650]

In the thorns of the tree in the courtyard the ladies hung their laundry out to dry, crowding beneath the dripping cloth to seek shelter against the burning sun.[651] Some probably attempted, with whatever black cloth they could find, to fashion widows' armbands in honor of their dead husbands. With their hair cut almost to the scalp against fleas and lice,[652] a few still wore the bonnets and sun hats they had brought with them from the Entrenchment.[653] Others covered their heads with wetted veils torn from the remnants of their gowns and petticoats.[654] Without any chairs or benches to sit on, some ladies learned to sit on their heels like Indian women, minimizing contact with the filthy ground. Most no longer had shoes to wear, and padded across the muck of the courtyard in their bare feet.

The deaths from disease continued. The Greenways, who with Mrs. Jacobi and her children were still sequestered from the other prisoners, suffered two losses in two days.[655] First their ayah died on the thirteenth, and then Rose's grown son Edward the next day, both dehydrated by severe bouts of diarrhea. So many women and children were ill by now that the Bengali doctor simply listed diarrhea as the cause of death instead of trying to differentiate among cholera, dysentery, and sepsis. The women and children watched and feebly mouthed their prayers as other corpses were dragged out of the yard: the emaciated remains of Mrs. Beestal, of Jimmy Leary, of one of the Brett girls—all dead of "diarrhea" by the fourteenth of July—the latest three of the twenty-three cadavers that had been dragged off by now from the Bibighar and carted to the river a quarter mile away.

The Begum had endeared herself to no one but her malicious lover, a Eurasian bodyguard named Sarvur Khan.[656] The Bibighar's sepoy guards, especially their jemadar Yusuf Khan, had grown to detest her queenly airs. Through swarms of flies the Begum paraded, officiously barking gratuitous commands at the servants and inmates, contemptuously averting her eyes from the children's wretchedness and covering her nose and mouth against their stench. By the dawn of July 15 she presided over two hundred prisoners. Of these the three burra sahibs from Fatehgarh were the only grown men; seventy-three were women; and 124 were children, including teenaged girls and boys.[657]

Early in the morning of July 15, while lying on the filthy grass mats that covered the Bibighar's floors, the ladies could feel the earth shake and hear the muffled pounding of artillery somewhere to the southeast. Shushing their children, they pressed their ears against the ground, listening for over an hour to the sporadic rumbling, like some distant echo of the Entrenchment barrages they had somehow survived. Outside the Bibighar the guards were also listening. Had the pounding approached or receded? the ladies asked themselves as the firing dwindled away. Had the rebels driven back the relief force that old Sir Hugh had promised for so long? Why, they would wonder for the next three hours, had the firing stopped?

But then the roaring started up again, closer and more intense, rolling through the station like a tide. Women seated by the Bibighar's windows could see that fewer guards were standing about, and those that remained were speaking excitedly, clustered in little groups and anxiously glancing back over their shoulders at the Bibighar and the Old Cawnpore Hotel beyond. Soon the rumbling was nearly drowned out by the rising clamor of panicked townspeople fleeing toward Nawabgunj. If any of the captive boys had had the energy to brave the thorns of the courtyard tree and climb into its branches, they would have seen a stream of carts and hackeries hurrying up the road to Bithur, forced off here and there by sowars and artillery wagons racing toward Aherwa from the magazine.

Some of the ladies no doubt rejoiced at the unmistakable noise of Havelock's advance, and many children must have been told that their rescue was at hand. But others must have dreaded the consequences of the sulking rebels' humiliation and worried as the Begum grew ever more hostile and agitated. As the gunfire dwindled again in the late hours of the morning, there was a burgeoning sense of expectancy in the humid noonday air, as if congested clouds were about to break.[658] A few prisoners may have asked the guards what was going on, but the rest would have seen the risk of provoking the Begum or the jittery, muttering guards and called for silence. They gathered their children around them, quieted them as if at church. The Bibighar must be inconspicuous, negligible, so that the Begum and the guards and Nana Sahib himself might, out of kindness or impatience or sheer absentmindedness, simply leave them behind for the advancing column. Certainly this would make tactical sense to the rebels, for two hundred women and children would inevitably stall the column at Cawnpore.

And so they whispered their prayers together in little groups, gathering around the few among them who had somehow managed through siege and massacre and their squalid imprisonment to keep hold of their sacred books. Some clung to Bibles, others to prayer books, while Mrs. Blair read from a veritable library of inspirational volumes that had belonged to her late daughter,[659] including the *Companion to the Altar*[660] and Charles Drelincourt's seventeenth-century *Preparation for Death: The Christians defense against the fears of death with seasonable directions how to prepare our selves to dye well.*[661]

✦   ✦   ✦

Colonels Smith and Goldie and the wounded Magistrate Thornhill still occupied a separate cell in the Bibighar's compound with the late Edward Greenway's teenaged son Frank. The three men did their best to comfort the boy, but there was not very much they could say. The survival of the three burra sahibs had depended entirely on an elaborate hoax: a fraudulent pledge to arrange the evacuation of Allahabad. Perhaps the three men hoped they might save themselves by stalling the rebels with gentlemanly expositions on the bureaucratic delays that would inevitably attend so massive an undertaking as the evacuation of a major Company station. But at its best their ruse had merely delayed the inevitable; at its worst it had so infuriated Nana's advisers as to further imperil the women and children.

If the three burra sahibs actually sent any memoranda to Calcutta or Allahabad, they do not survive in the public record. If they ever existed, perhaps they were suppressed as letters unworthy of Englishmen or they were so clumsily composed—ghostwritten, perhaps, by Azimullah—that Havelock's scouts had dismissed them as forgeries. But there would have been no use encoding them in Smith's schoolboy French, for by all accounts Azimullah's French was far superior to the colonel's.

After their audience with the furious Peshwa, the three burra sahibs must have known that they were doomed. Now in the stillness of the simmering afternoon, after the artillery fire from the Pandu River had died away, the three men prepared themselves for execution. Neither Smith nor Goldie were particularly pious, but Thornhill had sent a child away "to study for the glory of his Heavenly Father" and was given to composing inspirational verse, so it may have fallen to the young civilian to lead the old colonels in prayer.[662]

The Bibighar's triangular compound was surrounded by a low wall of brick and stucco that bounded the junction of two roads: one leading from the civil station to the magazine, the other from the river to the Assembly Rooms, which the rebels now employed as a warehouse for their plunder.[663] At about four o'clock in the afternoon, Nana Sahib led his entourage up to the northwestern perimeter of the Old Cawnpore Hotel's compound and sat under a neem tree with perhaps twenty courtiers around him.[664]

First the shackled Indian couriers were hustled out of a cell in the

Bibighar's yard and brought before the Peshwa. As spies they had been condemned not to be shot but to be cut down ignominiously by jullads.[665] A few yards away the three burra sahibs must have understood from the sighs and shouts of the gathering crowd that the spies had been beheaded. Now from the same direction the three men could hear the peculiar shuffling tramp of sandaled sepoys marching back into the compound. The tramping stopped, the gentlemen's cell door opened, and in a bloom of afternoon light stood a jemadar in his red coat[666] with a small squad of men in variegated dress.[667]

The jemadar ordered the gentlemen out.

Where are we going? one of them asked as he emerged from the dark room, squinting in the light.

To Nana, the jemadar replied.

Fourteen-year-old Frank Greenway may not have moved at first, expecting that the burra sahibs had been summoned for another of their meetings with the rebels. But the jemadar motioned to him as well, and soon the last four adult Englishmen in Cawnpore were walking up the footpath. A few women—Smith's and Thornhill's wives, perhaps, Goldie's daughter, Frank's mother and grandmother—hurried toward the Bibighar's entrance to see where the sepoys were taking them. But the guards ordered them back.

None of the four males spoke, but "their lips moved as if in prayer"[668] as they trudged through the compound gate and up to where Nana himself awaited them in a turban of gold lace.[669] By now a "great crowd"[670] had gathered that included Tatya Tope,[671] Baba Bhutt, Azimullah, Shah Ali, Jwala Prasad, the wounded Bala Rao and a number of landlords,[672] as well as a body of sowars posted among the roadside trees.[673] At the junction of the two roads the gentlemen's escort was ordered to a halt. The burra sahibs stood together against the wall of a nearby commissariat godown, looking out toward the theater and the Assembly Rooms, remarking, perhaps, the damage to the Christ Church tower.[674] One of them, probably Thornhill, held Frank Greenway's hand.[675] Tatya Tope waved to the jemadar, who gave his men the order to fire. Thornhill fell first, then young Frank; the two old colonels followed.[676]

✦ ✦ ✦

At the sound of the volley, cries could be heard from the Greenways' cell, and some of the ladies at the Bibighar rushed to comfort Goldie's surviving daughter and the two Marys: Thornhill and Smith. Perhaps, the other ladies suggested, only a second batch of Indians had been executed. Perhaps their husbands had indeed gone for another of their conferences with the Maharaja. The gunfire was probably mere musketry practice in the lines of the 1st Native Infantry camped at the commissariat.

As jullads dragged the four men's bodies into a ditch, Baba Bhutt ordered Hussaini Khanum to bring the rest of the prisoners to the road. An expectant crowd of young men and boys climbed the compound walls and stood along the top, jostling for a better view.

A little before five thirty, the double doors near the courtyard tree swung open, and in marched the Begum, ordering out the Bengali doctor, the cook, and the wife of Boodoo,[677] a sweeper who had escaped some days before.[678] The doctor protested, tried to scribble the names of the day's latest victims of disease, but before he could record the cause of their deaths he was shoved outside.[679]

Struggling to maintain her composure, one of the memsahibs approached the despotic Begum and asked what Nana Sahib intended to do with the women and children.

Hussaini Khanum snapped back that "the Nana had sent orders for their immediate destruction" and closed the doors behind her.

Some of the ladies raced frantically around the courtyard, calling for their children and lunging at the bolted window shutters. But others insisted to each other that this was just another of the Begum's hollow threats. Like Jonah, many of them had convinced themselves by now that God had saved them for a purpose: to testify to the rebels' barbarity, perhaps, or to prove to the heathen that the English and their faith were too strong and too stubborn to be wiped from the face of Hindustan. It was simply inadmissible that after three weeks of bombardments and eighteen days of captivity, after all their grief and suffering and fervent prayers, God now intended for them to be butchered within earshot of their rescuers' cannon.

By now the sun was low enough in the sky to cast the courtyard in shadows. It may have been at this dismal hour that Caroline Lindsay, one arm wrapped around her little sister Fanny, wrote the last entries in her family's chronology and tucked it into her clothes. Other ladies pinned names to their children's shirts and hid their infants and toddlers beneath what remained of their skirts. Through one window a burra memsahib—she may have been Mrs. Moore—spotted Jemadar Yusuf Khan and asked him if it was true that they intended to murder the children.[680] The jemadar replied that he had received no such orders "and that she was not to be afraid."

The jemadar hastily conferred with his men. They agreed that the British column seemed invincible, and their only hope of "[saving] their own lives" from British wrath was to protect the women and children.[681] And so when the Begum returned from the execution of the doctor and the servants and sharply ordered the jemadar to bring the women and children up to the road, Yusuf Khan told her that his men had vowed not to harm the memsahibs and their children.[682] The Begum berated them, warned them that if they did not cooperate she would have them killed.

But the sepoys seemed adamant. "Who are you to give us orders?" one of them snarled.

The outraged Begum stomped off to report the sepoys' traitorous defiance, and in a few minutes the stout Tatya Tope was impatiently leading a delegation of Nana's zemindars back into the Bibighar's yard and demanding an explanation from Yusuf Khan. By now the jemadar had begun to take the situation into his own hands. He liberated a number of musicians' families from his regiment and put them into a nearby shed for safekeeping,[683] and though a few sepoys had lingered in the Bibighar to look for plunder, it appeared as though the guards were determined to keep their pledge.

Tatya Tope demanded that they bring the ladies out, but Yusuf Khan told him "that they would not lift their hands against women, though they would kill every man."[684] Tatya Tope accused him and his men of working in league with the advancing Europeans. The jemadar denied this, but, as a crowd gathered, he began to falter, and when Tatya Tope threatened to shoot them if they did not obey, the jemadar conferred with his men. Though the rebel cause seemed doomed, it was still well within Tatya Tope's power to make good on such a threat. Perhaps it was wiser to trade certain death for possible capture and execution by the British.

Angrily, reluctantly, the sepoys formed ranks and followed the Begum to the Bibighar's door. From the direction of the commissariat yard there was another shout as Nana's executioners cut down the doctor and the two servants.[685] Many of the women and children shrieked and tried to shrink away from the doors and windows.[686] Women and children prostrate with cholera and dysentery crawled in among the others as they pressed themselves along the walls. The strongest ladies locked arms around the verandah pillars and pledged never to let go, never to allow the rebels to drag them away, while a few feeble boys, in solemn observance of their late fathers' dying admonitions, prepared to defend their mothers and sisters.[687]

Someone stood with her *Book of Common Prayer* and tried to lead the others in the Litany.[688]

> . . . From our enemies defend us, O Christ.
> *Graciously look upon our afflictions.*
> Pitifully behold the sorrows of our hearts.
> *Mercifully, forgive the sins of thy people.*
> Favorably with mercy hear our prayers.
> *O Son of David, have mercy on us* . . . [689]

The double doors at the end of the courtyard were flung open again, and the ladies ordered out. But they refused to move and tightened their grips on the verandah pillars and on each other's arms and waists, trying to keep from crushing their weeping children underfoot.[690] The Begum ordered a few sepoys into the courtyard to drag the ladies away. They halfheartedly pushed and pulled at the huddled groups of women and children, determined now to get this over with. But the women shrieked and wailed and held their ground. Disconcerted by the crush and the terrible din, the sepoys declared it "impossible to separate [them] or drag them out of the building," and backed out into the yard, shutting the door behind them.

A ray of pained hope must have flickered through the huddled prisoners then, and a brief thrill of pride at having faced their captors down. Someone suggested that they secure the doors from the inside, and several women ran over and, tearing strips of cloth from their gowns, frantically bound the door handles together.[691] A few ladies raised their quaking voices in a hymn.

Tatya and the Begum berated the sepoys for failing to budge these sickly women and half-starved children. Finally they decided that if the memsahibs would not move and the sepoys could not drag them out, then they must all die where they stood.

Hearing this, Nana apparently left his place under the neem tree and returned to his hotel, leaving his officers to see the matter through.[692] He still had little stomach for such slaughter, nevertheless Azimullah had achieved at the Bibighar what the past weeks had not: his prince's complete immersion in the tide of rebellion. At long last shrugging off the crippling languor and irresolution that had defeated his adoptive father forty years before, Nana Sahib Peshwa Bahadur prepared to depart for Aherwa on his chestnut horse and turn back the "God-Forgotten."[693]

Now the jemadar ordered his men to stand outside the doors and windows on one side of the Bibighar and directed the crowd of onlookers to move away "as they were going to fire."[694] The crowd obeyed, dropping down behind the low walls. At a signal from the jemadar, his men thrust the barrels of their muskets through the window shutters along the one wall of one long room.

With a great cry the women and children tried to move across the courtyard to the far verandah and seek cover behind the pillars and the tree, but there was hardly any room.[695] The courtyard was only sixteen feet wide, the verandah five feet, the long room ten feet deep, so most managed only to compress themselves up toward the opposite verandah while the remainder, including some of the sick and wounded and orphaned children, crouched helplessly on the courtyard ground.

Twenty sepoys aimed their muskets into this wave of bodies and at Yusuf Khan's command opened fire at point-blank range.[696] The first volley pared some of the foremost layer of women and children away, and may have wounded a few beyond.[697] The sepoys backed away from the smoking windows, and a second squad moved in to take their places. But the sight and sound of what their comrades' volley had achieved was apparently too much for some of them to bear, and when the havildar gave the order to fire, a few merely emptied their muskets into the air and staggered back.[698]

By now many of the survivors of the two volleys had probably found cover in the sleeping rooms and behind the pillars, and it may be that, shooting from the doors and windows, the sepoys simply could not find their targets. Or perhaps they were sickened and shamed by the shrieks and pleas from within. For whatever reason, they refused to return to the windows. Let Tatya Tope blow them from guns if he wished. Yusuf Khan and his men had had enough.

The Begum taunted them, cursed them as cowards, traitors, eunuchs. But it was no use. They merely stepped back a few paces more and stood shamefaced with their smoking muskets.[699] Hussaini Khanum told them she would find real men for the job, and sent word to her lover, Sarvur Khan, to assemble his own execution squad.

Sarvur Khan had been a barrack boy, and in some ways the malignant antithesis of Jonah Shepherd. His mother was a Pathani prostitute who had serviced "the regimental bazaar of the Eighty-Seventh Royal Irish," and Khan claimed "the whole regiment, including the sergeant-major's cook, for his father." A childhood spent in the "snarling animal world" of British regimental lines had induced in this sullen, hirsute, burly half-caste a lethal hatred of the British, a fundamental contempt for womankind, and a savage self-loathing that he freely extended to small children.

A little before sunset,[700] Sarvur Khan appeared, walking out of the setting sun in his red bodyguard's uniform and trailing four companions, each with a tulwar in his hand.[701] Two of his recruits were aproned Moslem butchers: both tall; one dark, pockmarked, and stout.[702] The other two appeared to some witnesses to be Hindu villagers of low caste,[703] but one of these was evidently a half-blind and heavily mustached Brahmin swordsman named Souracun.[704]

As they approached the Bibighar the onlookers resumed their places along the compound wall.[705] Inside, some of the women dragged the dead to one side and tried to tend to the wounded. A few soldiers' wives and daughters were determined to fight. "Quite capable of making a stout resistance, and holding their own against any single native," Mrs. Jacobi and Mrs. Probett, both squarely built daughters of artillerymen, prepared to defend the nine children they had somehow managed thus far to keep alive.[706]

Now they could hear the bolt sliding back. The burra memsahib who had first spoken with Yusuf Khan stepped foward now as if to answer the door. There were angry mutterings from the other side, and then someone heaved against the doors, and the cloth strips between the handles began to strain and break. The doors burst open and slapped against the walls.

Stepping out from under the dark shadow of the mulsuri tree,[707] the burra memsahib opened her mouth to speak. Sarvur Khan felled her with one stroke.[708]

"Fearful shrieks" rose from the courtyard into the clear, dim sky. Closing the doors behind them, the five men fanned out and worked their way forward, slashing at the straggling wounded crawling along the floor. From behind a pillar the stout Mrs. Jacobi suddenly lunged toward one of the butchers and knocked him down with one blow. But as the other women shrank back, his comrades came to his rescue. First they hung her daughter Lucy on a hook by her chin[709] and then silenced her mother by cutting her throat.[710]

Five against perhaps 180 souls, however feeble and hysterical they may have been, would have been fearful odds if so many of them had not already been wounded or rendered helpless by disease. Like the jullads, the five men saw their job as finishing up what the sepoys had started. They knew that stabbing was inefficient, that hacking at their victims' necks would be the quickest means of accomplishing their mission.[711] If the ladies protected their necks with their arms then their arms would simply be severed as well; the effect was the same: they would bleed to death. Slashing right and left at all who were standing, chopping downward at the fallen with their heavy blades, the five men proceeded methodically, like reapers, through a spreading pool of blood.

"Some of the helpless creatures in their agony," Jonah was told, "fell down at the feet of their murderers, clasped their legs, and begged in the most pitiful manner to spare their lives, but to no purpose."[712] Others tried to dodge the men's swords by ducking into the doorways and around the pillars, and so often did the clumsy, muscular Sarvur Khan strike the walls that he broke two swords and twice emerged to fetch new weapons from his fellow bodyguards.[713]

Though the shutters of the doors and windows remained opened, none of the women or children tried to escape out of the building, surrounded as it was by sepoys and Indian onlookers—by an India from which every hope and refuge had now completely vanished. The few defiant boys were cut down quickly, as was every child who tried to make a run for it through the phalanx of swordsmen. Mothers kept pulling their children close to them and pushing them back into the corners of the building, and in the sweltering heat and the crush of bodies, children suffocated to death under their dying mothers' skirts.

It took something less than an hour for the chorus of wailing to die away into a few individual voices, and then even these were stilled.[714] In that single hour seventy-three women had fallen, including the pious Mrs. Blair, still clinging to her prayer books. Caroline and Fanny Lindsay, the last of William's maidenly wards, died in terrible fulfillment of Caroline's tearful "presentiment" at Calcutta over a year before.[715] Old Rose Greenway and her family reached the end of their game, all hope of ransom exhausted. The brave, phlegmatic Mrs. Moore had been struck down;[716] and Mrs. Prout, the major's new bride; and Mrs. O'Brien, who had begged Jonah to take her with him out of the Entrenchment.[717] The fecund and ferocious Mrs. Probett may have died in a counterattack on the butchers, for by one account her body, like Mrs. Jacobi's, was left that evening tied to a pillar.[718] A Mrs. Walker lay among the dead: at sixty-five probably the oldest of the victims at the Bibighar. They cut down the late

Louisa Chalwin's pet project, Miss Isabel White, who, just before the uprising, had been coming into her own at last as one of Cawnpore's most eligible spins.[719] Here lay the scrofulous but gallant Fanny Williams and her wounded mother.[720] There lay Colonel Goldie's daughter; and Mary Smith, the colonel's wife; and the beautiful Mary Thornhill, all following their burra sahibs to their fates.[721] Over a hundred children lay dead, and native Christian nursemaids like Mrs. Prout's Mary Cheeters and Nancy Lang of Fatehgarh. And somewhere in the carnage lay Captain Seppings's widow, to whom Thomson had given the late Lieutenant Harrison's rings at the river, "as I thought the women might perhaps excite some commiseration, and that if any of our party escaped, it would be some of them."[722]

At candlelight the few remaining onlookers could hear an occasional exhausted swordstroke as the five men searched through the gloom for vagrant signs of life, drawn to this or that corner by a rustling or a groan. At last Sarvur Khan and his cohorts could do no more in the darkness and emerged into the courtyard with their arms and feet and clawed clothing covered in blood. At the sight of them panting and staggering out of the Bibighar's yard with their smeared swords, the remaining onlookers jumped down from the compound wall and fled. The Begum locked the doors, and her lover and his armweary helpers returned to their homes to bathe.

Early that night a few soldiers and townspeople crept back to peek through the windows and doors.[723] But they did not linger long. In the dull light from the waning moon, they glimpsed impossible tangles of pale limbs and dark heaps of clothing leading into the verandah's shadows and heard the first of the spectral groans and half-suffocated cries that would interrupt the insect song of the long and sweltering night.

THE FATAL WELL

The Bibighar: July 16, 1857

By dawn of Thursday, July 16, word of the previous night's massacre had spread throughout the district. Despite the general exodus from the city, hundreds—some said even thousands[724]—of spectators assembled at the Bibighar to view the carnage. Cityfolk, villagers, sepoys, opportunistic boys stood along the walls and crowded around the compound gates to see if what they had heard was true.[725]

Around eight in the morning the crowd parted to make way for a burial party of scavengers and four jullads led by a resourceful executioner named Aitwurya.[726] By now they were masters of this sort of thing; indeed Aitwurya had already amassed a small fortune from the plunder and disposal of English bodies at Sati Chowra and Savada House.[727] But his mission today was unusual in one respect: the bodies were to be dumped not into the Ganges this time but down an irrigation well some forty feet south of the Bibighar. The cavity of the well was nine feet wide[728] and fifty feet deep;[729] three steps led to the rim, and nearby a shallow channel had been worn into the ground by the bullocks that used to haul sackloads of water up from below.[730]

The burial party reached the main entrance of the Bibighar and opened the doors onto a nightmare of flies and blood. Even Sarvur Khan himself would have been shocked by the scene, for he and his men had accomplished all this in semidarkness. In the sharp morning light bodies lay everywhere, heaping up along the wall of one long room as though someone had tilted the building in the night.[731]

The veteran jullads and scavengers set to work, dragging the uppermost bodies out from under the mulsuri tree. But suddenly the venturesome Aitwurya, stepping into one of the sleeping chambers,[732] made an alarming discovery: three or four ladies[733] and perhaps as many children sitting huddled in the shadows, still alive after a night of lying on the floor, "saturated with the blood of their late friends and companions, and surrounded by their mangled bodies. . . . Scarcely credible is it," wrote a later investigator into the slaughter at Cawnpore, "that any could outlive the terrors of such a night, and yet retain their reason; but only truly would such seem to have been the case."[734]

The burial squad backed away as if from ghosts, but now they could hear whimpering, rustling, sickly moaning from among the piles of corpses. Aitwurya hurried off to the Old Cawnpore Hotel for further instructions.[735] Perhaps it was Baba Bhutt who paused from his duties to consider the question. But the answer was obvious. The rebels had not annihilated all these witnesses only to let others escape. The survivors must be killed at once.

Aitwurya returned to the Bibighar and joined his brethren at the door. Whether the ladies heard him give the command, or whether the jullads simply stepped toward them with their swords upraised, two of the women rushed past Aitwurya and his men, stumbling over the low sill of a side window and running into the yard. Surrounded on all sides by walls, spectators, and guarded gates, they must have known they could never escape. But perhaps they had already resolved in the night to kill themselves, for they lunged straight to the lip of the well and jumped in, one after the other, falling some fifty feet to the bottom.[736]

The children, all aged between five and six years, followed the women into the yard but only ran around the well, reported one witness, for "where else could they go to?" At first a few jullads chased after them, but the shrieking children eluded them, and perhaps the indignity of this, or the rising heat, or the jeers from the crowd got the better of them.[737] Eventually they decided to let the children run themselves out while they went about their business.[738]

The jullads and scavengers returned to the Bibighar and brought out the bodies of the dead and near dead, grabbing many of them by the hair and dragging them through the grass. "Those whose clothes were worth taking were stripped" before they were rolled over the rim.[739] Aitwurya "was foremost in stripping the dead of their garments and taking as booty all he could get upon their persons."[740] But there was not much left to loot. Most of the Cawnpore women had already been plundered at Sati Chowra; only the Fatehgarh ladies had been permitted to retain their valuables, and these Sarvur Khan and his men had probably plundered the night before.

Aitwurya searched disappointedly through work boxes and knitting bags, casting aside hats, books, and stockings. But a few of his men snatched up the laundry the ladies had left still drying on the branches of the mulsuri tree,[741] and occasionally someone would find a ring worth wrenching or cutting from a lady's finger, or a few rupees in a lady's boot.[742] Here and there they found daguerreotypes in the ladies' clothes and, marveling at the silver images of their victims, popped them from their blood-caked cases.[743]

Several severely wounded women were still breathing when they were dragged out. Three could even speak and "prayed for the sake of God that an end might be put to their sufferings."[744] One spectator remembered that a "very stout" Eurasian woman "who was severely wounded in both arms . . . entreated to be killed." She and the two others were set down on the bullock ramp[745] and left to stare up into the whitening sky.[746]

As the burial party continued to drag corpse after corpse through the bloody grass and dump them into the depths of the well, it became obvious that at this rate not all the dead were going to fit. So the jullads went to work, severing with their swords the stiffening limbs of the dead and tucking them into the interstices of the half-choked well.[747]

At last the time came to dispose of the children who still darted desperately about the yard. Reports differ regarding their fates. By one account the children simply kept running around until at last they were caught and flung alive into the well.[748] But Jonah was told that several jullads were assigned to hide behind a corner of the Bibighar while a mehtar, approaching the children as an apparent friend, urged them with furtive gestures to hide behind the building. The children obeyed, and the jullads decapitated them as soon as they turned the corner, priding themselves "in their skill in taking the head clean off at one stroke."[749] In any case, "there was none to save them," one witness testified. "No, none said a word or tried to save them."[750]

With the death of the children the crowd began to melt away. Despite the jullads' surgery, the bodies had completely engorged the cold throat of the Bibighar's well, and the rest of the corpses had to be piled into the back of a scavenger's cart.[751] As the cart creaked off toward the river, Aitwurya and his jullads collected their sacks of gewgaws and heaps of bloody cloth and headed for their homes. By noon the only living souls at the Bibighar were three neighborhood sweepers toting buckets and rags into the littered courtyard. Their job was not to try to wipe up the blood from the floors and walls—there was no time for that—but merely to erase any damning inscriptions the women and children may have left behind.[752]

The Bibighar

◆ ◆ ◆

After his defeat at Aherwa that evening, Nana entirely circumvented the city. "Drenched in perspiration, mounted on a chestnut horse, [and] looking greatly alarmed," he led his shattered army up the Grand Trunk Road to Bithur.[753] Hundreds of mutineers swept through the city to gather their kits and dig up their plunder before rejoining the sowars on their lathered mounts, the lascars hauling what was left of Nana's artillery, the exhausted officers wavering atop Nana's war elephants, the straggling trail of sepoys and match-lockmen, camp followers, villagers, and city folk "rushing away as far as possible towards the west."[754]

All day long the city had been emptying out, and now as the rum-ble and clatter of Nana and his army receded up the road, the sepoys who had been left behind to look after the station began to pack their things and flee. At the jail at Putkapur, over half a mile northwest of the Bibighar, Jonah Shepherd and three hundred other prisoners watched the guards "bringing out their clothes and traps and making them into bundles." The prisoners shouted through the bars that the guards could not just leave them here. If they were not released im-mediately, shouted one desperate prisoner, the sepoys would "for ever be cursed." Mounting his horse, the kindly subhedar who had protected the secret of Jonah Shepherd's identity replied that the best he could do was to leave them in the care of an armed policeman with instructions to release them if, by morning, Nana had not triumphed.

Out of the chaos of that hour, Jonah dared to hope that he might yet be rescued from Putkapur and the stubbornly malicious Nowgong captain who still menaced him. "So you seem overjoyed that your brethren are coming to your rescue," the captain sneered. "Be assured you will not be allowed to leave this alive; for, bear in mind, I shall batter your head against the wall before I go away hence."

But by now Jonah had allied himself with a motley group of loyalists, including the musician Mendes; the Entrenchment cook Chaday Khan; and an unfettered Hindu named Kuloo who had "promised, together with his brother, to follow me wherever I might go." In the dark of the cell that night they kept Jonah hidden from his muscular nemesis until, in the small hours of the morning, the Indian constable abruptly abandoned his hopes for Nana's triumph and unlocked the door to the jail.

Three hundred prisoners pushed forward "in a fearful rush," and Jonah tumbled out into the night air. Gathering up his chains, he followed after his companions, staggering half a mile eastward to the Orderlies Bazaar, just shy of the Ganges Canal. "The streets were almost entirely deserted in some places, at other people were still rushing along with bundles on their backs and heads. Many stopped out of curiosity to see us, but we waited for nobody, fearful of falling into the hands . . . of the followers of Nana, or a stray sepoy."

The road was so quiet as they hurried past the Assembly Rooms that their fetters "became very audible," and Jonah proposed that they deaden the sound by wrapping their chains in strips of cloth. "But there was no help for it— we could not linger a moment on the public road,—on!—on! was the word." Evading small bands of mutineers, Jonah and his friends reached the blacksmith's shop only to find that the smithy had buried his tools and fled.

Deciding that his best hope lay in linking up with the advancing British force, Jonah led the others across the canal bridge and searched through Generalgunj for another blacksmith. Everywhere "the inhabitants were up," debating what kind of treatment they could expect from the British. Posing as unoffending villagers, Jonah and Mendes begged passersby to help them remove their fetters.

> The people heartily cursed the Nana and the sepoys for all they
> had done, and pointed out to us where to go; but the blacksmiths
> had all shut up their shops and would not acknowledge them-
> selves to be such. The fact was, that they did not know how mat-
> ters would end; that if by any chance the Nana should again come
> in possession, he would punish them for taking off our fetters;
> therefore, to pass it off, each would point out to his neighbour,
> who in his turn would direct us into another street.

Bleeding now from his shins and ankles and thoroughly exhausted, Mendes declared he could go no farther. But Jonah, Kuloo,
and Kuloo's brother continued down the road to the tank where
Jonah had first been captured. They retraced his escape route back to
the ruined barracks, across a parade-ground sprouting grass from the
weeks of rain.

The sight of the Entrenchment in the first dim light of morning reduced Jonah to tears as his companions continued on to investigate
an overturned cart. He gazed at the scorched barracks and the
picked-over litter in the cratered yard and his infant daughter's grave
in a trench now filled with rainwater. What had become of the rest
of his family? Unaware of what had just transpired only half a mile
from his cell, he still clung to the hope that they might be safe at the
Bibighar.

Drying his tears, Jonah left the Entrenchment and had begun
walking painfully toward his companions with his chains in his
hands when he heard someone calling to him from several hundred
yards away. "Stop you, prisoner—stop! Where are you running?"

Jonah glanced back and saw a Moslem "holding a sword in his
hand, making towards me, with long strides," like a specter from
Jonah's capture over three weeks before. Jonah walked as fast as he
could in his bloody fetters, but the Moslem broke into a run and
began to gain on him, "bawling away all the time as loud as possible,
and threatening to cut off my head the moment he overtook me."

Jonah shouted to his companions, and they came running to his
assistance armed with clubs. Why was the Moslem bothering this
poor shackled villager? they asked. Why was he stopping him from
returning to his village?

The Moslem halted. "What village?" he demanded to know.

Kuloo and his brother faltered, but Jonah managed to blurt the
name of a local settlement and kept walking away. Then why, called

out the Moslem, was Jonah heading toward the burned-out Field Artillery Hospital when the village was more to the right?

Jonah kept walking.

The swordsman turned to Kuloo. "Tell him not to go in the direction he is proceeding," he said, "for the Nana has caused a strong force to lie in wait in a ditch not far from hence, with a view to surprise the Europeans when they march in this morning. Some four thousand troops," he said, "are now coming down from the magazine with heavy guns, and a desperate battle will be fought presently."

The Moslem probably believed this, having been told as much by Nana's retreating troops. Jonah pressed on, but halted between the 56th and 53rd Native Infantry lines when he heard "a suppressed noise" and to his "horror perceived an immense army, as it appeared at dawn, covering the whole of the low ground in the front. . . .

"My first impulse was to get into the empty lines and hide myself," Jonah would recall, "but that would not do, for if the force really belonged to the enemy, the sepoys would naturally like to come under the shelter of the lines during the day." Standing paralyzed on the open plain, with his companions far behind him, Jonah was struck by "the regular and steady movement of the footmen.

"Can these be the rebel sepoys?" Jonah asked himself as the army began to move. "Surely they would not proceed so steadily." Just then he saw an officer remove what had appeared to be a turban and hold it at his side, and it at last dawned on him that it was not a turban but a cap and that the soldiers approaching him were not mutineers but the British. And that is when William Jonah Shepherd lurched forward in his shackles, shouting "Hurrah! Hurrah!" into the brightening sky.

✦   ✦   ✦

As Captain Ayton's detachment hurried forward, Jonah cried out "Thanks be to God, I am saved—I am saved!" and stood before them in his filthy rags and scraggly beard, feebly weeping with relief. After listening to his breathless account of "all that had happened to me, and to the European community at Cawnpore," the soldiers and officers "pitied me very much" and tried without success to pry his shackles loose with a bayonet. But they could not offer him a horse, and with his chains in his hands Jonah had to walk behind Ayton's horse and guide the detachment into a station to which both officers and men were "perfect strangers."

Jonah warned Ayton to expect an abandoned city from which fully three quarters of the population had fled, swept up in the rebels' panicked retreat. But Ayton and his men, already "quite done up" from their forced marches and terrible battles, were not prepared for the extent of the ruins they were passing.[755] Hugging the shadows of battered walls, they gazed at the charred and tumbled remains of European bungalows in compounds littered with "broken furniture and crockery [and] leaves of books" surrounded by scorched trees, their jagged branches stark against the hot morning haze.[756] To their right they passed close by the ruins of St. John's, "unroofed and dismantled," its memorial slabs and monuments destroyed.[757]

Opposite the church Jonah pointed out the "mere furrow"[758] of the Entrenchment surrounding "a couple of oblong buildings"[759] whose roofs had fallen in. "Not a square yard in either of the buildings [was] free from the scars of shot."[760] Ayton and Moorsom cantered over, alarming the adjutant birds and engorged vultures who waddled and bickered among bones[761] and "broken bottles, old shoes, pieces of chairs"[762] and rain-mottled papers blowing around the "torn and scored" trunks of shattered trees.[763] Along the echelon of mud walls that were all that remained of the unfinished barracks, Ayton's horse startled pigs feeding on little piles of human excrement,[764] stumbled over half-submerged round shot, kicked up "fragments of sepoy skeletons."[765]

They passed along a collapsed sapper's mine dug at right angles to a deep ravine now littered with snipers' leavings and regained the road near the blackened, roofless shell of the cavalry riding school.[766] Even for men who had ridden in Renaud's savage wake, the devastation was astonishing. It appeared as though everything south of the Ganges Canal had been demolished: barracks, stables, storehouses; even the doors, windows, shutters, gates had been ripped away and all the compound walls laid low.[767]

A few Indian inhabitants could be seen advancing uncertainly from the grain market at Generalgunj. Eager to demonstrate their loyalty to the British, they reported that a number of rebels had slept that night in a rest house by the canal. Ayton sent twenty-five men at double-quick march to flush them out, but as they reached the rest house they saw that perhaps two hundred rebels had already crossed the canal and were now running out of town as fast as they could.[768]

The detachment returned and fell back into step with their comrades as they crossed the canal. A bold Indian vendor obtained permission from Ayton to sell his sweetmeats to the soldiers as they tramped along, and eventually scores of peddlers rushed forward, pressing liquor, chupatties, and jars of milk into the soldiers' grimy hands.[769] A local merchant named Elahee Buksh stood by the road, handing out cheroots, and after the soldiers had filled their shrunken stomachs they happily puffed away, their grins flashing from their bearded, sunburned, and powder-blackened faces as they marched a mile through the civil station.[770]

Beyond the ruins of the telegraph office they saw several buildings still standing: the Old Cawnpore Hotel, the theatre, the Masonic Lodge, and the celebrated Assembly Rooms, where only two months before the garrison had gathered for candlelit banquets and glittering balls.[771] By now Ayton's detachment had attracted a large straggling crowd of townspeople, including Mendes who, like Jonah was still heavily shackled. As they neared the Assembly Rooms, Wheeler's principal spy, the cattle contractor Lalla Bhudree Nath, emerged from hiding and out of the soldiers' earshot conferred with Ayton and Moorsom, pointing sorrowfully toward the river.

The two officers stared for a moment and then spurred their horses rightward along the curving road. Tossing aside their cheroots, the men hurried after them, double-stepping past the commissariat office and bearing right, parallel to the river. As the sun's glare spread over heaps of dust and ashes and tottering brick, they now caught a whiff of something in the dull waft from the Ganges: a "meat-yard" odor that seemed magnified by the oppressive silence of the place.[772] Slowing now, as if passing through some enfeebling miasma, the Highlanders watched the retreating figures of Ayton and Moorsom as they galloped into the compound of Sir George Parker's large charred bungalow.

Immediately they were joined by Lieutenant Richard Charles McCrae and a detachment of Highlanders and 64th Foot coming up from the direction of the severed Bridge of Boats. A trio of Indians—servants by the look of them—flitted anxiously around the compound gate, pointing toward the Bibighar and loudly whispering, "Sahib! Sahib!" as if "they wished, yet half dreaded, that the soldiers should enter the compound."[773] By now the smell was overpowering, but Ayton and McCrae pressed on through the trampled grass, leaning forward slightly in their saddles as if against some unseen, contrary force.

Though Jonah still clung to the hope that his family might be safe inside, "a strange indescribable something hovered round the place which impressed one with awe, and the deepest melancholy," and "I could not prevail upon myself to advance."[774] Standing spellbound by the gate, he watched Ayton, Moorsom, and McCrae dismount and saw the latter heave his shoulder against the doors of the main entrance. As they swung open on their shrieking hinges, a swarm of plump flies rose like swirling cinders from the floor.[775] McCrae gasped, covered his mouth, and gaped at the dark crimson sheen that had splashed up on the walls, windows, and broken shutters. The bark of the mulsuri tree was glossy with blood, and its branches scintillated with bits of tattered linen.[776] Ladies' bonnets and broad-brimmed sun hats;[777] children's shoes, papers, long tresses of ladies' hair lay all about, and the gore trailed and smeared and spattered through the pillared rooms "as if a hundred bullocks had been killed there."[778]

McCrae tried to step backward but the blood tugged with congealed insistence at the soles of his boots. He turned away, only to find bloody handprints on the hacked walls, and the door handles tied from the inside with the strips the ladies had torn from their dresses.[779] Choking, fumbling, he staggered back out into the compound and wandered toward the gate, where Jonah stood paralyzed in his rags and fetters.[780]

Afraid that McCrae had found his family slaughtered, Jonah asked the captain if there were any bodies inside. McCrae feebly shook his head. Moorsom followed McCrae to the Bibighar's door and willed himself inside, determined to find some trace, if possible, of the Lindsay family he had visited at Cawnpore only a few months before. "I went through the rooms strewn with Bibles and prayer books, and other religious works," he would write his sister, "with torn towels and clothing, with shoes, some of little children, certainly not three inches long, and amidst all these, fearful stains and pools of innocent English blood. Each room I entered, I peered into, expecting to see their bodies, but thank God I was spared that sight."[781] At last he backed his way out of the courtyard and rushed for the gate, teetering on his boots and tracking blood through the tall grass.

A look at these mute and ashen-faced young officers erased the pained hope from their soldiers' faces as they ventured into the compound yard. One after another the Highlanders crept toward the Bibighar and stood a moment at the threshold, gazing at the bloody desolation "with wet eyes and quivering lips." Pushed forward by their crowding comrades, a few staggered into the courtyard, where the matting "oozed spongily under their tread, for it was soaked with blood. Wherever there was a depression there stood a pool of blood, slowly soddening into the matting."[782] Some said it was two inches deep in places, others that it slopped over their boots as they walked.[783] A few paused by a hook protruding from the wall. It was covered with blood, and on the wall around it were the gory foot- and handprints of a child.[784]

But where were the women and children? Joining Ayton and Jonah at the gate, McCrae managed to stammer "that the scene he saw was the most awful that eye could witness."[785] He was mistaken. For now three Highlanders were following a bloody trail through the crushed grass and brush, forty feet from the Bibighar to the tangled roots of a clump of trees, where they found Bhudree Nath covering his mouth with his shawl and leaning quizzically over the smeared lip of the well as if listening for a loved one's dying whisper.[786] Bhudree Nath put his hands together and stepped back with a shudder as the Highlanders approached and peered bloodshot over the rim into "a mass of gory confusion."[787]

"I looked down," one of Ayton's comrades later wrote, "and saw such a sight as I hope never to see again. The whole of the bodies were naked, and the limbs had been separated . . ."[788] From under this "mangled heap, with an arm or leg protruding here and there," several children's corpses stared sightlessly at the unanswering sky.[789] They seemed to be in a less advanced stage of decomposition than the others, suggesting to some who saw them that they had not expired until after the well had claimed them.[790] The rest were already putrefying, the flesh greening on their limbs and faces, the hair working loose from their skulls.[791]

One Highlander stepped aside and hurried into the bushes to vomit up the milk and sweetmeats he had just ingested. Other soldiers gathered and gazed over the bloody coping of the well and reeled back, mumbling curses, tightening their fists, and glaring with insatiable, promiscuous rage at Elahee Buksh, Bhudree Nath, and the Indian servants who stood at some distance now, wringing their hands in sorrow and fear.

◆　◆　◆

Across the river in a village called Ooghu, a pair of sallow Hindus with caste marks rode up to the stall of a peddler named Punchum and commanded him to fetch them the best quality betel leaf he could find. "Otherwise," they told him, "we'll take your head off."

Punchum found some betel leaf from another stall and asked ten pice. The two men replied that they would only pay two. When Punchum would only lower his price to eight, one of the men rose to his feet and threatened to kill the peddler with his sword.

"We showed no pity to the ladies and children we just massacred who clung to our feet," the other snarled, flourishing a bloody blade. "Why should we show any pity to you?"

As Punchum backed away a group of soldiers gathered around the two men and asked how much they had been paid for their evening's work.

Twenty-one rupees, they boasted: one for each victim.[792]

PART FOUR

♦ ♦ ♦ ♦ ♦ ♦ ♦ ♦ ♦

RUM AND REVENGE

Cawnpore: July 17, 1857

Other detachments of Havelock's force now proceeded into the city. Old Phlos himself camped across the parade-ground from the Entrenchment, in the stables of the 2nd Native Cavalry: the first shelter his men had found since they left Allahabad. Here Havelock could command the Grand Trunk Road, count his casualties, and write up his triumph at Aherwa.

As Ayton's party marched off to inspect the magazine, Jonah wondered aloud if the rebels might be lying in wait. Ayton immediately ordered his men to camp opposite Jonah's old house and sent a trusted Indian to the magazine to scout. Jonah proceeded into the city with Mendes and at long last found a blacksmith to remove his fetters, and "Oh! with what light steps I returned to join the Europeans!" But no sooner had he left the bazaar than the ground seemed to roll underfoot and there was a tremendous roar from the direction of the magazine, where "a volume of flame gushed upwards, succeeded by clouds of dense smoke and dust."[1]

Immediately Jonah guessed that the rebels had left a slow fuse burning in the powder godowns of the magazine, hoping to destroy the British as soon as they entered. Thanks to Jonah, Ayton and his men had remained on the parade-ground, where Jonah found them still gazing in astonishment at the enormous mushroom of dust that receded on the faint river breeze like a storm retreating.

✦ ✦ ✦

So far the British entry into Cawnpore had been attended by none of the retributive atrocities the townspeople had been led to expect. Now about a quarter of Cawnpore's Indian residents emerged from their homes, hailing "with joy the advent of the British," as Jonah put it, and "blessing their stars for being once more permitted to behold the European countenance."[2]

"On entering the City," wrote Miss Sutherland, "I will never forget the reception we met with from the peaceable inhabitants who congratulated one another that the Nana's reign of terror was at an end."[3] As Havelock's troops spread out through the station other fugitives from the rebels' rule now emerged from their hiding places in "remote lanes and alleys."[4] Thomas Farnon, the Eurasian telegraph clerk who had crept away from the Entrenchment; Eduard Williams, whose wife and children had been killed in the streets of Cawnpore; William Maling, who had converted to Islam, now announced themselves. Maling staggered into the road with his mother and brothers, all clothed in Indian dress. Soldiers looking through the ruins of the Free School found Mrs. Bradshaw and Mrs. Letts and their children, half-starved from the fugitive existence they had been leading since escaping from the massacre at Sati Chowra Ghat.[5] Mrs. Spiers, wife of the bandleader of the 53rd Native Infantry, turned up with her son and four daughters. Rose Greenway's widowed sister-in-law, whom the rebels had spared on account of her age, came out of hiding to learn that Rose and the rest of the family had been annihilated.[6]

Exhausted, almost faint from the stifling heat, Sherer turned his horse down Avadh Road and entered the native city,[7] where he and his assistant, Captain John Bews,[8] were greeted "by a man with a small kettle-drum" shouting, "The World is God's; the Empire, the Company's; the Sahibs are in command."[9]

Sherer and Bews dismounted at the abandoned police station and climbed to the balcony. "The rebel flag," wrote Jonah, "which was still waving at the kotwallee [police station], was thrown down, and proclamation issued throughout the city, of the arrival of the British force, calling upon the inhabitants to settle down peaceably and to render every assistance to the Europeans with regard to supplies, &c."[10] Within a few minutes the street below was filled with supplicants, many of them Bengali babus who, having managed to elude Nana Sahib's jullads, now desperately feared that they might be mistaken by the British soldiers for rebels. Sherer and Bews assured them that, "as far as we knew, no indiscriminate punishment was at all likely to be inflicted; and told them the best way of showing their loyalty would be to offer their services for useful work." But the babus had heard of the slaughter at Allahabad and Benares, and one of them produced some "improvised paper, an inkstand, and a table" and began to write the first of series of placards he intended to post on his brethren's houses: *"This house belongs to one* (Mukerji), *a very loyal subject. Please not to molest."*

As Sherer was signing these "talismans" against British wrath, he enlisted "a rather energetic Baboo" who now led them out of the native city to Nur Mahomed's hotel, whose proprietor had just bid Nana Sahib and his retinue farewell and now equably welcomed the British.[11] Sherer was shown to Nana Sahib's abandoned suite, including a bedroom that had been fitted with clay stoves for the preparation of the Brahmin's food.[12]

From the Old Cawnpore Hotel it was a short ride to the Bibighar. Partaking of the milk and sweetmeats Indians kept thrusting at him as he rode through the streets, Sherer had been gratified up to now by the reception he had received and amused by the babus' anxiety. But the crowd fell back and the very air seemed to change as he and Bews rode across the hotel compound and passed through a gate into the Bibighar. The scene "was so unspeakably horrible," recalled Sherer, "that it would be quite wrong in any sort of way to increase the distressing circumstances which really existed. . . . The whole of the pavement was caked with blood," and there were "long tresses of hair glued with clotted blood to the ground."[13] Sherer marveled at how few things were littered about the Bibighar, but he had been preceded by Ayton and Moorsom and his men, many of whom had already taken relics with them.[14] Nevertheless, there were still "torn towels and clothing" scattered about the floor "with shoes, some of little children, certainly not three inches long," and "collars, combs, . . . caps, and little round hats,[15] . . . and these large hats now worn by ladies."[16]

Sherer and the pallid Bews staggered out of the Bibighar and forced themselves to look at the "map of naked arms, legs and gashed trunks" in the nearby well.[17] As he stood gaping at the women's and children's remains, Sherer "heard a low cry of pain," and turned to find Bews doubled over "with a sickening anguish."[18]

Sherer climbed back onto his horse and sought out Havelock in the cavalry lines, where the old general sat in the shade of an umbrella tallying up his casualties from the previous evening's battle.[19] Sherer reported that the well "would soon become very pestilential," and asked if something might be done.

"Please," agreed Havelock, "at once procure coolies, and have it filled up with earth."[20]

Riding back with an escort of volunteer horsemen, Sherer scrawled an exhausted note to Cecil Beadon, the Home Secretary in Calcutta. "What with the row, heat and flies," he wrote, "I really do not know what I am writing.

> But I must tell you an awful thing. The night the news of our crossing the Pundoo reached this place—the Nana had all the ladies whom he had saved from the former massacre—murdered in cold blood. May God in his mercy, my dear Beadon, prevent me from ever intruding again [on] such a sight as I have seen this day. . . . My nerves are so deadened with horror—that I write this quite calmly—it is better you should hear the worst—I am going this very moment to fill the well up—and cover its mouth with a mound. Let us mention the subject no more—silence and prayer alone seem fitting.[21]

The well was later filled "in a rough manner," Sherer later wrote, "and not a moment too soon, for the effluvia was becoming excessively bad."[22]

✦ ✦ ✦

"Vaunting, eager, maddened," officers and soldiers staggered through the Bibighar's dismal, fetid rooms all morning, searching for relics among the bloody refuse that littered the coagulated floor.[23] There were "many little bits of paper carefully folded up" inscribed with "'dear Willy's hair,' 'Ned's hair with love,' and such like endearing epithets";[24] there was also a spatula, a manicure set, and "bottles and water vessels, broken and unbroken, were to be seen strewn all about the place, dotted thickly with blood."[25]

Jonah Shepherd searched the walls for some message from his family among "the marks of bullets and sword cuts on the walls and pillars in the room and on the door posts" into which "long tresses of ladies' hair had been carried by the edge of the weapon and there hung." But the sweepers had wiped away all but a few words "scrawled over here and there with charcoal, or the fragment of a broken earthen vessel, such as, 'Arrived here on the 4th July, Saturday,' then below it . . . —'5th, Sunday'; and so on, up to the 14th July."[26]

In the courtyard, near the mulsuri tree, an officer picked up a piece of paper sprinkled with blood. It was Caroline Lindsay's chronology of the death of her family that accounted for the terrible fate of everyone but herself and her little sister. Other chronologies turned up, as though the women had decided among themselves to write their histories and hoped that at least one of them might be found. Elsewhere Mrs. Blair's note turned up with its truncated history. "27th June," it said. "Went to the boats. 29th. Taken out of boats. 30th—Taken to Sevadah Kothi, fatal day."[27] Another note was found among the heaps of bloody clothes that had apparently been appended to a map.

> We went into the barracks on the 21st of May. The 2d Cavalry broke out at two o'clock in the morning of the 5th of June, and the other regiments went off during the day. The next morning, while we were sitting out in front of the barracks, a twenty-four-pounder came flying along, and hit the intrenchment, and from that day the firing went on till the 25th of June, when the enemy sent a treaty, which the General agreed to, and on the 27th we all left the B (intrenched barracks) to go down to A (Allahabad) in boats; when we got to the river, the enemy began firing on us, killed all the gentlemen, and some of the ladies; set fire to the boats, some were drowned, and we were taken prisoners, and taken to a house, put all in one room.[28]

Many officers made bloody vows.[29]

> One officer we met coming out, with a small article of female dress dabbled with blood in his hand.
> "I have spared many a man in fight," he said; "but I will never spare another. I shall carry this with me in my holsters, and whenever I am inclined for mercy, the sight of it, and the recollection of this house, will be sufficient to incite me to revenge."[30]

The disappointment of arriving too late to save the women and children "cast a deep gloom over the conquerors. In every face sorrow and sadness was depicted."[31] "Stalwart, bearded men, stern soldiers of the ranks," wrote another officer, "have been seen coming out of that house perfectly unmanned, utterly unable to repress their emotions. From them there will be no mercy for these villainous assassins."[32]

Major Bingham of the Ross-shire Buffs looked down at the bodies lying "in heaps" and "very much [feared] that there are some of my friends included in this most *atrocious fiendish* of murders. A Mrs. Lindsay her daughters and son who was in the 1st Regiment Bengal

Native Infantry. I trust in God it may not be the case," added the major, "but I much fear it is."[33]

It is perhaps impossible for a twentieth-century sensibility to conceive of the effect that the sight of the ladies' naked and mutilated bodies had on even these most hardened British soldiers of nineteenth-century India. Anglo-Indian men entertained Arthurian notions of the inherent purity and virtuousness of English womanhood. Despite the inevitable hardships of life in India, few women outside of the royal families of Europe had been as sheltered as the memsahibs of John Company. The paramount mission of men like Willie Halliday and Charles Hillersdon had not been to promote commerce or administer justice or reform Indian society but to make India—especially its cantonments and thoroughfares—safe for their womenfolk. And at no place more than at Cawnpore had Anglo-Indian manhood so utterly failed to accomplish this fundamental mission. The soldiers' grief and outrage thus mingled with an intolerable sense of humiliation and guilt.

Though almost twice as many children as women died in the Bibighar massacre, it would always be known as the Massacre of the Ladies, or the Slaughter in the House of the Ladies, for though the children's corpses were hard enough to bear, the nakedness of the ladies' corpses was simply intolerable: seemingly incontrovertible evidence that their women had been raped.[34] Anglo-Indian men had always darkly suspected Indian males of sexual depravity. The image of fair English women in the clutches of dark sensualists trespassed dangerously into untraveled regions of the Victorian imagination, played on their own apprehensions of sexual inadequacy and on the bedeviling irreconcilability of animal lust and Victorian virtue.

Those who suggested that the stripping and mutilation of the women and children had been almost entirely postmortem were attacked as apologists for inhuman fiends. And anyone who dared to suggest that most Indian men found British women repulsive were indignantly shouted down as naive, perverse, and—to the extent to which Anglo-Indian men prized their ladies as possessions—insulting as well. British men, after all, had not found Indian women repulsive; certainly not in John Company's palmier days.

Officers and men searched the Bibighar for inscriptions that might prove their worst fears, and, finding none, invented their own:[35] "Your wives and children are here in misery," a soldier scrawled in theatrical letters, "and at the disposal of savages."[36] "We are at the mercy of savages," read another, "who have ravished young and old."[37] "My child! My child!" "Think of us." "Avenge us!"[38] "Country men and women, remember the 15th of July, 1857. Your wives and families are here in misery and at the disposal of savages, who has [sic] *ravished* both young and old, and then killed. Oh, oh! my child, my child. Countrymen, revenge it."[39] And in several places, daubed in broad and clumsy strokes, "Remember Cawnpore!"[40] which would become the British battle cry for the remainder of the rebellion.[41]

Soldiers stoked each other's flames with stories of finding "at the corners of streets, and in all parts of the town, . . . English ladies, stripped stark-naked, lying on their backs, fastened by the arms and legs,"[42] and the corpses of children who had been "pinned to the wall with bayonets . . . in the presence of the mothers who were compelled to look on . . . in a state of nudity."[43] The effluvia seemed to coil outward from the Bibighar's well like a poisonous fog, trailing after the soldiers as they erected their two-poled tents and explored the ruined station.

✦ ✦ ✦

Havelock's medical officers established a surgery in the same room in Savada House where the women and children had first been incarcerated. All day long the sick and wounded arrived in bullock carts, among them the bloody-minded Major Sydenham Renaud, who would lose his shattered leg to a surgeon's saw and die soon afterward of sepsis.[44]

But by late morning discipline had almost entirely broken down. Havelock, convinced by now that he had led his men too far too fast "in a fruitless attempt to accomplish what was beyond their strength," was too despondent to keep his men in check, and after touring the Bibighar his officers were not inclined to control them either.[45] When their men "began to break bounds"[46] and stumbled upon the "toddy godowns" that Azimullah had left untapped behind the cattle yard, there was no one to stop them from filling first their stomachs and then their canteens with champagne, beer, and rum.[47]

The bogus inscriptions and atrocious fictions acted like torches on the murderous blend of outrage and alcohol that coursed through the soldiers' veins, and in bands of a dozen or more they raged off into the native quarter to descend, wrote Archibald Forbes, "into intoxication, plunder and rapine."[48] What acts they committed as they rampaged through Cawnpore's Indian homes and shops that first night remains obscured by the protective veil of imperial piety.[49]

"The scenes which followed," wrote even the iconoclastic Montgomery Martin, "may well be passed over in silence."[50] But Kaye at least indicated that with enough provocation, British soldiers could be roused to such "passions" that they spared "neither sex nor age, yielded to no pity, and abstained from no crime." The provocations of Sati Chowra and the Bibighar, Kaye continued, were almost unprecedented in the history of British arms, and were "enough to madden even sober-minded men, and to stimulate them to acts of fearful retribution." Thus it was perhaps inevitable that "the first days of the re-occupation of Cawnpore [were] stained by excesses on the part of our soldiery—far greater than any which are recorded against them."[51] What emerges from between these lines is an Old Testament night of an eye for an eye: murder repaid with murder and suspected rape with rape.[52]

As soldiers of the 64th and Highlanders of the 78th marauded drunkenly through the city, the opportunistic Sikhs, let loose in the homeland of the Oudh men who had only a decade before helped the British wrench the Punjab from them, stormed into the bazaars to loot the shops of the Indian merchants who, only hours before, had pressed refreshments upon Ayton and Sherer and the Highlanders.[53]

Two Indians hanged by the British

✦ ✦ ✦

The first actual mutineers the British captured at Cawnpore were a couple of soldiers who had been wounded too severely during the siege of the Entrenchments to make their escape. When asked their identity, they answered proudly that they were "fighting men," which so enraged the soldiers that they had to be restrained by their officers from killing them. Eventually the two mutineers—one a sowar and the other a corporal in the 53rd Native Infantry—were "placed out in the sun as a preliminary punishment." But even then these two brave men would "occasionally console themselves by uttering sundry abuse and curses upon the English, and by saying that the *kaffirs* would yet be destroyed. On such occasions," wrote Jonah, "the Europeans would reward them with a kick or so for their pains."[54]

Even a beating before hanging was not enough to assuage British wrath, however. The deliberate and elaborate defilement that would soon become the stock-in-trade of British commissioners and provost-marshals may have been inspired by the infuriatingly noble conduct of the first rebel prisoners—most of them wounded—that the soldiers dragged in from the battlefield at Aherwa. Almost as soon as these few survivors of the soldiers' summary battlefield executions arrived in the camp at Savada House, they were tried collectively and perfunctorily by drumhead court-martial and immediately hanged. Officers and soldiers hungry for revenge waited eagerly to see their captives plead and grovel as they were dragged to the hastily erected gallows.[55] But in this they were to be thoroughly disappointed. Not one of the rebel prisoners attempted to appeal their verdict or struggle with their executioners. In fact "the demeanor of many of these wretches when in the unrelenting grasp of the provost-marshal," conceded the jingoist historian Charles Ball, "has been described as worthy of men suffering in a righteous cause."[56]

The Duke of Wellington had observed long before that in comparison with their European counterparts, Indians were strangely impervious to the prospect of execution. "There is a contempt of death in the natives, high and low," he wrote, "occasioned by some of the tenets of the religion of both sects, which makes the punishment a joke, and I may say an honour, instead of what it is in our country."[57] This stoicism infuriated Havelock's men, who had completely invested themselves in the belief that Indian men were degenerate cowards. So they ascribed their composure not to bravery, exactly, but to their wayward religious conviction that by dying for their faiths the Moslems among them were assured of entering paradise, the Hindus of embarking on an eternity of felicitous incarnations.

Sending the rebels to paradise was not the column's idea of revenge, however, so the hanging parties devised means of defiling and degrading them before death. Many captives were not permitted to call witnesses or testify in their own defense; some were even gagged. It probably would not have mattered if they had spoken up, for few of Havelock's men could have understood them anyway. Their judges were reduced to seeing if the charge fit the accused's demeanor, and in the passion of the hour it almost always did.

Condemned prisoners were often flogged, a spectacle appreciated especially by the soldiers of Her Majesty's regiments who, unlike the sepoys, were still subject to floggings themselves. Soldiers then forced beef down the throats of the Hindu captives, pork down the throats of the Moslems. Prisoners were daubed with animal fat; some Moslems were even sewn into pig skins before hanging. Sweepers were employed to execute Brahmin prisoners, many of whom were first smeared with cow's blood.[58]

The executions themselves were often ad hoc, carried out by untrained bands of soldiers who maliciously mistied nooses or employed inadequate rope so that captives might strangle slowly or have to be dropped repeatedly.[59] Nothing usually prevented soldiers from stepping forward as a bound prisoner passed and delivering a blow or two with his musket stock. The soldiers even made a point of informing their victims that all Moslems would be incinerated and all Hindus buried "to their certain damnation" in graves that they themselves were sometimes forced to dig.[60]

All this was supposed to break the rebels' faith in their own redemption. Yet the majority of them, if they were conscious by the time they had passed through the gantlets of ham-fisted soldiers, still met their deaths with dignity and defiance. "I have put my head into the mortar," ran an old Hindu saw. "It is useless to dread the sound of the pestle."[61] Nevertheless, for Indian prisoners and onlookers alike these measures constituted a grotesque, nightmarish affirmation of the very fears that had incited them to rebellion in the first place: that the Feringhees intended to destroy their caste and their religions.[62]

On the morning of July 18, General Havelock declared that his soldiers' drunken marauding had exceeded "the disorders which supervened on the short-lived triumph of the miscreant Nana Sahib." What had become of his vaunted "Saints"? As horrified by his soldiers' drunkenness as by their other excesses, the old Baptist ordered that every drop of liquor be bought up and carted off to a remote location with a small and preferably teetotaling guard; otherwise, as he explained to Patrick Grant, "it would require one-half my force to keep it from being drunk by the other half, and I should scarcely have a sober soldier in camp."

To keep his men out of the native quarter, Havelock moved his camp up to the ruined premises of poor Reverend Haycock's mission station, and warned that his provost-marshal would "hang up, in their uniform, all British soldiers that plunder. This shall not be an idle threat," he added. "Commanding officers have received the most distinct warnings on the subject."[63] But it was an idle threat. "We have had one European hung," wrote a soldier, "but they are very loth to do anything to the Europeans."[64] Havelock could not afford to hang his soldiers, the provost-marshal was already too busy stringing up natives, and small parties of soldiers continued to sneak off into the city to maraud.

In the meantime, the news of the massacres at Cawnpore seeped down the country like a stain. Henry Fane had found refuge in the riverside house of the magistrate of Mirzapore, almost two hundred miles downriver from Cawnpore. For several days Fane watched as bodies from the Sati Chowra slaughter came drifting down the Ganges. "In some cases 6 or 8 soldiers were tied together with their accoutrements on," he wrote, "but the heads cut off. One officer's body had nothing on it but a cloth tied round with the hands fastened inside the cloth—he had apparently been stripped, his hands tied down to his side, and shot—there appeared to be a bullet mark near the mouth." Contemplating these bloated corpses as they drifted on to Calcutta, Fane feared that if Havelock succeeded in dislodging the rebels from Lucknow they would simply descend on the smaller stations like Mirzapore. Would it not be wiser, he anxiously suggested, if Havelock were to leave them alone until he had amassed a force sufficient to assure the rebels' annihilation?[65]

STRANGE LAW

Neill: July 15–September 25, 1857

At noon on the seventeenth, Captain Spurgin and the steamer *Burrampoota* caught up with Havelock's column at Cawnpore, towing five native craft filled with Fusiliers, pensioned gunners, and two nine-pounders.[66] The sight of the steamer astonished Havelock. "Well," he told Spurgin," "I never expected to see *you* again!"[67] It also stunned the townspeople who had been led to believe that Havelock's little column was all that remained of the Company's British troops and that Calcutta—indeed, England itself—could not spare another man. Spurgin's mission had been to reach Cawnpore in advance and rescue the women and children.[68] But the Captain had spent a lot of his energies on firing at the landlords, friendly and unfriendly, who lived along the river.[69]

Ever since entering Cawnpore, Old Phlos had assumed that Nana would regroup and counterattack with five thousand troops. But late in the night of the eighteenth, he received a note from Narain Rao, son of Baji Rao's chief adviser, reporting that the "Bithoor Rajah had destroyed himself in despair, that the Sepoys had all fled towards Delhi, and that Bithoor was evacuated."[70] On Sunday, July 19, Havelock sent a Major Stephenson with a small force of Sikhs and Madras Fusiliers up the road to Bithur.[71]

They marched into a ghost town. On the night of July 16, after his flight from Aherwa and while his heralds were still proclaiming victory through the streets of Cawnpore, Nana Sahib had rushed past Cawnpore up the Grand Trunk Road and turned onto Bithur Road to secure his family and treasure at Saturday House.[72] Nana's retreat had been almost as hasty as his father's. Even after his four defeats he still had an army of "about 12,000 or 13,000 men, but [they were] without a leader, and each one followed his own course."[73] Many of the men Nana left behind at Cawnpore had no idea where he had gone.[74] Declaring that "there was no safety for them on earth,"[75] the retreating mutineers gathered up their families[76] and advised passersby "to flee too, if they did not want to be killed or deprived of their religion."[77] They said "it was quite in vain" to fight the British because their Enfields "carried so far that [the rebels] were killed before they heard the noise of the discharge."[78] A few mutineers, despairing of outrunning the British column and terrorized by Neill's and Renaud's depredations, apparently killed their wives and children rather than leave them at the mercy of Havelock's troops.[79]

When the mutineers tried to cross the Ganges into Oudh, the ferrymen charged them the extortionate rate of a rupee a head. Once across, many of Nana's soldiers "pitched away their muskets, coats, pantaloons, &c., and dispersed in different directions," loaded down with gold Moghul coins they had purchased at inflated prices from the bankers of Cawnpore.[80]

The mutineers who did follow Nana to Bithur spent the seventeenth excoriating him and his advisers and demanding their pay.[81] Retreating into the great rooms of Saturday House, Nana ordered his most cumbersome treasures secretly dumped into one of the palace wells and entrusted tens of thousands of rupees' worth of his family's jewels to the safekeeping of his concubine Adla.[82] Nana's elephants, hackeries, and property were loaded onto boats and ferried across into Oudh, but he released all his other animals, including the largest of the wild beasts in his vast menagerie.[83]

All day long Nana's agents spread the news that Nana intended to kill himself and his family by sailing his barge into the middle of the Ganges and ripping a plank from its hull. His followers were to watch for his barge's lamps to go out, the signal for his Brahmins to go into mourning. Late on the night of July 17, the Peshwa rode down to the ghat and with Bala Rao, Rao Sahib and the women of his family boarded his barge, bidding farewell to the panicked townspeople who stood along the ghats. To the beat of kettle drums and the whine of horns, Nana's boat pushed off into the stream and everyone watched as the lamplight on his boat receded into the gloom and flickered off.

The Brahmins loudly bewailed the death of their patron and the end of their world.[84] But their patron was dry as a bone and quite safe, having merely tossed his lamp overboard and proceeded to the far bank of the Ganges to spend the remainder of the night in a little pavilion he had ordered erected some weeks before.[85] For Nana Sahib was no penitent but Peshwa Bahadur, leader of the Mahratta nation, whose defeats were always illusory. Had not his own father eluded the British for seven months? Had not Sivaji himself lost battles and abandoned his capital, only to return to the field with a vengeance? Nana Sahib was not retreating but slipping the bonds of his dynasty's exile.

✦ ✦ ✦

On the nineteenth, Major Stephenson's troops raged through the littered rooms of Saturday House, searching for liquor, breaking the
mirrored walls of Nana's dingy zenana, destroying his "foot stools,
musical-boxes, and elegantly bound books, writing-desks, work-
boxes, plated dishes, sugar-basins, and teapots."[86] A lieutenant of the
Fusiliers was astonished to find Nana's walls "were decorated with
pictures of young children, English beauties and our noble Queen."
Here an officer carried off a saddle, there a soldier tucked Nana's
betel box[87] into his pouch before setting a part of the palace ablaze
and apparently burning to death at least one serving girl who had
fled to the roof.[88]

In a remote room of the old Residency, they made a horrifying discovery. When Nana left Bithur he had dragged Baji Rao's widows
along with him, thus removing the sole protectors of Joseph Carter's
young widow and her month-old daughter. Her sowar guards killed
these last of Nana's prisoners in Nana's name; Havelock's grimy
knights had again arrived too late to the rescue.[89]

The Sikhs and Fusiliers descended on the defenseless town, shooting any Indian they caught on the streets.[90] After removing eighteen
cannon and all the powder his men could carry, Stephenson deto-
nated Nana's arsenal, and they all marched back to Cawnpore with
their arms filled with plunder. "As we returned," a lieutenant wrote
with grim satisfaction, "we saw the flames spreading in all directions."[91]

That they did not burn down the entire town that day may have
been due to the tremulous intercession of Narain Rao. Fluent in English, he informed Major Stephenson that he had been imprisoned
by Nana Sahib and suggested that nothing would be gained by killing
the residents of the town now that Nana had made his escape.[92]
Though the British suspected Narain Rao of having assisted in Nana's
escape, he was now left in charge of Nana's establishment at Bithur
and eventually rewarded for his services with a substantial estate.

✦ ✦ ✦

By this time news of the Bibighar had raised the hysteria at Calcutta
to a fevered pitch. When Canning heard of the massacre he stayed
up all night, walking the halls of Government House, tormented by
the thought that he might have saved them.[93] Out in the city men
dispensed poison and pistols to their womenfolk in case the city peo-

ple rose up, and the few women who dared to venture out now saw Nana Sahibs lurking in every salaaming noble and shopkeeper.

The news of Wheeler's capitulation was greeted with astonishment and contempt. "Had it not been for the ladies," wrote a Calcutta trader and volunteer named Arthur Peppin,

> the general exclamation on receipt of the news would have been "serve them right." British soldiers, however few in numbers, however disheartened, however weakened, surrender to nigger rebels, to brutes who have committed the most atrocious cruelties on their countrymen!!! . . . It is to be hoped that [Wheeler] did not live to see the disgrace brought upon the troops he commanded. The absurd idea too, to believe in a nigger's word! . . . The bad effects of this will be incalculable; we are no longer invincible. . . . Another Cawnpore, and it is my firm belief that we shall be driven into the sea or massacred, and then India will be lost to the English.[94]

On July 15, Colonel James Neill received a letter from Calcutta announcing his promotion to brigadier general. Henry Havelock's "health was not strong," it said, and Neill was to make haste to Cawnpore to take command, if necessary, of the relief of Lucknow. Elated, Neill eagerly set off the next morning for Cawnpore. Over the next four days Neill's officers had to hold their handkerchiefs to their noses as they passed the half-eaten corpses hanging from the wayside trees and the rebel dead that still littered the battleground at Fatehpur, Aong, Pandu Nadi, and Aherwa. But the stench "appeared to have no effect upon the general," who could think of nothing but leading his Fusiliers into glorious battle against massed formations of rebel troops and liberating the garrison at Lucknow.[95]

But when he reached Cawnpore he was disappointed to be greeted by a vigorous and peremptory General Havelock. "Now General Neill," the old man told him, "let us understand each other. You have no power or authority whilst I am here, and you are not to issue a single order."[96] But, as Neill confided to his diary, Havelock did not appear to exercise much power or authority either: most of the old man's orders were still going "unattended." Havelock's encampment had turned into a swamp, littered now with plunder from the city. Hundreds of inebriated soldiers passed out in the rain or caroused about the station, firing off their pistols and guns. "There is a great plundering going on by the troops," Neill wrote.

Most disgraceful—And on the part of Commandants, more particularly the Sixty-Fourth, a disinclination to prevent their men misconducting themselves. All have taken to plundering, and the example set by officers has been very bad indeed; the plundering of the merchants and shopkeepers in the city by bands of soldiers and Sikhs has been most outrageous, and there has been no check to it. I should have adopted very decided steps with all these regiments, and this force at first, but this has been neglected.

". . . The want of attention to orders by Commandants of Corps and others is disgraceful," Neill concluded, as if preparing a brief against his elderly commander, "and I see it plainly. I suppose no force ever marched with a set of so inferior commanding officers."[97]

Havelock announced his intention to ferry a small force across the Ganges and fight his way to Lucknow, leaving Neill with three hundred men to hold down the fort at Cawnpore. The fort in question had been under construction for only the past twenty-four hours, but an army of Indian coolies, supplemented by disarmed Irregular cavalrymen and overseen, for the time being, by liberated Eurasian fugitives, had made remarkable progress. It was already more substantial than Wheeler's Entrenchment; in the wet weather coolies could dig deeper and build walls thicker and higher and ram them into "a solid mass, and of a thickness which no cannon shot could ever penetrate."[98] The fortification stood just north of the canal, on a rise in the Ganges cliff adjacent to the site of the severed Bridge of Boats, demarcated now only by a road and the grass that swirled to the turbulent surface of the Ganges from a string of submerged islands.[99]

✦ ✦ ✦

By July 17 Lucknow was threatening to become an even graver disaster than Cawnpore. Chief Commissioner Lawrence had been sitting on a powder keg with seven hundred soldiers and a garrison that included over 220 women, 230 children, and 120 sick and wounded. Thousands of native soldiers and constables roamed the neighborhood, and thousands more poured in from other stations. Perhaps no other population in India was so disaffected: outraged first by annexation and then by the Company's overassessments and "Summary Settlement" that had resulted in the systematic dispossession of vast numbers of landholders.[100]

Guided by "firmness, promptness, conciliation, prudence," and betraying "no bustle, no appearance of alarm, still less of panic," Lawrence had managed to keep an all-out revolt in abeyance even after the insurgents' first stab at rebellion on May 30.[101] But, exactly a month later, the powder keg finally exploded when seven thousand rebels, exhilarated by the fall of Cawnpore, marched on the city. Against his better judgment, an ailing Lawrence agreed to a plan proposed by his financial commissioner, Martin Gubbins, to ride out to meet the insurgents with a mixed band of Indian and British troops. In the battle that followed, many of Lawrence's native soldiers deserted, and some of his hard-drinking British troops, hung over and breakfastless, collapsed from the heat. Cutting his losses at two hundred men and several guns, Lawrence had blown up his arsenal and fled back into a complex of buildings in the civil station that he had been fortifying since the middle of May.

Lawrence's preparations had been prescient and ingenious, and even after the rout on June 30 he still had twenty-five guns at his disposal, but "the enemy are very bold," he wrote that evening, "and the Europeans very low."[102] His position was threatened on three sides by towering native buildings from which the rebels poured a devastating fire. On the first day of the siege a rebel shell had exploded in Lawrence's room, but, unharmed, he laughed it off as a lucky shot: a rebel gunner could never hit the same place twice. For once in his life, Lawrence was mistaken. The next day, July 2, a second shell exploded in his room, shattering his thigh.

It took Wheeler's old friend, and perhaps the most brilliant and durably sympathetic of all the Company's men, two days to bleed to death, and the specter of Cawnpore haunted him to the last. "No surrender," he commanded his grieving subordinates as they gathered around his bed. "Let every man die at his post; but *never* make terms. God help the women and children."[103]

The siege of Lucknow was almost as terrible as the bombardment at Cawnpore. Indeed, had it not been for Lawrence's preparations it might have been even worse, for the rebels, spurred on by the very able Begum Hazrat Mahal and the Maulvies of Fyzabad, fired from protected positions in greater numbers and at much closer range. Unlike Wheeler's garrison, however, the Europeans at Lucknow had a two-and-a-half-months' supply of food, plenty of water, some substantial protection from enemy fire, some degree of privacy in the various buildings, and a churchyard in which to bury their loved one's shrouded corpses. Some of Lucknow's upper crust—notably

Martin Gubbins—had prepared for the siege with stocks of liquor and tinned delicacies that they apparently reserved for themselves and their friends. As the rebel fire roared and whined about them, a few families actually ate at table together, led the children in rounds, bid extravagantly at auctions on the effects of the dead, including Lawrence's victuals. Nevertheless, by the twentieth of July their situation was desperate, and after the massacre of Wheeler's garrison and the death of Lawrence, Calcutta held out little hope for the garrison's survival.

✦ ✦ ✦

In his order of thanks, Havelock had reminded his soldiers that not only was Lucknow still imperiled but "Agra is besieged" and Delhi was "still the focus of mutiny and rebellion." Great as his warriors' efforts had been thus far, they would all have to make more "great sacrifices" to obtain "great results. Three cities have to be saved, two strong places to be disblockaded. Your General is confident that he can accomplish all these things, and restore this part of India to tranquillity, if you only second him with your efforts, and if your discipline is equal to your valour."[104]

But the death of Lawrence had taken some of the starch out of Havelock, who had dreamed of liberating his old friend. By July 28 his expeditionary force consisted of only 1,200 British troops, three hundred Sikhs, no tents, and ten "imperfectly equipped and manned" guns. The difficulties of relieving the garrison were "hourly multiplying" against him.[105] Exhausted by their long, hot marches and bloody battles and dissipated after their week of drink and rapine, his men were sickening with cholera and heat stroke. Forty miles of hostile rebel territory lay ahead of them, and the sustaining hope they had once entertained of saving the women and children had been displaced by a brooding, retributive rage.

It took Spurgin and his steamer four days to ferry Havelock's force across the swollen Ganges.[106] On the morning of July 29, the old general treated his troops to another of his high-pitched perorations, congratulating them for "so nobly volunteering to assist your country in the hour of great peril," at which point one of the pensioned artillerymen who had come to Cawnpore on Spurgin's steamer stepped forward to beg the general's pardon, but "we ain't no volunteers at all," he said. "We only come 'cos we was forced to come!"[107]

By the end of July, many of the mutineers who fled Cawnpore had joined with the Oudh rebels to fortify a string of villages along the

Lucknow Road, the first of which, Unao, lay only three miles from Havelock's landing place.[108] On July 29, Havelock's force charged through Unao's flaming streets and gardens, shouting, "Remember Cawnpore!" and fighting hand-to-hand with some of the most ferocious sepoys of Oudh, many of whom died at their posts, shooting through loopholes even as their clothes caught fire. When the rest of the rebels fell back to high ground beyond the village, Havelock's men waded waist-deep through fields inundated with rainwater, concentrating their fire on the road, down which the rebels advanced "in solid bulk, and with great show of resolution."[109] Maude's guns eventually drove the sepoys back with point-blank charges of grape, but the rebel gunners stood their ground, falling in heaps by the smoking muzzles of their cannon.

Havelock's men had fought ferociously so far, but at a walled village called Bashiratgunj, six miles further up the road, the 64th held back from attacking the fleeing rebels. Havelock accused them of fighting "as if the cholera had seized your minds as well as your bodies." But he could hardly blame them. A sixth of his men had been killed, wounded, or utterly debilitated by cholera, sunstroke, and exhaustion.

The mathematical improbability of ever reaching Lucknow began to stare Havelock in the face. He had only gone a third of the distance to Lucknow and could expect even stiffer resistance as he proceeded. As his men hanged captured rebels and local village men from the roadside trees, Havelock, perhaps out of simple frustration, now asked Maude, his artillery commander, if he would execute two captured sepoys by blowing them from guns. Maude said he would try. The British would later defend this mode of execution as relatively painless and trace its origins to the Indians themselves. But like such defilements as forcing pork down the throats of Mahomedan captives, execution by cannon was intended to strike a special terror in the hearts of the rebels, for among Hindus "the dissipation of the mortal remains of a man thus executed would necessarily render its importance impossible, and so expose the disembodied ghost, in their opinion, to a wandering, indefinite condition in the other world, which they regard as dreadful . . ."[110]

Nevertheless, reported one of Havelock's officers, "the fortitude with which [the sepoys] met this punishment was remarkable, and worthy of a better cause." Maude recounted how he "moved one of my guns on to the causeway, unlimbered it, and brought it into " 'action front.' "

The first man led out was a fine-looking young sepoy, with good features, and a bold, resolute expression. He begged that he might not be bound, but this could not be allowed, and I had his wrists tied tightly each to the upper part of a wheel of the gun. Then I depressed the muzzle, until it pointed to the pit of his stomach, just below the sternum. . . . The young sepoy looked undauntingly at us during the whole process of pinioning; indeed he never flinched for a moment. Then I ordered the port-fire to be lighted, and gave the word 'Fire!' There was a considerable recoil from the gun, and a thick cloud of smoke hung over us. As this cleared away, we saw two legs lying in front of the gun, but no other side of what had, just before, been a human being and a brave man. At this moment, perhaps from six to eight seconds after the explosion, down fell the man's head among us, slightly blackened, but otherwise scarcely changed. It must have gone straight up into the air, probably about 200 feet.[111]

Another officer remembered the "peculiar muffled report" of the gun, and how a "sickening effluvium tainted the atmosphere as his head was flung aloft far into the blue æther," all within sight of "two wretches who had suffered death by hanging."[112]

Even this grisly diversion could not distract Havelock from his dilemma. A rebel force was menacing him somewhere on his left, and at Dinapur, between Benares and Calcutta, a recent mutiny of Indian troops threatened to cut him off from reinforcements. There was nothing for it, he reluctantly concluded, but to retreat to his landing place and ferry his sick and wounded back to Cawnpore. The next morning his soldiers limped nine miles back to the river "in a dogged gloom."[113]

◆ ◆ ◆

The British camp was pestilential. "There was the gloom of the weather," wrote Sherer, "gloom of the news—for Delhi was not taken—gloom of death. We thought the soaking neem trees smelt of the blood of the massacres."[114] Cawnpore was "literally alive with all sorts and sizes of flies," wrote an officer, "some of them sleek and others bloated, apparently gorged with putridity, and thriving on this pestilential atmosphere, which swelters with mortality."[115]

The monsoon rains had reduced the camp to a vast muddy sea that hatched a plague of frogs.[116] Weeks of camping in the rains in tiny, double-poled tents had exacerbated the cholera that had followed the column to Cawnpore on its squelchy progress up the Grand Trunk Road. Neill installed as many men as he could in barracks, but even these became inundated by the torrential rains and "curiously enough," wrote Sherer, "we observed that several who took off shoes and stockings and paddled about got cholera."[117] During the first days of Havelock's occupation burial parties had escorted the dead to the pipers' wail of "The Flowers of the Forest."[118] Now the deaths had become so frequent that funerals were eventually conducted "in perfect silence; neither volleys were fired, nor bands played, lest the frequency of the sepulchral rites should cause a panic among the men."[119]

Neill had taken full charge at Cawnpore, imposing an unaccustomed discipline on the little remnant Havelock had left behind. He blew through the flooded camp like a crisp winter breeze, ordering sullen, drunken soldiers to their feet; confiscating their plunder; reinforcing the new entrenchment; ordering the well at the Bibighar bricked over; organizing games for the ambulatory, and doing his best by the sick.

During one of his frequent inspections Neill was greeted by a young medico anxious to show how he had sprinkled antiseptic over the hospital curtains and set cauldrons boiling to produce a "healing steam" in the middle of July. "How long have you been out?" Neill finally inquired.

"Oh, sir," said the surgeon, "I have only lately arrived."

"I thought so," replied Neill. "That accounts for your talking such damned nonsense."[120]

The men adored him. Where Havelock had been fussy, pious, and loquacious, Neill was decisive, audacious, and taciturn: a man's man and a soldier's soldier.[121] "Since I arrived here," he wrote from the ruins of Wheeler's Entrenchment, "I have been hard at work to get order re-established." He could not afford to make good on Havelock's promise to hang every plundering soldier, but he managed to rein in most of them by organizing a native police force and commanding the Indian residents of the city, on pain of death, to deposit all plundered British property into the streets. People living along the ghats dumped their loot into the river, but the next morning the narrow lanes of the native city were littered with chairs, music boxes, rugs, and other furnishings. These Neill ordered collected and stored in the vast Assembly Rooms so that "any which can be recognized" could be "handed over to the owners or put up to auction for the benefit of deceased estates, and the rest sold."[122]

He sent a detachment to Bithur to rescue Narain Rao's daughters from an advancing body of rebels, sent a steamer off to harass Nana Sahib, paraded his men to build up the confidence of the townspeople, visited the bazaars every morning to reassure the shopkeepers that they would not be plundered if they opened their shops.[123] "Police and Intelligence departments sprung up in no time," remembered Jonah. "A native corps of sweepers and other castes (held in abomination by the Hindoos and Mahomedans) was speedily formed into battalions, to bring down the pride of the Pandies, and paraded morning and evening."[124]

✦   ✦   ✦

On his arrival at Cawnpore, Neill had made straight for the Bibighar and received from his junior officers an embellished account of the slaughter of the ladies and children.[125] Neill was as predisposed as his nemesis Havelock to conceive of himself as God's avenging instrument. His "Scottish Bible-training," wrote an admiring reverend, "had taught him that justice was as absolute an attribute of Deity as mercy,—that magistracy was 'an ordinance of God,' and expressly designed to be a 'terror to evil-doers.'"[126] "It must be remembered," cautioned Sherer, "that he had been greatly praised. Everywhere it was noised abroad that Neill was the man for the emergency—Neill would not stand any nonsense, and so on. And of course he could no[t] but suppose that whatever position he was in, something marked would be expected of him . . ." Compulsiveness was "a facette, so to speak, of that general boldness which made Neill what he was."[127]

"No-one who has witnessed these scenes of murder, mutilation and massacre," Neill wrote to a friend, "can ever listen to the word 'mercy' as applied to these fiends. . . . Who could be merciful to one concerned? Severity at the first is mercy in the end. I wish to show the Natives of India that the punishment inflicted by us for such deeds will be the heaviest, the most revolting to their feelings, and what they must ever remember. . . .

"One cannot control one's feelings," Neill wrote, and he did not try.[128] On July 25, only a day after Havelock's departure, Neill issued the "strange law," as he called it, that for all his attributes and accomplishments would entirely subsume his reputation. In defiance, he said, of "our Brahminized infatuated elderly gentlemen" in Calcutta, he proclaimed that the blood on the floors of the Bibighar was "not to be washed or cleaned" by the victims' countrymen, but cleared up and wiped out, previous to their execution, by such of the miscreants as may be hereafter apprehended, who took an active part in the mutiny, to be selected according to their rank, caste, and degree of guilt. Each miscreant, after sentence of death is pronounced upon him, will be taken down to the house in question, under a guard, and will be forced into cleaning up a small portion of the blood-stains; the task will be made as revolting to his feelings as possible, and the Provost-Marshal will use the lash in forcing any one objecting to complete his task. After properly cleaning up his portion, the culprit is to be immediately hanged, and for this purpose a gallows will be erected close at hand.[129]

"All the Brahmins will be buried," he commanded, "and the Mohammedans burned . . .[130]

"The first to be executed," Neill reported, "was an infantry subahdar, a huge brute of the highest caste." Neill described how "a broom was given him by a sweeper. At first he refused to use it, but the provost-marshall's lash descended so energetically on his shoulders, that he screamed like a madman, and accomplished his task in hot haste. He was hanged afterwards, and buried under the road."

Another of Neill's early victims was a deputy collector who had earlier offered his services to Sherer. Ruling that he had "flaunted his disloyalty in the face of the whole district and displayed zeal in behalf of the Nana's cause" by forcing the Indian clerks to sit in Baba Bhutt's court, Sherer ordered him hanged and all of his property confiscated.[131] Neill pronounced him "a vile wretch, and one of the leaders of the revolt." Indeed the rumor among the soldiers was that he had "taken two of our ladies for his own ends" and killed them when the British returned. After being dragged off to the Bibighar, the deputy "attempted some resistance, but the lash soon brought him to his senses, and he cleansed with his tongue the stain of blood apportioned to him."

"We stuffed pork, beef and everything which could possibly break his caste down his throat," wrote Major Bingham, and "tied him as tight as we could by the arms and told the guard to be *gentle* with him . . . The guard treated him *gently*. I only wonder he lived to be hung which I had the pleasure of witnessing."[132] "His death was, accidentally, a most painful one," wrote another witness, "for the rope was badly adjusted, and when he dropped the noose closed over his jaw. His hands then got loose, and he caught hold of the rope and struggled to get free; but two men took hold of his legs and jerked his body until his neck broke."[133] A soldier standing by "had the pleasure of laughing in his countenance as he swung in front of our camp. He was an ugly-looking scoundrel."[134]

"Many high caste Brahmins among the captured rebels," wrote Jonah, were

> compelled to collect the bloody clothes of the victims and wash up the blood from the floor. After [they underwent] these degradations, which includes loss of caste, sweepers of a peculiar class called *domes* (the mere touch of whose hand to a Brahmin is pollution of the highest degree, and death from whom is to be attended by awful consequences, namely, transmigration of the soul into seven several forms of miserable reptiles and horrible monsters, each time dying most terrible deaths) received orders to hang the infatuated wretches.[135]

"This is not a measure to be judged by ordinary rules," Neill cautioned the public, "but it is well adapted for the present emergency, and I trust no one will interfere with me before the place is entirely cleansed"[136]—all two thousand blood-spattered square feet of it.[137] Neill was especially outraged by the behavior of the garrison's Indian servants, who, he claimed, had "behaved shamefully, and were in a plot, all but the lowest caste ones. They deserted their masters and plundered them."[138] He had little evidence of this, of course, for their sahibs and memsahibs were dead. A great many of them had risked their lives to hide or serve their masters and protect their possessions after Nana came to power, and they could hardly be blamed for laying claim to a few of their employers' effects after their masters had been killed and the British defeated. Nevertheless, nothing appalled and alarmed Anglo-Indians more than the treachery of servants, and kitmutgars, bearers, and watchmen were among those hanged every day at the Bibighar.

Almost every one of them died with grace. A sepoy of the 10th was dragged to the Bibighar and forced to kneel down and lick a square foot of bloody mat for over ten minutes while a soldier lashed him with a cat-o'-nine-tails. But the sepoy salaamed to the gallows as he took the stairs. Gazing out over the grave that low-caste coolies had prepared for him, he spoke to an immense crowd of Indian and European onlookers. "He was satisfied to die," an officer recalled him saying, "and we need not think we were going to beat the Sepoys because they would yet beat us."[139]

His face smeared with the Bibighar's blood, his back striped from the provost-marshal's whip, Cavalry Sergeant Suffar Ali Khan was dragged to the gallows, charged with having struck off General Wheeler's head. Protesting his innocence, the sergeant turned to the crowd as a noose was looped around his neck and shouted, "Oh Prophet! In due time transpire my infant son Mazur Ali of Rohtuck that he may avenge this desecration on the General and his descendants."[140]

"As a rule," recalled Sherer, "those who had to die died with extraordinary, I was going to say courage, but composure is the word; the Mahomedans, with hauteur, and an angry kind of scorn; and the Hindoos, with an apparent indifference altogether astonishing." Sherer recalled how one condemned Indian "positively under the shadow of the fatal tree, with only three or four minutes to live," objected "peevishly enough" to the soldiers plundering his jujubes.[141]

"I cannot help seeing that His finger is in all of this," Neill told his friends in England. "We have been false to ourselves so often."[142]

WHOM THOU HAST SPARED

Survivors: July 17–August 30, 1857

In the afternoon of July 17, various merchants had presented Jonah Shepherd with some readymade but ill-fitting English clothes, and his old dhobi invited him to his house for a bath and a shave. Several of his servants sought him out, bringing with them his two dogs, which they had managed to save. Bedecked in his clean clothes, he set off to offer his services to Havelock's chief commissariat officer, Colonel Fraser Tytler, whose subordinates "did not well understand the natives." Only five days earlier Jonah had marched through these same streets in irons, and the townspeople had "pointed at me with the finger of contempt. But now what a change!—every individual I met, whether high or low, bowed almost to the ground the moment he saw me, and made his obeisance—not to me, as I thought, but to the English clothes I had on, which only a day ago would have brought sure death to the wearer."[143]

That night Jonah bedded down in the house of his Bengali clerk, but he could not sleep. His mind reeled with the conflicting accounts of what had transpired at the Bibighar. He was still convinced that his family had been among the victims at the Bibighar, that his brother Daniel had been killed with the burra sahibs of Fatehgarh. He was "beside myself," he wrote his brother at Agra the next day, and wished "I had not been spared to hear of such dreadful accounts. Oh, my poor Polly! how must they have killed you!"[144] It would be some days before he would learn that his loved ones' names did not appear on the native doctor's list, and he could conclude that "they must have all been together in one boat and perished at the same time."[145]

On the eighteenth Colonel Tytler arranged for Jonah to receive his back pay as head clerk and asked him to reestablish the Cawnpore Commissariat "which I had no difficulty in doing, as the whole of the Bengalees composing the English Department were present, and were but too glad to be taken back."[146] But Jonah himself "hardly knew what I myself did." His babus "strained every nerve, from excessive regard for me, to have everything done satisfactorily" but "the world appeared to me a blank," Jonah recalled. ". . . I could only look upwards to heaven, and wish I had also joined the dear souls that had gone before me."[147]

✦   ✦   ✦

For the past two weeks Lieutenants Mowbray Thomson and Henry George Delafosse and privates Murphy and Sullivan had been recuperating from their escape under the care and protection of the elderly Raja Dirigibijah Singh of Moorar Mhow, drowsing through the long hot days "as if we had been fed upon opiates." The raja's cook prepared them three meals a day, a local healer visited them regularly to apply poultices of neem leaves; the raja's tailor measured them for clothes of Indian cut; "and when Hindustani shoes were added to our toilet," wrote Thomson, "we felt quite respectable again."[148]

The raja himself visited often and promised to send his four dependents to Allahabad as soon as it was safe. But the news they received was discouraging. "We were told that the Muchee Bhowan [at Lucknow] had blown up with two hundred Europeans in it. One day the Punjaub was lost, another day Madras and Bombay were gone into mutiny; then a hundred thousand Sikhs were said to be marching south to exterminate the English."

Nana Sahib knew the Raja was protecting Europeans, and ordered him to give them up. But when "a sowar of the 2d Cavalry and some Sepoys of the 66th Native Infantry brought the demand," the Raja replied that he was a tributary to the King of Oudh, and did not recognize Nana's raj. "There is this charm about thackoor hospitality," wrote Thomson, "—once claimed, it is not to be dishonoured by a trifle."

Though the rebels who roamed through the countryside did not dare attack the Raja's guards, a few occasionally entered his fort and visited his English prisoners. Among these were soldiers of the lieutenants' own regiment, the 53rd Native Infantry, who declared the Company's rule at an end. Thomson told them "they were talking nonsense, for in a short time reinforcements would arrive." But the sepoys insisted that Nana had sent "a sowar on a camel to Russia for assistance." Thomson roared with laughter and ridiculed their sense of geography. "Suppose you gain the country, what shall you do with us?" he asked one soldier.

"The Nana will send you all down to Calcutta and ship you home, and when he has conquered India, he will embark for England and conquer that country."

"Why, you Brahmins will not go to sea, will you?"

"Oh, yes," he said, "only we shall not cook upon the voyage."[149]

Azimullah had also convinced the sepoys that the Russians were all Moslems, and that "the armies of the Czar are to liberate the faithful and their land from the yoke of the Feringhees."[150]

Around the twentieth of July, news reached the raja that Spurgin's *Burrampoota* had passed by. An Indian who had once worked for the railroad convinced the Raja that if he did not move the four Englishmen out of his fort the British might accuse him of imprisoning them. So the Raja packed his guests on an elephant, and, recalled Thomson, "with abundant expressions of thanks, and some regret, we said farewell to the old brick," and proceeded to a little village by the river.[151] There, protected by a Rajput guard and supplied with two meals a day, they occupied a small hut, waiting for more British steamers to come heaving up the river. One morning they saw English furniture floating downriver: some of the plunder that the frightened inhabitants of Cawnpore had discarded at Neill's command. A guard managed to scoop something from the stream: a book "bearing the well-known inscription, *'53d Regiment, Native Infantry Book Club.'*"

But no more steamers appeared on the river, and on July 29 the Raja finally decided to send the four soldiers across the Ganges to a friendly landlord of Fatehpur, who greeted Thomson "with a rupee upon the palm, the native intimation of fidelity to the state. We touched the coin, and the covenant of hospitality was thus in simple formality settled."[152] Two days later, the four men set off in a hackery for Allahabad. Ten miles down the Grand Trunk Road, they were challenged by a British sentry who, judging from the four fugitives' "bronzed countenances, grim beards, huge turbans, and *tout ensemble*" took them for Afghans. Thomson demanded to be taken to the sentry's commanding officer, but, still uncertain what to make of them, the soldier kept his musket trained on him until Private Murphy waved to a comrade from the 84th in the gathering crowd of soldiers, who now greeted them all "with a truly British cheer."

The soldiers were part of a relief force headed up the road to Cawnpore, and at first none of them could believe that Thomson and his comrades could have possibly escaped from Cawnpore. But "the whole camp was impatient for our story, and we equally impatient to partake of English fare. Never was the beer of our country more welcome; and that first meal, interspersed with a fire of cross-questioning about the siege and our subsequent history, inquiries after lost comrades and relatives, and occasional hints at the masquerade style of our accoutrement, made a strangely mingled scene of congratulation, humour, lamentation, and good-will."

The four fugitives now found themselves "once more on the road to the centre of the war and the site of our old calamities." The route was punctuated by "the bodies of natives hanging to the trees, sometimes two or three, and in one instance seven hanging from one tree, in various stages of destruction from jackals and vultures." Along the roadside they passed the remains of Havelock's battles: gun carriages, remains of hastily improvised entrenchments, and two spiked guns.

After three jittery days of false alarms the column reached Cawnpore, and as soon the old Entrenchment came into view Thomson went off "to survey each well-remembered post of anxious observation." He paused over the sepulchral well "and its unutterable memories" and toured his enemy's positions in the mess house and the ruined church. At last he and his fellow fugitives stumbled into the new entrenchment by the Bridge of Boats, from which an astonished General Neill himself summoned them.

At his headquarters in Nawabgunj the general listened to their amazing adventure over supper. "Thomson," recalled Sherer, "though his ample ruddy beard showed maturity, had the bright face and laughing eyes of an undergraduate in his first term. Both [he and Delafosse] struck me very much in one way: they took the events which had happened to them, events almost surpassing the most romantic adventures of fiction, as if they were ordinary circumstances to be looked for in the day's work of life."[153]

The general assigned Delafosse to the police, where he could assist with "executions, raising native police, and the sale of plunder." Murphy returned to his regiment, and the "most intelligent"[154] Sullivan was appointed to the Ordnance Department of Cawnpore, where, with another fugitive, Ensign Brown, he would soon succumb to cholera.[155] Thomson, "being a handy fellow," volunteered to work on the new entrenchment "rushing after the coolies any morning," Sherer recalled, "as if he had been born to it."[156] Over the next months Thomson would oversee thousands of coolies in the new entrenchment.

> In less than a month these black, ant-like navvies, threw up earthworks of very considerable dimensions. They reared a wall seven feet high, eighteen feet thick, and half a mile in length; turfed over to prevent its being washed away by the rains; it was fitted with sally-ports and gates; field magazines, both expense and permanent; embrasures, and platforms for the guns, made of brick-on-edge, set in concrete by native masons. Besides this inner line of circumvallation, the outworks, . . . included a mile of parapet, and these were connected with the *enceinte*, by a covered way.

It also fell to Thomson to lead tours of the old Entrenchment for "brother officers who had lost friends and relatives on that carnage-ground" and for various dignitaries, including, eventually, Lady Canning.[157] Thomson's first blurted accounts of the siege and massacre at Sati Chowra condemned Wheeler's feeble preparations and distracted command as well as his pickets' near mutiny just before the capitulation. One officer who heard Thomson's and Delafosse's initial report wrote home in high dudgeon. "General Wheeler did nothing, was never wounded early in the siege as was stated, and never took any active part in the defence. He hardly ever showed himself outside the small barrack which sheltered almost all, and never but once went out to the defences. The heroes of the wonderful siege were Ashe (Artillery), Moore (32d) & Halliday."[158] But Thomson's account gradually softened with the retelling, until, perhaps at the urging of superior officers and in deference to the garrison's grieving relatives, it settled into the discreet and gentlemanly narrative he would eventually publish as *The Story of Cawnpore*.

✦ ✦ ✦

Over the next weeks other fugitives from the Doab came stumbling into camp. Under the increasingly grudging protection of the zemindar Hardeo Baksh Singh, William Edwards of Budaon, and George Probyn of Fatehgarh with his wife and four children had huddled together in a village twelve miles east of Fatehgarh: a tiny cluster of filthy huts surrounded now by a sea of inundated fields.[159]

"The only incident which marked these weary days," wrote Edwards, "was Probyn and myself, one morning, hearing distinctly a military band playing English airs in Futtehghur; the wind carrying the sound across the water, and reminding us of the near proximity of those who were, we knew, thirsting for our blood."[160]

But at dawn of August 2 the tedium was broken by "a tall spectral looking figure standing before me," wrote Edwards, "naked except a piece of cloth wrapped round his waist, much emaciated and dripping with water." It was Gavin Jones, the planter's son who, on account of his shoulder wound, had refused to press on with the second Fatehgarh flotilla and had spent the past month living under the protection of a friendly landlord. Jones "burst into tears at hearing his own language again and seeing one of his own countrymen," and told Probyn and Edwards what he knew of the fate of the Fatehgarh garrison. He had heard both that the second flotilla had reached Allahabad and that it had been seized at Bithur and all the passengers massacred. The latter possibility "he, as well as we ourselves, feared was the most probable story: we strove, however, to hope for the best, and to believe that nothing so terrible could have happened."

✦ ✦ ✦

But worse had already happened. On July 5, the seven children and six adults who had survived the attack on Major Robertson's boat at Manpur had been carted back to Fatehgarh.[161] The Nawab of Farrukhabad now held dizzy sway there, punctuating his endless ceremonials with visits to his newly widowed Eurasian inamorata, Bonny Byrne, whom he still kept safely ensconced in his harem with

The ruins of Wheeler's tiled-roof barracks

her enterprising mother. Bonny was pregnant by now, possibly by the Nawab, which posed a direct threat to his principal and formidable wife, the "Bigga Begum."[162] To annihilate this menace to her own ambitions, Bigga Begum plotted the slaughter of every one of the Nawab's Christian prisoners, hoping to sweep Bonny Byrne into the maelstrom.

Bigga Begum's chief co-conspirator was Wazir Khan, the Nawab's coachman, who before the rebellion had driven His Highness to his rendezvous with Bonny Byrne. After the uprising he had absconded with the jewels of the Nawab's late European instructor in watercolors whose wife was now among the Nawab's captives. There were thirty-two prisoners at Fatehgarh, excluding two Indian Christians whom the Nawab released so they might pray for his recovery from a case of the pip. Besides the survivors of the attack on the boats at Manpur they were Eurasians and Indian Christians the rebels had captured in the district. The women and children had been kept in the Nawab's palace at first, then moved to his stables, while the men subsisted on parched gram in a nearby row of sheds.

These prisoners now began to send messages to Wazir Khan demanding the return of the ladies' jewels. The coachman instead forged a document, passing it off as a letter from one of the prisoners to Henry Havelock and flourishing it in front of the sepoys of the 41st Native Infantry. The Nawab at first dismissed the letter as a fake, but eventually his sepoys wore him down, and he agreed to follow Nana's example and annihilate his captives.

On the gloomy morning of July 23, the prisoners were ordered out of their cells. The men were marched and the women and children carted off to the parade-ground where a large crowd was waiting in the rain. A sepoy tried to intercede on behalf of the sister of the same Miss Sutherland whom another sepoy had rescued at Bithur. He was pushed aside. The men were bound and led into a bungalow. One by one they were summoned out into the rain and cut down by two sepoys wielding scimitars. Their victims included Reverend John Edgar Freeman's loyal catechist, Dhaukal Pershad, the headmaster of the Mission High School, who "met his death calmly, bowing his head to receive the stroke of the sword."[163] When all the men's corpses lay together in a rain-drenched heap, the women and children were ordered out of their carts and made to sit along the walls of a row of mud huts facing a cannon loaded with grape.

"A little boy begged them hard not to kill him, and gave them something valuable," wrote a native Christian in the crowd, "which he had in a tin case, in hopes of being spared. The savages, of course, took what he gave, but would not let him off. When they were about to kill him, the poor thing ran here and there, and at last crept under some bedsteads which were there, where he was pierced through and cut to pieces."[164]

The cannon misfired once, twice in the torrential downpour and then finally discharged with a roar that carried all the way to Probyn's hiding place across the river. But the first blast did not kill everyone, and several more rounds were required. At the last Miss Sutherland was the only prisoner left alive. A sepoy fired a pistol at her but missed. Raising her arms to the rain, she cried out that God had protected her and so they must spare her, but another sepoy closed in and killed her with his sword. All of their corpses were left where they lay until next morning, when they were dumped down a nearby well: thirty-two of the 237 Fatehgarh Christians who died in the uprising of 1857.[165] But the Bigga Begum be damned, Bonny Byrne and her mother were not among the victims. The Nawab would not permit their execution, and they survived the rebellion.

◆   ◆   ◆

Gavin Jones remained with Probyn and Edwards, reducing them to tears with his evening renditions of "Old Folks at Home," sung in his "fine Welsh voice."[166] But their situation was desperate. Their diet was sparse, and Hardeo Baksh Singh had obscurely forbidden Probyn to keep milk goats for his children. Wasting away on the pestiferous little island that passed for their village haven, two children died and had to be buried in the mud.

When the Begum of Oudh set a price of one thousand rupees each on the heads of the two collectors, Probyn sent Havelock a request for instructions. Many days later a messenger returned with Havelock's answer, which was to stay put. But they could not survive much longer where they were, and so they decided to press on anyway. On the thirtieth of August, with eight oarsmen and a guard of eleven matchlockmen, they boarded a native boat and pushed off into the rapid current of the Ramganga and made for Cawnpore. At the junction with the Ganges they were challenged by a ferryman, but they merely floated past, pretending not to hear. That night they were joined by an ally of Hardeo Baksh Singh, a well known Rajput of the region named Dhanna Singh. On the strength of his reputation they managed to race past other ferrymen who shouted to them from along the riverbank. As they neared Bithur, bathers warned them that the British were downriver and would certainly kill them; Dhanna Singh thanked them for their advice. But at Bithur a man informed them that the rebels had reoccupied Bithur, and the British had fled to Cawnpore. At last they reached the site of the old magazine, where a detachment of Sikhs commanded them ashore. Mistaking them for rebels, Dhanna Singh ignored them as well and continued floating downriver until they came upon Spurgin's *Burrampoota*, where, on the thirty-first, a guard of soldiers from the 84th welcomed them with open arms.[167]

Edwards, Jones, Probyn, and his "wonderfully brave and calm" wife and two children took their lodgings in Nur Mahomed's seedy hotel, which seemed to them the height of luxury.[168] "A curious physical experiment worked itself out," wrote Sherer. "Edwards was of a mercurial temperament, capable of going through anything, whilst his nerves were braced by hope and expectation. Probyn, less excitable, looked in poor health from insufficient food. As soon, however, as he was restored to English diet, he picked up at once. But the other, when the tension was relaxed, was visibly enfeebled and worn down."[169]

THE MISCHIEFS OF CREATION

Amy Horne: June 27–December 1857

After her abduction from the riverbank, Amy Horne had awakened in the kindly African's tent near the Assembly Rooms to find her abductor, Ismail Khan of the 2nd Cavalry, towering over her.[170] He was dressed in white: a sallow, pockmarked Pathan with a beard parted in the center and combed outward in luxurious sprays.[171] Ordering Amy to her feet, he led her into the glare of the afternoon, past a jumble of huts and through the flaps of a large, sparsely furnished English mess tent the rebels had stolen from the cantonments at Cawnpore.

In the center of the tent Amy was ordered to squat down before Liaqat Ali, a Moslem sage who had led the revolt in Allahabad.[172] He was a dark, round-faced, thin-lipped man with whiskers to his breastbone and a penetrating gaze that he now directed at Ismail Khan's Eurasian captive while a man with a bared sword took up a position behind her and "a horde of wildlooking, fanatical Moslems" straggled into the tent.[173] So it had been decided, she thought. She was to be executed. But now Liaqat Ali silently brought out a pomegranate and broke it in two, handing one half to Amy. She stared at it for a moment, and the sage nodded to her, taking a few seeds from his half and popping them into his mouth. Amy numbly followed suit. Sherbet was produced, and again Liaqat Ali ate half and Amy was told to eat the rest. At that he and another sage began to recite prayers in loud voices, as a woman padded into the tent, grasped Amy's wrist and led her through the crowd, some of whom were "expressive of sullen indifference, others of religious frenzy and cruelty, and a few of vulgar curiosity at the sight of an English 'Missee' being placed so entirely in their power."

The woman led her into a hut near the Assembly Rooms and ordered her to undress. With trembling hands Amy pulled off her *chudder* and squatted down into an improvised tub as the woman briskly scrubbed her scratched and bruised body. Thus purified, Amy donned a new suit of Moslem clothes and returned to the sage's tent, where she was told to bow her head and recite a prayer called the *kulma*.

In the name of God, the Compassionate, the Merciful,
I betake me for refuge to the Lord of the Daybreak
Against the mischiefs of His Creation . . .

When she was done the sages nodded approvingly, and her abductor led her back to his hut. A bandmaster's wife anxiously brought Amy her meals of lentils and chupatties, afraid to converse with her lest she enrage the sowars, and Amy spent the next weeks in concealment, awaiting with dread the sowar's evening return and praying to Jesus to forgive her apostasy.

On July 11 the sowar brought her with him on what was supposed to be an expedition to capture Allahabad from the atrocious Colonel Neill. The uprising had made the sowar a man of substance, and he could afford to provide his converted concubine with a palanquin and a set of bearers to tote her through the wide pools that had submerged the Grand Trunk Road. When the force fled from Havelock at Fatehpur, Amy had remained with the baggage, and "what anguish it was," she remembered, "to be so near our soldiers, and not to be able to effect my escape!" Riding back toward Cawnpore she caught a glimpse of "an exceedingly fair girl with light hair and blue eyes"—Miss Sutherland, perhaps—stranded by the roadside.

At last she returned to her hut, where she "often heard the booming of guns and musketry, accompanied by the heartrending shrieks of the poor victims and the fiendish yells of the sepoys and the rabble" that the screaming of jackals would evoke for her ever after. On July 16 Ismail Khan led her out of Cawnpore on his Arab, determined to join the rebel army at Delhi. But a false rumor that the British had retaken Delhi sent him and his comrades veering off to Farrukhabad, where the Nawab had executed all of his Christian captives three days before.

Word of Amy's approach had already circulated among the sepoys of the 41st, who declared her conversion a fraud and threatened to kill her with even greater cruelty than they had shown their previous victims. "I was to be blown from the cannon's mouth! One hundred cavalry and the same number of infantry were to be paraded to see the unique spectacle of an English girl being consigned to perdition in the quickest possible manner." But Liaqat Ali was offended by the sepoys' challenge to his authority and arranged to smuggle Amy off to Lucknow with the sowar and a native woman who would show her hand through the curtains of their palanquin whenever they were challenged by rebel sentries.

At Lucknow Amy was kept secluded for two months in a "most wretched hovel" where she "would have died of suffocation" except for the few minutes every night when she was allowed to step outside. But Ismail Khan was right to hide her, for the forces at Lucknow were led by another Moslem sage who had massacred every European at Fyzabad and remained determined to wipe out every Christian he could find. Shortly before Amy's arrival, English fugitives who had been unable to reach the Residency had been "dragged out by a mob, barbarously served, and then shot, after which their bodies were hacked to pieces and left to be devoured by vultures."

✦ ✦ ✦

When, on July 31, General Havelock reported his withdrawal to the river, an appalled Neill wrote the general from Cawnpore that he "deeply" regretted his falling back "one foot. The effect on our prestige is very bad indeed. . . . It has been most unfortunate your not bringing back any of the guns captured from the enemy. The natives will not believe that you captured one. The effect of your retrograde movement will be very injurious to our cause everywhere. . . . You ought not to remain a day where you are," he concluded, ". . . You ought to advance again, and not halt until you have rescued, if possible, the garrison at Lucknow."

Havelock exploded. "There must be an end of these proceedings at once," he fired back from across the Ganges.

> I wrote to you confidentially on the state of affairs. You send me back a letter of censure of my measures, reproof and advice for the future. I do not want and will not receive any of them from an officer under my command, be his experience what it may. Understand this distinctly, . . . that a consideration of the obstruction that would arise to the public service at this moment alone prevents me from taking the stronger step of placing you under arrest. You now stand warned. Attempt no further dictation.

Neill had nevertheless gotten under the old man's skin, and four days later Havelock recklessly attempted another advance, despite a force so depleted by cholera that even the addition of a half battery and a company of foot soldiers could not raise it back to its original strength. A day later he routed another rebel force, but failed to capture their guns and the men "were dying so fast of cholera" that the next halt had to be spent "digging graves for its victims." As the bod-

General Henry Havelock

General Colin Campbell
(Lord Clyde)

ies were lowered into the ground, news arrived that the mutinous Gwalior Contingent, the formidable European-trained force that the British had maintained to keep watch over Scindia's Mahratta court, had joined with a force under Nana's general, Tatya Tope, and was about to march on Cawnpore. Over the lonely objections of his son, Old Phlos once more retreated to the river.

Now Neill's tone changed from reproach to apprehension. He urged Havelock to return immediately to defend Cawnpore against the menacing contingent. To keep the rebels from attacking while he crossed over to Cawnpore, Havelock chased a body of rebels "whirling in rout up the road." But his telegraph to the commander-in-chief was disconsolate. "I must prepare your Excellency," he said, "for the abandonment, with great grief and reluctance, of the hope of relieving Lucknow."

By August 13 he was back in Cawnpore, where wounds combined with cholera knocked out a quarter of his troops. Havelock's surgeon demanded that the men rest, otherwise at this rate he would have no able-bodied soldiers left. But Havelock could not rest, for thousands of rebels were said to be regrouping just northwest of the station. On the sixteenth he ordered his feeble troops to their feet and led them up to Bithur, where five regiments of sepoys, two regiments of sowars, and two guns awaited him a few hundred yards in front of Saturday House.

Some of the rebels lay entrenched in two villages, the rest poised among the vast surrounding stands of corn and wheat. Havelock ordered his men to lie flat on the simmering ground while Maude's artillery went to work. But his fourteen cannon hardly made a dent in the rebels' earthworks, and the mutineers fought with extraordinary bravery, inflamed, no doubt, by Neill's retributions at Cawnpore, but also heartened by the advance of the formidable Gwalior Contingent. The rebel gunners fired back with unexpected skill, and in the corn fields sepoys of the 42nd Native Infantry crossed sabres with the Fusiliers, refusing to withdraw until over sixty of them lay dead. By the time Havelock had driven the rebels off and returned to Cawnpore, the sepoys had killed or wounded over fifty of his men, and another dozen Europeans had dropped dead from heat stroke.

By now command of Wheeler's vacated Cawnpore Division had been assigned to fifty-four-year-old Major General Sir James Outram, perhaps the most popular general in the Indian Army. He had started out as a creature of the Bombay Army and from Afghanistan to Hyderabad he had fought in scores of engagements against rajas, bandits, tribals, and clansmen. A ferocious sportsman, he was once regarded as the best pig-sticker in India and in nine years "was at the deaths of 191 tigers, besides many other large animals."[174] In 1856 Dalhousie had appointed him first chief commissioner at Lucknow, where, with remarkable tact and sympathy, he oversaw the annexation of Oudh. He was a genial, clubby man: informal, generous, and unprepossessing, with a smooth baby's brow and thinning hair that tangled about his ears.

Technically, Outram now outranked Havelock, who was merely a field-force commander. But shortly before setting off for Cawnpore with a relief force of his own, Outram won the admiration of the British public by declaring that he did not intend to command the relief of Lucknow but would serve as a volunteer horseman, leaving to Old Phlos the glory for which he had already "so nobly struggled." This was the sort of gentlemanly gesture that the public loved, and Havelock himself was deeply moved. But many wondered how someone of Outram's dimension could possibly restrain himself from interfering with Havelock's command. He could not, as it turned out. As soon as he arrived at Cawnpore on September 5, Havelock's son was complaining that Outram was already interfering with the old man's orders. Though Havelock learned to forbear Outram's bright ideas and helpful suggestions, they ate away at his confidence, much to General Neill's mordant delight.

On September 19 a spy brought a message from Colonel Inglis, Lawrence's successor at Lucknow, that had been written in Greek, rolled up into a quill, and embedded in a ball of mud. "I must be frank," it said, "and tell you that my force is daily diminishing from the enemy's fire and our defences grow daily weaker. Should the enemy make any really determined effort to storm this place I shall find it difficult to repulse them."

Havelock and Outram now had three thousand men at their disposal. That very afternoon they began to cross the Ganges; two days later they were marching back into Oudh with Neill and a Colonel Hamilton commanding two brigades. Within six miles of the river Havelock met a large rebel force that had cleverly positioned itself to frustrate the old general's favorite stratagem of attacking his enemy's flanks. During the engagement that followed, Havelock's horse died from sword cuts—the sixth of seven horses to be killed under him. But the sheer momentum of the British attack sent the mutineers fleeing, with Outram galloping after them, striking at their turbans with his Malacca cane.

Havelock's column proceeded across the well-worn battleground along the Lucknow road, wading through flooded fields under torrents of monsoon rain. On the night of the twenty-fourth they could hear the guns booming at the Residency, and the next day they reached the outskirts of the city and began one of the fiercest battles of the rebellion. The citizens of Lucknow had been warned that the English would come among them with "vermillion applied to some member of their bodies" in order to enchant them. But their enchantment could be dispelled simply by repeating "Allah-Akbar"—God is great. Besides, the "execrable English," led by that "ill-starred, polluted Bitch" Queen Victoria, were "low people like the shoemakers and spirit sellers, and have but a small body of troops." The people were exhorted to wipe out the English with

guns, pistols, and carbines and with swords, arrows, daggers, poignando, etc. Some [should] lift them up on spears, some dexterously snatch their arms and destroy the enemy, some should wrestle and through the stratagem break the enemy to pieces, some should strike them with cudgels, some slap them, some throw dust in their eyes, some should beat them with shoes, some

attack them with their fists, some scratch them, some drag them
along, some tear out their ears, some break their noses.[175]

Above the city's lethal maze of alleys, rebels and townspeople lined
the rooftops "discharging their muskets, hurling down bricks and
stones and even spitting" on the British below.[176] By the time they
had beaten their way to the Residency so many men had been lost to
Havelock's mulish refusal to circumvent the enemy's strongest positions that Outram, now slightly wounded in the arm, would regret
ever afterward that he had not taken command. Over a fifth of his
men had been killed or wounded—including one in three of the
Highlanders who had led the charge to the Residency gates. Lieutenant Henry Delafosse, only partially recovered from his escape
from Sati Chowra, suddenly found himself in the grimly familiar
predicament of defending a garrison of starved and shellshocked
men, women, and children against an engulfing foe.

The garrison was jubilant, however, and as the Sikhs and Highlanders staggered into the Residency grounds they were surrounded
by women and children. This was how it should have been when
they reached Cawnpore two months before, and at the sight of the
children some of the soldiers burst into tears. "God bless you, Mis-
sus," a Highlander said to one lady as she brought him some tea.
"We're glad we've come in time to save you and the youngsters."[177]
But actually, Havelock had only managed to entrap his column in
the Residency, and it would not be long before some in the garrison
would look on his troops as just more mouths to feed.

Beyond the Residency the mutineers rejoiced that one of their
number, holding his musket at arm's length, had managed to fire a
ball through the brain of Brigadier General James Neill.[178] His men
had taken to calling him "Butcher Neill,"[179] but fondly, and his
"blood-lick law" had been applauded by Calcutta Anglo-Indians who
had been inundated with stories, real and imagined, of rebel atrocities.[180] Later writers would try to excuse his excesses. "It is easy now
at this distance of time," Garnet Wolseley reminded his American
readers many years later, "to argue about 'the quality of mercy' & in
sententious phrases. The blood is now cool. . . . But it was not so
then, and as I look back to those days, I am now lost in amazement
mingled with a sort of national pride at how small was the retribution we exacted & how much mercy seasoned our justice."[181]

George Campbell visited Cawnpore when the blood was still hot,
however, and condemned Neill for doing things "almost more than

massacre, putting to death with deliberate torture in a way that has never been proved against the natives. . . . Neill is one of those people who have been elevated into a hero on the strength of a feminine sort of violence. . . . There was not much more in him" concluded Campbell, who could "never forgive Neill for his very bloody work."[182]

Havelock's reputation fared far better. Despite blunders and terrible losses, Old Phlos had at last relieved or at least reinforced the Lucknow garrison and probably saved the women and children from the fate of their compatriots at Cawnpore. When the news reached Calcutta, he would be promoted to major general, appointed Knight Commander of the Bath, and hailed as the greatest hero of the day, the subject of hundreds of hagiographic books, prints, speeches, and songs.

Nevertheless, his "short bright day" was over, and during the long months of siege that followed, his old bones would sag under Outram's command.[183] He lived long enough to see the garrison evacuated by Colin Campbell, who informed Havelock of his knighthood by greeting him with, "And how do you do, *Sir* Henry?" A few days later Sir Henry was dead of dysentery.[184] His last words were to his son. "Harry," he said, "see how a Christian can die."[185]

✦ ✦ ✦

During the siege of Lucknow, Amy Horne used to overhear the rebels revile Canning, whose "brainless" head, they said, was not worth the ten thousand rupees the British had put on Nana's. Henry Lawrence was the only Company man they had ever respected, they said, and now that he was dead India would soon be theirs.

In late October, as the guns still boomed around the Residency, some local women learned of Amy's existence, and Ismail Khan moved her into the kitchen of an Englishman's abandoned bungalow. Here she became the virtual slave of one of the King of Oudh's mothers-in-law, a relative of Ismail Khan who promised to look after her but once alone with Amy called her an infidel pig who did not deserve to live. She even asked Hazrat Mahal's son, the newly coronated boy-king of Oudh, to arrange for Amy's execution.

But Amy was saved by a deep division in the ranks of the rebels at Lucknow between the followers of Hazrat Mahal and the Maulvie of Fyzabad. Ismail Khan brought Amy into the Maulvie's presence and she did her best to convince him that her conversion had been genuine. The Maulvie produced a piece of candy, ate half and gave the other to her, declaring her his disciple, "bound to follow him wherever he went, to observe all their festivals, and rigidly keep every fast. It was with considerable loathing and repugnance," she added, "that I went through the above ceremony, being, as I have been all through my life, a devout Christian; but life is sweet to the young, and the end justified the means."

For the next month she lived in the Maulvie's palace on a bank of the river Goomtee, reciting "endless petitions as lustily as my lungs would permit." In an adjacent building the Begum of Oudh herself held court, sitting over the hatch to a basement vault containing "the treasure of the King of Oudh, consisting of personal and State jewelry, money and other valuables, amounting to . . . roughly, four hundred and fifty million pounds sterling." The Maulvie treated Amy kindly, with a private room and three meals a day, and conversed with her in English. He said he had visited England, but blamed the British for taking Bombay from his family. When he conquered England, he declared, he would not deign to marry Queen Victoria but would employ her as one of his "meanest slaves."

The Maulvie had no scruples about massacring captives; in fact he made their execution a condition of his command. But he apparently grew fond of Amy, and when he suspected his subordinates of plotting her death, he spirited her back to the king's mother-in-law, who had been enjoined once more to protect her. Amy hardly cared any longer, "for what was life to me, bereft of home, parents, friends, and the comforts and even the necessities of life?"

WINDHAM'S MESS

Cawnpore: August–December 1857

John Walter Sherer did what he could as temporary magistrate to reestablish a police force at Cawnpore, but he was having trouble finding suitable personnel. It had been Neill's idea to appoint a police battalion composed of sweepers to horrify the high-caste Indians Neill's squads kept dragging to the gallows, but it was Sherer's idea to appoint a jullad to establish order at Bithur. This particular jullad had assisted at the execution of scores of suspected rebels and seemed an unusually resourceful man, with a bottomless pool of recruits to draw from. "With a tremendous shout of praise, and 'bole bala' (long life) to General Neill," the jullad donned a silver badge on a lace belt and rode off with a hundred of his followers to Bithur, where, "to the utmost horror and astonishment" of that Brahminical enclave he and his fellow jullads busily set about extorting bribes from the townspeople.

Soon there were so many complaints of graft and extortion brought against him that Sherer sent off the head of his battalion of sweeper police, a "covetous" man named Pursunnarain who spent his first night at Bithur drinking with his low-caste escort and a Kashmiri dancing girl. After they had all but passed out from wine, he and his men were attacked by a body of rebel horsemen who had been lurking in the vicinity. Pursunnarain was hacked to pieces, and the jullads fled back to Cawnpore.

In the investigation that followed, a grieving relative of Pursunnarain led Sherer's police to the jullad's home, where they dug up pots full of "European articles of clothing and ladies' jewels, also money." His neighbors now came forward and identified him as none other than Aitwurya, the enterprising jullad who, only a month before, had mopped up at the Bibighar, killing the survivors and plundering the dead. Aitwurya was seized and dragged off to the Bibighar. "His mates turned on him, when ordered, with a readiness that must have been very bitter to him," said Sherer, "and led him, bound and trembling, to the scaffold on which he had himself stood so often as executioner. I was . . . in the verandah of a little house which he had to pass, and, seeing me, he cried at the pitch of his voice, 'Dobai Collector Sahib,' and entreated his guardians to allow him to stop and speak to me. But they were inexorable, and hurried him to his fate."[186]

Finally Neill declared an end to Sherer's attempts to police the district, leaving it to bodies of European troops to keep the rebels at bay. Fed up with his pool of native personnel and horrified by the constant hangings, Sherer was pleased to hand such duties to the "colourless" Captain Bruce of the military police.[187] Despite rumors to the contrary "there was never the least misunderstanding between red-coats and black-coats."[188] Perhaps there should have been, and would have been if Sherer had been more rigorous.

In his spare time Sherer gloomily toured the ruins of the station, including the Hillersdons' house, where he and his wife had been entertained only a few months before by Lydia's accomplished artistry on the piano. "I . . . went into the room we occupied," he wrote to his wife, "and the long narrow out where the children were—then into the drawing-room. As I pointed down to a mass of burnt bricks and rubbish . . . my stick turned up a solitary scrap of music paper stained or sodden with the wet—it had on it 'con molto spirito'—and was a bit of that difficult sort of music she liked so much."[189]

After Neill's departure the district was relatively quiet. A few petty zemindars roiled around the countryside, attacking outposts along the Grand Trunk Road, and a few villages had been plundered between Cawnpore and Bithur, beyond which the rebels remained in control. Reports came in that Nana was in the neighborhood, joining forces with this or that faction. On October 18 six hundred British soldiers were sent up the river to Sheorajpur to capture him. But they met with "hardly more than nominal resistance," and never laid eyes on the Peshwa.

At the time Nana and Azimullah were busy formulating a plan to escape to the vestigial little French colony of Chandernagore in Bengal and secure the protection and assistance of Emperor Napoleon III, who, Azimullah assured him, still intended to fly to the Peshwa's assistance at a propitious moment. Evidently the moment never arrived, for the emperor had already opened a land route through France to hasten British troops to India, and never replied to Nana's letters asking for "aid against the English [who] had invaded all the most cherished customs of the Hindoos"[190] and reminding the emperor, somewhat disingenuously, that "the ancestors of Nana Sahib were in close ties with France."[191]

✦ ✦ ✦

In August Patrick Grant had been replaced as commander-in-chief by Sir Colin Campbell, whose service reached all the way back to a tour with Wellington in Spain during the Napoleonic War. His voluble, restive manner belied a sometimes plodding hesitancy that derived, it was said, from his longing for a peerage. En route to Cawnpore he paused to punish rebel landlords and, after firing various villages, his officers sent horsemen out "to cut up any fugitives who may be found in the fields." "I think we polished off almost all the Thakoors' followers, and the refugee Mahommedans from Coel, etc.," Campbell wrote Agra, but he was running into Neill's old problem. "We have established such a terror," he said, "that it is impossible to get any one to come in."[192]

When Campbell reached Cawnpore on November 3, one of his first acts was to abolish the late General Neill's notorious blood-lick law as "unworthy of the English name and a Christian government." But executions continued, and many of his troops, inflamed by their visit to the Bibighar, pledged to inflict further reprisals when they got the chance.[193] Shortly after Sergeant William Forbes-Mitchell arrived at Cawnpore with his company of the 93rd, he visited the Bibighar and found his regimental surgeon, Dr. Munro, inspecting the bloody hook and the child's bloody handprints "with tears streaming down his cheeks. He was a most kind-hearted man, and I remember [that] when he came out of the house, . . . he cast a look of pity on the three wretches about to be hanged, and I overheard him say to another officer, . . . 'This is horrible and unchristian to look at; but I do hope those are the same wretches who tortured the little child on the hook inside that room.'"[194]

Campbell arrived determined to evacuate the British garrison at Lucknow as soon as possible so he could then concentrate his energies on the Gwalior Contingent that had combined forces with Tatya Tope and was now massing at Kalpi, only forty-six miles away. By now the Bridge of Boats had been restored, and on November 9 Campbell pressed on to Lucknow, leaving five hundred men at Cawnpore under forty-seven-year-old Major General Charles Ash Windham.[195]

It was Windham's first independent command.[196] "A short man of prepossessing appearance," he had recently been elected an M.P. from East Norfolk on the strength of his bravery in the Crimean War.[197] After volunteering rather noisily for service against the rebels, he had declared on the ship over that he "was going to take Delhi in 10 days, put the army on an entirely new footing and ignite India in six weeks."[198] Sherer thought him "a fine specimen of a hearty English soldier."[199] As with Neill, the public expected much of him, and by trying to rise to those expectations he would soon sully his reputation at Cawnpore.[200]

Before setting off for Lucknow, Campbell instructed Windham to place his force in the position Thomson had been busily expanding and fortifying and not to attempt an attack on the enemy except in defense of the new entrenchment. With the exception of a party of Madras Fusiliers due the next day, Windham was not to detain any troops that came in from Allahabad without the express permission of Campbell himself.[201]

After fighting in the shadow of hapless fools and greedy prima donnas, Tatya Tope had now stepped forward to lead the rebel army: a stout, audacious, and impatient man with a flat nose, pockmarked face, and a commanding gaze that burned beneath the smoky gray arches of his bristling eyebrows.[202] With a steady supply of intelligence from his spies in Cawnpore and Oudh, he cannily tracked Campbell's movements from afar, and then as soon as the commander-in-chief entered Oudh, crossed the Jumma with thousands of troops and began deploying them along a string of riverside villages until they occupied every principal town from Akbarpur to Sheorajpur, twenty miles northwest of Cawnpore, where they would remain poised until Campbell was bogged down in the narrow, murderous lanes of Lucknow."[203]

Afraid he might be unable to defend his position if the rebels took the city, General Windham nervously ordered houses demolished within a broad parameter of his entrenched fortification and reduced the groves of mango and banyan trees to stumps. He continued to relay incoming detachments of British troops to Lucknow, however, until on November 14 he received Campbell's permission to retain as many men as he deemed fit to defend Cawnpore. He now detained parts of four regiments, including a body of the 27th Madras Native Infantry, southern sepoys Calcutta had trepidatiously introduced to the fray. Windham stationed these extra men on the outskirts of the city, hoping to mislead Tatya's agents into thinking his force was larger than it really was.

Soon Windham had accumulated about 1,400 bayonets in the field, plus another three hundred in the entrenchment. It seemed such a substantial force that Windham began to itch to put it to use. The most obvious course was to sit tight in the entrenchment and continue strengthening his position, safeguarding not only the fort but the army's stores in the Assembly Rooms and the various bungalows that had been repaired and furnished for the women and children of the Lucknow garrison. But Windham had already deployed his reinforcements beyond the city, and now intended to take bolder action against Tatya's advancing force, large bodies of which had occupied two villages lying on either side of the Ganges Canal, about fifteen miles from town. Windham hit on the idea of floating 1,200 of his men down the canal in native boats and landing them halfway between Tatya's two positions, either of which he could then attack at will. So he gathered some boats together, and wrote for permission from the commander-in-chief.

On the nineteenth a note arrived informing Windham that Campbell's army had taken the Residency and ordering him to await further instructions. They were not forthcoming. All contact with Lucknow ceased and Windham grew fretful. What if Campbell, like Havelock and Outram, had merely managed to entrap himself at Lucknow? Abandoning his canal plan, Windham decided to deploy his force on a series of brick mounds on the outskirts of Cawnpore, between the town and the gathering contingent.

On the twenty-second communications with Lucknow flickered on for a moment with a note from a commissariat officer at Lucknow to his brother at Cawnpore, asking Windham for ten days' provisions. But the general decided to ignore it, for he could not afford to provide an escort. Two days later he received word that the Oudh rebels were now crossing the river and joining with the Gwalior Contingent. His own forces were stationed just outside the city, near the junction of the Delhi and Kalpi Roads, and now he ordered them further forward, to the bridge where the Kalpi Road crossed the Ganges Canal. From there he intended not only to keep an eye on the bridge but revert to his original plan, if he wanted, and send his flotilla up the canal.

On November 25 Tatya began to move. Interpreting Campbell's instructions as broadly as possible, General Windham decided to lead an assault on the contingent's leading division at the Pandu Nadi. In the small hours of November 26 he ordered 1,200 men forward with a battery of eight guns. "The enemy were found in considerable numbers," reported an officer, "and the clouds of dust betrayed the movement of troops. They could be distinguished dressed in their scarlet uniforms."

The British troops advanced "cheerfully" until six heavy rebel guns opened fire with grape. Beating their way through fields "encumbered with high standing corn, topes of trees, walls &c.," the troops encountered some three thousand unusually determined rebel soldiers who retreated only grudgingly through a nearby village, killing sixteen men in the process and wounding seventy-eight more. Windham halted to rest his troops and savor his victory, but was startled to find the main body of contingent troops advancing in good order and great numbers, evidently undismayed by their advance guard's defeat. Windham drew his troops back to their positions around the city and, on returning to the entrenchment, found a letter announcing that Campbell was on his way back to Cawnpore.

Windham moved his troops to the Kalpi Road, just in front of their old positions at the brick kilns. He found the clearest ground he could, but several groves of trees stood nearby. Early the next morning his troops were relieved to find that one detachment of the contingent had still not crossed the canal. But in fact Tatya Tope had astutely determined that if Windham's force was truly formidable it would not have fallen back after its victory.[204] At 10 A.M. his artillery opened fire on two fronts, preparing the way for an all-out assault. The two British positions were held by six hundred men each and commanded respectively by Colonels Watson and Walpole. They formed a demicordon "as far as the limited number of troops allowed," but in a few minutes two battles were simultaneously waging, with Walpole's foremost position bearing the brunt of the rebels's seemingly inexhaustible fire.

Windham's bullock drivers deserted in droves, and along the plain to their rear his men saw that their tents had been struck and their kits scattered across the ground. As their ammunition ran out, the troops in front began to stumble backward. Windham belatedly shifted some of his men to reinforce Walpole's position, but Tatya Tope ingeniously sent a body of rebels charging Windham's now depleted right flank. Windham tried to draw out their infantry with two companies of the 64th, but Tatya continued to press them with artillery, holding his infantry in reserve.

Now it began to occur to Windham's men that they were not only outgunned and outnumbered—nothing new to British troops in India—but outmaneuvered. In Tatya Tope the rebels had finally found their mastermind. By now Windham had brought almost all of his reserves to the fore, and he became "naturally very anxious to assure himself the safety of the fort" now that rebels had made "a circuit through the enclosures on the river's banks" and entered the city.[205] Leaving General Dupuis in command of the main body, Windham galloped back to inspect the entrenchment and his threatened flank. But before he had gone more than a few yards an officer rushed up to report that the rebels were in possession of the lower part of the city, "had just fired a volley in his face," and were laying siege to the fort. Windham immediately ordered Dupuis to abandon the brick kilns and withdraw to the fort to avoid being surrounded, while Windham himself took immediate command of a newly arrived detachment of British riflemen who chased the audacious rebels through the city streets.

Officers estimated the enemy force at about twenty-five thousand men with perhaps fifty guns.[206] As the full dimension of their enemy's army sank in, Windham's men rose from their posts and fled through the city to the fort with rebel infantry in hot pursuit. Most rushed into the entrenchment, but two officers managed to post their men in a chain of intermediate outposts with the theater at its center. Windham's defenders would insist that the rest of the force retreated in an orderly fashion, but other witnesses described a rout. Their officers tried to rally their men with floggings so numerous that two men were said to have gone over to the enemy; in any case they were never seen again.[207] "The men got quite out of hand after their retreat," a chaplain would later tell William Howard Russell. "They broke open the stores, took the wine provided for the sick, smashed open the officers's boxes."[208]

The Sikhs in the fort were amazed and disgusted by the British troops' panic. "An old Sikh, who was standing at the gate of the work, lifted up his hands in wonder when he saw the men running past in disorder, and said aloud, 'You are not the brothers of the men who beat the Khalsa (Sikh empire)!'"[209] Others "patted the fresh arrivals on the back, saying, 'Don't fear! Don't fear!'"

"Ah," gasped a Highlander as he hurried through the gate, "and sure they were too strong for us!"[210]

"In disastrous retreats," observed one officer, "men lose their lives and, more, their confidence and discipline, from their inability to load their firearms quickly when pressed by a pursuing foe."[211] This day the soldiers' Enfields became so foul after seventy or eighty shots that bullets had to be bored out of their barrels.

"The sound of the retreat threw a panic into the whole neighborhood," wrote Thomson. "From the native city came merchants with their families and treasure, seeking the protection of the fort; from the field, helter-skelter, in dire confusion, broken companies of English regiments, guns, sailors, soldiers, camels, elephants, bullock-hackeries with officers' baggage, all crowding at the gates for entrance"[212] and, wrote Jonah, rivaling "the chaos that existed before the fiat of creation went forth."[213]

Like Delafosse at Lucknow, Jonah Shepherd and Mowbray Thomson thus found themselves living in nearly the same nightmare they had so narrowly escaped: huddled in an entrenchment under heavy rebel bombardment and awaiting rescue from Allahabad. "It was not difficult now to convince those few grumblers who previous to this attack were in the habit of speaking disparagingly about the late General Sir Hugh Wheelers' management during the fearful siege of June last," wrote Jonah, "for here we were with upwards of two thousand European soldiers in almost as bad a predicament as that unfortunate General was with but two hundred and ten men."[214] "But," Thomson insisted, "very, very different was the position of General Windham from that of Sir Hugh Wheeler five months previously."[215] There were ample provisions and no English women and children to look after, and thanks to Thomson the fortification was far stronger than Wheeler's had been, with high, impenetrable walls to deflect the rebels' barrage.

For some men the real hero of the second siege of Cawnpore was a hero of the first. "To the indefatigable exertions and almost superhuman self-abnegation of the gallant Captain Thomson (the survivor of the former catastrophe at this place) we owe these entrenchments," wrote an officer on December 7. "But for his working hand-to-hand with his men and officers from dawn to dark, day by day, and daily clad in shirt and trousers as though he had a frame of iron, nerves of steel, and an indomitable will, the most important works would have remained unfinished when the late fearsome storm broke upon us."[216]

The next day Windham deployed his men in a string of outposts between the entrenchment and the town, holding a large body of the 88th Regiment in reserve. At noon of the twenty-eighth the enemy launched an attack, concentrating, as Windham should have expected, on his right flank, which guarded his army's stores in the Assembly Room. But the general had not concentrated his soldiers on the right, and was now slow to reinforce it. Instead he ordered three bodies of his men to advance against the rebel guns, which they did, despite a continuous "shower of grape." "I see thousands of red-coated Sepoys firing away at us," wrote a soldier, "and I get into a rage, and shout, 'Come along my boys, remember Cawnpore!' but in a feeble voice, trying to fancy myself brave, fail totally in the attempt."[217] One party under a Brigadier Wilson rushed a battery of six guns, unfortunately the officers charged too far ahead of their men and by the time the soldiers caught up most of their superiors, including Wilson, had been killed or mortally wounded. All this while Windham had remained with his less beset left flank, and his right flank, under a Brigadier Carthew, gradually and reluctantly fell back against bolder and bolder rebel attacks. Among those who stuck most stubbornly to their guns was Captain H. F. Saunders, who fought with special fury a few yards from where his brother, Captain F. J. G. Saunders of the eighty-fourth, had been crucified and hacked to pieces five months before. "Please Goodness, I hope never to see such a hailstorm of bullets again," wrote one of his soldiers. "I saw men fall on every side of me, . . . splinters hit me, pieces of earth from bullets, &c, . . . while a hurricane of balls passed through us."[218]

By nightfall Windham had suffered 315 casualties, and the rest of his force had retreated into the fort, entirely abandoning the civil station, including the theatre and the Assembly Rooms and the bungalows that the quartermaster had prepared for the reception of the women and children from Lucknow. In an insinuating dispatch Windham hastily tried to blame his brigadiers for the defeat: Wilson for overextending himself on his own initiative, Carthew for withdrawing prematurely. But many in the camp took to calling the debacle "Windham's mess." The general and his officers "had an overweening degree of self-reliance and contemptuous undervaluation of the enemy," wrote one soldier, "who have indubitably shown us they are by no means so contemptible or despicable as they had been assumed to be."[219] According to one officer Windham had been "the biggest braggart" he had ever met; now after his defeat he was "so piano" dining at mess that "I should not have known him for the same man who came out on the same ship with me."[220]

On the morning of November 29 the rebels opened up a blistering fire, the heaviest anyone—even Thomson and Shepherd—had ever experienced. "The rain of balls was thick enough to intercept sight," reported one witness, "and the thundering noise of the cannon did not rest even for a moment."[221] A few round shot came lobbing in to smash the furniture and livestock jammed into the yard, but Thomson's parapets deflected most of the enemy's fire,[222] and a few men ventured out to attend the sale of dead officers' effects, shouting their bids to the auctioneers over the din of the rebel batteries.[223]

The rebels scoured the city for stragglers from Windham's retreat, posting rewards for captured Europeans and searching the city for loyal sepoys. It was widely reported in the British camp that two wounded officers of the 64th[224] had been captured and carted off to the Bibighar where, with grim irony, the rebels hanged them from a three-hundred-year-old banyan tree Neill had employed as a gallows.[225] But the rebels reserved their special rage for the Sikhs, looting the local Gurdwara and murdering the wives of several of the Sikh soldiers who had accompanied Campbell to Lucknow.[226] Any native they suspected of treachery was subjected to amputation, and "several men natives in our employ . . . came into the entrenchment with both arms and their noses cut off."[227]

Nana Sahib and Azimullah kept their distance northwest of Bithur, but otherwise the old cast of characters returned—Bala Rao, Hulas Singh, Jwala Prasad, and Rao Sahib.[228] This time there was no pretense of an administration, however. Raked over by rebel and Highlander alike, Cawnpore had become nothing more than a military position in a worthless ruin. Shopkeepers were ordered to close their shops until further notice, and only the vegetable markets remained open. "Low caste men looted the roti godown [bread storehouse]," wrote Nanak Chand. "Some servants marched about armed with matchlocks, looting on behalf of their [landlords]." But aside from making off with sugar and stacks of sacks with which to fortify their position, the contingent did not plunder the bazaars—perhaps, as Nanak Chand unkindly speculated, because they had been well supplied with money after their uprising at Gwalior.[229]

✦　✦　✦

On the night of November 28 an appalled Colin Campbell came galloping across from Oudh. By funneling their way down a narrow approach to the Residency, Campbell's men had been nearly swallowed up by the teeming tenacious rebel force at Lucknow. But with almost lunatic bravery they had pressed on, the Sikhs and Highlanders vying with each other as they bayoneted their way along the river from one shell-pocked stucco edifice to another with hoarse cries of "Remember Cawnpore!"[230]

At last they had clambered over heaps of rebel dead and burst into the Residency for a rather anticlimactic reception. "What an entry compared with the one we had promised ourselves!" an officer reported home. "We expected to march in with colours flying and bands playing, and to be met by a starving garrison, crying with joy; ladies waving handkerchiefs on all sides and every expression of happiness; but instead of all that we entered as a disorganized army, like so many sheep, finding the whole of the garrison at their posts, as they always remained, and a few stray officers and men only at the gate to meet us."[231]

Indeed, some of the women had seemed rather ungrateful as they emerged from their hiding places, and Campbell's officers gradually recognized, as if coming out of a dream, that the women they had risked so much to rescue were not the noble abstractions they had

beatified on their pilgrimages to the Bibighar but a lot of discom-
posed memsahibs. For the past five months, the garrison had endured horrible deprivations and terrible losses: four hundred had
been killed, including twenty-three women. But how could Campbell expect them to quit their months-long home with only two
hours' notice and without sufficient carriage to transport their furnishings, boxes of silver, books, and "all our glass and crockery?"[232]
As Richard Collier wrote, "It was as if Sir Colin, like an untimely
groom, had brought the carriage round too early."[233]

By the time they had departed, many of the ladies had donned
their best gowns and bonnets. "Whether 'Betty gave the cheek' a little touch of red or not, I cannot say," wrote Russell, "but I am assured
the array of fashion, though somewhat behind the season, owing to
the difficulty of communicating with the Calcutta *modistes*, was very
creditable."[234] Soldiers expecting to see ragged martyrs stumble
melodramatically out of the Residency found that they "looked quite
well, dressed up with white kid gloves."[235]

Hours had been lost to endless negotiations about "these few little
clothes-trunks" the ladies asked to take with them, requests that
were nearly incomprehensible to so austere an old Scottish warrior
as Campbell (although his officers apparently did find room to carry
the King of Lucknow's treasure and £240,000 worth of gold and silver).[236] After he thought he had finally cleared the Residency, two
young ladies "came trippingly in, whisked about the Residency a
short time, and then, with nods and smiles, departed," graciously informing the General that they would be back "presently." At that the
general finally lost his temper. "No, ladies, no," he snapped back.
"You'll be good enough to do nothing of the kind. You have been
here quite long enough, I am sure, and I have had quite enough
trouble in getting you out."[237]

The operation was compared to turning a sock inside out, for the
women had to proceed by night and under fire down the same narrow passage their rescuers had struggled through.[238] A few ladies
played their parts nobly, giving up their doolies or draped litters for
the wounded.[239] But the evacuation was chaotic. Disoriented soldiers, panicked camp followers, wounded men in excruciating agony
filled the air with their shouts and screams as rebel shells burst
among them, illuminating their motley caravan in nightmarish vi-
gnettes. Here and there they had to leave their transport and run
along the trenches the soldiers dug for them when no other cover
was available, after which men would hurry them back into the carts

and doolies; one stout woman required three men and a chair each time she climbed back onto her horse.[240]

They proceeded down the Lucknow Road in a nine-mile caravan through dust so thick they could not see "the children in their arms."[241] In the chaos of their camps they could hardly sleep for all the shouting and confusion, and some temporarily lost their way in the darkness. Six days later they finally reached the river, vastly relieved to find, after Windham's bulletins of his defeat, that the Bridge of Boats was still intact but dismayed to see, in the evening light, that their refuge had become a pandemonium of smoke and flames.

In the morning Tatya Tope caught sight of the British tents across the river and began firing at the Bridge of Boats, but Campbell fired back from the entrenchment with everything he had, including a battery of naval guns manned by a naval brigade under Captain William Peel, son of the former Prime Minister. Their guns managed to silence the rebel artillery for the thirty hours it took to get the women, children, and hundreds of wounded men across.

"Amongst those who returned from Lucknow was my friend Lieut. Delafosse," wrote Thomson, "reduced to a most emaciated condition from the continued effects of fever and dysentery."[242] He counted himself lucky. "Doolie after doolie, with its red curtains down, concealing some poor victim, passed on to the hospitals. The poor fellows were brought in shot, cut, shattered, and wounded in every imaginable way; and as they went by, raw stumps might be seen hanging over the sides of doolies, literally torn like butcher meat."[243]

The rebels now sullenly set fire to all the surrounding buildings, including the Assembly Rooms, which contained the kits of most of the men who had marched to Lucknow with Havelock and Campbell.[244] "Those few houses in cantonments that had escaped hitherto," recalled Jonah, "were on this occasion reduced to ashes."[245] Campbell could only watch, for he would not risk more casualties until he had managed to evacuate the women and children to Allahabad. "Five hundred new tents, and a great quantity of clothing, . . . a large quantity of spare ammunition, and saddlery" went up in smoke, as well as heaps of material historians still mourn: most of the mementos, books, letters, and records that the soldiers had salvaged from the ruins of Cawnpore.

"Nothing could look more wretched and miserable," wrote one of the Lucknow ladies, "than this dreadful place as we came in by the light of the moon." The station of Cawnpore, once so familiar, was a desolation. . . . Burnt bungalows, broken gates, the remains of gun-carriages, trees lying on the ground with their leaves and branches stripped off, and more than all, the thoughts which arose in our minds of the fearful scenes so lately enacted here, depressed and saddened us altogether."[246]

The ladies were "thoroughly miserable" in their battered and besieged haven, but it was the wounded who suffered most.[247] "Grape and round shell have been falling on the tree close to our tent," wrote a soldier. "Some shells, I believe, have fallen on the hospital, which is unfortunately much exposed. Every square foot of the floor and verandah of the General Hospital is covered with wounded officers and men."[248]

"I had tremendous work," wrote a young surgeon.

> . . . The first day I amputated eight limbs, dressed more than 80 wounded men, scarcely knowing night from day, eating beef and biscuit and drinking tea and water whenever I could get a chance. Three round shots passed through my hospital roof, bringing down plenty of tiles and dirt, but injuring no one. . . . All my clothes are spoilt with blood. I went about in my shirt-sleeves, bareheaded; my hair was matted with blood; my arms and hands covered. Blood spurted from arteries into my mouth and eyes; I was indeed all blood. . . . In one week I saw more surgery than most surgeons see in a lifetime, and I trust I have improved myself.[249]

Finally, under the cover of the night of December 3, Campbell assembled all of his transport and set the women and children on the road to Allahabad. "It was miserable and so cold," wrote an officer, that the four-mile-long convoy[250] could only move "at the rate of two miles an hour."[251] The garrison at Allahabad had designated "heroine" as the password to announce their arrival, but when they finally reached the station on December 7, they did not quite rise to expectations. People had expected to see women suffering from malnourishment, grief, the horrors of their ordeal. Instead, they "seemed a most cheerful party," and it was "so strange" to see them stroll off to listen to the band in the evenings.[252]

But after the siege and the long dusty march the familiar routines of garrison life finally brought the shock and unreality of what they had endured into stark relief. Many women could not credit their newfound security and continued to carry their valuables sewn lumpily into their skirts. They gasped as if suffocated in the presence of servants; stared vacantly at their suppers; could scarcely follow conversations; wandered sleepless along the bungalow verandahs, afraid that in the strange silence at Allahabad the rebels were mining the cantonment.[253]

A month later they sailed for Calcutta on flats towed by the steamer *Madras*. The authorities urged their countrymen to allow the survivors to enter the city in peace. "No one will wish to obtrude upon those who are under bereavement or sickness any show of ceremony which shall impose fatigue and pain. The best welcome which can be tendered upon such an occasion is one which shall break in as little as possible upon privacy and rest."[254] But no one paid any mind of course, and, when the *Madras* chugged into view, hundreds of townspeople lined Prinsep's Ghat, cheering and waving as guns fired salutes from the ramparts of Fort William.[255] But as soon as the women began to emerge from the boats in their newly fashioned widows' weeds,[256] leading their children by the hand, the cheers subsided into a sorrowing silence, as if these survivors of the Lucknow garrison were trailing the ghosts of Wheeler's Entrenchment, Fatehgarh, Sati Chowra, and the Bibighar's well.[257]

NO SPORT

Retribution: December 6, 1857–January 26, 1858

Sir Colin Campbell reluctantly waited three days before launching an attack on the Gwalior Contingent.[258] Nana Sahib had kept his distance somewhere in the country northwest of Bithur,[259] but Tatya Tope was firmly in command at Cawnpore, where his army of about thirteen thousand men now occupied a semicircle only two hundred yards from the outer defenses of Campbell's fort. The Gwalior Contingent was camped astride the Kalpi Road that led westward out of the city, while a miscellany of mutineers and matchlockmen had joined Bala Rao on the road to Bithur.

By now reinforcements had swelled Campbell's army to six hundred cavalry, five thousand infantry, and thirty-five guns. On the morning of December 6 he ordered his batteries to fire on Bala's forces as if to soften up the enemy's left for an assault; for two hours "houses fell, trees disappeared," wrote one of Peel's artillerymen, "and the air rang with the whistling of shot, fizzing of shells, etc."[260] But Campbell's real target was the contingent's position along the Ganges Canal.

Leaving Windham with a small force to hold down the fort, Campbell sent two brigades to Generalgunj, just northwest of Wheeler's Entrenchment: one to hold its ground and the other to cross the canal and march around behind the native city, cutting the contingent off from Bala Rao's force and blocking a retreat down the road to Kalpi. Two other brigades crossed the Grand Trunk Road and launched the main assault, marching toward the brick kilns as the rebels arrayed along the canal opened a tremendous fusillade. But they were overwhelmed by Peel's naval brigade and a body of horse artillery. With the approaches to the city shut off, the retreating contingent began to flee along the Kalpi Road with Campbell's cavalry in hot pursuit.[261] In their rush to escape, the rebels threw down their weapons and abandoned their ammunition. "The slaughter was great," wrote an officer. The rebels "dispersed over the country on each side, and flying into the jungle and the cultivation, shrouded themselves in its thick cover from the red sabres and lances of the horsemen." (The lance was "an admirable weapon for pandies," wrote one officer at the time, for "they lie on the ground, and it is difficult to reach them with a sword.")[262]

In the rebels' abandoned camp the British found chupatties still simmering on their griddles and scores of rebel wounded lying in hospitals. "Many rose too late, for the conquerors spared none that day; neither the sick man in his weakness, nor the strong man in his strength."[263] "All the men, native and European," wrote another participant, "got no end of plunder and rupees off the dead men that were shot and cut down. It was a wonderful sight."[264]

By nightfall the remainder of Tatya's army, cut off from the Kalpi Road, began to withdraw in the gathering dusk, fleeing toward Bithur. Through some blunder no one pursued them, but the next morning Campbell's men patrolled the city "from end to end, east, west, north, and south"; not only did they not meet any resistance, "but many of the townspeople brought out food and water to our men, appearing very glad to see us."[265] Campbell's men spent most of the day "hanging those who had disguised themselves as natives, and hid in the town. We soon found them out," wrote an officer in

Torching a village in Cawnpore district

Peel's brigade, "and it did not take even a magistrate to hang them."[266]

✦ ✦ ✦

It was the last the ruined city would ever see of the rebel army. As the contingent fled back to Kalpi, the rest raced to Bithur, where Nana was frantically and vainly attempting to recover his treasures from the wells at Saturday House. But on the morning of December 8 British troops under the command of General Hope Grant closed on his shattered army, and Nana was forced to give up on his treasure and flee up the riverbank to Serai Ghat, where boats had been assembled to ferry his army into Oudh.

As Nana boarded his craft and pushed off into the stream, his elderly Mahratta sowars, the last living relics of Baji Rao's glory, galloped out on their bony horses and gallantly charged a combined cavalry force of British lancers and sowars led by that dashing young executioner of Moghul princes, Lieutenant William Hodson. The Mahrattas were outnumbered and soon cut down, and as the dust whirled away the rest of Nana's army heard a chilling skirl of bagpipes and saw a broad line of British infantry advancing through the town.

The rebels broke for their boats, leaving behind all but two of their seventeen guns[267] and a train of carts loaded with Cawnpore plunder sinking in the quicksand along the river's edge.[268] The British opened fire with their Enfields, but Nana Sahib's boat had pushed off first and was already reaching the Oudh side of the Ganges before the artillery could bring their guns to bear on the retreating fleet. Nevertheless, they soon raked the river with grape and round shot, swamping many of the native boats and drowning hundreds of rebel soldiers in Nana's wake. The sepoys who had been wounded in the assault or managed somehow to scramble out of the current and back to the riverbank were executed. "I never let my men take prisoners," wrote Hodson, "but shoot them at once."[269]

"It would have been impossible for the Europeans to have guarded their prisoners," explained Forbes-Mitchell, "and, for that reason, it was obvious that prisoners were not to be taken; while on the part of the rebels, wherever they met a Christian or a white man, he was at once slain without pity or remorse. . . . It was both horrible and demoralising," he concluded, "for the army to be engaged in such a war . . . The inhuman murders and foul treachery of the Nana Sahib and others put all feeling of humanity or mercy for the enemy out of the question, and our men thus early spoke of putting a wounded Jack Pandy *out of pain*, just as calmly as if he had been a wild beast; it was even considered an act of mercy."[270]

Nevertheless firing on Nana's boats "was some return for [Nana Sahib's] treachery at Sati Chowrah *ghat* six months before." The parallel was not lost on a few of the rebels' wives and children who had been left on the bank with their baggage. "They evidently expected to be killed," Forbes-Mitchell recalled, "but were escorted to a village in our rear, and left there. We showed them that we had come to war with men—not to butcher women!"

After bathing and washing their filthy shirts in the Ganges, Grant's men camped at Serai Ghat for two days of rest. "From the date of the defeat of the Gwalior Contingent," wrote Forbes-Mitchell, "our star was in the ascendant, and the attitude of the country people showed that they understood which was the winning side."[271] They seemed "not so frightened," recalled a lieutenant of the Madras Army, and "bring us milk and fruit."[272]

The peasants' confidence proved premature. On the eleventh of December, Grant's column was ordered to march into Bithur to drag Nana's palace wells for treasure. In one of the nearly deserted settlements along the road they passed a lone villager sitting in his doorway, idly watching the troops march by.[273] He was shot "for the fun" by a Highlander.[274]

At Bithur the men were promised a share in whatever treasure they could dredge up, and in the cool December weather they labored with a will. At first they found nothing but a lot of rubbish, but after hauling out a rotting log they came upon two pewter vases and, scooping around in the muck, began to discover gold and silver *objets* of "extreme antiquity": pots, plates, lamps "which seemed of Jewish manufacture and spoons of barbaric weight."[275] Everyone remarked on the disappointing workmanship of these first objects which, "in mean material, would not have attracted attention, if discovered in a South Sea Island."[276]

The crews worked night and day, for "if they do not work at night the water rises to the original height."[277] Sappers were lowered thirty feet[278] down into the well in one-hour shifts to stand waist deep in the frigid water and heave treasures into the huge leather buckets.[279] Two million rupees[280] were recovered "which had been packed in ammunition-boxes."[281] The Peshwa's silver howdah emerged, tarnished black from the muck of the well.[282] There seemed to be no end to Nana's treasures. "What beautiful gold chatties, plate and goblets were brought up today from the well," exclaimed one soldier.[283] A solid gold bowl weighing forty pounds emerged, along with hundreds of more pounds of gold and silver.[284]

Shivering sappers and Highlanders worked straight through Christmas, expecting they would each be rewarded with a thousand rupees. But in the end they never saw a pice of the treasure; the Company decreed that most of the treasure was simply Nana's loot from the Cawnpore garrison and should therefore revert to the state.[285] "We even had to pay from our own pockets for the replacement of our kits," one soldier bitterly recalled, "which were taken by the Gwalior Contingent when they captured Wyndham's camp."[286]

During these excavations the rest of Grant's force was busy plundering the town, but the take was disappointing. There was "scarcely anything worth looting," wrote an officer, "this operation having successfully been performed by Havelock's force some time since."[287]

"Our own Sappers and Miners with the Seikhs ones," wrote Francis Grant, "are blowing up and burning the Hindoo temples and large houses. On one large temple of beautiful construction with a marble altar and flooring they are making four large bores to blow it at once into atoms." This had been Baji Rao's temple, inlaid with semi-precious stones that the soldiers now pried out with their bayonets. Sappers laid nine thousand pounds of powder in the bore holes and in a few seconds reduced it to gravel.[288]

Soldiers searched the ruins of Saturday House for a store of jewels Nana was rumored to have left behind. But they found only a lit-ter of bric-a-brac and a stack of Azimullah's letters from Lucie Duff Gordon and his deluded fiancée from Brighton. "Such rubbish I never read," fumed Lieutenant Fred Roberts. They were "partly in French, which this scoundrel seems to have understood. How English ladies can be so infatuated. Miss ___ was going to marry Azimula, and I have no doubt would like to still, altho' he was the chief instigator in the Cawnpore massacres. You would not believe them if I sent home the letters."[289] Roberts kept the letters for him-self, but for some years versions of them circulated through British camps as *Love Letters*, probably racy inventions along the lines of *The Lustful Turk*.[290]

The Sikh raja whose family had contributed the land for Baji Rao's estate managed to convince the soldiers not to destroy his family's house. Otherwise all the large houses, including Tatya Tope's, were destroyed. Roistering through Nana's menagerie, British soldiers car-ried off two English bulldogs, an enormous squirrel and a "wan-deroo" monkey that later took to leaping from tent pole to tent pole in Cawnpore camp, stealing potatoes for its new master. The squirrel died in Sherer's keeping; the monkey, dubbed Nana, would end up at the Zoological Gardens in London, where schoolboys came to jeer him.[291]

◆   ◆   ◆

On November 1 at Allahabad, Canning read a proclamation by Queen Victoria addressed to the "Princes, Chiefs and People of India" in which she resolved "to take upon ourselves the government of the territories in India heretofore administered in trust for us by the Hon. East India Company."[292] She appointed Canning her Viceroy, adopted all Company personnel as her employees, intended to abide by all of the Company's treaties, and expressed her determination not to extend her territory.

> We hold ourselves bound to the natives of our Indian territories
> by the same obligations of duty which binds us to all our other
> subjects; and those obligations, by the blessing of Almighty God,
> we shall faithfully and conscientiously fulfill. . . . We desire to
> show our mercy by pardoning the offences of those who have
> been thus misled but who desire to return to the path of duty. . . .
> Our clemency will be extended to all offenders, save and except
> those who have been or shall be convicted of having directly
> taken part in the murder of British subjects. With regard to such
> the demands of justice forbid the exercise of mercy.[293]

So there was an end to *Kampani Jehan* after all, just as the Brahmins had predicted. The Mahrattas, Moslems, Santals, Brahmins, and outcastes could now take their place with the English, Irish, and Welsh as the baba logue of Her Majesty the Queen. The impersonal rule of the Company had been displaced by the regency of a living, breathing human being.

But despite the Queen's clemency, the British reoccupation of Cawnpore was marked by more destruction and bloody reprisals. Robert Napier of the engineers, who would win fame as Napier of Magdala for his campaign against Theodore of Ethiopia, busied himself blowing up temples at Buxee Ghat. "A deputation of Hindu priests came to him to beg that the temples might not be destroyed," recalled one witness.

"Now, listen to me," replied the colonel.

> You were all here when our women and children were murdered,
> and you also well know that we are not destroying these temples
> for vengeance, but for military considerations connected with the
> safety of the bridge of boats. But if any man among you can prove
> to me that he did a single act of kindness to any Christian man,
> woman, or child, nay, if he can even prove that he uttered one
> word of intercession for the life of any one of them, I pledge myself to spare the temple where he worships.[294]

The Brahmins backed away.[295]

The men of the 64th had been especially provoked by the hanging of two of their officers, and the Sikhs were enraged by the murder of their wives.[296] But it was Peel's stout little sailors who proved the most enthusiastic if not the most skillful hangmen. At Calcutta they had already manifested a special loathing of natives; Lady Canning had once observed them from Government House drunkenly beating a native policeman to death.[297] According to Fred Roberts, Indians thought the Highlanders in their kilts were "the ghosts of the murdered women, but the sailors astonish them most—'4 ft. high, 4 ft. broad, long hair, and dragging big guns!!' They can't make them out."[298]

One officer saw them hang three men at Cawnpore with tent ropes "which proved too weak, as, on the drop being removed, two of the three broke and the men came to the ground, one of them breaking his leg. The third man did not die for nearly ten minutes, but hardly struggled at all. As soon as he was dead the other two were hanged; this time without mishap."[299]

Sherer saw another sort of execution. "Mr. Gregson and I were present," he recalled,

> when a noisy crowd approached the bank overhanging the lower plateau and we found, in the centre of it, two men being roughly handled by some sailors and others. They were really bullock-drivers employed by our side, and, having got wounded, were in search of medical aid. But being ragged chaps, and smeared with dust and blood, they were set down at once, by the lawless party with whom they had fallen in, as rebels. No remonstrance or explanation that Mr. Gregson or I could make was of any avail, and the unhappy fellows lost their lives, and were precipitated head-foremost to the level below. The tumult and confusion prevented us from distinguishing the actual perpetrators of the outrage; and under the circumstances, it seemed scarcely desirable to lay our information before the authorities against men we recognised as members only of the crowd—illegal assembly though it undoubtedly was.

When Captain Bruce of the military police condemned one of Nunne Nawab's brothers to death, the sailors demanded that they be allowed to hang the man themselves. Bruce ordered them to stand aside. "The condemned man was timid, but not without self-possession. He said something which I understood to be that Jesus was a forgiving prophet; and that even if he had committed a fault, it would be over-looked for the sake of Jesus. He spoke very low, and it was not easy quite to make out his words. But the sacred name was certainly mentioned more than once."[300]

The dignity and bravery of the condemned men continued to confound many onlookers. "They have in effect the most supreme indifference to death," wrote an officer who had looked on as one victim "watched the process of fastening the rope to a tree, talking all the time to people near him about the mutiny, had his arms pinioned and walked under the bough just as cool as if he had been going to dinner." Another sepoy took the gallows with ferocious defiance, declaring, "You are all a nation of pigs," as the drop was sprung.[301]

The looting of what little must have remained at Cawnpore also had fatal results. "There was a tent-maker, in the bazar," recalled Sherer, "named Choonee Lal, a man who had throughout taken the British side very loyally, and had been of great service in many ways.

> Naturally handsome, he had by grain diet and simple habits obtained a certain look of benevolent content. . . . He saw, near his house, two soldiers enter a shop, and compel its keeper to give up his money. Choonee Lal knew English perfectly, and spoke to the men, telling them they were protectors, not oppressors of the poorer citizens. An aphorism so gentle might have passed, but he unfortunately added that if any officer knew what they were doing, they would be punished. This sounded like a threat, and the knowledge of English, too, was calculated to create some alarm; and so the two fellows turned on their monitor, and one of them, putting his musket absolutely against Choonee Lal's side, discharged it. The poor body, with face uncovered, and the pleasant smile still lingering in death, was brought to my tent by the murdered man's nephew, who was present when the event occurred—and a truly sad sight it was.[302]

Captain Archibald Impey reported that two soldiers killed "Salik Rasi the great contractor" and the plundering got so out of control that officers were "obliged to have [roll] called every hour to keep the troops from looting the town."[303] Nevertheless the hanging parties at Cawnpore gradually ran out of candidates. Working from captured papers from Baba Bhutt's court, Sherer learned the names of various landlords who had paid Nana Sahib their respects. A number of them were hanged, 144 were forced to forfeit their estates, and a fine was levied on the townspeople. But the hanging parties looked elsewhere for victims.

♦   ♦   ♦

To open communication between Cawnpore and Agra, Campbell moved next on Fatehgarh, which for the past six months had been ruled by the rebel Nawab of Farrukhabad. Preoccupied with his harem and his watercolors, the Nawab allowed his privy councillor to manage things, but his retainers proved capricious administrators. The administration of justice was marked by extreme severity and leniency; theft was punished by amputation, but rapists were fined only two rupees, and a Hindu convicted of murder was released when he converted to Islam. The Hindu sepoys of the 41st Native Infantry interceded to prohibit the slaughter of cows or their use in the carting of garbage, but commandeered bullocks from local farmers to carry their plunder home and levied fines on villagers to make up for their arrears in pay. Local landlords declared their independence, raising their own banners and charging fines and tolls, and dacoits rampaged through the district, plundering villagers. The result was that a lot of fields were left uncultivated, and the Nawab's coffers began to run dry.[304]

Over the past months the Nawab had been thrice defeated by British forces at Kanauj, Kasganj, and Patiala. Now Campbell sent a force of two thousand men under Brigadier Walpole with orders to link with a force of 1,900 men proceeding from Delhi under Colonel Seaton, who had recently taken the town of Mainpuri at the junction of the Delhi, Agra, and Cawnpore roads. The two forces converged at nearby Bewar. In the meantime Campbell himself proceeded with five thousand troops from Cawnpore, determined now to march in perfect order and with great deliberateness to impress on the natives the coherence of the Company's overwhelming might.

Campbell had not intended to attack Farrukhabad until Seaton and Walpole could join him, but when he reached the iron suspension bridge across the Kali River he found that the rebels had removed all the planks. Fearing they might destroy the bridge completely before his force could cross, he immediately set about repairing it. Astonishingly, the Nawab's force, also five thousand strong, did not fire on Campbell's men until after the planks had been replaced, and it was not until Campbell's men had begun to trot across the river that the Nawab finally brought four battalions of the 41st Native Infantry plus cavalry and eight guns forward to block the bridge.

Leading the way across, Campbell and Hope Grant were both struck by spent bullets, and one small rebel gun in particular sent many men toppling into the river, but Peel's brigade put it out of commission with three rapid shots.[305] Campbell's force eventually crossed the bridge, sending the Nawab's men flying down the road to

Fatehgarh. Campbell's cavalry set off after the Nawab's troops with Hodson in the lead, and when the rest of the force marched to Fatehgarh on January 2 they found the road and the surrounding fields "strewn with dead bodies, some of old men, some of young and some even of boys, covered with ghastly wounds, and one could trace the tracks through the fields of the flying sepoys pursued by the relentless Sikhs, and see the trampled ground where the short, final struggle had taken place. Some of the wells we passed were choked with corpses."[306]

More slaughter was to follow, for the return to British civil law simply meant that "the hangman's noose was to be substituted for rifle-bullet and bayonet."[307] The Nawab himself had escaped, but a relative named Najir Khan was found in the city, and though he hosted Campbell and his officers at supper that evening, the newly reinstated magistrate, Mr. Power, arrested him the next morning and hanged him the following day "with some circumstances of needless cruelty," wrote one officer. He was first "forced to eat hog's flesh, and flogged severely at first—deeds unworthy of a great and victorious people."[308]

Magistrate Power issued an order to the townspeople of Farrukhabad that if they did not turn over their rebel collector, he would give the town over to the soldiers to sack. As Campbell's Highlanders marched toward the city gates, the townspeople surrendered the collector. After a few minutes' trial he was "brought out," wrote Forbes-Mitchell, "bound hand and foot, and carried by *coolies* on a common country *charpoy*. . . . I fear he had neither jury nor counsel, and I know that he was first smeared with pig's fat, flogged by sweepers, and then hanged. Both Sir Colin Campbell and Sir William Peel were said to have protested against the barbarity."[309]

But the barbarities continued. It was in this district, after all, that the Nawab's prisoners had been put to death: gentlemen decapitated, ladies and children lined up along the walls and fired upon with cannon. On January 6 Brigadier Adrian Hope was sent out into the countryside to round up rebels and incinerate their property. The magistrate, whom the Highlanders had by now admiringly dubbed "Hanging Power," followed along, and at every halt lived up to his name. At one village an old man who had declared himself the new Nawab of Farrukhabad was given over to Sir Colin Campbell in exchange for not bombarding their town. "Poor wretch!" wrote Oliver Jones, "he only enjoyed his usurpation for a very few hours." In the middle of a broad avenue Jones found a tree being rigged as a gallows, and a large crowd of inhabitants and camp followers. The self-styled Nawab

> was tied down to a *charpoy*—a sort of native bedstead—and carried under the fatal tree, upon which he cast an anxious look when he saw the noose suspended therefrom. He was then stripped, flogged, and hanged. He had on a handsome shawl, which an officer took possession of on the spot—an action which requires no comment. The man behaved with great firmness. While the rope was being adjusted, a soldier struck him on the face; upon which he turned round with great fierceness, and said—"Had I had a sword in my hand, you dared not have struck that blow": his last words before he was launched into eternity."[310]

It fell to Forbes-Mitchell to guard Power as he processed over one hundred of the natives Hope's men kept dragging in. "They were marched up in batches, and shortly after marched back again to a large tree, which stood in the centre of the square, and hanged thereon. This went on from three o'clock in the afternoon till daylight the following morning, when it was reported that there was no more room on the tree, and by that time there were one hundred and thirty men hanging from its branches."

Captain Hodson, who had executed the Delhi princes in cold blood and slaughtered scores of retreating rebels, had finally had enough. "I'm sick of work of this kind," he said, mounting his horse. "I'm glad I'm not on duty."[311] But the commissioner was so insatiable that when the Nawab's mistress Bonny Byrne was found and brought before him, Power telegraphed the governor-general for permission to string her up as well.[312]

"The proposal is not sanctioned," Canning wired back. "There has been enough bloodshed of this kind."[313]

AS TO DISHONOR

The Abducted: 1858

Campbell now longed to press southward and conquer all of Rohilkhand, reserving the final occupation of Lucknow for the next run of cool weather. But Canning insisted that he conquer Lucknow next. He was anxious that a campaign in Rohilkhand would give the rebels at Lucknow too much time to consolidate, but the fact was that British public opinion, not to mention the Queen's, demanded no less than the immediate conquest of the capital of Oudh. Even after the women and children had been successfully evacuated and Outram left on the city's outskirts with three thousand men, Lucknow had attained enormous symbolic significance, the antidote to the terrible sorrows of Cawnpore.

For the next weeks Campbell built up his army until it was the largest British army ever seen in India: 164 guns and some thirty-one thousand men.[314] They proceeded with excruciating slowness in a column that stretched for twenty-five miles: Highlanders, Fusiliers, Gurkhas, Sikhs, and the murderous little sailors of Peel's brigade trailing guns and ammunition wagons and a city's worth of coolies, tradesmen, camp followers, loath bullocks, blustering camels, and shambling, gentlemanly elephants holding their trunks above the dust. Their slow, mechanical approach terrorized the rebels who had gathered at Lucknow. Hazrat Mahal, tearing away her veil to shame her soldiers "for their indifference to the wrongs and sufferings of their countrywomen," had begged her generals to drive Outram away before Campbell could reach the city.[315] The rebels tried to storm Outram's stronghold, but all they had to show for it were their comrades' already bare and bleached skeletons lying around the battleground in their uniforms' rotting shreds.

It took Campbell two weeks of brutal fighting to capture the city. The old retributive fires still raged, especially among the young recruits who had recently arrived at Cawnpore and paraded at their officers' orders through the ruins of the Bibighar. One injured rebel was dragged out of a bombarded house and deliberately wounded by a united squad of Sikhs and Englishmen; they first tried to draw and quarter him, but when that did not work they stabbed him in the face with bayonets and then pinned him down in a small fire until he burned to death.[316] In room after room, rebels died by the hundreds, shot down "in files" until "no living enemy was left to kill."[317] One hundred and twenty-seven of Campbell's men were killed and over five hundred wounded: among the dead was Captain Hodson, shot in the chest by a roomful of rebels as he turned a corner in a darkened hallway.[318]

The looting of Lucknow was second only to the sack of Delhi. Wading through rooms two feet deep in smashed mirrors and chandeliers, officers packed their kits and ammunition pouches with jewels and gold mohurs snatched up from the burning houses of Oudh's aristocracy. In the heat of plunder a soldier offered William Howard Russell a silver casket full of gems for two gold mohurs and a bottle of rum. Russell, in accord with Anglo-Indian custom, did not carry any cash, but the soldier gave his companion a diamond and opal pin that a London jeweler would later buy for £7,500.[319] The total take from Lucknow's palaces and vaults and wells was estimated at over one million pounds. Officers would later contrive any excuse they could find to get home to England to sell them; in their homebound trunks they secreted treasures worth "estates in Scotland and Ireland, and snug fishing and shooting boxes in every game-haunted or salmon-frequented angle of the world."

Once the worst of the looting was over the citizens of Lucknow began to return, "but tens of thousands will never return," wrote Russell, "for the court, the nawabs, and rajahs who maintained them are gone forever, and their palaces are desolate."[320] The Mutiny was the end of Lucknow's nobility. The Begum, fighting as she went, fled into the Nepalese wilderness. Her husband, Wajid Ali Shah, remained in splendid exile at Garden Reach. He finally decided to accept the pension he had scorned since annexation and lived until 1887, indulging his enthusiasm for women, opium, wild animals, and the arts.

Lucknow itself never regained its former glory, not even when it was made the capital of the North-Western Provinces, redubbed the United Provinces in 1902. The subcontinental center of Moslem culture moved to Hyderabad and Delhi, only to flee India completely with Partition, and many of the old Nawabi edifices crumbled to the ground. But strangely enough the British victory at Lucknow proved a godsend to the dispossessed talukdars, even some of those who had rebelled, for Lord Canning had learned from Oudh that Dalhousie never should have tampered with the existing landed aristocracy. To their own astonishment, the Rajput talukdars of Oudh were restored to their old estates and found themselves more powerful than they had ever been under Wajid Ali Shah. Grateful and relieved, they would eventually become "a pillar of the British Raj."[321]

✦ ✦ ✦

Amy Horne's abductor, Ismail Khan, did not wait for Campbell's army, but resolved to flee with her from Lucknow to his village near Allahabad, not many miles from the plantation of a great uncle of hers named Flouest. By now Amy had been a captive for nine months "that seemed as many lifetimes—of horror, grief, and heartrending anguish, . . . and every living, breathing cell in my frail body seemed to shout out the query 'How long, O Lord, how long?'"

Another month passed at Ismail Khan's village: weeks of endless alarms that rebel bands or British hanging parties were approaching. At last came the Government's proclamation that any rebel who voluntarily surrendered Christian captives would be pardoned automatically. Ismail Khan initially dismissed the offer as a ruse, but little by little Amy managed to convince him that his best hope of surviving the new Raj was to release her. At last he consented, "provided I gave him a solemn undertaking to act as his advocate, and obtain for him a free and full pardon for the part he had played in the rising."

Amy agreed, and the sowar made her put her vow in writing, passing it by a moonshi to make sure it said what he intended. At last, still dressed in Moslem clothing, Amy took leave of Ismail Khan and stumbled to a nearby village that was now under British control.

> I interviewed the native official in charge, informing him that I was an English lady, and—at the same time placing my hand inside the bosom of my jacket—that I was the bearer of an important despatch to the General Sahib in charge of the Fort at Allahabad; and requesting that a dooly [palaquin] be placed immediately at my disposal, to convey me thither. With a promptitude that astounded me a *dooly*, with a relay of bearers, was in a few minutes in attendance.

By midday of April 7, 1858, Amy reached Allahabad, and found her way to the house of her great-uncle. At first the Flouests could hardly recognize her. "It would be superfluous to dwell on the warmth of their reception of their grand-niece, and my aunt very kindly placed her entire wardrobe at my disposal. I was glad indeed to discard my hateful native dress with its still more hateful associations, and to habilitate myself once more in the garb of civilisation."

As the Bengal *Hurkaru* reported, Amy was "in great distress of mind, often in tears," had "forgotten much of the English language, and [looked] prematurely aged." Flouest immediately found her a berth on a steamer bound for Calcutta, where two of her aunts resided. When the steamer arrived at Calcutta the riverbank was crowded with curiosity seekers come to lay eyes on this survivor of the massacre at Sati Chowra and ten months' unimaginable captivity with a rebel sowar. But she was spared "the ordeal of a reception" by one of her aunt's friends, who took her further downriver in his launch and delivered her to her aunts. At the end of that month she wrote a very brief account of herself to the Calcutta authorities. "The whole of our family must have been cruelly killed," she said, "and of course all our property lost. I take the liberty of thus addressing you," she continued, "as I am given to understand that Government has graciously allowed two thousand Company's Rupees compensation to all persons situated like myself." Here was one of the women Canning, Havelock, and Neill had risked everything to try to save, but the Government replied with a chilly little note informing her solicitor that no such compensations had been contemplated, suggesting that she apply for a pension like anyone else,[322] and advising the readers of the *Times of London* not to donate any money to her welfare until her story had been investigated thoroughly.[323]

People occasionally tried to interview her about the individual destinies of the Cawnpore garrison. Canning's secretary hoped she might be able to account for the fate of the Lindsays.[324] A Baptist minister reported however that she was only "able to give a very connected account of things up to the massacre, but whenever she reached that point she becomes mad."[325] So mad that her uncle never credited her tale of a vast treasure hidden under the Begum's floor. But by then of course, it had already been found, for much of the plunder of Lucknow simply disappeared, and the cabal of officers who made off with it had no interest in entertaining her addled claims to a share.

By August she had been granted a pension of one hundred rupees a month. "I need hardly add," she wrote, "that I am as happy and comfortable as I could wish to be."[326] Under the pseudonym of Amy Haines, she managed to write an account of her experiences in 1859 for an Indian newspaper, and testified to a committee investigating the reports of mutilations that now appeared to have been apocryphal. She was the sole prosecution witness at the trial of Maulvie Liaqat Ali who had, for whatever reason, saved her life. But evidently Ismail Khan was never brought to trial.

The Anastasia of the Cawnpore massacres was not Amy Horne, however, but Margaret Wheeler, the general's youngest daughter.[327] Amy had last seen her by the river, riding behind the saddle of a sowar. It was widely reported that on the night of June 27, before her abductor could have his way with her, Miss Wheeler had produced either a pistol or a sword, killed him and his family, and then thrown herself down a nearby well.[328] Her gallant end became a staple of Victorian theatricals and the subject of the most popular of the melodramatic engravings that were collected eventually in Ball's *The History of the Indian Mutiny*.

But no one who looked into the story believed it. During his investigations into the massacres Colonel G. Williams, commissioner of military police for the North-Western Provinces, was told by two musicians who had followed the mutineers' flight to Farrukabad that

Miss Wheeler slays her captors

they had seen Miss Wheeler with the troops "in a native dress, silk pyjamahs and a chudder over her head." One witness reported that she "was riding on a side saddle. I heard it was General Wheeler's youngest daughter. The sepoys were talking about her. I saw her every day during the march to Futtehgurh" and again "when the mutineers marched for Bithoor."[329]

Three years later a Hindu traveler asked some local people to show him the well into which Miss Wheeler had jumped, but no one could point it out. "Many people suspect this to be a trumped-up sensation-story," he wrote, "and believe her to be living quietly in the family of her captor, under a Mahomedan name. But she has not turned up, for all the enquiries made about her,—and we would fain believe her to have put an end to her life, that had before it the dreary prospect of a life-long ignominy."[330] Perhaps it was in this same spirit that G. O. Trevelyan suggested in his classic history of Cawnpore that Miss Wheeler may have died with Nana's forces in the malarial swamps on the Nepalese border.[331]

In 1874, however, it was reported that she was "still alive in one of the northern frontiers of India, and has no desire to change her condition in life."[332] Four years later the local amateur historian R. Macrae insisted that Miss Wheeler was living in Cawnpore as a Moslem. But evidence of Miss Wheeler's residence did not surface until sometime after 1880, when a Mrs. Emma Clarke settled in the city with her husband and through an ayah became acquainted with an Englishwoman who lived in the bazaar. Mrs. Clarke regularly invited her for Sunday visits, during which the woman entered the house in a Moslem *burka* and proceeded to Mrs. Clarke's bedroom, where she enjoyed donning Western clothes and admiring herself in the mirror.

The woman either confided that she was Miss Wheeler or her hostess recognized her as such, for Mrs. Clarke had been a contemporary of General Wheeler's daughters.[333] Mrs. Clarke often urged her visitor to tell her surviving brothers that she was alive: five of Wheeler's sons lived into the twentieth century, three of them as major generals.[334] But she replied that she was too ashamed and would not risk the life of Ali Khan, who, for whatever reasons but nevertheless at considerable and prolonged risk to himself, had rescued her from slaughter. Perhaps Ali Khan was dead and safe from prosecution when, some fifty years after the rebellion, an old lady was reported to have summoned a missionary doctor and a Roman Catholic priest to her deathbed in the native city and, speaking in cultured English, revealed at last that she was General Wheeler's long-lost daughter.[335]

✦ ✦ ✦

During the uprising, young Fred Roberts came upon a case similar to Miss Wheeler's: a Eurasian girl who had been abducted by a mutineer and taken to his village. The girl declined Roberts's offer to rescue her—her family had been massacred, she explained, her abductor had been kind, and if she returned to "decent society" it would be only to a life of disgrace.

Roberts quite understood, and acceded to her wishes. Her reasoning—and his—was grounded, of course, in the Victorian belief that rape was literally a fate worse than death. Any white woman who had been raped by a black man was believed better off dead than alive. Since Eurasians occupied the middle of this spectrum, it was almost to be expected that Eurasian women like Amy Horne and Miss Wheeler—who were regarded as sensualists to the same extent to which their blood was Indian—would survive their despoliation, whereas the experience would necessarily kill their pure-blooded English counterparts.

That some Eurasian women were not murdered by their Indian abductors was also believed to be a function of racial contamination. By way of explaining Miss Wheeler's possible survival, G. O. Trevelyan felt called upon to remind his readers that "she was by no means of pure English blood. To some the very statement of the fact may appear heartless, but truth demands that it should be made."[336] "All over the country," wrote H. Dundas Robertson of the civil service, "there are a few scattered Eurasian women who were permitted to live after dishonour."[337]

After the war was all but won, Canning directed William Muir, the head of the Intelligence Department at Agra, to inquire into the persistent stories that English women and girls had been raped by the rebels. The rumors were obstructing his attempts at reconciling the ruling and subject races of Queen Victoria's Indian Empire. The Queen herself had urged Canning to "ascertain *how* far these [stories] are true.

> Of course the mere murdering—(I mean shooting or stabbing) innocent women and children is very shocking in itself—but in *civil* war this will happen, indeed I fear that many of the awful insults

&c, to poor children & women are the inevitable accompaniments
of such a state of things. . . . What I wish to know is whether there
is any *reliable evidence* of eye witnesses—of horrors, like people
having to eat their children's flesh—& other unspeakable and
dreadful atrocities which I could not write? Or do these not rest
on *Native* intelligence & witnesses whom one cannot believe im-
plicitly.[338]

Canning disbelieved the rumors and was confident that every alle-
gation would disintegrate under careful scrutiny. Already some of
the earliest stories were coming unstuck. When the *Bombay Times* reported that all of the ladies massacred at Jhansi had been raped by
order of the Rani, the Superintendent of Jhansi wrote back that on
the contrary they "were not brought before the Ranee and stripped,
their faces were not blackened, nor were any of them dishonored,"
though it was certainly true that "after the murder, the bodies were
stripped, and left in Jakim Bagh."[339] It turned out that Mrs. Chambers of Meerut, whose fetus was supposed to have been cut out of
her and then killed before her "dimming eyes," had been immediately shot and "did not suffer any protracted pain, torture, or indignity."[340] And a child who was reported to have been "cut in pieces by
little and little, with every refinement of gradual torture, . . . was actually killed with one blow of a tulwar" while fast asleep.

The "blood and scalp" school of journalism, declared one civil servant, had published such exaggerations "to inflame the feelings of
our countrymen and turn them into fiends," and it was in this hysterical atmosphere that William Muir began to canvass his fellow civil
servants all across North India. A civilian at Meerut believed that
only the dead had been "grossly insulted," first by the sweepers who
stripped them and then by the Moslems who believed they would
gain entry into paradise by trying their swords on infidel corpses.[341]
In any case, asked C. B. Thornhill, brother of the late magistrate of
Fatehgarh, who could testify to these supposed rapes? "All the European sufferers were massacred, and the natives most positively deny
their existence in fact."

E. A. Reade of Agra theorized that "the colour of European females
is repugnant to Oriental taste." But Muir wondered if Indian squea-
mishness, "even if admitted," really fit the case. Though he did not
agree with those who were already anticipating the late twentieth-
century theory that rape was not a sexual but a political act, he be-

lieved that the object of the rebels was "not so much to disgrace our name as to wipe out all trace of Europeans, and everything connected with foreign rule."

Thornhill explained that "Hindoos, except of the lowest grades, would have become outcasts had they perpetrated this offence. Neither would Mahomedans have done so in the unconcealed manner which has been supposed by some." All Indian witnesses firmly denied that rape was ever perpetrated and were shocked even to be posed the question.[342] "Sahib," a rebel answered, "you are a stranger to this country or you would not ask such a question. Any one who knows anything of the customs of this country and the strict rules of caste, knows that all such stories are lies, invented to stir up race-hatred, as if we had not enough of that on both sides already. That the women and children were cruelly murdered I admit, but not one of them was dishonoured."[343] Muir pointed out, however, that there was nothing in Moslem law that forbade a soldier "from taking females seized at the general outbreak to their homes with sinister designs." And yet "all the evidence . . . is entirely opposed to the supposition that ladies of English blood were anywhere reserved for that disgrace," due perhaps "to the awe with which Europeans have always been regarded by the natives of India."

One officer in the field had another explanation. "From what I have seen of the mutineers," he said, "I should think that *instant* death had been the fate of those who fell into their hands, when they rose anywhere, because plunder being their primary object, they could not resist the impulse of murder."[344] "Fanaticism and idolatry are equally cruel, but Indian lust," wrote Reade, "is almost always the lust of bloodshed and plunder only."

Nevertheless, everyone Muir consulted agreed that Indian and Eurasian women had probably been dishonored. A commissioner in Rohilkhand reminded Muir that "the Hindoos have suffered in this way wherever the Mahomedan rabble soldiery have had their sway." Citing Roberts's story of the Eurasian girl and mentioning, though not naming, Amy Horne, he was "inclined to believe that women or girls have been taken to Zenanahs."[345]

A. H. Cocks, Special Commissioner of Aligath, could "hardly hope that the captives escaped violation" at Cawnpore, where even Maharaja Scindia of Gwalior believed that women had been dishonored. Though Muir had to concede that Cawnpore may have been "a peculiar case" owing to the ladies' extended detention, he hastened to point out that the ladies had been equally in the power of the sepoys at Gwalior, where their captors did insult and menace them to the point of putting swords to their throats "to extract even their wedding rings. Yet the shadow of an attempt at their honour there was not." After his extensive inquiry, the newly promoted Major G. Williams, Superintendent of Police Battalions, concluded that there were no European women dishonoured "anywhere," including Cawnpore.[346] "There was cold and heartless bloodthirstiness," agreed Muir in his final report, but it had been "at the farthest remove from the lust of desire."

Canning was grateful to Muir for dispelling the rumors, and most twentieth-century historians would embrace Muir's conclusions as eagerly as many Anglo-Indians believed the most atrocious of the fictions that the soldiers contrived. But Muir was a gifted bureaucrat mindful and supportive of Canning's conciliatory agenda, and all along the civil service's line of command men shared the viceroy's desire to put the matter behind them. The truth may lie closer to the conclusions of a man Muir did not consult, H. Dundas Robertson, the magistrate at Saharunpore who later tried rebels with singular restraint.[347] "As to dishonor," Robertson wrote,

> so far from its not taking place, my investigations firmly convinced me that it was as a general rule the case whenever the prisoners were not too emaciated by hardships to become objects of passion, as—it may be thought fortunately—was almost always the case with those of European extraction. The localities were, indeed, few in which European ladies fell into the hands of the rebels, and those who did so were in general eventually exterminated, though evidence in some cases exists of their treatment.

Most investigations of rape had broken down, Robertson contended, "in consequence of the impossibility of procuring a satisfactory recognition of the guilty parties" and because "the investigators themselves are unwilling to inquire minutely, or dwell longer on such humiliating subjects." ("I had felt distaste," wrote one civil servant, "to make enquiries on the subject from natives.")[348] "Where the victims had been personal acquaintances or friends," Robertson continued, "and there appeared to be no hope of discovering the guilty parties, all proceedings were invariably quashed, as productive of no other result than pain to the relatives."[349]

It seems likely that the vast majority of the stories of rape were fabrications based on the appearance of the corpses the soldiers came upon or their own tormented prurience. But even a correspondent for the *Times* who tried to "take a more cheerful view of things," could not rule out the possibility that some rape occurred.

> I do not assert that no unnecessary cruelty in the course of murder and no dishonour occurred—it would be opposed to human nature if, in this saturnalia of blood, it had been so—but I *do* express my strong belief that, under the known circumstances of the outbreak, there is rather to be remarked the absence, so far as we can discover, of the amount of female dishonour which might have been anticipated, than an excessive tendency that way.[350]

Thus, whether rape is an expression of power or lust or both, a few of the hundreds of stories of rape were probably true, for even the proprieties of caste and religion have never entirely protected Indian women from communal rape: not in feudal times, not in the rebellion of 1857, not during Partition. Nor, of course, could they protect Indian women from rape at the hands of Company soldiers at Delhi, Lucknow, Cawnpore, and along the Grand Trunk Road. As the men of the Raj rebuilt their cantonments and raised the walls of their compounds even higher than before, rape festered at the heart of the imperial anxiety far enough into the twentieth century to act as the fulcrum for three of British India's most distinguished novels: E. M. Forster's *A Passage to India*, John Masters's *Bhowani Junction*, and, of course, Paul Scott's *The Jewel in the Crown*, in which poor Miss Manners is raped by *hooligans* in a place called the "Bibighar Gardens."[351]

THE MOST PAINFUL
UNCERTAINTY

England: May 1857–July 1859

For the relatives of the Cawnpore garrison who tracked the Mutiny in the *Times of London*, the delay in communications between England and the Doab was excruciating.[352] "The lag of time between the Mails is *very* trying," wrote Queen Victoria, "& must be harrowing to those who have (& *who* has not amongst the gentry & middle Classes in England—Great Britain I should say?) relations in uncertain & dangerous places?"[353]

In the middle of May, as refugees were swelling Wheeler's Entrenchment, the *Times* was assuring its readers, after the disturbing news of Mungal Pandy's outburst at Barrackpore, that however discontented the Brahminical sepoys might be, "now that the whole of India has been thoroughly subdued, and that from Afghanistan to the borders of Siam there is no Power which even aspires to oppose us, we may be humane while we are politic, and be content to punish disobedience by loss of pay and pension, without a resort to artillery or a charge of the bayonet."[354]

Sometimes it seemed that the *Times*'s advertisers had a more urgent sense of the magnitude of the catastrophe. In patriotic response to the crisis in India, A. Davis of 33 Strand begged "to call the attention of officers and gentlemen proceeding to India of the large STOCK of INDIA SADDLES he has always on hand." Other enterprising merchants purveyed sheet music with a Mutiny theme,[355] premature disquisitions on the causes of the uprising,[356] maps of Delhi,[357] and journals like the *Indian Mail* and the *Indian War Chronicle*. Messrs. Jay of the London General Mourning Warehouse kindly offered "the lowest possible prices, to those families who, in consequence of the late deplorable events in India, may require mourning attire."[358]

When, on the day of the massacre at Sati Chowra, the news reached London of the uprisings at Meerut and Delhi, the *Times* snapped out of its Olympian torpor and took notice. "This mutiny," it said, "has assumed a very serious character."[359] Cawnpore was first mentioned two days later, but the news was hopeful. "Sir Hugh Wheeler," wrote the *Times* correspondent from Bombay, "reports from Cawnpore that everything there is in a satisfactory state,"[360] and for the next several weeks dispatches continued to portray Wheeler holding his own.[361]

By early August soldiers on the scene invited the British public to "give full stretch to your imagination. Think of everything that is cruel, inhuman, infernal, and you cannot then conceive anything so diabolical as what these demons in human form have perpetrated."[362] The Great Globe on Leicester Square accepted the soldier's invitation by featuring a bloody diorama of the "Insurrection in India."[363] "If our soldiers knock down every filthy idol they see," wrote "An Anglo-Indian," "and lay every *musjid* level with the ground, and if they pollute every shrine and plunder every one which is worth plundering, I shall not be sorry."[364] "Those blood-thirsty fiends have placed themselves in the same relation to their fellow man as that of a rabid dog to his kind," wrote an officer. "Nothing but extermination will cure the malady and preserve the race."[365]

On the fifteenth came a report of the first massacre of Fatehgarh fugitives, which "surpassed in atrocity all that has hitherto been perpetrated" and, weeks before England would hear of Sati Chowra or the Bibighar, established Nana Sahib's reputation in England as the most bloodthirsty of the rebel leaders.[366] "His last act of butchery was of a wholesale nature, and it is a pity he has not a thousand lives to make expiation for it."[367] But it was not until August 22, almost two months after the fact, that the *Times* finally learned of the massacre at Sati Chowra.[368] Even then it chose to believe that Nana could only be in possession of "the open city, and not the military position occupied by Sir Hugh Wheeler."[369] Six days later the *Times* finally confirmed the fall of Wheeler's garrison. "We cannot help wishing it may turn out," it editorialized, "that Sir Hugh Wheeler had been killed before the capitulation, and that he finished his long and brilliant career still as a soldier, and not as the helpless victim of a hideous butchery." Be that as it may, "Nena Sahib has released us from all obligation," and "what we have to teach the followers of Mahomet and the worshippers of Vishnu is that, whatever their creed or their caste, we treat murderers as we do dogs, and in all moral respects rate them a great deal lower."[370]

In the middle of September the *Times* first hinted at still greater horrors at the Bibighar.[371] "There now, we are sorry to say, remains no room for doubt that the most fearful stories and fiendish cruelties perpetrated there by the ruffian Nena Sahib are entirely true. . . . The name of Nena Sahib will hold rank among . . . the greatest enemies of the human race to the end of the world."[372] The Cawnpore massacre was "the crowning atrocity—for it can hardly be surpassed—of native India, comprising in one deliberate act its pagan and infidel rulers and conquerors."[373]

On September 21 came the news of Neill's blood-lick law, and though the *Times* quoted the Bengal *Harkuru* as stating that "its infliction has gained him great credit," British officialdom began to pause. The horrors of Cawnpore seemed to be seeping indelibly into Britain's soul. "Never since she became a nation has England been so outraged in the persons of her sons and daughters as she has been in

THE MOST PAINFUL UNCERTAINTY • 513

the tremendous rebellion now raging in her Indian possessions," observed a reverend of Middlesex.[374] Some began to fear that the nation was being brutalized by its own insatiable rage.

"I *execrate* the tone of everybody in England on the whole affair," wrote Lucie Duff Gordon, Azimullah Khan's hostess and sponsor only two years before. She ached to hear what had become of her

> very amiable, charming young Mussulman Mahratta. I am quite unable to believe that he could approve or endure the atrocious conduct of Nana Sahib & yet he must be too much in his power not to be hanged either by him or the English. The real truth of the whole outbreak, I believe, we shall never know—I mean the native side of the question. . . . Who will pity the poor, helpless mass of people guilty of the offence of a dark skin and a religion of their own? What a vista of disaster & hatred is before us and them![375]

The anti-Orientalist Thomas Babington Macauley, who had devised India's penal code and Anglicized Indian education, noted with satisfaction that "Peace Societies, and Aborigine Protection Societies, and Societies for the Reformation of Criminals" had been silenced by "one terrible cry for revenge." But he was disturbed by the delight with which he read about the hangings and blowings from guns. "The Indian troubles," he wrote, "have affected my spirits more than any public events in the whole course of my life. . . . I may say that, till this year, I did not know what real vindictive hatred meant." He feared he would greet the annihilation of the entire population of Delhi with "equanimity," and asked himself, "Is this wrong? Is not the severity which springs from a great sensibility to human suffering a better thing than the lenity which springs from indifferences to human suffering? The question may be argued long on both sides."[376]

When a few liberal-minded missionaries and nostalgic old Company men publicly urged their countrymen not to believe everything they read nor to condemn an entire subcontinent for the transgressions of the Bengal Army, parliamentarians attacked them for "false sentimentality" and "mawkish, maudlin philanthropy." But at the end of September Benjamin Disraeli, budding champion of the imperial ideal, publicly condemned his countrymen's calls for vengeance. "I am persuaded," he said, "that our soldiers and our sailors will exact a retribution which it may, perhaps, be too terrible to pause upon." But he protested "against taking Nena Sahib as a model for the conduct of the British soldier. I protest against meeting atrocities by atrocities. I have heard things said and seen things written of late which would make me almost suppose that the religious opinions of the people of England had undergone some sudden change, and that instead of bowing before the name of Jesus we were preparing to revive the worship of Molech."[377]

Finally, Queen Victoria declared October 7 a Day of Humiliation, "so both we and our people may humble ourselves before Almighty God, in order to obtain pardon of our sins, and . . . send up prayers to the Divine Majesty for imploring His blessing and assistance on our arms for the restoration of tranquility."[378] Of all the fallen stations, Cawnpore loomed largest that day. The minister at All Souls, Langham-Place, had heard "a wail . . . come across the ocean from the well of Cawnpore." A Congregationalist at Pentonville Hill could assure his flock that Christ had heard the victims at the Bibighar because "their last moments were spent in praying to Him, as we learnt from their journals, the scattered leaves of their prayer-books, and the *Preparation for Death* found on the bloody floor at Cawnpore."

Many were in a retributive frame of mind. Speaking at the Crystal Palace to "the largest audience that has assembled in modern times to listen to the exhortations of a minister of the Gospel," the Reverend C. H. Spurgeon declared that the Company "should never for a moment have tolerated the religion of the Hindoos," which was "the vilest filth." The rebels must be hanged, he said, "for both Heaven and Earth demanded it."[379] But a few clergymen sounded a note of caution. Reverend Marchmont of Lower-Street Chapel, Islington, believed in "the absolute necessity of just retribution" but warned against "the indulgence of the vindictive passions so likely to be roused even beyond the limits of justice by the vile treachery of the insurgents." And Reverend Henry George Liddell reserved his special prayers for the British soldiers in India, "that they might not lose the vantage ground which . . . Christians ought ever to maintain above heathens," lest "the innocent be merged in one common destruction with the guilty, without reference to age or sex."[380]

The Day of Humiliation apparently temporized the *Times*'s Mutiny coverage somewhat, for it began to disassociate itself from the "savage and vindictive" public feeling in India, excusing some of the Calcutta papers' invective only as "a vent to outraged humanity, just as ejaculations are to bodily pain, rather than deliberate statements."[381]

✦ ✦ ✦

No one left a more complete record of the special anguish of the victims' families than the Lindsays. At her home in Rochester, William
and Kate Lindsay's sister, Mary Drage, kept a vigil for her siblings
while caring for the major's three small children. The last letter she
had received from Cawnpore was a note from Caroline dated May
31. "I hope next mail," she had written, "I will be able to give a better and more avowable account of our proceedings."

Traveling in Genoa, William's brother Martin received a letter from
Caroline dated May 19. "We are most anxious to hear more," he
wrote home. "By this time they are either in safety or in a state [too]
fearful & distressing to contemplate or think of. I fear much—even
for the consequences to their future health."[382] "What has become of
the women and children God knows," William's cousin Alexander
wrote from India. "It is hoped that they were removed some time
previous. [The Lindsays] were there I know at the end of May."[383]

Over the next few months Mary devoured the news of Cawnpore
that appeared in dribs and drabs, culminating in the August 22 report of the garrison's massacre at Sati Chowra. On August 29, the
Times published a roll of casualties at Cawnpore that listed only
a "Colonel" Lindsay. "We fear," the editors apologized, "we can
do nothing to relieve the anxiety which must exist until it is known
definitely who is the Lindsay returned as killed. The list is evidently quite incorrect with regard to both names and military ranks;
and as in the Bengal service there are several of the name Lindsay,
the most painful uncertainty must be endured until the arrival of
details."[384]

Mary's hopes for William were dashed a few days later when the
Times published a letter by Henry Lawrence listing "Major Lindsay"
among the dead at Cawnpore. But it seemed possible that one of the
others had survived when, on September 1, the news arrived that
Ensign Browne had escaped the massacres. If he had escaped perhaps
young George or one of his sisters could have as well. But a week
later the Times published a clarification: Browne had been on detached duty during the siege. On September 15 the Times had to
admit that in all likelihood Nana Sahib had massacred everyone in
the station. A week later the Bengali doctor's list appeared with the
names of "Mrs. Lindsay (wife of Major Lindsay), Nancy Lindsay, Caroline Lindsay," and recording the deaths of a "Miss Lindsay" and
"Mrs. Lindsay." Four days later the publication of Caroline's chronology—the closest she ever came to the "better and more avowable ac-

count" she had promised—cleared up some of the mystery. The "Mrs. Lindsay" at the Bibighar had been Kate, not Lilly, and "Nancy" had been Fanny.[385]

"All all gone," groaned Mary's husband Henry, "without one word, no memento of them. What a sad sad reverse to all dear William's promised happiness in this country. Poor unhappy Kate dearly has she paid the penalty of seeking for happiness in India and sadly must she have lamented not having left at least Caroline who wished to stay & Fanny who ought to have been at school."

"What shall I say for the poor dear orphans," wrote Lilly's brother from Bombay, "thus early & ruthlessly bereft of both their parents, & scarcely able to realize their loss—[though] the eldest boy surely will." But he didn't. Willie was ten years old, Charlie was eight, Mary Anne almost seven; it had been five years since they had seen their father and a year and a half since their mother had left them in Rochester. When Mary Drage and her husband Henry gathered the three children around them and broke the news, Mary was shocked to find that Mary Anne did not have a very "clear remembrance of either Father & Mother—and Charlie a faint one of either—But Willie distressed me—after the first cry which he took when I told him—he never seemed to mind, and to me the sound of them laughing, whistling, singing & romping when all around here are sorrowful has been painful & mystifying." It would not have surprised their late father. The consequence of the separation of Anglo-Indian parents and their children, he had sadly observed, was "no mutual or natural affection between them and little interest in either in after life."[386] It was the old subcontinental case of death and absence differing "but in name."[387]

William, Charles, and Mary Anne Lindsay remained in the Drages' care. Willie went on to serve as private secretary to four parliamentary undersecretaries of state, including one undersecretary for India. Charles joined the artillery and returned to India to do battle on the Northwest Frontier before dying at the age of forty a major with two clasps. His fey little sister, Mary Anne, died of heart failure at the age of thirty-two, having survived her Aunt Mary, the only mother she could remember, by less than six months.[388]

✦   ✦   ✦

Robert Garrett, the stranded Anglo-Irish engineer who had been killed serving with his fellow railway men in the outer barracks of

Wheeler's Entrenchment, had last written his partner William Doyne on May 28, when it seemed to him "that the worst is over at least in this district." Three months later, Doyne, who had lost his own brother in the rebellion, wrote Garrett's brother "that there is no longer any hope left that even one of the Europeans at Cawnpore is alive." J. McClean of the India Board was not so sure. "I believe that if anyone has escaped he will *be the one* unless there were defenceless women, whom I know he *could* not leave. He was too good a man to leave one woman unprotected." But "he had *Pluck* to overcome anything if free to act." But Garrett had not been listed simply because no one had known him at Cawnpore. Even Mowbray Thomson could not recall him, the surest evidence that he had died "very early in the affair"—before Thomson had been assigned to the outer barracks. Within a year and a half of Garrett's death, his partner and his brother were squabbling over the few hundred pounds he had left behind.[389]

✦ ✦ ✦

Major Edward and Emma Vibart's son Butcher had remained at Meerut through the month of June, listening to the *"fearful* rumours . . . brought in here daily by the natives [that] almost deprive me of all *hope* and drive me to despair." As he camped before Delhi in August, he wrote that "nothing can be heard of that awful calamity but that *all* are killed—all murdered by those *miscreants*." He tried to convince himself that his parents managed somehow to flee to Calcutta, but it was a faint hope. "Oh, I am driven *wild* and I Vow *vengeance* on these wretches—*murderers* & fiends." He had "lost everything I cared for in the world," and believed that God had spared him "to *avenge* my parents—my *darling* Mother—my little *brothers and sisters*—my *poor Father*."

In September Edward took part in the sack of Delhi, bloodier even than the retributions at Cawnpore and Lucknow. "The town presents an awful spectacle now," he wrote. "Heaps of dead bodies scattered throughout the palace, & every house broken into & sacked—

> But they are the townspeople now who are falling victims to the infuriated soldiery, and wherever you go you see some unfortunate man or another being dragged from his hiding place and barbarously put to death—Heaven knows *I* feel no pity—but when some old grey headed man perhaps is brought & shot before your

very eyes: hard must be that man's heart I think who can look on with indifference. And yet, it *must* be so, for these black wretches *shall* atone with their blood for our murdered countrymen. . . . *Slay* on & *spare not* ye soldiers—*Remember Cawnpore.*

◆　◆　◆

Emma Halliday's father blamed himself for having allowed his favorite daughter to go off to India with a Company man. "He is most terribly cut up by this terrible affair in India," his sister reported. ". . . His poor wife's death was no shock in comparison to what he has now had to undergo."[390] A year after Emma's death, her younger brother Spencer arrived at Cawnpore as a soldier and visited Wheeler's Entrenchment and the sepulchral well, where "poor Emma, Willie & child are buried."[391] For some time the family dared to hope that little Mabel had survived, like the "baby Macansh" who was supposed to have been smuggled out of the garrison before the capitulation on June 27. But evidently the story was apocryphal; the baby Macansh turned out to be the orphaned daughter of a surgeon who had died of fever after escaping the rebels in the Punjab hills.[392]

THE CURSE OF CAIN
Nana Sahib

After the fall of Lucknow most of the fighting shifted to central India, where Sir Hugh Rose fought for five months in terrible heat, defeating the Rani of Jhansi and pursuing the elusive Tatya Tope. But for many months Oudh remained in turmoil. Rebel landlords still rampaged with ragtag corps of freelances and matchlockmen, and thousands of mutineers surged through the jungles of northern Oudh, starving, ragged, beset by villagers, their bayonets dull with rust, desperately seeking chieftains who might feed them, arm them, or lead them to safe haven in the foothills of Nepal.

No one could blame them for fleeing. British expeditions set off from Cawnpore in hot pursuit, slaughtering any stray rebels they could find. An officer in the Oudh Field Force recounted how in one engagement in April the local villagers turned fugitive sepoys over to the soldiers, nearly one hundred of whom were killed singly or in twos and threes as the British hurried through. When the officer caught up with the rebel rear guard, some sepoys tried to hide in the trees, whereupon "our men amused themselves by what they called 'rock shooting' and the sepoys came down with a 'squelch' from trees 20 and 30 feet high: others hid themselves under bundles of straw or faggots and were bayonetted by the men: 18 men were found under one bundle." At another village one hundred sepoys who had cast away their weapons to pass for villagers were all killed.[393] Before long all that remained of an army that had once numbered twenty-eight thousand men were a few desperate and scattered bands seeking refuge in the hills and jungles.[394]

Of all the fugitives none was pursued more hotly than Nana Sahib. Public opinion demanded his capture and execution. Dubbed the "Fiend of the House of the Ladies" and the "Butcher of Bithur," he had displaced Napoleon in the corridors of the imperial nightmare, an all-purpose bugaboo in his bloodstained robes. But among the high crops and tangled jungles of Oudh he was proving hard to find. Some said it was no use looking, for "rather than be taken," Nana would first "abandon his family, and retire to some monastery or temple in Thibet for the remainder of his days."[395] Others maintained that he had "a diamond for a bosom friend, which when *in extremis* he will powder and swallow to commit suicide!"[396]

After his ignominious flight from Serai Ghat, Nana had proceeded with Rao Sahib and Bala Rao to Lucknow, where he apparently received some supplies from Hazrat Mahal. He then turned around, crossed the Ganges again, and marched to Kalpi to collect a column of Oudh rebels with which he intended to reconquer Cawnpore.[397] But the force encamped at Cawnpore was too daunting, and he crossed back into Oudh with two regiments of mutineers and thousands of matchlockmen. "He is said to be almost alone and without money," one British officer reported hopefully, and would shortly "fall into the hands of the villagers to whom the reward for his apprehension"—£5,000—"would be a great object."[398]

In February, Rao Sahib crossed from Oudh just north of Bithur and destroyed a police station. Nana encamped at a little settlement on the Ganges called Fatehpur-Chaurasi, where he evaded capture by the British by a matter of hours. He next slipped north to Shahjahanpur and finally Bareilly, where Khan Bahadur Khan, head of the insurgent forces of Rohilkhand, offered him command of his troops. Soon after arriving at Bareilly he ordered that a man accused of sympathizing with the British be blown from a gun.

Things did not go well, however. Perhaps after months of putting up with the endless demands of his Moslem sowars, he let his Concanist intolerance get the better of him, and not only prohibited the slaughter of cows but actually executed nine Moslem butchers for violating his ban. "He has prevented bovicide," declared the *Hindoo Patriot*, "and the reins of affairs are in his hands." But when he ordered one of the town's mosques closed, the Moslems rioted. Nana decided to move on.

In April he led five hundred sowars southeast toward Lucknow, but after a skirmish with Hope Grant[399] he retreated to Shahjahanpur,[400] forty miles northwest of Lucknow, where he kept "a horse saddled night and day ready to fly."[401] It was rumored—probably falsely—that one of his wives had given birth to a son. When the British closed in on him he ordered the cantonment destroyed to deny shelter to his pursuers and galloped off into the countryside.[402]

Running low on funds and trying to keep his men from bolting, Nana appealed to his fellow princes.[403] "Seeing the faith perishing I have girt my loins to defend it," Nana Sahib wrote to Raghuraj Singh of Rewa on April 23rd, "and I have suffered much for it. But this is no man's doing. It is God's design; I have done my utmost; . . . the faith is the faith of us all. I have endeavoured to support and defend it; all chiefs, and monarchs, Hindoo or Mussulman who assist the English, the destroyers of faith, destroy their religion with their own hands."[404] Nana appealed to the *bheels*, tribesmen with a well-earned reputation for banditry. If the Rajas of the Bheels would "destroy the Kaffirs," Nana wrote, "the Sircar will be highly pleased, and when our enemies are at an end, the Sircar will come in person and will make arrangements for you in perpetuity."[405]

By now his pursuers had wearied of chasing him about. "I do not think we have the slightest chance of catching him," wrote one officer, "as the country is so covered with clumps of trees and high crops that a mounted man can disappear in a few minutes."[406] Despite all the defeats and the bounty on his head, the rebels still acted "in the name of Nana Peishwa, whose rule they proclaim wherever they go; and the cruelties they practice on all parties suspected of siding with the British Govt. cause the greatest terror even on police who cannot be induced to face them even for an hour."[407]

When Campbell marched on Bareilly, Nana was able to send a

body of troops into the fray and escape after their defeat. His fortunes seemed to rise in June when the Gwalior Contingent chased Scindia to Agra and Nana's old childhood playmate, the Rani of Jhansi, proclaimed him Peshwa. But only a few days later the Rani was killed in battle, and Nana was forced to flee with a large body of soldiers and camp followers to Bahraich, about sixty miles north of Lucknow, where he was joined by the Begum of Oudh and her son, the boy-king Birjis Qadr. In September he issued another of his proclamations, this time to the princes of the Deccan, promising aid from the French and the Russians and reminding his countrymen that "to submit to and live under such wicked 'Kaffurs' is disgraceful. . . . Do not suffer the stain of being effeminate and foolish to attack the people of the South."[408] His letters to the British remained almost giddily defiant. "As you have taken Bithoor and my jewels set with precious stones, gold and silver, to the value of seven crores [70 million] of Rupees," he wrote to Canning, "I humbly beg you to return them to me at an early period. I will wait three months more when, should you refuse, I will take your life and hang your [Commander] Sahib."[409]

On December 17, 1858, Nana and the Begum fled together from Campbell's force, moving inexorably northward toward the Nepalese border and conscripting villagers to act as coolies along the way.[410] By now his force was a motley assemblage of matchlockmen and mutineers. The core of his army was Jwala Prasad's 1st Native Infantry, prime instigators of the uprising at Cawnpore who had pledged to remain faithful to Nana to the last. Many of their co-conspirators, Teeka Singh's 2nd Native Cavalry, had been killed in an ill-considered attack on Etawah in December; the survivors were now "the most poverty-stricken and dejected" of all the rebels in Nana's camp.[411]

"Whenever our force approaches," wrote Russell, "the recriminations and reproaches of one to another are only silenced by the opening of our fire. 'Where will you fly to now?' they ask [each other]. 'What a fine example you set the other day!'

"'It was you who brought me to this; but for your advice I should have been well clad and fed and my family looked after. Now I am hungry and in rags, and no chance of escaping death.'

"The new year, which opens upon us full of hope," concluded Russell, "to them presents no prospect but of disgrace, suffering, and death."[412]

On December 27 Campbell—now Lord Clyde—opened fire on

Nana's camp at the mud-walled bastion of Mejidaih, killing several mutineers, but again Nana escaped and proceeded across the Nepalese border to the town of Banki, ninety-three miles northeast of Lucknow. Here with his back to the hills, Nana's army tried to make a stand, but after a brief exchange of fire across a deep swamp his men fled in disorder to the river Rapti. Nana's gunners managed to cover his flight across the river with a cannonade, but Campbell's Hussars caught up to the stragglers and killed scores of men struggling in the Rapti's current.

Nana fled into the Terai, the pestilential swamps that lay between the plains and the Himalayan foothills.[413] By now the bounty on Nana's head had been raised to £10,000 and garnished with a full pardon for any native informant who was not implicated in atrocities,[414] though Canning thought it likely "that difficulty may arise in establishing the Nana's identity even if taken alive, and this would be greatly increased if the reward were payable for his head alone. It is known that the Nana has taken measures to mislead his pursuers and to escape recognition."[415] Charles Raikes heard that Nana had "engaged many men resembling him in face and figure, and is always in disguise. To ask whether he is in the camp is punishable by death."[416]

It was astonishing that Nana had managed to stay ahead of the British with all of his encumberances: elephants loaded with treasure, incantating Brahmins, ragtag soldiers, camp followers, plus his wife Kasibai, a sister, Baji Rao's widows, and the no doubt desolate but always scheming Azimullah Khan. Defiant to the last, Begum Hazrat Mahal and Birjis Qadr still remained with Nana, rejecting British offers to maintain them at Lucknow as state prisoners.[417]

The Nepalese Terai was regarded as so pestilential as to be uninhabitable. From April to October even the monkeys were said to desert the area, and "not the monkeys only," Bishop Heber was told, "but everything which had breath of life instinctively deserts them. . . . The tigers go up to the hills, the antelopes and wild hogs make incursions into the cultivated plain . . . and not so much as a bird can be seen in the frightful solitude."[418] The Terai brought out the worst in everybody, including Nana's pursuers who, among other "outrages,"[419] set fire to villages to warm themselves.[420] All year round a virulent malaria known as the *ayul* infested the dense, spongy jungles; as soon as Nana Sahib stepped into the Terai rumors began to slip down the damp slopes that he had succumbed to the disease.

But in February, joined now by Bala Rao and his battered army of five hundred troops,[421] Nana Sahib was still very much alive and urging Jung Bahadur of Nepal to allow him and some twenty thousand followers to pass through his kingdom to Tibet.[422] Addressing Jung Bahadur as "the sun in the midst of a cluster of stars," because he had not "refused to give your aid even to the British, who are opposed to you in everything," Nana could not resist a certain bitter irony. Such generosity, he said, "makes me hope confidently that [you will] not fail to give us your aid. As a poet says, 'You, who are kind to your enemies cannot make your friends . . . hopeless. I have no hope from anyone in the world but from you—in all respects you are master of my acts. Do what you think best for me. With such hopes I have determined to come with a view to gain the object of my desire."[423]

A contemporary of Nana Sahib, Jung Bahadur ruled Nepal somewhat like a Peshwa: as prime minister to a puppet king. On his 1850 tour of England (with Azimullah's future guide, Mohamed Ali Khan), he had been knighted, decorated, and feted as the "lion of the London season."[424] But even after Sir Jung had provided Campbell with nine thousand of his Gurkha soldiers, his Resident suspected him of sneaking rupees into Nana's camp,[425] and the commander of the force pursuing Nana Sahib even feared Jung Bahadur intended to provide Nana with troops "to fight against the British."[426] Determined to prove his loyalty to the triumphant Queen, Jung Bahadur noisily threatened to attack Nana's camp if he tried to cross "the snowy ranges,"[427] and urged Calcutta to send him troops to chase the rebels from his country.[428] "As the Hindoos and Mahomedans have been guilty of ingratitude and perfidy," he told the rebels, "neither the Nepal Government nor I can side with them."[429]

Thus trapped at the border, Nana sent a letter to the nearest British camp that would be his most comprehensive testament. "You have forgiven the crimes of all Hindoostan and murderers have been pardoned," he said. ". . . It is surprising that I who have joined the rebels from helplessness have not been forgiven. I have committed no murder." He claimed that the sepoys had disobeyed his orders and murdered the Europeans, and that "by means of entreaties" he had "saved the lives of 200 English women and children," who were killed "by your sepoys and [hooligans].

> *You are well aware that I am not a murderer, nor am I guilty*; neither have you passed any order concerning me. You have no enemy besides me, so, *as long as I live I will fight*. I also am a man. . . . It is

strange that you, a great and powerful nation, have been fighting with me for two years and have not been able to do anything; the more so when it is considered that my troops do not obey me and I have not possession of my country. . . . With all this you have not been able to do anything. You have drawn all to your side, and I alone am left but you will see what the soldiers I have been preserving for two years can do. *We will meet, and then I will shed your blood and it will flow knee deep. I am prepared to die. If I alone am worthy of being an enemy to so powerful a nation as the British it is a great honor to me, and every wish of my heart is fulfilled;* death will come to me one day. What then have I to fear? *But those whom you have taken to your side will on the day fixed turn upon you and kill you.*[430]

A cavalry major named Richardson replied the next day

that the Proclamation which has been issued by Her Majesty the Queen, . . . was not for any one party or person, but for all, and the identical terms under which the Nawab of Farrukabad, the Nawab of Banda and other chieftains and Rajahs of Oude, laid down their arms and surrendered themselves to Government. Those terms are open to you and all those who may wish to surrender. In writing as you do that you have not murdered women and children, it becomes you to come in without fear.[431]

Two days later Nana wrote back that he could not "surrender myself in this manner." But "if a letter, written by Her Majesty the Queen and sealed with her seal, and brought by the Commanding Officer of the French or the second in Command, reaches me, I will, placing reliance on these officers, accept the Terms without hesitation.

Canning was enraged by this exchange. Richardson had implied that the Queen's clemency might conceivably be extended to include the "arch fiend" of the rebellion, and invoked the Nawab of Farrukhabad, who had just surrendered on exactly the same terms and now appeared to be on the verge of escaping the hangman's noose. They would have to hang Nana Sahib if they caught him; public opinion would still demand it. But in order to hang him they would have to be able to try him for sedition because the murder charges at Cawnpore would be hard to prove against him. Richardson was to tell Nana only "that he will have a fair trial and nothing more. ·

Whether he surrenders or be taken he will be tried for the crimes of which he stands charged."[432]

Bala Rao remained encamped at some distance from Nana Sahib, no doubt to protect his brother from capture. But he seemed to be distancing himself from his brother in other ways, and proposed a separate deal, claiming that he had been coerced into serving his brother.[433] Jung Bahadur's emissary replied that if Bala gave up all his European prisoners Jung Bahadur would protect Bala's family.

"It is true," conceded Bala, "that a daughter of the Judge of Furruckabad, the only European with me, who has received a bullet wound, which I caused to be cured *was* with me, but she has lately been made over to Colonel Bird." This would have been the wounded infant daughter of Robert and Mary Thornhill whom the golundaz rescued from the reeds.[434] The child had reportedly been recovering from her wounds when General Havelock reached Cawnpore, whereupon the golundaz had taken her with him. According to Nunne Nawab the golundaz was eventually imprisoned by Teeka Singh for proposing to adopt the child, and the little girl was probably murdered.[435]

Bala confessed that in his camp there was still the family of a Eurasian musician of the 1st Native Infantry named William Allen who had converted to Islam and then died of the ayul. "His sons and his wife are here," he said. "Take them away with you if you please." Mrs. Allen and her children appeared in the tent and knelt down in front of Bala Rao. He had saved their lives, she said, and "they were ready to jump into wells and forfeit their lives, if he wished it."

Jung Bahadur's emissary arranged for the evacuation of Bala's and Nana's womenfolk, but was at a loss as to what to do with the Allens. "Where am I to keep them?" he asked his liege. "And what am I to do regarding their clothes and expenses?"[436]

Calcutta worried that Jung Bahadur may have made the same vague promises of clemency to Bala that Richardson had extended to Nana Sahib and reminded his officers that "Bala Rao shall, upon submission, be brought to trial, of which he should be clearly informed."[437] But soon it was a dead issue. In a few days Nana was kneeling by his brother's bed, begging the Nepalese to send for a Moslem physician.[438] Not long after, Bala was dead. The British did not believe it at first, because the Ghurkas were making so much money selling the rebels provisions "that they were now protecting them from capture."[439] But apparently it was true.

✦ ✦ ✦

Reports of Nana's death soon followed. First came the news that he was "very sick,"[440] though evidently not too sick to threaten the locals that anyone who menaced or betrayed him would be "deprived of caste and killed."[441] Then in August he released twelve more musicians[442] who appeared near Gorakhpur with a Gurkha escort and reported that on their way to the border, "they saw an elephant and horses which were being sent by the Nana's family to the Brahmins on the occasion of his death."[443]

A general stationed on the upper Gogra River reported that in September 1859 "two of my Subadars were always at me to allow them three or four days leave to capture [Nana].

> They kept me informed of his movements like a court circular. I always told them that I was on duty for a certain purpose, and it was impossible I could give any man leave. One Thursday Ram Singh came to me begging me still more strongly than before, saying the Nana was getting much worse—he was as you know suffering from the fever and ague and had an enlarged spleen—and he told me that the Nana had had his little finger cut off, and had burnt it as an offering to Kali, with a view of propitiating the goddess. Two days after this Ram Singh & the other Subadar came and said: "No one will get the reward now! He died and was burnt yesterday."[444]

The Resident of Nepal wrote Calcutta that he had received a report from the Nana's camp in the Deokur Valley that according to the females in his family Nana had died on the twenty-fourth of September.[445] Indeed, one of Baji Rao's widows had supposedly sent one of Nana's bones down to the Ganges for immersion.[446]

"He had suffered previously from repeated attacks," wrote the *Friend of India*, "and at one time was so ill that his attendants believed him to be dead, and the usual gifts were distributed amongst the Brahmins; he however recovered partially and did not die till the 24th September. His dead body is said to have been seen by creditable witnesses, and to have been burnt in their presence with the usual Hindoo rites."[447]

Such men as Canning and Hope Grant believed the story of Nana's death, but not everyone was convinced. In 1860 a long-missing tenant farmer turned up at his sahib's plantation near Gorakhpur, dying of fever and starvation. He claimed that he had been kidnapped by Nana Sahib and his men and had followed them past a line of boundary pillars and into what was probably Tibet, where the people "never shave their heads, have long hair, wear thick cloth of dog's hair and kept large dogs with long shaggy hair," details a tenant farmer would have been hard put to invent.[448] Shortly thereafter a convicted mutineer named Ramdeen claimed that in November 1860 he visited Nana Sahib's dismal camp in southern Tibet.[449] "There are no horsemen in the force," he said. "The soldiers armed with swords and guns carry their baggage on their own shoulders. Nana pays for their food but issues no pay. He rides on a mule and that is the only carriage procurable. But few of even the more noted rebels have even this. . . . He had no guns or cavalry, having lost them in a hill fight with a mixed force of English and native troops. . . .

"The report of the Nana's death was wrong," Ramdeen insisted. "He had burnt only a finger to discharge the funeral ceremonies of himself in his lifetime, as he had no heir. . . . The Nana gave out that he was dead—and all Brahmins were fed. . . . He has a ranee with him (I don't know who) but no child. He cannot adopt, as he has nothing left."

Ramdeen claimed that he had remained with Nana "three months under the hills where a little snow fell, then went further north to where there was much snow." He said Nana had some twenty-three thousand men, "many of them from Nepaul and Behar—4,000 are old sepoys. . . . General Teeka Singh daily serves out rations, company by company."[450]

In 1861 a mendicant gave a very detailed account of an encampment in the Nepalese hills guarded by sentries. "I was bathing one day in the Banganga," he testified, "when a person dressed like a [holy man], with long hair plaited round his head passed close to me on an elephant attended by from 15-20 followers, all very dirtily dressed and looking like [holy men]." The first holy man gave him "ten Company rupees," and some villagers said he was "a great Mahratta Rajah" and "the brother of Bala Rao." Other pilgrims corroborated the story, which convinced the Resident at Nepal that Jung Bahadur had assisted in Nana Sahib's deception and permitted him to roam the kingdom as a mendicant.[451] In fact Jung Bahadur himself hinted that Nana was still alive and had headed back to the plains.[452]

The Nana Sahib sightings persisted, nagging the Government's efforts to lay the rebellion to rest. In 1862 the authorities at Karachi, convinced they had found the Beast of Bithur, shipped their hapless suspect to Calcutta, but before he could be taken to Cawnpore for identification the poor man died. He turned out to have been a writer of religious works who had lived respectably and in the same place for over twenty years.[453] In 1863 another man was seized at Ajmer in Rajputana, purportedly with "plans of extensive conspiracy" in his possession. The man was a little on the scrawny side, but he seemed to fit the description Dr. Tressider and Mowbray Thomson had provided, all the way down to the lancet mark on one of his toes.[454] But slowly the story unraveled. His "plans of extensive conspiracy" turned out to be a packet of prayers and songs that the police deemed "rubbish," and no one who had known Nana Sahib at Bithur saw much resemblance. The press began to backpedal and despite grave suspicions that the man had been one of Nana's entourage, he was eventually released.

After yet another suspect was trundled forward, examined, and released, Calcutta assigned two native spies to creep into Nepal and investigate the rumors of Nana's existence. The spies could find only one man in Nepal who still insisted that Nana Sahib was alive: a holy man addicted to hemp. Another man who had lived in China contended that Jung Bahadur had allowed Nana Sahib and a band of rebels to pass through to China, and that some rebels had found sanctuary there, but Nana Sahib had died and his rebel followers had broken up, many to live out their days as mendicants in the hills. Evidently Jung Bahadur had taken to sleeping with Nana Sahib's wife and laying claim to her serving girls, replacing them with "five old ones instead." The residents of Kathmandu regarded this as positive proof that Nana Sahib was dead. Kasibai, Nana Sahib's teenaged wife, lived in a house just outside Jung Bahadur's garden, and it is impossible to know for certain whether she never wore the white robe of a widow because she considered herself too young for such austerities or because Nana Sahib was still alive and, as was rumored, visited her annually during the Shivaite festival of *Sivaratri* dressed as a mendicant.[455]

In 1874 the Maharaja of Gwalior was approached by a mendicant who claimed to be Nana Sahib. When the Maharaja surrendered the man to the British his subjects raised such a protest that His Highness felt called upon to issue a proclamation reminding his subjects that "the Nana Saheb is an enemy of both Governments and was the originator of the mutinies." But soon "Nana" recanted his confession, and neither Dr. Tressider nor a middle-aged Thomson could "go so far as to swear" that he was Nana. Some said that the man who had first turned himself in had indeed been Nana, but the Maharaja had handed someone else over to the British; others maintained that Nana had in fact come to Gwalior but had brought along a look-alike to test the Maharaja's intentions. The mendicant was eventually released.

In 1877 the Bombay money market staggered slightly when a newspaper at Indore reported that Nana was about to invade with a Russian army and reestablish a Mahratta empire. And in April 1879 a letter signed "Nana Sahib of Bithoor" arrived at Calcutta, outlining Nana's purported plan "to rid the country of Christians," and bequeathing his treasure to a claimant to the throne of Jaipur.[456] Some were convinced that Nana Sahib did not die until 1881, almost a quarter century after the rebellion, when two of Nana's old servants returned to their homes in Cawnpore.[457] They claimed that Nana had died in Nepal, from whence they had just returned, "as their services were no longer required . . . Their hands not being polluted with Christian blood," wrote Macrae, "they returned to their families, from whom they had been separated since 1857."[458]

Fifteen years later a Major Maxwell stationed in Manipur reported "that a [holy man] named Poorum Dass, has lived in Manipur Pât for over 30 years, and that he suspects that the Fakir is an 1857 Mutineer." The foreign secretary, Colonel Henderson, called this "vague" and asked the viceroy's secretary what to do. "It *is* rather vague," agreed the secretary. "A detective could ascertain . . . whether he is an Oudh man or not," but that "would not advance matters much. And if the man turns out to be a 1857 Mutineer what after all would be done to him?" By May the authorities at Manpur had convinced themselves that not only was the holy man a mutineer but very likely Nana Sahib himself. Major Maxwell asked for a detective from Oudh to assist in identifying the suspect, but his superior wondered "what use he is to be when he gets there, for I don't suppose there is any man who could (. . .) identify the Nana or any other Mutineer." The secretary dismissed the whole business as "rather a wild goose chase" and the Foreign Office agreed, although it felt that "if there is any real reason to suppose that he was an instigator or leader of revolt, or a murderer of our people, we should push the matter. We ought to hunt down such men." But in the end, no detective was sent, and by

December the authorities had given up their watch on the aged mendicant and reported to Calcutta with some relief that "nothing more has transpired or is likely to."[459]

By the time yet another suspect was arrested in 1894, the government was thoroughly fed up with the whole business. Even supposing that he was Nana Sahib, asked the viceroy, Lord Elgin, "on what charge can we try him?" The relatives of the people massacred at Cawnpore would demand he be tried and hanged for murder, but there was no evidence that could be brought against him that would stand up in a court of law.[460] The suspect was released.

There were more sightings, of course. For many years rumors would flutter through the bazaars of North India that the English had been defeated by the French, that Queen Victoria had poisoned herself, or that Nana Sahib was about to descend from Nepal.[461] Nana Sahib was said to have moved to Mecca, where he lived with a European woman. And there are people in Cawnpore who believe Nana lived in the Deccan until 1896 in the guise of a Hindu saint named Jaja Maharaj. According to local tradition he used to return to Bithur year after year to observe Baji Rao's funeral rites. On one of these visits Nana is said to have drawn his sword and chopped off the head of a local pundit he suspected of conspiring to betray him to the British.[462]

The British decided as a matter of policy that it was best to let Nana Sahib die, if he still lived, "old, discredited, half-witted, . . . still clawing to the horrible honor of being himself."[463] But one more claimant remained. In 1895, when Nana Sahib would have been seventy years old, an addled old man dressed as a *sadhu* was found in a station in Gujerat, staggering around the bazaars, pestered by children. He was placed in protective custody, where he confided to a young British police officer that he was the Nana Sahib and wished to place himself under the protection of the King of Nepal. The police officer eagerly telegraphed district headquarters. "Have arrested the Nana Sahib," he declared. "Wire instructions."

"Release at once," came the weary reply.[464]

◆   ◆   ◆

"When the massacre became generally known," wrote Sherer, "the Nana grew positively into a European notoriety.

> The French, with their taste for melodrama, and their perception
> of the artistic value of contrast, seized on the idea of concocting

his personality out of cruel instincts, exceeding those of ordinary barbarism, on the one hand, but with delicate and luxurious habitudes on the other. So that, in their hands, the Nana became a scented sybarite, who read Balzac, played Chopin on the piano, and, lolling on a divan, fanned by exquisite odalisques from Cashmere, had an English child brought in occasionally, on a pike, for him to examine with his pincenez.

But in England "the desire was rather to make out the Nana to have been one of those extraordinary monsters of ferocity and slaughter who were favourite characters in the earliest dramas." In 1860, Sherer returned to England to find "a large canvas daub in a show at a fair, which was said to represent the Nana, and he really was a terrific embodiment of matted hair, rolling eyes, and cruel teeth."[465] Madame Tussaud's found room for Nana in their chamber of horrors, posed miserably in the "winter costume of his country," according to their catalogue, in which he "died, it is said, the coward's death, despised and forsaken."[466]

In 1858 a painting titled "In Memoriam" and dedicated to "the Christian heroism of the British ladies in India during the Mutiny of 1857" caused quite a stir at the Royal Academy Exhibition in London. In the original version the Scot iconographer Sir Joseph Noel Paton depicted "maddened Sepoys, hot after blood" skulking toward a tableau of prayerful and strangely well-fed and well-scrubbed British women and children. But many visitors found this obvious reference to the Bibighar so excruciating that after Campbell evacuated the women and children from Lucknow, Paton replaced the crazed rebels with Highlanders coming to the rescue in the nick of time.[467]

CONDEMNED AND TRANSPORTED

Rebel Fugitives

As for the rest of Nana's court, Rao Sahib put together a force of six to seven thousand men and continued to seek assistance from France, Afghanistan, and China. He sometimes claimed he was Bala Rao or Nana Sahib "to distract attention," it was said, "and partly to keep up the belief that Nana Rao and Bala Rao were still [alive], in order to increase his *prestige*." At Gwalior he referred to Scindia as his slipper bearer. But eventually his troops dispersed and he wandered around the country disguised as a mendicant, winding up eventually at Jammu, north of the Punjab.

Acting on a tip, an officer named James MacNabb climbed into a palanquin disguised as a native woman and eagerly set off to capture Rao Sahib, under the misapprehension that he was the more notorious rebel Bala Rao. MacNabb's Sikh escort beat him to Rao Sahib's door, and by the time MacNabb arrived they had tied Rao Sahib's long hair "around a post and five or six of them to each hand and foot. It was most amusing to see them stare at me for even the dhooly bearers did not know they were not carrying a woman. The Rao confessed at once—I found some £4000 worth of property in the house—gold, diamonds and pearls."

The charges against Rao Sahib included sending the heads of the three officers off to Cawnpore in a basket and ordering the death of Joseph Carter, the tollkeeper whose pregnant wife was kept in the palace at Bithur. Though the native jury could only find enough evidence to convict him of "modified rebellion," the rebellion at Cawnpore was just five years past, and this was the only one of Nana's adoptive brothers the British would ever have the chance to execute. The judge exceeded the jury's verdict and ordered him hanged.[468]

✦ ✦ ✦

The other rebel the British desperately longed to capture was Tatya Tope, not only for his complicity at Sati Chowra and the Bibighar but for his extraordinary gifts as a guerrilla leader. Frustrated by their futile pursuit of this ferocious Mahratta, the British burned down his mansion at Bithur and incarcerated his family at Gwalior, where, to gain information about his whereabouts, they tied his twenty-year-old brother to a wheel and flogged him.[469]

After the Rani of Jhansi's death Tatya knew he could never defeat the British in open battle, but, like Sivaji, he managed to harass and humiliate them. Toward the end of his struggle his own countrymen had begun to disgust him. "This is the country of my grandfather and my great grandfather," he once complained, "and yet no one gives me supplies—All the people of my country, Hindoos or Mussulmen, have become Christians."[470]

In 1859 he was betrayed by a turncoat raja and captured by a detachment of Bombay sepoys. He was immediately tried and condemned to be hanged. The wife of General Meade protested on the grounds that Tatya deserved respect for eluding the British so long and defeating them in open battle. Someone might have argued that he could not be tried for rebellion or mutiny because he had always been the servant of the Peshwas, to whom he had proved ferociously loyal. They hanged him anyway. "The rope broke the first time," an eyewitness told his son, "but they swung him up again, and that time there was no hitch in the proceedings."[471]

✦ ✦ ✦

Nana's brigadier, Jwala Prasad, was captured in late 1859 and "sent to Cawnpore, a close prisoner." Sherer saw that his fetters were bothering him and ordered them adjusted. "He was not afraid," said Sherer, "and answered readily when I spoke to him. He told me, if I remember his words rightly, that he was not present when the Nana died, but that he attended when the body was burned. He spoke apparently without intention to deceive, and I fully believed him."[472] Jwala Prasad was hanged from a tree at Sati Chowra.[473]

According to the descendants of the boatmen of Sati Chowra, most of their brotherhood was wiped out by the British: the heads of the guild were flogged and hanged beside the river, and the village burned to the ground, although there is not much evidence of the latter in the photographs of the time. Be that as it may, their era had come to an end, for the Grand Trunk Road and the railway would soon destroy their business, and the canals the British continued to dig would drain the Ganges to a ghost of its former self.

The former police chiefs Shah Ali and Hulas Singh were hanged, but many of their subordinates, including the clerks who attended

Clockwise: Tatya Tope, shortly before his execution on April 18, 1859

Jwala Prasad, Nana Sahib's commandant

Rao Sahib, Nana's nephew

Baba Bhutt's court, were reinstated by Sherer because he found they had been "coerced"; more likely he simply could not afford to lose so many experienced personnel.[474]

Nunne Nawab, Nana's Moslem rival, was found to have fired on the Entrenchment, but he had become so estranged from Nana Sahib and remained such a revered figure among Cawnpore's Moslems that he was merely banished to Mecca in 1861, where the local people apparently confused him with Nana Sahib himself.[475]

In early 1859 the Nawab of Farrukhabad turned himself in on the guarantee of an eager young officer that he would not be hanged for sedition. He was tried in February for the "wholesale murder of Europeans," but his lawyers put the blame on the 10th Native Infantry.[476] One witness, David Churcher, was still too addled from his ordeal to provide very convincing testimony of the Nawab's guilt.[477] Though the Nawab was convicted and sentenced to be hanged, the officer's promise of clemency had so muddied the waters that even though he appeared "indifferent to his fate" he too was exiled to Mecca.[478] In August, he was let loose in the port of Aden at the mouth of the Red Sea, and died a few years later.[479]

Maulvie Liaqat Ali eluded the British for fourteen years, traveling freely to Baroda, Bombay and even, he said, to Baghdad. He was captured with seditious documents and a hollow cane filled with two thousand rupees' worth of tiny gold ingots. At Allahabad he was greeted with "hootings, hissings, and groanings" and pleaded guilty to leading the mutineers. But in mitigation he insisted that Nana had forced him to command, and he asked the court to consider that he had saved the lives of several ladies and gentlemen at Allahabad and of Amy Horne at Cawnpore. The judge denounced him as a cowardly rebel and sentenced him to life at the penal colony of Port Blair.[480]

◆　◆　◆

The last time Nana Sahib's older brother Baba Bhutt was sighted he was hurrying toward Calcutta with an ailing Azimullah Khan. Perhaps Baba reverted to his old mendicant ways and died an ascetic.[481] Some say Azimullah died of smallpox on this same trip,[482] but others believe he fled the country in the company of a "Miss Clayton" and eventually moved to Istanbul as an emissary of the Sherif of Mecca. According to this story he was murdered after Miss Clayton had died of old age. The Turks thought he was actually Nana Sahib, but if he was anyone in the Peshwa's court, and he probably was not, he would have been the Turkophile Azimullah Khan.[483]

Whatever became of him, Azimullah Khan had been one of "a few designing men" who worked on the "haziness of popular conceptions" to turn "a little grain of truth to account in generating a harvest of lies."[484] He was an extraordinary man, but only one of many fanatics who would try to palliate with genocide his own subjugation and the alienation and dislocation of the modern world.[485]

Azimullah's "European mother," Lucie Duff Gordon, never could reconcile the "enthusiastic Englishman" she had championed in London society with the monster the British press portrayed, nor could she forgive her countrymen their vengeful excesses. She moved to Egypt and died in 1869.

✦ ✦ ✦

The prostitute Azizun, whom Nanak Chand pictured "on horseback in male attire decorated with medals, armed with a brace of pistols," testified years after Havelock's death that she was in a Mahajun's keeping throughout the Mutiny and never showed her face.[486] Nevertheless a legend persists that "on the reconquest of Kanpur she was arrested by General Havelock who promised to spare her life if only she relented. But the brave Azeezun declined. As the bullets of the firing squad pierced her body, she remembered her master and cried *Nana Saheb Ki Jai!*"[487]

Adla, Nana's favorite concubine, tried to get his jewels to him, but was captured by Mowbray Thomson's police and returned as a prostitute to Cawnpore, where, on the strength of her former intimacy with the Raja of Bithur, she was sometimes summoned to identify the various "Nana Sahibs" the authorities kept dragging in.[488] As for Adla's servant, Hussaini Khanum, the murderous Begum of the Bibighar apparently fled to the hills with Nana's entourage.

In February 1858, William Forbes-Mitchell of the 93rd Sutherland Highlanders was seated in his tent at Cawnpore when "a very good-looking, light-coloured native in the prime of life" walked up hawking plum cakes. He informed Forbes-Mitchell, in fluent English, that his name was Jamie Green, and that he had been mess *khansama* (cook) for an extinct regiment, and that he had Sherer's permission, as well as General Adrian Hope's, to sell his wares in camp. Forbes-Mitchell did not like the look of Jamie's coolie, a "villainous-looking" Eurasian named Mickey, but he admired the way Jamie cheerfully shamed the troops into paying for his wares, and lent the little peddler some Anglo-Indian papers he had been saving. The next day

Green and his coolie were arrested and condemned to death: the first for spying for the Lucknow rebels and the second for having been identified as none other than Sarvur Khan, lover of the Begum of the Bibighar and leader of her execution squad.

Standing guard over Green and Sarvur Khan as they awaited execution, Forbes-Mitchell prevented his fellow Highlanders from procuring "pork from the bazaar to break their castes" and provided the condemned men with a last meal and a hookah. Out of gratitude, Green confessed to Forbes-Mitchell that he was no native Christian but Mohamed Ali Khan, the Rohilkhand nobleman who had accompanied Azimullah to London and Constantinople, where together they had "formed the resolution of attempting to overthrow the Company's Government.

"Thank God," Mohamed Ali said, "we have succeeded in doing that, for from the newspapers which you lent me, I see that the Company's rule has gone, and that their charter for robbery and confiscation will not be renewed."[489]

He and Sarvur Khan were hanged the next morning.

✦　✦　✦

The slaughter of mutineers naturally waned as the rebellion drew to a close, but no one knows how many tens of thousands of them were shot, hanged, blown from guns, run down by lancers, or chopped down by Sikhs by the time the rebellion was over in 1859. Not every mutineer was killed, of course. A great many found refuge in the foothills, and others were tried by more temperate commissioners and magistrates and sentenced to transportation.

As early as August 1857 some Englishmen had suggested that slaughtering so many excellent physical specimens was a terrible waste of manpower. Why not transport them to the West Indies? asked one correspondent to the *Times*. "Transportation to the high-caste East Indian is, in anticipation, as dreadful a punishment as death. . . . In the British West Indian colonies, far from the scenes of their horrible crimes, these misguided men, dangerous in their own country, would in due course of time become useful members of the community." It was the perfect solution, he continued, since the severe manpower shortage on British sugar plantations had resulted from "ultrahuman restrictions" and "anti-slavery suspicion," both of which could naturally be waived in the case of "these miscreants."[490] In November a committee of Western Australian "gentlemen, landowners and others" kindly volunteered to receive transported rebels and employ them in their "healthy" climate, "not very dissimilar to that of some of the northern provinces of Bengal."[491]

Politely declining these offers, Canning elected to exile the rebels to a penal colony at Port Blair, one of the Andaman Islands in the Bay of Bengal. The British had nearly given up on settling it, for hostile tribes occupied the dense surrounding jungles and massacred sailors who ventured ashore. It was a terrible, swampy place, and many of the first rebel prisoners who were dumped there succumbed almost immediately to cholera and malaria. Two hundred and twenty-eight of them tried to escape from their prison; of these twenty were overtaken by fever or killed by the aborigines. When the rest voluntarily staggered back into custody, the superintendent, a Dr. Walker, hanged eighty-one of them.[492] Every rebel prisoner who was not wounded or maimed was transported to Port Blair,[493] along with any condemned rebels who agreed to turn informer.[494] Because they were political prisoners they were not "as a general rule" to be fettered.[495] As the colony took shape, thirty sepoys were allowed to send for their families, though marriages were to be discouraged for long-term prisoners and lifers.[496]

In exchange for a reduction in their sentences, some European prisoners were sent to Port Blair on an experimental basis, but they suffered "excessive mortality."[497] Since it was to remain primarily a sepoys's colony, the authorities wisely denied the Church Missionary Society permission to establish an outpost at Port Blair.[498]

In the 1860s a superintendent's plan to make Port Blair "a prosperous and profitable colony" was not considered feasible,[499] nor was elephant breeding allowed.[500] So the convicts were employed in draining the surrounding swamp. When in 1872 Lord Mayo, Viceroy of India, came to inspect the colony, he was so impressed that he foresaw a day when two million people might live there. A few hours later His Excellency was stabbed to death by an inmate, a hillsman who preferred hanging to imprisonment for killing a blood-feud enemy. "Among men I have no accomplice," the assassin told the judge. "God is my partner." He was hanged on the gallows on Viper Island.[501]

✦ ✦ ✦

At Augur in Central India in March 1887, a sowar named Mazar Ali raised his musket at parade and shot his major dead. The crime seemed to make no sense; neither did Mazar Ali at his trial. He said he had been trying to kill a pigeon, then claimed that a spirit had commanded him to kill his adjutant. Since the major had always been kind to Mazar Ali, the authorities ascribed his crime to one of those inscrutable fits of temper to which Indian troops were believed to be prone and hanged him for murder.

But shortly afterward a leaflet appeared in the bazaars explaining that Mazar Ali had been the son of Suffar Ali Khan, a 2nd Native Cavalry sergeant who had been flogged, desecrated with pig's fat, and forced to lick the bloody mat at Cawnpore thirty years before. Standing on the gallows at the Bibighar, Suffar Ali Khan had shouted to the crowd to tell his son that he must someday wreak a terrible vengeance on General Neill, by whose orders he had been so cruelly and unjustly treated. Since General James Neill had been killed long ago in the streets of Lucknow, Mazar Ali had shot Major A. H. S. Neill, the "Butcher's" only son.[502]

ALL SOULS

Epilogue

I f an Indian who remained loyal to the British managed to survive not only the rebels' depredations but the indiscriminate killings of Neill and the Highlanders and Peel's rabid little sailors, he was apt to be rewarded. The Mahajun Ishwari Prasad was given a village worth over seven thousand rupees for supplying both Wheeler's and Wind-ham's entrenchments[503] and for saving the life of an unnamed European.[504] Sheo Prasad was also rewarded, but for some reason committed suicide in 1895 by swallowing a diamond.[505] Narain Rao of Bithur received a village worth 4,500 rupees.[506] Dirigibijah Singh, who hosted Thomson and his party, was rewarded with a pension, and Hardeo Baksh Singh, who had gingerly protected Probyn and Edwards, was made a raja. Eventually 140 villages or portions of villages in Cawnpore district were taken from rebel landlords and redistributed.[507] Loyal sepoys such as Khoda Bux and Gobind Singh who remained with Wheeler's garrison were rewarded with high ranks in the Indian police, chasing down their old comrades and dragging them to the gallows.[508]

The noisiest loyalist had been Nanak Chand, the mooktear who emerged from hiding with Ishwari Prasad to join the British camp. In August he presented a grateful John Walter Sherer with a long list of rebels. In December he topped it with his famous "diary," a journal which had been "commenced before the Mutiny, and . . . brought down to the day on which the rebellion was extinguished, and . . . corrected after minute inquiries made, since the reoccupation of Cawnpore by the British, to prove to the authorities that I have been a loyal subject, and also to establish a good name."

Nobody questioned Nanak Chand's loyalty, but his good name was another matter. Charles Hillersdon was not the last collector to throw Nanak Chand out of his office. Eventually Sherer barred him from the Collectorate on suspicion of collecting extortion from townspeople in exchange for leaving their names off his list of disloyal townspeople. In 1861 Nanak Chand tried to sell some information about Nana Sahib's whereabouts to Sherer's replacement, and a year later claimed he deserved a reward for helping the British find Nana's treasure at Bithur.[509] But he was again thrown out of the Collectorate as "a common informer [who] had disgusted everyone that has had anything to do with him."[510]

✦ ✦ ✦

Of the four men from the Cawnpore garrison who managed to escape down the Ganges, one—the "most intelligent" Gunner Sullivan—died of cholera soon after Neill assigned him to the ordnance department.[511]

"Most emaciated . . . from the continued effects of fever and dysentery," Lieutenant Henry George Delafosse of the 53rd Native Infantry nevertheless survived to receive a medal with two clasps, and the thanks of the governor-general in council for his service at Lucknow, where an advance battery bore his name. Permitted by the army to count two years' extra service—one for Cawnpore and a second for Lucknow—on March 10 he sailed for England on the *Ava* with his old friend Thomson.

Six nights later the *Ava* struck a rock off the coast of Ceylon and sank. As water poured into the engine room "the crew were ordered to clear away boats to land the passengers, which was done without any accident. An officer was put in charge of each boat, and all the ladies and children, and then the gentlemen were embarked, with orders to lie by the ship until daylight." This time Thomson and Delafosse remained with the women and children, and since the surf was too high on the beach they made for a nearby settlement, where they all arrived safely. (Like the burning of the Assembly Rooms, the wreck of the *Ava* was a disaster for future historians, taking with it Martin Gubbins's journals, Thomson's notes, Teddy Vibart's letters, and one of Russell's dispatches.)[512]

Delafosse published a brief and clumsy narrative of the siege in the *Times of London*, but never seems to have attempted a full-fledged account. In 1860 he returned to India and was decorated again for service in Sikkim and the Frontier War. He became a major general in 1887, having in the meantime held Colonel Acklom Smith's old command at Fatehgarh for two years.[513] He lived to be seventy years old, and when he died in 1905 a plaque in his memory was installed at All Souls, where, with his friend Thomson's, it still frames the chancel.[514]

In 1858 Lieutenant Mowbray Thomson published his own narrative of the events at Cawnpore, upon whose skeleton some of this book has been built.[515] Stalwart, magnanimous, daring, he seemed to regard life as a wonderful, headlong adventure; though his narrative is harrowing, the horror of the siege and the massacres never seemed to seep into his bones. A banker once dined with Thomson after he returned to London, "and I shall never forget an answer he made to a question of mine. I asked: 'When you got once more amongst all your countrymen, and the whole terrible thing was over, what on earth was the first thing you did?'

"'Did?' cried he, 'why, I went and reported myself as present and ready for duty.'"[516]

By the time of his death in 1917, Thomson was the last of the Cawnpore survivors. He died a general, but never received the decorations that Sherer always insisted he deserved. Delafosse had had the good fortune to serve at Lucknow, whose relief served as an antidote to the horrors of Sati Chowra and the Bibighar. But Thomson's achievements remained enmired in Wheeler's capitulation, the officers' flight from the ghat, and even the disaster of "Windham's Mess."[517]

◆ ◆ ◆

Eventually Amy Horne gave up her pension to marry a railway surveyor named Bennett, for whom she bore several children. She might have done better to keep the pension. As an elderly widow she supported herself by giving piano lessons in Howrah, a dreary suburb of Calcutta, where she waxed tiresome about the treasure "that would have made me rich for life, instead of leaving me the pauper I now am." Though her "flesh crept at the recollection of the horrors I had gone through," she revised her initial account with the help of R. Macrae and in 1913 published her story in *Nineteenth Century* magazine as "Ten Months' Captivity After the Massacre at Cawnpore," which "made me live my sufferings over again," she wrote, "reviving scenes and incidents that I would give the world to forget. None know how bitter are my remembrances, nor the desolation that presses so heavily upon my spirits."[518]

✦   ✦   ✦

Perhaps the most anguished of all the Cawnpore survivors, however, was William Jonah Shepherd. Jonah remained with the Commissariat for some months, and assiduously tried to account for all of the victims at Cawnpore, amassing in the process a voluminous file of letters from their relatives in England and working with Doctors De Facien and Tressidar to produce a definitive list of Cawnpore casualties.[519] But his nerves were frayed, and he longed to leave the scenes of his family's massacre. "My impaired memory," he wrote, "and loss of power to *fix my attention*, compelled me often to put aside work that required immediate attention, and I laboured under a perpetual and unaccountable . . . apprehension which was exceeding distressing, the fear of something going wrong."

Relieved of his duties in December, Jonah left Cawnpore.[520] For the next three years he lived with his elder brother at Agra, where, in 1860, he accepted a position in the Executive Commissariat Office. But as a result of "exposure to the sun, and mental anxiety both before and after the mutiny," Jonah was granted medical leave in 1862. At the age of thirty-five he sat down to write *A Personal Narrative of the Outbreak and Massacre at Cawnpore*, whose "charm is *simplicity*," wrote the reviewer for the Delhi *Gazette*, and whose "value truth."[521]

But his memory continued to fail him, and he finally retired to a small estate in Oudh, bestowed for his Mutiny services by Lord Elgin. Gratefully dubbing his estate "Elgingurh," Jonah applied himself to its management, but his best efforts were unavailing. He spent the money from his late brother-in-law's estate on improving his tenants' living conditions, but he lost twenty acres to the Oudh and Rohilkhand Railway, and the remaining land was so poor that after a series of disastrous harvests and epidemics, he was compelled to order his starving tenants to go elsewhere for work.

William Jonah Shepherd

Lieutenant Mowbray Thomson in his mutiny whiskers

Charlotte Jacobi, whose father sent her to Calcutta in May

Gavin Jones, who rebuilt Cawnpore

Destitute, Jonah accepted a low-paying position with the chief engineer's office of the Oudh and Rohilkhand Railway in 1873 and three years later sold off his calamitous estate. But he could never put the Cawnpore massacre behind him, and in 1878, drawing on the Indian depositions collected by Colonel Williams, he revised his *Personal Narrative*, which was republished a year later.

That same year he published a second book composed of a series of tracts he was probably advised by his publisher to leave out of his narrative. Titled *The Guilty Men of 1857: Failure of England's Great Mission to India*, it blamed the uprising on the government's scorning of Christianity. Jonah wrote of a day when India would be ruled by Eurasians who would combine the best of both cultures and spread Christianity across the entire subcontinent. But for the present, Jonah bitterly observed, "no status, no prospects, no interest in the soil of India" seemed to be their lot under the new British Raj, while "natives who are not in the remotest degree connected with Europeans by blood, are received as orphans, or converts, and Baptised with European names."[522] Though Jonah's dream of a ruling Eurasian race was never realized, his people's devotion to the British, wrote Edward Thompson in 1925, remained "beyond any loyalty that [the British] get from the free races of our world-wide Commonwealth."[523] As a people they remained adrift: disdained by Indians and British alike, scorned by each for the contaminant of the other's blood.

William Jonah Shepherd died in 1891 at the age of sixty-six, and though his descendants believed he was buried at Lucknow, his grave has disappeared. Because "Uncle Jonah" had such bad luck, the family would never name a child after him.[524] Evidently nothing remains of his extensive collection of letters from the relatives of the Cawnpore dead. "You must understand, Mr. Ward," one of his descendants told me when I inquired after Jonah's files, "he was a very insignificant man."

✦ ✦ ✦

The identity of the baby who was supposed to have been spirited out of the Entrenchment by her ayah remains a mystery. The ayah is said to have eventually brought the baby girl to Calcutta, from where she was shipped to relatives in Australia. Whatever the truth of the story, in June 1858 one of Emma Halliday's aunts referred to "the Macansh baby" as "the sole survivor" at Cawnpore. The story became a schoolroom staple in New South Wales. It may well have been a fable to palliate the horrors of Sati Chowra and the Bibighar from which not a single child is believed to have survived, and for this same reason it is hard to accept that it is not true.[525]

✦ ✦ ✦

Of the Fatehgarh survivors, David Churcher, who had tended to the dying Major Robertson in their hiding place near the Ganges, declined to join Edwards, Probyn, and Jones on their journey downriver and remained in hiding for several more months. By the time his brother found him in January 1858, Robertson was dead and Churcher was living in sugarcane fields, reduced to a bearded skeleton whose "scared and vacant looks" would haunt his brother for the rest of his life. Shattered by his ordeal, David returned to Fatehgarh to cultivate indigo, but died a pauper in 1908, the last planter in the district. At his request he was buried with the little towel he had worn during his escape from the Manpur Massacre.

The only American missionary in Fatehgarh's vicinity to survive the rebellion was the Methodist William Butler who, after wisely declining his Presbyterian brothers' invitation to join them in their doomed flight to Cawnpore, led his family to safety in the hill station of Nainital and wrote about his harrowing experiences in *The Land of the Veda*.

Miss Sutherland's account of her rescue from the riverbank was first published in the *Indian Planter's Gazette* but never verified. Whatever the truth of her story, Miss Sutherland did not repay her savior's kindness. The subhedar who cared for her was eventually caught and prosecuted for mutiny at Allahabad. Miss Sutherland, by then a wife and mother, was subpoenaed by the defense to testify that the subhedar had risked his life to preserve hers. She refused, and the subhedar was hanged.[526]

After her release from "Hanging" Power's custody, Bonny Byrne, the Nawab's eighteen-year-old former mistress,[527] married a Sub-Collector of "prodigious abdominous dimensions"[528] named Chandler, who had been widowed three years before.[529] She gave her newborn son the name of Byrne, and died two years later, "a sincere friend," so says her tombstone, "and an attached wife."[530]

Calcutta evidently forgave George Probyn his flight from Fatehgarh and appointed him magistrate of Fatehpur. His fellow fugitive, the prescient and mercurial William Edwards, went on to sit behind

George Lindsay's old magisterial bench at Benares. He wrote of his Mutiny experiences in *Personal Adventures during the Indian Rebellion in Rohilcund, Futtehghur, and Oude.*

Gavin Sibbald Jones spent the rest of the rebellion recovering from his wound and testifying against the mutineers and villagers who attacked the second Fatehgarh flotilla. In 1859 the railway finally reached Cawnpore, and when the American Civil War increased the demand for cotton, Hugh Maxwell, who had ridden out the uprising in Calcutta, asked Jones to manage the Elgin Cotton Spinning & Weaving Company Limited, which had been established to process the heaps of cotton bales that poured into Cawnpore from neighboring districts. Restive and ingenious, Jones eventually went on to establish a woolen mill, boot and shoe factory, and engineering works that first established Cawnpore's enduring if not always enviable reputation as the "Manchester of the East." Before his death in Southsea in 1913, Jones was known as the "Father of Cawnpore," but the Anglo-Indian community never warmed to him; he was too vaunting and probably too bright. His chilliness did not extend to everyone, however, for even at the height of his glory, whenever he was visited by the village headman who had protected him from the rebels and nursed him back to health, Jones would always seat the old man in his desk chair and sit down at his feet.[531]

♦ ♦ ♦

Cawnpore's resurrection was long in coming. "The aspect of this once beautiful station of Cawnpore," Shepherd wrote in 1858, "is entirely changed.

> Residents, who were absent when the mutiny broke out in June, now returned and looked at the place in bewilderment, and shook their heads in sorrow. Houses, gardens, large shady trees, bazars and huts, all had disappeared—every thing, to the extent of a mile all round the new fort, was . . . cleared away. The spot where once stood the splendid assembly rooms, the shops of Brandon and Company and J. D. Hay, merchants, had become dreary waste. The House of Slaughter of the helpless women and children had likewise been dismantled; and the trees round the well and the court-yard all cut down.[532]

There was plenty of bustle about the place. "Thousands of men," wrote an officer, "are employed making tents, saddlery, harness, and preparing guns and ammunition for the Troops."[533] But always there was a haunted atmosphere of death. Men on their morning rides returned "hot, stuffy, and powdered all over with impalpable, but visible leg-bones and skulls, and mud, and nastiness, which the bath could scarcely clear away."[534]

European women and children were not permitted to return until July 27, 1858, a year after the Bibighar massacre, but no one flocked to move there.[535] "Ruins; dust, flies, evil odours and general misery and distress were all one could see," wrote a visitor in 1859.[536] An Indian traveler in 1860 was saddened "to see the desolate houses, some windowless, others roofless, of the European residents. In the wrecks of gardens and flower-beds, 'roses contended in vain with choking weeds.'"[537]

Later that year Canning came to Cawnpore to hold a Grand Durbar, but under the circumstances, Sherer said, it could not be "a splendid one." Canning assured the assembled talukdars and "minor monarchs of mid India" that their titles and estates would be restored and protected under the rule of Queen Victoria, who now deigned to rule the subcontinent as Empress of India.[538] During the ceremony "one of the small Rajpoot chieftains had brought an old grey and toothless courtier, who had got himself up in a ferociously warlike manner, and carried a portentous sword of the pantomimic scimitar description." In a loud voice the old man declared that if Canning's enemies "ever gave him any trouble, he had only to say the word and this sword should be drawn in his defence." Eventually the viceroy's aides hustled the old man away, and Canning "burst into uncontrolled laughter."[539] Empress or no empress, Raj or no Raj, the elderly warrior had sung the swan song of the old feudal order.

The countryside around Cawnpore remained desolate, and along the ravaged Grand Trunk Road, "whole villages [were] in ruins, without one human being. The walls of mud-huts stand thatchless and rain-beaten. The roads, untrodden by any footsteps, are overgrown with weeds and brambles. Thick bushes hide these villages from the view. There is no stir—no sound of life in them—not even the baying of a dog to break in upon the silence."[540] In 1860 the district was visited by another famine, and after the interrupted harvests of the mutiny years there was no surplus to feed the thousands of people who wandered in from Bundelkhund.[541] Cholera plagued the native city, into which soldiers were no longer allowed to venture.

Some thought it might be best simply to destroy Cawnpore altogether and let it drop back into its former obscurity. But the East Indian Railway and such visionaries as Hugh Maxwell and Gavin Jones would not allow it. By 1892 the city boasted chemists and druggists, wine and general merchants, clothiers, printing presses, several hotels, four banks, a government saddlery and harness factory, Cooper & Allen's and the Foy brothers' boot factories, a government flour mill, a jute mill, and five textile mills, where tourists found it "very interesting to watch the *Indian* children, with their parents, working in the Mills on *English* principles."[542]

"On the 6th December, 1857," wrote William Forbes-Mitchell, now an elderly veteran of Campbell's campaign, "I advanced across the Canal with *thirty-six*, well served, heavy [rebel] guns pouring shot and shell through our ranks. On the 19th of August, 1892, I stood on the top of the Cawnpore Woollen Mills, and counted *thirty-six* chimneys . . . belching smoke from more than three times that number of steam boilers."[543]

✦ ✦ ✦

In late 1857 Reverend Willis, the only surviving missionary from the Society for the Propagation of the Gospel's Cawnpore Mission, returned to the station from Calcutta, where he had gone before the outbreak for his ordination. He could not find secure lodgings, since what was left of the S.P.G.'s mission was four miles from the British encampment and still subject to rebel raids. So he took up residence in an end room of the tile-roofed barracks in the ruins of the Entrenchment. After several months he moved to a renovated bungalow, and when the district was secure he visited the missionary complex to find that the schoolhouse was still in one piece. But all the wood had been removed from the chapel and dwellings, and the landlord to whom Haycock had entrusted the communion plate had absconded. Willis preached every Sunday to a congregation of about thirty people "in one of the aisles of Christ Church with the bright blue sky open to the view."[544] Within two years Soldiers' Church was repaired and, at Canning's insistence, Christ Church roofed over.

The missions of North India lost seven hundred thousand rupees worth of property to the rebellion,[545] and for a time their reestablishment seemed in doubt.[546] But veteran missionaries believed that if their brethren did not return to the field India would descend into a nightmare of hatred and bitterness. "Where has Christ been more humbled and shamed than in India?" wrote the *Colonial Church Chronicle and Missionary Journal*. "What will be the case now, between races embittered by bloodshed and mutual fear? What a tremendous peril is before us now, lest the dews of Christian love, that fell so scantily before, should utterly be dried up from those waste places of Hindostan!"[547]

"During the course of 1858," the S.P.G. reported, "frequent discussions were raised as to whether Cawnpore should be retained as a missionary centre." But after the Mutiny India-mission boxes swelled with cash all over the Western world. A full-fledged mission station was reestablished, in time to minister to the orphans of yet another terrible famine.[548]

The native Christians at Fatehgarh gradually returned to the ruins of their mission. A Reverend Fullerton labored to reestablish the American Presbyterian Mission, and an All Saints Memorial Church was eventually erected in honor of Colonel Smith's doomed garrison. "I sometimes think," Mrs. Freeman had written on the eve of her fatal voyage down the Ganges, "our deaths would do more good than we would do in all our lives."

Despite all the native Christians who lost their lives in the Mutiny, their number doubled between 1851 and 1861 to 3,717, probably due to the number of orphans the rebellion and the famine of 1860 generated.[549] Nevertheless the North Indian missions never really took hold, and the evangelicals had to content themselves with their educational contributions to Indian life and a few individual converts. Of the latter, perhaps none better pleased his sponsors than a boy of Pathan ancestry who converted to Christianity after the rebellion and survived into the next century. "He worked at Banda and Karwi and Cawnpore," wrote Reverend Hill, "and was a good man and a thorough Christian." He was also the son of Azimullah Khan.[550]

✦ ✦ ✦

The well at the Bibighar proved an unquiet grave. Over Sherer's "thin covering of earth" soldiers deposited the women and children's discarded clothing, which later visitors mistook for the cadavers themselves. And in the monsoon rains the earth kept washing down among the corpses, so that the well had to be covered over with brick and mortar. Eventually "a draft of recruits of the 32nd" erected a little monument in front of the well.[551] "It is in the shape of a cross," wrote Jonah, and inscribed, "I believe in the resurrection of the body."[552] "One or two other small tombs and inscriptions have since sprung up in its vicinity, . . . the only marks that indicated the place of slaughter to a stranger at that time."[553]

When Canning came through for his Durbar he ordered the surrounding landscape cleared of all ruined buildings. The Bibighar itself had already been demolished and its surrounding trees cut down by the occupying army, and after a while people lost track of exactly where it had stood. But in 1860 the well was still covered with "ordinary brick," though "the decay of the bodies had caused the top to sink a few inches."[554]

People wondered if perhaps a church might be built over the spot, with a crypt in the middle. But Lady Canning sketched a memorial she thought might be more appropriate, consisting of a stone screen and an angelic central figure.[555] Several leading sculptors were asked to contribute designs. A leading contender proposed a sculpture consisting of dead children lying at the feet of an English woman leaning against a cross pierced with a sword. Appalled by this graphic reminder of the "horrors of 1857" which Canning "wished to avoid," the viceroy chose instead a figure sketched by Lady Canning's girlhood friend, Baron Carlo Marochetti. It began as "a sort of Britannia" figure that reminded Canning of "a half penny," but evolved into a downcast marble angel holding palm fronds in its crossed arms.[556]

The Cannings personally commissioned the memorial, but they were both dead by the time it was completed in 1865.[557] To finance the vast surrounding park, the inhabitants of Cawnpore were required to pay a punitive fine of £30,000 for their unresisting submission to Nana Sahib's rule.[558] The memorial proved a great inconvenience to the native residents of Cawnpore who were not allowed inside without a pass. Even for the British "no games or amusements are allowed," wrote a visitor, "and carriages must go at foot pace."[559]

The sepulchral well near the Entrenchment was boarded over during the Mutiny, and a cross erected upon it. (The nearby echelon of unfinished barracks that Thomson and the railway men defended were eventually finished and function today as army barracks.) The Entrenchment was memorialized in 1862 by a vast Romanesque Church called All Souls, whose walls were eventually studded with plaques and memorial stones and whose clerestory windows bore the names of all the garrison's officers except Wiggins.[560]

The pages of the *Times* had been full of debate over what denomination should administer it; eventually it was deemed Anglican, and consecrated in 1875 by the Bishop of Calcutta.[561] A year later Prince Edward of Wales visited the Entrenchment and ordered that stones be placed to mark its boundaries. In 1883 his mother the Queen donated a baptismal font on a stout marble pedestal "as a token of her deep sympathy."[562] Four years later Lord Dufferin ordered the shell-pocked Entrenchment well restored, complete with horse troughs and the cistern near which the gallant John MacKillop had been wounded while fetching water for the children.

But it was the Memorial Well at Cawnpore that became Anglo-India's most hallowed shrine, and a decade after the Mutiny it was visited more frequently than the Taj Mahal. Private Murphy of the 84th who had escaped with Thomson and Delafosse was appointed the guardian of the gardens, where he could be seen "daily," wrote William Butler, "accompanying visitors from many lands, who with sad thoughts and respectful steps approach the Ladies' Monument."[563]

One of Murphy's duties was "to indicate and bound off the spots having reference to the Mutiny at Cawnpore.[564] But some spots may have been marked off more accurately than others. "Poor fellow," wrote the historian A. Busteed, "[Murphy] was an inveterate drunkard and though he got several chances, nothing could be done with him. When drunk he would sometimes harangue and protest that Lord Canning ought not to be Viceroy of India while such a man as Mowbray Thomson was to the fore! He was a harmless poor devil ruined by the habit of the British soldier. At last he was remanded to the [84th Regiment] again as a full Private and a hopeless case. Then I believe he died."[565]

Murphy was not the only person to be haunted by the Memorial Gardens. Zoë Yalland, who was born in Cawnpore, recalled that a cousin who lived for a time in the garden cottage reported observing her dogs behaving oddly, watching and following the movement of the screen doors as if some unseen figure were crossing the room. She got up and looked out at the garden, where she claimed to see the ghosts of "two blonde boys running this way and that around the mouth of the well" as if "desperately trying to find somewhere to escape."[566]

◆   ◆   ◆

The Memorial Well and Gardens that were erected around the Bibighar.

Photographs of the Memorial Well were pasted into many an album of the Raj to remind the families posed on their verandahs, the memsahibs instructing the gardeners by the flower beds, the children riding ponies in the hill stations, the gentlemen at their *gymkhana* clubs or holding court al fresco in some dusty jungle hamlet of not only the martyrdom of their forebears but the underlying perils of the raj.[567] For the well at Cawnpore was never really covered over, and the women and children never laid to rest. They festered in the minds of every Anglo-Indian, haunted even their loftiest intentions. And whenever Indians dared propose to rule themselves, the British would flourish the bloody relics of the Bibighar as proof of Indian barbarity.

None of the many wells that the British filled with rebel corpses were memorialized. At Ujnalla in the Punjab, for instance, a deputy commissioner named Frederick Cooper executed 237 unarmed sepoys in batches of ten and suffocated forty-five more in a closed cell. He then threw all their bodies into "a deep dry well," as Cooper described it, whose "presence furnished a convenient solution as to the one remaining difficulty, which was of sanitary consideration." But despite Cooper's own breast-beating account of this massacre— "there is a well at Cawnpore," he crowed, "but there is also one at Ujnalla"—such wells were merely covered over.[568]

It was not until April 13, 1919, that the well at Cawnpore was displaced in India's moral imagination by another: the well at Jallianwallah Bagh in Amritsar into which Indian men, women, and children jumped to escape the volleys of a party of Gurkhas under the command of British General Dyer, who had resolved to evince the imperial will by blocking the only exit from the garden and firing on an assembly of Independence workers. Three hundred seventy-nine people were killed and another twelve hundred wounded.[569]

✦ ✦ ✦

Of all the Indian Mutiny sites at Cawnpore the ghat at Sati Chowra is the least changed. After years of drain-off the ravine down which Wheeler's garrison marched is deeper now, and the Ganges is shallower and narrower. But the boatman's temple still stands, as do the compound walls between which the rebels lay in waiting as the garrison embarked. In the shade of the tree from which Rao Sahib was hanged stood a small memorial cross inscribed, "In Memoriam/27th June/1857." But the cross was broken off after Independence, and was recently cast into the Ganges.[570] People have walked off with a few of the brick Entrenchment markers that Prince Edward commissioned, and local villagers keep trying to install a shrine in the stump of an extinct banyan tree on the grounds of All Souls. The church itself still stands, and every Sunday services are held for a dwindling congregation of local Christians, vastly outnumbered by the names of the victims that flank the apse on a row of marble tablets.

Today's visitor to Cawnpore will not find Marochetti's angel in the Memorial Gardens. After Independence a few young Indians climbed in, tarred the angel and broke one of its wings.[571] The Indian government graciously paid for its repair, and though Gavin Jones's son protested, the padre at All Souls was allowed to cart off a portion of the memorial to his church's compound for protection: there the angel now stands in a remnant of its former enclosure.

The Memorial Gardens, renamed Nana Rao Park, are no longer in mourning. The vast iron railing that encircles it has been painted in a rainbow of pastels. The remaining chunks of the memorial screen have been employed as benches and pot stands, and under one of the banyan trees a portion of its pedestal serves as a small Shivaite shrine. Near the blank sandstone circle that is all that remains of the Bibighar's well stands a rather hastily conceived monument to Tatya Tope, surrounded by four small marble frogs, evocative of the baleful creatures that used to drive Neill's men to distraction in their swampy camp.

I asked one of the schoolboys playing cricket nearby in an empty fountain basin if he knew what had happened here almost a century and a half ago. He did not, he said, and listened politely as I told him of the massacre at the Bibighar. "Quite impossible," he said, gazing at the sandstone slab beneath us. "The British would never have buried their dead so carelessly."

SOURCES

Anyone who tries to tell the story of Cawnpore must subsist on a sometimes sparse diet of questionable depositions, muddled accounts, dubious journals, and the narratives of shell-shocked survivors with axes to grind. I have tried not to burden this narrative with my own struggle to weigh this account against that, or my reasons for believing one witness versus another. The narrative is composed of the conclusions I have drawn; the process by which I have arrived at those conclusions I have reserved for the notes.

A great frustration for any historian hoping to write an objective history of Cawnpore is the dearth of primary material from the Indian side of the equation. The disposition of some Indians of the time to tell the British only what they wanted to hear was usually matched by the British inclination to hear only what they wanted to believe. So each native's testimony has to be judged on its own merits, independent of the elegant distillations that British imperialist and Indian nationalist historians have produced. My approach has been to believe the native accounts except where they contradict one another or are obviously compromised by a witness's desperate attempt to save his neck from the hangman's noose. But even in these cases there are facts hidden among the convenient falsehoods that illuminate the truth.

ARCHIVES

British Library (BL)
Many of the obscure books listed under published material were consulted at the British Library. See also the Oriental and India Office Collections, which is a branch of the British Library.

British Museum (BM)
Anonymous, *The Mahomedan in India*. [Mss.41996.]
Horne, Amelia. *Narrative*. [Mss.7158]
Sutherland. "The Story of Miss Sutherland." Transcribed by R. Macrae from the *Indian Planter's Gazette*, no. 15, Oct., 1890, p. 454. [Mss.7158]

Cambridge Center of South Asia Studies (CCSAS)
Bradshaw, A. F. *Letters*. Lenox-Conyngham Papers.
De Wend, Captain Douglas. *Journal*.
Fortesque-Brickdale, Lt. J., *Letters*.
Monckton Papers.
Reid Papers.

Clwyd
Glynne-Gladstone Manuscript. [Ms.2481] Letter regarding David Lindsay, a cousin of the major's.

Devon
Seymour Papers. [1392M/Family/Literary/1]. Contains a journal of the final relief of Lucknow in 1858

Durham
Blackett, J. S. *Papers*. [Add.MSS835/1–3]

East Sussex
Campion, William Henry. *Letters*. [DAN 477–85]
Wolseley, Garnet. *From England to Cawnpore for the Great Indian Rebellion*. Manuscript. Hove Reference Library of the East Sussex County Council. [W/W/2/1]

Gloucester
Mactier, Mrs. Colonel, regarding the Fatehgarh massacre. [D245/V.21.]

Humberside
Denison Letters. [DDSA 1077]

Isle of Wight (IW)
Oglander, Col. Henry. He signs one letter written in May 1837 "General Henry Oglander Col. 26th Foot." Isle of Wight County Record Office. [OG/CC/43293/182–210]

Kent
Garrett, General Robert. *Papers*. [U888/016]

Leicestershire
Eyrl, Henry of HM 19th Foot. *Diary*. Leicestershire County Council Record Office.

Lincolnshire
Fane, Henry Edward Hamlyn. *Letters*. Lincolnshire County Council. [6/9/1/4a–b]

National Archives of India (NAI)
In addition to the Foreign (FDP), Military (MDP), Home (HDP), and Governor-General's Proceedings (GGP), Foreign and Secret Correspondence (FSC), and Foreign Correspondence Supplement (FCS) I consulted the following sources:
Atchison, C. V. *A Collection of Treaties, Engagements and Savads Relating to India and Neighbouring Countries*. Vol. 6. Calcutta, 1909.
Zillah Cawnpore: 1848–1854. Cawnpore, 1848–1854 and 1855. Records of the district court that include Narain Rao's suit and several mentions of Nanak Chand.

National Army Museum (NAM)
In addition to the Bengal lists and the photography collection I consulted the following sources:
Bingham, General G. W. *Diary*. [5903–105]
Cafe, W. M. *Papers*.
Dinwiddie, C. *Life and Adventures*. Privately printed. 1864.

Oliver, J. R. *Recollections of the Indian Mutiny Campaigns. Volume XIII. April 1846 to September, 1896*. London, 1896.

National Library of Scotland (NLS)
Heathcote. *Papers*. [Ms.20206]
Keene, Henry George. *Papers*. National Library of Scotland. [MS 4132]

Northern Ireland (PRONI)
Garrett, Robert. *Papers*. Public Records Office of Northern Ireland. [MsT.2235]
Scott/Transcript Letter dated 8 Nov. 1857 from C. Scott in Cawnpore to his parents, Reverend George and Mrs. Scott in Dungiven County, Londonderry. Public Record Office of Northern Ireland. [D.1698.5]

Nottingham
Anonymous notes written among the pages of a copy of the pamphlet published as a tract containing extracts from the letters of Rose C. Monckton. The letters were privately printed by a lady of Edinburgh unacquainted with the Moncktons. "Rosa" Catherine Monckton was the daughter of Thomas Taylor of Clifton and granddaughter of Sir John Cottrell, Baronet. In 1854 she married John Rivas Monckton (born 1833), who was superintendent of a section of the Grand Trunk Road. University of Nottingham, Department of Manuscripts & Special Collections. [Ga 2D 1230]

Oriental and India Office Collections of the British Library (OIOC)
In addition to the records of the East India Company, the Board of Control, the India Office, Parliamentary papers, the Proceedings of the Government of India, and the Presidencies and Provinces, and the photography collection, I consulted the following sources at the OIOC:
Alexander, Captain. Letter in Vibart, Edward Daniel Hamilton. *Papers: 1854–1933*. [Mss.Eur.F.135/19]
Ames, Frederick. *Letters: August 1857–December 1858*. Lieutenant Ames served with the Oudh Field Force under Gen. Sir Colin Campbell. He was a lieutenant in the 2nd Battalion, the Rifle Brigade. [Mss.Eur.B.236]
Bartrum, Katherine. *Diary*. Indian Office Library. [Eur.Mss.A.67]
Biddulph, Lieutenant Robert. *Letters: 20 Sep 1857 to 1 Jan 1860*. [Photo.Eur.47]
Board's Collections 1857–1858. [f/4/2703. 193490]
Chalwin, Louisa Parsons. *Letters: 1851–1870*. Louisa was the wife of Edmund George Chalwin of the Bengal Army Veterinary Service. [Mss.Eur.B.344/2]
Chevers, Norman. *Papers*. [Mss.Eur.C506]
Clowes, Major George. *Letters*. [Photo.Eur.54]
Collins, Francis. *Letters: 1857–1858*. Assistant surgeon in the 5th Fusiliers, Collins took part in the first and second reliefs of Lucknow. [Photo.Eur.59]
Eckford, *Letters*. [Mss.Eur.F240/23]
Ewart, Emma. *Letters: May–June 1857*. Emma S. Ewart was the wife of Lt. Col. J. Ewart, 1st Bengal Native Infantry. The Ewarts died at Cawnpore en route to the boats. [Mss.Eur.B.267]
Fitzgerald, Patrick Gerald. *Diary*. Fitzgerald was an assistant surgeon in the Madras Medical Service and served at Cawnpore, Lucknow, Gorakhpur and with the Central India Field Force. [Mss.Eur.A.140]
Gilliland, Mary. [Photo.Eur.251]
Grant Family. *Letters: June 1857 to April 1858*. Letters from Lieutenant John Anderson Grant of the Madras Army, who died of cholera at Cawnpore in August 1857, and Grant, Ensign Francis William, who served at Cawnpore, Bithur, and Lucknow. [Mss.Eur.C.323]
Johnson, Chardin Philip. *Journal*. Johnson was a captain in the 9th (Queen's Royal) Regiment of (Light) Dragoons (Lancer). In 1858 he acquired the army rank of major.

Eventually, like his friends Grant and Little, he became a lieutenant-colonel. [Mss. Eur.A.161]

Larkins, Emma. Letter, dated 9 June 1857, written to her sister Henrietta Coffin. Emma was the wife of Major George Larkins of the Bengal Artillery. [Photo.Eur.233]

LeBas, Charles T. *Journal*. [Mss.D.1157] LeBas was in the Bengal Civil Service and escaped the massacre at Delhi. He was the son of Charles Webb LeBas, the Principal of the East India College at Haileybury.

Lyveden. Vernon Smith. *Correspondence Book*. [Eur.Mss.F231/6]

MacNabb Family. *Letters*. [Mss.Eur.F.206]

Martineau, Lt. E. M. to Sir John Kaye regarding his interactions with Azimullah. [HM725]

Mason, Edward Montgomery. *Diary*. [Mss.Eur.C.330]

Money, Gilbert Pocklington. *Papers*. Money was magistrate and collector at Shahjahanpur. [Photo.Eur.151]

Moorsom, Lt. William Robert of the 52nd Light Infantry. Moorsom was killed in the relief of Lucknow. He was an old friend of Major Lindsay. [Mss.Eur.E.299/43]

Morris, Mrs. Monica. *Letters*. [Mss.Eur.B.309]

Morris, William Albert. *The Story of Cawnpore*. [Mss.Eur.B.309]

Oliver, John Ryder. *Campaigning in Oude*. Oliver was in the Horse Brigade of the Royal Artillery. He died 10 Feb. 1909, at the age of seventy-four. Privately printed, ca. 1859. [Mss.Eur.A66]

Pearse, Lieutenant George Godfrey. *Papers: 1857–1858*. [Mss.Eur.E417/6&7]

Pearson, Lt. Hugh Pearce. *Letters: 1856–1859*. [Mss.Eur.C.231]

Peppin, Arthur Joseph Reginald. *Letters*. Peppin (1838–90) was a Calcutta trader and a member of the Calcutta Volunteers during the Mutiny. [Mss.Eur.C4/88]

Polehampton, Rev. Henry S. *A Memoir, Letters and Diary of the Rev. Henry S. Polehampton*. Ed. the Rev. Edward Polehampton and the Rev. Thomas Stedman Polehampton. London, 1858. [T36815]

Poore, Major Robert. *Letters*. Poore served in the 8th Hussars. [Photo.Eur.54]

Seaton, Ensign William John of the Madras Infantry. *Letters: 1855–1858*. [Mss.Eur.A.166]

Sneyd, Elizabeth. *Account*. Sneyd, who escaped from Fatehpur to Calcutta, was the mother of Captain Henry Sneyd of the Bengal Army who was killed, with his sister Anna and her husband, at Aurangabad. Her account was written when she was an old lady and her Mutiny dates are confused. [Photo.Eur.44]

Thornhill, Robert Bensley. *Papers*. [Mss.Eur.B.298]

Vibart, Captain Edmund. [Mss.Eur.F.18/11] and [Mss.Eur.F.135/21]

Vibart, Edward Daniel Hamilton. *Papers: 1854–1933*. [Mss.Eur.F.135/19–23]

Warner, Ashton Warnel, and Ensign Wynyard. *Letters: 1857–859*. Served in the 7th Bengal Light Cavalry. [Mss.Eur.C.190]

Wilkie, Private William. *Memoirs*. 1890–1891. [Mss.Eur.B.221]

Wimberley, Captain Douglas. *Some Account of the part taken by the 79th Regiment (Cameron Highlanders) in the Indian Mutiny Campaign in 1858*. Inverness, 1891. [Photo.Eur.58]

Wonnacott, William. *Letters*. Wonnacott served with 1st Company, 8th King's Regiment as a schoolmaster. Volume 4 of his letters cover the period from 1872 to 1874 in Cawnpore. [Mss.Eur.C.376 v.4]

Orkney (OA)
Lillie, Arthur to F. W. Burroughs dated Cawnpore, 31 Aug. 1848. [D19/8/6/3]

Presbyterian Church (U.S.A.), Department of History
Material relating to the Fatehgarh mission.

Scottish Record Office
Dalhousie, Marquis of. *Letter-Books*. [GD45/6/1–18]
"Notes of a March into Oudh." [GD1/633/7]

Suffolk
Smith, Thomas. *Letters*. Suffolk County Council. [HA13/C/9]

Warwickshire
Newdigate, Henry R. L. *Letters*. Warwickshire County Council. [CR136/A284]

West Sussex
Plans of Wheeler's Entrenchment and Plan of European Barracks. West Sussex Record Office. [7124,7126]

Yale Divinity School Library Special Collections
Alter, James. *Presbyterians in Farrukhabad, a "Half-Way House," 1838–1915*. Manuscript. [84/19/397]
Archives of the Presbyterian Church in the U.S.A. Board of Foreign Missions. Film Ms. 11. Reels 5–9.

Zoological Society of London
Reports of the Council and Auditors of the Zoological Society of London. London, 1859.

Newspapers
Bengal Harkuru
Bombay Gazette
Englishman
Friend of India
Illustrated London News (ILN)
London Daily News
Mofussilite
Overland Mail
Phoenix
Statesman
Times of London (TL) Contains Delafosse (16 Oct. 1857, p. 7); Thomson, Reply (11 Sept. 1858, p. 7); Shepherd's account (7 Nov. 1857, p. 7); account of Mary Ann (16 Oct. 1857, p. 8); Mrs. Murray's account (3 Sept. 1858, p. 5).

Periodicals
Bennett, Amelia [Amy Horne]. "Ten Months' Captivity after the Massacre at Cawnpore." *The Nineteenth Century*, June, July 1913.
The Colonial Church Chronicle and Missionary Journal.
Hunter, Reverend. "A Mutiny Martyr," *The Presbyterian Banner*, 6 July 1911.
Mukherjee, Rudrangshu. "'Satan Let Loose upon Earth': The Kanpur Massacres in India in the Revolt of 1857." *Past and Present: A Journal of Historical Studies*, no. 128, Aug. 1990.
Mukherjee, Rudrangshu, (reply) and English, Barbara (comment). "Debate: The Kanpur Massacres in India in the Revolt of 1857." *Past and Present: A Journal of Historical Studies*, no. 142, Feb. 1994.
Ward, Andrew. "Stalking the Nana Sahib." *Military History Quarterly* 1,2 (Winter, 1989).
Yalland, Zoë. "Early Kanpur Bungalows." *Inside/Outside*. New Delhi. Dec./Jan. 1987.

Private Collections
Angelo, Helen. Diary.
Chalwin, Louisa. Letters.
Cracklow, George. Letters.
Duff Gordon, Lucie. Letters.
Halliday Papers.
Lansdowne Letters.
Lindsay Family Papers. The Lindsay letters are numbered, but not consecutively, and so I have identified them as follows: Sender/Recipient: date. WL is William Lindsay; MWL

is Martin William Lindsay, William's older brother; MD and JC are William's sisters Mary (Lindsay) Drage and Jane (Lindsay) Clement, wife of GC, George Clement. WL(Sr) is William Lindsay of Dundee, the major's father. LDL is Lillias Don Lindsay, William's wife.

Lindsay, Alexander. Letters.

Macansh Letters.

P. J. O. Taylor. Genealogy of Wheeler family and miscellaneous Mutiny photographs.

Wyndham Family Papers.

Collection of Zoë Yalland, including Cracklow letters; Angelo Diary; Chalwin letters; Peppé, Humphrey, letter; Thomson, Mowbray, *Cawnpore: Report to the Commander-in-Chief: 9th March, 1858* (referred to as Thomson, *Report* in notes).

PUBLISHED WORKS

Aberigh-Mackay, G. R. ed. *The Times of India Handbook of Hindustan.* Bombay, 1875.

———. *Twenty-One Days in India.* London, 1880.

Adam, H. L. *The Indian Criminal.* London, 1909.

Adams, W. H. Davenport. *The Makers of British India.* London, after 1894, before 1907.

Adye, John. *The Defence of Cawnpore, by the Troops under the Orders of Major General Charles A. Windham, C.B. in Nov., 1857.* London, 1858.

[Aitken, E. H.] "EHA." *Behind the Bungalow.* Simla, 1929.

Ali, Mrs. Meer Hassan. *Observations on the Mussulmauns of India: Descriptive of their Manners, Customs, Habits and Religious Opinions Made During a Twelve Years' Residence in their Immediate Society.* Bombay, 1917.

Ali, Salim. *The Book of Indian Birds.* Bombay, 1955.

Allen, Charles. *Raj: A Scrapbook of British India.* New York, 1979.

Allen, Charles, ed. *A Glimpse of the Burning Plain: Leaves from the Indian Journals of Charlotte Canning.* London, 1986.

———. *A Soldier of the Company: Life of an Indian Ensign 1833–43: Captain Albert Hervey.* London, 1988.

Alter, James Payne. *In the Doab and Rohilkhand: North Indian Christianity 1815–1915.* Rev. by John Alter. Delhi, 1986.

Anonymous. *British India: From Queen Elizabeth to Lord Reading, by an Indian Mahomedan.* London, 1926.

———. *Despatches and General Orders Announcing the Victories Achieved by the Army of the Sutlej over the Sikh Army at Moodkee, Ferozshah, Aliwal, & Sobraon in December, 1845, & January & February, 1846.* Rep. Patiala, 1970.

———. *Glimpses of India.* (Damaged. Pub. and date unknown: ca., 1908.)

———. ("A Hindu"). *The Mutinies and the People or Statements of Native Fidelity Exhibited during the Outbreak of 1857–58.* Calcutta, 1859.

———. "Madras Staff Officer." *What Is History and What Is Fact? or Three Days at Cawnpore in November 1857 Under the Command of Major General C.A. Windham, O.C.B.* Madras, 1866.

Anthony, Frank. *Britain's betrayal in India: the story of the Anglo-Indian community.* Bombay, 1969.

Atchison, C. V. *A Collection of Treaties, Engagements and Savads Relating to India and Neighbouring Countries.* 6 vols. Calcutta, 1909.

Ball, Charles. *The History of the Indian Mutiny.* 2 vols. London, n.d.

Bamfield, Veronica. *On the Strength: The Story of the British Army Wife.* London, 1974.

Barr, Pat. *The Memsahibs.* London, 1976.

Barr, Pat, and Ray Desmond. *Simla: A Hill Station in Northern India.* New York, 1978.

Bartholomew, J. G., ed. *Constable's Hand Atlas of India.* Westminster, 1893.

Battye, Evelyn. *Costumes and Characters of the British Raj.* Exeter, 1982.

Bayly, C. A., ed. *The Raj: India and the British: 1600–1947*. London, 1990.

Beames, John. *Memoirs of a Bengal Civilian*. Columbia, 1984.

Beaumont, Roger. *Sword of the Raj: The British Army in India, 1747–1947*. New York, 1977.

Begley, W. E. *Taj Mahal: The Illumined Tomb*. Seattle, 1989.

Bell, Evans. *The English in India: Letters from Nagpore*. London, 1859.

Bernier, François. *Travels in the Mogul Empire: A.D. 1656–1668*, trans. Archibald Constable. Repr. of 1891 ed. Delhi, 1968.

Bernstein, Henry T. *Steamboats on the Ganges*. Hyderabad, 1960.

Beveridge, Henry. *A Comprehensive History of India: Civil, Military, and Social*. Vols. 2–7. London, 1858.

Bhargava, Moti Lal. *Architects of Indian Freedom Struggle*. New Delhi, 1981.

Bhatnagar, O. P., ed. *Private Correspondence of J. W. Sherer, Collector of Fatehpur (19th May, 1857 to 28th July, 1857)*. Allahabad, 1968.

Bidwell, Shelford. *Swords for Hire: European mercenaries in eighteenth-century India*. London, 1971.

Björnstjerna, Count. *The British Empire in the East*. London, 1840.

Blanford, W. T. *The Fauna of British India, Including Ceylon and Burma: Mammalia*. London, 1891.

Blunt, E. A. H. *Christian Tombs and Monuments in the United Provinces*. Lucknow, 1911.

Bond, Ruskin. *Mussoorie and Landour: Days of Wine and Roses*. New Delhi, 1992.

Bowie, John. *The Empire at War*. London, 1989.

Brett, Charles. *Long Shadows Cast Before: 9 Lives in Ulster, 1625–1977*. Edinburgh, 1978.

Broehl, Wayne G. *Crisis of the Raj: The Revolt of 1857 through British Lieutenants' Eyes*. Hanover, 1986.

Broughton, Thomas. *Letters from a Mahratta Camp During the Year 1809*. Repr. of 1813 ed. Calcutta, 1977.

Bruce, George Ludgate. *Six Battles for India: The Anglo-Sikh Wars, 1845–6, 1848–9*. London, 1969.

Bruce, George. *The Stranglers: The Cult of Thuggee and its Overthrow in British India*. New York, 1969.

Buckland, Charles. *Bengal under the Lieutenant Governors*. 2 vols. Repr. of 1902 ed. New Delhi, 1976.

———. *Dictionary of Indian Biography*. London, 1906.

Buckle, E. *Memoir of the Services of the Bengal Artillery from the Formation of the Corps to the Present Time*. London, 1852.

Bull, H. M., and K. N. Haksar. *Madhav Rao Scindia of Gwalior: 1876–1925*. Gwalior, 1926.

Burgess, James. *The Chronology of Modern India: 1494 to 1894*. Edinburgh, 1913.

Busteed, H. E. *Echoes of Old Calcutta*. London, 1908.

Butler, William, D. D. *The Land of the Veda*. New York, 1872.

Buyers, Rev. William. *Recollections of Northern India*. London, 1848.

Campbell, George. *Memoirs of my Indian Career*, ed. Charles E. Bernard. 2 vols. New York, 1893.

Campbell, Walter. *My Indian Journal*. Edinburgh, 1854.

Capuchin Mission Unit. *India and Its Missions*. New York, 1923.

Cardew, Francis Gordon. *A Sketch of the Services of the Bengal Native Army to the Year 1895. Compiled in the office of the Adjutant General in India*. Repr. of 1903 ed. Faridabad, 1971.

Carey, W. H. *The Good Old Days of Honorable John Company: Being the Curious Reminiscences Illustrating Manners and Customs of the British in India during the Rule of the East India Company from 1600 to 1858. With Brief Notices of Places and People of those Times &c., &c., &c.* 2 vols. Calcutta, 1906.

Chan-Toon, Mabel Mary Agnes. *Love Letters of an English Peeress to an Indian Prince*. London, 1912.

Chaudhuri, S. B. *Theories of the Indian Mutiny: 1857–59*. Calcutta, 1965.

Chunder, Bholanauth. *The Travels of a Hindoo to Various Parts of Bengal and Upper India*. 2 vols. London, 1869.

Chunder, Pratap. *The Sons of Mystery*. Calcutta, 1973.

Clark, F. *East-India Register and Army List for 1858*. 2d ed. Comp. F. Clark. London, 1858.

Clemons, Mrs. Major. *The Manners and Customs of Society in India; including Scenes in the Moffusil Stations Interspersed with Characteristic Tales and Anecdotes: and Reminiscences of the Late Burmese War. To which are added Instructions for the Guidance of Cadets, and Other Young Gentlemen, During their First Year's Residence in India*. London, 1841.

Colesworthy-Grant. *Anglo-Indian Domestic Life: A letter from an Artist in India to His Mother in England*. Calcutta, 1862.

Collier, Richard. *The Sound of Fury: An Account of the Indian Mutiny*. London, 1963.

Congregational Publishing Society. *History of Missions of American Board of Commissioners for Foreign Missions in India*. Boston, 1874.

Cook, Hugh C. B. *The Sikh Wars: the British Army in the Punjab, 1845–1849*. London, 1975.

Cosens, F. R., and C. L. Wallace. *Fatehgarh and the Mutiny*. Repr. of 1932 ed. Karachi, 1978.

Cotton, Arthur. *The Famine in India*. London, 1866.

Critchely, J. S. *Feudalism*. London, 1978.

Crooke, W. *The Northwestern Provinces of India*. London, 1897.

Crump, Charles Wade. *A Pictorial Record of the Cawnpore Massacre, Three Original Sketches Taken on the Spot*. London and Calcutta, 1858.

Cunningham, H. S. *Earl Canning. (Rulers of India* series.) Oxford, 1891.

Dangerfield, George. *Bengal Mutiny: the story of the Sepoy rebellion*. New York, 1933.

Darton, F. J. Harvey, ed. *The Life of Mrs. Sherwood (1775–1851): from the Diaries of Captain and Mrs. Sherwood*. London, 1910.

De Gaury, Gerald, and H. V. F. Winstone, eds. *The Road to Kabul: An Anthology*. New York, 1982.

Depositions of native witnesses. See Forrest.

Dewar, Douglas. *Bygone Days in India*. London, 1921.

De Wend, Captain Douglas. *Journal*. Centre of South Asian Studies.

Dickinson, John. *The Famine in the NW Provinces*. London, 1861.

Dictionary of National Biography, Oxford, 1964.

Dodwell. *Alphabetical List of Officers of the Indian Army*.

Drelincourt, Charles. *The Christians defense against the fears of death with seasonable directions how to prepare our selves to dye well*. London, 1675.

Dube, S. C. *Indian Village*. New York, 1967.

Dubois and Beauchamp. *Hindu Manners, Customs and Ceremonies*. Written from 1812–17. Oxford, 1906.

Duff, Alexander. *The Indian Rebellion*. London, 1858.

Dulles, John W. *Life in India; or, Madras, the Neigherries, and Calcutta*. Philadelphia, 1855.

Dunbar, Janet. *Golden Interlude: The Edens in India: 1836–1842*. Gloucester, 1985.

Dunbar, Janet, ed. *Tigers, Durbars and Kings: Fanny Eden's Indian Journals: 1837–1838*. London, 1988.

Dunlop, Robert Henry Wallace. *Service and Adventure with the Khakee Ressalah; or Meerut Volunteer Horse*. Repr. of 1858 ed. Allahabad, 1974.

Dutt, Romesh C. *Famines and Land Assessments in India*. London, 1900.

Dyson, Ketaki Kushari. *A Various Universe: A Study of the Journals and Memoirs of British Men and Women in the Indian Subcontinent: 1765–1856*. Delhi, 1978.

Eastwick, Edward B., ed. *Autobiography of Lutfullah: A Mohamedan Gentleman and his Transactions with his Fellow-Creatures*. London, 1858.

Eden, Emily. *Up the Country*. 2 vols. London, 1866.

Edwardes, Herbert Benjamin, *The Life of Sir Henry Lawrence*. London, 1873.

Edwardes, Michael. *Bound to Exile: The Victorians in India*. New York, 1969.

————. *Raj: The Story of British India*. London, 1969.

————. *Red Year: The Indian Rebellion of 1857*. London, 1973.

Edwards, William. *Personal Adventures during the Indian Rebellion in Rohilcund, Futtehghur, and Oude*. Repr. of 1858 ed. Allahabad, 1974.

Elliot, Henry. *Memoirs of the North Western Provinces of India*. London, 1869.

Elphinstone, Mountstuart. *The History of India: The Hindu and Mahomedan Periods*. Notes and additions by E. B. Cowell. London, 1874.

Embree, Ainslie T. *1857: Mutiny or War of Independence?* Boston, 1963.

Fane, Henry Edward Hamlyn. *Five Years in India Comprising A Narrative of Travels in the Presidency of Bengal, A Visit to the Court of Ranjeet Sing, The Late Expedition to Cabul and Afghanistan, Voyage down the Indus, and Journey Overland to England*. 2 vols. Repr. Punjab, 1970.

Farwell, Byron. *Armies of the Raj: From the Mutiny to Independence, 1858–1947*. New York, 1989.

————. *Eminent Victorian Soldiers: Seekers of Glory*. New York, 1985.

————. *Queen Victoria's Little Wars*. New York, 1972.

Fayrer, J. *Recollections of My Life*. Edinburgh, 1900.

Featherstone, Donald. *Victoria's Enemies: An A–Z of British Colonial Warfare*. London, 1989.

Fitchett, W. H. *The Tale of the Great Mutiny*. London, 1912.

Forbes, Archibald. *The Afghan Wars: 1839–42 and 1878–80*. London, 1896.

————. *Havelock*. London, 1891.

Forbes, James. *Oriental Memoirs: A Narrative of Seventeen Years Residence in India*. 2 vols. 2d ed., rev. the Countess Montalembert. London, 1834.

Forbes-Lindsay, C. H. *India: Past and Present*. 2 vols. Philadelphia, 1903.

Forbes-Mitchell, William. *The Relief of Lucknow*. Repr. of *Reminiscences of the Great Mutiny*, 1893. Ed. Michael Edwardes. London, 1962.

Forrest, G. W. *A History of the Indian Mutiny: Reviewed and Illustrated from Original Documents*. 2 vols. London; 1904.

Forrest, G. W., ed. *Selections from the Letters Despatches and Other State Papers Preserved in the Military Department of the Government of India: 1857–58*. Vols. 2 and 3. Calcutta, 1902.

Forsyth, Douglas. *Autobiography and Reminiscences*. Ed. his daughter. London, 1887.

Foster, Joseph. *Men-at-the-Bar: A Biographical Hand-list of the Various Members of the Various Inns of Court including her Majesty's Judges, etc*. London, 1885.

Fowler, Marian. *Below the Peacock Fan*. London, 1988.

Frank, Katherine. *A Passage to Egypt: The Life of Lucie Duff Gordon*. Boston, 1994.

Fraser, E. G. *Remarks on the Education of East Indians with Especial Reference to the Missionary Work*. Allahabad, 1851.

Fuhrer, Rev. *A List of Christian Tombs and Monuments of Archaeological or Historical Interest and Their Inscriptions in the North-Western Provinces and Oudh*. Allahabad, 1896.

Ganguly, Anil Baran. *Guerilla Fighter of the First Freedom Movement*. Patna, 1980.

Gardner, Brian. *The East India Company*. New York, 1990.

Germon, Maria. *Journal of the Siege of Lucknow*. London, 1870.

Gibbs, M. E. *The Anglican Church in India: 1600–1970*. Delhi, 1972.

Gilliat, Edward. *Heroes of Modern India*. London, 1911.

————. *Heroes of the Indian Mutiny*. London, 1922.

Gimlette, G. H. D. *A Postscript to the Records of the Indian Mutiny: An Attempt to Trace the Subsequent Careers and Fate of the Rebel Bengal Regiments, 1857 to 1858*. London, 1927.

Godden, Rumer. *Gulbadan: Portrait of a Rose Princess at the Mughal Court*. New York, 1980.

Gordon, Andrew. *Our India Mission: A Thirty Years' History of the India Mission of the United Presbyterian Church of North America, together with Personal Reminiscences*. Philadelphia, 1886.

Gordon, Charles Alexander. *Recollections of Thirty-Nine Years in the Army*. London, 1898.

Gordon-Alexander, Lieutenant-Colonel W. *Recollections of a Highland Subaltern during the Campaigns of the 23rd Highlanders in India under Colin Campbell, Lord Clyde*. London, 1898.

Gough, Sir Hugh. *Old Memories*. London, 1897.

Gowing, Timothy. *A Soldier's experience, or, a voice from the ranks: showing the cost of war in blood and treasure: a personal narrative of the Crimean campaign from the standpoint of the ranks, the Indian mutiny and some of its atrocities, the Afghan campaigns of 1863: also, sketches of the lives and deaths of H. Havelock and Hedley Vicars, together with some things not generally known by one of the Royal Fusiliers*. Privately printed. Nottingham, 1895.

Grant, Hope. *Incidents in the Sepoy War: 1857–8*. Edinburgh, 1873.

Grant, James. *Cassell's Illustrated History of India*. 2 vols. London, 1890.

Grant Duff, James Cuninghame. *A History of the Mahrattas*. 2 vols. London, 1921.

Greathed, H. H. *Letters written during the Siege of Delhi*. Privately printed. London, 1858.

Greenwood, Joseph. *Narrative of the late victorious campaigns in Affghanistan, under General Pollock; with recollections of seven years' service in India*. London, 1844.

Grenard, Fernand. *Baber: First of the Moguls*. New York, 1930.

Griffin, Lepel. *Ranjit Singh and the Sikh Barrier between Our Growing Empire and Central Asia.* (*Rulers of India* series.) Oxford, 1905.

Gubbins, Martin Richard. *An Account of the Mutinies in Oudh, and of the Siege in Lucknow*. London, 1858.

Gupta, Pratul Chandra. *Baji Rao II and the East India Company: 1776–1818*. Oxford, 1939.

———. *The Last Peshwa*. Calcutta, 1944.

———. *Nana Saheb and The Rising at Cawnpore*. Oxford, 1963.

Hall, Montagu. *Reminiscences of the Indian Mutiny: 1857–1858*. Privately published from his diary.

Hallissey, Robert C. *The Rajput Rebellion Against Aurangzeb: A Study of the Mughal Empire in Seventeenth-Century India*. New York, 1977.

Hamilton, Walter. *East India Gazeteer*. 2 vols. London, 1828.

Hankin, Nigel. *Hanklyn-Janklin or a Stranger's Rumble-Tumble Guide to Some Words, Customs and Quiddities Indian and Indo-British*. New Delhi, 1992.

Haq, Syed Moinul. *The Great Revolution of 1857*. Karachi, 1968.

Hardy, P. *The Muslims of British India*. Cambridge, 1972.

Harris, Mrs. G. *A Lady's Diary of the Siege of Lucknow*. New York, 1858.

Hastings, Michael. *Sir Richard Burton: A Biography*. New York, 1978.

Havelock, Henry. *Narrative of the War in Afghanistan in 1838–39*. Karachi, 1976.

Heathcote, T. A. *The Afghan Wars, 1839–1919*. London, 1980.

———. *The Indian Army: The Garrison of British Imperial India, 1822–1922*. London, 1974.

Heber, Reginald. *Heber's Journal: Narrative of a Journey Through the Upper Provinces of India from Calcutta to Bombay, 1824–1825*. 3 vols. London, 1828.

Hervey, Gen. Charles. *Some Records of Crime: Being the Diary of a Year, Official & Particular, of an Officer of the Thuggee and Dacoitie Police*. 2 vols. London, 1892.

Hewitt, James, ed. *Eye-Witnesses to the Indian Mutiny*. London, 1972.

Hibbert, Christopher. *The Great Mutiny: India 1857*. New York, 1978.

Higginbotham, J. J. *Men Whom India Has Known: Biographies of Eminent Indian Characters*. Madras, 1874.

Hill, J. R. et al. of the Society for the Propagation of the Gospel in Foreign Parts. *The Story of the Cawnpore Mission*. Westminster, 1909.

Hilton, Edward H. *The Mutiny Records: Oudh and Lucknow (1857)* Repr. by Sheik Mubarak Ali. Lahore, 1911.

Hilton, Richard. *The Indian Mutiny: A Centenary History*. London, 1957.

Hodgson, Pat. *Early War Photographs*. Boston, 1974.

Hodson, V. C. *List of the Officers of the Bengal Army: 1758–1834*. London, 1947.

Hodson, W. S. R. *Twelve Years of a soldier's life in India: Being extracts from the letters of the late Major W.S.R. Hodson, including a personal narrative of the siege of Delhi and Capture of the king and princes*. Boston, 1860.

Holmes, F. M. *Four Heroes in India*. London, n.d.

Holmes, T. Rice. *A History of the Indian Mutiny.* London, 1913.

Howarth, Patrick. *The Year is 1851.* London, 1951.

Hughes, Derrick. *The Mutiny Chaplains.* London, 1991.

Hunter, W. V. *Annals of Rural Bengal.* London, 1897.

———. *Dalhousie. (Rulers of India series.)* Oxford, 1895.

———. *The Earl of Mayo.* Oxford, 1891.

———. *Imperial Gazeteer.* London, 1885.

Hunter, W. W., ed. *Imperial Gazeteer.* London, 1881.

Hutchinson, David. *Annals of the Indian Rebellion: 1857–58,* comp. N. A. Chick. London, 1974.

India, Government of. *Selections from the Records of the Government of India Foreign Department No. XXXIV: Report of the Operations in the Thuggee and Dacoity Department During 1859–1860.* Calcutta, 1861.

Innes, McLeod. *Lucknow and Oude in the Mutiny.* London, 1895.

INTACH (Indian National Trust for Art and Cultural Heritage). *Preliminary Unedited Listing of Cawnpore. Uttar Pradesh, Unprotected Monuments, Buildings and Structures Listed for Conservation.* Cawnpore, 1992.

Iyer, C. S. Ranga. *Father India: A Reply to Mother India.* New York, 1928.

Jacquemont, Victor. *Letters from India: 1829–1832. Being a Selection from the Correspondence of Victor Jacquemont,* trans. Catherine Alison Phillips. London, 1936.

Jeffrey, Robin. *People, Princes and Paramount Power: Society and Politics in the Indian Princely States.* Oxford, 1978.

Jha, Kamal Narain. *Nana Sahaba.* [Lekhana] *Kamalanarayana Jha 'Kamelsa' Prakkathanalekhana SriGanagananda Singha.* Patna, 1962.

Jones, Oliver. *Recollections of a Winter Campaign in India in 1857–1858.* London, 1859.

Kavanagh, Henry. *How I Won the Victoria Cross.* London, 1860.

Kaye, John William. *A History of the Great Revolt.* 3 vols. Repr. of 1880 ed. Delhi, 1988.

———. *The History of the War in Afghanistan.* London, 1851.

Keeling, William, ed. *Liturgiae Britannicae or the several editions of the Book of Common Prayer of the Church of England from its Compilation to the last revision; together with the Liturgy Set Forth for the Use of the Church of Scotland: Arranged to shew their respective variations.* 2d ed. London, 1851.

Keene, Henry George. *Fifty-Seven: Some Account of the Administration of Indian Districts During the Revolt of the Bengal Army.* London, 1883.

———. *Handbook to Allahabad, Cawnpore, Lucknow and Benares.* Calcutta, 1896.

———. *A Servant of 'John Company': Being the Recollections of an Indian Official.* Calcutta, 1897.

Knaplund, Paul. *The British Empire: 1815–1939.* New York, 1941.

Knighton, William. *The Private Life of an Eastern King.* London, 1855.

Landon, Percival. *Nepal.* 2 vols. London, 1928.

———. *Under the Sun: Impressions of Indian cities: with a chapter dealing with the later life of Nana Sahib.* London, 1906.

Lane-Poole, Stanley. *Aurangzib. (Rulers of India series.)* Oxford, 1893.

Lang, John. *Wanderings in India and Other Sketches.* London, 1859.

Lawrence, John, and Audrey Woodiwiss, ed. *The Journals of Honoria Lawrence: India Observed 1837–1854.* London, 1980.

Lear, Edward. *Edward Lear's Indian Journal (1873–75).* London, 1953.

Leasor, James. *The Red Fort: The Story of the Indian Mutiny of 1857.* New York, 1957.

Lee, [Joseph]. *The Indian Mutiny and in Particular A Narrative of Events at Cawnpore June and July 1857.* Cawnpore, 1895.

Lee-Warner, William. *The Life of the Marquis of Dalhousie K.T.* 2 vols. Rep. of 1904 ed. Shannon, 1972.

———. *The Protected Princes of India.* London, 1894.

Lejeune, Anthony, and Malcolm Lewis. *The Gentlemen's Clubs of London.* London, 1984.

Lewin, Thomas L. *A Fly on the Wheel, or, How I Helped to Govern India.* London, 1885.

Llewellyn-Jones, Rosie. *A Fatal Friendship: The Nawabs, the British and the City of Lucknow.* Bombay, 1992.

Long, James. *Hand-Book of Bengal Missions, in Connexion with the Church of England together with an Account of General Educational Efforts in North India.* London, 1848.

Long, James, and J. H. Stocqueler, *British Social Life in Ancient Calcutta (1750 to 1850).* ed. Thankappan Nair. Calcutta, 1983.

Loveday, A. *The History and Economics of Indian Famines.* London, 1914.

Lucas, J. J. *Memoir of Reverend Robert Stewart Fullertón: American Presbyterian Missionary in North India: 1850–1865: Compiled from his letters during fifteen years in India, and his Narratives of the trials, faith and constancy of Indian Christians during the Mutiny of 1857.* Allahabad, 1928.

Lutfullah. *Autobiography of Lutfullah: An Indian's Perception of the West.* Repr. of 1857 ed. New Delhi, 1985.

Lutfullah, Syed. *Azimullah Khan Yusutzai: The Man Behind the War of Independence: 1857.* Karachi, 1970.

Mackay, J. *From London to Lucknow.* 2 vols. London, 1860.

Mackenzie, Mrs. Colin. *Life in the Mission, the Camp and the Zenana.* London, 1854.

Maclagan, Michael. *"Clemency" Canning.* London, 1962.

MacMillan, Margaret. *Women of the Raj.* London, 1988.

MacMunn, Sir George. *The Indian Mutiny in Perspective.* London, 1931.

———. *The Martial Races of India.* London, 1932.

Macrory, Patrick. *Signal Catastrophe: The Story of the Disastrous Retreat from Kabul: 1842.* London, 1966.

Majendie, Vivian Dering. *Up Among the Pandies: A Year's Service in India.* London, 1859.

Majumdar, Dhirendra Nath. *Social contours of an industrial city; social survey of Kanpur, 1954–56.* Bombay, 1960.

Malcolm, Thomas. *Barracks and Battlefields in India; or, The experiences of a soldier of the 10th Foot (North Lincoln) in the Sikh wars and Sepoy Mutiny.* ed. Caesar Caine. Punjab, 1971.

Malgonkar, Manohar. *The Devil's Wind: Nana Saheb's Story.* London, 1988.

Malleson, G. B. *Essays and Lectures on Indian Historical Subjects.* London, 1869.

———. *The Indian Mutiny of 1857.* London, 1906.

Malleson, G. B., ed. *Kaye and Maleson's History of the Indian Mutiny of 1857–8.* 6 vols. Repr. of 1898 ed. Westport, 1971.

Marsden, B. A. *Genaeological Memoirs of the Family of Marsden.* Birkenhead, 1914.

Marshman, J. C. *Abridgement of the History of India.* London, 1905.

Martin, R. Montgomery. *The Indian Empire.* Vol. 2. London, n.d.

Mason, Philip. *A Matter of Honour: An Account of the Indian Army, Its Officers and Men.* New York, 1974.

Mead, Henry. *The Sepoy Revolt: Its Causes and Consequences.* London, 1857.

Medley, Julius George. *A Year's Campaigning in India.* London, 1858.

Mehta, Asoka. *1857: The Great Rebellion.* Bombay 1946.

Metcalfe, Henry. *The chronicles of Private Henry Metcalfe, H.M. 32nd Regiment of Foot, together with Lieutenant John Edmonstone's letter to his mother of 4th January, 1858, and other particulars collected and edited by Sir Francis Tucker.* London, 1953.

Mills, Arthur. *India in 1858.* London, 1858.

Ministry of Information and Broadcasting, Government of India. *1857: A Pictorial Presentation.* New Delhi, 1957.

Misra, A. S. *Nana Saheb Peshwa.* Lucknow, 1961.

Mohammad, Noor. *Slum Culture and Deviant Behaviour.* Delhi, 1983.

Mollo, Boris. *The Indian Army.* Poole, 1981.

Molund, Stefan. *First we are people—: the Koris of Kanpur between caste and class.* Stockholm, 1988.

Moorehead. *Researches on Disease in India*. London, 1860.

Moorhouse, Geoffrey. *India Britannica*. New York, 1983.

Morris, James. *Farewell the Trumpets*. New York, 1978.

———. *Heaven's Command*. New York, 1973.

———. *Pax Britannica*. New York, 1968.

Morris, Jan. *The Spectacle of Empire*. New York, 1982.

Morris, Jan, and Simon Winchester. *The Stones of Empire*. Oxford,

Muir, William, ed. *Records of the Intelligence Department of the Government of the North-West Provinces of India during the Mutiny of 1857*. Vol. 1, Edinburgh, 1902.

Mukherjee, Rudrangshu. *Awadh in Revolt: 1857–1858: A Study of Popular Resistance*. Delhi, 1984.

Murdoch, John. *Indian Missionary Manual: Hints to Young Missionaries in India*. London, 1889.

Murphy, Ray, ed. *Edward Lear's Indian Journal*. London, 1953.

Murray et al. *Murray's Handbook: Bengal. Northwest Provinces & Burmah*. London, 1890.

———. *Murray's Handbook for Travellers in India, Burma and Ceylon*. London, 1859.

———. *Murray's Handbook for Travellers in India, Burma, and Ceylon*. London, 1898.

———. *Murray's Handbook for Travellers in India, Burma and Ceylon*. London, 1920.

Murray, A. H. Hallam. *The High-Road of Empire: Watercolour and Pen-and-Ink Sketches in India*. New York, 1905.

Nagar, Ishwardas. *Futuhat-I-Alamgiri*, trans. and ed. Tasneem Ahmad. Delhi, 1978.

Narasimhan, Sakuntala. *Sati: Widow Burning in India*. New York, 1992.

Nevill, H, R. *Cawnpore: A Gazetteer. (Volume XIX of the District Gazetteers of the United Provinces of Agra and Oudh.)* Allahabad, 1929.

Newton, John. *Historical Sketches of the India Missions of the Presbyterian Church in the United States of America, known as the Lodiana, the Farrukhabad, and the Kolhapur Missions: from the beginning of the work, in 1834, to the time of its fiftieth anniversary, in 1884*. Allahabad, 1886.

Noel, Baptist Wriothesley. *England and India: An Essay on the Duty of Englishmen towards the Hindoos*. London, 1859.

North, Major Charles. *Journal of an English Officer in India*. London, 1858.

Oliphant et al. *Cassell's Life and Times of Queen Victoria*. 4 vols. London, n.d.

Owen, Arthur. *Recollections of a Veteran of the Days of the Great Indian Mutiny Being an Autobiographical Sketch of his Life and Work During Sixty Years in India by Arthur Owen (The Blind veteran of the Delhi Durbar)*. Simla, 1914.

Owen, Rev. William. *Memorials of Christian Martyrs in the Indian Rebellion*. London, 1859.

Padfield, J. E. *The Hindu at Home*. Madras, 1896.

Page, Jesse. *Henry Martyn: His Life and Labours: Cambridge—India—Persia*. London, n.d.

Parks, Fanny. *Wanderings of a Pilgrim in Search of the Picturesque*. 2 vols. Repr. of 1850 ed., annotated by Esther Chawner. Karachi 1975.

Pearse, Hugh. *The Hearseys: Five Generations of an Anglo-Indian Family*. London, 1905.

Pearson, J. D. *A Guide to Manuscripts and Documents in the British Isles Relating to South and Southeast Asia*. 2 vols. London, 1990.

Peggs, James. *India's Cries to British Humanity*. London, 1832.

Pemble, John. *The Raj, the Indian Mutiny and the Kingdom of Oudh: 1801–1859*. Sussex, 1977.

Pemble, John, ed. *Miss Fane in India*. Gloucester, 1985.

Pincott, Frederic. *Analytical Index to Sir John Kaye's History of the Sepoy War and Col. G.B. Malleson's History of the Indian Mutiny*. London, 1896.

Prater, S. H. *The Book of Indian Animals*. Bombay 1965.

Prinsep, Val C. *Glimpses of Imperial India*. Repr. of 1879 ed. Delhi, 1979.

Raikes, Charles. *Notes on the Northwest Provinces*. London, 1852.

———. *Notes on the Revolt in the North-western Provinces of India*. London, 1858.

Ramsay, Balcarres Dalyrimple Wardlaw. *Rough Recollections of Military Service and Society*. 2 vols. Edinburgh, 1882.

Rao, P. Setu Madhava. *Eighteenth Century Deccan*. Bombay, 1963.

Rawlins, J. S. *The Autobiography of an Old Soldier: 1843–1879*. Privately printed, n.d.

Read, Rev. Hollis. *India and Its People*. Columbus, 1858.

Rees, L. E. Ruutz. *A Personal Narrative of the Siege of Lucknow from Its Commencement to Its Relief by Sir Colin Campbell*. London, 1858.

Rice, Edward. *Captain Sir Richard Francis Burton*. New York, 1990.

Richards, D. S. *The Savage Frontier: a history of the Anglo-Afghan Wars*. London, 1990.

Roberts, Emma. *The East India Voyager or Ten Minutes Advice to the Outward Bound*. London, 1839.

———. *Scenes and Characteristics of Hindustan*. 2 vols. London, 1837.

———. *Views in India*. London, 1838.

Roberts, Fred. *Letters Written During the Indian Mutiny*, ed. Countess Roberts. Repr. of the 1923 ed. New Delhi, 1979.

Robertson, H. Dundas. *District Duties During the Revolt in the North-West Provinces of India in 1857: with Subsequent Investigations during 1858–9*. London, 1859.

Roper-Lawrence, Walter. *The India We Served*. London, 1927.

Rousselet, Louis. *India and Its Native Princes*, ed. Lt. Col. Buckle. London, 1878.

Russell, William Howard. *My Diary in India in the Year 1858–9*. 2 vols. London, 1860.

———. *My Indian Mutiny Diary*. Michael Edwardes, ed. London, 1957.

———. *The Prince of Wales' Tour: A Diary in India*. London, 1878.

Saintsbury, George. *East India Slavery*. Repr. of 1829 ed. Shannon, 1972.

Sale, Florentia. *A Journal of the Disasters in Afghanistan, 1841–2*. London, 1843.

Sardesai, G. S. *New History of the Marathas*. Vols. 1–3. Bombay 1957.

———. *Poona Affairs*. 15 vols. Bombay, 1961.

Sargent, John. *A Memoir of Rev. Henry Martyn, B.D.* New York, n.d.

Sarkar, Sir Jadunath. *A Short History of Aurangzib*. Calcutta, 1962.

Satow, Michael, and Ray Desmond. *Railways of the Raj*. London, 1980.

Savarkar, Vinayak Damodar. *Indian War of Independence*. Rep. of 1909 ed. Bombay 1947.

Scholberg, Henry. *The Indian Literature of the Great Rebellion*. New Delhi, 1993.

Schwendinger, Julia R., and Herman Schwendinger. *Rape and Inequality*. Beverly Hills, 1983.

Scidmore, Eliza Ruhamah. *Winter India*. New York, 1903.

Scott, H., ed. *Fasti Ecclesiae Scoticanae*. Edinburgh, 1928.

Scott, Paul. *The Jewel in the Crown*. New York, 1966.

Sears, Stephen W. *The Horizon History of the British Empire*. New York, 1973.

Seaton, Thomas. *From Cadet to Colonel*. London, 1893.

Sen, Ashoka Kumar. *The Popular Uprising and the Intelligensia: Bengal between 1855–73*. Calcutta, 1992.

Sen, Surendra Nath. *Eighteen Fifty-Seven*. New Delhi, 1957.

———. *Military System of the Marathas*. Calcutta, 1928.

Sharar, Abdul Halim. *Lucknow: The Last Phase of Oriental Culture*. Harcourt, E. S. and Hussain, Fakhir trans. and ed. Boulder, 1975.

Sharma, S. R. *The Founding of Maratha Freedom*. Bombay, 1964.

Shepherd, W. J. *Guilty Men of 1857: England's Great Mission to India*. Repr. of 1879 ed. Delhi, 1987.

———. *A Personal Narrative of the Outbreak and Massacre at Cawnpore During the Sepoy Revolt of 1857*. Repr. of 1879 ed. New Delhi, 1980.

Sherer, John Walter. *Cawnpore Narrative*. Calcutta, 1859.

———. *Daily Life During the Indian Mutiny*. Repr. of 1910 ed. Allahabad, 1974.

———. *Havelock's March on Cawnpore: A Civilian's Notes*. London, 1910.

———. *At Home and In India: A Volume of Miscellanies*. London, 1883.

Sherring, M.A. *The Indian Church during the Great Rebellion: An Authentic Narrative of the Disasters that Befell It; Its Sufferings; and Faithfulness unto Death of Many of Its European and Native Members*. London, 1859.

Singh, Sheo Bahadur, ed. *Letters of Sir Henry Lawrence*. New Delhi, 1978.

Skinner, Thomas. *Excursions in India, including a walk over the Himalaya Mountains, to the sources of the Jumna and the Ganges*. 2 vols. London, 1832.

Sleeman, William. *A Journey through the kingdom of Oude in 1849–1850, with private correspondence relative to the annexation of Oude to British India*. London, 1858.

——. *Rambles and Recollections*. Repr. of 1844 ed. Karachi, 1973.

Smith, R. Bosworth. *Life of Lord Lawrence*. 2 vols. New York, 1883.

Spear, Percival. *The Nabobs: A Study of the Social Life of the English in 18th Century India*. Oxford, 1963.

Stark, Herbert Alick. *Hostages to India, or; The life story of the Anglo-Indian race*. Calcutta, 1936.

Stocqueler, J. H. *The Handbook of India: A Guide to the Stranger and the Traveller and a Companion to the Resident*. London, 1845.

Stokes, Eric. *The Peasant Armed: The Indian Revolt of 1857*. Oxford, 1986.

Stone, Julia A. *Illustrated India: Its Princes and People*. Hartford, 1877.

Tahmankar, D. V. *The Ranee of Jhansi*. Bombay 1960.

Taylor, Bayard. *A Visit to India, China, and Japan in the Year 1853*. New York, 1885.

Taylor, Meadows. *A Student's Manual of the History of India*. London, 1871.

Taylor, P. J. O. *A Star Shall Fall*. New Delhi, 1993.

——. *Chronicles of the Mutiny*. New Delhi, 1992.

Taylor, William. *Four Years' Campaign in India*. Written in 1875. New York, n.d.

Thackery, Edward T. *Biographical Notices of Officers of the Royal (Bengal) Engineers*. London, 1900.

Thapliyal, Hari Prasad. *The Life and Work of Peshwa Nana Saheb*. Delhi, 1985.

Thayyur, R. S. *Achievements of Indian Raj*. New Delhi, n.d.

Thomas, P. *Hindu Religion, Customs and Manners*. Bombay, n.d.

Thompson, Edward. *The Other Side of the Medal*, ed. Mulk Raj Ranand. Repr. of 1925 ed. London, 1989.

Thomson, Mowbray. *Report to the Commander-in-Chief*. Calcutta, 1858.

——. *The Story of Cawnpore*. London, 1859.

Tod, James. *Annals and Antiquities of Rajasthan: Or, The Central and Western Rajpoot States of India*. 2 vols. Repr. of 1914 ed. New Delhi, 1978.

Trevelyan, G. Otto. *Cawnpore*. Repr. of 1866 ed. Delhi, 1992.

——. *The Life and Letters of Lord Macaulay*. New York, 1876.

Trevelyan, Raleigh. *A Pre-Raphaelite Circle*. London, 1978.

——. *The Golden Oriole: A 200-Year History of an English Family in India*. New York, 1987.

Trotter, L. J. *The Earl of Auckland*. London, 1893.

Tuker, Francis. *The Yellow Scarf: An Account of Thuggee and Its Suppression*. London, 1961.

Tuker, Francis, ed. *The Chronicle of Private Henry Metcalfe. (Together with Lieutenant John Edmondstone's Letter to his Mother)*. London, 1953.

Tussaud et al. *Madame Tussaud and Sons' Catalogue*. London, 1861.

United Grand Lodge of Antient, Free and Accepted Masons of England. *The Lodge Harmony: 1836–1936*. Cawnpore, 1936.

Uttar Pradesh (U.P.), S. A. A. Rizvi, and M. L. Bhargava, ed. *Freedom Struggle in Uttar Pradesh*. 6 vols. Kanpur, 1957.

Valbezen, E. de. *The English and India*. London, 1883.

Venn, J. A. *Alumni Cantabridgienses: A Biographical List of all Known Students, Graduates and Holders of Office at the University of Cambridge from the Earliest Times to 1900*. Part 2. Cambridge,1940.

Verney, G. L. *The Devil's Wind: The Story of the Naval Brigade at Lucknow from the Letters of Edmund Hope Verney.* London, 1956.

Vibart, Col. H. M. *Addiscombe: Its Heroes and Men of Note.* Westminster, 1894.

Von Orlich, Leopold. *Travels in India: Including Sinde and the Punjab.* 2 vols. London, 1845.

Walker, Benjamin. *The Hindu World.* New York, 1968.

Wallace, C. L. *Fatehgarh Camp: 1777–1857.* Lucknow, 1934.

Waller, John H. *Beyond the Khyber Pass: The Road to British Disaster in the First Afghan War.* New York, 1990.

Ward, Andrew. *The Blood Seed.* New York, 1985.

Ward, F. De W. *India and the Hindus: Being a Popular View of the Geography, History, Government, Manners, Customs, Literature and Religion of that Ancient People; with an Account of Christian Missions Among Them.* New York, 1850.

Warren, Joseph. *A Glance Backward at Fifteen Years of Missionary Life in North India.* Philadelphia, 1856.

Waterfield, A. J. *Children of the Mutiny: A Record of Those Now Living Who Were in India During the Sepoy War, 1857–9.* Worthing, 1935.

Welch, Stuart Carey. *Room for Wonder: Indian Painting during the British Period: 1760–1880.* New York, 1978.

Wheeler, George. *India 1875–6: Chronicle of the Visit of the Prince of Wales.* London, 1876.

Wheeler, J. Talboys. *India and the Frontier States of Afghanistan, Nipal and Burma.* 2 vols. New York, 1899.

Wightman, A. J. *No Friend for Travellers.* London, 1959.

Wilder, R. G. *Mission Schools in India of the American Board of Commissioners for Foreign Missions.* New York, 1861.

Wilkinson, Johnson, and Osborn Wilkinson. *The Memoirs of the Gemini Generals: Personal Anecdotes, Sporting Adventures and Sketches of Distinguished Officers.* London, 1896.

Williams, H. M. *Indo-Anglian Literature: 1800–1970: A Survey.* Bombay, 1977.

Woodruff, Philip. *The Men Who Ruled India: The Founders and The Guardians.* 2 vols. London, 1971.

Worswick, Clark, and Ainslie Embree. *The Last Empire: Photography in British India, 1855–1911.* Millerton, N.Y., 1976.

Yalland, Zoë. *A Guide to the Katcheri Cemetery and the Early History of Kanpur from 1750.* London. 1983.

———. *Traders and Nabobs: The British in Cawnpore 1765–1857.* Salisbury, 1987.

Younger, Coralie. *Anglo-Indians: neglected children of the Raj.* New York, 1987.

Yule, Henry, and A. C. Burnell. *Hobson-Jobson: A Glossary of Colloquial Anglo-Indian Words and Phrases.* Repr. of 1886 ed. London, 1986.

NOTES

Note: The native testimony collected by Colonel G. Williams and published in the third volume of Forrest's *Selections from the Letters Despatches and Other State Papers Preserved in the Military Department of the Government of India: 1857–58* are identified as "Deposition(s) of, etc." In the references I have retained Williams's anachronistic spelling of witnesses' names though some have been changed in the text.

PART ONE

1. Allen, *A Glimpse of the Burning Plain*, p. 66.
2. Much of this material is based on Emma Roberts's *Scenes and Characteristics of Hindustan* and Fanny Parks's *Wanderings of a Pilgrim in Search of the Picturesque*. The ultimate authority on Cawnpore's growth during this period is Zoë Yalland's *Traders and Nabobs*.
3. Pemble, ed., *Miss Fane in India*, p. 141.
4. Roberts, *Scenes and Characteristics of Hindustan*, 1:55. Another indictment came from General J. S. Rawlins, who was stationed there in the 1840s. "Cawnpore was always a hateful place," he said, "famed for being the hottest hole in India, and was looked upon as a sort of penal settlement." Rawlins, *Autobiography of an Old Soldier*, p. 95.
5. Hunter, *Imperial Gazeteer*, pp. 340–41.
6. Chunder, *Travels of a Hindoo*, p. 337.
7. The first Lord Massy.
8. Wheeler would not have had to pay a commission; he simply applied to the Company. "This is why the Company's service attracted the less-affluent new recruits." NAM/the author, 24 Nov. 1993.
9. J. H. Stocqueler in Edwardes, *Bound to Exile*, p. 6; and Hastings, *Sir Richard Burton*, p. 48.
10. Dulles, *Life in India*, p. 25.
11. Seaton, *From Cadet to Colonel*, p. 3.
12. Gordon, *Our India Mission*, p. 38.
13. Gordon, *Thirty-Nine Years*, p. 10.
14. Allen, ed., *A Soldier of the Company*, pp. 14–16.
15. When the 72nd Highlanders landed at Madras in 1781, sickness reduced them in three weeks from five hundred to fifty effective men. Reverend John Murdoch theorized that this "frightful mortality among European troops . . . was due partly to their being despatched without the slightest reference to their time of arrival. . . . From mere thoughtlessness" they were sometimes required "to land at Madras when the scorching winds of

the Carnatic are setting in; or to disembark at Calcutta when the whole of Bengal is a steaming swamp." In the 1820s the chance of living to old age in India was deemed "nearly 100 per cent worse than in England, at least until the age of fifty, when the proportion rather improves." In 1826, 205 of the 260 people buried in a single cemetery at Calcutta were under the age of forty. A twenty-one-year-old was charged £1.13.10 for insurance in England, £3.13.7 in India. Mason, *A Matter of Honour*, p. 138; Murdoch, *Indian Missionary Manual*, p. 31; Carey, *Good Old Days*, 1:347, 351.

16. For a pathetic description of an ensign's lonely death in a traveler's bungalow see Lang, *Wanderings in India*, pp. 121–22.

17. Gresley MSS, 15 Nov. 1834, Manchester City Archives Department (803M/F114), in Pearson, *A Guide*, 2:101b.

18. Before his assignment Wheeler studied native languages at the "most riotous" Cadet College at Baraset near Calcutta, where amid hundreds of cadets newly liberated from their parents' care, "it was necessary for a young man to show that he was not devoid of spirit to defend himself from being insulted." The college was so tumultuous that at one point the Chief Justice threatened to hang or transport any cadet caught dueling or playing pranks, which apparently included burning down the huts of their native servants.

19. The boats were fitted with two square sails and fearful figureheads carved and painted to look like Europeans, each "with a black hat, a bright blue coat, and a yellow waistcoat." Carey, *Good Old Days*, 1:230.

20. The Company's pay; by accepting its salt a native soldier pledged his fidelity to the British.

21. Heber, *Narrative*, 2:5.

22. Mason, *A Matter of Honour*, pp. 125–26.

23. Allen, ed. *A Soldier of the Company*, pp. 36–41.

24. Mason, *A Matter of Honour*, p. 202.

25. Yalland, *Traders and Nabobs*, p. 146.

26. Medley, *A Year's Campaigning*, pp. 209–10.

27. Clemons, *Manners and Customs*, pp. 338–39.

28. Yalland, *Traders and Nabobs*, pp. 144–46, 235–36. One officer went so far as to raise his cane and strike a Moslem sepoy on the rump as he was kneeling down to say his prayers. The sepoy killed him and was hanged. Knighton's *Tropical Sketches*, cited in Dyson, *A Various Universe*, p. 317.

29. Regimental officers tended to be young and inexperienced because age and experience garnered them staff positions. "Thus," wrote Napier, "the regiments are constantly commanded by lieutenants." Indeed, he knew of one artillery troop that was commanded "by a cadet of 15." Leasor, *The Red Fort*, pp. 118–19.

30. The civilian was Henry George Keene. Keene, *A Servant of 'John Company,'* p. 133.

31. An officer named Cradock who issued the orders was backed up by William Bentinck, the Governor of Madras. After the mutiny at Vellore both men were recalled to England.

32. In the Vellore Mutiny apocryphal reports circulated that were eerily similar to the rumors that would follow the massacres at Cawnpore: the dishonoring of English women and "the braining of little children before their mother's eyes." Kaye, *A History of the Great Revolt*, 1:232nn.

33. "He finds his wife and children alive; he *may* find, if she is not pretty, that she has remained faithful among his friends of the village; but it is as common to find that one of the European magistrate's uncovenanted native people has taken her." Napier in letter dated 31 May 1850 in TL, 17 Aug. 1857.

34. Heber, *Narrative*, 2:19.

35. Halliday Letter 34, 22 Oct. 1854.

36. Dewar, *Bygone Days in India*, p. 232.

37. Bishop Heber observed that one reason so many men chose Indian wives was because "ladies going out are not always permitted to take white maids, and always under bond, that in a year or two they shall be sent back again." Heber, *Narrative*, 1:42.

38. Rice, *Captain Sir Richard Francis Burton*, p. 47.

39. In the early days respectable European ladies were called *bibis;* the wife of a Mr. Cunningham, for instance, would have been referred to by her servants as "Cunningham bibi." But when the term was applied to native mistresses, British wives preferred instead to be called *memsahib*, a combination of "ma'am" and "sahib" that is still in use. Ibid., p. 49; Dewar, *Bygone Days*, p. 156.

40. In 1810 *The East Indian Vade Mecum* described concubinage as "a matter of ordinary necessity," and advised griffs (newcomers) on how to establish their own zenanas or seraglios.

41. Mason, *A Matter of Honour*, p. 177; Long and Stocqueler's *British Social Life in Ancient Calcutta*. Mutton clubs were cooperatives organized to buy cheap meat on the hoof. Chawner in Parks, *Wanderings*, 1:488nn.

42. Carey, *Good Old Days*, 1:472–73. Some smitten officers built lavish *bibighars* in their compounds and even remembered their mistresses in their wills. Richard Burton, who made a study of bibis and learned from them the sexual techniques with which he annotated his translations of the *Ananga Ranga* and *Kama Sutra*, admired their "subtlety, . . . their wonderful perceptive powers, their knowledge, and their intuitive appreciation of men and things." And one Anglo–Indian found native women "so amusingly playful, so anxious to please a person," that an Englishman, "after being accustomed to their society, shrinks from the idea of encountering the whims or yielding to the furies of an Englishwoman." But Malcolm wrote that "the dancers are all slaves, condemned to a life of toil for the profit of others; female children and grown up young women are bought by all ranks. . . . Numbers date their condition from a famine or scarcity, when men sell their children for bread; and others are stolen from their parents by brinjarries or grain carriers. Female slaves, in almost every instance, are sold for prostitution." Samuel Sneade Brown in Rice, *Captain Sir Richard Francis Burton*, p. 48.

43. A rupee was worth sixteen annas, therefore the appellation "eight-annas" meant half English, "four-annas" a quarter English, and so on. For a time during and after the Mutiny, most people of mixed Indian and European ancestry preferred to be called Eurasians, a name first officially applied to them by the Marquis of Hastings. But eventually the community's leaders decided that this appellation was too inclusive, and at a convention in 1883 they declared that henceforward they would demand to be called Anglo-Indians. After a time the term stuck and remains in use to this day. But its shifting meaning continues to confuse twentieth-century students of British India. Material relating to these appellations is from Long and Stocqueler, *British Social Life in Ancient Calcutta*, p. 227; Yule and Burnell, *Hobson-Jobson*, p. 344; Dewar, *Bygone Days in India*, p. 156.

44. In 1837 there were approximately thirty thousand Eurasians and forty-one thousand Europeans in India out of a population of about one hundred and seventy million. Edwardes, *Bound to Exile*, p. 12. Even in the age of the nabobs few English officers actually married native women, but a good many married Eurasians.

45. Dyson, *A Various Universe*, p. 324.

46. "The prejudice against 'dark beauties' . . . are daily gaining ground," wrote Emma Roberts, "and in the present state of female intellectuality, their uncultivated minds form a decided objection."

47. Regarding Frances's mother's religion, my guess may be farfetched but is based on the name of her first child, Osman Daniel Marsden, who was brought to my attention by Zoë Yalland. Most officers' native wives and mistresses were Moslem (see Wallace, *Fatehgarh Camp*). The latest Osman could have been conceived was in about June of 1809 when, by my estimation, Frances would have been approximately fourteen years old. Osman is

probably a Moslem name, which suggests that Frances's mother was Moslem, for if Frances had not been entirely abandoned, she was probably living with her mother, and few Hindu women would have permitted even their illegitimate grandchildren to adopt a Moslem name.

48. Carey, *Good Old Days*, 1:264–65.

49. Yalland, Interview.

50. Cardew, *Bengal Native Army*, p. 111.

51. Oliver's illegitimate children and the names of their mothers are from notes provided to a meeting of Kanpur Historians in January 1993, by P. J. O. Taylor.

52. But it is more likely that the mother was one of Oliver's mistresses, for over the course of the next seven years he would find the time to sire three children by three different women: a "native woman," a certain "Mary Elizabeth," and a third named Elizabeth Cherry, a widow from Fatehgarh.

53. Though Francis John Wheeler was conceived out of wedlock in 1841, he was born after his parents married; I thus count him as a legitimate child.

54. Taylor, *A Student's Manual*, pp. 604–12; Burgess, *Chronology*, p. 322.

55. Gupta, *Baji Rao II*, pp. 202–3.

56. Waller, *Beyond the Khyber Pass*, pp. 137, 148; Farwell, *Queen Victoria's Little Wars*, pp. 4–11; Morris, *Heaven's Command*, pp. 100–112; Cardew, *Bengal Native Army*, pp. 167–91.

57. Conspicuous in this assault was Captain Henry Havelock, the austere and fearless Baptist warrior who eighteen years later would arrive at Cawnpore too late to save Wheeler and his garrison.

58. Sale, *Journal*, pp. 116, 121.

59. The Doctor was the luckless William Brydon, who would later find himself besieged in the Residency at Lucknow. In recognition of his services he was later made a Companion of the Bath.

60. Waller, *Beyond the Khyber Pass*, p. 222; Macrory, *Signal Catastrophe*.

61. "I have witnessed a marked change in the conduct of the Bengal Sepoys," Charles Raikes noted, "from the period of our Cabool disasters." "At Cabul we lost an army," Henry Lawrence would write, "and we lost some character with the surrounding States. But I hold that by far our worst loss was in the confidence of our native soldiery." Lawrence in Innes, *Lucknow and Oude in the Mutiny*, pp. 333–34.

62. Farwell, *Queen Victoria's Little Wars*, pp. 37–60.

63. Cook, *The Sikh Wars*; Morris, *Heaven's Command*, pp. 181–86.

64. Cardew, *Bengal Native Army*, pp. 205–42.

65. Wheeler was compensated for his wound, which the surgeons deemed "fully equal to the loss of a limb," with an annual pension of three hundred rupees. General Letter to the Court of Directors dated 11 May 1847 in E/4794, no. 952, p. 967; Fort William Military Consultation of 19 March 1847, no. 158 in L/Mil/3/406, p. 126 (OIOC).

66. DNB.

67. FPC in 4:722–74.

68. At both Aliwal and at Kangra one of his subordinates, Major Alexander Jack, distinguished himself. Jack would die in the uprising at Cawnpore as Wheeler's brigadier.

69. Henry Lawrence, the eldest of the Lawrence brothers who would die commanding the Residency at Lucknow, was appointed chief political agent at Dhuleep Singh's court in Lahore.

70. Who in turn ceded it to the King of Jammu.

71. Burgess, *Chronology*, p. 348; the expedition is explained in Cook, *The Sikh Wars*, p. 109.

72. Wilkinson, *The Gemini Generals*, pp. 20–21.

73. Dalhousie: December 1848 in Lee–Warner, *Life of Lord Dalhousie*, pp. 200, 273–74; Napier's estimation of the Jullunder Doab is from pp. 319–20.

74. "I endeavoured," wrote Wheeler, "to console myself with the Poet's lines, that

"Honor and Fame from no condition rise/Act well your part in that true honor lies." Embarrassed by his oversight, Gough told Dalhousie that Wheeler had "exercised his command with judgment and sound discretion, worthy of himself as one of the best officers of his rank in this army," FDP, SC, 29 Sept., 1849 (NAI).

75. Scottish Record Office: GD45/6/5/1, pp. 233–34.

76. Rees, *The Siege of Lucknow*, p. 358.

77. The first recorded double drought struck in 1345, under the cruel reign of Tughlak Shah, and turned the fertile Doab into wilderness. Beginning in 1631, the whole of Asia was parched dry for two years, and during another famine in the 1660s, Aurangzeb rescued the region from starvation by importing vast quantities of grain from Bengal. In 1770, the first double famine under Company rule had claimed nearly a third of the North-Western Province's population. It was worsened by the "corruption and rapacity" of the Company's servants, which Warren Hastings would also blame for a 1784 famine that helped prompt not only Pitt's Bill for the Better Government of India but the appointment of Lord Cornwallis to the governor-generalship. Though famine also struck during Cornwallis's administration, his Permanent Settlement was credited with the near elimination of famine in nineteenth-century Bengal. Keene, *A Servant of 'John Company,'* pp. 103, 183; Nevill, *Cawnpore*, pp. 58–59.

78. Hill, *The Story of the Cawnpore Mission*, p. 18.

79. N.W.P. General Proceedings, 214/32, no. 15, Agra, 28 Oct. 1837, courtesy of Zoë Yalland.

80. Nevill, *Cawnpore*, p. 61.

81. Wallace, *Fatehgarh Camp*, p. 62.

82. Eden in Hill, *The Story of the Cawnpore Mission*, p. 18.

83. "Sometimes, when they see a [sepoy] eating they rush upon him to take his food," Mrs. Parks reported from nearby Kanauj. "Sometimes they fall one over the other as they rush for it, and having fallen, being too weak to rise, they die on the spot. . . . The wretched inhabitants tear off the bark of the wild fig tree . . . and pound it into food; in the course of four or five days their bodies swell, and they die in agonies."

84. *The Englishman* quotes and the estimate of fatalities are from Loveday, *The History and Economics of Indian Famines*, p. 41

85. The wolves are from Fane, *Five Years in India*, p. 33, and Forbes, *Oriental Memoirs*, p. 438. Some of these wolves were said to have suckled the babies they dragged off, and supposed "wolf boys," upon whom Kipling's Mowgli was based, were periodically found in the jungles. "These boys when caught struggle to get back to the wolves," wrote Baptist Noel, "and, with an angry snarl, try to bite those who hold them." Noel, *England and India*, p. 29.

86. N.W.P., General Proceedings, Range 214/32 1837, no. 15 Agra 28 Oct., courtesy of Zoë Yalland. A large-hearted old subhedar induced his comrades to subscribe to a fund to pay famine victims to dig a second reservoir that came to be known as the Subhedar's Tank; every native officer stationed at Cawnpore donated a month's wages, which, combined with the subhedar's own donation of ten thousand rupees, amounted to thirty thousand rupees. The result was "a handsome tank" filled with "excellent water" that long remained "a monument to native liberality." Rawlins, *The Autobiography of an Old Soldier*, pp. 95–96.

87. Trotter, *The Earl of Auckland*, p. 22; Loveday, *The History and Economics of Indian Famines*, p. 41.

88. Yalland, *Traders and Nabobs*, p. 155

89. Keene, *A Servant of 'John Company,'* p. 278.

90. Nevill, *Cawnpore*, p. 61.

91. The date of Azimullah's first appearance is from Shepherd, *A Personal Narrative*, p. 14. Shepherd calls the reverend who took Azimullah Paton, but there is no record of a Reverend Paton at Cawnpore, and Azimullah's appearance jibes with Carshore's tenure.

Three years later a Reverend Perkins succeeded Carshore—perhaps Shepherd mistook his name for Paton.

92. Hill, *The Story of the Cawnpore Mission*, pp. 16–17.

93. "Had it been possible to preserve the lives of even half of these unfortunate children after receiving them into our asylums, it would have caused us to have now much larger nominal Christian communities; but they became so debilitated and diseased that the greater part of them died, although attended to most kindly and assiduously. . . . The number of people that died of starvation and famine-fever during the prevalence of the scarcity, great as it was, probably did not nearly equal those who died slowly afterward in consequence of disease and debility contracted then." Warren, *A Glance Backward*, pp. 68, 246.

94. Russell described his complexion as "dark olive," which may be how he appeared among the pallid soldiers in the Crimea. But Russell is contradicted by the description the government put out during the Mutiny, according to which he was fair complexioned, "tall and well-made" with a "flat nose." Russell, *My Diary in India*, 1:165; N.W.P. Political Department: Jan.–June 1864 in U.P., 3:700nn; Morris, *The Story of Cawnpore*, p. 3 (OIOC). (Lieutenant Colonel William Albert Morris was Senior Medical Officer at Cawnpore from 1909 to 1911.) I say Azimullah was only "possibly" a Pathan because by the 1830s "Khan" was so indiscriminately adopted by Indian Moslems that it was no longer a definite indicator of Pathan ancestry. See Yule and Burnell, *Hobson-Jobson*, pp. 479, 570; Hill, *The Story of the Cawnpore Mission*, p. 47.

95. Roberts, *The East India Voyager*, p. 28.

96. Hill, *The Story of the Cawnpore Mission*, p. 47; Shepherd, *A Personal Narrative*, p. 14.

97. Perkins once baptized an elderly Hindu who had read the New Testament and had approached him for further instruction. Perkins christened him Simeon, but was later distressed to find that the old man had not informed his family for fear they would disown him. Perkins insisted he must, and finally accompanied Simeon to his house. Sure enough, the family was horrified by the old man's announcement and banished him forever from their home. "After some little time had passed," Perkins recalled, "Simeon turned to me, and with his eyes filled with tears said, 'Well, sir, now I trust that you are satisfied. Why should we stay here longer? We can do no good!' And being fully satisfied," Perkins cheerfully concluded, "and sensible that our work was done, I returned with my aged friend, now more deeply bound to me than ever." Hill, *The Story of the Cawnpore Mission*, pp. 26–28; Gordon, *Our India Mission*, p. 19.

98. Raikes, *Notes on the Revolt*, p. 137.

99. Mrs. Sherwood remembered how the wife of an Arab convert to Christianity berated her husband for abandoning Islam, telling him that even if Christ assured him a place in heaven she would sooner go to hell. The convert was a man named Sabat who helped Henry Martyn produce an Arabic translation of the Bible. Eventually his wife prevailed; after Martyn's death Sabat reverted to Islam. Darton, *The Life of Mrs. Sherwood*, p. 343.

100. Shepherd, *A Personal Narrative*, p. 14.

101. It is possible Azimullah lost siblings to the famine as well.

102. Shepherd, *A Personal Narrative*, p. 14. In Calcutta in the mid-1850s, kitmutgars were paid from six to ten rupees a month; three rupees was probably low even for Cawnpore in the early 1840s. Colesworthy-Grant, *Anglo-Indian Domestic Life*, p. 106.

103. Roberts, *Scenes and Characteristics of Hindustan*, 1:64.

104. MacMillan, *Women of the Raj*, p. 144. Yalland disagrees, and believes that the British simply chose not to speak English to their servants. Even this was a major difference between the British and the American sahibs and memsahibs of my boyhood, who were completely at a loss with the indigenous language.

105. By the 1930s, however, sweepers deigned to eat British leftovers. Yalland/ASW.

106. Shepherd, *A Personal Narrative*, p. 14.

107. Gough/Dalhousie: 13 Feb. 1846; Talbot-Rice/ASW: 26 Jan. 1944; anonymous diary by a visitor to Cawnpore who dropped in on the Scotts in January 1850 in collection of Zoë Yalland.

108. "Bengal is a low lying country," the British used to say, "full of low, lying people." Farwell, *Armies of the Raj*, p. 179.

109. Aberigh-Mackay, *Twenty-One Days in India*, pp. 50–51. "One, two thing I do," Honoria Lawrence heard one tell her husband Henry, "no mistake can make, multiply, sine, cosine. Sir, you are my sucking father, Sir." (Lawrence and Woodwiss, *The Journals of Honoria Lawrence*, p. 74.) But it was amazing how well the babus performed their duties, considering that the first English/Bengali dictionary was not published until 1815. Carey, *Good Old Days*, 1:294.

110. He may have been merely imitating the Anglo–Indian drawl. The French botanist Victor Jacquemont was proud of his naturalness in society, but among Anglo–Indians found he had to "drawl my speech and make myself heavy after their fashion." N.W.P. Political Department: Jan.–June 1864 in 3:700nn.

111. Shepherd states that Ashburnham succeeded Scott, but Ashburnham's predecessor was an officer named Baldeston. Perhaps Scott had been acting brigadier in the meantime. Rice/Ward: 7 Jan. 1994.

112. Temple in Sardesai, *New History of the Marathas*, 1:40–41.

113. Heber, *Journal*, 2:548, 560.

114. Temple in Sardesai, *New History of the Marathas*, 1:40–41. Some theorized that their name came from *Mär*, meaning to strike, and *hûtna*, meaning to duck. Be that as it may, strike and duck, hit and run was the essence of their military genius. Marshman, *Abridgement of the History of India*, p. 76.

115. Unfortunately, he was not a Kshatriya, really, as some of his Brahmins pointed out, but Sivaji hired one of the most distinguished pundits in Benares to concoct a Kshatriya lineage for him and recapitulate Vedic coronation rituals. The pundit determined that Sivaji's mother was a Yadava, a descendant of ancient kings.

116. Grant Duff, *A History of the Mahrattas*, 1:10–11nn.

117. MacMunn, *The Martial Races of India*.

118. Sivaji's son Sambhaji was captured by Aurangzeb, who had him executed with particular cruelty, cutting off first his tongue and then his sputtering head. Aurangzeb later captured Sambhaji's son, but his brother put up a good fight, as did his wife, Tara Bai, one of the great female military leaders of all time and a later inspiration to the Rani of Jhansi.

119. Yule and Burnell, *Hobson-Jobson*, p. 215.

120. Lutfullah, *Autobiography*, pp. 35–36.

121. It was a disgrace for a king "to die of old age, in bed, of disease." Kings were supposed to fight with each other, to make peace with their superiors and war with their equals, and always to conquer the weak. The *Arthashastra* of Kautilya said that "all neighboring states were to be regarded as concentric rings of hostility and alliance." The ideal kingdom was surrounded by subordinate kingdoms, "like bamboos surrounded by thorns." Kautilya, *Arthashastra* in Mason, *A Matter of Honour*, p. 43; Critchely, *Feudalism*, pp. 92–93.

122. Atchison, *A Collection of Treaties*, vol. 4.

123. Gupta, *Baji Rao II*, p. 14.

124. *Kampani Jehan*, a title the Company adopted to evoke the Moghuls Jehangir and Shah Jehan, appeared on the earliest coins the British minted in India, and eventually became the nickname "John Company." "'What is the Company?'" wrote Mowbray Thomson, "is a question often discussed in the villages, and various and conflicting are the answers that have been promulgated in reply." It was said that the "Company was a nondescript brute, that swayed their destinies with a resistless sceptre; its species, genus, habitat all unknown." Thomson, *The Story of Cawnpore*, p.194.

125. Elphinstone's characterization of Baji Rao was probably accurate. "He is eager for power," he wrote Calcutta, "though he wants the boldness necessary to acquire it, and tenacious of authority though too indolent to exercise it. Though capricious and changeable in his humours, he is steady in his serious designs." Woodruff, *The Men Who Ruled India*, 1:216.

126. Grant Duff, *A History of the Mahrattas*, 2:477nn.

127. Woodruff, *The Men Who Ruled India*, 1:218.

128. Wheeler, *India and the Frontier States*, 2:570–71.

129. Malcolm in Gupta, *Baji Rao II*, pp. xii, 159.

130. Governor-General Hastings was appalled by Malcolm's generosity, but accounting for administrative costs and various distributions of portions of Baji Rao's empire to friendly chiefs, the Peshwa's defeat garnered the Company an initial annual dividend of five million rupees. According to Beveridge, Malcolm later argued that at the time of Baji Rao's surrender the Peshwa could easily have bolted and protracted the war for another six months. Grant Duff, *A History of the Mahrattas*, 2:512–13; Gupta, *Nana Saheb*, pp. 2–3; Beveridge, *Comprehensive History of India*, 7:105.

131. Some accounts maintain that Benares was Baji Rao's first choice but that Hastings reneged on it as too dangerous a location for Hinduism's deposed king. But according to John Low, who oversaw the negotiations, Baji Rao rejected Benares because he would have gone broke supporting Mahratta pilgrims. On the journey to Bithur, His Former Highness groused and balked at every step, erecting shrines and praying for deliverance from his captors. (A civil officer reported disgustedly that Baji Rao "made every halt that he could possibly obtain.") Baji Rao crossed the Nerbudda on June 12, 1818, and "before he entered Northern India more than 8000 of his people were granted passports by the British Government." Much to Baji Rao's disappointment, his "progress through Rajpootana and the Doab to the scene of his exile excited scarcely any sensation among the people." But the approach of his Brahminical establishment alarmed Bithur's resident pundits. Though a number of Baji Rao's followers were "low men" and mere "ministers of his pleasure," many of the swarm of Brahmins now staggering toward Bithur were Concanists with priestly and diplomatist pretensions: subtle, cultivated men accustomed to ministering to emperors and princes. He paused at the holy city of Mathura for six weeks of "devotional exercises," and pleaded for permission to remain, but by now the governor-general had determined that since Baji Rao had not yet been weaned "from the expectation of a change in his favour" it might be dangerous to station the last of the great Hindu monarchs in one of the most visited of Hindu cities. The British made way for Baji Rao by moving their district headquarters out of Bithur and into Cawnpore. Sardesai, *Poona Affairs*, 13:453, 462, 483–84, 512; Landon, *Under the Sun*, p. 277; Misra, *Nana Saheb Peshwa*, p. 108; Gupta, *Baji Rao II*, pp. 193–94; Grant, *Cassell's Illustrated History of India*, 1:526; Yalland, *Traders and Nabobs*, p. 119.

132. Misra, *Nana Saheb Peshwa*, p. 124.

133. *Poona Gazetteer* in Misra, *Nana Saheb Peshwa*, pp. 97–98; Lutfullah, *Autobiography*, pp. 215–16.

134. Misra, *Nana Saheb Peshwa*, pp. 122, 124–25.

135. Baji Rao had spent enormous sums on his extravagant charities and reputedly licentious entertainments, but when the time came to pay his troops he always pleaded poverty. Grant Duff, *A History of the Mahrattas*, 2:430.

136. Anund Rao Jaswant to Malcolm in Sardesai, ed. *Poona Affairs*, 13:467. These were among the items found by Havelock's forces in the palace wells at Bithur after the Nana fled.

137. Among these pilgrims, refugees, and opportunists there were very few Moslems. At Poona Baji Rao had "incurred the dislike of the Mohamedans," wrote a Moslem traveler, "by prohibiting them from appearing in his sight till ten o'clock in the morning every day, in order that his eyes might not be defiled by seeing them." Baji Rao even forbade

Moslems "of whatever rank or station from even passing through those streets which were overlooked by his palace." Lutfullah, *Autobiography*, pp. 104–5.

138. The Brahmins were only one of eighty-four castes in the district (not including subcastes), but Brahmins accounted for over fifteen percent of the population in the 1920s. With the flight of Nana Sahib and the destruction of the establishment at Bithur, many Brahmins had left the area; it is therefore likely that the proportion of Brahmins was far higher at Bithur in the early 1800s. Nevill, *Cawnpore*, pp. 101–3.

139. Evidently Baji Rao's mother crossed out the word "capture" in her husband's order and changed it to "kill." Wheeler, *India, 1875–6*, p. 419.

140. The story of Vanayak's appointment was told to me by his grandson, the late Narain Rao Tope of Bithur. Field notes.

141. Misra, *Nana Saheb Peshwa*, p. 120b; he mentions the calligraphers for which Bithur became famous on p. 121.

142. Captain Robert Smith in Yalland, *Traders and Nabobs*, p. 204. In 1837 Charles LeBas encountered Baji Rao and his medieval guard as he set forth on a pilgrimage to Benares. "His Highness rode a magnificent Elephant, the largest I ever saw, superbly equipped, and was followed by a number of closed Palanquins, which must have contained the beauties of his harem. They are almost entirely surrounded by a guard of cavalry, evidently picked men, as was fitting, seeing that to them is entrusted the difficult task of watching some dozens of ladies belonging to an old gentleman on the wrong side of 60." LeBas, *Journal* (OIOC).

143. Malgonkar, *The Devil's Wind*, p. 11.

144. LeBas, *Journal* (OIOC).

145. Keene, *Handbook*, p. 19.

146. Thomson was describing the palace during Nana Sahib's occupancy, but if such rooms existed they were more likely to have been the creation of Baji Rao than Nana Sahib, of whose lechery there is less credible evidence. Thomson, *The Story of Cawnpore*, p. 48.

147. Grant Duff, *A History of the Mahrattas*, 2:253, 430.

148. The life expectancy of Peshwas was generally brief: Narain Rao was eighteen when he was murdered, his successor had jumped to his death at the age of twenty-one, Baji Rao's own father never reached the age of fifty.

149. Misra, *Nana Saheb Peshwa*, p. 127.

150. Gupta, *Baji Rao II*, p. 214.

151. Yalland, *Traders and Nabobs*, p. 202. His handmaidens were so stunning that a band of usually remorseless stranglers allowed one of them to pass unmolested with one hundred thousand rupees in her possession. "We had talked to her," one Thug later sighed, "and felt love towards her, for she was very beautiful." Tuker, *The Yellow Scarf*, p. 194.

152. Gupta, *Baji Rao II,*. p. 204.

153. Kaye, *A History of the Great Revolt*, 1:70.

154. Nana Sahib's birth date has been calculated from his horoscope, unearthed by Shri Krishnaji Haripatankar of Rajapur. See Thapliyal, *Nana Saheb*, p. 69.

155. Misra, *Nana Saheb Peshwa*, p. 131. The honorifics "Sahib" and "Rao" were later added to each of the names of the Peshwa's adopted boys. Bala's formal name was Gangadhar. Pandurang, one of Mahadev's grandsons, appears in Baji Rao's will as yet a third adoptive son; he was later known as Rao Sahib. But the relationship appears to have been informal. Indeed, Hindu law provides for the adoption of only one son, unless the first dies. Only Nana Sahib was legally regarded as Baji Rao's son. Misra, *Nana Saheb Peshwa*, p. 130nn.

156. Landon, *Under the Sun*, p. 275.

157. Baji Rao and Mahadev bore the same *gotra* or caste name. Thapliyal, *Nana Saheb*, p. 65. Dhondu Pant had also been the name of Baji Rao's most able general. U.P., 5:698.

158. By Hindu law, eldest sons could not be adopted.

159. Lang, *Wanderings in India*, p. 410.

160. Though in later years some writers assumed that Tatya Tope's last name derived from his adoption of a solar topi hat such as the British wore, it was evidently a family title meaning "commander." He actually always wore a *chukridar* turban. U.P., 3:580; Mr. Narain Tope.

161. The people of Bithur insist that the Rani of Jhansi grew up at Baji Rao's court and fell in love with Nana Sahib but that they were forbidden to marry by Baji Rao, who married her off to the aged Maharaja of Jhansi. This story also appears in Malgonkar's *The Devil's Wind*, a novel so convincing that portions of it have crept into many ostensibly nonfiction accounts of Nana Sahib's life.

162. Yalland, *A Guide to the Katcheri Cemetery*, p. 25.

163. Misra, *Nana Saheb Peshwa*, p. 134.

164. Gupta, *Nana Saheb*, p. 4

165. Thorens in Yalland, *Traders and Nabobs*, p. 341.

166. Misra, *Nana Saheb Peshwa*, p. 140.

167. Ibid., p. 149.

168. *The Englishman and Military Chronicle*, 11 Feb. 1851 in Gupta, *Nana Saheb*, p. 5.

169. M. Court, former magistrate of Cawnpore, in TL, 30 Nov. 1874.

170. Misra, *Nana Saheb Peshwa*, pp. 127–28, 132.

171. Kaye, *A History of the Great Revolt*, 1:104–9.

172. Gupta, *Nana Saheb*, pp. 3–4, 18–19. "A native of any rank," wrote John Lang, "considers it a disgrace to sell property." Lang, *Wanderings in India*, p. 117.

173. Misra, *Nana Saheb Peshwa*, p. 140.

174. Gupta, *Nana Saheb*, pp. 3–4.

175. U.P., 1:12–13.

176. Misra, *Nana Saheb Peshwa*, pp. 146, 152.

177. NWP, PP, 15 Dec. 1853, 14–16.

178. FDP, FC, Dec. 1853, nos. 155–57.

179. Misra, *Nana Saheb Peshwa*, pp. 141, 145.

180. U.P., 1:18–19.

181. FDP, FC, 16 Dec. 1853, nos. 155–57.

182. Nana was still discussing the possibility of going to London himself when John Lang visited him in 1854. Lang, *Wanderings in India*, pp. 110–19.

183. Kaye, *A History of the Great Revolt*, 1:67, 109–11.

184. Bhonsley's Nagpore connection may have accounted for Azimullah's apparent interest in Nagpore's case with the British Government during his later visits with Captain Martineau. HMS, 725 (34).

185. According to Forbes-Mitchell, Mohamed Ali Khan, Azimullah's assistant, recalled that they had spent £50,000 in England, which was equivalent to the *Telegraph*'s figure. The precise date of Azimullah's departure from India is not known. Mohamed Ali Khan in Forbes-Mitchell, *The Relief of Lucknow*, pp. 110–11.

186. Thapliyal, *Nana Saheb*, p. 95.

187. Lutfullah covered a lot of ground on his visit. He tried out the diving bell at the Polytechnic Institution on Regent Street; attended trials; enjoyed the dancing horses at Astley's Theatre with the Russian Prince Soltikoff; and observed some visiting Native Americans on exhibit at Egyptian Hall who looked and sounded to him like Mahrattas. Lutfullah, *Autobiography*, pp. 406, 409–33.

188. Lucie Duff Gordon in Frank, *A Passage to Egypt*, ms. copy.

189. *Chambers Journal*, April 3, 1858.

190. Kaye, *A History of the Great Revolt*, 1:109–11. The only Biddles I have found who were practicing law at this time were William, who worked out of Oxford, and Sydney, who was not admitted to the bar until 1856. The Law Society/ASW: 2 and 5 April 1993; Foster, *Men-at-the-Bar*, p. 37.

191. I surmise Mill's introduction of Azimullah to LDG from Mill's position at the Company and his relationship with LDG; there seems to be no record of exactly how Azimullah and Lucie met. Frank, *A Passage to Egypt.*

192. George Meredith in *EB*, 11th ed.

193. LDG's first references to Azimullah are dated 4 Jan. 1854, but her account of him suggests that he may have arrived somewhat earlier. Perhaps she took him in so that he could witness an English Christmas celebration. Azimullah's delight in the snow is from LDG/Lord Lansdowne: 4 Jan. 1854. Courtesy of the Earl of Shelburne. See Frank, *A Passage to Egypt*, p. 179.

194. Ms. of Frank, *A Passage to Egypt.*

195. LDG/Lansdowne: 11 Jan. 1854, courtesy of the Earl of Shelburne. See also Frank, *A Passage to Egypt*, p. 181.

196. LDG/Bayley: 15 June 1854, courtesy of Mrs. Carintha and Antony Beevor. Azimullah was not a Mahratta.

197. LDG/Lord Lansdowne: 11 Jan. 1854. Courtesy of the Earl of Shelburne.

198. Burgesss, *Chronology*, p. 350.

199. Kaye, *A History of the Great Revolt*, 1:109–11.

200. Lang, *Wanderings in India*, p. 118.

201. "Tantalizing the assembly," Lutfullah had sniffed, "was their principal aim by such a violation of decorum." Lutfullah, *Autobiography*, pp. 338, 409.

202. Thomson, *The Story of Cawnpore*, pp. 58–59.

203. Keene, *Fifty-Seven*, p. 69.

204. Azimullah in Russell, *My Diary in India*, 1:166.

205. Ricketts in Taylor, *A Star Shall Fall*, p. 59. Misra says that "not a few English girls showed their keen desire to marry him," but provides no substantiation. Certainly that was the rumor at the time. Misra, *Nana Saheb Peshwa*, p. 557.

206. Roberts, *Letters*, pp. 120–21.

207. Keene, *Handbook*, p. 24.

208. Thomson, *The Story of Cawnpore*, p. 55. No doubt Azimullah was a polygamist by faith but in fact there is no evidence that he had more than the one wife who bore him a son. Hill, *The Story of the Cawnpore Mission*, p. 49.

209. Keene, *A Servant of 'John Company,'* p. 162nn.

210. Forbes-Mitchell, *The Relief of Lucknow*, p. 110.

211. Lutfullah, *Autobiography*, p. 406.

212. Most historians scoff at Azimullah's theory that Britain's military was dangerously depleted, but by August 17, 1857, the *Times* was alarmed that Britain now had "38,000 fewer armed men in this country than we had during the Crimean war, and that when, on all ordinary rules, we are much more exposed to European attack than we were then; for however much the Crimean alliance gave us to do in the East of Europe, that very alliance protected us completely in the West, whereas now we are thrown back upon ourselves again, and have only our own army to depend on, and our ordinary relations with our neighbours on which to rely." Lord Ellenborough had proposed that India would require yearly reinforcements of fifteen thousand men but "where is this reinforcement to come from? Why, one year, upon this calculation, will swallow up the greater part of the whole army at home, regular and Militia too, which united only amount to 25,000." TL, 17 Aug. 1857.

213. Farwell, *Queen Victoria's Little Wars*, p. 69. "The Indian view of that war is (or rather, was)," wrote Reverend Hill of Cawnpore, "that when the Emperor of the World (*i.e.*, the Sultan of Turkey) was offended with the Czar of Russia, he ordered his subject chieftains of France and England to punish the offender!" Hill, *The Story of the Cawnpore Mission*, p. 48.

214. If he needed any encouragement he did not have to look any farther than the agents of the Czar, the Shah, the Emperor of France, and the Sultan of Turkey who haunted the drawing rooms of Belgravia, always on the lookout for the Company's disil-

lusioned vassals and whispering vague and confidential promises of diversionary actions and military support. None of their employers entertained any real hope of ridding India of the British and conquering it for themselves, but all of them had a stake in at least keeping things stirred up. "There is no room to doubt," wrote the *Illustrated London News* in 1854, "that whenever disaffection has been excited against our rule on our Indian frontier, Russian emissaries have had something to do with it." ILN, no. 664, vol. xxiv, 21 Jan. 1854, p. 54.

215. *Chambers Journal*, 3 April 1858.

216. The date of Azimullah's departure is surmised from his having received word of the defeat of the British at Sebastopol on June 18 while his ship paused at Malta. Gupta mistakenly places his departure "in 1856, during the Crimean War," but by June 1856 the war was over. There is some controversy over when Azimullah returned to India. Martineau claimed to have traveled with him from Suez to Aden in October 1856 (Home Miscellaneous, 725 [34]). But it seems doubtful that he spent over a year getting home, and by one account he visited the King of Oudh at Cawnpore on his way to exile in February or March 1856. Perhaps Martineau confused him with Ali or met Azimullah on another trip. Russell, *My Diary in India*, 1:165; Hill, *The Story of the Cawnpore Mission*, p. 48.

217. NAM and Boyden/ASW: 31 Jan. 1994. Doyne would later join in a partnership with a young engineer named Robert Garrett, who, while in India to conduct a survey for the Oudh Railway, would become stranded at Cawnpore and die in the defense of the Entrenchment.

218. Sherer, *Daily Life*, p. 152.

219. "Now," Russell later asked his readership, "is it not curious enough that he should have felt such an interest to see, with his own eyes, how matters were going on in the Crimea? It would not be strange in a European to evince such curiosity; but in an Asiatic, of the non-military caste, it certainly is. He saw the British army in a state of some depression, and he formed, as I have since heard, a very unfavourable opinion of its morale and physique, in comparison with that of the French." Russell slightly overstated his case; in fact a North Indian Moslem, especially of Afghani extraction, cannot be regarded as belonging to a "non-military caste." Russell, *My Diary in India*, 1:165–67.

220. Keene, *A Servant of 'John Company,'* pp. 162–63.

221. Forbes-Mitchell, *The Relief of Lucknow*, pp. 110–11.

222. Roberts, *Scenes and Characteristics of Hindustan*.

223. Yalland, *A Guide to the Katcheri Cemetery*, p. 17. Up to then plays had been performed in "a dirty little house," complained one visitor, "and so cold." Pemble, ed., *Miss Fane in India*, p. 143.

224. INTACH, *Preliminary Unedited Listing of Cawnpore*, p. 100.

225. Nevill, *Cawnpore*, p. 168. (Nevill is not always reliable about construction dates.)

226. INTACH, *Preliminary Unedited Listing of Cawnpore*, p. 118; Nevill, *Cawnpore*, pp. 121–22.

227. Roberts in Yalland, *Traders and Nabobs*, p. 167.

228. Though most people continued to rely on the Calcutta papers for their news, Samuel Greenway established a printing press and began to publish the *Cawnpore Advertiser* and a "not very sightly quarto sheet" called the *Omnibus*. Carey, *Good Old Days*, 1:447.

229. Roberts, *Scenes and Characteristics of Hindustan*.

230. Nigam/ASW: 29 Dec. 1993.

231. Heber, *Narrative*, 1:104; Russell, *My Diary in India*, 2:44; Ali, *The Book of Indian Birds*, p. 97.

232. Parks, *Wanderings in India*, 1:160–61.

233. Russell, *My Diary in India*, 1:202.

234. Heber, *Narrative*, 1:129.

235. Pemble, ed., *Miss Fane in India*, p. 141.

236. LeBas, *Journal*, OIOC.

237. Fortesque-Brickdale: 18 March 1846 (CCSAS).

238. Yalland, *Traders and Nabobs*, p. 171.

239. Nevill, *Cawnpore*, p. 4.

240. Grant, *Letters*, OIOC.

241. Ball, *History of the Indian Mutiny*, 1:304–6.

242. Several former residents of Cawnpore wrote to various newspapers after the Mutiny to insist that Nana Sahib never ventured into Cawnpore, never showed himself at his parties, and that the only Europeans he would meet with were civil servants on official business. Cawnpore Magistrate M. H. Court made this claim, and Henry George Keene embraced it. This may well have been the case immediately after Baji Rao's death, when Nana was still smarting from his humiliation at Dalhousie's hands. It is also likely that in some accounts of his visits to Cawnpore Nana was confused with his brothers, with Narain Rao (also called "Nana"), and even with the Moslem Nunne Nawab of Cawnpore. But Lang's description demonstrates that by 1854 Nana was quite at ease with Europeans and did ride his carriage into Cawnpore. There are enough specific accounts of his visits to suggest that his initial insularity changed, perhaps under Azimullah's influence. The "pic-nic" party was described in an anonymous letter to the *Times*, written at the time of Nana Sahib's supposed capture at Gwalior in 1874, which politely refuted Court's contention. The anonymous writer—possibly Harvey Greathed—also attended the party; Greathed mentions attending the party in his *Letters*, p. 138; TL, 31 Oct. 1874, p. 7.

243. Ball, *History of the Indian Mutiny*, 1:304–6.

244. INTACH, *Preliminary Unedited Listing of Cawnpore*.

245. United Grand Lodge, *The Lodge Harmony*, pp. 27–28, courtesy of Zoë Yalland.

246. Butler characteristically attributed all this to the Indians being "utterly strangers" to Christianity. Butler, *The Land of the Veda*, p. 58.

247. Rajnikant Gupta in Misra, *Nana Saheb Peshwa*, p. 134.

248. Ibid.

249. Thapliyal, *Nana Saheb*, p. 253; Malgonkar, *The Devil's Wind*, p. 38; U.P., 1:699; Landon, *Under the Sun*, p. 278. Landon says she was also known as Kasi Bai and Kaku Bai. But Kasi (Kashi) Bai was Bala Sahib's wife. Thus it is not entirely clear that Landon got her age and the date of her wedding right. Some accounts would later refer to Nana's widows, but it appears that these witnesses may have mistaken Rao Sahib's wife for Nana's. There is a mention of the father of Nana Sahib's third wife in Anderson/Beadon, 11 July 1859, in HDP, Public, 29 July 1859, nos. 40–41 (NAI). But most accounts suggest that by the time of the Mutiny Nana had only one wife. FDP, PC, March 1864, nos. 151–54 (NAI).

250. Thapliyal, *Nana Saheb*, p. 82.

251. Bond, *Mussoorie and Landour*, pp. 49–51.

252. Grant, *Cassell's Illustrated History of India*, 2:184–85; Grant mistakenly gives his name as Long. For his services Pershad gave Lang an honorarium of three hundred thousand rupees and a portrait of himself that was later mistaken for Nana Sahib. Misra, *Nana Saheb Peshwa*, p. 137.

253. Lang often found something "peculiarly quaint about the arrangement of European furniture in the house of a native gentleman. . . . The furniture has, for the most part, been purchased at various sales, and has belonged to officers of all grades, civil and military. There are the tent-table and the camp-stool of the dead ensign, in the same room with the marble-topped table and crimson damask-covered easy chair of some luxurious judge. On the mantel-piece you will find a costly clock of the most elegant design and workmanship, and on each side of it, a pair of japan candlesticks, not worth half-a-crown."

254. Ball, *History of the Indian Mutiny*, 1:305.

255. TL, 29 Oct. 1874; 31 Oct. 1874, p. 7; Yalland, *A Guide to the Katcheri Cemetery*, p. 72; Muir, *Records of the Intelligence Department*, vol. 1; Gupta, *Nana Saheb*, p. 4 (illus); Misra, *Nana Saheb Peshwa*, p. 133; Thomson, *The Story of Cawnpore*, p. 46; N.W.P. Political Department: Jan.–June 1864 in U.P., 3:700nn.

584 ◆ NOTES TO PART ONE

256. Lang noted here that "a native of any rank considers it a disgrace to sell property," a belief Nana Sahib himself often invoked in his memorials to the Company.

257. Ball, *The History of the Indian Mutiny*, 1:304–6.

258. Gupta, *Nana Saheb*, pp. 13–14.

259. Lang, *Wanderings in India*, pp. 110–19.

260. "He had either been wronged by the government, or by some judge, whose decision had been against him. In the matter of the government, it was sheer love of oppression that led to the evil of which he complained; in the matter of the judge, that functionary had been bribed by the other party."

261. "Why will not Lord Dalhousie pay a visit to the King of Oudh?" he wanted to know. "Lord Hardinge did so." And would Colonel Sleeman, the Resident at Lucknow, persuade Lord Dalhousie to seize Oudh? "So far as I could glean," continued this visitor, "Nana Sahib wished for the annexation of Oude—albeit he expressed a very decided opinion that, in the event of that measure being resorted to, there would be a disturbance, and perhaps a war."

262. Marshman, *Abridgement of the History of India*, p. 99.

263. Pemble, *The Raj, the Indian Mutiny, and the Kingdom of Oudh*, pp. 4–5.

264. Lee-Warner, *Life of the Marquis of Dalhousie*, p. 304.

265. Kaye, *A History of the Great Revolt*, pp. 116–17.

266. Sharar, *Lucknow*, p. 54.

267. The neglected Begums of Lucknow were among the kingdom's most ferocious protectors of religion.

268. Russell, *My Diary in India*, 1:257.

269. The sheer spectacle of the Lucknow Court was such that Europeans from Cawnpore used to attend the king's monthly public breakfasts just to gape at the cascading jewels that glittered from his corpulence, and to marvel at his menagerie (which reputedly included a man-eating horse); his vast collections of steam engines, hot air balloons, and windup toys; his swarms of bucklered attendants and the hundreds of state elephants that used to devour the harvests of entire districts. Pemble, *The Raj, the Indian Mutiny, and the Kingdom of Oudh*, p. 27; Kaye, *A History of the Great Revolt*, 1:114.

270. Pemble, *The Raj, the Indian Mutiny, and the Kingdom of Oudh*, pp. 51–52.

271. Large landholders of Oudh.

272. Kaye, *A History of the Great Revolt*, 1:134–36, 136nn.

273. He became the first Marquis of Dalhousie in 1849 for defeating the Sikhs.

274. DNB; Hunter, *Dalhousie*; Lee-Warner, *Life of the Marquis of Dalhousie*.

275. The same was true of his successor, George Canning.

276. DNB.

277. General James Outram confessed that though he had met Wellington, Peel, and most of the leading statesmen of England, he "never felt so awed, so stricken by his own inferiority, as in his interviews with Lord Dalhousie." Hunter, *Dalhousie*, p.32.

278. Hibbert, *The Great Mutiny*, p. 25.

279. Kaye, *A History of the Great Revolt*, 1:74.

280. Lee-Warner, *Life of the Marquis of Dalhousie*, 2:11, 179.

281. Kaye, *A History of the Great Revolt*, 1:75–78, 91–93. John Lang couched her protests for her in his appeals to the Company.

282. Woodruff, *The Men Who Ruled India*, 1:190–91.

283. Yalland, *Traders and Nabobs*, p. 219; Kaye, *A History of the Great Revolt*, 1:81.

284. Pemble, *The Raj, the Indian Mutiny, and the Kingdom of Oudh*, p. 109. On January 24, 1856, Lindsay reported a major buildup of troops in anticipation of the annexation of Oudh: some twelve to fourteen thousand men at Cawnpore alone. "No fighting is expected," he wrote, "but I daresay several independent chiefs will not give up their Forts or Independence without having a few shells thrown into [their strongholds]." WL/MD: 23–25 Nov. 1855.

285. William Sleeman reported that the desperation in the countryside was such that his soldiers were tearing the roofs off villagers' huts to provide shelter at their campsites. Sleeman in Lee-Warner, *Life of the Marquis of Dalhousie*, 2:319.

286. Home Miscellaneous, v. 828 in Pemble, *The Raj, the Indian Mutiny, and the Kingdom of Oudh*, p. 95.

287. Sleeman's early career is from Tuker, *The Yellow Scarf*, pp. 1–28. Born in Cornwall in 1788, Sleeman studied Indian languages before enlisting in the Bengal Army, and eventually mastered not only Hindi and Urdu but Persian, Pushtu, and Gurkhali.

288. Kaye, *A History of the Great Revolt*, 1:136nn.

289. Pemble, *The Raj, the Indian Mutiny, and the Kingdom of Oudh*, pp. 96–101.

290. Kaye, *A History of the Great Revolt*, 1:143.

291. Mukherjee, *Awadh in Revolt*, p. 35.

292. Taylor, *A Star Shall Fall*, p. 216.

293. "So our gracious Queen," Dalhousie declared, "has 5,000,000 more subjects and £1,300,000 more revenue than she had yesterday." Pemble, *The Raj, the Indian Mutiny, and the Kingdom of Oudh*, p. 111.

294. Ibid., pp. 92, 99, 100.

295. Yalland, *Traders and Nabobs*, p. 224.

296. Collier, *The Sound of Fury*, p. 71.

297. Horne, *Narrative* (BM); and Bennett, "Ten Months' Captivity."

298. TL, 27 Oct. 1874, p. 8; and Sharar, *Lucknow*, pp. 68–75.

299. Foreign Political Consultations in U.P., 4:776; Duff-Gordon/Lansdowne: 11 Jan. 1854, courtesy of the Earl of Shelburne (there is no record of such a portrait among Phillips's works, which leads me to conclude that Azimullah brought it back with him to India); Lutfullah, *Azimullah*, p. 113; Taylor, *A Star Shall Fall*, p. 60; TL, 17 Sept. 1857, p. 9. (Evidently a check for £50,000 was wired to Azimullah, but he must have been given a good deal of money on his departure from Bithur.) Azimullah maintained his cordial relations with Lucie to the last, and in October 1856 his prince sent her a bolt of kincob; a diamond, emerald and pearl necklace; and the following letter: "Dear Madam, Permit me to express to you my most sincere gratitude for the extreme kindness that you have shown my representative during his stay in England. Since the death of my father H.H. the late Peshwa nobody else has obliged me so much as you have done and I do hope that your ladyship will not fail to command my services in this country and ever think me to be / Your Ladyship's most respectful Serv. / Nana Sahib."

300. Misra, *Nana Saheb Peshwa*, p. 201nn.

301. E. M. Martineau/John Kaye: 20 Oct. 1864, HM 725 (OIOC).

302. The only documented letter from Azimullah to Nana Sahib was the one Nana showed Lang during his visit, but there must have been many others. See Lang, *Wanderings in India*, pp. 110–19.

303. In 1849 a prisoner at Bithur named Kishen Dixit sent a petition to the Commissioner, in which he accused Nana Sahib of conspiring against the Company. He claimed that Nana had imprisoned him to shut him up, and produced a document purporting to be a letter from Nana Sahib to Golab Singh, the restive Maharaja of Jammu and Kashmir. But the Commissioner declared the letter a forgery and supported Kishen Dixit's imprisonment, though he hoped that "no vindictive feelings toward the prisoner should lead to his harsh or improper treatment." Sitaram Bawa, one of Nana Sahib's emissaries, deposed before the Judicial Commissioner of Mysore that his employer had, as Kishen Dixit claimed, written to Golab Singh, who received his letter from the hands of a fruit seller [Mohammed Ali?], and that Nana Sahib had not only written to but received a reply from the Imperial Government of Russia, which advised him that they could not assist him unless he took Delhi. U.P., 1:12, 307.

304. Proprietory landholders, similar to zemindars except that in Oudh they were originally subcontractors who collected revenues on behalf of large landholders.

305. Many of the Bengal Army's native soldiers came from the districts hardest hit by the new British regime. Mukherjee, *Awadh in Revolt*, pp. 57, 62.

306. Heber, *Narrative*, 2:106. There appears to be no record of where native soldiers were recruited, but Mukherjee (*Awadh in Revolt*, p. 78) cites a list of deserting noncommissioned officers of the 22nd N.I., 95 percent of which came from this area. It may be, however, that this list reflects simply the increased disaffection in these areas or the traditional recruiting ground of a particular regiment, rather than a general pattern of recruitment.

307. Edwards, *Personal Adventures*, p. 70.

308. She was not the king's chief wife (whose first name, Khas, meant "favorite"), but Hazrat Mahal's first name, "Highness," indicates that she was highly regarded, and her last name, "Palace," meant she was so highly regarded as to warrant a house of her own. Sharar, *Lucknow*, p. 251nn.

309. Pemble, *The Raj, the Indian Mutiny, and the Kingdom of Oudh*, pp. 210–11; Sharar, *Lucknow*, pp. 64, 251.

310. Keene, *A Servant of 'John Company,'* pp. 162–63. In his paraphrase of the letter Keene states that the Begum had recently returned from London, but Keene's memory must have failed him. Hazrat Mahal does not appear to have gone to London. Wajid Ali Shah's mother headed the delegation, and, ashamed of her profligate son's complete capitulation to the British, died in Paris after the Mutiny. See Sharar, *Lucknow*, p. 70.

311. U.P., 1:302; and Lutfullah, *Azimullah*, p. 113.

312. N.W.P., P.D.P., Jan.–June 1864: 30 Jan. 1864, P.D.A., pp. 19–20.

313. U.P., 1:12.

314. Trevelyan, *Cawnpore*, p. 54. In his *Cawnpore Narrative* Sherer states there were three guns, but the *Times* correspondent in Calcutta reported that after denying the Nana Sahib his father's pension, Lord Dalhousie had allowed him to keep six guns "at his castellated palace at Bithoor. These guns turned the scale against our unhappy countrymen at Cawnpore." TL, 2 Sept. 1857.

315. Gupta, *Baji Rao II*, p. 130.

316. After 1819 the Native Cavalry regiments were called "Light Cavalry," but for clarity's sake I have reverted to the original term. Mollo, *The Indian Army*, p. 17; Gimlette, *A Postscript*, pp. 39–45.

317. Diary of Nunne Nawab. Rissaldar Major Bhowani Singh, was also a Hindu.

318. Jehanigar Khan, sowar of the 2nd Native Infantry in Lucknow Collectorate Records in U.P., 4:501–2.

319. Trevelyan, *Cawnpore*, p. 54; Deposition of Kunhye Pershad.

320. Raikes, *Notes on the Revolt*, pp. 18–19.

321. Keene, *A Servant of 'John Company,'* pp. 162–63.

322. A junior clerk named Henry Kavanagh noticed about the new commissioner that "a good straightforward native gentleman was sure to be treated with courtesy, and with a cordiality that filled him with pleasure; but woe to the intriguer or deceiver—these, Captain Lawrence met with a stern aspect, and sent sneaking away in fear and trembling."

323. Gubbins, *Account*, pp. 30–31.

324. Kavanagh, *How I Won the Victoria Cross*, pp. 3–4.

325. WM/MWL: 22 Dec. 1827 and 12 May 1833.

326. Hodson, *List*, pp. 54–55.

327. WL/MD: 7 Nov. 1851.

328. *Life in Bombay* in Edwardes, *Bound to Exile*, p. 41.

329. Maitland, *Letters from Madras by a Lady* in ibid., p. 40.

330. Roberts, *Scenes and Characteristics of Hindustan*, 1:28–29.

331. Lalik Ram is mentioned in a fragmentary memo written by Henry Drage in the fall of 1857 and included among the Lindsay Family Papers.

332. Roberts, *Scenes and Characteristics of Hindustan*, 1:61. Nevertheless, Roberts believed that ladies had a solemn duty to improve the morality of cantonments. "Where the ladies

of a station patronize public amusements, and encourage social visiting," she wrote, "the gentlemen seldom or ever abandon themselves to gambling, or any other destructive pursuit; and a ready concurrence with any scheme proposed for the furtherance of harmless entertainment, forms one of the best means of keeping society together." Roberts, *The East India Voyager,* p. 31.

333. Haycock graduated from Bishop's College in 1850 and was ordained two years after the death of his wife Ellen in 1852 when the Bishop of Madras passed through the North-Western Provinces. Kay in Sherring, *The Indian Church during the Great Rebellion,* p. 167.

334. Willis in ibid., p. 178.

335. TL, 7 Sept. 1857.

336. The bishop's note is from a memo by Captain W. R. Moorsom written in August 1857.

337. No one could understand the Anglo-Indian's delight in receiving mail "but those who have been for years in a foreign land, separated from all the dear objects of youth, those who still hold with freshness the memory of past days, who feel that neither time nor change of circumstances have lessened the heart's warm glow. It is in those moments that we forget that seas divide us, and that we may never in this world meet again." Clemons, *Manners and Customs,* p. 54.

338. P. G. Thacker, Spink & Company advertisement in backpaper of Keene's *Handbook.*

339. Long and Stocqueler, *British Social Life in Ancient Calcutta,* pp. 200–201. (They added a third variety of spin: namely the legitimate and illegitimate daughters, many of them orphaned and Eurasian, of Company men.)

340. Keene, *A Servant of 'John Company,'* p. 80.

341. Long and Stocqueler, *British Social Life in Ancient Calcutta,* p. 24.

342. Roberts, *Scenes and Characteristics of Hindustan,* 1:14.

343. Edwardes, *Bound to Exile,* p. 34.

344. Their mothers "thought they had better roam/Than die, *perhaps,* old Maids at home;/Where men considered it so rash/To think of Hymen without cash,/That many an accomplished fair,/Saw little hope of marrying there." Whereas in India they might: "Select their own protectors/Amongst the Judges and Collectors,/And if they wished might e'en aspire/To marry in a rank still higher;/Perhaps, oh charming words to utter,/Be *Burrah Beebees* of Calcutta!" Dewar, *Bygone Days in India,* pp. 116–17.

345. LL/MD: 1 Sept. 1856. It began to dawn on the Lindsays that they too might be unhappy in England; certainly they would not be able to live in the style to which they had become accustomed in India. Though they wanted their children to acquire an English education, not to mention English accents, Lilly worried that they could not afford to live in Rochester. "I fancy our means must take us to Scotland if nothing else will, indeed we sometimes feel rather frightened by the letters Indian friends write about want of means & fear we are trying it at too low a figure." Nevertheless, she insisted, "we do not waver in our resolution." LL/MD: 6 Nov. 1856.

346. Carey in Long and Stocqueler, *British Social Life in Ancient Calcutta,* p. 66.

347. Robert Henry Dunlop, a civil servant at Meerut, used to make the band play on the verandah owing to his "insurmountable objection to dancing in the presence of 'niggers.'" Dyson, *A Various Universe,* p. 323.

348. Roberts, *Scenes and Characteristics of Hindustan,* 1:20, 46.

349. His name has a certain ring to it: Balcarres Dalyrimple Wardlaw Ramsay. He was married to one of Lilly's cousins.

350. Ramsay, *Rough Recollections,* 1:264.

351. WL/MD: 7 Dec. 1856.

352. They were never honored for their part in this battle. By an oversight the 1st Madras European Regiment was authorized to put "Condore" on their colors despite the fact that not a man from that regiment took part. The government had evidently confused them with the 1st Bengal Native Infantry, but the mistake was never corrected.

353. Mason, *A Matter of Honour*, pp. 79–80, 88–90, 97.

354. Cardew, *Bengal Native Army*, pp. 86, 153, 164.

355. At the heroic but unsuccessful siege of Bhurtpore in 1805 the colors of the 31st were so torn by Jat gunfire that it was decided to cremate them and replace them with new silks in the morning. The two standards were left to spend a night together, so that the honor of the old might be transferred to the new. But when it came time to cremate the old standard it could not be found, and would not reappear until 21 years later when the descendants of the sepoys who died at Bhurtpore returned under Lord Combermere to take the fort, and, rushing through a breach in the doomed fort's walls, drew forth pieces of the old standard they had lovingly preserved and tied them to the new colors to honor "the fruitless valor of their fathers." Mason, *A Matter of Honour*, pp. 23, 66–67, 129–30.

356. Thomson, *The Story of Cawnpore*, p. 109.

357. Ewart's fluency derives from his listing in Hodson, which shows that he served as interpreter to various regiments beginning in 1835. Ewart's strict discipline is surmised from his death at the hands of his men, who mocked his stern parade–ground manner before cutting him down. Ewart addresses his sepoys as his "children" in Kaye, *A History of the Great Revolt*, 2:307.

358. TL, 16 Oct. 1857, P. 7.

359. He was born November 28, 1826, sixteen years before his parents married.

360. Three of Godfrey's brothers—Frederick, Patrick, and Robert—went on to become major generals. Taylor, genealogy distributed to a meeting of Kanpur historians in January 1993.

361. Supple had been a classmate of Burney of the artillery, who would die with him in the uprising. Hardcastle/ASW: 13 Nov. 1992.

362. Diary of Nunne Nawab.

363. R. Bernal Osborne in TL, 26 Sept. 1857, p. 10.

364. Caroline Lindsay/Jane Boase: 5 Feb. 1857.

365. LL/ML: 1 Aug. 1856, Lindsay Papers.

366. Thomson, *The Story of Cawnpore*, pp. 140–41.

367. Morris, *The Story of Cawnpore* (OIOC).

368. Wheeler/Lawrence: 4 June 1857. BM.

369. LL/MD: 20 Sept. 1856, Lindsay Papers.

370. Drawing by Reverend Moore in BM.

371. Lee-Warner, *Life of the Marquis of Dalhousie*, 2:203.

372. Hill in *The Story of the Cawnpore Mission*, p. 37.

373. "Private houses," says the *Cawnpore District Gazetteer*, "depended on their own sweepers, who emptied all filth into large excavations in the suburbs. Sullage found its way into the streets, and we are told that before drains were made the state of the city was disgusting. . . . Many large excavations filled with decomposing animal and vegetable matter added to the general impurity of the atmosphere, matters being rendered worse by the narrowness of the streets and the congestion of the population, factors which cause grave concern even at the present [1926] day." Nevill, *Cawnpore*, p. 175–76.

374. MDP, 30 Jan. 1857, nos. 77–78 (NAI).

375. Strachey/Oldfield in MDP, 16 Jan. 1857, nos. 324–25, NAI.

376. MDP, 30 Jan. 1857, nos. 77–78 (NAI). Shepherd's map of the military cantonments shows nine such barracks; the 56th and 53rd N.I. were stationed close to each other at the easternmost extremity of the cantonments, the lines of the 1st (Gordon Wheeler's regiment) were over a mile off toward the general's house. The 2nd Native Cavalry were stationed south of the 1st N.I. lines, half a mile from Generalgunj, and were not mentioned in the quartermaster's order, probably because they were already in what he considered a suitable position.

377. The Jack memorial at All Souls gives his name as Andrew William Thomas Jack, but in *Fasti Ecclesiae Scoticanae* (1:367) his middle names are reversed.

378. DNB and Cardew, *Bengal Native Army*, pp. 215, 220. In 1846 Jack had received a medal fighting the Sikhs at Aliwal, and succeeded in dragging artillery into position for the siege of Kangra against obstacles even Wheeler had deemed insurmountable. He was again decorated for his bravery at Chilianwalla and Goojerat, receiving a medal and two clasps and, like Wheeler, the ceremonial title of Commander of the Bath.

379. DNB.

380. Portrait in Yalland, *Traders and Nabobs*, p. 264.

381. This was "hunting money" known as the Sind Allowance. Lee-Warner, *Life of the Marquis of Dalhousie*, pp. 327–28. The 13th, 22nd, 32nd, 41st, and 66th all manifested various degrees of disaffection. The 66th actually mutinied and some tried to seize the fort at Govindghar, where they had just been stationed.

382. Higginbotham, *Men Whom India Has Known*.

383. Lawrence had first distinguished himself as a revenue surveyor, and, despite his distaste for the intrigue of native courts, later served with distinction as Resident at Nepal and Lahore. Though he had opposed the annexation of the Punjab, he had been so instrumental in the defeat of the Sikhs that Dalhousie appointed him head of a board of administration that was to govern the new territory. He was a foe of Westernization and battled with Dalhousie to protect the rights of the Sikh aristocracy. Two years later the Marquis replaced him with Lawrence's more amenable brother John and sent Henry off to supervise the royal houses of Rajputana.

384. As far back as 1843 Lawrence had envisioned a rebel force making quick work of the Company's feeble defenses at Delhi. "Let this happen on June 2nd," he theorized, "and does any sane man doubt that twenty-four hours would swell the hundreds of rebels into thousands, and in a week every ploughshare in the Delhi States would be turned into a sword? And when a sufficient [British] force had been mustered, which would not be effected within a month, should we not then have a more difficult game to play than Clive had at Plassey or Wellington at Assaye? We should then be literally striking for our existence at the most inclement season of the year, with the prestige of our name tarnished. . . . The enemy who cannot reach us with his bayonets, can touch us more fatally if he lead us to distrust ourselves, and rouse our subjects to distrust us; and we shall do his work for him if we show that our former chivalrous bearing is fled."

385. Morris, *Heaven's Command*, p. 231.

386. Sitaram Bawa in Kaye, *A History of the Great Revolt*, 1:645–46. This theory at least accounts for the story that lotus blossoms were in circulation at this time, when in fact lotus blossoms were not in season. William Edwards of Budaon thought the chupatties originated at Barrackpore, but Theophilus Metcalf and the Emperor of Delhi's physician believed that the chupatties began in Lucknow. William Howard Russell, cited in the *Friend of India*, 10 Mar. 1859, mentioned a story similar to the story about Dassa Bawa, except that the prince in question was Raja Madhoo Singh. See Kaye, *A History of the Great Revolt*, 1:632, 636–37; Gupta, *Nana Saheb*, p. 34.

387. "The leaders and promoters of the great rebellion, whoever they may have been," recalled William Edwards "knew well the inflammable condition . . . of the rural society in the North–Western Provinces, and they therefore sent among them the chupaties, as a kind of fiery cross, to call them to action."

388. Cave-Browne in Kaye, *A History of the Great Revolt*, 1:638.

389. U.P., 1:391.

390. Ibid., 1:389–90.

391. Mason, *A Matter of Honour*, pp. 264–65. Indeed, the cartridges were "abundantly offensive to the Feringhees as well as the faithful," recalled Lieutenant Thomson of the 53rd Native Infantry, "and from the nauseous odor which accompanied them quite equal to breeding a pestilence, if not adequate to the task which has been attributed to them of causing the mutiny." Thomson, *The Story of Cawnpore*, p. 25.

392. Kaye, *A History of the Great Revolt*, 1:652.

393. Hearsey in Martin, *The Indian Mutiny*, 2:137.

394. Hibbert, *The Great Mutiny*, p. 64.

395. Despite his plea that heavy doses of hemp and opium had simply gotten the better of him, Pandy was hanged. "Pandy" became synonymous among the British with Indian mutineers.

396. Mason, *A Matter of Honour*, pp. 269–73; Hibbert, *The Great Mutiny*, pp. 65–69.

397. Deposition of Sheo Churran Das.

398. Kaye, *A History of the Great Revolt*, 1:242nn.

399. Trevelyan, *Cawnpore*, p. 98.

400. Wheeler in Pearse, *The Hearseys*, pp. 396–400.

401. Halliday letters courtesy of Dr. Colin Forbes, plus a letter courtesy of Raleigh Trevelyan. The letter numbers referred to below were assigned by Dr. Forbes, and the dates refer to the specific entries within the letters, some of which were written in journal form. See also Colesworthy-Grant, *Anglo-Indian Domestic Life*; Dewar, *Bygone Days*; MacMillan, *Women of the Raj*.

402. Charlotte Mary Wright, courtesy of Peter Wright in the *Journal* of the Dalwood Restoration Society, no. 9, Sept. 1987. Mrs. Wright evidently kept a letter written by Emma as a young girl reporting the gypsy's prophesy. Mrs. Wright also mentioned that Emma married Willie "after much opposition on the part of her family." Emma Laetetia Wyndham was named after her mother Emma and her father's sister, Laetetia Wyndham, who married Charles Codrington.

403. The 56th had been raised in 1815 as the 2nd Battalion of the 28th Regiment and when the Presidency armies were reorganized in 1824 became the 56th Bengal Native Infantry.

404. Haughty and overconfident, sepoys were especially susceptible to the flattery and humble deceptions of the brotherhood of stranglers, and it was the disappearance of sepoys on leave that led eventually to the Company's campaign against Thuggee and the murderous brotherhood's downfall in the 1840s.

405. Kaye, *A History of the Great Revolt*, 1:276.

406. Halliday Letter 85: 22 Feb. 1857.

407. Halliday Letter 18: 12 June 1853.

408. Memsahibs were advised to ensure that their cooks were using "wholesome" clay pots and cooking vessels by going into the kitchen every few months and breaking them with a stick. Clemons, *Manners and Customs*, p. 189.

409. Halliday Letter 60: 20 Oct. 1855.

410. "Some bearers in Calcutta will not snuff a candle if it be on the dinner-table," wrote Fanny Parks, "but a khidmatgar having put it on the ground, the bearer will snuff it, when the other man replaces it." Parks, *Wanderings in India*, 1:144.

411. "The [Santals] used bows, arrows, and large sharp axes," wrote a sepoy who fought against them, "but they always dispersed when we fired on them."

412. Halliday Letter 60: 12 Oct. 1855.

413. Halliday Letter 68: 12 Feb. 1856.

414. Halliday Letter 85: 22 Feb. 1857. Even though some milestones dated back to the Moghuls, they were regarded as symbols of European rule, and in many places during the Mutiny the rebels—some of them under the misapprehension that the stones had something to do with the telegraph—would dig them up and break them into pieces.

415. Halliday Letter 94: 21 Aug. 1857.

416. Halliday Letter 86: 1 March 1857.

417. Kaye, *A History of the Great Revolt*, 1:479.

418. A primary source for this chapter is Murdoch's *The Indian Missionary Manual*, an encyclopedic compilation of advice to missionaries assembled from hundreds of sources, both British and American.

419. For such a desultory station Fatehgarh was unusually well served by two historians: C. L. Wallace and Lieutenant Colonel F. R. Cosens. Writing in the 1930s they produced *Fatehgarh and the Mutiny*, the definitive treatment of the uprising there, and two years later Wallace wrote a municipal history of the station titled *Fatehgarh Camp: 1777–1857*. Both books are marked by meticulous research and a vigorous style. Wallace was Magistrate and Collector of Farrukhabad District; Cosens served with the 10th Battalion of the 7th Rajput Regiment, also known as the "Lucknow Regiment."

420. Wallace, *Fatehgarh Camp*, p. 1

421. Including that of a Captain Marsack, the disputatious illegitimate son of none other than George II.

422. In 1796 Sir John Shore wrote that the officers at Fatehgarh were "more unanimous in adopting violent resolutions than those at Cawnpore."

423. Kaye, *A History of the Great Revolt*, 3:292.

424. Probably the most incorrigible bandit of all time was Prithi Singh of Fatehgarh district. Even after both his hands and his feet were chopped off and his eyes gouged out by a local zemindar, he persisted somehow in holding people up on the public roads until the government finally confiscated all his property in 1809. Wallace, *Fatehgarh Camp*, pp. 14–15, 200.

425. By the dawn of the nineteenth century the Nawab Vizier had fallen so far behind in his annual contributions of 2,300,000 rupees to the maintenance of the Company's troops that he was forced to cede to the British vast holdings that included Gorakhpur, Rohilkhand, and the Doab. His district governor, the Nawab of Farrukhabad, in turn ceded his powers to the Company in exchange for a pension. But almost immediately the British had to protect their acquisitions against the great Holkar, who set out from Indore to attack western Bengal and, if possible, chase the Feringhee from Calcutta itself. For two November days in 1804 he briefly occupied Fatehgarh Fort, before he and his inebriated troops were defeated in a surprise attack by the 8th Royal Irish Dragoons and eventually chased off to Lahore.

426. Taylor, *Student's Manual*, p. 68.

427. *Hindoo Patriot* in U.P., 5:915.

428. Thornhill Papers (OIOC). The verse was later found in the wreckage of Fatehgarh Fort, where it must have found an unappreciative audience among the rebels. Three out of the six Thornhills serving in India at the time died in the Mutiny, two of them murdered. Cosens and Wallace, *Fatehgarh*, p. 17.

429. Harriet survived the Mutiny and for the next thirty-five years lived in Fatehgarh on a small pension, pathetically trying to win back the affection and respect of the European community with little gifts of sweets and mangoes. She died at eighty-one in 1892.

430. Wallace, *Fatehgarh Camp*, p. 167; Cosens and Wallace, *Fatehgarh*, pp. 10–13; and Taylor, *A Star Shall Fall*, pp. 123–31.

431. One landlord remembered that Probyn had always treated him "as a gentleman, gave him a seat, and conversed with him with affability."

432. Kaye, *A History of the Great Revolt*, 3:293.

433. The Board had previously been called the Western Foreign Missionary Society, which was founded in Pittsburgh, Pennsylvania, in 1833. In several accounts the American missionaries at Fatehgarh are said to have been sponsored by the American Board of Missions, but the Board of Foreign Missions of the Presbyterian Church in the United States was a separate entity. By 1850 there were twelve major Protestant missionary societies at work in India, five of them American: The American Board of Commissioners for Foreign Missions, The American Baptist Board of Foreign Missions, The Board of Foreign Missions of the Presbyterian Church in the United States, The Free Will Baptist Foreign Missionary Society, and The Lutheran Missionary Society.

434. Warren, *A Glance Backward*, pp. 13–14.

435. Among the idealistic young American clergymen who came to India in the 1830s was my own great–great–grandfather, Ferdinand De Wilton Ward of Rochester, New York, who thus described his duties in his 1850 tract, *India and the Hindus*.

436. Dyson, *A Various Universe*, pp. 165–66, 231.

437. Murdoch, *Indian Missionary Manual*, p. 346

438. Allen, ed., *A Soldier of the Company*, p. 44. When the first Anglican bishop arrived in India, the Brahmins of Calcutta feared that he might be so religious and virtuous a man that he would carry all of India before him. So they delegated one of their number to scout him out. The Brahmin returned to report that they had nothing to fear from the Bishop for he lived in a mansion, rode in a carriage, and practiced no austerities. Field notes.

439. Murdoch, *Indian Missionary Manual*, p. 215.

440. Warren, *A Glance Backward*, pp. 80–82, 108, 115, 141–43.

441. Ward, *India and the Hindus*, pp. 292–94.

442. Missionaries who were themselves permitted an occasional alcoholic beverage for medicinal purposes were advised never to serve liquor to their Indian Christian guests. "Mere nominal Christians are not more honest than heathens, and sometimes drink, which the latter as a rule, do not. Drunken nominal Christians ought above all others to be avoided." At Cawnpore Samuel Greenway baptized a compositor named Husain Bakhsh, a Persian who proved "a drunkard, quarrelsome, and dishonest." After Campbell's colleague, Reverend Warren, fired him for drinking, he returned to Cawnpore, where Reverend Perkins refused to baptize him. Murdoch, *Indian Missionary Manual*, p. 63.

443. M. A. Laird in Dyson, *A Various Universe*, p. 167.

444. One of its architects was the father of Field Marshall Lord Roberts. It was mined by the mutineers in 1857. Wallace, *Fatehgarh Camp*, pp. 178–81.

445. Ibid., p. 222.

446. Ibid., pp. 14, 46, 216.

447. Warren, *A Glance Backward*, pp. 68, 246.

448. The mission thrived at a time when Fatehgarh itself had fallen on hard times. The golden age of indigo planting had ended around 1840, probably as a result of overproduction, and land in the district became so useless that it could not be sold off. Seaton, *From Cadet to Colonel*, p. 76; Wallace, *Fatehgarh Camp*, pp. 207, 223.

449. "One of the first lessons which an 'old Indian' seeks to impress upon a griffin, as they sit together after dinner, with cheroots and brandy and water is, 'Don't take native Christian servants, they are all great rascals.'" Murdoch, *Indian Missionary Manual*, p. 4.

450. Not that Americans were incapable of fanaticism. In September 1857, when Delhi was retaken by the British, the magistrate at Saharunpore had to threaten an American missionary named Woodside with imprisonment before he would stop haranguing the Moslems of the station. Butler, *The Land of the Veda*, pp. 424, 427; Robertson, *District Duties*, pp. 172–73.

451. Portrait, AC 1925, Dept. of History, Presbyterian Church (U.S.A.).

452. Warren, *A Glance Backward*, p. 69.

453. "John Edgar Freeman and the Indian Mutiny," *The Presbyterian*, 9 Oct. 1912, p. 10.

454. Sherring, *The Indian Church during the Great Rebellion*, p. 121.

455. The nineteen were comprised of two orphan schools, seven bazaar schools, and ten village schools supported by Duleep Singh. Martin, *The Indian Empire*, 2:322.

456. Born in Cadiz, Ohio, in 1833, the slight and high-strung Johnson was a graduate of Jefferson College and Western Theological Seminary in Pennsylvania. Immediately upon graduation he had married Amanda Gill, a professor's daughter educated in England. Within two months the two had set sail for India, arriving at Fatehgarh in December 1855. Butler, *The Land of the Veda*, p. 293, and Cosens and Wallace, *Fatehgarh*, p. 33. The names of the wives of Johnson, Campbell, and McMullin are from Alter, *In the Doab*, p. 113; Hunter, "A Mutiny Martyr," *The Presbyterian Banner*, 6 July 1911, pp. 12–13.

457. Sherring, *The Indian Church during the Great Rebellion*, p. 121.

458. Butler, *The Land of the Veda*, p. 293.

459. Gordon, *Our India Mission*, p. 85.

460. Murdoch, *Indian Missionary Manual*, p. 586.

461. Blunt, *Christian Tombs*, p. 115.

462. Keene, *A Servant of 'John Company,'* pp. 101–2.

463. One of the frustrations of the job was hacking through the verbiage of Indian nobility. Here, for instance, is the Raja of Dholpur addressing the Lieutenant-Governor of Agra in a letter sprinkled with gold leaf and bordered with flowers: "Nawab Sahib, of high dignity, appreciator of merit, affectionate and kind to me, your humble servant, may your dignity increase! After paying such respects as a suppliant should offer, and expressing my desire for the honour of serving you (your service having the virtue of changing the base into the noble), which is the dearest wish of my heart, I beg to submit to your exalted mind of sunlight splendour the following information . . ." Muir, *Records*, 1:397.

464. Roberts, *The East India Voyager*, pp. 81–82.

465. "Strange must that man's character be," wrote one, "and dull his sympathies, who, in the midst of occupations like these, does not find his heart accompanying and lightening his labours. He sees the people in their fairest light; he witnesses their ceaseless industry, their contented poverty, their few and simple pleasures, their plain sense of justice, their general faithfulness to their engagements." Bird in Woodruff, *The Men Who Ruled India*, 1:300.

466. Henry Sherer in Keene, *A Servant of 'John Company,'* p. 127.

467. Edwards, *Personal Adventures*, p.17.

468. Hunter, *Annals of Rural Bengal*, p. 243.

469. EB, 11th ed.

470. "There was to my mind always something tragic about Lord Canning's countenance," wrote a civil officer. "The brow was as fine almost as that of his father; but the lower part of his face was weak. There was, too, a look about him of Hamlet distraction: that he, the muser, should have fallen on days demanding masterly action." Sherer, *Daily Life*, pp. 178–79.

471. EB; DNB; Cunningham, *Earl Canning*; and Allen, ed., *A Glimpse of the Burning Plain*. In his private life Canning was not so noble. His wife Charlotte was a humane and empathetic woman, a gifted watercolorist, and former Lady of the Bedchamber to Queen Victoria. But before their departure for India Canning had betrayed her with at least two mistresses; it was even rumored that Canning had been nominated as governor-general by Lucie Duff Gordon's friend Lord Lansdowne in order to "get him away from the spell of his *inamorata*." But the affairs of the Company and the Indian Empire of which Canning would later become the first viceroy precluded such flirtations, and for Lady Canning their last years together were "almost a reminiscence of the perfect happiness of her married life." Allen, ed., *A Glimpse of the Burning Plain*, pp. 8, 158.

472. Stocqueler in Edwardes, *Bound to Exile*, p. 3.

473. Emma Ewart: 18 May 1857.

474. Shepherd, *A Personal Narrative*, p. 26.

475. Emma Ewart: 18 May 1857.

476. Bhatnagar, ed., *Daily Life*, p. 81nn; *Private Correspondence of J. W. Sherer*, p. 13.

477. Woodruff, *The Men Who Ruled India*, 1:356.

478. Martin, *The Indian Empire*, 2:246.

479. Thomson, *The Story of Cawnpore*, p. 16.

480. Ibid.; Mollo, *The Indian Army*, p. 28.

481. Keene, *Fifty-Seven*, p. 71.

482. Thomson, *The Story of Cawnpore*, p. 38; Gimlette, *Postscript*, pp. 168–70.

483. "This shows," wrote Henry Keene, "that ticklish topics were not avoided in intercourse with the men." Keene, *Fifty-Seven*, p. 71.

484. Indeed, a few sepoys of the 53rd had gone to Umballa to receive instruction in the use of the Enfield rifle, and one of them returned with samples of the suspected cartridges to demonstrate that they contained no animal fat. These sepoys had been "amicably received" by their comrades, "and allowed to eat with their own caste." Deposition of Ram Buksh; Thomson, *The Story of Cawnpore*, p. 25.

485. "The writer," said a correspondent to the *Times*, "has seen [Nana Sahib] and shot in his company." TL, 2 Sept. 1857. See also, *The Land of the Veda*, p. 185. It seems to me likely that if Thomson of the 3rd attended parties at Bithur his commanding officer must have as well, and that Charles Hillersdon's readiness to accept Nana's offers of help must have been predicated on some past association and not simply blind desperation. Lydia Hillersdon: May 16 in TL, 10 Sept. 1857, p. 7; Thomson, *The Story of Cawnpore*, p. 48; Bennett, "Ten Months' Captivity." Amelia does not specifically mention the Hillersdons, but they would have topped the list of Nana's invitees.

486. Captain Montagu, who would flee Cawnpore just before the uprising, only to lose his children from "want and exposure" en route from Allahabad to Calcutta.

487. ILN, no. 882, vol. xxxi, 10 Oct. 1857, p. 354.

488. Read, *India and Its People*, p. 73.

489. Chalwin, Letters, courtesy of Zoë Yalland.

490. Gough, *Old Memories*, p. 6.

491. Hillersdon in TL, 10 Sept. 1857, p. 7.

492. Sherer, *Daily Life*, p. 7.

493. Muir, *Records of the Intelligence Department*, 1:4.

494. "The Story of Miss Sutherland."

495. Hill, *The Story of the Cawnpore Mission*, p. 46.

496. Louisa Chalwin: 11 April 1857, courtesy of Zoë Yalland.

497. Martin, *The Indian Empire*, 2:245–46.

498. Butler, *Land of the Veda*, p. 294.

499. WL/MD: 4, 7 May 1857.

500. Louisa Chalwin: 11 April 1857, courtesy of Zoë Yalland; obituary of Henrietta Vibart, collection of Dr. Colin Forbes; Vibart family tree, courtesy of Alan C. Hardcastle.

501. The Vibart's son Edward later married Emma's cousin, Emily Trevelyan. The relationship between the Vibarts and the Hallidays was close. Edward's sister, Henrietta, who with two other Vibart daughters spent the period of the Mutiny in England, spent the rest of her life at the Hallidays' estate at Chapel Cleeve, caring for Willie's grieving mother and playing the organ at the parish church every Sunday under a stained-glass memorial to the Hallidays and the Vibarts. She died in 1926 at the age of eighty-seven. Henrietta Vibart's undated obituary, courtesy of Dr. Colin Forbes.

502. Emma Halliday/Jane (Halliday): 20 May 1857, courtesy of Raleigh Trevelyan.

503. Lieutenant Moorsom, Lindsay papers.

504. Leasor, *The Red Fort*, pp. 17–93; Hibbert, *The Great Mutiny*, pp. 75–119; Morris, *Heaven's Command*, pp. 218–29.

505. Aberigh-Mackay, *Twenty-One Days in India*, pp. 119, 121, 123.

506. Quoted in Long and Stocqueler, *British Social Life in Ancient Calcutta*, p. 227.

507. Even after the Mutiny, in which they proved utterly loyal and among the first of the rebels' victims, the deputy adjutant general declared that "half-castes" as he called them, were fit only to serve as musicians, owing to their "want of stamina." And native soldiers were "for the future" not to have anything to do with "a gun or its arrangement in the field." MDP, 8 Jan. 1858, nos. 149–150, NAI.

508. "Cranny" was evidently derived from *Karanah*, Hindi for the mixed-caste children of *Sudra* women and *Vaisya* men. Yule and Burnell, *Hobson-Jobson*, p. 273.

509. Most genealogical information regarding Jonah Shepherd is from material kindly provided by Keith Shepherd, from which I have made a number of assumptions. It seems to me likely that John married a native woman, as there were very few European women

available to English soldiers in India at the time of his young manhood. There were only about two dozen ladies in Calcutta in 1780. One Miss Campbell had been so bold as to proceed to Calcutta without a Company permit, and upon her arrival she was sent back to England. Three other ladies were refused permits because the directors believed there were enough ladies at Calcutta as it was. "The Court allowed no one out to India without a pass, and were rather chary of increasing the number of European ladies." (Long and Stocqueler, *British Social Life in Ancient Calcutta*, pp. 13, 47.) I therefore believe that James was Eurasian. At the time of James's enlistment some Eurasians joined the Company's army as sergeants: the rank of quartermaster sergeant, with its clerkish aspects, would have been regarded as suitable for the son of a Company soldier. See Spear, *The Nabobs*, p. 64. James retired to Cawnpore in 1837 and died four years later in Lucknow, where he was buried.

510. Jonah was the same age as Nana Sahib. Shepherd, *A Personal Narrative*, p. 67; appendix A, p. x.

511. Shepherd, *England's Great Mission*.

512. Jonah once asked another officer whether he would prevent Wheler from preaching to his regiment. "I shall," replied the officer. "I will not have him near my men." "Well," Jonah told him, "you must take the consequence. Remember that he is doing the work of God, and if a punishment is sent by the Almighty for your so doing, I shall not be surprised." "Well," replied the officer, "I will risk that." Wheler became a hero to the evangelicals of England, but others took a dim view of his proselytizing, which they believed contributed at the worst possible time to the native troops' suspicion that the Company was out to convert them. "The gallant colonel," said the *Illustrated London News*, "had entirely missed his calling." Wheler was eventually censured by Lord Canning. Shepherd, *England's Great Mission*. p. 15; ILN, no. 872, vol. xxxi, 8 Aug. 1857, p. 154.

513. Aberigh-Mackay, *Twenty-One Days in India*, p. 121.

514. The date of his marriage is derived from Shepherd's statement on p. 47 of his *Personal Narrative* that one of his children was killed on June 18, his seventh wedding anniversary; he describes his wife on p. 8.

515. Her kindness is testified to by the character of her child Polly, and by the unusual devotion of her ayah, Thakurani.

516. Ellen's age at the time of her marriage is derived from her age—twenty-two years, six months—at the time of her death in June 1857.

517. Shepherd says that Ellen was of "European parentage," but had she been entirely European (by which he may in any case have meant Portuguese ancestry, which by this time was sometimes a euphemism for Eurasian) he would not have gone on to remark about her fairness. It was extremely unusual for European girls in the 1840s to marry Eurasian men; had Ellen been entirely European, it seems likely that Shepherd would have stated it more emphatically, for he cared about these distinctions more than we should. Probably her father was European and her mother Indian or Eurasian.

518. Nevill, *Cawnpore*, p. 31.

519. One was founded by a banker and commissariat contractor named Ram Narain, after whom one of Cawnpore's bazaars is still named, but his heir was a sterile dimwit, and the family's fortunes rapidly declined. Another clan was founded by Lalla Thantinal, whose son Sheo Prasad (often spelled "Pershad" in contemporary accounts) was a *khazanchi* or treasurer at various government stations. At his office at Sursyea Ghat, Sheo Prasad had a lucrative lock on the local manufacture of "gentlemen's dresses, caps, &c." as well as coats and uniforms for the Cawnpore garrison. A third family was that of Lalla Ajodhya Prasad, on whose behalf John Lang had successfully sued the East India Company. Dr. Munishwar Nigam.

520. Ishwari's brother Joti Prasad of Agra was one of the wealthiest men in India and in a separate suit filed on his behalf by John Lang claimed that the East India Company owed him thirty million rupees that he had loaned in order to finance the Afghan War. The case

was a great scandal, for not only did the Company try to wriggle out of paying him his due, they forced him to loan additional funds for the First Sikh War and, when he pressed his suit, prosecuted him for fraud and forgery. He was cleared of all charges and the Company condemned from the bench. A portrait of Ishwari Prasad showed a fat man with a fancy mustache and one of those odd donut–shaped caps the Mahajans of the time affected; a descendant described him as looking like "a typical capitalist." Grant, *Cassell's History of India*, 2:184–85; Kailash Nath Wahal.

521. His house stood on the current site of Indira Gandhi Park. Nanak Chand records two occasions when high British officials played evening billiards at Ishwari Prasad's house. The Cawnpore *zilla* (district) court records at the National Archives record many cases involving local Mahajuns, including several brought by and against Nanak Chand himself.

522. Dr. Munishwar Nigam; Mr. Kailash Nath Wahal. (In my novel *The Blood Seed* I mistakenly portrayed Nanak Chand as a Bengali babu.)

523. Ishwari Prasad to Beadon: 28 Jan. 1858 in Sen, *Eighteen Fifty-Seven*, pp. 164–5.

524. During the last one hundred years of British rule in India the incorruptibility of district magistrates was an article of faith (though in remote stations there were evidently exceptions). If the virtue of British justice was impartiality, the virtue of Indian justice was flexibility and accommodation. The result was that though many Indians preferred to be heard before British magistrates, at least as many found them unduly harsh and brittle.

525. By 1929 this was "no longer the case owing to the diminution in the volume of the water as the result of the demands on the rivers for the supply of irrigation canals." Nevill, *Cawnpore*, p. 91.

526. "The pinnace, which, with its three masts and neat rigging, might have passed for a ship; budgerows—the clumsiest of all clumsy things—with their sterns several times higher than their bows; and bauleahs, ugly enough, but lightly skimming along like gondolas, compared with the heavy craft about them; the drifting haystacks, which the country boats appear to be when at a distance, with their native crews straining every nerve upon their summits, and cheering themselves with a wild and not unfrequently sweet song; panchways shooting swiftly down the stream, with one person only on board, who sits at the head steering with his right hand, rowing with his foot, and in the left hand holding his pipe. A ferry-boat constantly plying across the stream adds to the variety of the scene, [with] its motley collection of passengers,—travellers, merchants, and faquirs (sic) camels, bullocks, and horses, all crowded together. The vessels fastened to the shore are so closely packed, that they appeared to be one mass, and, from their thatched roofs and low entrances, might easily pass for a floating village." But by the 1850s this traffic had been somewhat reduced by the completion of the Grand Trunk Road; today it is almost nonexistent. Skinner, *Excursions in India*, 2:244.

527. Most accounts state that the Hardeo Temple at Sati Chowra Ghat, from whose terrace Tatya Tope oversaw the attack on the boats on June 27, was a fishermen's shrine. But Nand Kumar, a resident of Sati Chowra and a descendant of one of the boatmen who supplied vessels to the rebels, states that the Hardeo Temple was in fact a boatmen's temple.

528. The system was changed in 1888. Roberts, *Letters*, p. 5nn.

529. The messengers the British employed at Lucknow were primarily Pasis. "They crossed the Ganges at Cawnpoor," wrote Martin Gubbins, "though the ferry was strictly guarded by the enemy, and conveyed Sir Henry Lawrence's despatches under the enemy's fire into Sir Hugh Wheeler's camp and brought us back his replies." Shepherd, *A Personal Narrative*, p. 6.

530. Captain W. Williamson, D.A C.G., was born in Saugor in 1822 and joined the service in 1843. Blunt, *Christian Tombs and Monuments*, p. 110; Shepherd, *A Personal Narrative*, p. 59.

531. Accounts say that two hundred *maunds* were sent down. In Upper India in 1857 a maund was equal to about eighty-two pounds. Thus this shipment was a little over eight tons.

532. The official account of the flour panic states that it was a sepoy who spread the rumor, but this may have been the generic use of the term, for at the time the sowars of the 2nd Cavalry appear to have been the most active agents of rebellion at Cawnpore. The account is from Carey in U.P., 1:395–96.

533. Shepherd, *A Personal Narrative*, pp. 1–2.

534. Ball, *History of the Indian Mutiny*, 1:75.

535. Bennett, "Ten Months' Captivity."

536. Nanak Chand's diary.

537. Emma Ewart: 18 May 1857 (OIOC).

538. Bennett, "Ten Months' Captivity."

539. Deposition of Kunhye Pershad.

540. Bennett, "Ten Months' Captivity."

541. Deposition of Lalla Bhudree Nath.

542. *The Mofussilite*, 15 May 1857 in Yalland, *Traders and Nabobs*, p. 247.

543. Malleson, *Mutiny of the Bengal Army*, p. 126.

544. Captain LeFons in TL, 16 Sept. 1857 in Noel, *England and India*, p. 54.

545. Lydia Hillersdon in TL, 10 Sept. 1857, p. 7.

546. Statement of Tatya Tope in Kaye, *A History of the Great Revolt*, 2:300nn.

547. Another resident described Wheeler as "old and tried," and "our farseeing energetic General." Anonymous letter in the *Mofussilite*, 29 May 1857.

548. Thomson, *The Story of Cawnpore*, p. 29.

549. Lawrence in Morris, *The Story of Cawnpore*, p. 5 (OIOC).

550. Gough, *Old Memories*, p. 6.

551. Jervis in Hunter, *Annals of Rural Bengal*, p. 248.

552. Gough, *Old Memories*, p. 6.

553. Ball, *The History of the Indian Mutiny*, 1:299.

554. Wheeler/Hearsey: 10 May 1857 in Pearse, *The Hearseys*, pp. 398–400.

555. Emma Larkins in Home/Miscellaneous 814, pp. 302–12 (OIOC).

556. Leasor, *The Red Fort*, p. 17.

557. Parliamentary Return, 9 Feb. 1858, p. 3 in Martin, *The Indian Empire* 2:246.

558. WL/MD: 19 May 1857.

559. KL/JB: 19 May 1857.

560. WL/MD: 19 May 1857.

561. "There was also an optimism displayed by the civil authority [i.e. Colvin at Agra and Hillersdon at Cawnpore] where a prudent caution would have served better, which misled Sir Hugh Wheeler." Morris, *The Story of Cawnpore*, pp. 5–6 (OIOC).

562. Shepherd, *A Personal Narrative*, pp. 2–3.

563. "Cawnpore is an unusually hot station and the fort is the hottest part of it," wrote Lieutenant Colonel William Albert Morris, who was senior medical officer at Cawnpore between 1909 and 1911. "In June the temperature averages over 95°, and some times reaches 112° and even more. . . . General Wheeler was right in preferring his position in Cantonments to the Fort." Morris, *The Story of Cawnpore*, p. 10 (OIOC).

564. Ball, *The History of Indian Mutiny*, 1:300.

565. The often fanciful Joseph Lee contended that Nana Sahib himself helped choose the site of Wheeler's Entrenchment. "The General suggested the magazine, but Nana replied that it was too dangerous and he would take care of it. Then the store-house, where the ordnance stores were, was mentioned. The Nana however remarked that if the building was selected he felt it only right to point out that there was a bungalow close by which commanded it and that should rebels be so minded they could take shelter there and fire upon any exposing themselves. It was then that the General selected the open plain for the entrenchment, where the enemy could have little or no cover afforded them." Lee, *The Indian Mutiny*, p. 8.

566. Shepherd, *A Personal Narrative*, p. 18.

567. Pemble, ed., *Miss Fane in India*, p. 145.

568. Hibbert, *The Great Mutiny*, p. 46.

569. MacMunn, *The Indian Mutiny in Perspective*, p. 100.

570. Yalland, *Traders and Nabobs*, pp. 225, 252–53.

571. Perhaps the other merchants hoped he might represent their concerns to General Wheeler more persuasively because Hay's house stood near the Ganges Canal, within a mile of Wheeler's proposed refuge. Hay Senior had been uniquely upstanding among Cawnpore's merchants, and the only one of his day not to deal in illicit liquor. To auctioneering he had added the equally lucrative trades of undertaking and cabinet-making, probably patterning his furnishings after the heat-cracked and dust-scuffed old pieces that accumulated between auctions at his warehouse. Yalland, *Guide to the Katcheri Cemetery*, p. 33.

572. Shepherd, *A Personal Narrative*, p. 5.

573. A Swiss coachmaker named Frederick Jacobi also approached Wheeler, representing himself and a Eurasian merchant named Eduard Williams who, "seeing this state of things," was considering fleeing with his family to Calcutta. But Wheeler told him "that there was no fear," and advised Jacobi and Williams not to remove their families. Deposition of Eduard Williams.

574. "Well-informed and sympathetic Indians in the city had another story. It was the month of June and the General was well over 70 [*sic*] years. Lady Wheeler they said, knowing that her old soldier would be riding there at all hours in the sun to watch preparations, urged him to decide on the hospital site, close to his own residence pointing out how the Nana had assured him that the sepoys would go straight to Delhi." MacMunn, *The Indian Mutiny in Perspective*, p. 100nn.

575. At Addiscombe engineers had to pass examinations in "logarithms, practical geometry, plane trigonometry, the use of chain box, sextant and theodolite," and after fourteen months of training each was required to prepare "a well-finished plan of a system of fortification drawn by himself." Mason, *A Matter of Honour*, p. 147.

576. EB, 11th ed. 10:680.

577. Testimony of Nerput, *Opium Gomashta*, FSP, in U.P., 4:502–3.

578. Nanak Chand's diary.

579. EB, 11th ed. 10:72. To clear the surrounding terrain, Wheeler ordered a number of other bungalows and native buildings torn down, and set aside £10,000 to compensate their owners. Wheeler might have considered demolishing the half-completed barracks as well, several of which would provide the rebels with sniper's roosts. Cawnpore Collectorate Records in Collier, *The Sound of Fury*, p. 73.

580. Later strategists would argue for the lowest parapets possible—eighteen inches or less—and depended on obstacles like barbed wire for defense against all-out attacks. EB: 11th ed. 10:719.

581. Nerput, *Opium Gomashta*, in U.P., 4:502–3.

582. My source for this is Shepherd's careful map, which shows that the Entrenchment was about 150 by 275 yards.

583. A kind of rampart consisting of two walls jutting out toward the enemy at an angle.

584. According to Nerput the Entrenchment was "undermined," but he was probably referring to the powder magazines. Nerput, *Opium Gomashta*, FSP, in U.P., 4:502–3.

585. Worswick and Embree, *The Last Empire*, p. 17.

586. TL, 29 March 1858, p. 8.

587. Gupta, *Nana Saheb*, p. 56.

588. Thomson, *The Story of Cawnpore*, pp. 54–57.

589. Khoda Bux of the 56th Native Infantry. Deposition of Khoda Bux.

590. Wheeler/Canning: 21 May 1857 in Ball, *The History of the Indian Mutiny*, 1:300.

591. Emma Ewart: May 28, 1857 in TL, 22 Oct. 1857, p. 7. In some accounts Wheeler ordered every officer to sleep in his regiment's lines that night, but Ewart states that only

two officers slept in their regimental quarter guards that night: her husband and Major Hillersdon. Wheeler was evidently so impressed by the effect of this gesture that he subsequently ordered every officer to do the same.

592. Tuker, *The Yellow Scarf*, pp. 156,177. "They were accompanied by a squadron of Gall's Irregular Cavalry and a second of Daly's Cavalry, under command of Lieutenant Barbor, and the brother of the Residency Surgeon, Mr. R. Frayer, volunteered to help him. The party was also accompanied by Captain Fletcher Hayes, military secretary to the Chief Commissioner, who went by Sir Henry Lawrence's desire to communicate personally with Sir Hugh Wheeler." Fletcher Hayes had been one of Sleeman's proteges: a handsome, brilliant man with an extensive oriental library. Everyone agreed he was destined for great things: a worthy successor to men like Sleeman and the Lawrences, and certainly the perfect choice to be Henry Lawrence's eyes and ears at Cawnpore.

593. The tents employed in the *mofussil* were sometimes palatial affairs, and it seems likely that a number of the tents erected at Cawnpore would have been the best available. "All the mofussilites are accustomed to spend a large portion of their time under canvas," wrote Emma Roberts, "and in consequence of the necessity of providing a moveable habitation, there are tents which do not boast more comfort than can be easily imagined by those who are only acquainted with a European marquee. All are double, the interior and exterior covering being about a foot and a half apart; those which are double poled contain several commodious apartments, and are furnished with glass doors to fit into the openings. They are usually lined with some gaily-coloured chintz; the floors are well covered with *settringees*, and they have a convenient space enclosed at the rear by *kanauts* [a wall of canvas], for out-offices and bathing-rooms." Roberts, *Scenes and Characteristics of Hindustan*.

594. LL/JB: 27 May 1857, Lindsay Papers.

595. Tatya Tope's testimony in U.P., 4:510–11.

596. Lydia Hillersdon: 18 May 1857 in TL, 10 Sept. 1857, p. 7.

597. Ewart: 27 May 1857, OIOC.

598. Some accounts say these were Nana's elephants, but Kalka Prasad states they were government animals. I think Nana's elephants did not arrive until Nana and his force arrived on the morning of May 22, and that the accounts that say they were Nana's elephants simply confuse the two separate incidents. Hillersdon had plenty of his own elephants from the Commissariat to do the job. Deposition of Kalka Prasad.

599. Nerput, *Opium Gomashta*, FSP, in U.P., 4:502–3.

600. Mowbray Thomson stated that the treasury contained £100,000 or about a million rupees, but Commissariat Clerk Shepherd (p. 6) would have had a more accurate idea.

601. Deposition of Kalka Prasad. He places this before Nana Sahib's arrival at Cawnpore.

602. Shepherd, *A Personal Narrative*, p. 5.

603. Deposition of Lalla Bhudree Nath.

604. Ball, 2:300; Nerput, *Opium Gomashta*, FSP, in U.P., 4:502–3.

605. Keene, *Handbook*, p. 20.

606. Keene, *Fifty-Seven*, p. 71.

607. Deposition of Tatya Tope.

608. He was apparently the son of another adopted son of Baji Rao named Raghunath Rao.

609. According to Gubbins, Wheeler sent a note dated May 22 that Nana's force had come in that morning; they must have set out the night before.

610. Deposition of Hulas Singh.

611. Estimates of Nana's force ranged from two hundred to six hundred men. See "Statement of Information" in TL, 16 Oct. 1857, p. 8; and Shepherd, p. 6; Thomson. pp. 32–33. Wheeler himself reported to Lawrence that "two guns and three hundred men, cavalry and infantry, furnished by the Maharaja of Bithoor, came in the morning." See

Gubbins, p. 31. But it is possible Wheeler never knew the extent of the force that would camp five miles from his Entrenchment, and so I base my figure on the statement of Tatya Tope, who probably helped to make Nana Sahib's arrangements. See Tatya Tope's testimony in U.P., 4:510–11.

612. The date of Hillersdon's request and Nana Sahib's arrival is deduced from the letters of Lydia Hillersdon in TL, 19 Sept. 1857, p. 7. Hillersdon's assurance that Agra would pay Nana's men is from the Statement of Tatya Tope in Kaye, *A History of the Great Revolt*, 2:300nn. According to Tatya Tope, Agra agreed.

613. As a small boy Chimnaji had actually occupied the Peshwa's throne for a few weeks until his adoption by the preceding Peshwa's widow was invalidated. Gupta, *Nana Saheb*, p. 9.

614. Nanak Chand's diary.

615. Shepherd, *A Personal Narrative*, pp. 4–5.

616. Hibbert, *The Great Mutiny*, p. 46.

617. Llewellyn-Jones, *A Fatal Friendship*, p. 33. She refers to the Lucknow garrison, but it was equally true at Cawnpore.

618. The goojur rumor conveniently enabled Wheeler to appear as though he were preparing not for mutiny but an external threat. The goojurs were as apt to loot and burn the sepoys' villages as the cantonments; perhaps Wheeler hoped that the sepoys would make common cause with their European officers against a foe they mutually despised.

619. Deposition of Jokhun.

620. Nanak Chand's diary.

621. Halliday Letter 92: 22 May 1857. A havildar was a sergeant. Khoda Buksh, his subhedar, said the havildar's name was Khan Mahomed, but Jonah calls him Jann Mahomed. Deposition of Khoda Buksh.

622. Deposition of Khoda Buksh. Shepherd (p. 5) states that this all transpired on the twenty-first, but Emma Halliday (Letter 92: 22 May 1857) reported that the trial was still going on on May 22 and that she and the Vibarts still did not know the outcome on the twenty-third; certainly Major Vibart would have been among the very first to find out. I suspect the verdict was handed down on the twenty-first but sentencing and Wheeler's decision to postpone the hanging came later.

623. Shepherd, *A Personal Narrative*, p. 5.

624. Halliday, Emma: 21 May 1857 from a letter by William Halliday dated 27 May 1857 in collection of Raleigh Trevelyan.

625. This is the same rumor of an uprising mentioned in a letter from an unknown officer of the 53rd N.I. dated 24 May 1857 in Ball, *The History of the Indian Mutiny*, 1:307.

626. Wheeler/Hearsey: 22 May 1857 in Pearse, *The Hearseys*, pp. 396–97.

627. Martin, *The Indian Empire*, 2:246.

628. Lydia Hillersdon: 23 May 1857 in TL, 10 Sept. 1857, p. 7.

629. WLH/JH: 20 May 1857.

630. Lydia Hillersdon: 18 May 1857 in TL, 10 Sept. 1857, p. 7.

631. Halliday Letter 92: 22 May 1857.

632. Lydia Hillersdon: 23 May 1857 in TL, 10 Sept. 1857, p. 7.

633. Letter dated 28 May 1857 in TL, 22 Oct. 1857, p. 7.

634. Ewart: 27 May 1857, OIOC.

635. Hayes in Kaye, *A History of the Great Revolt*, 2:300.

636. Lydia Hillersdon: 23 May 1857 in TL, 10 Sept. 1857, p. 7.

637. Hayes/Edmonstone in Kaye, *A History of the Great Revolt*, 2:300.

638. Unknown officer of the 53rd N.I.: 24 May 1857 in Ball, *The History of the Indian Mutiny*, 1:307.

639. Emma Ewart: 28 May 1857 in TL, 22 Oct. 1857, p. 7.

640. John Ewart: 31 May 1857 in Ball, *The History of the Indian Mutiny*, 1:312.

641. Thomson, *The Story of Cawnpore*, p. 30; "All the officers had to sleep in the Lines last night [the twenty-second]." Halliday, Emma, extracts dated May 21 and 23, 1857, in a letter by William Halliday dated May 27; 1857, in collection of Raleigh Trevelyan.

642. Ball, *The History of the Indian Mutiny*, 1:300.

643. CL/JB: 31 May 1857.

644. Shepherd, *A Personal Narrative*, p. 5.

645. Wheeler/Canning: 22 May 1857 in Ball, *The History of the Indian Mutiny*, 1:301.

646. WLH/JH: 21 May 1857.

647. Martin, *The Indian Empire*, p. 179.

648. The only conceivable consolation was that the sepoys at Aligarh "did not harm their officers or any one," wrote Emma Halliday, "in fact the men were most polite to the Ladies, handing them into their carriages and advising them to go down country." Halliday, Emma, Extracts dated May 21 and 23, 1857, in a letter by William Halliday dated May 27, 1857, in collection of Raleigh Trevelyan.

649. Their correspondence was already a communion between ghosts: unbeknownst to Emma her mother had just passed away, and before Emma's letters reached England she too would be dead.

650. Halliday Letter 92: 22 May 1857.

651. WLH/JH: 21 May 1857.

652. WLH/JH: 23 May 1857.

653. Tatya Tope's testimony in U.P., 4:510–11. The bungalow was evidently one to which the Resident at Bithur retired after Baji Rao's death. Yalland/ASW.

654. Thomson, *The Story of Cawnpore*, p. 33

655. Keene, *Handbook.* p. 20. "The relations we had always sustained with this man," wrote Thomson, "had been of so friendly a nature that not a suspicion of his fidelity entered the minds of any of our leaders; his reinforcements considerably allayed the feverish excitement caused by our critical condition." Thomson, *The Story of Cawnpore*, pp. 32–33.

656. Nanak Chand's diary.

657. Ball, *The History of the Indian Mutiny*, 1:302.

658. Lucknow Collectorate Records in U.P., 4:500.

659. Nanak Chand's diary.

660. Keene, *Fifty-Seven*, p. 72.

661. Hayes in Kaye, *A History of the Great Revolt*, 2:300–301.

662. Emma Ewart: 28 May 1857 in TL, 22 Oct. 1857, p. 7.

663. Wheeler to Henry Lawrence, 4 June 1857, BM (Add Ms 39922, Folio 10).

664. Hayes in Kaye, *A History of the Great Revolt*, 2:301. The depiction of Mrs. Wiggins is from Lydia Hillersdon: 31 May 1857 in TL, 10 Sept. 1857, p. 7.

665. Emma Halliday: May 21 and 23, 1857, in William Halliday: May 27, 1857, in collection of Raleigh Trevelyan.

666. As a senior military wife Mrs. Ewart could have claimed space for herself in the pucca barrack, but she had decided instead to erect a tent for herself and the very pregnant Lydia Hillersdon and their children on the grounds of the Entrenchment because it was "more private and comfortable for the night." Ewart: 27 May 1857, OIOC.

667. Emma Ewart: 28 May 1857 in TL, 22 Oct. 1857, p. 7.

668. Ball, *The History of the Indian Mutiny*, 1:306.

669. Sherer, *Narrative*.

670. Hayes in Kaye, *A History of the Great Revolt*, 2:301.

671. Wheeler in ibid., 2:303–4.

672. Shepherd, *A Personal Narrative*, p. 6.

673. It is hard to know if this was true or another of Joe Lee's fabrications. Lee, *The Indian Mutiny*, p. 7.

674. Gubbins, *Account*, p. 32

675. Sherer, *Narrative*.

676. Horne, *Narrative*.

677. Lydia Hillersdon: 25 May 1857 in TL, 10 Sept. 1857, p. 7.

678. Sherer, *Narrative*.

679. Ball, *The History of the Indian Mutiny*, 1:307.

680. Halliday, Emma: 24 May 1857, in a letter by William Halliday dated May 27, 1857, in collection of Raleigh Trevelyan.

681. WLH/JH 26 May 1857.

682. Emma Halliday says they were "Mahrattas," but she had probably mistaken the Oudh Irregulars for Nana's men, as in no other account are Mahrattas mentioned as guarding the Entrenchment. They apparently remained five miles upriver at Nawabgunj.

683. MacMillan, *Women of the Raj*, p. 80.

684. These officers were Lieutenant Chalmers and Ensign Browne.

685. Halliday Letter 93: 30 May 1857.

686. Horne, *Narrative* (BM).

687. WLH/JH: 26 May 1857.

688. Lindsay letters and entries in a letter by Emma Ewart dated May 22–23, 1857.

689. Thomson, *The Story of Cawnpore*, p. 31.

690. "The Government dawk, and the dawk companies," Canning continued, "are fully engaged in carrying a company of the 84th to Benares, at the rate of 18 men a dawk." Gubbins, *Account*, p. 37.

691. The date on which Wheeler ordered the provisioning of the Entrenchment is not known, but I assume that since he stipulated that he wanted enough food to last twenty-five days it was probably in response to Canning's wire to Lucknow that it would take twenty-five days for the relief force to reach Oudh.

692. Thomson, *The Story of Cawnpore*, pp. 30–31.

693. His name was Chunna Mull. Shepherd's account, dated August 29, 1857, published in TL, 7 Nov. 1857, p. 6.

694. Trevelyan, *Cawnpore*, p. 50.

695. Literally *soldier*, but more usually denoting a departmental employee of the army, especially laborers connected to the artillery. MacMunn, *The Indian Mutiny in Perspective*, p. 100.

696. Depositions of Gobind Singh, Sheik Elahee Buksh, and Ghouse Mohomed.

697. Mowbray Thomson's answer, dated September 8, 1858, to Mrs. Murray's account. TL, 11 Sept. 1858, p. 7.

698. It is impossible to say for certain who this was, but Lieutenant Dempster shared command of the "half battery" with eighteen-year-old Lieutenant John Nickleson Martin of the Bengal Artillery.

699. Hayes in Kaye, *A History of the Great Revolt*, 2:305nn.

700. Ball, *The History of the Indian Mutiny*, 1:306–7. The telegram was dated May 25.

701. Hayes in Kaye, *A History of the Great Revolt*, 2:305nn.

702. Emma Ewart: 28 May 1857 in TL, 22 Oct. 1857, p. 7.

703. Nanak Chand's diary.

704. Undated extract from a letter by Lieutenant Charles Crump, Lindsay Family *Papers*. Crump's drawings of the Mutiny sites at Cawnpore became famous; he may have been related to William Crump, the local wine merchant.

705. In addition he handed over his small collection of "oriental works" to "the mission pundit": an Indian catechist, perhaps, or a moonshi. Willis in Sherring, *The Indian Church during the Great Rebellion*, pp. 179–80.

706. Yalland, *Traders and Nabobs*, p. 260.

707. Emma Ewart, *Letters*.

708. Shepherd, *A Personal Narrative*, p. 7.

709. Ibid., p. 54.

710. Ibid., p. 8.

711. Wheeler even found comfort in the entire absence of crime. "Not a single robbery," he marveled to Lawrence, though nothing could have been more ominous. It could only mean that either the native police were no longer reporting to their superiors or the *bad-mashes* of the district were awaiting their cue to plunder. Ball, *The History of the Indian Mutiny*, 1:307; Sherer, *Daily Life*, p. 7; Raikes, *Notes on the Revolt*, pp. 18–19.

712. Gubbins, *Account*, pp. 44–45.

713. Thomson, *The Story of Cawnpore*, p. 28.

714. Yalland, *Traders and Nabobs*, p. 356.

715. Helena Angelo, *Journal*, in ibid., p. 356. Helena and her daughters survived the rebellion.

716. A year later her oldest daughter, tortured by visions of a monument and a tree by a river on the wall over her bed, died of a fever, after which Mrs. Sneyd and her remaining daughter Anna had been awakened one night by the sound of ghostly wailing.

717. Sneyd, *Account*, p. 38 (OIOC).

718. Yalland, *Traders and Nabobs*, pp. 231–32, 261.

719. Charlotte Jacobi's departure for Fort William is from material supplied by her descendant, Mrs. A. Regan. Charlotte later married an apothecary named Hogan, and though they were to have eight children and prosper in Rawalpindi running a chemist's shop and a tonga line, according to family legend Charlotte always panicked at the sound of native drumming. Frederick Jacobi the coachbuilder would have understood his great-great-grandson, Gerald Fisher, who is, of all things, a coachman in, of all places, San Jose, California.

720. Yalland, *Traders and Nabobs*, p. 261.

721. ILN, no. 882, vol. xxxi, 10 Oct. 1857, p. 354.

722. Deposition of Eduard Williams. The luckiest man in the Doab that season was a cousin of Amy Horne named Frederick Briant, who managed to outrun the uprising all the way to Calcutta, beating it by a nose. He left Bareilly with his family two days before the outbreak there, arrived at Fatehgarh two days before the outbreak there, and reached Cawnpore a day and a half before the outbreak there to find his in-laws huddled in the Entrenchment with Amy's mother, Mrs Cook. For a moment he considered remaining with them, but Mrs. Cook advised against it. "Look around you," she said, "and judge of our insecurity. Do you think we can hold out here with but a handful of men?" So Briant and his family bade farewell to the Cooks and proceeded with his wife, children, and in-laws down the Ganges to Allahabad, from which they would catch the last steamer less than an hour before the outbreak there, possibly on the same steamer as Mrs. Sneyd. Briant and his family survived their flight to Calcutta and returned to Fatehgarh after the Mutiny to prosper. Rees, *The Siege of Lucknow*, pp. 358–59; Cosens and Wallace, *Fatehgarh*, p. 22; Bennett, "Ten Months' Captivity."

723. Yalland, *Traders and Nabobs*, p. 345.

724. Horne, *Narrative* (BM). She says it was the head of the office, which would have been Ramsey. One misconception held by some Indians was that the telegraph wire stretched all the way to England and that if you yanked on it a bell went off in Queen Victoria's apartments.

725. Sherer, *Letters*, p. 2.

726. Her husband was Sergeant-Major Tom MacMahon of the 53rd.

727. Thomson, *The Story of Cawnpore*, p. 29. On the twenty-seventh Agra printed another of its feeble proclamations in the *Government Gazette*. "The Governor General of India in Council has warned the Army of Bengal, that the tales by which the men of certain regiments have been led to suspect that offence to their religion or injury to their Caste is

meditated by the Government of India are malicious falsehoods. The Governor General in Council has learnt that this suspicion continues to be propagated by designing and evil-minded men, not only in the Army, but amongst other classes of people." Chevers, *Papers* (OIOC).

728. Nanak Chand's diary.

729. Ibid.

730. Moti Singh of Nanamow.

731. Emma Ewart: 28 May 1857.

732. See Nanak Chand's entry for 31 May.

733. Emma Larkins, Home/Miscellaneous 814, pp. 314–20.

734. Emma Ewart: 30 May 1857.

735. Garrett was a partner of the same William T. Doyne who had introduced Azimullah Khan to William Howard Russell on the roof of Missirie's Hotel in Constantinople.

736. Yalland, *Traders and Nabobs*, p. 346. Like the telegraph and the Ganges Canal, the railroad terrorized many Indians. There was the noise and smoke, but Brahmins were also horrified by the carriages in which people of all castes were forced to mingle, and Indians unaccustomed to such impossible speed or the concept of fixed track were killed or lost their livestock under the engines' wheels. Others saw the tracks that crisscrossed their country as chains upon the breast of Hindustan.

737. Shepherd, *A Personal Narrative*, p. 45 illus. "From the peculiar manner in which bricks are manufactured in India, these brick-kilns always become considerable mounds, the excavations round them generally becoming large deep pools, at times almost lakes, of water." Robertson, *District Duties*, p. 109nn.

738. Thomson, *The Story of Cawnpore*, pp. 69–70.

739. Garrett, *Papers*, PRONI.

740. Sherer, *Daily Life*, p. 70. The letter was written to a man named Bews at Fatehpur. Two months later all Bews could find of his friend and his family was a miniature of the engineer's wife at an abandoned sowar outpost across the river from Cawnpore. The engineer may have been sub-engineer Grey, the only engineer whose wife died with him in the Entrenchment.

741. Emma Ewart, *Letters* (OIOC).

742. Ewart: 27 May 1857 (OIOC).

743. Louisa Chalwin: 29 May 1857, courtesy of Zoë Yalland.

744. Thomson, *The Story of Cawnpore*, p. 29.

745. Bennett, "Ten Months' Captivity."

746. Emma Ewart: 28 May 1857 in TL, 22 Oct. 1857, p. 7.

747. LL/MD: 27 May 1857.

748. One "Cawnpore Devil," wrote Fanny Parks, "arose in clouds of dust which, sweeping over the river from the Lucknow side, blow directly on the windows of the drawing-room; they are all fastened, and a man at every one of them, or the violence of the wind would burst them open." Parks, *Wanderings in India*, 1:136.

749. The punkah was supposedly introduced sometime between 1784 and 1790, but evidently this was merely the time when the British adopted it. *Hobson-Jobson* includes mentions of such contraptions in use in Arabia in 1166, and Bernier mentioned seeing them in Indian courts in 1662. Some say the punkah was invented by a Eurasian clerk so demented by the heat that he hung half his camp table overhead and ordered his servant to pull it back and forth. Sometimes punkahs sported painted landscapes, and often their rigging was ornate, with intertwined ribbons, brass rosettes, and clasp-hands.

750. But punkahs did not always accomplish much and depended on coolies, who, tugging gently on their ropes out on the verandah, were always and understandably falling off to sleep. The British were driven mad by this arrangement, and kept trying, without success, to devise self-perpetuating punkahs with pulleys, gears, and weights. By 1830 some houses at Cawnpore were cooled by loud and ungainly contraptions called ther-

mantidotes: hollow mango–wood affairs by which air, fanned into a draft by teams of ped-aling coolies, was sucked through wetted grass screens and blown up a funnel and into the house. But they were noisy and expensive— keeping the screens wetted required a second team of coolies—and though fresh *khuss-khuss* screens initially gave off a "fragrant, deli-cious, and refreshing scent," they quickly mildewed and had to be replaced. Eventually thermantidotes fell out of favor; they looked awful bolted to the side of a bungalow, the sight and sound of teams of coolies pedaling in the heat was unseemly or in any case an-noying, and the dank draft proved unwholesome.

751. Emma Ewart, *Letters*, (OIOC).

752. Emma Ewart: 1 June 1857.

753. Chalwin: 31 May 1857.

754. Bennett, "Ten Months' Captivity."

755. CL/JB: 31 May 1857.

756. Emma Ewart: 30 May 1857 in TL, 22 Oct. 1857, p. 7.

757. John Ewart: 31 May 1857, in TL, 22 Oct. 1857, p. 7.

758. I surmise this from the fact that after the outbreak on June 5 Halliday went off to Savada House to collect the weapons of furloughed sepoys and the furniture and posses-sions of the Christian gunners who had crowded into the Entrenchment.

759. Emma Ewart: 31 May 1857.

760. Shepherd, *A Personal Narrative*, p. 9.

761. Emma Ewart: 30 May 1857 in TL, 22 Oct. 1857, p. 7; and 1 June 1857.

762. Emma Ewart: 31 May 1857 in TL, 22 Oct.1857, p. 7.

763. Halliday Letter 94: 21 August 1857.

764. Malleson, *Essays and Lectures*, 6:79.

765. Durgah Prasad Misur.

766. Lucknow Collectorate Mutiny Basta in U.P., 4:668.

767. Willie's return and all remaining material is from WLH/JH: 1 June 1857.

768. Emma Larkins in HM 814, pp. 302–12.

769. Martin, *The Indian Empire*, 2:179.

770. This was their nickname. Heathcote, *The Indian Army*, p. 156.

771. Wheeler in Kaye, *A History of the Great Revolt*, 2:303–4.

772. Malleson, *Essays and Lectures*, 6:79, 174–75; WLH/JH: 1 June 1857; Ensign Browne. Letter dated 24 July 1857 in TL, 21 Sept. 1857, p. 6. I am conservatively estimating that each company consisted of eighty men. As many as three hundred men may have been away on furlough, if the number of their muskets left behind at Savada House is any indi-cation. (Deposition of Khoda Buksh.) "The Sepoys here are not to be depended on more than at other places," wrote Mrs. Larkins, but she believed they remained staunch at Cawnpore because "they are kept in fear as their numbers are not great." Emma Larkins in HM 814, pp. 314–20.

773. No one knows why they did not immediately ride the eight miles to see for them-selves.

774. Cosens and Wallace, *Fategarh*, p. 25.

775. Lord Roberts often cited Hayes's death as proof of the necessity of teaching every officer good horsemanship, but Mowbray Thomson saw it as an example of the folly of sending British officers out with native troops whom they had never before commanded. Ibid., p. 27.

776. A Sikh zemindar turned up at the magistrate's house in the afternoon with the bodies of Fayrer, Barbour, and Hayes laid out in a cart while the faithful native officer who had tried to warn Hayes and Carey galloped back to Lucknow to report their fates. Ibid., pp. 24–26.

777. Gubbins says there were two guns, Thomson says three. Both were working from memory (both had lost their notes in the wreck of the *Ava*) but Thomson would have re-membered, as the number was critical to him in the Entrenchment.

778. He was the son of Lieutenant Colonel Benjamin Ashe of the 62nd N.I. and was born at Sitapur in 1830. He attended Addiscombe from 1846 to 1848, and was a classmate of Ashburner, who died on their sortie at the beginning of the siege. Ashe also overlapped with Swynfen Jervis of the Light Bengal Artillery and had seen service in Burma.

779. Gubbins, *Account*, pp. 35–36; Shepherd, *A Personal Narrative*, p. 10.

780. Lieutenant F. H. Tomkinson, whose name appears mistakenly on Shepherd's list of Cawnpore casualties, was away at Urai with Captain Alexander of the 53rd, and after being politely abandoned by his troops, hid in a village for some months; he was killed on 23 Oct. while trying to blow up a rebel encampment. Kaye and Malleson, *History*, 6:174–75.

781. Malleson, *Essays and Lectures*, 6:174–75; TL, 7 Sept. 1857, p. 9; Thomson, *The Story of Cawnpore*, pp. 225–27.

782. Pearse, *The Hearseys*, pp. 396–97.

783. Thomson, *The Story of Cawnpore*, pp. 30–31, 63–64. According to Buckle's *Memoir of the Services of the Bengal Artillery*, this 3-pounder was the first rifled gun ever used by the British in war. Buckle, *Memoir of the Services of the Bengal Artillery*, p. 147nn.

784. Acting Deputy Paymaster Captain E. J. Seppings of the 2nd Native Cavalry. He was thirty-one years old and the son of a Calcutta surveyor. MDP, 20 Feb. 1857, nos. 209–11; Shepherd, *A Personal Narrative*, p. 93.

785. Shepherd, *A Personal Narrative*, p. 10; Deposition of Ajoodea Pershad.

786. The Mahajun Kunhye Prasad called this place "Sooka Mullah's Ghat"; a "Sukha Ghat" appears on a map of Cawnpore in Bartholomew, *Constable's Hand Atlas of India*, pl. 46.

787. N.W.P., P.D.P., Jan.–June 1864: 30 Jan. 1864, P.D.AG, pp. 19–20.

788. Depositions of Sheo Churran Das and Kunhye Pershad.

789. Nanak Chand's diary; Shepherd, *A Personal Narrative*, p. 20.

790. Deposition of Kunhye Pershad.

791. Shepherd, *A Personal Narrative*, p. 20.

792. Nanak Chand's diary.

793. Deposition of Kunhye Pershad.

794. Nanak Chand's diary.

795. Forrest, *Selections*, appendix A, pp. ii–iii.

796. Thomson, Reply.

797. I base these numbers on Shepherd's roll. Shepherd, *A Personal Narrative*, pp. xii–vi.

798. Wheeler in Trevelyan, *Cawnpore*, p. 56.

799. Wheeler in Kaye, *A History of the Great Revolt*, 2:303–4.

800. Trevelyan, *Cawnpore*, p. 56, says he was a subaltern. Other accounts merely say he was an officer. Hodson, *List*, NAM.

801. L/Mil/10/59, 61, 65; L/Mil/5/335; L/Mil/1/24, NAM.

802. Kaye, *A History of the Great Revolt*, 2:307nn.

803. It is not entirely clear that Cox missed. By the time the news reached Ajodhya Prasad the story was that a sowar may have been killed or at least wounded. But the sowars who spoke to Shepherd said only that they had been fired upon and did not garnish their grievances with any mention of a casualty, which it seems to me they would have if they could. Perma Nund also said that "some sahib had fired at a sowar" and Lalla Bhudree Nath, Wheeler's chief native spy, stated that Cox (he called him Christie) had missed. Shepherd, *A Personal Narrative*, p. 11; Depositions of Ajoodea Pershad, Perma Nund, and Lalla Bhudree Nath.

804. Hodson, *List*, NAM.

805. Nanak Chand's diary.

806. Shepherd, *A Personal Narrative*, p. 9.

807. According to Sherer's narrative, these troops were Sikhs and represented only a portion of the original force. Delafosse in TL, 16 Oct. 1857, p. 7, gives the title as shown.

He says that the troops had mutinied on the Fatehgahr Road on the fifth of June, and returned on Sunday afternoon (which would have made it the sixth), but the garrison was already under siege by that date. Shepherd specifically says his confrontation with the sowars occurred in front of his house on the third of June at 5 P.M., as he was eating supper with his family. Since he and his family would have already moved into the Entrenchment by the fifth, his dates, and not Delafosse's, must be correct.

808. Delafosse, TL, 16 Oct. 1857, p. 7.

809. Shepherd, *A Personal Narrative*, pp. 9–10.

810. Ibid., p. 10.

811. Shepherd translates this as "Make a clearance."

PART TWO

1. Parks, *Wanderings in India*, 1:167. The corpses were sometimes hard to make out. "I fancied I saw the corpse of a European floating down the Ganges just now," wrote Mrs. Parks in the 1830s, "but, on looking through the telescope, I beheld the most disgusting object imaginable," a corpse that, for reasons of economy, had been only partially incinerated. "Fire enough had been allowed just to take off all the skin from the body and head, giving it a white appearance.... It floated almost entirely out of the water, whilst the crows that were perched on it tore the eyes out."

2. Nanak Chand's diary.

3. Italics mine but probably intended by Wheeler, who wrote Grant's rank twice.

4. Patrick Grant had actually served in many battles, including Maharajpur, Mudki, Firozhsahr, Sobraon, Chilianwalla, Gujerat, and the North West Frontier. But he was only acting commander-in-chief. Unpopular with the Bengal Army, he was soon succeeded by Sir Colin Campbell.

5. Martin, *The Indian Empire*, 2:275.

6. Wheeler / Henry Lawrence: 4 June 1857, BM (Add Ms 39922, Folio 10).

7. U.P., 4:501–2

8. Kaye, *A History of the Great Revolt*, 2:302nn.

9. Shepherd, *A Personal Narrative*, p. 16.

10. Deposition of Bhola Khan, who stated that "Teeka Singh, subadar, ... with about 50 sowars, was on picquet duty near the entrenchments."

11. ILN, no. 875, vol. xxxi, 22 Aug. 1857, p. 203.

12. Nerput, *Opium Gomashta*, FSP, in U.P., 4:503–11.

13. According to Trevelyan, Teeka Singh was on picket duty that night, but Jehangir Khan did not mention him as being one of his picket's number.

14. Wheeler to Lawrence, 24 June 1957; Singh, *Letters of Sir Henry Lawrence*, pp. 32–34.

15. Deposition of Khoda Buksh.

16. Deposition of Perma Nund.

17. Depositions of Gobind Singh, Sheik Elahee Buksh, and Ghouse Mohomed.

18. "No one in his senses," wrote a British officer of the time, "could suppose that the old Subahdars and Jemadars, who were most of them only fit for the pension list, would be any assistance to Government in a crisis. They were simply so many old men, rewarded for having served a certain number of years." Medley, *A Year's Campaigning*, pp. 211–12.

19. The trooper's name was Dabi Deen.

20. Deposition of Ewuz Khan; Thomson, *Report*.

21. Shepherd, *A Personal Narrative*, p. 15.

22. Depositions of Gobind Singh, Sheik Elahee Buksh, and Ghouse Mohomed. The riding master was a Mr. Walsh.

23. They evidently spared some of the stables, for six weeks later they would provide the only shelter available for the British relief force under Henry Havelock.

24. Bennett, "Ten Months' Captivity."

25. Deposition of Perma Nund.

26. Trevelyan, *Cawnpore*, p. 58.

27. Shepherd, *A Personal Narrative*, p. 16.

28. Shepherd's account.

29. Horne, *Narrative* (BM).

30. Shepherd, *A Personal Narrative*, p. 15.

31. Nanak Chand's diary.

32. Deposition of Lalla Shunker Doss, who says the looting began before the sepoys marched to Kalyanpur.

33. "Statement of Information" in TL, 16 Oct. 1857, p. 8.

34. Shepherd, *A Personal Narrative*, p. 16; Trevelyan, *Cawnpore*, p. 58.

35. Shepherd says that the officers of the 1st were sleeping that night in their lines, and before departing the sepoys begged their officers to flee to the Entrenchment (Shepherd, *A Personal Narrative*, p. 16), but both Delafosse and Thomson state that the officers of the 2nd Cavalry and the 1st and 56th N.I. were ordered not to sleep in their lines. Delafosse in TL, 16 Oct. 1857, p. 7; Thomson, *Report*. That the officers of the 1st went to the lines at the first alarm and were not sleeping in the lines is further testified to in Forrest, *Selections*, appendix A, p. iv.

36. I have slightly paraphrased the translation of the deposition of Ajodhya Prasad (Ajoodea Pershad), the Mahajun: "Baba logue! Baba logue! This is not as usual, do not act thus!" Trevelyan has: "My children! My children! This not your usual conduct. Do not so great a wickedness!" Trevelyan, *Cawnpore*, p. 58.

37. Thomson states that Ewart was severely wounded "early in the proceedings" and took no part in the defense; it is possible he may have been wounded as he rode among his men. Thomson, *The Story of Cawnpore*, p. 109.

38. Ibid., pp. 63–64.

39. Depositions of Gobind Singh, Sheik Elahee Buksh, and Ghouse Mohomed.

40. Deposition of Khoda Buksh; Depositions of Gobind Singh, Sheik Elahee Buksh, and Ghouse Mohomed.

41. Deposition of Khoda Buksh.

42. Depositions of Gobind Singh, Elahee Buksh, and Ghouse Mohomed.

43. Thomson, *Report*.

44. Dr. W. R. Boyes.

45. Thomson, *Report*.

46. Depositions of Gobind Singh, Elahee Buksh, and Ghouse Mohomed.

47. Deposition of Bhola Khan.

48. Depositions of Khoda Buksh and Bhola Khan.

49. Deposition of Bhola Khan.

50. Thomson, *Report*; Deposition of Bhola Khan.

51. Delafosse in TL, 16 Oct. 1857, p. 7; Thomson, *Report*.

52. Deposition of Lalla Bhudree Nath.

53. Nerput, *Opium Gomashta*, FSP, in U.P., 4:503–11. Thomson thought he heard the guard at the treasury fire their muskets at the rebels and grieved that he was not allowed to go to their assistance. But it seems likelier that he heard the firing of muskets in celebration of the outbreak. One of their jemadars, Dulgunjun Singh, was a leader of the rebellion. Thomson, p. 40; Deposition of Ram Buksh.

54. Nanak Chand's diary.

55. Trevelyan interpreted this to mean that they would not let the other soldiers in until the 53rd had arrived to claim its share of the spoils, but the officers of the 53rd believed that their men were under attack at the treasury and asking for aid. Trevelyan, *Cawnpore*, p. 59.

56. It may have been these officers who, according to Shepherd, never came back but returned to their villages to sit out the Mutiny. Shepherd's account.

57. Nerput, *Opium Gomashta*, FSP, in U.P., 4:503–11.

58. Deposition of Khoda Buksh.

59. Deposition of Bhola Khan.

60. Deposition of Ram Buksh; Sheo Churran Das.

61. In his narrative of the uprising Mowbray Thomson would write that he was "at an utter loss" to account for Ashe's firing on the 53rd. But in a more candid account he wrote for the commander-in-chief, he stated that Ashe had fired in order to commit his native gunners to the Entrenchment's defense. Thomson, *The Story of Cawnpore*, p. 39; Thomson, *Report*.

62. Deposition of Bhola Khan; Ram Buksh.

63. Thomson, *The Story of Cawnpore*, p. 39.

64. Wheeler in Kaye, *A History of the Great Revolt*, 2:303–4.

65. Chalwin, *Letters*.

66. Thomson, *The Story of Cawnpore*, p. 103; Blunt, *Christian Tombs and Monuments*, p. 115.

67. Mirzapore Collectorate Records in U.P., 4:78. In his letter the Christian asked the Magistrate of Mirzapore for "temporary aid" as he was "without a fraction." In this account I am trusting that he was not merely one of a number of swindlers who applied for relief from the fund established for the sufferers from the Mutiny. According to Mrs. Angelo a "French Colonel" from Cawnpore arrived at Allahabad on June 11; perhaps this was Lafout. He may have been a former officer in the King of Oudh's forces and the Christian his Eurasian or native secretary.

68. Nanak Chand's diary states Murphy was killed "by the lake," which was probably a mistaken translation of tank—there are no lakes per se at Cawnpore; Shepherd, *A Personal Narrative*, p. 17, states that Murphy was killed while returning from his bungalow on the railway line; Thomson, *The Story of Cawnpore*, pp. 64–65. Trevelyan, p. 72, states, I think mistakenly, that Murphy was among those killed in Ashburner's sortie. His name is spelled *Murphey* at All Souls Church.

69. Deposition of Lalla Bhudree Nath; Thomson, *The Story of Cawnpore*, pp. 77–78; Shepherd, *A Personal Narrative*, map 1.

70. Delafosse and Master. Lieutenant G. A. Master's father was commanding the 7th Native Infantry at Lucknow. The family's roots in India extended back to an ancestor who served as governor of Fort St. George in the 1600s. Many Masters had served the Company since, most of them as soldiers.

71. Deposition of Bhola Khan.

72. Shepherd, *A Personal Narrative*, p. 17.

73. Deposition of Bhola Khan.

74. Deposition of Ram Buksh.

75. Based on Shepherd's map.

76. Deposition of Bhola Khan; Thomson, *Report*.

77. Deposition of Bhola Khan.

78. Thomson, *Report*.

79. Rigor mortis sets in about three to four hours after death, but can set in earlier if victims had been exerting themselves strenuously at the time they expired.

80. Shepherd, *A Personal Narrative*, p. 17.

81. Trevelyan, *Cawnpore*, p. 72; Shepherd, *A Personal Narrative*, p. 17; Thomson, *The Story of Cawnpore*, pp. 64–65.

82. "Events showed," wrote Sherer, "that [Wheeler] was right in every respect. He weathered the outbreak in safety, the mutineers *did* make off for Delhi, and the Nana was clearly not in league, previously, with the native soldiery, or it would not have been necessary for him to pursue them down the road, and entreat them, with lavish promises, to return. The treachery of the Nana disturbed all calculations. Now that we know what the Nana was, it may seem very blind and credulous to have relied upon him at all. But have

we not relied on the Nawab of Rampore? Have we not relied on the Raja of Chirkaree, and not been deceived? It has been well said, there are prophets of the past, as well as the future. There is a danger, surely, to be avoided here." Sherer, *Narrative*.

83. Tatya Tope testified that "the three Regiments of Infantry and the 2nd Light Cavalry surrounded us and imprisoned the Nana and myself in the treasury and plundered the magazine and treasury of everything they contained leaving nothing in either. . . . The Nana was also under charge of these sentries and the sepoys which (*sic*) were with us also joined the rebels." Some historians discount Tatya Tope's version of events as mere special pleading, but he was a brave man and by the time he gave his testimony he knew that, whatever he might tell the British, he was going to be hanged.

84. Deposition of Ram Buksh.

85. Nerput, *Opium Gomashta*, FSP, in U.P., 4:503–11.

86. Nana Sahib in Foreign Political Consultations in ibid., 4:772–74.

87. Deposition of Kunhye Pershad (Prasad), who paid Ramdeen, one of Nana's attendants, to provide him with intelligence about Nana's machinations. Kunhye Prasad was a Mahajan and speaks with glib authority: "the facts are these," etc. He does not seem to have witnessed much of anything directly, however Mahajans often employed agents to keep track of their debtors' affairs. Kunhye Prasad feared Jwala Prasad because he had bought some land out from under the brigadier.

88. Deposition of Lalla Bhudree Nath; Wheeler/Henry Lawrence: 24 June 1857 in Singh, *Letters of Sir Henry Lawrence*, pp. 32–34.

89. Forrest, *Selections*, vol. 2, appendix A, p. iv.

90. Testimony of Jehangir Khan, Khan, Lucknow Collectorate Records in U.P., 4:501–2.

91. Nerput, *Opium Gomashta*, FSP, in ibid., 4:503–11.

92. Shepherd, *A Personal Narrative*, pp. 20–21.

93. Thomson, *Report*.

94. TL, 16 Oct. 1857, p. 8.

95. Shepherd, *A Personal Narrative*, p. 21.

96. TL, 16 Oct. 1857, p. 8.

97. Deposition of Ajoodea Pershad.

98. Trevelyan, *Cawnpore*, p. 65; Shepherd, *A Personal Narrative*, p. 21; Testimony of Mary Ann; Thomson, *Report*; Depositions of Jokhun and Ajoodea Pershad. Tatya Tope is vague and unconvincing in this part of his story. "In the morning the whole army told him (the Nana) to go with them towards Delhi. The Nana refused and the army then said, 'Come with us to Cawnpoor and fight them.' The Nana objected to this, but they would not attend to him and so taking him with them as a prisoner they went towards Cawnpoor and fighting commenced there." This contradicts too many other accounts to be plausible. "Everybody in the city said it was the Nana who brought the troops back from Cawnpore. It was a general belief in which I likewise participated." Deposition of Sheo Pershad; Tatya Tope's testimony in U.P., 4:510–11. "There can be no doubt but that troops when they had mutinied and gone off to Kullianpore were brought back from thence by the Nana and Baba Bhut. Hundreds of men saw this. I can give no one's name in particular." Deposition of Hulas Singh.

98. Gambling that the rebels would proceed to Delhi, a railway foreman named Farnon had taken his fiduciary responsibilities so seriously as to venture out of the Entrenchment on June 5 to pay his crew camped far to the north of town. Rather than return to Cawnpore that night, he decided to sleep in his hut and proceed in the morning. But on hearing the sowars trotting toward Kalyanpur, he jumped out of bed and fled into the countryside disguised as a native, where he would wander for two weeks before returning to Cawnpore and waiting out the Mutiny in the house of a Moslem childhood friend who himself was in hiding to protect his Christian wife. Deposition of Thomas Ambrose Farnon.

100. Deposition of Mr. Eduard Williams.

101. Diary of Nunne Nawab.

102. Testimony of Nerput.

103. Diary of Nunne Nawab and contemporary map of Cawnpore by Thomason College of Roorkee. The house was owned by David Duncan, proprietor of Duncan's Hotel.

104. Nanak Chand's diary.

105. Depositions of Narain Kachee; Appa Shastri; Appajee Luchman; Nundeedeen; Nana Ubbhunker.

106. Depositions of Appajee Luchman and Appa Shastri.

107. Evidently the sowars, who were not much use against the Entrenchment, were assigned the task of hunting for Christians and Europeans. Depositions of Ajoodea Pershad; Kalka Pershad; Bajay Lall; Lalla Shunker Doss; Muir, *Records*, 1:443.

108. Shepherd, *A Personal Narrative*, p. 21.

109. Thomson, *The Story of Cawnpore*, p. 61.

110. How Cawnpore's Christians were rooted out is not told, but in Aligarh the Mohammedans suspected the sweepers of hiding Christians, and hundreds turned out to kill the sweepers "with their naked swords" if they did not point out the Christians. All the huts were searched, but no European or Christian was found. Muir, *Records*, 1:443.

111. Depositions of Lalla Bhudree Nath and Seo Pershad Panday.

112. Testimony of Nerput; Sherer, *Narrative*.

113. Diary of Nunne Nawab.

114. Deposition of Futteh Singh.

115. Deposition of Lochun.

116. Nevill, *Cawnpore*, p. 264. I wonder if any of Nana's fellow Masons, particularly J. R. Brandon, may have remained hidden in Lodge Harmony during the first days of the siege.

117. Testimony of Nerput; Sherer, *Narrative*.

118. Deposition of Bhudree Nath.

119. Depositions of Seo Pershad Panday and Eduard Williams.

120. INTACH, *Preliminary Unedited Listing of Cawnpore*, p. 122.

121. Deposition of Futteh Singh.

122. Trevelyan, *Cawnpore*, p. 70; Nanak Chand's diary.

123. Deposition of Futteh Singh.

124. Much as Baji Rao's diwan had been rewarded for arranging a loan from Baji Rao.

125. Shepherd, *A Personal Narrative*, p. 21; Trevelyan, *Cawnpore*, p. 70; though no mention in Nunne Nawab's diary.

126. Diary of Nunne Nawab; Deposition of Lalla Shunker Doss; Nevill, *Cawnpore*, p. 119.

127. Shepherd, *A Personal Narrative*, p. 21; Deposition of Moonshee Zuhooree.

128. Rest house.

129. Diary of Nunne Nawab; Shepherd, *A Personal Narrative*, p. 21.

130. Deposition of Futteh Singh; Shepherd's account.

131. Thomson, *The Story of Cawnpore*, p. 62.

132. Wheeler/Lawrence: 24 June 1957 in Singh, *Letters of Sir Henry Lawrence*, pp. 32–34.

133. Deposition of Bhola Khan.

134. TL, 16 Oct. 1857, p. 7.

135. Thomson, *The Story of Cawnpore*, p. 61.

136. Thomson, Ibid., pp. 62–63.

137. Shepherd, *A Personal Narrative*, p. 18.

138. According to Captain Douglas De Wend, who lived in Cawnpore in the 1830s, most bungalows "had their roofs first thatched and then tiled, a roof which is found to exclude the heat of the sun better than any other, while it is less exposed to the accidents to which a mere thatched roof is liable." De Wend, *Journal*.

139. Shepherd, *A Personal Narrative*, 19.

140. Thomson, *Report*.

612 • NOTES TO PART TWO

141. Shepherd, *A Personal Narrative*, p. 18.

142. Shepherd's account.

143. Fragment of *The Scotsman* dated Thursday, September [indecipherable], 1857, Lindsay Family Papers.

144. Deposition of Bhudree Nath.

145. To destroy enemy cannon, soldiers drove iron spikes through the torch holes and jammed them inextricably into the barrels.

146. Depositions of Bhola Khan and Ram Buksh. Bhola Khan says there were three officers, but Ram Buksh says four, and names them: Bridges [mistakenly transcribed as Burgess], Delafosse, Masters, and Thomson. The extra carriages may explain the discrepancies in various accounts about the number of cannon that were out of commission at various stages of the siege; they were probably used to replace carriages destroyed by rebel fire.

147. Presumably including several of the eight bachelor lieutenants of the 2nd Native Cavalry.

148. He was the son of W. P. Ashburner of Wesbury and was born at Longford in 1829. In 1848, for health reasons, he had withdrawn from Addiscombe, where he had been a classmate of St. George Ashe. Alan Hardcastle/ASW 13 Nov. 1992; Blunt, *Christian Tombs and Monuments*, p. 111.

149. Testimony of Mary Ann in TL, 16 Oct. 1857. p. 8; Thomson, *Report*.

150. TL, 16 Oct. 1857, p. 7; Wheeler / Henry Lawrence: 24 June 1857 in Singh, *Letters of Sir Henry Lawrence*, pp. 32–34.

151. Thomson, *The Story of Cawnpore*, p. 65; Depositions of Eliza Bradshaw and Elizabeth Letts. Thomson does not mention the kitmutgar, but he was stationed to the northwest. The position of the kitchen is consistent with the trajectory he describes; the kitchen was one of the few places servants could find shade.

152. Shepherd, *A Personal Narrative*, p. 23.

153. Thomson, *The Story of Cawnpore*, p. 65.

154. There were three buglers in the Entrenchment: John Bradshaw of the 56th; Warrel of the 1st Company, 6th Battalion, Bengal Artillery; and J. C. Warcoat of the 1st Native Infantry.

155. Thomson, *The Story of Cawnpore*, pp. 65–66.

156. Cracklow Letters.

157. Not all the cannon that would be brought to bear upon the Entrenchment came from the magazine; some were native cannon like those Collector William Edwards of Budaon was coming upon, including "a fine 18-pounder gun" that had been dug out of a wall "where it had been concealed since the proclamation issued last year by the Resident at Lucknow to the Thalookdars of Oude requiring them to give up all their ordnance. A 24-pounder was at the same time produced from a field, where it had been concealed about fifty yards from a Neem tree, which marked its position. The wheels and other portions of the carriages of these guns were fished up from wells, where they had been hidden. Four other guns of different calibres were brought in from the chief villages in the neighbourhood, where they had been concealed. . . . We heard that there were many more guns which could be produced if need be." Edwards, *Personal Adventures*, pp. 70–71.

158. Deposition of Eduard Williams; Shepherd, *A Personal Narrative*, p. 22.

159. Thomson, *The Story of Cawnpore*, p. 68. Thomson states that they did not receive military officers until June 9.

160. Shepherd, *A Personal Narrative*, p. 24.

161. Sherer, *Narrative*.

162. Testimony of Nerput.

163. Sherer, *Narrative*. Sherer is careless about these things; he claims that the rebels brought in fourteen guns on June 6. But all the native testimony suggests that the num-

ber of guns remained small during the first day of the siege, and the worst of the cannon-ade did not begin until the next day.

164. Thomson, *Report*.

165. Thomson, *The Story of Cawnpore*, pp. 41–42.

166. Shepherd, *A Personal Narrative*, p. 22.

167. Lindsay, Papers.

168. A series of holes dug in front of a fortification to obstruct cavalry charges.

The noise was such that when John Walter Sherer walked out of his bungalow in Fateh-pur fifty miles east of Cawnpore, he could hear the distinct sound of guns. "The firing had been going on since mid-day," he calculated, "but we had not known of it in the muffled house; and every now and then the deep rumble of heavy ordnance came rolling over the fields." Sherer, *Daily Life*, p. 10.

169. TL, 29 Aug. 1857; Blunt, *Christian Tombs and Monuments*, p. 113.

170. Thomson, *The Story of Cawnpore*, pp. 102–3; All Souls memorial tablet.

171. The son of the 32nd's paymaster, for three and a half years he had languished in the West Indies as an ensign before entering his father's regiment as a lieutenant in late 1846. NAM: WO31/900, 992; Swiney, *Historical Records of the 32nd (Cornwall) Light Infantry*.

172. Thomson, *The Story of Cawnpore*, pp. 64–65, 140–42.

173. Shepherd, *A Personal Narrative*, p. 22.

174. Thomson, *The Story of Cawnpore*, p. 66. Punctuation mine.

175. Collins Letters, 1 Nov. 1857.

176. Testimony of Nerput.

177. Shepherd, *A Personal Narrative*, pp. 22–23.

178. Sherer, *Narrative*.

179. Nanak Chand's diary.

180. According to Nunne Nawab he was under house arrest at the time, but according to Eduard Williams he was already at his battery. Even giving the Nawab every benefit of the doubt, I am assuming that he was brought not from his house but from his battery at St. John's.

181. Diary of Nunne Nawab. Foggy on dates and contradicted by many more neutral witnesses, the Nawab's diary should be employed with great caution.

182. Deposition of Moonshee Zuhooree.

183. Deposition of Bajay Lall.

184. Depositions of Ajoodea Pershad and Jowahri Singh. "He was not under any re-straint, but appeared to be the commander and master of the place: every one obeyed the orders given by him. . . . He had a sword and telescope by him, and used to go to the guns and direct the artillerymen what to do." Deposition of Seo Pershad Panday.

185. Depositions of Seo Pershad Panday and Bajay Lall.

186. Deposition of Moonshee Zuhooree. This act nearly cost his family their lives. Other sweepers turned them in to the rebels, condemning them as Christians, but the towns-people interceded, and they were released.

187. Shepherd, *A Personal Narrative*, p. 23.

188. Thomson, *Report*.

189. Thomson, *The Story of Cawnpore*, p. 31.

190. Shepherd's account.

191. Nanak Chand's diary.

192. Shepherd, *A Personal Narrative*, p. 23.

193. Kaye, *A History of the Great Revolt*, 2:317.

194. This is my surmise.

195. Shepherd, *A Personal Narrative*, p. 22.

196. Bennett, "Ten Months' Captivity."

197. Nanak Chand's diary.

198. Shepherd, *A Personal Narrative*, p. 24.

199. Ibid., p. 27; Yalland, *Traders and Nabobs*, p. 257.

200. Bennett, "Ten Months' Captivity."

201. Shepherd, *A Personal Narrative*, pp. 25–26.

202. Captain E. J. Seppings left an inscription on the wall that read, "The following were in this barrack on the 11th June, 1857. Captain Seppings, Mrs. Ditto, 3 children; Mrs. Wainwright, Ditto infant; Mrs. Cripps, Mrs. Halliday." Shepherd, p. 34. (I also found a letter containing transcriptions by a Captain Alexander of the inscriptions on the Entrenchment walls; it had been tucked into a copy book containing the letters of Edward Vibart at the OIOC. They jibe substantially with Shepherd's transcriptions.) Since Mabel is not listed and Emma would not otherwise have allowed herself to be parted from her, it seems to me likely that Mabel was dead by the eleventh. Thomson also does not mention Mabel, again suggesting that she had died. The Wyndham family believed, however, that Mabel had survived up to the ghat massacre and had been cared for by Mrs. Cripps (see above transcription; Letter by Ella Wyndham to her sister dated November 2, 1857, courtesy of the Historic "Dalwood" Restoration Association of New South Wales). But according to Shepherd she too died in the bombardment, and in a later letter Emma's father reported that "Emma and Captain Halliday died at Cawnpore, the former from small pox and the Captain and their baby killed by the mutineers" (Margaret Kelly/ASW: 29 Aug. 1993). Knowing how fragile Mabel was and how excitable, it seems to me extremely doubtful that she would have survived the first shock of the cannonade.

203. "We ought not to blame Hillersdon for not knowing [Azimullah's plots]," wrote Henry George Keene, "or for thinking that it was best, in his perplexed situation, to endeavour to outbid the sepoys for the only alliance that had a chance of safety in it." Keene, *Fifty-Seven*, p. 72. My account of Charles Hillersdon's death is based on Shepherd, *A Personal Narrative*, pp. 26, 36–37, and Thomson, *The Story of Cawnpore*, p. 107. In his list Shepherd says Mrs. Hillersdon died on the ninth; Thomson states that this was "two or three days" after her husband died. Shepherd says in his list that Hillersdon died on the thirteenth, and though he is generally reliable, the specificity of Thomson's account induces me to accept his version. Shepherd states that Mrs. Hillersdon was buried "very early" on the tenth in the cooking pit and remembers burying Mrs. DeRussett the next day in the same pit. I assume that Hillersdon took his wife outside either because there was a lull in the fighting or because he thought he had found a safe spot to do so, not figuring on a rebel battery opening up from the south.

204. Shepherd's account.

205. Thomson, *The Story of Cawnpore*, p. 109.

206. Newenham of the 1st Native Infantry was the son of a functionary of the excise department.

207. Shepherd, *A Personal Narrative*, pp. 24–25.

208. Thomson, *The Story of Cawnpore*, p. 70.

209. Garrett/Garrett: 28 May 1857, item 13; Burgess/Smith: 7 June 1858, item 25; Doyne/Garrett: 14 April 1858, item 26, PRONI.

210. Thomson, *The Story of Cawnpore*, pp. 68–70.

211. Shepherd, *A Personal Narrative*, p. 27.

212. Thomson, *The Story of Cawnpore*, pp. 72–73.

213. Ensign Browne, letter dated July 24, 1857 in TL, 21 Sept. 1857, p. 6.

214. Thomson, *The Story of Cawnpore*, p. 226.

215. Ensign Browne, letter dated July 24, 1857 in TL, 21 Sept. 1857, p. 6.

216. Cosens and Wallace, *Fatehgarh*, p. 29. Henry Rees of Lucknow told a variation on this story: "Lieutenant Boulton had already made preparation for escape, for he was less confident than his brother officers. His horse had been tied to a tree at a distance, and accompanied by Captain Staples, whom he had persuaded to join him, he arrived safely at

the tree, favoured by the darkness of the evening. Unfortunately, they had but one horse, for Staples had only at the eleventh hour determined on quitting. They mounted the same animal, and galloped off. They were seen, fired at, and Staples, who was behind, was shot through the back and fell. The other officers were all killed while at dinner, but Boulton effected his escape. He was pursued by seven of his men, and a bullet sent him wounded in the wrist. He rode for six miles for his life, and, jumping a broad ditch, left his pursuers behind." Rees, *The Siege of Lucknow*, pp. 45–46; Depositions of Chuni Lal, Maun Singh, and Mungna.

217. Deposition of Mungna.

218. Deposition of Chuni Lal.

219. Depositions of Narain Kachee, Nundeedeen Aheer, Appajee Luchman, and Appa Shastri.

220. Deposition of Narain Kachee.

221. Deposition of Nundeedeen Aheer.

222. Thomson, *The Story of Cawnpore*, p. 104.

223. Deposition of Jokhun.

224. Depositions of Bradshaw and Letts.

225. Gubbins, *Account*, p. 225.

226. Thomson, Reply.

227. Shepherd, *A Personal Narrative*, p. 26.

228. Emma Ewart: 1 June 1857.

229. Shepherd, *A Personal Narrative*, pp. 26, 36–37; Thomson, *The Story of Cawnpore*, p. 107.

230. Three of them were in the employ of Lieutenant Bridges of the 53rd. Thomson, *The Story of Cawnpore*, pp. 111–112.

231. Shepherd, *A Personal Narrative*, p. 26.

232. Thomson, *Report*.

233. Emma Larkins said there were only forty men left by June ninth, but this appears to have been an exaggeration. Emma Larkins, letter dated 9 June 1857 (OIOC).

234. Shepherd's account, dated August 29, 1857, published in TL, 7 Nov. 1857, p. 6.

235. Testimony of James Stewart, Pensioner of the 56th Native Infantry in *The Friend of India*, 27 Aug. 1857. Stewart survived the massacre at the ghats.

236. "He was brought into the thatched barrack quite unconscious, and died at my feet, leaving a widow and two daughters. At dusk the body was dragged out by the legs, the head bumping down the barrack steps, and his remains were then cast into a well just outside the entrenchment, where all our dead were thrown. His death affected us very much, especially on account of the pitiless way in which the body was disposed of." Bennett, "Twenty Days' Captivity."

237. Lee, *The Indian Mutiny*, p. 5.

238. Thomson states that this was the depth of the water well in the Entrenchment; I surmise that the depth of the nearby burial well was about the same. Thomson, *The Story of Cawnpore*, p. 86.

239. Shepherd, *A Personal Narrative*, p. 28.

240. Thomson, *The Story of Cawnpore*, p. 57.

241. Ibid., pp. 140–41.

242. Lieutenant Glanville. His father was an officer in the Grenadier Guards. Glanville was born in 1831 at St. German's in Cornwall and attended Bedford Grammar School. Blunt, *Christian Tombs and Monuments*, p. 111.

243. Captain Edward John Elms of the 1st Native Infantry served for a brief interval before Moore assigned him elsewhere. Elms was the son of the rector of Itchingfield, Sussex. Born in 1823, he had been a soldier for sixteen years. According to Delafosse he died in the Entrenchment.

244. Thomson, *The Story of Cawnpore*, p. 96.

245. Sherer, *Daily Life*, pp. 102–3.

246. Thomson, *The Story of Cawnpore*, pp. 84–85.

247. Shepherd, *A Personal Narrative*, p. 27.

248. Thomson, *The Story of Cawnpore*, pp. 71–72. Stirling was born in Perth, Australia, and was the son of Rear Admiral Sir J. Stirling of the Royal Navy.

249. Thomson, *The Story of Cawnpore*, pp. 67–68, 70–71, 74–75, 77, 84–85.

250. Thomson guessed he was an Irishman.

251. Jonah says it was two hundred yards from Nana's headquarters, but on his map the battery shown was closer to four hundred yards away. It is possible that the original battery was nearer Duncan's house.

252. Testimony of Nerput; Shepherd, *A Personal Narrative*, p. 28.

253. "Nizam-Ood-Dowlah, however, from fear still continued to attend the Nana." Testimony of Nerput.

254. Forbes, *Havelock*, p. 139. Some guessed it had been built by a Portuguese named Salvador, though there is now some evidence that it had been the home of a Lucknow noblewoman known as the Savada Begum. "The Savada House, where the massacres took place [*sic*], was occupied by the Nawab Golam Hossein, who frequently entertained the officers of the garrison to a grand dinner, and afterwards we were amused by a 'Nautch,' and a fine display of fireworks." In any case, it had been abandoned for a time, used as an asylum to house the orphans from the great famine, and then abandoned again after an epidemic in 1846. Nevill, *Cawnpore*, p. 121; Rawlins, *Autobiography*, p. 95; Dr. Munishwar Nigam.

255. Shepherd, *A Personal Narrative*, p. 29; Deposition of Hulas Singh; contemporary map of Cawnpore by Thomason College, Roorkee.

256. Deposition of Hulas Singh; contemporary map of Cawnpore by Thomason College, Roorkee.

257. For a brief period Hollings had also been editor of the *Delhi Gazette*. Carey, *Good Old Days*, 1:448.

258. Deposition of Kalka Pershad.

259. In the "Statement of Information" in TL, 16 Oct. 1857, p. 8, there is some question as to whether they were captured by neighboring zemindars or sowars from the 2nd Cavalry, and her zemindaree at Nujjubgurh was fourteen miles from Cawnpore. The statement also says that part of the money was paid, and they were confined until they came up with the rest, after which they would be permitted, ostensibly, to go to Allahabad.

260. Shepherd says the Greenways were set out because of "the money not being forthcoming immediately." Shepherd, p. 32; "Statement of Information" in TL, 16 Oct. 1857, p. 8. Over the next weeks the Greenways' servants would be dragged before Nana and pressured to reveal the whereabouts of the Greenways' fortune, but they insisted that all of their money was in Calcutta. Deposition of Kalka Pershad.

261. Shepherd, *A Personal Narrative*, pp. 32–33.

262. Deposition of Ajoodeea Pershad; he ascribes this speech to Mrs. Greenway, but Shepherd was told by witnesses that it was Mrs. Jacobi who shamed Nana Sahib into sparing her family.

263. Deposition of Ajoodea Pershad.

264. Shepherd, *A Personal Narrative*, p. 32.

265. Deposition of Futteh Singh; "Statement of Information" in TL, 16 Oct. 1857, p. 8, states they were killed "by the cavalry troopers." Their remains were kicked into a nearby drain, where they would lie for three months until another of his sons returned to Cawnpore and buried them.

266. Nerput witnessed her execution and said her head was placed under her arm. Shepherd states it was placed on her breast. It may have been moved there later. Shepherd, *A Personal Narrative*, p. 30; Testimony of Nerput.

267. Shepherd, *A Personal Narrative*, pp. 30–31.
268. Ibid., p. 31.
269. Testimony of Nerput.
270. Diary of Nunne Nawab.
271. Thomson, *The Story of Cawnpore*, pp. 143–46.
272. Deposition of Luchmun Pershad.
273. Depositions of Azizun and Jowahri Singh.
274. Deposition of Azizun.
275. Deposition of Jankee Pershad.
276. June 9 was a Tuesday, an especially auspicious day for worshippers of Hanuman.
277. Shepherd, *A Personal Narrative*, p. 29.
278. Deposition of Luchmun Pershad.
279. Shepherd, *A Personal Narrative*, p. 29.
280. Deposition of Jankee Pershad.
281. Nanak Chand's diary.
282. Deposition of Azizun.
283. Deposition of Lalla Gunga Pershad.
284. Shepherd, *A Personal Narrative*, p. 29.
285. Testimony of Nerput.
286. Ibid.
287. Muir, *Records*, 1:443.
288. Testimony of Nerput.
289. Shepherd, *A Personal Narrative*, p. 33.
290. Mir Wais Ali in Kanpur Collectorate Records in U.P., 4:519–20.
291. Nanak Chand's diary.
292. Shepherd, *A Personal Narrative*, p. 30.
293. Testimony of Nerput.
294. Fined.
295. Sherer, *Narrative*.
296. "You see," says Ishwari Prasad's descendant, Kailash Charan Wahal, "he was honest enough." Field notes.
297. Shepherd, *A Personal Narrative*, p. 33; Nanak Chand's diary.
298. Bennett, "Ten Months' Captivity."
299. Thomson, *The Story of Cawnpore*, pp. 82–83.
300. Thomson, *Report*.
301. *The Bombay Gazette Overland Summary*, 31 Aug. 1857, collection of Colin Forbes.
302. A presumably contemporaneous inscription was found in the Entrenchment by a Captain Alexander. It read, "Cap$^{n.}$ W. Halliday 56th N.I. Killed by a round shot on the 9th June 1857." Khoda Bux also stated that Halliday had been killed by a round shot. Willie's brother-in-law, Spencer Wyndham of the 88th Foot, wrote home that Halliday had been shot through the heart; and just before the massacre at the ghat Goad and Warde supposedly told a servant named Jokhun that Willie had been one of those who had died a "natural" death. But Thomson's story that Willie was killed between the puckah barrack and the main guard ". . . whilst carrying some horse-soup for his famishing wife," is probably the more reliable, though he states he was "shot dead," which suggests by a sniper. In this respect I tend to trust the inscription's report that Willie was killed by a round shot. In any case, the location Thomson gives indicates that by the ninth Emma had not yet been deemed ill enough to be moved to the hospital barrack, from whose burning wreckage she would later be dragged, which suggests that she sank dangerously after learning of Willie's death.

As for Emma's death, the newspapers in England published the following entry in the "native Doctor's list": "July 8th Miss Flascow, Mrs Halliday (from wounds) Mrs Halam and Col: Wiggen's son." The native doctor's list was a source of great confusion and frustration, for it represented a phonetic transliteration of probably grudgingly mumbled names into "Hindee" which had then been translated back into English. Relatives of victims were eager to find their loved ones' names on the list of those who died before the fifteenth of July so that they could imagine them spared the massacre at Bibighar, which they believed included rape and torture.

A translation was published in the September 21, 1857, issue of the *Times*, and under July eighth gives a "Mrs. Heles (name indistinct)" where the *Bombay Gazette* lists "Mrs. Halliday." But "Heles" is more likely to have represented either Mrs. Lydia Hillings, whose date of death was unknown (though this may have been a mistaken reference to Lydia Hillersdon), or Mrs. Mary Hill, whose death Shepherd in his not always reliable list places on the fifteenth of July.

Thus, after Willie's death on June eighth and the evident death of her daughter before June eleventh, it seems extremely unlikely that in the harrowing circumstances of the siege Emma could have survived the smallpox from which she was reported by Shepherd to have been suffering when she was dragged from the burning hospital barracks on July thirteenth. Emma simply could not have lived for another twenty-five let alone twenty-nine days, depending on which date one chooses. Edward "Butcher" Vibart wrote that "Poor Uncle Willie was killed before the capitulation, and poor Emma had died—better far have died thus—but I can write no more." (Edward Daniel Hamilton Vibart, *Papers*.) In my opinion, and in the opinion of her brother Spencer, who was later encamped at Cawnpore, Emma Halliday died of smallpox in the Entrenchment and was buried in the well beyond its walls.

303. Long and Stocqueler, *British Social Life in Ancient Calcutta*, p. 96.

304. "Henry dear boy," she told her apparently rebellious son, in lines that must have followed after him the rest of his life, "my heart grieves over you, oh dear boy if you saw the position your little brother and sisters are in at this moment you would weep over ever having pleased your own desires." But she tried to reconcile herself with her mother-in-law, who had evidently disapproved of the Larkins's life. "Dearest Mrs. Larkins," she said, "I got your last letter, it pained me but I feel with all our sins and difficulties I have been faithful to you and to Georgie, perhaps his best Earthly friend." Emma Larkins/Henrietta Coffin: 9 June 1857 (OIOC).

305. Thomson, *The Story of Cawnpore*, p. 66.

306. Ibid., pp. 91–92.

307. Deposition of Ram Buksh. A few were from the 1st and 56th but most from the 53rd Native Infantry.

308. According to Thomson, the general's concern was that he did not have enough food for them, not that he feared they might be treacherous. In any case, this is what the sepoys themselves were probably told.

309. Deposition of Ram Buksh; Thomson, *The Story of Cawnpore*, pp. 39–40.

310. Deposition of Bhola Khan.

311. Depositions of Gobind Singh, Sheik Elahee Buksh, and Ghouse Mohomed.

312. Some of them may have been among those loyal sepoys who were hanged by British commissioners in the retributive slaughter already under way at Benares and Allahabad.

313. Depositions of Bradshaw and Letts.

314. Shepherd, *A Personal Narrative*, p. 69.

315. Bennett, "Ten Months' Captivity."

316. Ibid.

317. Shepherd, *A Personal Narrative*, p. 57.

318. Thomson, *The Story of Cawnpore*, p. 67.

319. Ibid., pp. 120–21; Shepherd, *A Personal Narrative*, p. 27.

320. "In contemplating the circumstances of this emeute in which Lieutenant [Boulton] was concerned," wrote Thomson, "and which terminated in the death of several offi-

cers, I can but think it entirely attributable to a practice which I trust will from henceforth be for ever exploded from the Indian army, or at least from that portion of it which may consist of native troops; I refer to the detaching of officers from their own companies, and placing in their stead, for special service, those who have no knowledge of the men, and have never had the opportunity of gaining their confidence." Thomson, *The Story of Cawnpore*, pp. 122–23.

321. Trevelyan, *Cawnpore*, p. 115.
322. Testimony of Mary Ann.
323. Shepherd's account.
324. Thomson, *The Story of Cawnpore*, pp. 87–88.
325. Thomson, Reply.
326. A shilling was then worth half a rupee.
327. Shepherd, *A Personal Narrative*, pp. 25–26.
328. MacKillop was born in Calcutta in 1827 and educated at Bishopwearmouth and Haileybury and came to India upon his graduation in 1847. He was Joint Magistrate at Cawnpore. C. W. MacKillop, his brother, was also in the civil service in India. A plaque at All Souls reads: "To the Memory of John Robert MacKillop of the Bengal Civil Service who was killed at Cawnpore on or about the 25th of June 1857 in his 31st year. He nobly lost his life when bringing water from the well for the distressed women and children. His death was deeply lamented."
329. Shepherd, *A Personal Narrative*, p. 26.
330. Thomson said MacKillop was wounded in the thigh; the less delicate Amelia Horne stated he was shot in the groin. Bennett, "Ten Months' Captivity."
331. Cosens and Wallace, *Fatehgarh*, pp. 10, 13–15, 18, 77.
332. Blunt, *Christian Tombs and Monuments*, p. 112.
333. Trevelyan, *The Golden Oriole*, p. 315. Their brother Edward Vibart would later tour the ruined "walks and little paths" of his parents' compound "where it was the delight of those little brothers and sisters to take their 'Teddy' out, and run after him until he was out of breath, and show him all the flowers." Vibart Papers.
334. Edmund Vibart, *Papers* (OIOC).
335. Yalland, *Traders and Nabobs*, p. 264.
336. Heathcote/Heathcote: 16 May 1857, NLS (MS.20206).
337. Monckton Papers, (CCSAS.)
338. The future Lord Roberts would report that the women were braver than the men. "In this country," he wrote from Amritsar, "the [European] women are the only ones who have behaved properly. The men are positively disgusting, and make one ashamed of being a man." Roberts, *Letters*, p. 14.
339. "*Much* comfort have we in religion," wrote Rosa Monckton. William Edwards of nearby Budaon observed that there was "not a day on which we do not find something that appears as if written especially for persons in our unhappy circumstances, to meet the feelings and wants of the day" (Edwards, *Personal Adventures*, p. 147). The American Methodist William Butler, stationed at Bareilly, sixty miles north of Fatehgarh, found that in particular "the 'denunciatory Psalms,' which in a calm and quiet civilization seem sometimes to read harshly, were in our case so apposite and so consistent that we felt their adaptation and propriety against these enemies of God as though they had been actually composed for our special case" (Butler, *The Land of the Veda*, p. 267). "How precious are the Psalms!" exclaimed Reverend Campbell. "I always loved them, but how unspeakably precious are they at such a time as this!" (Fullerton in Sherring, *The Indian Church during the Great Rebellion*, pp. 150–52). "Though the heathen be raging around us," wrote regimental surgeon Thomas Godfrey Heathcote, "and the people may imagine a vain thing, He that sitteth in the Heavens shall laugh, & shall dust the devotees of Mahadeo, Devi, Kali, & the rest of them to pieces like a potter's repel." (Heathcote/Heathcote: 16 May 1857, NLS [MS.20206]).

340. Monckton Papers, CCSAS.

341. Hughes says this is from Sherring and that it occurred on the twenty-first of May, but that was a Thursday. The garrison found out about Meerut and Delhi around the fourteenth. Hughes, *The Mutiny Chaplains*, p. 63.

342. Monckton Papers, CCSAS.

343. Mrs. Freeman in Sherring, *The Indian Church during the Great Rebellion*, p. 125.

344. Dass in Sherring, *The Indian Church during the Great Rebellion*, pp. 134–35. Dass had been one of the "orphans" rescued from the 1837–1838 famine and became a distinguished author of tracts. Alter, *In the Doab*, pp. 105, 113.

345. Sherring, *The Indian Church during the Great Rebellion*, p. 126.

346. Fullerton in ibid., pp. 150–52.

347. Dass in ibid., pp. 134–35.

348. Freeman in ibid., pp. 124–25.

349. "I have but little doubt," Campbell's successor would write, "that they would have succeeded, if the effort had been made; but He who knows the end from the beginning, saw fit to order it otherwise." Fullerton in ibid., pp. 150–52.

350. They "could not be sure of any place," she explained to her mother, and "it would be worse to be murdered on the roads, and one, perhaps, left solitary. . . . We shall have been married three years on the 29th of this month. Think of us on that day. I am so thankful I came out to India to be a comfort to my beloved John; and a companion to one who has so given his heart to the Lord. And circumstances and positions in which we have been placed, during our sojourn in India, have made the promises of God's Word so sweet, and the consolations of religion so unspeakably great; besides endearing us to one another in a degree and way which a quiet English home might not have done." Monckton Papers, CCSAS.

351. Heathcote/Heathcote: 16 May 1857, NLS (MS.20206).

352. Wallace, *Fatehgarh*, pp. 155–56; Thornhill plaque at All Souls in Cawnpore.

353. Cosens and Wallace, *Fatehgarh*, p. 14.

354. "The Story of Miss Sutherland" (BM).

355. Cosens and Wallace, *Fatehgarh*, p. 31.

356. Ibid., p. 23.

357. "If the Reg^t [the 10th N.I.] be faithful," wrote Thomas Heathcote, "we hope to give you a good account, but if it sh^d fraternize with the insurgents, the Lord have mercy upon us, you will probably never receive another letter written by my hand." Heathcote/Heathcote: 16 May 1857, NLS (MS.20206).

358. Narrative of Gavin Jones.

359. Cosens and Wallace, *Fatehgarh*, pp. 28–29.

360. Ibid., pp. 30^n 33

361. Heathcote/Thornhill in FSC, U.P., 5:733–36.

362. Cosens and Wallace, *Fatehgarh*, p. 34.

363. Heathcote/Heathcote: 2 June 1857, NLS (MS.20206).

364. Freeman in Sherring, *The Indian Church during the Great Rebellion*, p. 126.

365. Cosens and Wallace, *Fatehgarh*, pp. 30–32.

366. Unless otherwise noted, my account is derived from Cosens and Wallace, *Fatehgarh*.

367. Newton, *Historical Sketches*, p. 127.

368. Owen, *Memorials of Christian Martyrs*, p. 88.

369. Reverend R. S. Fullerton in Sherring, *The Indian Church during the Great Rebellion*, pp. 152–53. The other wives were equally philosophical. "What is to become of us and the Lord's work in this land we cannot tell," wrote Mrs. McMullen, "but he reigneth, and in him we will rejoice." "Although we may be called upon to part with life for Christ and his cause," wrote Mrs. Johnson, "may we not glorify God more by our deaths than by our lives?" Owen, *Memorials of Christian Martyrs*, p. 88.

370. Reverend R. S. Fullerton in Sherring, *The Indian Church during the Great Rebellion*, pp. 152–53.

371. This was true enough, but a great many zemindars and petty rajas were to protect and assist fugitive Europeans. Writing of the fugitives from a station called Gogra, Innes stated that though "the villagers on the Gogra were hostile, . . . elsewhere they seem to have been more or less helpful; a singular circumstance when it is remembered to what turbulence and bloodshed and evil deeds they had long been accustomed. . . . The Rajahs of Bulrampore, of Bithur, and Gopalpore; Roostum Sah of Deyrah and Hunwunt Singh of Dharoopore; with the chiefs of Amethee and of the Byswara clans; besides many others . . . helped into security the fugitives from Gonda and Secrora, from Fyzabad and Sultanpore, from Salone and Rae Bareilly." Innes, *Lucknow and Oude in the Mutiny*, pp. 86–87.

372. Dass in Sherring, *The Indian Church during the Great Rebellion*, pp. 135–36.

373. Narrative of Gavin Jones.

374. For this and subsequent attacks on passing boats, twenty-eight villagers were later transported for life to the Andaman Islands, and the village itself was confiscated. Cosens and Wallace, *Fatehgarh*, p. 40.

375. Narrative of Gavin Jones.

376. Cosens and Wallace, *Fatehgarh*, pp. 42–43.

377. It appears to be four miles on Cosens and Wallace's map.

378. Deposition of Hingun.

379. Fullerton in Sherring, *The Indian Church during the Great Rebellion*, pp. 154–55.

380. The loot included four yards of black broadcloth; twenty pounds of nails; a telescope; a woolen carpet; a silk gown; eleven yards of silk; a silver sword hilt; and a package of English soap. Cosens and Wallace, *Fatehgarh*, p. 45.

381. Ibid., p. 44.

382. Heathcote/Thornhill in FSC, U.P., 5:733–36.

383. Ibid.

384. Fatehgarh Narrative, FPP, in ibid., 5:729–33. Smith confronted the Nawab about this second proclamation, demanding to know if it meant he had rebelled, but the Nawab replied that he was merely trying to keep the peace and Smith did not press him further.

385. "The Story of Miss Sutherland" (BM).

386. Dass in Sherring, *The Indian Church during the Great Rebellion*, p. 138.

387. Indian convicts endured the most appalling conditions without complaint, but they were every bit as meticulous about caste as their more law-abiding brethren. Thus the British had to separate high caste from low caste, Hindu from Moslem, and devise labor suitable to their prisoners' individual stations.

The most daunting proposition was keeping them fed. At first prisoners had been allowed to cook for themselves, thereby protecting their caste from contamination. But the system galled the British. "Men loitered over their cooking, and their eating," wrote Kaye, "and made excuses to escape work." So a new system of prison messes was devised, in which cooks were assigned to separate caste groups. This seemed sensible enough until the wrong cook prepared food for the wrong caste, or the wrong dish went to the wrong prisoner, and a prisoner's caste was lost, to be retrieved only after the most prolonged and arduous rituals and ablutions.

Then there was the business about the prisoners' water vessels. In order to insure the purity of his drinking water, each Hindu had his own brass lotas (water pots), which they occasionally employed as weapons, beaning each other or their guards. (Or even a magistrate: in 1845 a judge in Alipore was killed by a blow from a lota.) When the British confiscated the prisoners' lotas, or initiated any leveling measure to regiment prison life after the English model, it was taken as further proof that the Company intended to tamper with their religion. Kaye, *A History of the Great Revolt*, 1:195, 198, and nn.

388. Suspicions were also aroused by a policy of educating inmates, which a reviewer for the *Times of London* would later call "a perfect mania. . . . Burglars and murderers who

could distinguish themselves as teachers were passed on from gaol to gaol to act as instructors. Reading, writing, and arithmetic were required, and sometimes geography and the planetary system were taught, as, we infer, to vagabonds and dacoits by profession. Why were we doing all this? Surely not without some hidden purpose. . . . It was whispered, and extensively believed, that the object of our Government was to destroy the religion of the Hindoos and to convert them to our own." TL, 7 Sept. 1858, p. 10.

389. Dacoits, thugs, and poisoners were usually transported to Calcutta (though an average of fifty percent of them would escape along the way). But now the roads were too hazardous, and hardened criminals were intermingled with the usual petty thieves who served their time building roads, pulling punkahs in the courts and hospitals, and walking the defective treadmill at the jail. Wallace, *Fatehgarh Camp*, pp. 128–31.

390. Heathcote/Thornhill: 6 June 1857 in FSC, U.P., 5:733–36.

391. No doubt the sepoys would have argued, however disingenuously, that without an officer to command them they could not have been expected to intercede or to obey the panicky orders of the roughed-up superintendent. The sepoys had been assigned to reinforce the usual complement of prison guards whom Smith had judged unreliable, and if the rest of his performance is anything to go by, it is likely that Smith stationed them at the jail without laying out the line of command or preparing them for all possible contingencies.

392. Heathcote/Thornhill in FSC, U.P., 5:733–36.

393. Narrative of Gavin Jones.

394. After the Mutiny, Beloi, which stood on an island that was often submerged by the monsoon floods, was erased from official maps. Cosens and Wallace, *Fatehgarh, p.* 45.

395. The *churrs* or islands that appeared and disappeared in the dry and wet seasons were so fertile that their proprietorship had to be sternly regulated by the Company.

396. Fullerton in Sherring, *The Indian Church during the Great Rebellion*, p. 155.

397. Cosens and Wallace, *Fatehgarh*, p. 46.

398. Deposition of Hingun; Forrest, *Selections*, 3ccxiii–ccxv.

399. Fullerton in Sherring, *The Indian Church during the Great Rebellion*, p. 157.

400. Four of the sweepers were women. Cosens and Wallace, *Fatehgarh*, p. 48.

401. The subhedar ordered a native nurse to keep Miss Sutherland's presence a secret, for if Nana Sahib found out that one of his officers was protecting a European, it would mean death for all of them. Suffering from a fever that "nearly deprived me of my reason," she heard "nothing of what was going on in and around Cawnpore, but her nurse evidently brought her bulletins from time to time, including an evidently fanciful account of an unsuccessful attempt by Nana to have the wealthiest of the Fatehgarh party trampled by elephants. "Though the Nana appropriated all the money and valuables found in the boats of the fugitives, the male prisoners were subjected to the most cruel torture for the purpose of forcing them to confess where they had buried their wealth, for some of the merchants and traders were thought to be very rich. So when the Nana's instruments of torture failed to obtain the desired information, the arch fiend put it down to stubbornness and obstinacy on the part of the Englishmen and he ordered them to be bound hand and foot and trampled to death by Elephants. The Europeans were accordingly fettered and pinned to the ground. But when the Elephants, which had formerly belonged to the English Commissariat Department arrived, they refused to pass over the prostrate Christians. When urged on by the mahouts, the huge beasts lifted up the prostrate bodies in their trunks and put them aside but would not trample upon them. . . . The huge beasts instead of going forward retreated through the crowd, knocking down and injuring many who had come to see the hated Feringhee flattened into a pancake. After this orders were given to the men of the 2nd Cavalry to dispatch the Europeans." Trampling was a mode of execution under the Mahrattas, and was even practiced on occasion by Baji Rao himself. But this version is not corroborated by any of the other witnesses, all of whom agreed that the

entire party of refugees was inspected by Nana and then executed in a ditch between a half hour and an hour later.

402. This may have been the same kindly subhedar who later oversaw Shepherd's imprisonment.

403. The dialogue during the party's capture is from the testimony of native Christian witnesses quoted by Fullerton in Sherring, *The Indian Church during the Great Rebellion*, pp. 156–59 and a set of notes (Ga 2D 1230) at the University of Nottingham.

404. Deposition of Hingun.

405. "The Story of Miss Sutherland" (BM).

406. Cosens and Wallace, *Fatehgarh*, pp. 46–48.

407. Deposition of Hingun.

408. Cosens and Wallace, *Fatehgarh*, p. 48.

409. Deposition of Hingun.

410. Shepherd, pp. 38–39; Deposition of Futteh Singh.

411. That day Nana Sahib's retinue included Bala Rao, Azimullah Khan, Brigadier Teeka Singh, the Vakil Ahmed Ali Khan, an attorney named Akbar Ali, Shah Ali the former kotwal or police chief; and a number of zemindars. Hulas Singh, the newly appointed kotwal, was reported by one witness to have been present, but he later denied it to Colonel Williams.

412. Shepherd, *A Personal Narrative*, p. 33.

413. Ibid., p. 38–39; Deposition of Futteh Singh; Nanak Chand's diary.

414. Depositions of Hingun, Bukkee Singh, Futteh Singh, Golab Singh; Nanak Chand's diary. Only Hulas Singh, the rebel kotwal, claimed that Nana himself gave the order. Hulas Singh said he was not present when the decision was made, and based his assertion on the assumption that any order that momentous would have had to come from the Peshwa himself.

415. Shepherd defines *jullads* as belonging "to a very low caste of people generally employed as executioners and hangmen, as well as in killing dogs when they increase to a dangerous extent." Shepherd, *A Personal Narrative*, p. 119.

416. Depositions of Futteh Singh and Golab Singh; Shepherd, *A Personal Narrative*, pp. 38–39. "I heard some of the Sahibs tell the sepoys who they were, and ask them to give their names and salaams to the Nana. Some sepoys went away and soon returned saying that the Nana's orders were to kill them." Deposition of Sheo Churran Das.

417. Nanak Chand's diary.

418. One young lady, the daughter of an officer, was said to have refused to grovel. "No tyrant has ever been so cruel and blood-thirsty as you are," she told Nana. "In no religion is the killing of women and children authorized, but I know not what retribution you will meet with. Now consider well that however much you may kill and slaughter them in this barbarous manner, the English will never be diminished in numbers. If any one is left he will avenge our deaths." She was said to be the daughter of "some General." She may have been one of Colonel Tucker's daughters, but the anecdote is so similar to the story of Mrs. Jacobi's defiant speech that it may be a mere variation. Testimony of Nerput.

419. Deposition of Hingun.

420. Deposition of Bukhee Singh.

421. Deposition of Hingun.

422. Shepherd, *A Personal Narrative*, pp. 38–39. On the morning of the thirteenth Nanak Chand, a Bengali babu, "saw a number of corpses of ladies and gentlemen," at the river, "also the bodies of a number of natives. I cannot tell the exact number, but they extended here and there about a mile. I did not recognize any near the ghat. I saw the bodies of three young ladies. They all had their clothes on, but the low caste people had commenced to take the clothes from the bodies; and the animals had torn some of the corpses." Deposition of Nanak Chand.

423. TL, 16 Oct. 1857, p. 7; Shepherd, *A Personal Narrative*, pp. 42–43.

424. It is impossible to determine the exact location and size of the rebel guns for they were constantly being moved; also, some had been spiked, others replaced.

425. Testimony of Nerput.

426. Thomson, *The Story of Cawnpore*, pp. 136–37.

427. Shepherd's account.

428. Deposition of Hulas Singh.

429. Shepherd's account.

430. Shepherd, *A Personal Narrative*, pp. 34, 93.

431. Halliday letter 19: 10 July 1853; WLH/JH: 26 May 1857, collection of Raleigh Trevelyan.

432. I have been told that a collector possesses Willie's inscribed sword, which was evidently fished out of the well after the reoccupation of Cawnpore.

433. Shepherd states that Emma died of smallpox, and though in other cases he is sometimes mistaken or in any case contradicted in his statements of causes and dates of death, he would have seen Emma Halliday firsthand in Seppings's chamber.

434. Shepherd refers to Parker as "a sergeant or road overseer." Parker was the only sergeant overseer listed among the casualties at Cawnpore. Shepherd, *A Personal Narrative*, p. 35.

435. *Hickey's Gazette* recommended keeping a long bamboo with a triple iron hook close at hand to snag these oleaginous intruders. Carey, *Good Old Days*, 1:359; Long and Stocqueler, *British Social Life in Ancient Calcutta*, pp. 31, 76.

436. Shepherd, *A Personal Narrative*, pp. 34–35.

437. Deposition of Khoda Buksh; Shepherd, p. 5.

438. Trevelyan, *Cawnpore*, p. 85

439. She proved more effective than the picket who came to relieve her, for during the next watch they tried to escape. Thomson, *The Story of Cawnpore*, pp. 75–76.

440. Ibid., p. 77.

441. Ibid., p. 76.

442. Mason, *A Matter of Honour*, p. 299.

443. "In the night, on the housetop, [Major Banks] had asked me, as a Clergyman, what I should advise him to do, in case of its being certain that his wife would fall into the hands of the rebels, and that they would treat her as they had done the women at Delhi and Meerut. It was a difficult question: but I told him that, if I were certain that my wife would be so treated, I would shoot her rather than let her fall into their hands. (Colonel Inglis afterwards asked me whether I thought his wife would be justified in killing her own children, rather than let them be murdered by the natives. I said, no; for children could be but killed; whereas we had been told that at Delhi young delicate ladies had been dragged through the streets, violated by man, and then murdered.) //God forgive me, if I gave the wrong advice! but I was excited; and I know that I should have killed Emmie [his wife], rather than have allowed her to be thus dishonoured and tortured by these bloodthirsty savage idolators." Polehampton, *Memoir*, pp. 270–71 (OIOC).

444. Gubbins, *Account*, p. 149.

445. Shepherd, *A Personal Narrative*, p. 35.

446. Sherer, *Narrative*.

447. Shepherd, *A Personal Narrative*, pp. 42–43.

448. Thomson, *The Story of Cawnpore*, pp. 74–75.

449. Shepherd, *A Personal Narrative*, p. 36.

450. Thomson, *The Story of Cawnpore*, pp. 139–40.

451. Shepherd, *A Personal Narrative*, p. 36.

452. In a note folded into the blank back pages of a copybook of the letters of Edward Vibart at the India Office Library (OIOC Mss.Eur.F.135/19), I came upon a hitherto un-

known transcription of Shepherd's inscription that had been recorded after Cawnpore was reoccupied by Captain Alexander. It varies slightly from the version Shepherd included in his *Personal Narrative*. "Should this meet the eyes of any who know as in case we are all destroyed, be it known that we occupied this room for eight days under circumstances so distressing as has no precedent. The destruction of Jerusalem could not have been attended with distress so severe as we have experienced in so short a time./Signed R. [*sic*] J. Shepherd wounded in the back, his wife & children. Rebecca & her infant/Emma, Martha, old M^rs. Frost/M^rs. Osborne/Daniel Thacking * [Shepherd] /Conductor Burrill [Berrill] his wife and daughter/together with their friends 11 June 1857./ *Not sure whether it is J. Jackson or Thackson or Thicking."

453. Shepherd, *A Personal Narrative*, p. 69.

454. Horne, *Narrative* (BM).

455. Thomson, *The Story of Cawnpore*, pp. 90–91.

456. Ibid., p. 91.

457. I would not name Wiggins if he did not so exclusively fit Thomson's criteria. Wiggins was in his forties when he died, and is the only officer "of high rank" at Cawnpore whose name I could not find among the memorial stained-glass panes at All Souls Church. But the charge of cowardice is grave enough that a review of the other candidates is in order. It is unlikely that by Thomson's definition any of the captains in the garrison qualified as officers "of high rank"; in any case only one of the captains comes close to fitting the bill: Captain Kempland of the 56th. But Thomson specifically absolves him because he "suffered so much from the heat, that although not wounded, he was also utterly prostrate and non-combatant." No higher-ranking officer fits the bill either. Wheeler was certainly not "in the prime of life" and though he did withdraw from command toward the end of the siege, Thomson would not have said of him that he "never showed himself outside the walls of the barrack, nor took even the slightest part in the military operations." Thomson writes about the old general with respect and sympathy. The bachelor Brigadier Jack, like Williams and Prout, died of apoplexy early in the siege. The Queen's Captain Moore was "the life and soul" of the defense. The "brave and clever" Ewart, according to Thomson, "was severely wounded in the arm early in the proceedings, and was entirely disabled from any participation in the defence." Thomson's cowardly officer was shot in the boats; Major Lindsay died in the barracks. Hillersdon was a bachelor. Larkins might circumstantially seem to fit the bill, but artillery officers were famously brave, and Thomson excuses him: "in consequence of the shattered state of that officer's health, he was able to take but a small part in the defence." Vibart was one of the heroes of the Entrenchment, "active and robust to the last." Thomson mentions all of these officers in his narrative but never once mentions Wiggins, whose death in the boats and whose imprecating letter to Lucknow, written toward the end of the siege as he lay on the barrack floor, is consistent with Thomson's description of the skulking officer.

458. Lydia Hillersdon: 31 May 1857.

459. Lawrence in TL, 2 Sept. 1857.

460. Bennett, "Ten Months' Captivity."

461. Thomson, *The Story of Cawnpore*, p. 110.

462. Shepherd, *A Personal Narrative*, pp. 43–44.

463. Her name was Mrs. Darby. Thomson, *The Story of Cawnpore*, p. 104.

464. Bennett, "Ten Months' Captivity."

465. Shepherd, *A Personal Narrative*, pp. 3, 45; Yalland, *Traders and Nabobs*, pp. 225, 252–53.

466. These small remains, at least, "were gathered up in a sheet" before being thrown into the well. Horne, *Narrative* (BM).

467. Thomson, *The Story of Cawnpore*, p. 102.

468. Shepherd's account.

469. Bennett, "Ten Months' Captivity."

470. I surmise this from the fact that they were evidently not brought before Nana Sahib. The sepoys had instructions to bring all Europeans and Christians to Nana before executing them. Shepherd merely lists Mrs. Williams and her three children as among those killed outside of the Entrenchment.

471. Shepherd, *A Personal Narrative*, p. 57.

472. Ibid., pp. 100–101.

473. Deposition of Appajee Luchman; Shepherd, *A Personal Narrative*, p. 122.

474. Innes, *Lucknow and Oude in the Mutiny*, p. 89.

475. Lucknow Collectorate Mutiny Basta in U.P., 4:667.

476. Police chief.

477. Azizun's role in the uprising may be Nanak Chand's fantasy.

478. Deposition of Golab Singh.

479. Shah Ali would play a major role in negotiating the garrison's capitulation. Depositions of Hulas Singh and Sheo Prasad; Diary of Nunne Nawab; Nanak Chand's diary.

480. Deposition of Hulas Singh.

481. Deposition of Juggernath.

482. Anderson/Beadon: 11 July 1859 in HDP Public, 29 July 1859, nos. 40–41, NAI. "The inhabitants of the villages outside the city broke the telegraph posts and cut up the wire, and took the wood and wire to their own houses." Testimony of Nerput.

483. Lady Canning in Allen, *A Glimpse of the Burning Plain*, p. 84.

484. An evidently contemporary map of Cawnpore in the Mutiny, drawn for Thomason College, Roorkee, makes reference to an explosion in buildings near the church, but Nunne Nawab, who should have known, stated that this happened in Duncan's bungalow. Diary of Nunne Nawab.

485. Deposition of Lalla Shunker Doss.

486. He was "Reuz Ali, son of a one-eyed pensioner." Deposition of Hulas Singh.

487. Depositions of Bradshaw and Letts.

488. Depositions of Gobind Singh, Sheik Elahee Buksh, and Ghouse Mohomed.

489. Thomson, *The Story of Cawnpore*, p. 92.

490. Thomson, *Report*.

491. "It was perfectly impracticable to save any of the wounded or the medicine in consequence of the insurgents collecting in very large bodies in the adjacent compounds and buildings, with their muskets and swords, ready every moment to pounce down upon us, and the men were compelled to keep their places under the walls of the entrenchment, and could not bear a helping hand to those in the barracks." Shepherd's account.

492. Nevertheless, said Thomson, "though he suffered much, this neither suspended his endeavours at the time in question, nor kept him from constant service." Thomson, *The Story of Cawnpore*, pp. 96–97.

493. Thomson, *Report*. In his book he states that they were gunners. He may have simply been referring to the sick and wounded soldiers and not counting the deaths of the women and children of which, from his post in the unfinished barracks, he would have been less aware than Shepherd and Horne.

494. Bennett, "Ten Months' Captivity"; Horne, *Narrative* (BM). Sherer in his narrative of the Cawnpore uprising stated that "many" were burned alive. Sherer, *Narrative*.

495. Shepherd, *A Personal Narrative*, pp. 25, 45; Yalland, *Traders and Nabobs*, p. 344.

496. Shepherd, *A Personal Narrative*, p. 44.

497. Horne, *Narrative* (BM).

498. Trevelyan, *The Golden Oriole*, p. 313. Some say she was among the women and children who were later confined at the Bibighar; a name that loosely resembles hers appeared on a native doctor's list of the Bibighar's occupants, but it was later determined to have been another lady's. According to Major Vibart's son Edward, Thomson definitely maintained that Emma had died of smallpox while in the Entrenchment. Vibart Papers.

499. Trevelyan, *Cawnpore*, p. 101.

500. Halliday Letter 18: 3 July 1853, collection of Dr. Colin Forbes.

501. One curious aspect of Emma's death is that she is the only person in the Entrenchment said to have been suffering from smallpox, which is one of the most contagious of all diseases. Some of the others had probably been inoculated against smallpox, but it may be that those who succumbed to what Amy Horne called a "maddening fever" were sufferers so weakened by heat, shock, wounds, thirst, and starvation that they did not survive even its early stages.

502. Thomson says sixty to eighty yards. Thomson, *The Story of Cawnpore*, pp. 93–94.

503. Ibid., p. 140.

504. Ibid., p. 94.

505. Shepherd, *A Personal Narrative*, p. 44.

506. Thomson, *The Story of Cawnpore*, pp. 93–94.

507. Thomson, *Report;* Delafosse; Shepherd's account.

508. Thomson, *The Story of Cawnpore*, p. 93.

509. Shepherd, *A Personal Narrative*, p. 45; Shepherd's account.

510. Lee, *The Indian Mutiny*, p. 9.

511 Thomson, *The Story of Cawnpore*, pp. 99–100.

512. Horne, *Narrative* (BM); Sherer, *Narrative*.

513 TL, 16 October 1857, p. 7.

514. Shepherd's account.

515. Thomson, *The Story of Cawnpore*, pp. 99–100. Indeed, as George Otto Trevelyan would put it, "To have slept four in a cabin on board an outward-bound steamer; to have passed a night in a palanquin, or a day at a posting-house where there was no tea, and only milk enough for the little ones, had hitherto appeared to the Cawnpore ladies the last conceivable extremity of destitution and discomfort." Trevelyan, *Cawnpore*, p. 96.

516. Later, "when the ashes of the consumed barrack cooled, the men of the 32d Regiment, who had been stationed there, raked them over with bayonets and swords, making diligent search for their lost medals. A great many of them were found, though in most instances marred by the fire. The fact that they would explore after these treasures while the sepoys were firing on them, shows the high appreciation in which the British soldier holds his decorations." Thomson, *The Story of Cawnpore*, pp. 92–93.

517. Horne, *Narrative* (BM).

518. Bennett, "Ten Months' Captivity."

519. Horne said fully "half our number" had gone mad, but she may have been referring only to her own party. Bennett, "Ten Months' Captivity"; Horne, *Narrative* (BM).

520. This may account for the peculiar alternation between boyish jauntiness and despair that runs through Thomson's account.

521. Thomson, *The Story of Cawnpore*, pp. 84–85.

522. Shepherd, *A Personal Narrative*, pp. 44. Bennett also stated that two kits were saved; Thomson said "not one of the surgical instruments was saved."

523. Horne, *Narrative* (BM).

524. Thomson, *The Story of Cawnpore*, p. 94.

525. Ibid., p. 103.

526. Horne, *Narrative* (BM).

527. TL, 16 Oct. 1857, p. 8.

528. Thomson, *The Story of Cawnpore*, pp. 80–84.

529. Shepherd, *A Personal Narrative*, p. 24.

530. Thomson, *Reply.*

531. Shepherd's account.

532. Trevelyan, *Cawnpore*, p. 104.

533. TL, 16 Oct. 1857, p. 8.

534. Thomson, *Reply*.

535. Shepherd, *A Personal Narrative*, p. 56.

536. A sweeper named Moonshee Zuhooree hired thirteen men and two women to convey "a supply of eggs, sugar, bread, butter, &c., to Major Larkins of the artillery." All fifteen were taken prisoner the next day "and blown away from guns," but not before they had betrayed Zuhuri, who promptly fled the city with a message from Larkins and a "gold ring set with five diamonds given to me by the Major's lady," which he faithfully delivered to the garrison at Allahabad before turning right around and marching back to Cawnpore with Havelock's force. Trevelyan, *Cawnpore*, p. 100; Deposition of Moonshee Zuhooree.

537. James Stewart in *Friend of India*, 27 August, 1857.

538. Bennett, "Ten Months' Captivity."

539. After their appendages were severed boiling oil was applied.

540. Over the protests of his officers, Lawrence did not demolish the temples and mosques. Collier, *The Sound of Fury*, p. 100.

541. Gubbins, *Account*, p. 443.

542. Polehampton, *Memoirs*, p. 275 (OIOC).

543. Kavanagh, *How I Won the Victoria Cross*, pp. 16–17.

544. Gubbins, *Account*, p. 173.

545. Horne, *Narrative* (BM). Horne places this sortie before the fire and regarded the fire as a retaliation for it. But Thomson and Shepherd place it after the fire, which jibes with the special risk they took to put the battery that had set fire to the barrack out of commission. Horne may have been confusing this sortie with one of Moore's earlier sallies.

546. The mess is shown on Thomson's vague map; the distance is estimated from Shepherd's map.

547. Shepherd, *A Personal Narrative*, p. 44.

548. "Though some state that this amount was paid him as compensation for the loss sustained by him owing to the plunder of his house." Deposition of Lalla Shunker Doss.

549. Horne, *Narrative* (BM).

550. Thomson, *The Story of Cawnpore*, p. 112; Thomson, *Report*.

551. Shepherd's account.

552. North, *Journal*, p. 91.

553. North says Wheeler expected relief on the fifteenth; Sherer says it was the fourteenth.

554. I have projected the population of Cawnpore District in 1857 from the census of 1853, which showed a population of 174,566. This represented a jump of 18.2% from five years before. But any figure is approximate and fluctuated wildly when various regiments and their followers arrived or departed. Nevill, *Cawnpore*, p. 94.

555. Ibid., pp. 94, 102.

556. An entire community's religious affiliation could shift at the whim of a single zemindar: in Ghatampur, for instance, a community of Rajput Dikhits embraced Islam because their zemindar had promised God that they would do so if God granted him a son. Ibid., p. 120.

557. Ibid., pp. 100–101. The Hindu community at Cawnpore was unusually pragmatic and broad-minded for the period: census takers found that among the local Hindus "there is an aversion to disown the worship of any member of the pantheon."

558. Landon, *Under the Sun*, p. 276; Ball, *The History of the Indian Mutiny*, 1:304.

559. Shepherd, *A Personal Narrative*, pp. 105–109; and N.W.P., P.D.P., Jan.–June 1864: 30 Jan. 1864, P.D.A., pp. 19–20.

560. Diary of Nunne Nawab.

561. Four years later the Company banned amputations from its territories. *Calcutta Chronicle*, 19 Feb. 1789, in Carey, *Good Old Days*, 1:358. Shepherd states that the butchers were executed at Nana Sahib's order, but I surmise that such a case would have been brought before Baba Bhutt, and that Nana, surrounded as he was by Moslem advisers,

would probably not have condemned the butchers to death. Shepherd says that almost every execution at Cawnpore was by Nana's order, but it is hard to determine when he personally condemned people and when his officers acted under his name. Certainly his role is ambiguous in some cases in which he is specifically depicted as being present during executions or when orders for executions were given. He may not have intended to execute poor DeGama, and he may have opposed the execution of the first Fatehgarh fugitives, saved the Greenways and the Jacobis, apparently approved the sparing of Mrs. Carter at Bithur, and put an end to the killing of women and children at the ghats.

562. Shepherd, *A Personal Narrative*, p. 85.

563. Thomason College map of Cawnpore.

564. Shepherd, *A Personal Narrative*, pp. 85–86.

565. Nevill, *Cawnpore*, p. 101.

566. Ibid., pp. 214–16, 229–343.

567. Diary of Nunne Nawab.

568. Diary of Nunne Nawab; Shepherd, *A Personal Narrative*, p. 48.

569. Shepherd, *A Personal Narrative*, pp. 41–42.

570. Thomson, *The Story of Cawnpore*, pp. 112–13.

571. Deposition of Peer Bux.

572. Blunt, *Christian Tombs and Monuments*, p. 115; Gubbins, *Account*, pp. 127–28. Evans would eventually join the garrison at Lucknow and become a hero of the siege.

573. Hibbert, *The Great Mutiny*, p. 415nn. The remainder of this narrative is based entirely on Mrs. Sneyd's memoir at the India Office Library.

574. Mrs. Sneyd's account, written for her grandchildren, is a chronological puzzle. I surmise the date of her departure from Fatehpur and her arrival at Allahabad from two landmarks: the firing she heard at Fatehpur, and her description of Allahabad on the verge of rebellion. Certainly she describes Allahabad as of June 6, when mobs killed every European, Eurasian, and Christian they found, and "the flames from our burning bungalows," writes Kaye, "soon lit up the skies." (*A History of the Great Revolt*, 2:257). But in order for her to travel the more than seventy miles to Allahabad before the uprising on the sixth, she would have had to leave Fatehpur by at least the fourth. What guns, then, could she have heard from the direction of Cawnpore? The garrison fired an alarm gun when the sowars rose up on the night of the fourth or early in the morning of the fifth, and Ashe fired on the 53rd on the morning of the fifth, but unless a few guns were fired as the rebels gathered at the magazine, apparently they did not fire any artillery until the sixth, when Collector Sherer at Fatehpur, resting on his verandah after luncheon, heard the bombardment. "There was a purple haze in the distance," he wrote, "and a sound of guns was distinctly heard. The firing had been going on since mid-day, but we had not known of it in the muffled house; and every now and then the deep rumble of heavy ordnance came rolling over the fields." Sherer, *Daily Life*, p. 10.

575. It is entirely possible that some of these sepoys were not mutineers but loyal Sikhs whom Neill had set on the villages in the vicinity of Benares.

576. Canning in Hibbert, *The Great Mutiny*, p. 165.

577. "The great station of Cawnpore has been much agitated," the *Times of London* correspondent reported from Bombay on June 11. "There were till lately nothing but native troops, with the exception of one company of European artillery. . . . The Europeans of this station included not only civilians and officers with their families, but a number of non-residents who had either come in from parts of the country supposed to be less protected or had been stopped there on their way by the Mutineers in the Dooab [*sic*]. The tone of feeling in the native lines appearing to be very unsatisfactory, the Europeans took possession of a large barrack, allotting certain wards to the women and children, and proceeded to intrench themselves therein. All the guns they were able to move were placed in position, and the remainder were spiked." TL, 15 July 1857.

578. Kaye, *A History of the Great Revolt*, 3:4.

579. Ibid. Allen, ed., *A Glimpse of the Burning Plain*, p. 66.

580. Allen, ed., *A Glimpse of the Burning Plain*, p. 62.

581. Campbell, *Memoirs of my Indian Career*, pp. 282–83.

582. Marshman was an Englishman but he received his Doctorate of Divinity at Brown University in the United States. He died in 1837, leaving the *Friend of India* to his son John who was instrumental in virtually canonizing his brother-in-law. During the Mutiny the *Friend of India* promoted retribution and evangelism, and became a special target of Canning's suppression of the press. Buckland, *Dictionary of Indian Biography*, p. 276.

583. Martin, *The Indian Empire*, 2:276.

584. Lady Canning's journal in Allen, ed., *A Glimpse of the Burning Plain*, p. 71. His hair was gray, Havelock agreed, "but my soul and mind are young and fresh." Martin, *The Indian Empire*, 2:276.

585. Havelock in Hibbert, *The Great Mutiny*, p. 199.

586. According to an officer at Benares they killed 650 men. TL, 25 Aug. 1857. "All here bears traces of the insurrection," wrote an artillery officer who visited Benares; "roofless houses, ruined gardens, and the frequent rude gallows tell the tale of the outrages & the retribution that overtook it." Biddulph, *Letters* (OIOC).

587. Forbes, *Havelock*, p. 95.

588. These executions went on for months after Neill's departure from Benares.

589. Newton, *Historical Sketches*, p. 126.

590. The role of the Sikhs in suppressing the Mutiny was complicated. John Lawrence of the Punjab "perceived that whilst the Sikhs disliked subjection or any other foreign power, yet they hated these purabi [eastern] sepoys so intensely that, for the purpose of fighting them, he could safely entrust them with arms. Accordingly, he dared not only to muster in new recruits, but to enlist old soldiers who had actually fought against the British in the recent Sikh wars." Some British officers adored the Sikhs. "Their proud air and manly bearing, plainly stamped them as belonging to the aristocracy and chivalry of the northern countries of Asia; and on all occasions in this war, well and nobly have they seconded the gallantry and daring courage of their dashing leaders." Oliver Jones was clearly smitten by these "stern, wiry, dark-looking men, tall and straight of limb, their broad brows overhanging piercing black eyes—their noses rather aquiline and well chiselled—their not too full lips, which, when parted, showed teeth rivalling the whitest ivory, and which were shaded by jet-black mustachios, proudly curled, and their chins covered with silky black beards, carefully parted in the middle, and combed outwards—their voluminously folded blue or red turbans—their grey tunics and bright-coloured vests—their silver-mounted fire-arms, curved scimitars, and lightly-poised lances—the gap caparisons of their well-bitted and often thorough-bred horses—the ease and grace with which they sat and managed them."

They were spirited soldiers, it was said, who required a spirited commander. "A mere easy, good-natured man, who can only be *nurum* [soft], and never *gurrum* [hot], will not do for the Sikhs," wrote one Company man, but "the mixture of quiet benevolence and justice, with an ardent spirit, chains them to a leader for ever." But other officers viewed them with suspicion and worried that the loot they brought home to their villages would foment a rebellion in the Punjab. The governor-general reported that some Sikh soldiers were demanding gratis supplies from merchants. "There is reason to fear that these men have become impressed with the notion that their assistance is indispensable to us; and if this is not checked, it is likely to become the source of much future trouble and embarrassment." Neill himself had thrown them out of the fort at Allahabad because they had been merely "coaxed into loyalty" and besides getting dangerously drunk had become "very overbearing, and knew their power." "There is no sympathy between us," an officer would write. "We despise niggers, they hate us . . . Everyone expects we will have to polish off the Sikhs and Punjabees, when we have done with the Pandies." Gordon, *Our India Mission*, p. 141; Jones, *Recollections*; Raikes, *Notes on the Revolt*, p. 135; Muir/Beadon: 21 Oct.

1857 in Muir, *Records*, 1:209; *Further Parliamentary Papers*, encl. no. 1 in no. 7, no. 5 (cont.), p. 3, vol. 44; Neill in Martin, *The Indian Empire*, p. 298; Johnson, *Journal* (OIOC).

591. Chunder, *Travels of a Hindoo*, pp. 324–25.

592. Martin, *The Indian Empire*, 2:282.

593. Deposition of Perma Nund.

594. Rees, *The Siege of Lucknow*, p. 29.

595. Letter to the Court of Directors: 11 May 1847 in E/4794, no. 952, p. 967; and the Fort William Military Consultation of 19 March 1847, no. 158 in L/Mil/3/406, p. 126 (OIOC).

596. Deposition of John Fitchett.

597. A good deal of mystery surrounds the names of the Wheeler daughters. Some think there were three: Margaret, Eliza, and Ulrica. A birth record exists for Eliza, a baptismal record for Margaret, but the only mention of a daughter named Ulrica comes from Amy Horne, who claimed to recognize her and speak to her on the bank of the river after the ghat massacre. Whether this name came from her or from R. Macrae, who assisted Mrs. Bennett, is not known. I think it may be either mistaken or a nickname, and that the Miss Wheeler who would figure so prominently in the myths surrounding the massacres at Cawnpore was Margaret. Eliza would have been twenty-six years old; Margaret's age is not known. The date of her baptism in 1842 does not indicate her age because it was the date of her parents' wedding and the simultaneous baptism and legitimatizing of a number of their children. Her brother Francis, the Wheelers' youngest child, was born in May 1842, so Margaret would have to have been born at least ten months before, but very likely earlier—perhaps ten months after Patrick Wheeler's birth in July 1835. Either daughter could have lived, as has been claimed, until 1907, when Eliza, the oldest, would have been seventy-six. The Miss Wheeler who was evidently abducted from the ghats was said to have been about nineteen, which suggests that she was probably Margaret, though the similarity of the names Eliza and Ulrica—names that could be mistranscriptions of each other—is worrisome. Both Amy Horne and the Wheeler daughters were Eurasian, but the general's daughters would not have associated much with a merchant's daughter like Amy. Amy may have met them at a ball—although she does not mention attending balls at Cawnpore—or seen them on the course, but she was quite new to the station and might not have known one from the other. Thus Ulrica may have been a very shaken Amy Horne's mistaken stab at Eliza, which in turn was a misidentification of Margaret, the younger of the two.

598. My description of Wheeler is based on a rather clumsy watercolor of him—the only representation of Wheeler I have seen—by Lieutenant Charles D'Oyly. Though some state that Wheeler was inactive during the siege, it appears from his own letter to Lawrence that he took an active part in the defense on June 23 and that it was after his son was killed that the stuffing went out of him and command devolved upon Moore and Vibart. There is an early report published in the *Bombay Gazette* written by someone who interviewed Thomson and Delafosse after they returned to Cawnpore. "General Wheeler did nothing," the story said, "was never wounded early in the siege as was stated, and never took any active part in the defence. He hardly ever showed himself outside the small barrack which sheltered almost all, and never but once went out to the defences." But all subsequent reports indicate that he was somewhat more active. *Bombay Gazette*, Overland Summary, 31 Aug. 1857.

599. Thomson, *The Story of Cawnpore*, p. 102; All Souls memorial tablet; Blunt, *Christian Tombs and Monuments*, p. 111.

600. TL, 29 Aug. 1857; Blunt, *Christian Tombs and Monuments*, p. 113.

601. "A sickening stench arose from the dead, and the corpses of horses and other animals that had been shot at the commencement of the siege drew swarms of flies." Shepherd, *A Personal Narrative*, 49.

602. Bennett, "Ten Months' Captivity."

603. Roberts, *Letters*, p. 91

604. Bennett, "Ten Months' Captivity."

605. Thomson, *The Story of Cawnpore*, pp. 101–2.

606. Moorsom in the Lindsay Papers.

607. Thomson, *The Story of Cawnpore*, p. 88.

608. Butler, *The Land of the Veda*, p. 332.

609. Thomson, *The Story of Cawnpore*, p. 103. He called the snipers "incarnate fiends," but some were firing from such a distance that they probably could not distinguish an adult from a child.

610. Shepherd, *A Personal Narrative*, p. 45.

611. Thomson, *Report*.

612. Thomson, *The Story of Cawnpore*, p. 101.

613. Shepherd, *A Personal Narrative*, p. 52.

614. Ibid.

615. Thomson, *The Story of Cawnpore*, pp. 87–89. According to Thomson a gunner came upon "three large masses of silver in the ruins, supposed to be worth about three hundred pounds. He communicated his secret to only one of his companions, and by night they buried the spoil just outside Eckford's battery. Sullivan, the confidant, was not to touch this treasure unless anything happened to the finder. Sullivan lived to escape with Lieutenant Delafosse, private Murphy, 84th Foot, and myself; he came back to Cawnpore, was immediately seized with cholera, and died." Thomson does not specifically say what became of the treasure, but compliments the people of Cawnpore for their incredibly thorough excavations of the Entrenchment after the British departed. Thomson, *The Story of Cawnpore*, p. 95.

616 Kaye, *A History of the Great Revolt*, 2:320.

617. Jervis was the son of Captain W. Jervis, Bengal Native Infantry, and was born in Neemuch in 1830. Halliday's contemporary, he attended Addiscombe from 1846 to 1874, a classmate with Ashe and Ashburner and a friend of Chalmer's, with whom he shared the following adventure. "Mʳ Jervis & Chalmers went to a village," Emma Halliday wrote. "Mʳ [Jervis] had a native bow from which he shoots round mud balls with him. As they were going on they were charged by a cow buffalo with her calf. He turned & hit her above the eye with a ball which made her pause during which Mʳ C. climbed a house above 8 or 9 feet hight [*sic*] & stood on the roof & Mʳ J jumped a ditch & then a low wall rᵈ which he dodged her shooting at her all the time till she ran after some one else round a stack where he got away. Mʳ J had tea with us & sang 'A Baby was sleeping' so very nicely." Hardcastle/ASW: 13 Nov. 1992.

618. Shepherd, *A Personal Narrative*, pp. 46, 57–58, 62.

619. The absence of amputating saws and knives actually prolonged a few lives, at least briefly: almost no one survived amputation in the Mutiny. Trevelyan, *Cawnpore*, p. 98.

620. "One, belonging to Lieutenant Goad, 56th Native Infantry, was crossing to barrack No. 2 with some food in his hand, and was shot through the head." Thomson, *The Story of Cawnpore*, pp. 111–12.

621. Ibid., pp. 31–32.

622. Diary of Nunne Nawab.

623. Bennett, "Ten Months' Captivity."

624. Thomson, *The Story of Cawnpore*, pp. 137–38; Butler, *The Land of the Veda*, p. 298.

625. Thomson, *The Story of Cawnpore*, p. 137–38.

626. Collins, *Letters*, 1 Nov. 1857 (OIOC).

627. "How I now *execrate* the treacherous Sepoys—Good God!" he was now exclaiming in a letter to his older sisters in England. ". . . I only wish I could hear something from Cawnpore—they have got Europeans with them by this time, however. Still, I am very anxious, as the Lucknow Sepoys have risen, & that is close by Cawnpore, you know." Vibart, Edward Daniel Hamilton, *Papers* (OIOC).

628. Halliday letter 29: 1 May 1854.

629. Trevelyan, *The Golden Oriole*, p. 313.

630. Lieutenant Redman of the 1st N.I. came from a line of parliamentarians, officers, and bishops. He was the fourth son of George Clavering Redman of Saint Peter's, Isle of Thanet, Kent. His family motto was *Si ne sanguine nulla trophea*. ILN, no. 880, vol. xxxi, 26 Sept. 1857, p. 314.

631. Thomson, *The Story of Cawnpore*, p. 108.

632. His wife Sophie would die at the ghats, but their beautiful daughter Charlotte, recuperating from an illness at Fort William, would survive the Mutiny. (OIOC N/1/119, p. 271); Thomson, *The Story of Cawnpore*, pp. 100–101; Mrs. A. Regan/ASW: 21 Feb. 1994.

633. Thomson, *The Story of Cawnpore*, pp. 57–58, 106–7, 128–29, 142.

634. The only verifiably old and gray-haired officer was Wheeler, but unless Shepherd was being tactful, he probably meant someone else. The oldest of the remaining officers by this date was Ewart at fifty-four, Larkins and Vibart at fifty. Of the three, Larkins may be the likeliest candidate.

635. Shepherd, *A Personal Narrative*, p. 46.

636. Diary of Nunne Nawab; Tucker/Canning: 25 June 1857 in Ball, *The History of the Indian Mutiny*, 1:332.

637. OIOC Mss.Eur.F.135/19.

638. Bennett, "Ten Months' Captivity."

639. Shepherd, *A Personal Narrative*, pp. 46–47.

640. Thomson, *The Story of Cawnpore*, p. 111.

641. WL/G&J(L)P: 7 Jan. 1854.

642. GL/JB: 19 May 1857.

643. Shepherd states that even during the siege "station and division orders were issued with great regularity daily, announcing demises, promotions, &c., &c." Shepherd, *A Personal Narrative*, p. 59.

644. Thomson, *The Story of Cawnpore*, p. 114.

645. "Major Lindsay was struck in the face by the splinters caused by a round-shot," Thomson states. "He lay for a few days in total blindness and extreme pain, when death came to his relief. His disconsolate widow followed him a day or two afterwards, slain by grief." But Thomson served in the outer barracks and his account appears to be mistaken about the order in which Lilly and the major died and the number of days Lindsay suffered. According to his niece Caroline, whose chronology was found after Cawnpore was retaken, Lilly died before him, on the seventeenth (Kaye, *A History of the Great Revolt*, 2:326; Lindsay Papers). I rely entirely on Caroline's chronology regarding the order of death, and must assume that Katherine nursed William after he was wounded, or relieved Lilly when she died within hours of his receiving his wound. As to placing Lindsay's death on the seventeenth, Charles Crump stated in a letter to the Lindsay's relatives that "Lindsay was killed in his room by the splinters of brick work caused by the blow of a 24 pd. shot on the outside of the wall. He was lying down, with his head just close to the spot on the *inside*, the splinters blinded him & he died next day, from the effects. This young Delafosse told me." This all suggests to me that Lilly died after the major was wounded but before he died.

646. Thomson states that they did not suffer "the most frightful aggravations of epidemic disease, from the putrefying remains of the dead around us" because of "the kind services of the vultures and adjutant-birds, which effectually cleared the neighbourhood of all such dangerous and offensive relics." Thomson, *The Story of Cawnpore*, p. 77.

647. Shepherd says Mrs. Belson died on June 19.

648. Horne says Miss Campbell, but Shepherd lists a Mrs. Campbell and provides no date for her death.

649. The date of death of a Mrs. Yates is not given by Shepherd.

650. In his list Shepherd says Mr. Christie died on the twenty-first of June, but in his narrative states that he died two days before the twenty-fourth, i.e., the twenty-second.

651. Bennett, "Ten Months' Captivity."

652. Wiggins in Gubbins, *Account*, p. 446.

653. TL, 16 Oct. 1857, p. 7.

654. Thomson, *The Story of Cawnpore*, p. 109.

655. Officer's account in Ball, *The History of the Indian Mutiny*, 2:331.

656. Thomson states that the thermometers in the Entrenchment ranged from 120 to 138 degrees, but the thermometers had probably exceeded their capacity to measure accurately; the highest air temperature ever measured was in Libya and registered 136 degrees.

657. Fitchett, *The Tale of the Great Mutiny*, p. 406.

658. Thomson, *The Story of Cawnpore*, p. 77.

659. Shepherd, *A Personal Narrative*, p. 48.

660. Sherring said he was shot as he entered the Entrenchment, a comforting fiction embraced by his fellow missionaries to spare his children's feelings. But if Sherring embraced this version of Haycock's death his description of the Reverend's mental state must apply to the period before the siege began. Sherring, *The Indian Church during the Great Rebellion*, pp. 167–68.

661. Thomson, *The Story of Cawnpore*, p. 105. This was probably the same round shot that carried away the solar topi of Mr. O'Brien of the Collector's office. Shepherd, *A Personal Narrative*, p. 51.

662. Shepherd, *A Personal Narrative*, p. 51.

663. Horne, *Narrative* (BM); Bennett, "Ten Months' Captivity."

664. Thomson, *The Story of Cawnpore*, p. 106.

665. Lindsay: 25 Aug. 1855.

666. Thomson, *The Story of Cawnpore*, pp. 105–6.

667. Shepherd, *A Personal Narrative*, p. 54.

668. Ibid., p. 48.

669. Bennett, "Ten Months' Captivity"; Horne, *Narrative* (BM).

670. Thomson, *The Story of Cawnpore*, p. 110.

671. Shepherd, *A Personal Narrative*, p. 53.

672. Shepherd said he died of a "determination of blood to his head." Ibid.

673. Hibbert, *The Great Mutiny*, p. 187.

674. Gubbins, *Account*, p. 443.

675. Shepherd, *A Personal Narrative*, pp. 47, 56–57, 59.

676. Thomson, *The Story of Cawnpore*, pp. 103–4.

677. Shepherd, *A Personal Narrative*, pp. 49, 68.

678. Thomson, *The Story of Cawnpore*, pp. 114–15.

679. Diary of Nunne Nawab.

680. In the 1920s, writes MacMunn, "it was found that one of the two barracks has a huge underground chamber, capable of sheltering many, which was unknown to the garrison." MacMunn, *The Indian Mutiny in Perspective*, p. 114. This mysterious but by no means huge chamber is visible today. It would not have protected the residents of the thatched barrack from fire; indeed it might have trapped them there. Nowadays no one will venture into the chamber for fear of snakes.

681. One secret of the garrison's endurance was discipline. Even during the barrack fire, when flames had threatened to engulf their loved ones, the vast majority of pickets had remained at their posts, firing murderously into the advancing swarms of rebels. And Wheeler's gunners, despite the pounding they were taking at their batteries, had learned to save their ammunition for when the rebels advanced within range of their field pieces. Their casualties, especially among the women and children, had been appalling, but the dead had been carried off in timely fashion. The garrison evidently adhered to Wheeler's rationing, and some measure of order had been maintained.

682. Farwell, *Queen Victoria's Little Wars*, p. 69.

683. Nanak Chand's diary. This would have been news to Poona, which remained placidly under British control throughout the rebellion.

684. Shepherd, *A Personal Narrative*, p. 86.

685. Ibid., pp. 46–47.

686. Gubbins, *Account*, p. 444.

687. Shepherd, *A Personal Narrative*, p. 47.

688. Ibid., p. 50.

689. Diary of Nunne Nawab.

690. Deposition of Hulas Singh.

691. Thomson, *Report*.

692. Shepherd says Moore was chasing Khan Mahomed when he used this "dodge," but he was not present and may have confused the two forays. Though I have employed Thomson's account, I include Shepherd's rendering of Moore's mock commands, which seem more complete and convincing than Thomson's version: a simple, "Number one to the front." Shepherd, *A Personal Narrative*, pp. 55–56; Thomson, *The Story of Cawnpore*, pp. 124–25.

693. Thomson, *The Story of Cawnpore*, pp. 124–25.

694. Shepherd, *A Personal Narrative*, p. 50; Wheeler to Lawrence, 24 June 1957. Singh, *Letters of Sir Henry Lawrence*, pp. 32–34.

695. This description is from Dr. Francis Collins's description of the Battle of Kunch the following May, but having experienced the heat mirages at Cawnpore I safely surmise that the sowars looked the same at Cawnpore as at Kunch. Collins, *Letters* (OIOC).

696. Shepherd says six thousand rebels took part in this attack. This seems inflated.

697. Thomson, *The Story of Cawnpore*, pp. 126–27.

698. Shepherd's account.

699. Diary of Nunne Nawab.

700. Thomson, *The Story of Cawnpore*, pp. 126–29.

701. Shepherd, *A Personal Narrative*, pp. 50–51.

702. Wheeler to Lawrence, 24 June 1957 in Singh, *Letters of Sir Henry Lawrence*, pp. 32–34; Captain Alexander later transcribed the following inscription from Wheeler's room: "Below is the mark of the round shot by which young Wheeler was killed, his brains and hair scattered on the wall below." Alexander appended a note: "Young W. was wounded and his mother and Sister were bathing his wounds when R^d. shot took his head off." Alexander, letter in Edward Daniel Hamilton Vibart, *Papers*.

703. Thomson, *The Story of Cawnpore*, pp. 127–28.

704. Shepherd, *A Personal Narrative*, p. 86.

705. Thomson, *The Story of Cawnpore*, p. 128.

706. Ibid., p. 109.

707. Probably Whiting.

708. I have again slightly altered Shepherd's translation for the sake of clarity.

709. "Blenman was exceedingly courageous," wrote Thomson, "and, when he chose, one of the best men we had, but he was always fitful in temper, and at times difficult to manage." *The Story of Cawnpore*, p. 130.

710. Depositions of Gobind Singh, Sheik Elahee Buksh, and Ghouse Mohemed.

711. She was the most prominent of Nana's Christian prisoners.

712. Shepherd, *A Personal Narrative*, pp. 57–70.

PART THREE

1. Deposition of Kalka Pershad.

2. Thomson, *The Story of Cawnpore*, pp. 149–50.

3. Depositions of Peer Buksh, Sheo Churran Das, Khoda Buksh, and Futteh Singh; Shepherd's account.

4. Diary of Nunne Nawab. The content of Azimullah's conversation with Mrs. Green-way is my surmise.

5. R. Macrae in Bennett, "Ten Months' Captivity."

6. Rees, *The Siege of Lucknow*, p. 63.

7. Wheeler to Lawrence, 24 June 1957 in Singh, ed., *Letters of Sir Henry Lawrence*, pp. 32–34. To convey his letter to Lucknow, Wheeler now had to pay a native courier the in-flated price of five thousand rupees. In her later account Amy Horne raised the amount to six thousand. Horne, *Narrative* (BM).

8. Gubbins, *Account*, p. 445.

9. Ibid., pp. 444–45.

10. "We lost 250 men in the entrenchment in 22 days," wrote Thomson, "and a large number of these were killed by shells; certainly as many as a dozen on one fatal day that I remember." He was not counting the women and children. Thomson's answer, dated 8 Sept. 1858, to Mrs. Murray's account in TL, 11 Sept. 1858, p. 7.

11. Among the books Forbes-Mitchell found at the Entrenchment, "I picked up a New Testament in Gaelic, but without any name on it. All the blank leaves had been torn out, and at the time I formed the opinion that they had been used for gun-wadding, because, close beside the Testament, there was a broken single-barrelled duck gun, which had evi-dently been smashed by a 9-pounder shot lying near. . . . The Testament must have be-longed to some Scotch Highlander in the garrison." Forbes-Mitchell, *The Relief of Lucknow*, p. 23.

12. Shepherd, *A Personal Narrative*, p. 56.

13. In his published narrative of the siege Thomson indignantly disagreed with Shep-herd's contention that the garrison had a week's worth of food left; Thomson put it at three days' provisions in his book, four days in his letter to the *Times of London*. Thomson was concerned that people might condemn Wheeler's capitulation if they believed there were enough provisions for the garrison to have survived a week or more longer. (Thomson stated in his confidential account for the commander-in-chief that the garrison had a week's worth of quarter rations left at the time of the capitulation, which would have meant three to four days on half rations.) As a head clerk of the Commissariat Depart-ment, Shepherd probably had a better idea of the remaining supply, and though he em-ployed some of Thomson's account in later editions of his narrative, he did not choose to change his estimate. But reading these estimates in context it appears that Thomson was counting from the twenty-fourth or twenty-fifth when the officers were deliberating about Nana's offer, whereas Shepherd may have been counting from an earlier date, when he was still trying to determine whether to leave the Entrenchment on his mission; thus they were not so very far apart. (Wheeler believed as late as the twenty-fourth that the garrison had "provisions for 8 or 10 days at farthest" but evidently believed Moore when he told him that there were only three days' rations left. Thomson, *The Story of Cawnpore*, pp. 134, 150; Thomson's answer, dated 8 Sept. 1858, to Mrs. Murray's account in TL, 11 Sept. 1858, p. 7; Thomson, *Report*; Shepherd, *A Personal Narrative*, p. 56; Wheeler/Lawrence: 24 June 1857 in Singh, *Letters of Henry Lawrence*.

14. Horne, *Narrative* (BM).

15. Ibid.

16. Thomson, *The Story of Cawnpore*, p. 84.

17. Shepherd, *A Personal Narrative*, p. 71.

18. Deposition of Sheo Churan Das.

19. Testimony of Mary Ann in TL, 16 Oct. 1857, p. 8.

20. The note did not survive the Mutiny. Both Thomson and Shepherd give this ver-sion, but Sherer gives another: "All soldiers and others unconnected with the acts of Lord Dalhousie, who will lay down their arms and give themselves up, shall be spared and sent to Allahabad." Sherer, *Narrative*. Khoda Bux gives yet another: "My father was always

faithful to the British Government. I will take care that no native shall kill you. I will send eight troopers with you, if you will go to Allahabad and leave all the arms, ammunition, and stores in the entrenchments."

21. I surmise this from the testimony of Bradshaw and Letts, who said he stood near them when he read the letter. They were quartered near the Main Guard.

22. Thomson, *The Story of Cawnpore*, p. 152.

23. This is from a passage Thomson prudently crossed out of his *Report to the Commander-in-Chief*.

24. Depositions of Bradshaw and Letts.

25. This dramatic confrontation does not appear in Thomson's published account. According to P. J. O. Taylor, the threatened mutiny of the British troops in the garrison is corroborated in the letters of Elijah Impey, who served during the Mutiny in the Engineers, though it is likely Impey's source was also Thomson, with whom he spoke at Cawnpore. Taylor, "Deciphering the 'Unseen Letters,'" *The Statesman*, 16 July 1993.

26. R. Macrae in Bennett, "Ten Months' Captivity."

27. Deposition of Futteh Singh.

28. Thomson, *The Story of Cawnpore*, p. 150.

29. Pearse, *The Hearseys*, pp. 396–400.

30. Thomson, *Report*.

31. Bennett, "Ten Months' Captivity."

32. Though Jones was speaking humanely as a besieger and not as the besieged. EB: 11th ed., 10:724.

33. Shepherd's account.

34. Sherer, *Narrative*.

35. Thomson, *Reply*.

36. Thomson, *The Story of Cawnpore*, p. 150.

37. Malleson, *The Indian Mutiny*, p. 169.

38. TL, 16 Oct. 1857, p. 7.

39. Shepherd, *A Personal Narrative*, pp. 71–72.

40. Thomson, *The Story of Cawnpore*, p. 152; Shepherd's account; Nanak Chand's diary.

41. Thomson, *The Story of Cawnpore*, p. 153.

42. Thomson, *Report;* TL, 16 Oct. 1857, p. 7.

43. Horne, *Narrative* (BM); Thomson, *The Story of Cawnpore*, pp. 148–55.

44. Gubbins, *Account*, pp. 174, 446; Trevelyan, *Cawnpore*, p. 129. A somewhat doubtful letter bearing the same date was transcribed by Arthur Peppin, a trader and a particularly virulent member of the Calcutta Volunteers. "We are in a dreadful plight here; God only knows what is to become of us all. Our leader Sir H. Wheeler is now no more. He received a mortal wound in the sally the day before yesterday, and was brought into the entrenchments to breathe his last amongst his own race. Nobly he fought, and bravely he fell, most deeply and sincerely regretted by his gallant little band. . . . We are short of men, no provisions, no water and hardly any ammunition left. Now we are thinking of consulting together to capitulate to the enemy—our only and last resource. But are not 'the tender mercies of the heathen' cruel? I sent this letter by the trustworthy native servant of mine. I know not if it will ever reach you. However ere it reaches you my fate will be decided. Oh, the wretchedness around!"

"The servant remained at Cawnpore until the following day," wrote Peppin, "and saw the massacre consummated the day after the above letter was written." But the letter, or the version Peppin transcribed, was either a fraud or the correspondent was curiously ill informed for an officer of the garrison. Though Wheeler's fate remains obscure, all other sources agree at least that he lived long enough to reach the ghat. Perhaps the correspondent had just heard the news of Godfrey Wheeler's wounding and death and had confused him with his father. Peppin, *Letters* (OIOC).

45. Thomson, *The Story of Cawnpore*, p. 100.

46. "Situated as we were in the entrenchment, it was not possible to observe etiquette and decorum, for we had to witness sights that often shocked us." Bennett, "Ten Months' Captivity."

47. Shepherd, *A Personal Narrative*, p. 72; Lee, *The Indian Mutiny*, p. 11.

48. Horne, *Narrative* (BM).

49. Shepherd, *A Personal Narrative*, p. 72.

50. Thomson, *The Story of Cawnpore*, p. 161.

51. Russell, cited in Martin, *The Indian Empire*, 2:259, stated that the garrison was permitted to walk around the neighborhood that day, but according to Shepherd they were confined to the Entrenchment by a sepoy guard and none of the survivors' accounts indicate they saw anyone leave the Entrenchment before the evacuation.

52. Delafosse in TL, 16 Oct. 1857, p. 7; Thomson, *Report*.

53. Jokhun testified that the officers were "Goad, Fagan, and Warde, mounted on an elephant, and two Europeans whose names and regiments I don't know, mounted on another elephant." Deposition of Jokhun.

54. Thomson, *The Story of Cawnpore*, p. 156.

55. The ravine leading to the ghat was much deeper by the early 1890s, "owing to the overflow of water from the Cantonment drainage (not the main Canal) having worn a deep water course." Lee, *The Indian Mutiny*, p. 21.

56. Nevill, *Cawnpore*, p. 3.

57. Shepherd, *A Personal Narrative*, p. 61; Yalland, *Traders and Nabobs*, pp. 226, 232, 347; Yalland, *A Guide to the Kacheri Cemetery*, p. 66.

58. Halliday letter 37: 24 Nov. 1854.

59. Map by Thomason College, Roorkee.

60. Deposition of Bukkee Singh.

61. William Simpson in Keene, *Handbook*, p. 35. "The gardens, I think," wrote Keene, "replaced the village of Sati Chaura, which was destroyed."

62. Deposition of Lochun.

63. Depositions of Goordial and Lochun.

64. Deposition of Hulas Singh.

65. Depositions of Budloo, Goordial, and Lochun. For what it is worth, Nanak Chand believed Lochun; certainly Budloo's testimony is the less plausible of the two.

66. Nanak Chand's diary; deposition of Budloo.

67. Deposition of Lochun.

68. Heber, *Journal*, 1:150.

69. Thomson, *The Story of Cawnpore*, p. 165.

70. Deposition of Goordial.

71. Shepherd states that the boats were later hauled further into the shallows to delay the departure. Shepherd, *A Personal Narrative*, p. 75.

72. Thomson, *The Story of Cawnpore*, p. 165.

73. Depositions of Bradshaw and Letts.

74. Deposition of Jokhun.

75. Thomson, *The Story of Cawnpore*, pp. 156–57.

76. Ibid., p. 161.

77. This is my surmise, but I am certain the vigorous Moncrieff would have said prayers over the well, and Thomson states that families ventured out to view the outer barracks.

78. ILN, no. 877, vol. 31, 5 Sept. 1857, p. 234.

79. "In Captain Jenkins," wrote Thomson, "we lost one of the bravest and one of the best of our party." Thomson, *The Story of Cawnpore*, p. 129.

80. Shepherd, *A Personal Narrative*, pp. 137–38.

81. Deposition of Kalka Pershad.

82. This was told to me by Mr. Alward Wyndham, who heard it as a schoolboy in New South Wales.

83. Thomson, *The Story of Cawnpore*, pp. 155–56; Depositions of Goordial and Peer Bux.

84. Deposition of Khoda Buksh; Shepherd, *A Personal Narrative*, p. 72.

85. Deposition of Khoda Buksh.

86. Depositions of Gobind Singh, Sheik Elahee Buksh, and Ghouse Mohomed.

87. Deposition of Khoda Buksh.

88. Horne, *Narrative* (BM).

89. Thomson, *The Story of Cawnpore*, pp. 155–58; Shepherd, *A Personal Narrative*, p. 73.

90. "Jwala Pershad had caused a strong guard of cavalry and infantry to be placed all round, with the plausible excuse of guarding the place, though in reality it was done to prevent the possibility of any one escaping during the night." Shepherd, *A Personal Narrative*, p. 73.

91. Gordon, *Our India Mission*, p. 38. Anglo-Indians characterized the jackal's cry as "dead Hindu, where, where, where." Blanford, *Fauna*, p. 141.

92. Lee, *The Indian Mutiny*, p. 12.

93. Thomson, *The Story of Cawnpore*, p. 159, 161–62.

94. Deposition of Hulas Singh; Thomson, *The Story of Cawnpore*, p. 162.

95. Thomson, *The Story of Cawnpore*, p. 166.

96. The dog was part of the plunder taken after the massacre; I surmise it must have been brought by a servant. Even if it could have withstood the bombardment it could not have survived in the Entrenchment; it would either have starved to death or someone would have eaten it. Nanak Chand's diary.

97. Deposition of Jokhun.

98. Lee, *The Indian Mutiny*, p. 12.

99. Thomson, *The Story of Cawnpore*, p. 162.

100. Shepherd, *A Personal Narrative*, p. 73.

101. Thomson, *Report*. In his book, Thomson revised the sepoy's figure upward to "eight hundred to a thousand," and added that he believed "this estimate to have been under, rather than over the mark." Thomson, *The Story of Cawnpore*, p. 164.

102. Even after the massacre Thomson believed that his sepoy was sincere. Ibid.

103. Ibid., pp. 164–65.

104. Mary Ann in TL, 16 Oct. 1857, p. 8.

105. Lee, *The Indian Mutiny*, p. 12.

106. Thomson, *The Story of Cawnpore*, p. 163. It is possible this was the same incident Horne describes with Captain Kempland, but likelier that several sepoys attempted to disarm various men along the way.

107. Bennett, "Ten Months' Captivity."

108. Horne, *Narrative* (BM). Some dismiss Horne's account of the evacuation as hysterical. I do not. It seems to me that Thomson and Delafosse at the head of the procession would not have witnessed what occurred a quarter to half a mile behind them; that the scene in the Entrenchment was too confused and crowded for them to have witnessed everything that transpired; that even if the euphemistic Thomson and the reticent Delafosse had witnessed such things they would have been reluctant to recount them.

109. Shepherd, *A Personal Narrative*, p. 73.

110. Horne, *Narrative* (BM).

111. Shepherd, *A Personal Narrative*, p. 138.

112. Ibid., p. 73; Deposition of Peer Bux.

113. Here the various versions of Wheeler's death begin to collide. Peer Bux, perhaps the most reliable witness to Wheeler's departure, says he rode a horse part of the way, then dismounted and climbed aboard an elephant. But others say he rode in a palanquin the whole route. Shepherd says he rode a "galloway" or small horse. This seems likelier than

that he would ride in a palanquin. According to Ewuz Khan, who was in the Entrench-ment at the time of evacuation, several officers climbed on horses that morning. Deposi-tions of Peer Buksh and Ewuz Khan; Shepherd, *A Personal Narrative*, p. 73.

114. Diary of Nunne Nawab.

115. Nanak Chand's diary.

116. Halliday letter 44: 17 Feb. 1855.

117. Depositions of Bradshaw and Letts.

118. Shepherd said there were twelve, but Peer Buksh, who was an eyewitness, said there were eleven. It is not entirely clear, however, whether these men were left behind because they could not be moved or because there was not enough room. Shepherd, *A Per-sonal Narrative*, 73–74; deposition of Peer Buksh.

119. Bennett, "Ten Months' Captivity."

120. Shepherd, *A Personal Narrative*, p. 138.

121. Lee, *The Indian Mutiny*, pp. 12–13.

122. Account of Mary Ann.

123. Shepherd, *A Personal Narrative*, p. 138.

124. Bennett, "Ten Months' Captivity."

125. Deposition of Perma Nund. I say "absently" but perhaps he hoped she might carry intelligence for him. Hers was one of the first accounts of the Cawnpore massacres to be published.

126. Thomson, *The Story of Cawnpore*, pp. 161–62.

127. Bennett, "Ten Months' Captivity."

128. Thomson, *The Story of Cawnpore*, pp. 161–62.

129. Bennett, "Ten Months' Captivity." Some historians clung to Thomson's comforting assertion that the column was not molested. "Let who might incline to disown those war-worn men in their dingy rags," wrote Archibald Forbes, "their foes knew them for what they were; and made way for the white *sahibs* marching firmly, each man with rifle on shoulder and the fearless glance in the hollow eye." Forbes, *Havelock*, p. 92.

130. Thomson, *The Story of Cawnpore*, pp. 164, 166.

131. Lee, *The Indian Mutiny*, pp. 12–13; Fitchett, *The Tale of the Great Mutiny*, p. 410.

132. I surmise this from the fact that all of these officers were in the first two boats to push off. Ewart was left out because he was badly wounded and his bearers lagged behind. Major Hillersdon is unaccounted for in the various accounts of the march to the ghats. De-position of Perma Nund.

133. Thomson, *The Story of Cawnpore*, p. 164.

134. Deposition of Lochun.

135. Nanak Chand's diary.

136. Deposition of Khoda Buksh.

137. They were Ghouse Mohomed, Gobind Singh, Mitter Jeet Singh, and a native reg-imental doctor named Sahibdad Khan. The latter two were evidently killed. Depositions of Gobind Singh, Elahee Buksh, and Ghouse Mohomed.

138. Shepherd, *A Personal Narrative*, p. 99.

139. Delafosse in TL, 16 Oct. 1857, p. 7.

140. Bennett, "Ten Months' Captivity."

141. Ewart, *Letters* (OIOC).

142. Gupta found this story unlikely because he believed a banker unfamiliar with war-fare would not have stood around watching such horrors. I think Gupta underestimates a civilian's capacity for such things and the difficulty of getting free of a large crowd. In any case, it would be a far unlikelier incident for a banker to invent than to witness, especially the line about the parade. Depositions of Ajoodea Pershad, Ewuz Khan, and Perma Nund; Shepherd, *A Personal Narrative*, p. 74.

143. Mary Ann in TL, 16 Oct. 1857, p. 8; deposition of Perma Nund.

144. Depositions of Gobind Singh, Elahee Buksh, and Ghouse Mohomed.

145. Thomson, *The Story of Cawnpore*, p. 96.

146. Shepherd, *A Personal Narrative*, 74. Futteh Singh testified that the corpses of only six soldiers had been left behind by the garrison: Golab Singh said there were only two or three, but Peer Bux's testimony is more specific: he saw eleven severely wounded soldiers "on quilts on the floor; some of them still breathing, though dying from severe gun shot wounds." Depositions of Futteh Singh, Golab Singh, and Peer Bux.

147. Depositions of Bradshaw and Letts.

148. Shepherd, *A Personal Narrative*, 75; deposition of Peer Bux.

149. Depositions of Bradshaw and Letts.

150. Thomson, *The Story of Cawnpore*, p. 166.

151. Depositions of Nundeedeen and Juggernauth. Hulas Singh understandably denied he was there but he must have been; he had arranged for the boats and the boatmen, and as chief police officer would have been present to keep watch on the enormous crowd.

152. Thomson, *The Story of Cawnpore*, p. 165.

153. Horne, *Narrative* (BM).

154. Depositions of Peer Bux and Perma Nund.

155. Thomson, *The Story of Cawnpore*, pp. 169–70.

156. Depositions of Bradshaw and Letts.

157. This was Shepherd's surmise. He believed they were all burned to death in one of the boats. Shepherd, *A Personal Narrative*, p. 134.

158. Collier, *The Sound of Fury*, p. 149.

159. Horne, *Narrative* (BM).

160. Bennett, "Ten Months' Captivity."

161. The two boats carrying Bradshaw and Letts contained at least twenty-nine people between them. Depositions of Bradshaw and Letts.

162. Mary Ann in TL, 16 Oct. 1857, p. 8.

163. Depositions of Bradshaw and Letts.

164. Germon, *Journal*, p. 66.

165. Horne, *Narrative* (BM).

166. Shepherd, *A Personal Narrative*, p. 75.

167. Delafosse in TL, 16 Oct. 1857, p. 7; deposition of Perma Nund.

168. Depositions of Narain Kachee and Bukkee Singh; diary of Nunne Nawab; testimony of Mary Ann in TL, 16 Oct. 1857, p. 8; Nanak Chand's diary; Sherer, *Narrative*.

169. Bennett, "Ten Months' Captivity."

170. "Statement of Information" in TL, 16 Oct. 1857, p. 8; Nanak Chand's diary.

171. Thomson, *The Story of Cawnpore*, p. 166.

172. Deposition of Peer Bux.

173. Deposition of Perma Nund; Nanak Chand's diary.

174. Thomson, *The Story of Cawnpore*, p. 168.

175. Ibid., p. 167.

176. Depositions of Lochun and Bukkee Singh.

177. "Statement of Information" in TL, 16 Oct. 1857, p. 8.

178. Shepherd, *A Personal Narrative*, p. 81; Shepherd, account.

179. Thomson, *The Story of Cawnpore*, p. 170.

180. Ibid., p. 166.

181. According to some Cawnpore natives, the boatmen who secreted the embers were from Bithur; but these witnesses may merely have been trying to protect their own relations from British retribution.

182. Depositions of Bradshaw and Letts; Sheo Churran Das.

183. Thomson, *The Story of Cawnpore*, p. 166.

184. Jankee Pershad and Juggernauth both testified that they fled when the firing began.

185. Deposition of Lochun.

186. Map by Thomason College, Roorkee; Delafosse in TL, 16 Oct. 1857, p. 7.
187. Horne, *Narrative* (BM); Bennett, "Ten Months' Captivity."
188. Testimony of Myoor Tewaree.
189. Thomson, *The Story of Cawnpore*, p. 170.
190. Thomson, *The Story of Cawnpore*, p. 167.
191. Deposition of Peer Bux.
192. Deposition of Jokhun.
193. Thomson, *The Story of Cawnpore*, p. 167.
194. Deposition of Nundeedeen.
195. Thomson, *The Story of Cawnpore*, p. 167.
196. Horne, *Narrative* (BM).
197. Thomson, *The Story of Cawnpore*, pp. 167–68.
198. Bennett, "Ten Months' Captivity."
199. Willis in Sherring, *The Indian Church during the Great Rebellion*, p. 178.
200. Thomson, *The Story of Cawnpore*, p. 110.
201. Deposition of Jokhun.
202. Blunt, *Christian Tombs and Monuments*, p. 113.
203. Bennett, "Ten Months' Captivity."
204. Thomson, *The Story of Cawnpore*, p. 168.
205. Depositions of Bradshaw and Letts.
206. Fitchett, *The Tale of the Great Mutiny*, p. 113.
207. Bennett, "Ten Months' Captivity."
208. Mary Ann in TL, 16 Oct. 1857, p. 8.
209. Thomson, *The Story of Cawnpore*, p. 168.
210. Deposition of Lochun; Horne, *Narrative* (BM).
211. Bennett, "Ten Months' Captivity."
212. Lindsay Family Papers.
213. At Lucknow that day, Henry Lawrence sent a reply to the Wheeler's desperate letter of the twenty-fourth. Havelock, Lawrence assured his old friend, *"must* be at Cawnpore within two days. . . . I hope, therefore, you will husband your resources, and not accept any terms from the enemy, as I much fear treachery. You cannot rely on the Nana's promises," he said. *"Il a tué beaucoup de prisonniers."* But in fact more than two weeks would pass before Havelock reached Cawnpore. Edwardes, *The Life of Sir Henry Lawrence*, p. 354.
214. Thomson, *The Story of Cawnpore*, p. 168.
215. Delafosse in Shepherd, *A Personal Narrative*, pp. 76–77. Neither Delafosse nor Thomson is clear about which boat they were in at first, though Thomson at least states that he abandoned the first boat he entered in order to swim after Wheeler's boat. It is possible that Delafosse let slip his disgust with the other officers in the other boats in order to make his success in budging Wheeler's boat appear to be the consequence not of luck, a better designed boat, or Wheeler's bribe to the boatmen but his fellow passengers' manly conduct. But Delafosse was terrifically brave, and may indeed have been disappointed by the rapidity with which many of his comrades—including Thomson—abandoned the women and children in the other boats. His disgust with this and perhaps other aspects of his comrades' behavior may explain his decision never to write about his experiences at Cawnpore.
216. Nanak Chand's diary.
217. Thomson, *Report*.
218. Thomson, *The Story of Cawnpore*, p. 190.
219. Ibid., pp. 169–70.
220. Ensign John Wright Henderson of the 56th had first served at Banda with the Hallidays. Blunt, *Christian Tombs and Monuments*, p. 114.
221. Thomson, *The Story of Cawnpore*, p. 169.

222. Deposition of Lochun.

223. Thomson, *The Story of Cawnpore*, pp. 171–72.

224. Deposition of Perma Nund.

225. Perma Nund claimed that Thomson and Delafosse were two of those who jumped from the boat at this point, but if they were on the boat they may not have been fleeing but jumping down to push the boat through the shallows. Deposition of Perma Nund.

226. Nanak Chand's diary; deposition of Perma Nund.

227. Keene, *Handbook*, p. 23.

228. I surmise this from the presence of his wife and children on Vibart's boat.

229. Thomson, *The Story of Cawnpore*, pp. 91, 171, 176.

230. Bennett, "Ten Months' Captivity." No one ever testified to the death of Lady Frances Wheeler nor her oldest daughter, Eliza, but they do not appear on the lists of survivors at Sati Chowra. Perhaps, like Wheeler's youngest daughter, Margaret, they dropped from the boat a few yards downstream when the round shot struck its stern. But unlike Margaret, Lady Wheeler evidently never reached the riverbank, falling in the same fusillade that claimed Moore, Ashe, and Boulton. There may have been something particularly unfortunate about the circumstances of Lady Frances's death, reflecting badly either on her or her protectors. But more likely the embarrassed silence derived from the troubled circumstances of her life and her ancestry, and the same Anglo–Indian proprieties that had so complicated and constricted her life now obscured her death forever. What became of her older daughter Eliza is more of a mystery. Shepherd firmly recorded that Lady Wheeler died on the twenty-seventh but went out of his way to record that Eliza's fate was "not known." She was probably killed with her mother at the ghat, but it is at least possible that like her sister Margaret she was captured, which might explain the divergent accounts of the fate of "Miss Wheeler." The *Bombay Telegraph and Courier* reported that when the 78th Highlanders arrived at Cawnpore on July 17 they found "the remains of one of General Wheeler's daughters," from which they removed a lock of hair and divided it among themselves, pledging that for every strand they would kill a mutineer. Citing a sergeant of the grenadiers named Macnab but not mentioning the Wheeler connection, Havelock's biographer, Archibald Forbes, claimed that the body was found in some shrubs at Savada House, and that she had been thrown from a window. "But it was not the fall that had killed the fair-haired girl," he wrote. "The rough soldiers tenderly straightened the still supple limbs," and buried her in the garden. Ball, *The History of the Indian Mutiny*, 1:379; Forbes, *Havelock*, p. 139.

231. Deposition of Lochun; Delafosse in TL, 16 Oct. 1857, p. 7; Shepherd, *A Personal Narrative*, pp. 76–77, 91; Testimony of Myoor Tewaree.

232. Some sowars were on foot, but many were evidently on horseback. Depositions of Bukkee Singh and Ajoodea Pershad; Testimony of Bhoondoo Singh in Lucknow Collectorate Records, 4:97–98.

233. In her later account, written when she was an old lady, Horne stated that this unfortunate man was John Kirkpatrick, a produce merchant, a version embraced in several historians' accounts. But in her earlier account, which in this instance I consider more reliable, she said Kirkpatrick was shot and did not name the man who was hacked to death. Horne, *Narrative* (BM); Bennett, "Ten Months' Captivity."

234. Lindsay Family Papers.

235. I presume this was so because the reverend's wife and child were not mentioned by Bradshaw and Letts. Moncrieff, who had been famously brave during the siege, would not have abandoned them unless they were already dead. Some said he stood with the "padre" or Roman Catholic priest or with another missionary. But Father Rooney had died of heatstroke in the Entrenchment, as had Haycock, the only other missionary in the station.

236. Depositions of Bradshaw and Letts. Mrs. Letts died three days later.

237. Mrs. Murray's account.

238. Shepherd, *A Personal Narrative*, pp. 74–75; deposition of Narain Kachee.

239. Deposition of Hannah Spiers.

240. Ibid.

241. Nanak Chand's diary.

242. Georgiana Williams is recorded by Shepherd as having been killed at the boats. Her other sisters, Mary (or May) and Fanny, died on the fifteenth of June and the fifteenth of July respectively. In Blunt, *Christian Tombs and Monuments*, p. 113, Fanny is described as the youngest daughter.

243. Depositions of Bradshaw and Letts; Shepherd, *A Personal Narrative*, p. 77.

244. Mrs. Murray's account.

245. Depositions of Bradshaw and Letts.

246. Horne, *Narrative* (BM).

247. The Christie family, or what was left of it, lost two hundred fifty thousand rupees in the Mutiny.

248. Bradshaw in Shepherd, *A Personal Narrative*, p. 78.

249. Nanak Chand's diary.

250. Horne, *Narrative* (BM).

251. Testimony of John Fitchett; Bhoondoo Singh in Lucknow Collectorate Records in U.P., 4:97–98.

252. Nanak Chand's diary.

253. It is possible that at the last minute some women were killed by their own fathers and husbands who, like some in the Lucknow garrison, had resolved to spare their womenfolk the special horrors that were said to have befallen European women and girls at Meerut and Delhi. But there may not have been time.

254. Horne, *Narrative* (BM).

255. I suspect that she could not have escaped if she returned to the shore near Sati Chowra and that she must have reached the riverbank somewhere near the sandbar where Wheeler's boat was grounded, otherwise she would not have met up with Margaret Wheeler.

256. Horne, *Narrative* (BM); Bennett, "Ten Months' Captivity."

257. Deposition of Golab Singh.

258. Depositions of Nundeedeen, Lochun, Narain Kachee, Goordial, Bradshaw, and Letts; Shepherd, *A Personal Narrative*, p. 77.

259. There has been some controversy as to whether Tatya Tope, who would later enter the rolls of Indian nationalist heros as a brave and able commander of Nana's dwindling army, commanded the attack at Sati Chowra. I had hoped to absolve Tatya Tope of his part in the massacre and embrace the claim that it was Bala Rao or Jwala Prasad who took the leading role. But my reexamination of the evidence suggests to me that Tatya Tope was indeed in charge. The claim regarding Bala Rao is based on the testimony of Goordial, who stated that Bala Rao and Azimullah gave the order to sound the bugle. And one of Futteh Singh's servants, Shuniker Singh, made a charge that was adopted not only by Futteh Singh but by his friend and erstwhile employer Nanak Chand. Futteh Singh stated that Bala Rao was the one who championed the plan to massacre the Europeans at the ghat, that Bala Rao and Azimullah commanded the sowars to attack, and that Azimullah and Bala Rao reported on the massacre to Nana. But Futteh Singh's other servant, Bukkee (or Bhikee) Singh, contradicted this account and identified Tatya Tope as the commander.

But the evidence against Tatya Tope is much more persuasive. Certainly he was present that morning; Jokhun saw him at the Entrenchments, dismounted, and Goordial later saw him pay off the boatmen. Lochun says Azimullah and Jwala Prasad gave the order for the boats to be fired, but otherwise he believed Tatya Tope commanded the operation. Lochun heard Tatya order the sowars to finish off the Europeans. "[Tatya Tope] was with the troops engaged in the massacre, and was seated near a temple at the Suttee Chowra Ghat, close to Mouzah Kooreea. . . . By his orders the bugle was sounded, and the guns fired. He also gave the order to the sowars to plunge into the river, and massacre the Europeans. All orders regarding the massacre, issued by the Nana, were carried into execution by Tantia Topee." Bukkee Singh said Tatya gave orders for the bugle to sound and that other orders came from men running from his direction. Narain Kachee, who was in the rebel camp, testified that Nana and Bala ordered Tatya to arrange the massacre and saw him give orders at the ghat. Nundeedeen, standing nearby, said Tatya ordered the bugler to blow the signal and saw him give orders. Shepherd's account also stated that Tatya, was the "principal" official at the ghat, assisted by Teeka Singh and Jwala Prasad.

260. Depositions of Ajoodee Pershad, Peer Bux, Bradshaw, and Letts; Shepherd, *A Personal Narrative*, p. 77.

261. Depositions of Bukkee Singh and Budloo.

262. Bradshaw and Letts in Shepherd, *A Personal Narrative*, p. 77. Depositions of John Fitchett, Thomas DeCruze, William Clarke. Nunne Nawab testified that only a few had escaped uninjured. Diary of Nunne Nawab.

263. Depositions of Fitchett, DeCruze, Bradshaw, and Letts.

264. These hats and bonnets were later found at Bibighar.

265. Lindsay Family Papers; native doctor's note.

266. I surmise this from her ferocious reputation.

267. Yalland, *Traders and Nabobs*, p. 245.

268. Thomson, *The Story of Cawnpore*, pp. 119–20.

269. Depositions of Bradshaw and Letts.

270. Deposition of Lochun.

271. Shepherd, *A Personal Narrative*, pp. 137–38.

272. Deposition of Jokhun.

273. Bradshaw in Shepherd, *A Personal Narrative*, p. 78.

274. Depositions of Bukkee Singh and Nundeedeen.

275. Deposition of Futteh Singh.

276. Shepherd, *A Personal Narrative*, p. 78.

277. Deposition of John Fitchett.

278. Deposition of Khoda Bux.

279. Depositions of Fitchett, DeCruze, and Thomas Clarke.

280. Horne, *Narrative* (BM).

281. Map of Cawnpore by Thomason College, Roorkee.

282. Lucknow Collectorate Mutiny Basta in U.P., 4:585.

283. Depositions of Futteh Singh and Mrs. Spiers.

284. Depositions of Lochun, Futteh Singh, and Bukkee Singh; Nanak Chand's diary.

285. Williams in Shepherd, *A Personal Narrative*, p. 91. Futteh Singh stated that one of the men's wives refused to be parted from him and died with him and her baby, but I assume he is confusing this with the massacre of the fugitives brought back to Cawnpore from Sheorajpur on the thirtieth.

286. Henry Fane, *Letters* (Lincolnshire Archives).

287. Nanak Chand's diary.

288. Horne, *Narrative* (BM).

289. HDP, Public, 14 May 1858, no. 1, NAI.

290. Horne, *Narrative* (BM).

291. My count, based on Thomson's and Delafosse's accounts, indicate that at least forty-four men, six women, and thirteen children were in the boat, though several died in the first hour trying to push the boat off the sandbar.

292. Bernstein, *Steamboats on the Ganges*, p. 12.

293. Testimony of Myoor Tewaree.

294. Bernstein, *Steamboats on the Ganges*, p. 12.

295. Thomson, *The Story of Cawnpore*, pp. 172–73.

296. Ibid., p. 27.

297. Testimony of Myoor Tewaree.

298. Delafosse in TL, 16 Oct. 1857, p. 7.

299. Testimony of Myoor Tewaree.

300. Thomson says it was a moonless night, but astronomical tables indicate that a new crescent moon was shining. It must have been obscured by rain clouds.

301. Thomson, *The Story of Cawnpore*, pp. 173–77.

302. Delafosse in TL, 16 Oct. 1857, p. 7.

303. With the exception of a Private Sullivan of the Madras Fusiliers, the rest were soldiers of the 84th and 32nd.

304. Delafosse in TL, 16 Oct. 1857, p. 7.

305. Ibid.

306. Thomson, *The Story of Cawnpore*, pp. 175–78.

307. Account of James Stewart in the *Friend of India*, 27 Aug. 1857. He says the other woman was a Mrs. Letts; apparently it was another Mrs. Letts who remained with Mrs. Bradshaw.

308. Depositions of Bradshaw and Letts.

309. Shepherd, *A Personal Narrative*, p. 79.

310. Military Department Memorandum in FD, 30 April 1858, nos. 178–79, NAI.

311. Grant, *Cassell's Illustrated History of India*, p. 286. "Mr Saunders was nailed down, hands, feet, and knees; . . . these barbarians the first day cut off his feet and ears and nose, and so left him until the next day, when some other pieces were cut off him, and he died." Letter from a noncommissioned officer of the 84th Regiment printed in TL, 29 Sept. 1857.

312. Nanak Chand describes this officer as "an officer of the grenadier company"; Angelo served with the 16th Grenadiers and was the only Grenadier officer at Cawnpore. He was captured near Nanak Chand's hiding place. Yalland, *Traders and Nabobs*, pp. 357–59.

313. Nanak Chand's diary.

314. Since Indians ate with their right hands only, reserving their left hands for their ablutions, this was for them proof of his desperation.

315. Deposition of Lalla Bhudree Nath.

316. A similar story is told about a man "believed to be Dr. Harris, Civil Surgeon," who was said to have been captured by a zemindar and taken immediately to Cawnpore, where Nana ordered a thakur to kill him. The thakur refused and Nana ordered others to kill Harris with their swords. Shepherd, *A Personal Narrative*, p. 147.

317. Angelo's son was born at Government House, and at his baptism Lord Canning himself stood as godfather.

318. Deposition of Lalla Bhudree Nath.

319. Shepherd, *A Personal Narrative*, p. 93.

320. Thomson, *The Story of Cawnpore*, p. 210.

321. Deposition of Jokhun.

322. Deposition of John Fitchett.

323. Myoor Tewaree testified that there were twenty-five women in the boat; but that would have swelled the number of people in Vibart's boat to about eighty people; far too many to have made its way even to Sheorajpur.

324. Shepherd, *A Personal Narrative*, p. 93.

325. Mrs. Boyes was named in several accounts as the heroic wife who died with her husband at Savada House. But Mrs. Boyes was listed on the native doctor's list as dying on July 7, and not of wounds but dysentery. In any case, Myoor Tewaree described her only as the wife of either the superintending surgeon or the medical storekeeper, positions that better fit Harris than Boyes, who was merely the surgeon of the 2nd Native Cavalry.

326. Diary of Nunne Nawab.

327. Shepherd, *A Personal Narrative*, p. 93.

328. In Myoor Tewaree's account the man who read prayers was a "padre," but in Shepherd's account Seppings was supposed to have "sued for a few minutes to pray." Rev-

erend Willis, who succeeded Haycock and Cockey at Cawnpore, was convinced that the
"padre" was Reverend Cockey. Willis in Sherring, *The Indian Church during the Great Rebellion*, p. 178.

In the firing squad was a Christian drummer named William Diddier whose family had
been killed by the rebels near Allahabad. To prove himself a sincere convert to Islam and
the rebel cause, he had volunteered to take part in the execution, thereby earning the
right to circulate freely through Nana's camp. "Thomas Clarke told him he ought not to
have fired at the Europeans; his reply was that his own family had been killed and he did
not care. After this Diddier was not kept in confinement; he went to the city and did duty
as a sepoy." Deposition of John Fitchett.

329. Testimony of Myoor Tewaree; deposition of Futteh Singh. There would be parallels
to this execution in the British punitive expeditions that followed the massacres at Cawnpore. A year later a detachment of the 84th rounded up about twenty sepoys and badmashes, and one woman "threw herself into a sepoy's arms just as one of our men fired;
the ball went through both of them." Pearson, *Letters*, p. 198 (OIOC).

330. Shepherd, *A Personal Narrative*, p. 93–94; Thomson, *The Story of Cawnpore*, pp.
176–77.

331. Letter from Nana Sahib to officers of 41st N.I. in U.P., 4:601.

332. I am increasingly convinced that Nana Sahib was a mere pageant at these events,
and that it was Bala Rao and Azimullah who issued these edicts and arranged these ceremonies.

333. Diary of Nunne Nawab.

334. Deposition of Goordial.

335. Deposition of Budloo.

336. Shepherd, *A Personal Narrative*, p. 83.

337. Ibid., p. 93.

338. Deposition of Hulas Singh.

339. Nanak Chand's diary.

340. Shepherd, *A Personal Narrative*, p. 85.

341. Ibid., p. 82.

342. Deposition of Kalka Pershad.

343. Shepherd, *A Personal Narrative*, p. 74.

344. Nanak Chand's diary.

345. Shepherd, *A Personal Narrative*, p. 75.

346. Depositions of Narain Kachee, John Fitchett, Hulas Singh, DeCruze, and Clarke.

347. FPP V/4, vol. 44, Inclosure E 21, no. 2, p. 60.

348. Deposition of Futteh Singh.

349. Kaye, *A History of the Great Revolt*, 2:348.

350. Shepherd, *A Personal Narrative*, pp. 79–82.

351. "He was really a good man," wrote Shepherd, "and in justice to him I must say that
it was entirely to his kindness I am indebted for not being exposed to the Nana." Ibid., p.
88.

352. Ibid., p. 84.

353. Hibbert, *The Great Mutiny*, p. 194.

354. Unless otherwise noted, all of the material in this section is from Thomson, *The
Story of Cawnpore*, pp. 179–90.

355. Shepherd's account.

356. Deposition of Khoda Buksh.

357. Shepherd, *A Personal Narrative*, p. 78.

358. Horne, *Narrative* (BM); testimony of Myoor Tewaree. The sepoys who taunted
Amy Horne and the nurse who brought Amy her meals told her that the ladies "were subjected, old and young, to horrors and cruelties, which the tongue may not name." But eyewitnesses maintain they were not physically abused.

359. Havildar Amundee Deen Misser.

360. Jokhun tried to find the colonel's son, but when he reached Lucknow the Begum imprisoned him for a month "on the suspicion that I was seeking employment among the British." He claimed to be still looking when he gave his deposition. Deposition of Jokhun.

361. TL, 29 Oct. 1857, p. 12.

362. Thornton in Hibbert, *The Great Mutiny*, p. 59.

363. Misra, *Nana Saheb Peshwa*, p. 250.

364. Shepherd, *A Personal Narrative*, p. 94.

365. FSC, 26 Nov. 1858 (27, 28).

366. Seating arrangements at court were also drawn up, with places reserved for ministers, generals, and the representatives of every nation and province. Out of all this bounty of tribute and revenue, the prime minister, presumably Azimullah, was scheduled to receive the astronomical salary of one hundred thousand rupees a month, his subordinates twenty-five thousand. Gupta, *Nana Saheb*, p. 87.

367. Kaye, *A History of the Great Revolt*, 2:673.

368. Ibid., 3:299nn, 669.

369. Sherer, *Daily Life*, p. 112.

370. Cosens and Wallace, *Fatehgarh*, pp. 42, 55.

371. Adams, *The Makers of British India*, p. 389.

372. Narrative of Gavin Jones.

373. Testimony of David Churcher at the trial of the Nawab of Farrukhabad, Farrukhabad Collectorate Mutiny Basta in U.P., 5:924–26; Fatehgarh narrative.

374. Dass in Sherring, *The Indian Church during the Great Rebellion*, p. 138.

375. Narrative of Gavin Jones.

376. Shepherd, *A Personal Narrative*, p. 111.

377. The relative sizes of the Entrenchment and Fatehgarh Fort are based on maps in Shepherd, *A Personal Narrative*, and in Cosens and Wallace, *Fatehgarh*.

378. Narrative of Gavin Jones.

379. Fatehgarh narrative.

380. Cosens and Wallace, *Fatehgarh*, pp. 60–62.

381. Dass in Sherring, *The Indian Church during the Great Rebellion*, pp. 139–41.

382. Fatehgarh narrative.

383. Cosens and Wallace, *Fatehgarh*, p. 69.

384. Fatehgarh narrative.

385. Smith mentioned one thousand in his letter, but this must have been based on observation. The sepoys alone numbered over one thousand, and they had been joined by almost as many Pathans, matchlockmen, and Oudh Irregulars. Perhaps only one thousand attacked at any one time. Cosens and Wallace, *Fatehgarh*, p. 82.

386. Narrative of Gavin Jones.

387. Fatehgarh narrative.

388. The two were Kale Khan and Surat Singh. Cosens and Wallace, *Fatehgarh*, pp. 93, 120.

389. Gavin Jones in ibid., p. 72.

390. Narrative of Gavin Jones.

391. Intelligence report received at Agra in Cosens and Wallace, *Fatehgarh*, p. 75.

392. Narrative of Gavin Jones.

393. Cosens and Wallace, *Fatehgarh*, p. 75.

394. Narrative of Gavin Jones.

395. Yalland, *Traders and Nabobs*, p. 233.

396. Dass in Sherring, *The Indian Church during the Great Rebellion*, p.143.

397. Narrative of Gavin Jones.

398. A native informant's report to William Edwards in Cosens and Wallace, *Fatehgarh*, p. 82.

399. Frederick Fisher had been chaplain at Fatehgarh for two years. Born in 1813, he was appointed to the Company Chaplains' Service in 1839, three years after graduating from Cambridge. He was now forty-four, and a full chaplain of some experience, having worked in five previous stations in various parts of the country. He was grandson of the Reverend Henry Fisher who had so impressed Bishop Heber when they had met in 1825, in Meerut. "He was thoroughly imbued with the tradition of the Chaplains' Service and its duties. He was not a missionary (although he seems to have been on good terms with the American missionaries in town)." Hughes, *The Mutiny Chaplains*, p. 63.

400. A more remote possibility was that they had heard of Havelock's advance and hoped he had cleared the rebels out of Cawnpore by the time of their arrival.

401. Shepherd, *A Personal Narrative*, p. 111.

402. TL, 9 Oct. 1857, p. 8.

403. Fisher/Heathcote: 2 Sept. 1857, NLS (MS.20206).

404. Fisher/Stevens: 16 Sept. 1857, NLS (MS.20206).

405. Robertson's boat was said to have been larger than Smith's, yet it carried a passenger weight that was only about 70 percent of Smith's. Unless the last-minute scramble had simply confused the embarkation and more people piled onto the lead boat to get away faster, perhaps Robertson's boat was carrying more baggage, or Smith's boat, like Vibart's at Cawnpore, had a lighter draft.

406. Dass in Sherring, *The Indian Church during the Great Rebellion*, pp. 143–44.

407. The Churchers had fallen on hard times at Fatehgarh. They had once owned Colonel Smith's house, which had been a refuge for the Fatehgarh garrison in May, but their plantations were floundering. Wallace, *Fatehgarh*, p. 157.

408. Phillott had had the prescience to send his wife off to the relative safety of Allahabad on May 23. He was born in 1810, the son of a banker, and joined the service in 1828. Cosens and Wallace, *Fatehgarh*, p. 21; Blunt, *Christian Tombs and Monuments*, p. 118.

409. Officer on Neill's staff in letter dated 1 Aug. 1857 in TL, 30 Sept. 1857, p. 6.

410. Testimony of David Churcher at Trial of Nawab of Farrukhabad in February, 1859, Farrukhabad Collectorate Mutiny Basta in U.P., 5:924–26.

411. Edwards, *Personal Adventures*, pp. 65, 135–36.

412. Cosens and Wallace say that twenty-seven out of the original forty-four perished at Manpur, but I think they miscounted. They list nineteen people as having survived the attack, and though they state that seven were taken captive, their list shows fourteen. The remaining five who escaped that day were Gavin Jones, David Churcher, Reverend Fisher, Major Robertson, and Bhairo, Gavin Jones's servant. The reverend and the major would die soon afterward.

413. The four heads belonged to one man and three ladies: Mr. Sutherland, Mrs. Jons, and two of her daughters. Trial of Babu Ram Bakhsh, U.P. 4:678–79.

414. Though they were only six miles from where Probyn and Edwards lay in hiding, the major was so weakened by his wound and a case of dysentery that he declined their invitation to join them. The loyal Churcher would not desert the major, and when Robertson finally died of sepsis two months later, Churcher buried him in their village hideaway.

415. Edwards, *Personal Adventures*, p. 136.

416. Narrative of Gavin Jones.

417. Fisher/Stevens: 16 Sept. 1857 (NLS).

418. Edwards, *Personal Adventures*, p. 190.

419. Yalland, *Traders and Nabobs*, p. 325.

420. Narrative of Gavin Jones.

421. Jones eventually beat the infection by coaxing a puppy to lick his wound every morning and evening.

422. Munro was born in Jamaica and had served thirty of his fifty-one years in India. Officer on Neill's staff in letter dated 1 Aug. 1857 in TL, 30 Sept. 1857, p. 6.

423. Deposition of John Fitchett.

424. Cosens and Wallace, *Fatehgarh*, p. 17.

425. The Fishers' account apparently confuses the various rebel attacks on Smith's boat, but according to Cosens and Wallace the Heathcotes were in Smith's boat, and so this incident must have occurred opposite Bithur, for it was the one time Smith's boat was boarded by rebels. Fisher/Heathcote: 2 Sept. 1857 (NLS); Chevers, *Papers* (OIOC).

426. The head boatman escaped and returned to Chauchpur to tell Jones of the party's fate. Narrative of Gavin Jones.

427. There may have been one escapee from Smith's boat. On the morning of July 10 a dhobi carrying his wash to the river came upon an insensible five- or six-year-old girl lying on the bank with a wound to her clavicle. He handed her over to a golundaz who brought the child before Nana, begging to adopt her as his own. Teeka Singh objected, but Nana overruled him. She was reportedly recovering from her wounds when General Havelock reached Cawnpore, whereupon the golundaz took her with him. According to Nunne Nawab the golundaz was imprisoned by Teeka Singh and the little girl was probably murdered. But when in 1859 an emissary from the King of Nepal demanded that Bala Rao, then in hiding and dying of malaria, return all of his European prisoners, Bala conceded that it was true "that a daughter of the Judge of Furruckabad, the only European with me, who has received a bullet wound, which I caused to be cured, *was* with me, but she has lately been made over to Colonel Bird," though apparently no record of such a transferral exists. Bala Rao's "Judge of Furrukhabad" would have been Robert Thornhill, who, according to his family memorial at All Souls, had two children with him at Fatehgarh: a "fat & rosy" little boy and a newborn whose gender was not recorded. (A third child, whom Mary called "My dear Georgie," evidently lived with Mary's sister in England.) Diary of Nunne Nawab; Shepherd, *A Personal Narrative*, p. 39; Thornhill Papers (OIOC); FDP, Pol. 15 July 1859, no. 230.

428. Deposition of Nana Ubbhunker.

429. Deposition of Narain Kachee.

430. Depositions of Appajee Luchman and Appa Shastri.

431. His name was Koosaba Khiranee Gir. Deposition of Nundeedeen Aheer.

432. Mutiny Narrative, Cawnpore District in U.P., 4:536.

433. The identity of the officer who asked to be announced to Nana Sahib is not given in the various accounts, only that he was one of the three senior men: Smith, Thornhill, or Goldie. Smith was of little account to the rebels, and Thornhill only slightly more valuable as a bargaining chip because his father had been a director of the Company and his brothers served throughout the Bengal Presidency. But Goldie was another matter. It seems to me likely that only the forceful Goldie could have convinced Nana to save these three senior men from immediate execution.

434. TL, 9 Oct. 1857, p. 8.

435. An account in the *Times of London* would deem this story "not worthy of belief, and must have been fabricated by the Nena Sahib with a view to induce the people to believe he was to obtain possession of those places in a short time." TL, 16 Oct. 1857, p. 8.

436. The Fisher family lost nine people in the Mutiny. "Not a relic has reached us or perhaps ever will reach us of our beloved ones," wrote Frederick's brother. "All has been burnt—pillaged and destroyed. They and all they had are as if suddenly blotted out of existence." Fisher/Stevens: 17 Aug. 1857 (NLS).

437. Edwards had been relieved to separate from the two planters. "I was satisfied," he wrote, "that as long as I was alone I could provide for my own safety, having numbers of friends in the district able and anxious to protect and shelter me; but they were unwilling in any way to compromise their own safety by granting an asylum to the others: more especially as some of the party were at feud with the people of the district, in consequence of having purchased estates, sold under harsh circumstances, by decrees of our Civil Courts." Edwards, *Personal Adventures*, p. 12.

438. Shepherd does not give the name of either the native Christian or the servant, but I surmise their identities from Cosens and Wallace's list. Humphreys was not a "Hindu," as Shepherd characterizes the servant, but may have appeared like one after their ordeal on the river.

439. Shepherd, *A Personal Narrative*, p. 112. Shepherd places the executions in the Commissariat Yard. The generally authoritative Cosens and Wallace place it at Savada House, but appear to have based this on the testimony of Futteh Singh and various other natives who were either not present or confused the second massacre of Fatehgarh fugitives with the first. Cosens and Wallace's account also seems to have confused the second massacre with the execution of the surviving men from Vibart's boat on June 30. In any case, by July 10 Nana had left Savada House and moved his headquarters to the Old Cawnpore Hotel, a few hundred yards from the Bibighar, in which he had installed the surviving women and children of the Cawnpore garrison on July 2. I therefore side with Shepherd's version, which he culled from his interviews with various eyewitnesses.

440. Leather shoes were especially effective hiding places in India, for only the lowest caste Hindus would touch them.

441. Shepherd, *A Personal Narrative*, p. 113.

442. Shepherd's account. A sweeper named Cheda testified that the house belonged to a Mrs. Batten. This may have been Mrs. Battine, wife of Lieutenant Charles Battine of the 14th Native Infantry, who was killed in Vibart's boat, but it is likely Cheda confused the house with another nearby. Deposition of Cheda.

443. I have based this description on a drawing made on the spot by a medical man named Norman Chevers (OIOC), a drawing by Charles Crump in his *A Pictorial Record of the Cawnpore Massacre*, and Shepherd's map on p. 112 of *A Personal Narrative*, modifying them somewhat with the few photographs that exist of it before it was demolished.

444. Shepherd, *A Personal Narrative*, p. 140.

445. Thomson, *The Story of Cawnpore*, p. 210.

446. Deposition of John Fitchett.

447. Thomason College map.

448. It is impossible to know how many were at the Bibighar, for the circumstances of the deaths of a great many soldiers' wives and children were not recorded. Even leaving them out, I count at least 177 women and children alive there on July 2.

449. Darton, *The Life of Mrs. Sherwood*, p. 379.

450. Deposition of John Fitchett.

451. Shepherd, map of Bibighar, p. 112ff. A native doctor's list is titled "List of those who arrived in this house on Tuesday, July 7th, 1857," but he may have been referring to the women who filed by to be recorded. Other accounts maintain that the women and children arrived before Nana's return on July 6. TL, 21 Sept. 1857, p. 6.

452. Shepherd, *A Personal Narrative*, p. 94.

453. Thomson, *The Story of Cawnpore*, p. 210.

454. Ibid., p. 142. Mrs. Vibart's fate is unknown, but she was frail and may not have long survived her husband's death.

455. The following rough calculation may give some idea of how cramped the Bibighar was: it amounted to some two thousand square feet, but if everyone had been allotted a two-foot-six-by-six-foot bed they would have initially taken up 2,700 square feet, and 3,300 square feet after the Fatehgarh survivors joined them. Each person would have then had approximately a two- by five-foot space.

456. Chevers, *Papers* (OIOC).

457. Deposition of Khoda Bux.

458. Deposition of John Fitchett. R. Macrae, a relative of Mrs. Wrixon, judged Mrs. Jacobi harshly for her part in the negotiations: "When this letter was entrusted to Mrs. Jacobi she was carefully instructed that, if she returned without the acceptance of the terms, of which she was informed, her children would be killed. Mrs. Jacobi was aware of the

treachery intended, as the Nana's Camp was in the Sevada Compound. Captain Mowbray Thomson mentions her extreme uneasiness at being detained in the Garrison. Though she allowed her feelings as a mother to remain in the ascendant, she ultimately met the same fate as the other prisoners."

But there is little evidence that she knew of any impending treachery, or even that Nana had contemplated it by this time. Bennett, "Ten Months' Captivity."

459. Deposition of DeCruze; Shepherd, *A Personal Narrative*, pp. 94–95.

460. Shepherd, *A Personal Narrative*, p. 94; Thomson, *The Story of Cawnpore*, p. 210. Henry Lawrence's wife was startled to discover "among Europeans the prejudices of caste" and to hear many of them object to low-caste natives "as much as a Hindoo would." Honoraria Lawrence in Mason, *A Matter of Honour*, p. 125.

461. Butler, *The Land of the Veda*, p. 267.

462. Psalm 11:5–6.

463. Isaiah 47:1–3, 5.

464. Shepherd's account.

465. Diary of Nunne Nawab.

466. Nanak Chand's diary.

467. Ibid.; Deposition of Lalla Shunker Doss.

468. Nevill, *Cawnpore*, pp. 214–16; Shepherd, *A Personal Narrative*, p. 101; Shepherd's account.

469. Deposition of Nanak Chand.

470. Deposition of Dabie Deen.

471. Shepherd, *A Personal Narrative*, p. 114.

472. Nanak Chand's diary.

473. TL, 29 Oct. 1857, p. 12.

474. Nanak Chand's diary; deposition of Appajee Luchman.

475. Nanak Chand's diary.

476. FSP in U.P., 4:608. The detachment's commanders proved unpopular at Lucknow, and were largely ignored by the Begum's troops who felt they had matters well in hand without them. Nanak Chand's diary.

477. Deposition of Futteh Singh; Nanak Chand's diary.

478. Nanak Chand's diary.

479. Depositions of Futteh Singh and Hulas Singh.

480. "Some rebels declared that the Nana would win against the Europeans advancing on Cawnpore, but others decided to return their plunder to their families before going off to meet them, just in case they lost." Nanak Chand's diary.

481. Shepherd, *A Personal Narrative*, p. 101.

482. Nevill, *Cawnpore*, pp. 214–16.

483. Shepherd, *A Personal Narrative*, p. 114.

484. Baba Bhutt's papers would later fall into the hands of the British. "It was entertaining to read his orders," wrote Sherer, "some of them exactly the sort of directions one had given one's self when in some doubt what to do next. In the margin of a report on some village disturbance, he would have written: 'Make strict inquiries and report again in three days.' Deliciously make-believe energetic!" Sherer, *Daily Life*, p. 95.

485. Interview with Keith Shepherd.

486. Shepherd, *A Personal Narrative*, pp. 97–100, 106.

487. Horne, *Narrative* (BM). Baba Bhutt did not condemn every man who came before him. On July 1, wrote Nunne Nawab, "one of the sepoys, who had been in the entrenchment and was seized and confined on the 27th June, had a son in the 2nd Light Cavalry, who first went to Baba Bhut, and menacing to kill him in case of non-compliance with his request, he was referred to Nana, to whom he went and repeated his request in the same threatening manner. Nana immediately liberated both his father and his comrades." Diary of Nunne Nawab.

488. At one point two amputated hands were brought in for Baba Bhutt's horrified inspection. Ibid., p. 108.

489. Shepherd, *A Personal Narrative*, p. 109.

490. Deposition of John Fitchett.

491. *Friend of India* in U.P., 4:700, probably based on Mary Ann's testimony in the *Times*. "Then the Nena wrote to Delhi, mentioning the number of women and children whom he had taken, and soliciting instructions regarding them. A reply was received that they were not to be killed." TL, 16 Oct. 1857, p. 8.

492. Yalland, *Traders and Nabobs*, p. 345.

493. Deposition of John Fitchett.

494. Depositions of Kalka Pershad and Peero.

495. "One day," testified Hulas Singh, "the cooks said, 'The ladies won't eat *dhall*. Let us have as much meat as can be procured at the cost of the *dhall*.'" Deposition of Hulas Singh.

496. Shepherd, *A Personal Narrative*, 94–95; Shepherd's account.

497. Butler, *The Land of the Veda*, p. 306.

498. Sherer, *Narrative*.

499. Deposition of Nana Ubbhunker.

500. Estimates of her age ranged from twenty-five to thirty-six.

501. Depositions of Appajee Luchman, Nana Ubbhunker, Hulas Singh, Futteh Singh, DeCruze, Khoda Bux, and Appa Shastri.

502. Deposition of Nana Ubbhunker.

503. Deposition of Futteh Singh.

504. According to Jonah, she had been instructed "to persuade the ladies to yield to the Nana's wishes. This message, I learn, was conveyed to them with great subtlety, accompanied by threats and hopes; but it is gratifying to find that it was received with just indignation by all, and with a firm resolve to die, or to kill each other with their own hands, should any forcible means be employed to dishonor them." But Jonah seems to have been understandably determined to cast all of Nana's actions in the worst possible light and may have misinterpreted Nana's "great subtlety." The evidence suggests that Nana simply wanted to try to keep his prisoners alive. Shepherd, *A Personal Narrative*, p. 94.

505. Deposition of Kalka Pershad.

506. Deposition of John Fitchett, who was the only witness to make this claim.

507. Shepherd, *A Personal Narrative*, p. 95.

508. Deposition of Peero.

509. Deposition of DeCruze.

510. Lieutenant Chalmers, who was killed at Cawnpore, was her relative.

511. The identity of the doctor is not recorded. Presumably he was a prisoner as well. Shepherd mentions a native doctor named Wali Dad Khan of the 56th Native Infantry who was imprisoned at the jail, but does not say if he may have been the same doctor who was assigned to look after the women at the Bibighar. The doctor was more likely the Bengali Mookerji. Shepherd, *A Personal Narrative*, p. 99.

512. Yalland, *Traders and Nabobs*, p. 244.

513. Thomson, *The Story of Cawnpore*, p. 27.

514. She may have been carried out of the Bibighar on the ninth to be cared for by the Bengali doctor, as he recorded her death on July 10.

515. Lindsay Family Papers.

516. One inscription was scratched into the wall behind a door by using "a nail in the point of a pair of slippers." According to a later visitor to the Bibighar it alluded to the ladies having "suffered the last indignities from their captors who were then going to murder them—and ended with a lament for her child—'alas, alas—4 months this day.'" Fitzgerald, *Diary* (OIOC).

517. *The Phoenix*, 8 Aug. 1857.

518. Depositions of Gobind Singh, Sheik Elahee Buksh, and Ghouse Mohomed.

519. HMS, 726 (23), NAI.

520. "The indiscriminate burning of villages," wrote Montgomery Martin, "and the pillaging of 'niggers,' was the most costly amusement Europeans in India could indulge in." Martin, *The Indian Empire*, 2:282.

521. Highlander of the 78th in ibid., 2:289–90.

522. Letter, 6 July 1857 in ibid., 2:296.

523. Railway official, 23 June 1857; *London Daily News*, 25 Aug. 1857.

524. One young Englishman was apparently deranged by the excesses at Allahabad. After Neill's arrival, "this strange man was bitten with a desire to become a pirate. He rigged up a boat, put on board a quantity of loot he found lying about, and cruised up and down the river in his mysterious bark, amusing himself, amongst other employments, with a piano he had picked up in some deserted bungalow. That he would have been heard of generally, for good or evil, seems certain, as he was out of the common run, but death from fever or cholera put an end to his whimsical career." Sherer, *Daily Life*, p. 56.

525. Fusilier officer in Martin, *The Indian Empire*, 2:301; Neill, letter dated 30 June in ibid., 2:303. Historians like Montgomery Martin and Edward Thompson point out that all these atrocities had been committed before Allahabad had learned of Sati Chowra and more than two weeks before the massacre at the Bibighar had even taken place. The atrocities committed by the volunteers did predate even the June 12 massacre of the first party of Fatehgarh fugitives, but a degree of the special wrath of Neill's commissioners may have been attributable to the news of this first slaughter, which included men, women, and children, including missionaries affiliated with the American Presbyterian establishment at Allahabad. Their massacre had already branded Nana Sahib a monster. According to the *Englishman* the massacre of the Fatehghur fugitives "surpassed in atrocity all that has hitherto been perpetrated."

"Of all the villains engaged in [the] congenial pursuits [of robbery and murder], Nana Saheb would appear to be the most bloodthirsty," reported the *Friend of India*, shortly after learning of the massacre of the refugees from Fatehgarh. "His last act of butchery [the massacre of the Futtehghur fugitives] was of a wholesale nature, and it is a pity he has not a thousand lives to make expiation for it." *Friend of India* in TL, 15 Aug. 1857; TL, 17 Aug. 1857; *The Englishman* dated 29 July in TL, 15 Aug. 1857; Allahabad civilian in TL, 25 Aug. 1857; *The Phoenix*, 30 June 1857, in TL, 14 Aug. 1857; "Ne Cede Malis" in a letter from Calcutta dated 4 July 1857, in TL, 15 Aug. 1857.

526. But he went on to assure his wife that "one of the Bands played merrily in the Fort last night—I ran down with Riddell and heard it." Sherer, *Letters*, p. 9.

527. Fusilier officer in Martin, *The Indian Empire*, 2:301.

528. Collier, *The Sound of Fury*, p. 165.

529. Kaye, *A History of the Great Revolt*, 2:274–75.

530. Sherer was born in 1823, graduated from Haileybury College in 1846, and rose in the ranks of the Bengal Civil Service as Assistant and then Joint Magistrate and Deputy Collector. By 1852 he had become Assistant Secretary to the North-Western Provinces Government. He was not known as a particularly meticulous civil servant, and after leaving the civil service he turned his hand to fiction. Dickens published some of his work.

531. Sherer, *Letters*, pp. 3–4.

532. Ibid., p. 13. Two months later a young Garnet Wolsely, fresh from the Crimea, would help collect Tucker's remains. "We found his skull, and collected as many of his bones as we could. The only coffin we could obtain was an empty brandy case, in which we buried him with military honors. The sole inscription upon the box that contained his bones was 'Old Cognac.'" Wolseley, *From England to Cawnpore*, East Sussex (W/W/2/1).

533. Kaye, 2:364–6. Dr. Duff reported that Tucker's head, hands, and feet were cut off, "and exhibited, all bleeding, to the fanatical and murderous multitude!" Duff, *The Indian Rebellion*, p. 35.

534. Kaye, *A History of the Great Revolt*, 2:274–75.

535. Neill in ibid.
536. Ibid., 2:283–84nn.
537. Russell, *My Diary in India*, 1:162.
538. Russell in Thompson, *The Other Side of the Medal*, pp. 33–34.
539. Gupta, *Nana Saheb*, p. 127.
540. Russell, *My Diary in India*, 2:402.
541. Chunder, *Travels of a Hindoo*, p. 335.
542. Taylor, *Chronicles of the Mutiny*, p. 32.
543. The enraged zemindar armed his retainers and sent them after the steamer, but it had floated out of range. Eventually the authorities at Allahabad apologized to him. Martin, *The Indian Empire*, 2:374.
544. HMS, 726 (23).
545. Lawrence in Martin, *The Indian Empire*, 2:373.
546. HMS, 726 (16).
547. Gupta, *Nana Saheb*, p. 128.
548. HMS, 726 (16).
549. Sherer, *Letters*, p. 10.
550. North, *Journal*, p. 30.
551. Sherer, *Letters*, p. 11.
552. Collier, *The Sound of Fury*, p. 167; Mason, *A Matter of Honour*, p. 85.
553. Collier, *The Sound of Fury*, p. 176.
554. Heber, *Narrative*, 2:495.
555. Mason, *A Matter of Honour*, p. 203.
556. Forbes, *Havelock*, p. 107.
557. Plaque at St. Giles, Edinburgh.
558. Forbes, *Havelock*, pp. 111–12.
559. Mason, *A Matter of Honour*, p. 308.
560. Martin, *The Indian Empire*, 2:374.
561. North, *Journal*, p. 32.
562. Collier, *The Sound of Fury*, p. 164.
563. Forbes, *Havelock*, p. 113.
564. Sherer, *Narrative*.
565. One of these was a Moslem holy man, a "stout, able fellow" who hardly deigned to reply to his interrogators. The soldiers were going to let him go, but searched him first and found a note addressed to a regiment that had not yet mutinied "directing the brigade to rise at once and kill their officers and the ladies and children of their station, and march immediately for Delhi to help the Emperor against the English. . . . He was at once told to prepare for death. They gave him five minutes," during which he prayed with his beads, "and then dropped him by the roadside with the bullet." A soldier later gave the fakir's beads to the American Reverend William Butler. Butler, *The Land of the Veda*, p. 206.
566. Hibbert, *The Great Mutiny*, p. 205.
567. Such swamps gave Fatehpur a reputation as an unhealthy posting.
568. Sherer, *Narrative*.
569. The spies confirmed the fall of Cawnpore. That same day Havelock would write, "'On the 28th of June, Cawnpore fell into the hands of the rebels, and that fine old man, Sir Hugh Wheeler, and his force, were all destroyed by an act of foul treachery on the part of the Nana." North, *Journal*, p. 37.
570. Martin, *The Indian Empire*, 2:375.
571. Deposition of Dabie Deen. The British estimated that the rebel force numbered about 3,500. Burgess, *The Chronology of Modern India*, p. 364.
572. Artillery officer in Ball, *The History of the Indian Mutiny*, 1:366.
573. Ibid.
574. Civilian volunteer's letter, 15 July 1857 in ibid., 1:368.

575. Ibid., 1:366.

576. Ibid., 1:362; Collier, *The Sound of Fury*, p. 166; deposition of Cheda.

577. Infantry officer in Ball, *The History of the Indian Mutiny*, 1:366; Collier, *The Sound of Fury*, p. 168.

578. Martin, *The Indian Empire*, 2:375.

579. Infantry officer in Ball, *The History of the Indian Mutiny*, 1:366.

580. Sherer, *Narrative*.

581. Civilian volunteer's letter, 15 July 1857 in Ball, *The History of the Indian Mutiny*, 1:368.

582. Sherer, *Narrative*.

583. Ball, *The History of the Indian Mutiny*, 1:363.

584. One officer became the only direct casualty of the day when a bullock "lashed to fury" by a wound charged into him and knocked him unconscious. North, *Journal*, p. 44.

585. Forbes, *Havelock*, p. 119. Sherer remembered seeing Havelock pass by in his hour of triumph. "General Havelock went by—the erect, slight figure, handsome features, grey hair, with the white covered and curtained cap, and the easy seat on the natty Arab—a vignette very familiar to us all afterwards." Sherer, *Daily Life*, p. 61.

586. Collier, *The Sound of Fury*, p. 168.

587. Forbes, *Havelock*, p. 120.

588. Ball, *The History of the Indian Mutiny*, 1:367.

589. All Sherer could find of his estate was his buggy, "which was much knocked about with the lining torn out." Sherer, *Letters*, pp. 12–13.

590. Sherer, *Narrative*.

591. Ball, *The History of the Indian Mutiny*, 1:367.

592. Artillery officer in ibid., 1:366.

593. A volunteer horseman made off with, in addition to Wheeler's cloth, "an English leathern vallise, two good durries, a Cashmere chola, a pistol, a lot of puggry [turban] cloth, some horse traps, and a pollparrot." Civilian volunteer's letter, 15 July 1857 in ibid., 1:369.

594. Ibid., 1:363.

595. Kaye, *A History of the Great Revolt*, 1:369; Sherer, *Narrative*.

596. North, *Journal*, pp. 143–44; Ensign Browne, letter dated 24 July 1857 in TL, 21 Sept. 1857, p. 6.

597. ILN, no. 882, vol. xxxi, 10 Oct. 1857, p. 354.

598. The first reports of Browne's survival led people to believe that he had survived the siege and the massacres. On September 1, 1857, the *Times* published a letter from one "J. B." in which it was reported that "one has survived from the (Cawnpore) garrison—an Ensign Browne. What a narrative he could give!" TL, 1 Sept. 1857. The narrative would have to await Thomson and Delafosse.

599. Nana Sahib in Collier, *The Sound of Fury*, p. 167.

600. Havelock, Telegraph to the commander-in-chief, 14 July 1857 in Ball, *The History of the Indian Mutiny*, 1:367.

601. Sherer, *Narrative*.

602. Forbes, *Havelock*, p. 121.

603. "The Story of Miss Sutherland" (BM).

604. Bingham, *Diary* (NAM).

605. Forbes, *Havelock*, p. 123.

606. Collier, *The Sound of Fury*, p. 170.

607. Sherer to Beadon in Reid Papers, CCSAS.

608. Collier, *The Sound of Fury*, p. 169; Kaye suggests the rebels may have broken them in frustration. Kaye, *A History of the Great Revolt*, 2:370.

609. Forbes, *Havelock*, p. 124.

610. Bingham, *Diary* (NAM).

611. Participant in Ball, *The History of the Indian Mutiny*, 1:372.

612. Kaye, *A History of the Great Revolt*, 2:377.

613. Participant in Ball, *The History of the Indian Mutiny*, 1:373.

614. TL, 16 Oct. 1857, p. 9.

615. " 'I've just got three of 'em out of the house, sir,' said a 78th man, with a grin, as I met him at a turn in the village." Participant in Ball, *The History of the Indian Mutiny*, 1:373.

616. A particular hazard in this country were village wells, some obscured by smoke and others flooded over, which the cavalry kept falling into. North, *Journal*, p. 44.

617. Officer in Ball, *The History of the Indian Mutiny*, 1:375.

618. Participant in ibid., 1:373.

619. Bingham, *Diary* (NAM).

620. Officer's letter in Ball, *The History of the Indian Mutiny*, 1:370.

621. Officer of the 64th in ibid., 1:374.

622. Forbes, *Havelock*, p. 136. In fact, Havelock was accused of playing favorites with this regiment, and short-shrifting the contributions of the 64th. He would later be accused of playing favorites with his son as well, recommending him for a Victoria Cross for leading the 64th while their commander, Major Stirling, was "dismounted." The slur on Stirling, who, like the general, died soon afterward, rankled the 64th, who later pointed out that his horse had been critically injured by rebel fire. Despite the younger Havelock's valor at Cawnpore, Sir Colin Campbell recommended against awarding him the cross. Martin, *The Indian Empire*, 2:394–95.

623. Officer in Ball, *The History of the Indian Mutiny*, 1:373.

624. Participant in ibid., 1:376. Evidently no prisoners were spared.

625. Officer in ibid., 1:375.

626. Ibid.

627. Their rations consisted of biscuits and shreds of dried beef they called "ding-ding," after the noise it was said to make when you tapped it with your fingernail. Dinwiddie, *Life and Adventures*, p. 30 (NAM).

628. Havelock in TL, 16 Oct. 1857, p. 9.

629. Forbes, *Havelock*, p. 144.

630. There is some controversy over who first saw the Bibighar. Macrae, the local Cawnpore historian who lost several relatives in the massacre insisted that an officer also named McCrae was the first; other accounts say it was Captain McBean, Havelock's chief commissariat officer. But according to Shepherd's account Ayton's detachment was the first to enter cantonments and took the most direct route to the Bibighar and had other soldiers preceded Ayton's party, Shepherd would have mentioned it. Certainly Ayton and Shepherd preceded Sherer, who was still outside of the city when the magazine exploded perhaps half an hour to an hour after Shepherd visited the Bibighar. Shepherd, *A Personal Narrative*, pp. 129–30; Sherer, *Narrative*.

631. Shepherd, *A Personal Narrative*, pp. 127–28.

632. Deposition of Ajoodea Pershad.

633. Nanak Chand's diary.

634. "The Story of Miss Sutherland" (BM).

635. Nanak Chand's diary.

636. Deposition of Hulas Singh.

637. Deposition of Lochun.

638. Depositions of Gobind Singh, Sheik Elahee Buksh, and Ghouse Mohomed.

639. Deposition of Futteh Singh.

640. Nanak Chand's diary.

641. Shepherd, *A Personal Narrative*, p. 117.

642. Henry Fane/Caroline Beresford: 29 July 1857, Lincolnshire Archives (6/9/1/4a–b).

643. A similar letter was forged at Fatehgarh to instigate the massacre of the Christian captives. Taylor, *A Star Shall Fall*, pp. 139–40.

644. "Statement of Information" in TL, 16 Oct. 1857, p. 8; Shepherd, *A Personal Narrative*, p. 117.

645. Further papers in U.P., 4:588.

646. Shepherd, *A Personal Narrative*, p. 116.

647. Nana's letter in Foreign Political Consultations in U.P., 4:772–74.

648. Tatya Tope's testimony in FPC, U.P., 4:510–11.

649. Forbes-Mitchell, *The Relief of Lucknow*, pp. 113–14.

650. Deposition of Cherunjoo.

651. Collier, *The Sound of Fury*, p. 183.

652. Shepherd, *A Personal Narrative*, p. 95.

653. Many visitors reported finding bonnets and sun hats at the Bibighar. Fisher/Stevens: 17 Aug. 1857 (NLS); Shepherd, *A Personal Narrative*, p. 136; Sherer, *Daily Life*, p. 79.

654. The Allahabad garrison employed this means of avoiding sunstroke; it would have been one of the few means remaining to the ladies at the Bibighar. Fusilier officer in Martin, *The Indian Empire*, 2:301.

655. Deposition of John Fitchett.

656. Shepherd, *A Personal Narrative*, p. 117.

657. These are the July 15 totals I have been able to verify, but there may well have been a few more or less than turn up in Shepherd, in the inscription at All Souls, and on the native doctor's list on which most of the Bibighar tallies were based. It is likely that some of those whose time and place of death at Cawnpore were unknown actually died on July 15, but it seems just as likely that some had already died during their initial incarceration at Savada House. My count includes three men, seventeen women and twenty-three children from Fatehgarh, fifty-six women and 101 children from Cawnpore. The relatively small number of grown women versus the large number of children may account for the apparent ease with which the prisoners were killed.

658. Sherer, *Narrative*.

659. Shepherd, *A Personal Narrative*, p. 137.

660. Moorsom, *Letters* (OIOC).

661. Drelincourt, *The Christians Defense*, title page.

662. Thornhill Papers (OIOC).

663. Thomason College map.

664. Kuloo claims to have seen Nana under a neem tree south of the Bibighar compound. Deposition of Kuloo. At the time he was interviewed, Kuloo was employed as a *chuprassy* by a Captain Bruce.

665. Shepherd, *A Personal Narrative*, p. 119; Shepherd's account.

666. Mollo, *The Indian Army*, p. 25.

667. Nanak Chand says they were from the 1st and 56th. Diary of Nanak Chand; Mohamed Ali said they were from the 6th and Nana's own bodyguard. Forbes-Mitchell, pp. 113–14; Clarke says the men who killed the five males were ten or twelve men from a volunteer regiment. Deposition of William Clarke; deposition of Cheda.

668. Deposition of John Fitchett.

669. Deposition of Kuloo.

670. Deposition of Jankee Pershad.

671. Forbes-Mitchell, *The Relief of Lucknow*, pp. 113–14.

672. Cheda says Nana was in the compound with Tatya Tope. Deposition of Cheda.

673. Deposition of John Fitchett.

674. The 1st Native Infantry occupied the commissariat complex during the mutiny. Thomason College map.

675. Fisher/Heathcote: 2 Sept. 1857 (NLS).

676. Cheda, an eyewitness, says there were four men taken out; other accounts, based on Colonel Williams's narrative, say five and include Edward Greenway. But according to the doctor's list, Edward, the only "Mr. Greenway" at the Bibighar, had died on July 14 of

diarrhea. It is my guess that Cheda's account is correct except that Thornhill was the one who comforted Frank, for he was of the right age to have been mistaken for Edward Greenway: the two colonels were too old. Nanak Chand stated three gentlemen were brought out but evidently did not know about Frank. Sherer accepted that there were four men taken out and executed. Deposition of Cheda; Nanak Chand's diary; Sherer, *Narrative*.

677. Shepherd, *A Personal Narrative*, p. 119; deposition of Cheda.

678. TL, 16 Oct. 1857, p. 8.

679. TL, 21 Sept. 1857, p. 6. I surmise this because these were the only victims whose cause of death was not recorded.

680. Williams in Shepherd, *A Personal Narrative*, p. 117.

681. Deposition of John Fitchett.

682. Sepoys "on guard," according to Fitchett, were men of the sixth. According to Fitchett they said they intended to save the women and children in order to save their own lives. Deposition of John Fitchett.

683. The musicians were from Yusuf Khan's (and Fitchett's) regiment. Fitchett would have known their identities. Ibid.

684. Ibid.

685. Testimony of Mary Ann in TL, 16 Oct. 1857, p. 8.

686. Deposition of Cheda.

687. Shepherd, *A Personal Narrative*, p. 119; Shepherd's account.

688. Thomson found a "mutilated Prayer-book" at the Bibighar opened to the Litany, "where I have but little doubt those poor dear creatures sought and found consolation, in that beautiful supplication. It is here sprinkled with blood." Thomson, *The Story of Cawnpore*, p. 216.

689. Keeling, *Liturgiae Britannicae*, p. 49.

690. Shepherd, *A Personal Narrative*, p. 119.

691. Account of Mary Ann.

692. Though there continues to be some talk of "by Nana's order," etc., in all the eyewitness testimony, even in Shepherd's account, Nana at this point ceases to play any part in the scene at the Bibighar. I think that when it was decided that the women and children were not to be executed ceremonially in the open he decided to withdraw. I do not accept Sherer's story that he presided over a nautch that night. Nana knew that his situation was desperate; even more desperate now that his prisoners were dead. By all accounts he spent the night in frantic preparation for battle and retreat. Nanak Chand's diary.

693. Ibid.

694. Deposition of Kuloo.

695. Shepherd reported seeing bullet holes in the stucco of the pillars and walls at the Bibighar. Shepherd, *A Personal Narrative*, pp. 79, 136.

696. In some accounts the sepoys merely fired into the ceiling, but a later visitor to the Bibighar could not find any bullet holes to prove it. Certainly a great many of the prisoners had already been debilitated by disease and wounds, nevertheless it seems to me unlikely that men armed merely with swords would have been sent in to kill 196 people unless a great many of the women and children had already been killed or wounded. Shepherd found bullet holes in the walls and pillars, indicating that at least some sepoys had fired at the prisoners. If none of the prisoners had been shot by the sepoys, and Sherer was right in guessing that the slaughter took only half an hour, that means that five men managed to kill thirty-six prisoners each, or something more than one prisoner every minute: indeed, during the time Sarvur Khan fetched new swords, the rate for the other four would have gone up significantly. Two of the men claimed to have killed only twenty-one between them; if they were representative, the five men killed only a few more than fifty people. I conclude that like the jullads who were sent in to finish off the wounded after the other massacres at Cawnpore, Sarvur Khan and his men were sent in to finish off the survivors of the sepoys' two volleys.

697. Interview, Dr. Robert Huntington III.

698. Deposition of Cheda. Cheda says they fired twice. Fred Roberts was also told by native witnesses that "when all had been wounded by shots from the Sepoys, butchers were sent in to finish the bloody business." Roberts, *Letters*, p. 87.

699. Deposition of John Fitchett.

700. Diary of Nanak Chand.

701. Deposition of Sheo Churran Das.

702. Deposition of John Fitchett.

703. Deposition of Cherunjoo.

704. Deposition of Gunga Bishen.

705. Fitchett described the five men as two butchers, one *Velaitee* (mixed blood), and two (Hindu) villagers. Sarvur Khan was a Moslem and apparently not a butcher. I therefore deduce that he must have been the hairy-handed *Velaitee* Fitchett remembered and Forbes-Mitchell later met. Forbes-Mitchell, *The Relief of Lucknow*, p. 105.

706. Macrae in Bennett, "Ten Months' Captivity."

707. Shepherd, *A Personal Narrative*, p. 140.

708. Deposition of John Fitchett.

709. Forbes-Mitchell, *The Relief of Lucknow*, p. 25.

710. This story appears in the notes R. Macrae appended to Amelia Bennett's revised account of her abduction in *The Nineteenth Century*. He claimed that a Captain McCrae (a relative?) was the first man to enter and that he found Mrs. Jacobi's corpse still tied to a pillar. According to every other account of the Bibighar massacre all of the bodies of the women and children had been deposited in the well, and it seems extremely unlikely that the sweepers who were sent in to clean up after the massacre would have left any bodies in the building. Nevertheless, I think it very likely that women like Mrs. Jacobi and Mrs. Probett and the indomitable Bridget Widdowson who had guarded the rebel prisoners in the Entrenchment would have at least attempted to put up a fight. Macrae in Bennett, "Ten Months' Captivity."

711. One officer in Havelock's column who looked into the well stated that the bodies had all been decapitated. Ball, *The History of the Indian Mutiny*, 1:380.

712. Shepherd's account; deposition of Punchum.

713. Deposition of John Fitchett.

714. Sherer says it "must have taken a considerable time." Shepherd says "a little before sun-set till dark." Kuloo says he heard "firing" until "candlelight." Sherer, *Narrative*; Shepherd, *A Personal Narrative*, p. 119; deposition of Kuloo.

715. Ramsay, *Rough Recollections*, 1:264.

716. Thomson, *The Story of Cawnpore*, p. 142.

717. Shepherd, *A Personal Narrative*, p. 59.

718. Macrae in Bennett, "Ten Months' Captivity."

719. Chalwin, *Letters*.

720. Halliday Letter 82: 17 Jan. 1857.

721. Keene, *A Servant of 'John Company,'* p. 119.

722. Thomson, *The Story of Cawnpore*, pp. 176–77.

723. According to Fitchett, DeCruze returned an hour later to look at the Bibighar but was too horrified to remain. DeCruze denied this. Some analyses discount Fitchett's testimony because both DeCruze and Clarke contradicted it. But neither DeCruze nor Clarke are particularly reliable either, and appear to have collaborated on their testimony, for their accounts sometimes employ identical language. When they were first interrogated at Allahabad they denied even being at Cawnpore during the uprising. They insisted that Fitchett had not been incarcerated with the ladies at Savada House, as Fitchett claimed, but had been as free to move around as they had been. They were determined to distance themselves from the Bibighar as much as possible, and so was Fitchett. But Fitchett's solu-

tion may have been to give a false image of himself as prisoner of the rebels. This does not necessarily mean that he did not witness the massacre. Any historian of Cawnpore must guard against embracing any one account too eagerly, but I think Fitchett portrayed himself as a helpless prisoner not in order to place himself at the Bibighar—for anyone who admitted to having observed the massacre would have made himself the object of intense British scrutiny and suspicion—but in order to obscure his probably voluntary attendance, his failure even to attempt to save any of the women and children, and his obviously fascinated observation of not only the massacre on the fifteenth but the burial of the bodies the next morning. In any case, Clarke's and DeCruze's testimony deserves to be treated with at least as much caution as Fitchett's.

724. Williams in Shepherd, *A Personal Narrative*, p. 118.

725. Deposition of John Fitchett.

726. DeCruze stated that the same men who killed the ladies and children disposed of their bodies. This seems unlikely, as at least one of them, Souracun, was a Brahmin and would not have participated in the burial of corpses. Kuloo, whose testimony in other respects contradicts DeCruze, states that the men who cast the women and children down the well "looked like sweepers"; Shepherd, in his account of Aitwurya's later arrest, states that they were all jullads. Shepherd, *A Personal Narrative*, p. 139.

727. Ibid.

728. Russell writing on 12 Feb. 1857 in TL, 29 March 1858, p. 8.

729. Butler, *The Land of the Veda*, p. 308.

730. Fitchett described this as a "cut by which bullocks go down in drawing water from the well." Deposition of John Fitchett.

731. Sherer, *Narrative*.

732. I surmise this because these chambers would have provided the only hiding place in the building.

733. Shepherd states that six or eight women were still alive, and "a few" children; Williams says three or four ladies and two or three children. I think the difference between Shepherd's and Sherer's numbers is that Shepherd was counting those who turned out to be alive when they were dragged away, and Sherer is counting only those who had not been severely wounded and were still ambulatory. John Fitchett stated that there were three children who ran around the yard. The exaggerating Mary Ann claimed that there were twenty–five women and children found alive. "Many wounded women were thrown into the well with the dead bodies and earth. . . . Many." But there was no earth thrown into the well. The bodies were left uncovered. Shepherd, *A Personal Narrative*, p. 119; Williams in ibid., p. 118; Mary Ann in TL, 16 Oct. 1857, p. 8.

734. Williams in Shepherd, *A Personal Narrative*, p. 118.

735. Nana was at Aherwa by now. No such order could have come from him so soon, but others may have issued it in his name. Deposition of John Fitchett.

736. Shepherd, *A Personal Narrative*, p. 119; the depth of the well is from Butler, *The Land of the Veda*, p. 308.

737. Deposition of John Fitchett.

738. Shepherd, *A Personal Narrative*, p. 119.

739. Deposition of John Fitchett; letter from an officer of the 1st Madras Fusiliers in the *Record*, 18 Sept. 1857, quoted in Noel, *England and India*, p. 66.

740. Shepherd, *A Personal Narrative*, p. 139.

741. Collier, *The Sound of Fury*, p. 183.

742. Shepherd, *A Personal Narrative*, p. 136.

743. ILN, no. 882, vol. xxxi, 10 Oct. 1857, p. 355.

744. Deposition of John Fitchett.

745. Evidently the jullads and sweepers, unlike the butchers, didn't have the heart or perhaps the means of killing them immediately. Ibid.

746. Deposition of Kuloo.

747. I surmise this from Sherer's description of the "map of naked arms, legs and gashed trunks" he saw at the top of the well. He guessed that the well was not large enough to contain 196 bodies, and believed some must have been carted off to the river. Also see Fisher/Stevens: 17 Aug. 1857 (NLS); Sherer to Beadon, Reid Papers (CCSAS).

748. Williams in Shepherd, *A Personal Narrative*, p. 118; depositions of Kuloo and De-Cruze.

749. Shepherd, *A Personal Narrative*, p. 119.

750. Deposition of John Fitchett.

751. Sherer, *Narrative*; Sherer, *Daily Life*, p. 80.

752. Fitzgerald, *Diary*, 11 Nov. 1857 (OIOC). One curious aspect of the Bibighar massacre is why the rebels did not attempt to cover the well with dirt. Had they intended to keep the women and children's fates a mystery or had they intended for the British to find the bodies? If the latter, they might simply have left the bodies where they were. Perhaps the jullads ran out of time.

753. Nanak Chand's diary.

754. Shepherd's account.

755. Shepherd, *A Personal Narrative*, pp. 123–31.

756. Mason, *Diary* (OIOC).

757. Collins, *Letters* (OIOC).

758. North, *Journal*, pp. 72–73.

759. Grant, *Letters* (OIOC).

760. Thomson, *The Story of Cawnpore*, p. 205.

761. Russell, *My Diary in India*, 1:169, 178.

762. Grant, *Letters* (OIOC).

763. Collins, *Letters* (OIOC).

764. Russell reported that "the intrenchment is used as a *cloaca maxima* by the natives, camp-followers, coolies, and others who bivouac in the sandy plains around it. The smells are revolting." I assume this practice began as soon as the Entrenchment was evacuated as both a convenience to the sepoys camped on the adjacent parade-ground and an insult to the garrison's memory. Russell, *My Diary in India*, 1:169, 178.

765. Thomson, *The Story of Cawnpore*, p. 205.

766. Shepherd, *A Personal Narrative*, p. 44 (insert).

767. Collins, *Letters* (OIOC); Crump, *A Pictorial Record of the Cawnpore Massacre*.

768. Shepherd, *A Personal Narrative*, p. 129.

769. "A nigger brought lots of beer, sodawater, and brandy, " wrote a teenaged volunteer, "which was a great haul, as we had only had a biscuit for breakfast." Letter dated 21 July 1857 in TL, 23 Sept. 1857, p. 7.

770. Shepherd, *A Personal Narrative*, p. 129.

771. The hotel and the Assembly Rooms were not destroyed until the Gwalior contingent attacked Cawnpore in November. The theater may have been somewhat damaged, but appears intact in General Neill's sketch drawn soon after the occupation. The Masonic Lodge, called the "ghost" or "magic" house by the locals and revered by Nana Sahib, was spared by the rebels.

772. Sherer, *Daily Life*, pp. 81–82.

773. Forbes, *Havelock*, p. 140.

774. Shepherd, *A Personal Narrative*, p. 129.

775. North commented on the flies at Cawnpore; I surmise they would have been concentrated at the Bibighar. North, *Journal*, p. 210.

776. Shepherd, *A Personal Narrative*, p. 137; Collier, *The Sound of Fury*, p. 183.

777. Sherer to Beadon: 17 July 1857, Reid Papers (CCSAS).

778. The "hundred bullocks" are from an eyewitness quoted in Collier, *The Sound of Fury*, p. 182.

779. According to R. Macrae three bodies were found in the Bhibigar: two women tied to the pillars with their throats cut, a child hanging by his chin from a hook. But Sherer, one of the first to see the Bibigar, did not believe it. "The stories of children found suspended on the trees, and of mutilated dead bodies lying in the enclosure," he wrote, "are entirely fabrications. There were no dead bodies, except in the well." Shepherd also specifically stated that the first officers who came out of the Bibighar reported that there were no bodies in evidence except in the well. Sherer, *Narrative*; Shepherd, *A Personal Narrative*, p. 129.

780. Shepherd, *A Personal Narrative*, p. 129.

781. Moorsom/His sister: Aug. 1857. Lindsay Papers. Moorsom stated that he was the second man to enter the Bibighar.

782. Forbes, *Havelock*, p. 141.

783. Shepherd wrote that the blood came over the observers' shoes when they stepped in. Sherer dismissed this and North's claim that the blood lay "ankle deep" as exaggerations. Shepherd also stated that the blood was two inches deep in places, as did a Highlander in the *Bombay Telegraph*, published in TL, 17 Sept. 1857 and Neill in *The Caledonian Mercury*, 1857, Lindsay Family Papers. If this was so, and not an illusion born of horror, alcohol, exhaustion, and rage, perhaps, as Yalland has suggested, it had been diluted in some places with the water that had poured out of the Bibighar's broken jars and that the sweepers had splashed around the morning before to erase the women's graffiti, and was later diluted further by the provost-marshal when he enforced Neill's "blood-lick" law. See also Shepherd, *A Personal Narrative*, p. 136; North, *Journal*. pp. 76–77; Sherer, *Daily Life*, pp. 79–80; Fitzgerald, *Diary*, 11 Nov. 1857 (OIOC).

784. Forbes-Mitchell, *The Relief of Lucknow*, p. 25.

785. Shepherd, *A Personal Narrative*, p. 129.

786. Deposition of Lalla Bhudree Nath.

787. An officer with Havelock's column, letter dated 17 July 1857 in TL, 30 Sept. 1857, p. 6.

788. Letter dated 21 July 1857 in TL, 24 Sept. p. 8.

789. Crump, *A Pictorial Record of the Cawnpore Massacre*.

790. Thomas Farnon testified that when he visited the well the children's bodies were still "quivering," and that the body of an old gentleman lay in the courtyard. The natives supposedly told him he was the "Judge of Futtehgarh," but more likely he would have been either Smith or Goldie. Other witnesses make no mention of any adult males found among the victims.

791. The description of the condition of the bodies is based on the professional opinion of Dr. Robert Huntington III, a medical examiner and pathologist at the University of Wisconsin. Sherer remarked that the bodies were in the early stages of putrefaction when he viewed them that morning. "I have looked upon death in every form," wrote one officer, "but I could not look down that well again." Sherer/Beadon: 17 July 1857, Reid Papers (CCSAS); letter dated 21 July 1857, quoted in TL, 24 Sept. p. 8.

792. Deposition of Punchum.

PART FOUR

1. The explosion, wrote one officer, was "a tremendous affair; the ground beneath us heaved and shook as if rent by the throes of an earthquake, and the air was darkened by the *débris*." "The doors of city houses fell off their hinges," wrote Nanak Chand, and "for some time all was confusion and alarm." North, *Journal*, pp. 79–85; Nanak Chand's diary.

2. Shepherd, *A Personal Narrative*, pp. 129, 132.

3. "This expression of feeling I believe was genuine for the sepoys used to help themselves to what they wanted and never paid a price for anything." "The Story of Miss Sutherland" (BM).

4. Sherer, *Narrative*.

5. Shepherd, *A Personal Narrative*, p. xviii.

6. All of the women, wrote one officer, were "more or less ill, . . . dreadfully weak," and "in a dreadful state of mind, as they [had been] afraid that their servants might be tempted to betray them. For once," continued the officer, "these natives did not. Ought they not to be rewarded?" Officer of 1st Madras Fusiliers, letter dated 18 July 1857 in TL, 16 Sept. 1857, p. 7.

7. This *chowk* or principal market street was the route the King of Oudh always used to take when he passed through Cawnpore. Field notes.

8. Sherer to Beadon, Reid Papers (CCSAS).

9. Sherer suspected that the drummer had probably greeted Nana Sahib with a paraphrase of this adaptable verse; in Banda the rebels had been welcomed with a different version, to the effect that God ruled the world, the King of Delhi ruled the empire, and the native army was in command. Sherer, *Daily Life*, p. 129.

10. Shepherd, *A Personal Narrative*, p. 132.

11. "I have often thought since that considering this man had not left his house when the Nana was there, that the building was close to the scene of the massacre, and that English feeling was not in its calmest mood, it showed wonderful presence of mind on his part to pursue his occupation exactly as if nothing had happened." Three years later Mahomed was still hotelkeeping. Sherer, *Daily Life*, pp. 77–78.

12. Ibid., p. 78.

13. "Surely this is enough," he wrote in answer to Major North's description, "without saying 'the clotted gore lay ankle deep,' which besides being most distressing, is absolutely incorrect." Sherer to Beadon in Reid Papers (CCSAS); Sherer, *Daily Life*, p. 79.

14. Moorsom stated that "I searched and caused everything to be collected." Moorsom/His sister: Aug. 1857 in Lindsay Papers.

15. Thomson, *The Story of Cawnpore*, p. 215.

16. Sherer to Beadon: 17 July 1857, Reid Papers (CCSAS).

17. Ibid.

18. Sherer, *Daily Life*, pp. 79–80. Captain Bews would later sicken with dysentery when Havelock fell back on Cawnpore. He soon left India, and died eventually as an officer of volunteers in New Zealand. Sherer, *Havelock's March on Cawnpore*, p. 186nn.

19. In his book Sherer states that the general was at the mission station near Nawabgunj when he approached him, but Sherer's letter to Beadon reporting his conversation with Havelock was written on the seventeenth, the day before Havelock moved his headquarters.

20. Sherer, *Daily Life*, p. 81.

21. Sherer to Beadon, Reid Papers (CCSAS).

22. Sherer, *Daily Life*, p. 81.

23. North, *Journal*, p. 76.

24. Shepherd, *A Personal Narrative*, p. 136.

25. Acct. no. 5112-46/Neg. no. 11389 and Acct. no. 6310-24/Neg. nos. 11390–11391 (NAM).

26. Shepherd, *A Personal Narrative*, pp. 36–37.

27. Thomson, *The Story of Cawnpore*, p. 215.

28. *The Phoenix*, 8 Aug. 1857.

29. Butler, *The Land of the Veda*, p. 313.

30. Officer in Ball, *The History of the Indian Mutiny*, 1:383.

31. "The Story of Miss Sutherland" (BM).

32. Officer in Ball, *The History of the Indian Mutiny*, 1:383.

33. Bingham, *Diary* (NAM).

34. Letter from a Highlander in the *Bombay Telegraph* in TL, 17 Sept. 1857.

35. Shepherd could only find one, and it was indecipherable.

36. Ball, *The History of the Indian Mutiny*, 1:377.
37. Forbes-Mitchell, *The Relief of Lucknow*, p. 113.
38. Ball, *The History of the Indian Mutiny*, 1:377.
39. The emphasis is in the original. TL, 16 Jan. 1858, p. 10.
40. Dangerfield, *Bengal Mutiny*, p. 206.
41. The only authentic inscriptions were found in the barracks in the Entrenchment. "Here a round shot came and killed young Wheeler. His brains and hair are scattered on the wall," read one. "This is worse than the siege of Jerusalem—My God, my God, when wilt thou deliver us?" read another. Masonic writing was found in places, and elsewhere Seppings's and Jonah's inscriptions were found, and this fragment by Postmaster Roche: "4th June, wounded in the thigh. 6th " " leg, bullet.————fractured.—shell——all this and still alive. L. Roche." Rees, *The Siege of Lucknow*, pp. 357–58; *Key to the Tablets in the Memorial Church Cawnpore*.
42. Ball, *The History of the Indian Mutiny*, 1:381.
43. Anonymous officer in Hibbert, *The Great Mutiny*, p. 213. The volume of stories of women and young girls' bodies found elsewhere in the station suggests that several other women beside Amy Horne, Margaret Wheeler, and Miss Sutherland may have been abducted. There was a rumor that one of Captain Kempland's little girls was kidnapped; a Miss Kempland was listed among those whose time and place of death were unknown. I have already alluded to the story of a Miss Wheeler's body (probably the eldest, Eliza) being found in the brush near Savada House, which appears in Forbes, *Havelock*, p. 139 and Ball, *The History of the Indian Mutiny*, 1:379. But Margaret Wheeler's abduction was the only one Colonel G. Williams deemed worthy of investigation during his inquiry into the uprising.
44. Renaud was brave "unto recklessness," but "those who knew him best," wrote Kaye, "deplored him most." Kaye, *A History of the Great Revolt*, 2:371.
45. Marshman in Forbes, *Havelock*, p. 144.
46. Ibid., p. 140.
47. Noncommissioned officer of the 84th, letter dated 1 Aug. 1857 in TL, 29 Sept. 1857, p. 8.
48. Forbes, *Havelock*, p. 145.
49. One measure of the hysteria of the time is a story George Campbell of the civil service told of a skeleton his party came upon during the Mutiny. Medical opinion was divided as to whether it had been that of a woman or a man; if it was a woman, it would have had to have been "a large and large-boned woman," Campbell pointed out, and, besides, there had been no word of any European woman having been killed in those parts. Nevertheless, the rumor spread that the skeleton of an English woman had been found. "A great cry for vengeance arose," and the commanding officer decided to attack a nearby village. The soldiers began to march out of camp, and it was only at the last moment, when Campbell informed the officer that he would have to take full responsibility, that the attack was called off. Campbell, *Memoirs of my Indian Career*, pp. 253–54.
50. Martin, *The Indian Empire*, 2:384.
51. Kaye, *A History of the Great Revolt*, 2:386–87.
52. Lady Canning suggested that rape had been perpetrated at Dinapur, where, after the British reoccupied it, "screams were heard in the night, & many Sepoys and women found killed. I feel not only horror at such a crime, but a most painful addition of *disgrace*, in thinking of it as committed by our own soldiers & countrymen, & Christians." Allen, ed., *A Glimpse of the Burning Plain*, p. 77.
53. Shepherd, *A Personal Narrative*, pp. 132–33.
54. Ibid.
55. Some were hanged from gallows, others from trees.
56. Ball, *The History of the Indian Mutiny*, 1:388. During the Mutiny Osborn Wilkinson was "present at the execution of a Sepoy taken in arms. He was ordered to be shot. The

soldier told off for this purpose coolly walked up to the culprit, and put the muzzle of his rifle close to the man's head; but the cap was damp and missed fire. This occurred twice before the rebel's brains were blown out. At each failure the wretched man stood perfectly firm. He was not fettered in any way, and he merely turned his head aside as the rifle was pointed at him. I think few Englishmen could have shown more unflinching resolution, or could have met their death more bravely." Wilkinson, *The Gemini Generals*, p. 304.

57. Wellesley, *Supplementary Despatches and Memoranda of Field-Marshall the Duke of Wellington*, in TL, 5 March 1858, p. 8. Though John Lang regarded capital punishment in England "a very wholesome terror," he believed that it was no deterrent in the East, where men feared death less than the extension of a wretched existence in prison. Lang, *Wanderings in India*, pp. 414–15.

58. Russell, *My Indian Mutiny*, pp. 161–62.

59. Ball, *The History of the Indian Mutiny*, 1:391.

60. Dangerfield, *Bengal Mutiny*, p. 206; Potiphar in Hibbert, *The Great Mutiny*, p. 211.

61. Parks, *Wanderings in India*, 1:479.

62. "As for hanging," wrote a noncommissioned officer of the 84h, "it is nothing. It is a quite common thing to have a few swung up every day; the least thing will do it. We have a provost marshall and his staff here, and they would hang a European if they found him plundering, or give him a dozen on the spot if they found him half-a-mile from his camp; but as for a native the least thing is sufficient to hang him." Noncommissioned officer of the 84th, letter dated 1 Aug. 1857 in TL, 29 Sept. 1857, p. 8.

Writing of the depredations of July, Canning himself would condemn the "indiscriminate hanging, not only of persons of all shades of guilt, but of those whose guilt was at the least very doubtful, and the general burning and plunder of villages, whereby the innocent as well as the guilty, without regard to age or sex, were indiscriminately punished, and in some cases sacrificed." Loyal Indian soldiers who had fled their mutinous regiments—including sepoys who had remained with the garrison at Cawnpore until Major Hillersdon sent them away—"were liable," said Canning, "to be involved in one common penalty," and by such brutal means the British "had given colour to the rumour . . . that the Government meditated a general bloody persecution of Mohammedans and Hindus." Governor-General in Council, 24 Dec. 1857 in Thompson, *The Other Side of the Medal*, pp. 37–38.

63. Kaye, *A History of the Great Revolt*, 2:388.

64. Noncommissioned officer of the 84th. Letter dated 1 Aug. 1857 in TL, 29 Sept. 1857, p. 8.

65. Henry Fane/Caroline Beresford: 29 July 1857, Lincolnshire Archives.

66. Taylor, *Chronicles of the Mutiny*, p. 32.

67. Ibid., p. 34.

68. Shepherd, *A Personal Narrative*, p. 133.

69. Martin, *The Indian Empire*, 2:374.

70. Other reports suggested something other than despair. "He is reported to have said he could now die happy," wrote another officer, "as he had killed 1,000 'Feringhees.'" Letter dated 6 Aug. 1857 in TL, 22 Sept. 1857, p. 10.

71. Kaye, *A History of the Great Revolt*, 2:397nn.

72. "Statement of Information" in TL, 16 Oct. 1857, p. 8.

73. Deposition of Clarke.

74. Deposition of DeCruze.

75. Depositions of Bradshaw and Letts.

76. Deposition of Lalla Bhudree Nath.

77. Deposition of Ajoodea Pershad.

78. Edwards, *Personal Adventures*, p. 128.

79. Horne, *Narrative* (BM).

80. Shepherd, *A Personal Narrative*, p. 122.

81. Sherer, *Narrative*.

82. Deposition of Nana Ubbhunker.

83. Deposition of Appajee Luchman.

84. Sherer, *Narrative*.

85. Rao Sahib in U.P., 3:684.

86. Lang, *Wanderings in India*, p. 111.

87. The betel box now resides at the National Army Museum. NAM/acc no. 5111-3/Neg. no. 8804.

88. Misra, *Nana Saheb Peshwa*, p. 298.

89. The rumor was that Nana's men had accomplished this delectatiously in the long afternoon of July 17, for she was said to have been found "naked, tied by her lovely long hair to the ceiling and the flesh cut in long strips down her body by the sword." But this was probably another of the morbid fictions that a Delhi memsahib named Gilliland enjoyed reporting home from the Punjab after she herself had escaped the rebels by hiding in a well. Mrs. Gilliland survived the Mutiny, incidentally, and lived to be one hundred. Gilliland (OIOC).

90. Though a large portion of the population had fled, local historians claim that "hundreds were killed." Misra, *Nana Saheb Peshwa*, p. 299.

91. Grant, J. A. *Letters* (OIOC).

92. Vyankatesh Vaman Subedar in Misra, *Nana Saheb Peshwa*, pp. 315–16.

93. *Dictionary of National Biography*.

94. Peppin, *Letters* (OIOC).

95. Pollock in Hibbert, *The Great Mutiny*, p. 208.

96. Kaye, *A History of the Great Revolt*, 2:397.

97. Neill's Journal in ibid., 2:406nn.

98. Shepherd, *A Personal Narrative*, p. 139.

99. Kaye, *A History of the Great Revolt*, 2:404.

100. Mukherjee, *Awadh in Revolt*, p. 62.

101. Lawrence in Dangerfield, *Bengal Mutiny*, p. 153.

102. Ibid., p. 165.

103. As he passed in and out of delirium, Lawrence was also heard to say that he had sinned in accepting the chief commissionership of Oudh, "that he had always disapproved of annexation—and that he should never have come there, but he had been actuated by 'pique.'" Mrs. Harris in Singh, *The Letters of Henry Lawrence*, p. 72.

104. Havelock in Kaye, *A History of the Great Revolt*, 2:383.

105. Havelock in Forbes, *Havelock*, p. 153.

106. Sherer, *Narrative*; Shepherd, *A Personal Narrative*, p. 133. Spurgin had difficulty finding a sufficient number of boatmen. "This class of men were shy of coming forward," explained Sherer, "in consequence of the complicity of some members of their craft in the [treachery] at Suttee Chowra Ghat." Sherer, *Daily Life*, p. 93; Martin, *The Indian Empire*, p. 384.

107. Taylor, *Chronicles of the Mutiny*, p. 35.

108. Innes, *Lucknow and Oude in the Mutiny*, p. 89.

109. Forbes, *Havelock*, p. 156.

110. Butler, *The Land of the Veda*, p. 314.

111. Maude in Fitchett, *The Tale of the Great Mutiny*, pp. 193–94. In his memoir Maude placed this incident in September, but North's *Journal* indicates that it occurred on July 30.

112. North, *Journal*, pp. 112–13.

113. Forbes, *Havelock*, p. 160.

114. Sherer, *Daily Life*, pp. 101–2.

115. North, *Journal*, p. 210.

116. "The number of frogs which luxuriate in this humid atmosphere is astonishing," wrote one unhinged officer. ". . . My presence does not seem to discompose them in the least. They either flounder about in the little pools on my floor to their heart's content, or

rest panting on the saturated earth; their round, shining eyes fixed on me at times, as if fascinated." Ibid., pp. 87–88.

117. Sherer, *Daily Life*, pp. 101–2.

118. Forbes, *Havelock*, p. 142.

119. Thomson, *The Story of Cawnpore*, p. 227.

120. Sherer, *Havelock's March on Cawnpore*, p. 220nn.

121. Fitchett, *The Tale of the Great Mutiny*, p. 190.

122. "Almost all of the former European residents having been murdered by the miscreant Nana Sahib," Superintendent of Police Bruce wrote to Calcutta, "and no one being forthcoming to recognize or give any information concerning the property that has been saved, it would aid us very much were some Europeans to return who may be acquainted with the former residents, or be able to point out the property of different owners." Bruce in *The Englishman*.

123. Kaye, *A History of the Great Revolt*, 3:341–43, 348.

124. Shepherd, *A Personal Narrative*, p. 138.

125. Kaye, *A History of the Great Revolt*, 2:397–98.

126. Duff, *The Indian Rebellion*, p. 245.

127. "It is . . . preposterous to suppose," continued Sherer, "that men in scenes of great excitement can behave exactly as they would on calm reflection in ordinary circumstances." Sherer, *Daily Life*, p. 89.

128. Kaye, *A History of the Great Revolt*, 2:398–99.

129. Ibid.

130. Neill in Collier, *The Sound of Fury*, p. 210.

131. Kanpur Collectorate Mutiny Records in U.P., 4:594–95. Sherer eventually reported that 189 in the Cawnpore collectorate had been implicated in the rebellion: nine of them were from the magistracy alone. Shah Alli, kotwal of the city, and Hulas Singh, thannadar were, according to Sherer, "proved to have taken active parts, held employments under or tacitly submitted to the rebel government." GGP, HDP Public, Feb. 1858–Jan. 1859, no. 67A, NAI.

132. Bingham in Hibbert, *The Great Mutiny*, p. 210.

133. Noncommissioned officer of the 84th. Letter dated 21 July 1857 in TL, 30 Sept. 1857, p. 6.

134. Noncommissioned officer of the 84th. Letter dated 1 Aug. 1857 in TL, 29 Sept. 1857, p. 8.

135. Shepherd, *A Personal Narrative*, p. 139.

136. Neill in a private letter in Valbezen, *The English in India*, p. 166.

137. Sherer would later claim that Neill's law was enforced only twice, but even Neill makes it clear that it was employed many times in just the first days of his occupation at Cawnpore, and accounts of such executions stretch all the way to November, when Colin Campbell finally put a stop to it.

138. Fragment of *The Caledonian Mercury*, 1857, Lindsay Family Papers.

139. Potiphar in Hibbert, *The Great Mutiny*, p. 211.

140. Misra, *Nana Saheb Peshwa*, p. 573.

141. "So sanguine were they that even the women have been known to volunteer to share the same fate as their husbands, their fathers, or brothers." Dinwiddie, *Life and Adventures*, p. 37 (NAM).

142. Kaye, *A History of the Great Revolt*, 2:400.

143. Shepherd, *A Personal Narrative*, pp. 130–34.

144. He signed it "Thine affectionate, but miserable, W. J. Shepherd." Shepherd in Ball, *The History of the Indian Mutiny*, 1:383. The letter was sent by a messenger who barely managed to get through the rebel lines. It was the first communication Agra received regarding the fate of the women and children. Shepherd, *A Personal Narrative*, pp. 134–35.

145. Ibid., p. 134.

146. Tytler was chief commissariat officer.

147. Ibid., p. 135.

148. Ibid., p. 134.

149. This was, wrote Thomson, "a great thing for a native house to accomplish, as the Brahmins, to whose company our friend belonged, only cook once a day, and all the feeding for the twenty-four hours is done with them at midday." Thomson, *The Story of Cawnpore*, p. 191.

150. Ibid., pp. 192–93.

151. "Nothing that could contribute to our comfort," wrote Thomson, "escaped the kind and minute thoughtfulness of Dirigbijah Singh. I wish he could read English, and peruse my humble effort to express the gratitude I owe to him." Ibid., p. 197.

152. Delafosse in TL, 16 Oct. 1857, p. 7.

153. Sherer, pp. 103–4.

154. Thomson in Board's Collections 1857–1858 f/4/2703.193490, p. 2.

155. But not before bequeathing to Thomson and Delafosse a mass of melted silver he had dug up from the burned barracks during the siege and buried in the Entrenchment. Thomson eventually found the burial place, but the silver was gone.

156. Sherer, *Daily Life*, p. 103.

157. She pitied Thomson "very much for finding his appointment in the Police has brought him back to this spot." Allen, ed., *A Glimpse of the Burning Plain*, p. 122.

158. The *Bombay Gazette Overland Summary*, report dated 31 Aug. 1857, but based on an earlier letter. Halliday Letters.

159. Edwards, *Personal Adventures*, p. 143.

160. Edwards had managed to send his wife safely to the hills before the uprising. While still in hiding, Edwards sent her a letter via a courier, who found her dressed in black. After reading her husband's note Mrs. Edwards politely excused herself "and put on a white dress." Ibid., p. 141.

161. Cosens and Wallace, *Fatehgarh*, p. 111.

162. Hibbert, *The Great Mutiny*, p. 215.

163. Scott in Sherring, *The Indian Church during the Great Rebellion*, pp. 145–46.

164. Dass in ibid., pp. 142–44.

165. Cosens and Wallace, *Fatehgarh*, pp. 111–19. The story of the Parade-Ground Massacre, as it came to be called, was the subject of many embellishments. Mrs. Eckford, for instance, was said to have been blown from a gun, and Miss Sutherland fastened similarly to the mouth of a gun; when it failed to fire she was "cut to pieces at the muzzle." Noel, *England and India*, p. 461. Amy Horne's version was even more excruciating. According to her the sepoys fired on Miss Sutherland "every now and then, using blank cartridges however, screaming with delight at the sight of her horror-stricken countenance after every round that was fired at her and she still found herself alive. Firing these blank cartridges at short range, they blackened her face with the powder and singed her lovely hair, and as quickly as she used to wipe the stains off with her pocket handkerchief, they used to fire again and blacken it afresh. Tired of this performance, they reopened fire on her with small shot, peppering her pretty face till it was nothing but a mass of blood and smut. When satiated with their cruelties, they cut her throat from ear to ear." Bennett, "Ten Months' Captivity."

166. Edwards, *Personal Adventures*, p. 184.

167. Hardeo Baksh Singh, Probyn's and Edwards's protector, was made a raja and a knight commander of the Star of India. Unless otherwise indicated, my account of Bonny Byrne and the Parade-Ground Massacre is from Cosens and Wallace, *Fatehgarh*, pp. 111–19; the account of the collectors' travails is from pp. 126–36.

168. Edwards, *Personal Adventures*, p. iv.

169. Sherer, *Daily Life*, p. 112.

170. HDP, Public, 4 May 1858, no. 1 (NAI). I have done my best to reconcile the two accounts Amy left behind. In the first she tells about the African and the horrific journey to the outskirts of Bithur. In the other she suggests that she was taken to a hut. In her letter to Beadon she said the hut was near the Assembly Rooms, which would account for her contention that she could have seen the surviving women and children taken to the Assembly Rooms.

171. Collier, *The Sound of Fury*, p. 237.

172. Ibid., p. 238.

173. Adam, *The Indian Criminal*, p. 171 (illus.).

174. Buckland, *Dictionary of Indian Biography*, p. 325.

175. U.P., 2:152, 160–61.

176. Hibbert, *The Great Mutiny*, p. 264.

177. Ibid., p. 265.

178. At a key point in the fighting that day Neill had refused to bring his infantry to the rescue of Maude's exhausted artillery. "I am not in command," he had primly replied to Havelock's son. "I cannot take the responsibility."

179. Lee, *The Indian Mutiny*, p. 6.

180. Bengal Hukaru, 5 Aug. 1857, quoted in TL, 21 Sept. 1857, p. 6.

181. Wolseley, *From England to Cawnpore*, East Sussex County Council.

182. Campbell, *Memoirs of my Indian Career*, pp. 281–82.

183. Forbes, *Havelock*, p. 215.

184. Eventually an obelisk was erected over the spot. It now sits in a besieged little park from which Sikh squatters were recently expelled. On my visit a group of children were using it as a backstop for a dusty game of cricket.

185. Hibbert, *The Great Mutiny*, p. 350.

186. Sherer, *Daily Life*, pp. 107–8; Shepherd, *A Personal Narrative*, pp. 139–40.

187. "The charges of undue severity that have been made against the executive in relation to the treatment of captured rebels, by no means attach to Mr. [Sherer], whose leniency and forbearance were proverbial." Thomson, *The Story of Cawnpore*, p. 243.

188. Keene, *Fifty-Seven*, pp. 77–78.

189. Sherer, *Letters*, p. 13.

190. Bowring in Gupta, *Nana Saheb*, p. 158.

191. Letter from Nana Sahib in Bibliotheque Nationale, Paris.

192. Muir, *Records*, 1:180.

193. Forbes-Mitchell, *The Relief of Lucknow*, pp. 26–27. The humane Forbes-Mitchell had opted for military service rather than imprisonment in Scotland for operating a still. He remained in India after the Mutiny, married an Indian orphan, and died of old age on the eve of departure for Britain. Interview, Anne Toll.

194. Ibid., p. 25.

195. Buckland, *Dictionary of Indian Biography*, p. 457.

196. Malleson, *The Indian Mutiny of 1857*, 4:175.

197. Fitzgerald, *Diary* (OIOC).

198. Johnson, *Journal* (OIOC).

199. Sherer, *Daily Life*, p. 131.

200. "Strangely fatal has been this servile war," wrote a correspondent to the *Times*, "to all who have held place and honour." Index in TL, 15 Jan. 1858, p. 8.

201. These convoys of troops made slow but steady progress. "They travel . . . in large covered waggons," wrote an officer on one such convoy on November 24, "drawn by bullocks, which are changed every 10 miles or so. They go night and day, only halting for a few hours to get the men's breakfasts and dinners. In that way they make about 40 miles a day, whereas on foot they would make only 10." TL, 15 Jan. 1858, p. 8.

202. Martin, *The Indian Empire*, 2:464.

203. Malleson, *The Indian Mutiny of 1857*, 4:161.

204. Ibid., 4:167.

205. Adye, *The Defence of Cawnpore*, pp. 22–25.

206. Malleson estimates that they actually numbered fourteen thousand. Malleson, *The Indian Mutiny of 1857*, 4:172.

207. Pearson, *Letters* (OIOC).

208. Russell, *My Diary in India*, 1:206. "British forces," observed one of Campbell's young officers, "carry all before them as long as they are *advancing*, but once give them the word to *retire* and they are worse than a *rabble*." Pearson, *Letters* (OIOC).

209. Russell, *My Diary in India*, 1:206.

210. Thomson, *The Story of Cawnpore*, p. 235.

211. "The quantity of distant popping that goes on, from the belief in the accuracy and long range of the arm, is absurd." Captain Jones in Cosens and Wallace, *Fatehgarh*, p. 178.

212. Thomson, *The Story of Cawnpore*, pp. 234–35.

213. TL, 28 Jan. 1858, p. 8.

214. Shepherd, *A Personal Narrative*, p. 153.

215. Thomson, *The Story of Cawnpore*, pp. 234–35.

216. TL, 28 Jan. 1858, p. 8.

217. This soldier was a "boy of 19." TL, 2 Feb. 1858, p. 8.

218. Ibid.

219. Officer in TL, 27 Feb. 1858, p. 9.

220. Men like Thomson defended Windham, but others were unimpressed. When someone described him as calm under fire, an officer sniffed that "you need more than calm to make a good commander." "A brave soldier," concluded Forbes-Mitchell, "but no General." Johnson, *Journal* (OIOC); Forbes-Mitchell, *The Relief of Lucknow*, p. 82.

221. *The Hindoo Patriot* in U.P., 4:707.

222. Letter from unidentified witness dated 3 Dec. 1857 in TL, 16 Jan. 1858, p. 10.

223. Thomson, *The Story of Cawnpore*, pp. 222–23.

224. Probably Lieutenants Gibbon and McKinnon.

225. INTACH, *Preliminary Unedited Listing of Cawnpore*, p. 145.

226. Oliver, *Campaigning in Oude*, p. 29 (OIOC).

227. Johnson, *Journal* (OIOC).

228. Deposition of Hulas Singh.

229. Nanak Chand's diary.

230. On the night after they entered Lucknow, Campbell's men could be heard crying, "Cawnpore," and "Cawnpore, you bloody murderers," even in their sleep. Collier, *The Sound of Fury*, p. 327.

231. TL, 2 Jan. 1858, p. 8.

232. Barr, *The Memsahibs*, p. 136.

233. Collier, *The Sound of Fury*, p. 328.

234. Russell in Martin, *The Indian Empire*, 2:470nn; TL, 13 April 1858, p. 10.

235. Goode in Martin, *The Indian Empire*, 2:470nn.

236. One memsahib, a Mrs. Brydon, did manage to bring a harp with her in one of Campbell's grain carts. Hibbert, *The Great Mutiny*, p. 351.

237. Russell in Martin, *The Indian Empire*, 2:470.

238. Collier, *The Sound of Fury*, p. 330.

239. I am assuming that Julia Inglis was not the only lady to make this sacrifice. Ibid., p. 331.

240. Germon, *Journal of the Siege of Lucknow*, p. 186.

241. Hibbert, *The Great Mutiny*, p. 351.

242. Thomson, *The Story of Cawnpore*, p. 240.

243. Letter from unidentified witness dated 3 Dec. 1857 in TL, 16 Jan. 1858, p. 10.

244. Collins, *Letters* (OIOC); TL, 27 Jan. 1858, p. 9.

245. Shepherd, *A Personal Narrative*, p. 158.

246. Adelaide Case in Barr, *The Memsahibs*, p. 137.

247. Hibbert, *The Great Mutiny*, p. 352.

248. Letter from unidentified witness dated 3 Dec. 1857, in TL, 16 Jan. 1858, p. 10.

249. TL, 11 Feb. 1858, p. 7.

250. Allen, ed., *A Glimpse of the Burning Plain*, p. 86.

251. Officer in TL, 1 Feb. 1858, p. 8.

252. Matilda Spry in Collier, *The Sound of Fury*, p. 338.

253. Allen, ed., *A Glimpse of the Burning Plain*, p. 89.

254. Beadon in TL, 16 Feb. 1858, p. 9.

255. Ibid.

256. Collier, *The Sound of Fury*, p. 339.

257. Lady Canning found them "strangely well," she guessed because "they lived in small parties together & hardly ever went out of their doors & were so busy with their children & their household work that they hardly knew the full extent of their peril." Lady Canning in Allen, ed., *A Glimpse of the Burning Plain*, p. 89.

258. "I am obliged to submit to the hostile occupation of Cawnpoor," he told Canning, "until the actual dispatch of all my incumbrances towards Allahabad has been effected. However disagreeable this may be, and although it may tend to give confidence to the enemy, it is precisely one of those cases in which no risk may be run." Campbell in Martin, *The Indian Empire*, 2:474.

259. Grant, *Incidents in the Sepoy War*, p. 242.

260. Garvey in Verney, *The Devil's Wind*, p. 95.

261. The dust was so thick in the contingent's wake that two officers galloped into a well; they survived, but the horses had to be left there to die. Johnson, *Journal* (OIOC).

262. Warner, *Letters* (OIOC). "It mattered little whom the red-coats killed," wrote Bholanauth Chunder three years later, "the innocent and the guilty, the loyal and the disloyal, the well-wisher and the traitor, were confounded in one promiscuous vengeance. To 'bag the nigger' had become a favourite phrase of the military sportsmen of the day. 'Peafowls, partridges, and Pandies rose together, but the latter gave the best sport." Chunder, *Travels of a Hindoo*, p. 322.

263. Colonel Alison in Martin, *The Indian Empire*, 2:475.

264. Hodson in TL, 31 Jan. 1858, p. 12. One officer, disregarding Campbell's warning not to drink the liquor the rebels left behind, passed out after a few swigs, whereupon a straggling rebel cut his throat. But his death hardly interfered with the festivities. "It was a horrid death for him," wrote a comrade, "but he is good riddance—nobody liked him—and he has not paid his mess bill." Johnson, *Journal* (OIOC).

265. Forbes-Mitchell, *The Relief of Lucknow*, p. 91.

266. Officer of the Naval Brigade in TL, 11 Feb. 1858, p. 7.

267. Thomson, *The Story of Cawnpore*, p. 241.

268. Grant in TL, 30 Jan. 1858, p. 8.

269. "I have made many a sepoy pay the penalty for mutinying and killing my brother officers and friend, and trust more will suffer ere I have done." Hodson in TL, 31 Jan. 1858, p. 12.

270. "It is now horrible to recall it, but what I say is true." Forbes-Mitchell, *The Relief of Lucknow*, pp. 31, 68.

271. Ibid., p. 93.

272. Grant, F. W., *Letters* (OIOC).

273. Johnson, *Journal* (OIOC).

274. His commander sternly stopped his grog for five days. Wilkie, *Memoirs* (OIOC).

275. Grant, *Incidents in the Sepoy War*, pp. 213–14.

276. Forbes-Mitchell in Misra, *Nana Saheb Peshwa*, p. 313.

277. Grant, F. W., *Letters* (OIOC).
278. Jones, *Recollections*, p. 51.
279. Grant, F. W. *Letters* (OIOC).
280. Gordon-Alexander, *Recollections*, p. 194.
281. Forbes-Mitchell, *The Relief of Lucknow*, p. 94.
282. Ibid.
283. Grant, F. W., *Letters* (OIOC).
284. Mackay, *From London to Lucknow*, 2:341.
285. Wilkie, *Memoirs*, p. 56 (OIOC).
286. Forbes-Mitchell, *The Relief of Lucknow*, p. 95.
287. Johnson, *Journal* (OIOC).
288. Grant, F. W., *Letters* (OIOC).
289. Roberts, *Letters*, pp. 120–21.
290. Lutfullah, *Azimullah*, p. 51.
291. Pearson, *Letters* (OIOC); Sherer, *Daily Life*, pp. 88–89. The monkey was evidently donated to the Zoological Society by George Campbell. Zoological Society, *Reports of the Council and Auditors*, p. 33.
292. It was read on November 1 all over India. TL, 15 Dec. 1858, p. 7.
293. TL, 6 Dec. 1858, p. 7. "There were no especial circumstances attending its promulgation at Cawnpore," wrote Sherer. "There was a parade, a sufficient but not remarkable collection of natives, and the senior civilian, Mr. Batten, the Judge, read the document out from a carriage." The night before an old Rajput who had joined in the attack on the Entrenchment entered the district in anticipation of the amnesty, but he was surrounded by the soldiers of a loyalist thannadar. The thannadar ran him through with a sword, but only after the old Rajput had mortally wounded him with a pistol. "They both fell dead in the court." Sherer, *Daily Life*, pp. 173–74.
294. Mohammed Ali Khan, in Forbes-Mitchell, *The Relief of Lucknow*, pp. 111–12; Russell, *My Diary in India*, 1:220.
295. "They contented themselves with scowling at us," reported Russell, "and I could not help being amused at the indifference with which they saw their horrible little deities examined by the Feringhees and pulled to pieces by profane fingers." Russell in TL, 13 April 1858, p. 10.
296. "The Sepoys have murdered a number of Sikh women in Cawnpore," an officer reported cheerfully. "I expect [the Sikhs] will fight like fiends after this." Oliver, *Campaigning in Oude*, p. 29 (OIOC).
297. Allen, ed., *A Glimpse of the Burning Plain*, p. 84.
298. Roberts, *Letters*, p. 91; Stone, *Illustrated India*, p. 229.
299. Oliver, *Recollections*, p. 189.
300. After his hanging a sailor stepped forward to harangue the native onlookers. "'First of all, understand," he said, speaking in English, "that you are all rascals! And now you have seen a rascal die. But what is one rascal? My opinion is that not only one black rascal should be hung but every black rascal in the country! And then you black rascals would learn how to behave yourselves." Sherer, *Daily Life*, pp. 110–11, 145.
301. Johnson, *Journal* (OIOC).
302. "General Windham, to whom the circumstance was at once reported, was greatly moved, and interesting himself extremely in the inquiries which were set on foot, managed to have the men identified and arrested; and the case was afterwards brought to a successful issue." Sherer, *Daily Life*, pp. 144–45.
303. Impey in Taylor, "Deciphering the 'Unseen Letters,'" *The Statesman*, 16 July 1993.
304. Cosens and Wallace, *Fatehgarh*, pp. 164–75.
305. In the rivalry among Campbell's various regiments, the bugler for Her Majesty's 53rd sounded the advance to beat out the Highlanders of the 93rd, whom Campbell was

suspected of favoring. After the 53rd secured the village across the bridge, Campbell galloped up to bawl them out, but every time he opened his mouth the Irishmen of the 53rd shouted, "Three cheers for the Commander-in-Chief." Finally Campbell gave up and rode away laughing. Verney, *The Devil's Wind*, pp. 110–11.

306. Edmund Verney in ibid., p. 113. The rebels had fled in such haste that they had not bothered to sever the Bridge of Boats nor fire the gun-carriage factory in the battered fort, where the British recovered £100,000 in Government treasure. Only a few workshops in the tope surrounding the parade-ground had been torched; they were still smoldering when Campbell's troops set up their tents.

307. Forbes-Mitchell, *The Relief of Lucknow*, p. 100.

308. Alison in Martin, *The Indian Empire*, 2:476.

309. Forbes-Mitchell, *The Relief of Lucknow*, p. 100. That same day the civilian Charles Raikes visited the houses of these two nobles. "Notwithstanding my indignation at the conduct of the Nawabs of Furuckabad, the sight was a sad one. A fine palace full of every luxurious appliance, mirrors, chandeliers, lustres, pictures, books, and furniture, suddenly deserted—not a human creature left—save one or two withered hags, in the Zenana; cats, parrots, pet dogs, clamorous for food. Outside, in the shady terraces and summer houses, and round the family mausoleum, wandered animals in quest of water or food, *nylghai* [blue deer], *barasingha* [twelve-horned deer], and other pet deer; on the wall a little black puppy yelping, and a dog howling piteously; in the poultry yard geese shut up, and making a frightful noise; at the stables grain for seven horses ready steeped and in separate portions, but the horses pawing, looking round, and starving, with food in their sight; monkeys, cockatoos, and an elephant, who had broken loose, and was helping himself to food—formed one of the strangest yet saddest pictures I ever saw. I took care that the animals were fed. As for the princes who so lately were masters of all this luxury, nobody had ventured even to claim their bodies, and it remained for strangers to give them decent sepulture." Raikes, *Notes on the Revolt*, pp. 107–8.

310. Jones, *Recollections*, pp. 89–90.

311. "Stating as an inducement that all valuables in the way of rings or money found on the persons of the condemned would become the property of the executioner," Power asked Jack Brian, "a big tall fellow who was the right-hand man of the company, if he would act as executioner. Jack Brian turned round with a look of disgust, saying, 'Wha do ye tak' us for? We of the Ninety-Third enlisted to fight men with arms in their hands. I widna' become yer hangman for all the loot in India!'" Forbes-Mitchell, *The Relief of Lucknow*, p. 101.

312. "The time is not wholly misspent," wrote an officer with the force, "as Power, the civilian, hangs an average 20 reprobates per diem." Johnson, *Journal* (OIOC), Forbes-Mitchell, *The Relief of Lucknow*, p. 101. Power was later suspended for "severity and other causes." TL in Martin, *The Indian Empire*, 2:476.

313. Canning in Taylor, *A Star Shall Fall*, p. 141.

314. Fitchett, *The Tale of the Great Mutiny*, p. 350.

315. Martin, *The Indian Empire*, 2:477.

316. Majendie, *Up Among the Pandies*, p. 196.

317. Russell, *My Diary in India*, 1:336.

318. Martin, *The Indian Empire*, 2:480.

319. Russell, *My Diary in India*, 1:324.

320. Russell in Martin, *The Indian Empire*, 2:479nn, 481nn.

321. Pemble, *The Raj, the Indian Mutiny, and the Kingdom of Oudh*, pp. 252–54.

322. HDP, Public, 14 May 1858, no. 1 (NAI); Bennett, "Ten Months' Captivity."

323. TL, 20 Aug. 1858, p. 8.

324. Beadon/Ellenborough: 5 July 1858 (NAI).

325. HDP, 14 May 1858, no. 1 (NAI).

326. TL, 11 Aug. 1858, p. 7.

327. I give Miss Wheeler's name as Margaret and not "Ulrica."

328. The story may have been circulated by Nana's agents to discourage the mutineers from keeping any English girls hostage.

329. Deposition of John Fitchett.

330. Chunder, *Travels of a Hindoo*, pp. 340–41.

331. Trevelyan, *Cawnpore*, p. 150.

332. Higginbotham, *Men Whom India Has Known*, p. 467.

333. In 1858, at the age of seventeen, she had married her first husband at Lucknow.

334. Taylor, handout prepared for the Kanpur Historical Society: January 1993.

335. Yalland, *Traders and Nabobs*, pp. 324–25.

336. Trevelyan, *Cawnpore*, p. 150.

337. Robertson, *District Duties*, pp. 181–82.

338. Queen Victoria in Allen, ed., *A Glimpse of the Burning Plain*, p. 81.

339. Pinckney/Erskine: 13 April 1858, GGP, HDP Public, Feb. 1858–Jan. 1859, no. 90 (NAI). The merest suggestion that English women were *not* raped outraged many Anglo-Indians. "It requires some courage now to venture to hint to Englishmen that perhaps their wives and daughters, and fathers and mothers and sons, have not been ravished and tortured and dishonoured to such an extent as they have lately asserted," wrote a correspondent to the *Times*. TL, 29 Jan. 1858, p. 12.

340. TL, 3 April 1858, p. 9. The Mrs. Chambers story was batted back and forth. A magistrate in Portsea named Smithers wrote the *Times* four days later about Mrs. Chambers, insisting that T.E.H.'s story was true, for he had heard it from Mrs. Chambers's own son, a lieutenant recently returned from India who had conferred with him about a robbery. (TL, 7 April 1858, p. 11.) But on 9 April E.E.C. wrote back to inform Smithers that Mrs. Chambers's lieutenant son was an imposter. Mrs. Chambers "could not have had any son a lieutenant in the army, because she was only married about two years" before her death on May 10. "She had only one child, and that died at the early age of seven months." Nor could she have had a stepson "as she was very young at the time of her decease," and her husband, Captain Chambers, was only thirty-eight years old and had never been married before. TL, 9 April 1858, p. 7.

341. Shepherd, *A Personal Narrative*, p. 113.

342. Except for one Indian (probably the ayah Mary Ann of Cawnpore) who had escaped the Entrenchment at Cawnpore but was not an eyewitness and was "apt to indulge in prurient imagination."

343. Mohamed Ali Khan in Forbes-Mitchell, *The Relief of Lucknow*, p. 113.

344. Biddulph, *Letters* (OIOC).

345. Two Eurasian ladies, probably the daughters of Mrs. Spiers, appeared at Sherer's *Cutcherry* one day in April of 1858 to complain that they had been treated with "great rudeness" by a group of European officers. "These poor creatures," wrote Russell, "had been carried off by the mutineers, and had escaped worse than death by ready compliance with the worst. They were quite willing to speak about their misfortunes. Neither of them was sixteen years old." Russell, *My Diary in India*, p. 382.

346. Muir, *Records*, 1:368–79.

347. Although Robertson was not as voracious a hangman as some of his colleagues, he was no doubt eager to justify the extent of British retribution. Nevertheless, his reasoning as to why some rapes were not reported or investigated seems to me sound.

348. A. H. Cocks in P. J. O. Taylor/ASW: 3 Nov. 1994.

349. Robertson, *District Duties*, pp. 181–82.

350. TL, 29 Jan. 1858, p. 12.

351. Scott, *The Jewel in the Crown*, p. 1.

352. The usual delays had been compounded by a thunderstorm between Trieste and Munich that knocked out the telegraph for a time, and then a glut of extended messages had overwhelmed the staff of the Submarine Telegraph Company. ILN, no. 872, vol. xxxi, 8 Aug. 1857, p. 151.

353. Queen Victoria in Allen, ed., *A Glimpse of the Burning Plain*, p. 79.

354. Moreover, it was "reassuring" to know that "the Government may always count on the votaries of Islam for support in any tumult arising from the teaching of an idolatrous creed." TL, 19 May 1857.

355. TL, 17 Oct. 1857, p. 14.

356. Ibid. In addition there were advertisements for Forbes' *Hindustani Dictionary* and the obsolete *Emigration to British India: Profitable Investment for Joint-Stock Companies.* TL, 24 Aug. 1857.

357. TL, 29 Oct. 1857, p. 12.

358. TL, 17 Oct. 1857, p. 14.

359. TL, 27 June 1857.

360. TL, 29 June 1857.

361. Men signing themselves "Anglo-Indian," "Index," and "Old Soldier," fired the opening salvos in the continuing debate about the causes of the rebellion. The *Times* blamed the headlong pace of reforms. "Now, when conquest has ceased, and conversion—not merely religious, but of morals, manners, and habits—must begin, we cannot wonder that [the natives'] minds should pass through a phase of disaffection." Others blamed the greased cartridges, the arrogance of British officers, the "fatal suicidal blundering in Calcutta," and the seniority system that produced such mediocrities as Anson, although it had to be pointed out that "at Cawnpore and Lucknow we have admirable officers in the persons of Sir Hugh Wheeler and Sir Henry Lawrence." TL, 29 June 1857; Major General H. T. Tucker in ibid.

362. TL, 3 Aug. 1857.

363. TL, 5 Aug. 1857.

364. "An Anglo-Indian" in TL, 3 Aug. 1857.

365. Lieutenant Colonel J. H. MacDonald in TL, 8 Aug. 1857.

366. Quote from *The Englishman* dated 29 July in TL, 15 Aug. 1857.

367. *Friend of India.* Quoted in TL, 15 Aug. 1857. A detailed account of the Fateghar massacre was greeted with skepticism. Since the native soldiers committed no violence at Fategarh why would the Europeans have fled? They could not have reached Bithur so soon after their departure from Fategarh, and they could not have been slaughtered at Bithur, which was only twelve miles from the safety of Cawnpore. Besides, had not Havelock assured Calcutta on the first of July that Fategarh was safe and in his hands? (He had not; the *Times* had confused it with Fatehpur.) "Putting all the circumstances together," concluded one correspondent, "it appears to me that those (of whom I am one) who have friends in Futtehghur may hopefully look forward to the receipt by next mail of an authoritative contradiction of the alarming rumours in question." TL, 19 Aug. 1857.

368. TL, 22 Aug. 1857.

369. TL, 24 Aug. 1857.

370. TL, 16 Sept. 1857, p. 7. From now on, wrote an officer, "if we are to hold India at all we must do so wholly and entirely as conquerors ruling by fear." TL, 28 and 29 Aug. 1857.

371. Anonymous officer, letter dated 17 July.

372. *Bombay Gazette*, 15 Aug. 1857 in TL, 16 Sept. 1857.

373. TL, 17 Sept. 1857, p. 8. "The feelings of every British soldier in India may . . . be imagined," wrote the *Englishman*, "and, if they should in future be accused of cruelty in their vengeance, it need only be replied,—Remember Cawnpore!" *The Englishman*, 8 Aug. 1857 in TL, 19 Sept. 1857, p. 6.

374. TL, 8 Oct. 1857.

375. Lucie Duff Gordon, Letters transcribed by Katherine Frank. Courtesy of the Earl of Shelburne.

376. There was of course a third choice, which was the lenity that springs from a great sensibility to human suffering, but even as liberal a thinker as Oliver Wendell Holmes ex-

pressed the same opinions. "The royal stronghold is in the hands of the babe-killers," he wrote. "England takes down the map of the world, which she has girdled with empire, and makes a correction thus: Delhi. *Dele*. The civilized world says, Amen!" Trevelyan, *The Life and Letters of Lord Macauley*, pp. 366–68.

377. TL, 1 Oct. 1857, p. 10.

378. TL, 28 Sept. 1857, p. 4. The event brought some eccentrics out of the woodwork, including a woman who wrote a letter to the *Times* to bawl out her sisters for their extravagant dress, "a sin" that, as much as "the blunders of the East India Company," had brought "down upon the land the chastisements of God." TL, 7 Oct. 1857, p. 7.

379. He preached for free, and elicited from the crowd a donation of £475 for the Indian Relief Fund. ILN, no. 883, vol. xxxi, 17 Oct. 1857, p. 400.

380. TL, 8 Oct. 1857, pp. 5–8.

381. TL, 24 Oct. 1857, p. 6.

382. Lindsay Papers.

383. Letters of Alexander Lindsay, ibid.

384. TL, 29 Aug. 1857.

385. "At the Military Club (in Calcutta)," recalled William's friend Balcarres Ramsay, "I took up the *Phoenix* newspaper and read in it what turned me quite sick—a scrap of a journal kept by Caroline Lindsay, a cousin of my wife's. She and two other sisters, with their mother and brother, a young officer, had only recently been staying with us, and had gone to Cawnpore in high spirits, except this poor girl, who cried bitterly and asked to be left with us, which we would have gladly consented to. From some presentiment she appeared afraid to go up country, but her mother would not hear of her remaining. At that time there was not even a shadow apparent of all that was to happen."
Ramsay, *Rough Recollections*, 1:264.

386. Lindsay Papers.

387. Roberts, *Scenes and Characteristics of Hindustan*, 1:29.

388. For my account of the three Lindsay children I am indebted to Alexander Binney, the major's great-grandson; and Sir Ronald Lindsay's researches into the family genealogy.

389. Garrett Papers, items 13–33 (PRONI).

390. Ella Wyndham/George & Margaret Wyndham: 2 Nov. 1857. Courtesy of Historic "Dalwood" Restoration Association.

391. Spencer Wyndham, Letter 11, courtesy of Dr. Colin Forbes.

392. Correspondence with Alward Wyndham, Margaret Kelly of the Historic "Dalwood" Restoration Association, and D. Blaxland.

393. Pearson, *Letters*, p. 150 (OIOC).

394. The savagery continued on both sides. In June a Major Poore would report that at a place called Pool-Baag "we saw three men hanging from a tree by their legs and one of them was certainly one of our men. . . . He had his head cut off and was cut about the body, but the most brutal thing I saw was a sergeant of the 71st who had lost his way and been cut off. . . . They had tied a torch lighted to his back and cut him about in a most fearful manner." Poore, *Letters* (OIOC).

395 *The Carnatic Telegraph and Madras Exchange Gazette* in U.P., 5:949.

396. Bradshaw, *Letters* (CCSAS).

397. Muir, *Records*, 1:340.

398. Johnson, *Journal* (OIOC).

499. Daily Bulletin, *Hindoo Patriot* in *Further Papers* in U.P., 5:426, 434–38.

400. Telegram of E. A. Reade in U.P., 5:937, 2:325.

401. Cracklow Letters.

402. Russell, *My Indian Mutiny Diary*, pp. 134–35.

403. *Bengal Hurkaru and India Gazette* in U.P., 5:433.

404. U.P., 3:367. "The Nana," sniffed a brigadier, must have been "under the influence of opium." FDP, FC, 27 May 1859, nos. 63–70 (NAI).

405. FDP, 28 May 1858, nos. 177–79 (NAI).

406. "Everything that can possibly insure secrecy as to our movements is put in force," wrote an officer. "No orders for marching are issued until about an hour before the time for starting and any possible precaution is taken to prevent the enemy knowing of our intended attack. Off we go to this blessed place before we have started an hour they manage to get information and decamp. On our arrival not a soul is to be seen in the shape of a fighting man but some dozens of old men women and children come out to look at us. . . . Well we halt a day at the place and get a few of the people together, who say there will be justice for them, that they have been plundered by the soldiers until they have nothing left and that the only thing they hope for is the re-establishment of the Company's rule. Well the commissioner tells them to be good people and asks if they have any revenue ready to pay, this of course bears absurdity on the face of it. . . . Well we leave half a dozen policemen and away we march to the next place and before our baggage is well off the ground back comes the army [that] had occupied the place before our arrival. . . . I can't see how this business is to end." Cracklow Letters.

407. Mayne in U.P., 4:853.

408. FDP, FC, 22 Oct. 1858, nos. 17–18 (NAI).

409. FDP, FC, 30 Dec. 1859, nos. 742–55 (NAI).

410. "Mrs. Yalland mentioning the Nana Sahib escaping to Nepal reminded me of a story my father told me, when I first went out with him in Oct. 1919. His father, William Peppé senior, had told him that many years after the Mutiny (perhaps 15 or 20 years) some of the inhabitants of villages of Birdpur area, returned to their villages, & from inquiries my Grandfather was convinced that many of them must have been taken by the Nana Sahib as carriers, convincing him that the escape must have been through the Birdput Grant [estate]." Peppé, Humphrey, letter in Yalland Collection.

411. Gimlette, *Postscript*, pp. 39–45.

412. Russell, *My Indian Mutiny Diary*, p. 271.

413. Once a refuge occupied by indigenous tribes and teeming with wildlife, the Terai was drained and opened up to cultivation, primarily to accommodate Punjabi refugees from Pakistan after Partition.

414. FDP, SC, 26 March 1858, nos. 74–78 (NAI). The proclamation read as follows: "It is hereby notified that a reward of One Lac of Rupees will be paid to any Person who shall deliver alive at any British Military Post or Camp the Rebel Nana Dhoondo Punt of Bithoor commonly called Nana Sahib. It is further notified that in addition to this reward a Free Pardon will be given to any Mutineer deserter or rebel who may so deliver up the said Nana Dhoondo Punt. By order of the Right Honourable the Governor General." The British quite consciously denied him any titles even on his wanted poster. FDP, Despatch to Secretary of State. 16 July 1859, no. 109 (NAI).

415. FDP, SC, 26 March 1858, nos. 74–78 (NAI).

416. Raikes, *Notes on the Revolt*, p. 117.

417. Gupta, *Nana Saheb*, p. 171.

418. Heber, *Journal*, pp. 250–51.

419. FDP, 15 Feb. 1859, no. 40 (NAI). The British dismissed these allegations as "grossly exaggerated." FDP, 5 April 1859, no. 43 (NAI).

420. Russell, *My Indian Mutiny Diary*, pp. 255, 257.

421. FDP, Despatch to Secretary of State. 4 March 1859 (NAI).

422. FDP, FC, 13 May 1859, no. 319 (NAI).

423. FDP, FC, 30 Dec. 1859, nos. 742–55 (NAI).

424. Buckland, *Dictionary of Indian Biography*, p. 221.

425. FDP, 21 March 1859 (NAI).

426. FDP, 9 April 1859, no. 46 (NAI).

427. FDP, FC, 13 May 1859, no. 319 (NAI).

428. Hibbert, *The Great Mutiny*, p. 373.

429. Jung Bahadur in Sen, *Eighteen Fifty-Seven*, p. 359.

430. Foreign Political Consultations in U.P., 4:772–74.

431. FDP, FC, 27 May 1859, nos. 63–70 (NAI).

432. Ibid.

433. Ibid.

434. FDP, Pol. 15 July 1859, no. 230 (NAI); Thornhill Papers. A third child, whom Mary called "My dear Georgie," evidently lived with Mary's sister in England.

435. Diary of Nunne Nawab.

436. FDP, Pol. 15 July 1859, no. 230 (NAI).

437. FDP, Political Index. 1859/vol. 2, part 2 (NAI).

438. FDP, 21 July 1859, no. 95/72 (NAI).

439. FDP, FC, 30 Dec. 1859, nos. 742–55 (NAI).

440. Ramsay to Edmonstone, 26 July 1859.

441. FDP, 1 Aug. 1859, no. 4698/255 (NAI).

442. FDP, 8 Aug. 1859, no. 102/37 (NAI). Sirdar Siddinau Singh was rewarded one thousand rupees for arranging the release of the musicians and their families. FDP, 19 Aug. 1859, no. 5113/4–37 (NAI).

443 *Friend of India* in U.P., 4:360.

444. Copy of a letter from General Harris, originally printed in the *Pioneer* in 1907, Yalland Collection.

445. In 1859, September 24 fell on a Saturday, which jibes with Harris's recollection.

446. Landon, *Nepal*, 1:161.

447. *Friend of India* in U.P., 4:782; "But . . . clear authentication" of Nana's death, wrote the Resident, "will be very desirable, as the Nana is a Brahmin and is reputed to be very wealthy, and, in the present temper and spirit of the local authorities in the [Terai], it is not at all unlikely that they may be connived at his escape into the mountains." FDP, FC, 4 Dec. 1859, no. 159 (NAI).

448. *Friend of India*, 22 Nov. 1860.

449. He was convicted of rape, but whom he was convicted of raping—Indian or European—is evidently not recorded.

450. FDP, PD, Jan. 1862, nos. 84–89 (NAI).

451. FDP, Oct. 1861, nos. 33–34 (NAI).

452. Gupta, *Nana Saheb*, p. 184.

453. Ibid., p. 185.

454. TL, 5 Aug. 1863.

455. FDP, 27 May 1859, no. 69 (NAI). Kathmandu became a repository of deposed Ranis. According to a map drawn by the two spies, a widow of the great Sikh Maharaja Ranjit Singh lived in a small palace in Jung Bahadur's garden; Ranjit's sisters were across the road; and the formidable and unrepentant Hazrat Mahal took up residence next door to an arsenal. She died in 1879. FDP, PC, March 1864, nos. 151–54 (NAI); Taylor, *A Star Shall Fall*, p. 223; Landon, *Under the Sun*, p. 283.

Around 1920 a forester named Joseph Veasy Collier was lumbering a stand of thick virgin forest a few miles over the Nepalese border from Gorakhpur when "he came across the ruins of a considerable settlement with the foundations of a large central building of European type." The forester was convinced that he had found "Nana Sahib's hide-out in Nepal." Peppé, letter in Yalland Collection.

456. It was written in such acidic ink that it has long since eaten through the paper, and only a few fragments are still decipherable: "Should fortune, which is right the__to see them noble with what sorrows it__evil any who fill their lives with mist. . . . I was afterwards to make known__. . . . Never live to show myself but you will most likely find scraps of papers in my study after I am gone and those scraps will be of inestimable value to the literary and historical nations at large and especially of England. . . . There are many malfactions alleged to me. . . . Naturally, when I was hunted through the. . . . Nothing and

naturally to live comfortably . . . that course would be wiped off__and it will be if the child is alive and is found. Farewell own brother. Farewell. Yours in affliction and decline. Nana Sahib of Bithoor."

The letter was almost certainly a hoax, if only because in representing himself as an unrepentant rebel Nana Sahib would never have signed his last letter without employing his seal and all the ancient titles he had lost so much to reclaim. FDP, GC, May 1879, no. 408 (NAI).

457. Keene, *Handbook*, p. 35nn.

458. Macrae in Bennett, "Ten Months' Captivity."

459. FDP, SC, Jan. 1892. nos. 57–59 (NAI).

460. Elgin in Gupta, *Nana Saheb*, p. 200–201.

461. Lucas, *Memoir of Reverend Robert Stewart Fullerton*, p. 114.

462. "It was quite proper," an Indian army officer later assured me. "He was a military man. It was a necessity." Field notes.

463. Landon in Gupta, *Nana Saheb*, p. 202.

464. Ibid., p. 202.

465. Sherer, *Daily Life*, pp. 84–86.

466. The exhibit was removed in 1878. Tussaud et al., *Madame Tussaud and Sons' Catalogue*, p. 30.

467. The critic for the *Illustrated London News* deemed "In Memoriam" "too revolting," but the *Critic*'s man was so moved, or so intimidated by the quote from the Psalms that Paton had inscribed around the frame, that he deemed it worthy of a chapel of its own. Bayly, *The Raj*, p. 241; and Martin, *The Indian Empire*, 2:378.

468. MacNabb Papers. A soldier who saw him pass said "he was a fine young man." Henry Eyrl, *Diary*, Leicestershire.

469. Field notes.

470. FDP, FC, 15 April 1859, nos. 488–96 (NAI).

471. NAM (Press no. 52-5-25, Photo Number 37590-37591). His coat was pulled off of his corpse and locks of hair collected. Misra, p. 492. A year later his family was released. Field notes.

472. Sherer, *Havelock's March*, p. 330.

473. Field notes.

474. GGP, HDP Public, Feb. 1858–Jan. 1859, no. 67A (NAI).

475. Nevill, *Cawnpore*, p. 119.

476. *Friend of India* in U.P., 5:951.

477. Farrukhabad Collectorate Mutiny Basta in ibid., 5:926.

478. *Friend of India* in ibid., 5:953.

479. Ibid., 5:955.

480. Adam, *The Indian Criminal*, pp. 169–77.

481. Note by A. Busteed written at the back of the OIOC's copy of Mowbray Thomson's *The Story of Cawnpore*.

482. Ibid.

483. The story was written up in G. Ward Price's *Extra Special Correspondent* and is quoted extensively in Misra, *Nana Saheb Peshwa*, p. 466.

484. Kaye, *A History of the Great Revolt*, 1:342.

485. Reliable information on the background of Azimullah Khan is scarce. His sole biographer, the Pakistani historian Syed Luftullah, was reduced to assembling a portrait of Azimullah from the same scraps upon which Western historians have relied: the brief and dismissive accounts by W. J. Shepherd, Mowbray Thomson, William Howard Russell, and G. O. Trevelyan. (A book purporting to be Azimullah's diary, championed by a man who claimed to be Nana Sahib's grandson, has been discredited.) William Forbes-Mitchell interviewed one of Azimullah's confidants, and Reverend J. R. Hill of the S.P.G. had the singu-

lar opportunity of learning more from Azimullah's son, who converted to Christianity and worked with Hill at Cawnpore. But Hill's account in *The Story of the Cawnpore Mission* betrays no special knowledge, and Forbes-Mitchell learned very little about Azimullah's background.

Even if we had Azimullah seated before us to interview I doubt we would learn very much. He passed himself off as a prince during his visit to London, and like most ambitious young men would not have been one to dwell on his true background. He was obviously a clever, audacious, and complicated man, and his rise to power was an extraordinary accomplishment. But it seems to me likely that he would have been more ashamed than proud of his humble origins. In this account I have attempted to produce at least a silhouette of Azimullah by filling in some of the space around him.

486. Deposition of Azizun.

487. "Long live Nana Sahib," Misra, *Nana Saheb Peshwa*, p. 557, frontis.

488. Ibid., p. 479.

489. Forbes-Mitchell, *The Relief of Lucknow*, pp. 104–11.

490. TL, 24 Sept. 1857, p. 8.

491. TL, 19 Nov. 1857, p. 10.

492. His superiors made "no charge of inhumanity" against Walker, but "deeply deplore[d] the result." Escape was "a natural impulse, to which it is impossible to attach moral guilt," they said; perhaps a ban on native boats and a "good flogging would have answered all purposes." HDP, 19 June 1858, p. 262 (NAI).

493. HDP, Judicial, 2 July 1858, nos. 12–14 (NAI).

494. Ibid., 25 June 1858, nos. 31–33 (NAI).

495. Ibid., 22 Oct. 1858, nos. 1–5 (NAI).

496. Ibid., 21 March 1861, nos. 65–74A (NAI).

497. HDP, Public, 16 Aug. 1862, nos. 66–75b, and HDP, Judicial, 18 Feb. 1859, nos. 19–21 (NAI).

498. HDP, Public, 17 July 1862, nos. 21–29a (NAI).

499. Ibid., 27 Jan. 1863, nos. 56–59a (NAI).

500. HDP Index, 1858–1864 (NAI).

501. Hunter, *The Earl of Mayo*, pp. 194–97.

502. Misra, *Nana Saheb Peshwa*, pp. 572–73. Misra cited Forbes-Mitchell, who evidently acquired a copy of the leaflet and verified the story from several sources. But according to P. J. O. Taylor, Major General W. A. Watson debunked the story by determining that Mazar Ali was born four years after Suffar Ali's death. See the Augier Papers (CCSAS).

503. Nevill, Cawnpore, p. 222.

504. HDP, Public, 12 Oct. 1860, nos. 48–49 (NAI).

505. Mr. Kailash Nath Wahal, descendant of Sheoprasad. Interview with the author.

506. Field notes; Misra, *Nana Saheb Peshwa*, p. 311.

507. Nevill, *Cawnpore*, p. 222.

508. Anonymous, "A Hindu," *The Mutinies and the People*, p. 160.

509. HDP, 4 Sept. 1861, no. 17(B) (NAI).

510. Sen, *Eighteen Fifty-Seven*, pp. 163–68.

511. Mowbray Thomson. Board's Collections 1857–1858 f/4/2703, 193490, p. 2. He was dead by 15 Jan. 1858.

512. TL, 7 April 1858, p. 10 (OIOC).

513. Vibart, *Addiscombe*, pp. 628–29; Sherer, *Daily Life*, pp. 102–3.

514. It reads: "To the Memory of General Henry George de la Fosse C.B. D.S.O. Who, after serving with conspicuous bravery in the beleaguered garrison of Cawnpore fought with distinguished gallantry in the relief of Lucknow and later on other fields. Born 24th April 1835. Died 10th February 1905."

515. Thomson acknowledges that an anonymous friend assisted him in its composition: I think it may have been his good friend Sherer, whose own *Daily Life*, one of the classics of the Mutiny literature, is often equally fulsome and casual with dates and details.

516. Sherer, *Daily Life*, pp. 102–3.

517. His memorial plaque was installed at All Souls opposite Delafosse's. It is both inaccurate—Thomson was a lieutenant, not a captain at the time of the siege—and incomplete; unlike Delafosse's memorial, Thomson's provides no account of his subsequent service: "To the Memory of General Sir Mowbray Thomson. K.C.I.E. The last survivor of Nana Sahib's Massacre at Cawnpore on June 6th 1857. He was at the time a Captain in the 53rd Native Infantry. Born. April 1st, 1832. Died. February 25th, 1917."

518. Bennett, "Ten Months' Captivity."

519. HDP, 25 June 1858, 54–58 (NAI).

520. By the same R. Macrae who later transcribed Amelia Horne's account. Macrae was the eldest son by a former marriage of Mrs. Wrixon, who was killed with her child at the Bibighar. (Yalland, interview with the author.)

521. It was greeted rather uneasily by Mowbray Thomson and treated dismissively by many subsequent historians, but Shepherd brought a clerk's fastidiousness to his narrative, and to the extent to which it can be corroborated by the contemporary letters that have emerged long since, *A Personal Narrative* is by far the most reliable of all the eyewitness accounts, including Thomson's, which is all the more remarkable considering how much more Shepherd had suffered and lost.

522. Shepherd, *Guilty Men of 1857*, p. 53.

523. Thompson, *The Other Side of the Medal*, p. 64.

524. Interview with Keith Shepherd.

525. Alward Wyndham and Margaret E. Kelly of the Historic "Dalwood" Restoration Association; and Mr. Russell Blaxland.

526. The story of the subhedar's trial is in a note appended to R. Macrae's transcript of Miss Sutherland's narrative, written in Lucknow on December 29, 1890. The subhedar was probably Ali Bux of the 2nd Cavalry, who was tried and hanged after the Mutiny. The sole source for Miss Sutherland's story is her own account (BM).

527. Taylor, *A Star Shall Fall*, p. 125.

528. Russell, *My Diary in India*, p. 381.

529. Wallace, *Fatehgarh Camp*, p. 120.

530. Taylor, *A Star Shall Fall*, p. 125.

531. Jones died in retirement in Southsea in 1913. His son, Sir Tracy Gavin Jones, continued in his stead through Independence. Shepherd, p. 39; Edwards, *Personal Adventures*, pp. 131–39, 184; Yalland, *Traders and Nabobs*, pp. 199, 201, 233, 286; Interview with S. P. Mehra.

532. Shepherd, *A Personal Narrative*, pp. 158–59.

533. Cracklow Letters.

534. Russell, *My Diary in India*, 1:183.

535. HDP, Public, 29 July 1859, nos. 40–41 (NAI).

536. Beames, *Memoirs*, p. 93.

537. Chunder, *Travels of a Hindoo*, p. 338.

538. Maclagan, *"Clemency" Canning*, p.236

539. Sherer, *Daily Life*, pp. 176–78.

540. Chunder, *Travels of a Hindoo*, p. 335.

541. Nevill, *Cawnpore*, p. 62.

542. Lee, *The Indian Mutiny*, p. ii.

543. Forbes-Mitchell in ibid. In contrast, Bithur never recovered from the Mutiny, and still bears evidence of British retribution. But after Nana Sahib's departure the Ganges, which had veered away from the town when Baji Rao moved there, returned to its former course along Brahmavarta Ghat.

544. Hill, *The Story of the Cawnpore Mission*, pp. 55–56.

545. Butler, *The Land of the Veda*, p. 261.

546. Canning was determined to keep the government out of missionary work and refused missionary demands that he confiscate on their behalf "the endowments of all temples and mosques." Lyveden, *Correspondence Book*, pp. 110–11 (OIOC).

547. *The Colonial Church Chronicle and Missionary Journal*, May 1859.

548. The number of converts "grew from 60 to 300," wrote Willis's successor, whose conversion threshold was evidently lower than the fastidious Henry Martyn's. "Over 100 being baptised at one time in Christ Church!" Hill exulted. "Our slaughtered dear ones, were thus avenged by the rescue from death and starvation of those who had deserted and slain them and their children!" Hill, *The Story of the Cawnpore Mission*, p. 57.

549. Murdoch, *Indian Missionary Manual*, p. 282.

550. Hill, *The Story of the Cawnpore Mission*, p. 49.

551. Bradshaw, *Letters* (CCSAS).

552. Butler, *The Land of the Veda*, p. 310.

553. Shepherd, *A Personal Narrative*, p. 159.

554. Keene, *Handbook*, p. 34.

555. Allen, ed., *A Glimpse of the Burning Plain*, p. 122. C. B. Thornhill, the late Farrukhabad magistrate's brother, was asked to pursue the project and Collector Lance, Sherer's successor, was put in charge of designing the surrounding garden, which eventually encompassed fifty acres. Keene, *Handbook*, p. 30.

556. Steggles/ASW: 5 Nov. 1994.

557. Keene, *Handbook*, p. 34.

558. Yalland, *Traders and Nabobs*, p. 279.

559. Many admired Marochetti's grieving angel, but Henry George Keene took a dim view of the memorial grounds. "Nothing can well be conceived more commonplace than the carpenter's Gothic of the surrounding wall, with its frivolous crocketted battlements, purposeless finials, and tedious rows of lancet-windows with their dull trefoiled mullions. The doorway and cast-iron doors are the only decent feature, and they were designed by Dr H. Yule, whose name appears in the inscription on the inside of the portal. The garden is well laid out . . . but it is much too large for the enclosure of a tomb. . . . The necessary observances of a cemetery render this large and ornamental piece of ground useless for the ordinary purposes of a public garden; even though the monument is not visible from any but the most central portion." Keene, *Handbook*, p. 26.

560. The church cost two hundred thousand rupees to build, its marble floor having been kindly donated by the Maharaja of Jodhpur.

561. Gibbs, *The Anglican Church in India*, p. 223.

562. All Souls inscription.

563. Butler, *The Land of the Veda*, p. 310.

564. Lee, *The Indian Mutiny*, p. 7.

565. Note by A. Busteed written at the back of the OIOC's copy of Mowbray Thomson's *The Story of Cawnpore*.

566. Yalland/ASW: 10 Oct. 1994.

567. In 1903 William Lindsay, the major's son, sent a postcard from Cawnpore to his niece. It showed the Memorial Well on one side; on the other William had scrawled, "Remember Cawnpore."

568. Thompson, *The Other Side of the Medal*, pp. 28–33.

569. Mason, *A Matter of Honour*, p. 448.

570. Its base now forms part of the counter of a *pahn* shop. Yalland/ASW: 24 Oct. 1994.

571. Steggles/ASW: 5 Nov. 1994.

Index

775 - 4939